F
F
ir

The Catholic Church and the Campaign for Emancipation in Ireland and England

The Catholic Church and the Campaign for Emancipation in Ireland and England

Ambrose Macaulay

FOUR COURTS PRESS

Set in 11 on 12.5 point Ehrhardt for
FOUR COURTS PRESS LTD
7 Malpas Street, Dublin 8, Ireland
e-mail: info@fourcourtspress.ie
www.fourcourtspress.ie
and in North America for
FOUR COURTS PRESS
c/o ISBS, 920 N.E. 58th Street, Suite 300, Portland, OR 97213.

A catalogue record for this title
is available from the British Library.

ISBN 978-1-84682-600-9

Printed in England
by Antony Rowe, Chippenham, Wilts.

SANCTI COLUMBANI
MONACHI BENCHORENSIS, PEREGRINI PRO CHRISTO,
ABBATIS LUXOVII, BRIGANTII ET BOBIENSIS,
<ULTIMI HABITATORIS MUNDI>
HONORI ET MEMORIAE
HOC ANNO MILLESIMO QUADRINGENTESIMO AB OBITU EIUS
HOC QUALECUMQUE OPUSCULUM
DICATUR

Bishop John Milner to Denys Scully (1810)

When I advocated the Veto between two & three years ago I honestly thought it meant nothing else but the degrading ceremony of giving a fresh test of civil allegiance: but now I find that it means the shackling & stifling of our Church, in order to appease the jealousy of bigotted [*sic*] unbelieving parsons & their unfortunate head which has been so long subject to a delirium.

Duke of Richmond to Robert Peel (1812)

I will write to the Attorney-General today, but I doubt his undertaking Parliament. The Solicitor is against the Catholics, on account of their violence, but certainly thinks their clergy should be paid, and some indulgences granted. I should be glad if they would accept of payment of their clergy, as that would place them in the hands of Government, but I am not for other indulgence.

Cardinal Consalvi to Cardinal Pacca (1814)

Il partito della lettera di monsignor Quarantotto [*sic*] che è quello del Bill, cioè di destinare un comitato di laici (non esprime se cattolici o non cattolici) i quali dovessero inquirere sulle qualità degli eletti e riferirne poi al governo, non è né decente né prudente, né salva nessun riguardo. [The decision in Monsignor Quarantotti's letter, which is that of the bill, namely to set up a committee of laymen (whether Catholics or non-Catholics he does not specify) who would be charged to enquire into the qualities of those elected to the episcopate and report back to the government, is neither seemly nor judicious and spares no one's reputation.]

Coleraine

Letterkenny Londonderry

RAPHOE Ballymena Larne

DERRY **CONNOR**

Donegal Antrim

AND Belfast

Omagh

Dungannon Lisburn

ARMAGH **DOWN**

Enniskillen Portadown

KILLALA Sligo **CLOGHER** Armagh **DROMORE** Downpatrick

Ballina Monaghan

Newry

ACHONRY **KILMORE**

Castlebar Ballaghaderreen Boyle Cavan Dundalk

Westport **ARDAGH**

ELPHIN **AND**

Longford

Roscommon **CLONMAC**

TUAM **-NOISE** Navan Drogheda

Clifden **MEATH**

Tuam Athlone Mullingar

Galway Ballinasloe Maynooth

GALWAY **CLONFERT** Tullamore Dublin

Loughrea Kildare Naas

Gort Portumna Birr **KILDARE**

Port Laoise **DUBLIN**

KILLALOE **AND**

Ennis Wicklow

Nenagh Carlow

OSSORY **LEIGHLIN** Arklow

Limerick Thurles Kilkenny

CASHEL Enniscorthy

LIMERICK **AND EMLY** Cashel

Tipperary **FERNS**

Tralee Clonmel Wexford

Dingle **LISMORE**

KERRY **CLOYNE** **AND** Waterford

Killarney Mallow Fermoy **WATERFORD** Dungarvan

Cahirciveen Youghal

CORK Cork Cobh

Bantry

Clonakilty 0 10 20 30 40 50 miles

Skibbereen

ROSS

The dioceses of the Catholic Church of Ireland

Durham ■

NORTHERN

● York

● Preston
● Manchester
● Liverpool

MIDLAND

■ **Wolverhampton**
● Birmingham

● Cambridge

WESTERN

Oxford

● Ware

Chepstow ●
● Swansea

● Bristol

■ **Bath**

London ■

LONDON

Canterbury ●

● Taunton

● Winchester
● Portsmouth

Districts of the vicars apostolic, 1688–1840

Contents

Abbreviations

AA.EE. SS.	Archives of the second section (relations with states) of the Secretariat of State (formerly the congregation for Extraordinary Ecclesiastical Affairs), Rome
ACDF	Archives of the congregation for the Doctrine of the Faith (formerly the Holy Office), Rome
APF	Archives of the congregation for the Evangelization of Peoples (formerly de Propaganda Fidè), Rome
Arch. Hib.	*Archivium Hibernicum*
ASV	Vatican Archives
AVEC	Archives of the Venerable English College, Rome
BDA	Birmingham Diocesan Archives
CaDA	Cashel Diocesan Archives
Cast. Corr.	Castlereagh Correspondence
CJ	*Catholic Journal*
ClDA	Clifton Diocesan Archives
CloDA	Cloyne Diocesan Archives
CM	*Catholic Miscellany*
Coll. Hib.	*Collectanea Hibernica*
Corn. Corr.	Cornwallis Correspondence
CRDA	Cork and Ross Diocesan Archives
DCh	*Dublin Chronicle*
DDA	Dublin Diocesan Archives
DEP	*Dublin Evening Post*
DrDA	Dromore Diocesan Archives
FJ	*Freeman's Journal*
HC	House of commons
IER	*Irish Ecclesiastical Record*
IHS	*Irish Historical Studies*
LDA	Leeds Diocesan Archives
NA	National Archives (London)
NHI	*New history of Ireland*
OJ	*Orthodox Journal*
PRONI	Public Record Office of Northern Ireland
SCA	Scottish Catholic Archives
WDA	Westminster Diocesan Archives

Preface

The campaign for Catholic emancipation, which reached its successful conclusion in 1829, is often described and analysed in the context of the political career of Daniel O'Connell. He was the engineer who designed and managed the political struggle for more than two decades, and his name has ever since been linked to the achievement of legal equality for Catholics. The issue was also fought out at the ecclesiastical level, and an attempt is made here to examine the complex relations between the bishops in Ireland, the vicars apostolic in England and the Holy See.

The governments both in Dublin and London long insisted that they could not grant Catholics equal rights until they were fully satisfied of Catholic loyalty. That satisfaction could only be guaranteed by the willingness of Catholics to take oaths of allegiance from which they could not be freed by the dispensing power of the pope or other prelates, to allow the state to scrutinize the official correspondence of the Vatican with the bishops, and to permit the monarch to veto the appointments of bishops whom he deemed unsuitable to hold such an office in his kingdom.

Differing reactions in Rome, Ireland and England to these concessions among Roman officials, Catholic committees and bishops led to misunderstandings and disputes throughout the campaign for emancipation. Changes of opinions and emphasis among those struggling for Catholic relief added to these misunderstandings. The religious and political repercussions of compromises took on different complexions in Rome, Dublin and London. Though the Holy See insisted that Protestant sovereigns could not be allowed to nominate or influence the nomination of bishops, it often found ways in practice of granting some of them this right. Through the primary sources of decisions taken at Rome and of letters to and from Rome, London and Dublin, these matters are here explored.

I am grateful to all those who have helped me in the preparation of this book. For permission to use archival material, I should like to acknowledge my indebtedness to the following: Cardinal Tarcisio Bertone, former secretary of state; Cardinal Ludwig Müller, former prefect of the congregation for the Doctrine of the Faith; Cardinal Fernando Filoni, prefect of the congregation for the Evangelization of Peoples, formerly known as Propaganda or, officially, as de Propaganda Fidè; Cardinal Raffaele Farina, former archivist and librarian of the Holy Roman Church; Cardinal Vincent

Nichols, archbishop of Westminster; Archbishop Diarmuid Martin of Dublin; Archbishop Kieran O'Reilly of Cashel; Bishop Arthur Roche, former bishop of Leeds; Bishop John Buckley of Cork and Ross; Bishop Declan Lang of Clifton; Bishop John McAreavey of Dromore; Bishop William Crean of Cloyne; Bishop Nicholas Hudson, former rector of the Venerable English College, Rome.

I wish to thank the librarians and staffs at the British Library, the National Archives (London), the National Library of Ireland, the Public Record Office of Northern Ireland, and the Derbyshire Record Office.

I am especially indebted to Monsignor Sergio Pagano, prefect of the Vatican Archives; to Monsignor Luis Manuel Cuña Ramos, archivist at the congregation for the Evangelization of Peoples; to Monsignor Alejandro Cifres Gimenez, archivist at the congregation for the Doctrine of the Faith; to Dr Johan Ickx, archivist at the Secretariat of State (second section); to Fr Nicholas Schofield, archivist of the archdiocese of Westminster; to Fr John Sharpe, archivist of the archdiocese of Birmingham; to Canon Anthony Harding, archivist of the diocese of Clifton; to Mrs Noelle Dowling, director of the Dublin Diocesan Archives; to Mr Robert Finnegan, archivist of the diocese of Leeds; to Mr Andrew Nicoll, former director of the Scottish Catholic archives; and to Dr Herman H. Schwedt, archivist of the diocese of Limburg.

For their kindness in reading my typescript and giving me much valuable advice, I am happy to record my thanks to Professor Sean Connolly, Dr Patrick Maume, Fr Joseph Gunn and Mr Leon McAuley. I would also like to thank Oula Jones for creating the index. Finally, I should like to express my gratitude to Mr Martin Fanning and his staff at Four Courts Press.

Belfast

23 November 2015

Introduction

Catholics in Ireland and England seeking relief from the penal laws in the second half of the eighteenth century were obliged not only to deal with their governments in Dublin and London but also with the papacy. The administrations required them to pledge allegiance in oaths which could be held to impinge on papal authority or papal claims, and also to agree to the interference of the crown in the appointments of their bishops. The Catholic prelates could not accept these terms without the permission and consent of the Holy See. And that permission depended upon the attitudes prevalent in Rome as well as on the extent of the requests made by their rulers. The responses of the Vatican were coloured by the *Weltanschauung* of the Catholic countries of Europe and by the philosophical and theological pressures which governments and prominent thinkers of these countries could exert on Rome.

Hostility to the church in these Catholic countries made the Vatican very cautious and sensitive to any diminution of its authority. And it was afraid that the Catholics of Ireland and England, as they struggled to establish a new relationship with their governments, might be induced to agree to a transmutation of that authority.

During the second half of the eighteenth century the Holy See was buffeted by a series of antipathetic theological and political opinions. In the wider atmosphere of the Enlightment the prevailing views were either deistic or agnostic. Deism acknowledged a supreme being who was kind enough not to interfere much in the workings of the world. It did not accept Christianity in any traditional sense. The *philosophes* and writers associated with the *Encyclopédie* generally poured scorn on Christian beliefs, and some Catholic priests were undoubtedly influenced by them.

Within the church the Jansenist movement aimed at infiltrating the thinking and behaviour of the clergy and religious. The Jansenists called for a return to the early church, for a stricter morality, greater simplicity, more rigorous discipline, less frequent communion and a diminution of papal power, especially when it came into conflict with private judgment. They saw themselves as an elite and bitterly resented the condemnation of the tenets of the movement in 1713. In 1786 the synod of Pistoia, influenced by the

Jansenists and the Grand Duke Leopold of Tuscany, promulgated a series of anti-papal resolutions, and advocated the abolition of religious orders and of several devotions.

The Gallicans upheld the rights of the church in France against papal authority, and in the classic expression of their claims in 1682 declared that the Holy See had no authority to interfere in French political questions, that general councils were superior to the pope, that papal interventions by formal communications in the affairs of the French church were subject to Gallican traditions, and that the pope was not infallible without the consent of the universal church.

Febronianism attributed most of the ills of the church to papal claims. The pope, Febronius (the pen name of a German bishop) argued, should be the mere executive of all the bishops of the world, who would legislate for the whole church. The ruler in his state should be the protector of the church and should be ready to reject papal injunctions and make the serious spiritual decisions for his own territory. Febronius also opposed the religious orders, especially the Jesuits.

The emperor of Austria, Joseph II, exercised so much control over the church in his empire that he gave the name Josephism to this form of dictation. Apart from nominating the bishops and regulating all communications to them from Rome, he closed down some seminaries and only allowed others to exist with his permission and did the same with religious orders. Order and discipline in the church were regarded as imperial concerns.

Against these forces and attempts to weaken the jurisdiction of the papacy stood the Jesuits. They upheld ultramontanism or the defence of the powers and prerogatives of the papacy. By virtue of their fourth vow, the services of their order were to be at the disposal of the pope, and they resisted the views of the Jansenists and others who wanted to restore the primitive purity of the church and minimize papal authority. They emphasized the traditional means of sanctification and contributed massively to the education of the youth of Europe. In their extensive missions in Latin America they also provided the plans for economic development. They became the butt of envy and were accused (falsely, as it transpired) of possessing vast wealth and of interfering in political affairs in various countries. Adherents of the Enlightenment regarded them as enemies to be attacked.

The attacks began in Portugal in 1759 when the prime minister, who was a rationalist, and a bitter opponent, helped bring about their expulsion. They were expelled from France in 1764 and from Spain and Latin America in 1767. At the papal conclave of 1769 pressure was put on the candidates for the papacy to commit themselves to the suppression of the society, and in 1773 Pope Clement XIV dissolved the society throughout the world. However, the empress of Russia and the king of Prussia, neither of whom was Catholic, refused to obey this command and the order survived in those countries.

The background to the queries from Ireland and England about the legitimacy of the oaths that were proposed to the Catholics was the abuse Rome had received from the Catholic powers. Roman officials who had come under pressure from Jansenists, Gallicans and the emperor, Joseph II, instinctively resisted any further diminution of papal authority and influence. Hitherto Ireland and England, on the edge of Europe, had caused few of the difficulties that France, Spain, Austria and some smaller states had caused in the eighteenth century. Until his death in 1766 James, the Old Pretender, had nominated almost all the Irish bishops, and there had been scarcely any disputes about his appointments. Otherwise he had made no effort to exert control over the poor and weak churches of his 'dominions'.

The problems of the oaths presented to Rome from Ireland and England in the second half of the eighteenth century were doubtlessly unwelcome. Faced with the bigger issues from the Continent, the oaths must have seemed an unnecessary and bothersome irritant. The problem of allegiance to the Hanoverians ended in 1766 with the death of the Old Pretender. The other issues in the oaths – the denial of the pope's power to depose sovereigns and of his ability to release subjects from obedience, the question of not keeping faith with heretics and even the right to kill them, the pope's power to dispense people from their oaths, the claim to temporal authority in countries – raise questions about the views both of those who drew up the oaths and of the Roman officials who examined them. It seems impossible to believe that governments could then have feared the deposing power of the pope or his possessing temporal authority in their states, much less his ordering the deaths of heretics. The Romans who examined these oaths would have made a case for the pope's right to dispense with the oaths or vows of members of the priesthood or religious orders, but this was not the dispensing power that concerned rulers. The canonists at Rome must have regarded these oaths as insulting to the papacy, and as the claims in them had never been formally repudiated they must not have wished to repudiate them.

Roman officials always upheld papal prerogatives, and the Irish bishops, who were educated in Rome, tended to do likewise. Thomas Burke, the bishop of Ossory, opposed the oath of 1758, and his successor, John Thomas Troy, at first opposed that of 1774. Troy's loyalty to Rome was unquestioned but he was later obliged to adjust his responses somewhat in the light of Irish requirements.

The outbreak of the French Revolution, with its devastating attacks on the church, shocked and horrified Catholics throughout Europe. Church property was nationalized, monasteries and convents were dissolved, apart from those dedicated to education and charitable work, and the taking of religious vows was forbidden. The number of bishops was reduced and dioceses were made to correspond to the civil departments. All bishops and clergy were to be elected by lay bodies and all beneficed clergy were obliged to take an oath of fidelity to the nation, king and law, and to uphold the constitution. Between 30,000 and 40,000 priests fled abroad, 5,000 of whom were welcomed in Britain.

Worse was to follow, as Paris instituted a policy of de-Christianization in 1793 which was widely imitated throughout the country. Attacks on parish churches and clergy increased, clerical dress in Paris was forbidden and all churches in Paris closed. And as the armies of the French republic moved westwards, spoliation of the church in Austrian and German lands followed. In 1796 Napoleon's army moved into Milan and thence took over much of the Papal States. In 1798 the French occupied Rome and applied the principles of the republic by plundering churches, dissolving fraternities, forbidding the taking of new monastic vows, and closing down religious houses. In 1798 Pope Pius VI was forced into exile in Siena and Florence, and the following year he was brought, after a long and difficult journey, to Valence in France, where he died on 29 August 1799. The death of the pope in French exile marked the nadir of papal power in the eighteenth century. Not surprisingly, many revolutionaries congratulated themselves on having finally put an end to the papacy.

At first the slogans of the revolution resonated with those seeking their rights in Ireland. The bishops, many of whom had been educated in France, were appalled by developments there, and denounced the views of those who espoused such democratic ideals. Those ideals were also to some extent appropriated by Ulster Presbyterians, and helped create an atmosphere conducive to rebellion.

Almost four months after the pope's death the cardinals met in conclave in Venice. After a prolonged conclave, Cardinal Chiaramonti was elected and took the name of Pius VII. He chose as his secretary of state the young, able and energetic secretary of the conclave, Ercole Consalvi. Pius was regarded as a gentle, pious, moderate man, and in Consalvi he had a very able and astute assistant, who guided him carefully through the political minefield which lay ahead.

Their first task was the restoration of the church in France. Napoleon, though personally indifferent about religion, was keen for reasons of public order and national cohesion to bring about a satisfactory religious settlement. Negotiations for a concordat proved difficult but Consalvi brought them to a successful conclusion. The first consul (Napoleon) was authorized to nominate the bishops, on whom the pope would, except for grave reasons, confer spiritual jurisdiction or canonical institution. Both bishops and clergy were to receive stipends from the state, and were obliged to take an oath of allegiance. Pius called on all bishops to resign their sees, and among those appointed to the new reduced hierarchy were some from the *ancien régime* and some from the constitutional church.

This was an extraordinary act of authority on the part of the pope. He overturned the Gallican church, which had vindicated its rights against Rome for centuries. Before the revolution no pope would have tried to exercise such control over the French episcopate, and by this action Pius showed that he would not hesitate to take drastic steps for the good of the universal church, should he decide it was necessary.

But when Napoleon promulgated the concordat as a law in 1802, he appended to it the so-called Organic Articles. These imposed some of the old Gallican restrictions in legal and disciplinary matters, and made arrangements for all communications between Rome and the French episcopate to be examined by the state. Professors in the seminaries were obliged to subscribe to the Gallican Articles of 1682. As well as in France, Napoleon also instituted a system of state control modelled on the Organic Articles over the church in what had been the Cisalpine Republic and had become the Republic of Italy. And in the reshaped church in German lands the papacy was also forced to accept the *exequatur* or right of the ruler to examine communications between the bishops and Rome.

In 1806 Napoleon took control of large parts of the Papal States but the pope resisted his attempts to make the Papal States join the continental blockade of Britain – something which won him British gratitude. The French entered Rome in 1808 and in the following year Pius VII was brought to Savona, near the French border. He already had been forced to dismiss Consalvi but he was accompanied by Cardinal Pacca, a tough, determined ultramontane, and several other cardinals. In 1812 the pope and his cardinals were brought to France and Pius did not return to Rome until Napoleon's defeat and surrender in 1814.

Communication with the pope and his immediate advisers was difficult and at times impossible during the years after 1809. In 1814 a major decision was taken at Rome by Monsignor Quarantotti, the vice prefect of the congregation of Propaganda, in the absence of senior prelates. By his rescript of that year he authorized the veto of the British monarch on episcopal appointments, an oath and the *exequatur*. On the pope's return later that year, that decision was cancelled.

As one of the contributors to the victory of the coalition against Napoleon, the pope was invited in 1814 to send a representative to a celebration of the victors in London, and then to the Congress of Vienna, where the map of Europe was to be redrawn. Cardinal Consalvi was welcomed in London and had his portrait painted by Sir Thomas Lawrence for the Waterloo Hall in Windsor Castle along with those of the other leaders.

After the final defeat of Napoleon, Consalvi reorganized much of the papal machinery of government. He drew up concordats with states which invariably gave them a significant input into the nomination of bishops. More than four-fifths of the bishops of the church were appointed by their rulers by the time of Pius' death in 1823.

Napoleon had bullied and insulted the pope, and in France had forced him to make concessions allowing the metropolitans (archbishops) to give canonical institution to bishops, when he had refused to do so. But in spite of all this abuse and discourtesy, which ended in 1814, the papacy emerged stronger from the oppressive treatment meted out by Napoleon to Pope Pius. He was greeted enthusiastically by crowds on his journeys, and this affection led to an increase of reverence for the Holy See and to a greater ultramontanism, which enhanced the role of the Roman congregations as reflecting the authority of the pope.

Pope Leo XII (1823–9) did not pass judgment on any bill or oath from London during his pontificate. Pope Pius VIII, who had taken office just before the act of emancipation was passed, expressed some dissatisfaction with the oath in the act but made no official statement about it. In the hour of their victory Catholics met no opposition from Rome.

THE CATHOLIC CHURCH IN ENGLAND

The Irish hierarchy, though often reduced in numbers when sees were left unfilled for lengthy periods, survived the Reformation in its traditional form. The English and Scottish hierarchies did not survive that religious upheaval. England was left without bishops and was served only by archpriests from 1599 to 1621. One titular bishop, as a vicar apostolic, had charge of the whole country from 1623 to 1624, and was followed by two others from 1634 to 1655 and from 1655 to 1688. In 1688 the country was divided into four districts and a vicar apostolic in episcopal orders and directly under the jurisdiction of Rome was placed over each district. These titular bishops often lived with relatives or landed families and by the early nineteenth century were based in London, Durham, Wolverhampton and Bath. Towards the end of the eighteenth century the Catholic population amounted to about 80,000 or 1 per cent of the population.

Five or six prominent Catholic landlords had held on to their estates in Ireland throughout the political and religious revolutions. In England a larger and more affluent body of aristocrats and gentry kept their lands. They allowed private chapels attached to their houses to be used by the local Catholic communities, and they maintained priests as chaplains. In London there were eight substantial chapels attached to embassies. Otherwise,

Catholics, as their numbers grew in the towns and cities, were served by small, simple chapels. The English Catholics were also subject to the penal laws designed to leave them weak and powerless.

Though attempts were made in the early eighteenth century to draw up an oath acknowledging allegiance to the Hanoverians nothing came of them. No movement towards relief for Catholics occurred until the American War of Independence. The need for more soldiers persuaded the British government to open negotiations with intermediaries about the possibility of recruiting Catholics from the Scottish Highlands. That intervention opened the way for Catholics to begin to seek relief from their most indefensible burdens.

The English Catholic aristocrats wanted to take their place in society alongside Protestant aristocrats. They wanted to get rid of the remaining penal laws which limited their scope for full participation in political and social life. Membership of both houses of parliament would have marked their full acceptance by their Protestant colleagues. Some of them were entitled to sit in the house of lords and others, such as baronets, could have hoped that those who controlled seats in the house of commons might consider them for promotion.

Unlike the middle-class leaders of the Catholic committees or associations in Ireland, they had no political fears about the policies of their government. They did not foresee the government acting against their interests if emancipation were passed. Many of them were prepared to accept the royal veto if it were the price to pay for emancipation. Some of them, accustomed to regard their chaplains in a proprietary way and to contribute to the living costs of the vicars apostolic, regarded their titular bishops as colleagues and friends (and perhaps dependants) who should support their aspirations. Several of the vicars apostolic, who until 1766 were nominated by the Stuarts, were themselves closely related to the aristocracy or gentry as brothers or cousins, and understood the aspirations of their class.

Bishop John Milner, the vicar apostolic of the Midland District from 1803 to 1826, was the son of a London tailor and was totally immune to the superior feelings, elite sentiments and lofty expectations of the aristocrats and gentry who dominated the Catholic committees. Milner believed that the vicars apostolic and not the members of the committee were entitled to give guidance to the Catholic people about what was and was not acceptable as the price of emancipation. For several years the struggle between the combative Milner and some equally combative members of the Catholic Committee dominated the campaign for emancipation. Milner sought the support of the Holy See but weakened his case by the intemperateness of his writings, and his opponents were able to make use of his excess in their communications with Rome.

In the parliaments of 1830 and 1831 English Catholics won seats out of proportion to their numbers.

THE CATHOLIC CHURCH IN IRELAND

In the wake of the Williamite victory in 1691, the parliament of Ireland, representing the propertied Protestants of the country, undertook to ensure that there would be stability in the nation and that the landed property of Protestants would be secure. Hence Catholics were forbidden to buy land and were forced to divide their estates among all the sons of the family (if the eldest became a Protestant he could claim it all). The danger to the Williamite settlement was the claim of the Stuarts to the throne, and when threats of Stuart invasions in 1708, 1717, 1719 and 1720–1 were heard and actual risings occurred in Scotland in 1715 and 1745, tensions rose markedly.

The laws banishing bishops, vicars general, regular clergy and secular clergy who exercised authority in 1697, had they been ruthlessly applied, would have put an end to the priesthood in thirty or forty years. A priest was allowed to register for each parish, and, though stricter laws threatening to impose further hardships on parish clergy were mooted, they did not materialize. By the second decade most of the dioceses were filled and by the 1730s, apart from an occasional incident, most of the clergy were allowed to carry on their pastoral work, quietly and discreetly. The laws forbidding foreign education were likewise not strictly enforced as priests continued to receive their education on the Continent, especially in France. Still, the fear of Irish merchants, soldiers and priests in France teaming up with the French forces to restore the Pretender remained with the Irish Protestant elites until after 1745.

As the bishops were nominated by James, the Old Pretender, their loyalty to the Hanoverians could always be called into question. In 1727 Archbishop Synge, the Protestant archbishop of Tuam, corresponded with Cornelius Nary, a graduate in canon and civil law of the University of Paris, about the terms of an oath which would give Catholics security and assure Protestants of their allegiance. Nary could not accept an oath abjuring the Stuarts though he could pledge allegiance to the Hanoverians. Other proposals for oaths of loyalty were made in the 1720s, and the papal nuncio in Brussels (who represented Rome to the churches in Britain, Ireland and the United Provinces), who held extreme views about pontifical authority objected to them.[1] But these proposals concerned only a few people. There was no public discussion about how Catholics could profess allegiance. The bishops,

---

1 Fagan, *Divided loyalties*, pp 56–70.

who wanted to keep a low profile, sought no such publicity, and, anyhow, they were trapped by the Stuart right of nomination to the episcopate.

Consequent upon the defeat of Prince Charles Edward Stuart in 1745 and the expectation of the final end of the Stuart challenge, the political and religious atmosphere became more relaxed. In 1756, bills were brought forward in the Irish parliament to register parish priests and to expel the regular clergy (who were thought to be more sympathetic to the Stuarts). An oath for the registered clergy was included. A more liberal bill in 1757 met opposition from the Catholic bishops because it authorized the lord lieutenant to fill parish vacancies. Lord Trimleston, a Catholic landlord, invited the archbishop of Armagh and five other bishops from that province to discuss the bill. From their discussions they produced a pastoral letter rejecting some of the claims about papal powers which had been mentioned in the oaths. Other bishops objected to the line taken by this group of bishops, and – led by the archbishop of Dublin – passed on their anxieties to Rome. The fear of starting an argument about papal prerogatives and of antagonizing the Stuart court probably explained the hostility of these prelates to the pastoral.

In 1766 part of these difficulties ceased with the refusal of Rome to allow the Old Pretender's son, Charles Edward, to maintain the right of nomination to Irish sees. The lead in proposing oaths for Catholic relief was taken thereafter by Protestants, and the Catholic bishops played a reactive role.

The revolutionary ideas emanating from France after 1789 duly influenced those campaigning in Ireland for Catholic relief. The Irish Catholic Committee, which had not been active for a few years, was reorganized in 1790. As a result of new electoral arrangements the Catholic aristocrats, who had played a predominant role in it, were replaced by a radical middle-class leadership, which was much more determined to push for the removal of the remaining penal laws.

Within the committee itself a radical group called the Catholic Society was formed and it called for full enfranchisement of Catholics. The conservative aristocrats, lords Kenmare, Fingall and Gormanston, lobbied for an expression of unconditional loyalty to the king. Failing to obtain this they and Archbishop Troy of Dublin, who deplored the excessively democratic theories imported from France, left the committee. With Troy's backing they presented an address seeking the favour of the government. Troy also requested other bishops to obtain signatures to loyal addresses but many of them found little support. The Catholic Committee accused those who seceded from it of creating divisions among the clergy, and published in 1792 its rejection of claims it believed Protestants falsely attributed to the papacy.

Archbishop Troy felt obliged to sign this declaration, realizing the influence and power of Catholic radicals on the committee, and agreed to obtain assistance for their arrangements in electing members to attend a Catholic convention. He and Bishop Moylan of Cork attended some of the sessions, and, on behalf of his colleagues, Troy signed the petition for full political rights that was ordered to be presented to the king. The bishops, realizing the influence and power of the committee, decided that they had no choice but to go along with the more radical demands of its middle-class leadership.

Some of the members on the committee were also involved with the United Irishmen, and as the Presbyterians of Ulster and the Defenders, a Catholic secret society, moved towards rebellion the bishops denounced the threat of violence and called for loyalty and gratitude to the king for the relief already given. The rebellion of 1798, though vehemently opposed by the bishops, was subsequently described by Protestant propagandists as a Catholic conspiracy. Six priests were executed for their parts in it, as were three Presbyterian ministers, but many of the charges made against others were flimsy and unreliable.

With the arrangements for the union of the British and Irish parliaments in the wake of the rebellion came proposals for the payment of the Catholic clergy by the state, and, as a quid pro quo, the right of the king to veto the choice of candidates for the episcopate. The issue of the royal veto was to dominate every move for Catholic emancipation for the next twenty-five years.

The king rejected any suggestion of emancipation in 1801. Catholics could therefore only appeal to parliament for it and they did so in petitions regularly and unsuccessfully. A bill for emancipation presented to parliament in 1813 by Henry Grattan was defeated, but in Rome the acting head of the congregation that had charge of ecclesiastical affairs in Ireland and England decided that its terms permitting the veto of the king could be accepted. This Quarantotti rescript was greeted with anger and contempt by the middle-class members of the Catholic Association, sentiments that quickly spread, and the few bishops who would have accepted the rescript found that they could not resist both the popular opposition and the opposition of their colleagues. The aristocratic members of the association, led by Lord Fingall, were prepared to accept a veto, and seceded from it. Daniel O'Connell and his friends feared that the government might try to use a veto to manipulate the hierarchy and make use of it for political purposes contrary to the interests of Irish Catholics.

In the bills of 1821 and 1825 the veto again met strong opposition, but in the act of emancipation it was not mentioned.

THE ROLE OF THE LEGISLATURES

The Irish parliament, all of whose members were Protestants, was determined to maintain in Protestant hands the land transferred to Protestants in the upheavals of the seventeenth century. It agreed reluctantly to the commissions that examined some of the Jacobite claims to land under the terms of the treaty of Limerick of 1691, but once those were settled the parliament regarded itself as the bulwark of the Protestant land settlement. Only 14 per cent of the land remained in Catholic hands. The Protestant minority considered itself 'the people of Ireland', and felt it had to be very vigilant lest the Jacobites and the French should attempt an invasion of Britain or Ireland.

The laws forbidding education – including education of the clergy – on the Continent were also designed to guard against clerics and Irish soldiers on the Continent stirring up French hostility to Britain. These laws also weakened the future leadership of the Catholic community. During the scares of Jacobite invasions in 1708, 1715, 1745 and to a lesser extent in other years the state paid special attention to rumours of clerical intrigues.

The attitudes of some members of parliament in London and Dublin relaxed after the failure of the rebellion of 1745. The likelihood of another such rebellion had become remote. The first very modest alteration in the law about landed property occurred in 1772 when Catholics were allowed to lease not more than fifty acres of bogland for a period of sixty-one years. And 'from the 1760s onwards the British government's support for the continued exclusion of Irish Catholics from full citizenship would be pragmatic and conditional rather than instinctive and ideological'.[2] In 1778 the British government passed a relief act for English Catholics, to encourage the Irish government to do the same. This allowed Catholics to lease land for 999 years and to inherit property on the same terms as Protestants, thereby ending the division of Catholic-owned estates among all the sons and the right of the eldest son who conformed to Protestantism to claim all the family's land.

Catholic addresses of loyalty to the king increased greatly after this concession. And in the atmosphere created by the Volunteers, with their demands for constitutional change and concessions to Catholics, an act in 1782 allowed Catholics to buy land on the same terms as others and to open schools with the licence of the local Protestant bishops. By the 1790s the British government was concerned to conciliate the Catholics, conscious of the dangers of union between Catholics and Dissenters in Ulster. The government in London, faced with the opposition of members of the Irish parliament to the concession of the franchise, got parliament in 1792 to open

2 Bartlett, *The fall and rise of the Irish nation*, p. 72.

all professions, trades and manufacturers to Catholics. In 1793, after war with France had broken out and the need for Irish manpower in the army increased, the British government got the parliament in Dublin, again reluctantly on the part of some members, to concede to Catholics the right to vote in county elections, to keep arms and to serve on juries. As it was the government in London that was responsible for these concessions, Catholics felt that when union was mooted they could win emancipation more easily from London than from Dublin.

However, they were to find that emancipation had to be wrested from the united parliament after a thirty-year struggle. English people feared the prospect of Catholics sitting in parliament and ultimately, perhaps, having a share in the government of their country, which was, – and they hoped would remain – solidly Protestant. English Protestants regarded the settlement of 1688, which they had drawn up after the expulsion of the Catholic king, as sacrosanct. The fear of Catholicism was perfervid:

> The prospect in the first half of the eighteenth century of a Catholic monarchy being restored in Britain by force, together with the recurrent wars with Catholic states, and especially with France [made it seem] that the old Popish enemy was still at the gates, more threatening than ever before. The struggles of the Protestant Reformation had not ended.[3]

Catholicism was un-English and was not a fitting religion for freedom-loving English people.

In 1780, shortly after the first relief bill for English Catholics was passed, an eccentric Protestant peer, Lord George Gordon, exaggerating the concessions which had been made, sparked off riots in London and to a lesser extent in other cities. Catholic churches and priests' houses were set on fire, and the vicar apostolic in Edinburgh saw his house go up in flames. The houses of some members of parliament who had supported the relief bill were also burned. Eventually the king ordered the army to put down lawlessness on the streets, and it did so by firing on the mob, killing one hundred rioters and wounding over two hundred others. That such a small minority, perhaps 1 per cent of the population, should have been subjected to such violence indicated how deep-seated the anti-Catholic virus could be among some Protestants.

It is against this background that the response of the government to petitions for emancipation has to be understood. That response was a demand for 'securities'. Securities meant taking an oath both of allegiance to

3 Colley, *Britons: forging the nation, 1707–1837*, p. 26.

the king and of renunciation of papal claims. Catholics had been mistrusted as supporters of the Stuarts in the early eighteenth century but after the failure of the rebellion in 1745 there was less reason for such mistrust. When the Vatican in 1766 refused to allow Prince Charles Edward to nominate the Irish bishops the link between the Stuarts and Catholics in Ireland and Britain was virtually broken. But if there was little need to swear to repudiate the Stuarts after Prince Charles' death in 1788, the members of the government favourable to Catholic relief kept insisting that Catholics should give other 'securities'.

The king was to be given the power to veto the appointments of their bishops, and Catholics were to repudiate all papal claims that could infringe the jurisdiction of the sovereign. They were to swear that no pope or foreign prince could have any civil jurisdiction in the realm, and to deny that the pope had any power to dispense subjects from oaths, especially of allegiance. There were other terms about the deposition of princes and the murder of heretics that only religious fanatics could have regarded as having any relevance to Britain. These oaths were seen by some of the bishops and by the officials in Rome as at least offensive and at worst irregular and therefore to be avoided.

The alleged dispensing power of the pope could still cause unease and disquiet. It could have been interpreted as enabling Catholics to give only nominal allegiance to their sovereign, and, when Pope Pius VII was virtually a prisoner of Napoleon, to imply that a national enemy by putting pressure on the pope could attempt to tamper with the loyalty of Catholics. This would have been a contorted conclusion, and, in fact, Pius VII had won British favour by refusing to take part in the Continental blockade of Britain. The Vatican's official policy was to refuse Protestant sovereigns the right of veto in episcopal appointments, and the *exequatur* or right to scrutinize correspondence from the Holy See to the local churches. But Rome could be pragmatic and accept ways of tolerating what it did not formally approve.

Officially, the government claimed that in demanding 'securities', it was merely making the same demands that Catholic states made of the church, but 'securities' were really a sop to the anti-Catholics of Britain; opposition to emancipation was widespread, coming as it did from the churches, the universities, the town councils and other public bodies. Hostility to Irish Catholic workers in the cities and towns in the nineteenth century also helped to swell the thousands of counter-petitions that flooded into Westminster. It took the threat of political upheaval in Ireland to nerve Wellington, the prime minister, and Peel, the home secretary, to face down the king, the Ultra-Tories and the multitudes of anti-Catholics, and push through the bill for emancipation.

1

The beginning of the campaign for
the relief of Irish Catholics

I

The penal laws in Ireland were designed to guarantee the political settlement and confirm Protestant ownership of property in the wake of
King William's victory. The various penalties imposed on Catholics were
framed to ensure that they were so weakened that they could not challenge
the power structure established by parliament in the last decade of the seventeenth century and the first of the eighteenth. The Stuart claimants to the
throne posed a threat to the establishment, and the connection of the Irish
Catholics with the Stuart family ensured that they could be regarded as a
fifth column in the state. The recognition by the papacy of the Stuarts as the
lawful sovereigns of Great Britain and Ireland, and the acknowledgment of
their right until 1766 to nominate the bishops of Ireland, weakened the
claims of Irish Catholics for some amelioration of their lot. But as Ireland
took no part in the rebellions of 1715 and 1745, the fears and suspicions
about their association with the Stuarts began to diminish.

Those fears could be and were occasionally reignited by scare stories of
Catholics collecting money for the Pretender, which would lead in turn to
demands that the anti-popery laws be more rigorously executed. 'Toleration
by connivance' was endangered by rumours of wars between France and
Britain which carried the threat of Stuart involvement. By the 1750s the
likelihood of a Stuart restoration had become remote, and some prominent
Protestants had begun to consider easing the burdens borne by the Catholics.

Taking advantage of this atmosphere and hoping to move beyond the
mere absence of physical oppression, a group of three of the most
prosperous Catholics formed the first Catholic Association in 1760. They
were Charles O'Conor, a landlord, antiquarian and Celtic scholar from
Ballinagare in Co. Roscommon, who was a member of the O'Conor Don
family and a descendant of the last high-king of Ireland;[1] Thomas Wyse, a
landowner, industrialist and entrepreneur from Waterford; and John Curry,
a historian and physician in Dublin whose father had been a wealthy Catholic

---

1 Gibbons and O'Conor, *Charles O'Conor of Ballinagare*, pp 20–7, 81–4; Leighton, *Catholicism
in a Protestant kingdom*, pp 112–27.

merchant. Curry and O'Conor had corresponded about proposals for Catholic relief and had already published pamphlets anonymously appealing for it.[2]

Before this development Lord Limerick had brought in a bill in the Irish parliament in 1756 to have the parish clergy registered by grand juries to regularize their position. (He had complained of the numerous regular clergy in the country, not realizing that in 1751 the Vatican had ordered all novitiates in Ireland to close and had thereby begun to limit their numbers.) Unregistered and regular priests were to be subject to the penalties imposed by the Banishment Act of 1697. This contained an oath requiring the priests to profess allegiance to the Hanoverian succession, to abhor the belief that heretics could be lawfully murdered, that no faith was to be kept with heretics and that anyone could absolve those who took the oath from its obligation. The pope's authority to depose sovereigns was also denied. The bill met opposition from nearly all the bishops of the established church and was, in effect, defeated – much to the satisfaction of many Catholics. A more liberal bill with a simpler oath requiring allegiance to King George and his heirs was brought into parliament the following year. Objections were raised by Catholic bishops and by O'Conor to the proposal that the lord lieutenant be petitioned for the admission of priests to fill vacancies, and to the absence of reference to the role of bishops. This bill was rejected by the Irish privy council, having again been opposed by the archbishops of the established church and other influential members.[3]

While this bill was under discussion Lord Trimleston, a prominent Catholic landlord, invited his friend Archbishop O'Reilly of Armagh, and the bishops of Clogher, Derry, Kilmore, Meath and Kildare to his home to discuss the bill, to anticipate possible developments and to clarify Catholic teaching for Protestants who misunderstood or misrepresented it. They wrote a pastoral letter explaining that their Protestant neighbours often had false views of their doctrines and principles, and, wishing to disabuse them of these notions, had drawn up a formal declaration on such matters, and requested the parish clergy to read both to their congregations. The declaration was the first formal attempt by a group of bishops to rid themselves of Protestant charges and to proclaim their loyalty and obedience to the reigning sovereign. The Seven Years War between Britain and France, begun in 1756, had softened the attitudes of the British government to the Catholics as the possibility of recruiting Catholic soldiers arose.[4]

The declaration, which may have been praiseworthy pastorally but was

---

2 Connolly, *Divided kingdom*, pp 393–4.   3 Fagan, *Divided loyalties*, pp 97–112.   4 The nuncio in Brussels informed the congregation of Propaganda in 1756 that the English minister had assured him that the viceroy was of 'sweet and human manners' and would guarantee protection to the Catholics, if they remained tranquil (APF, SC(Ibernia) 10, ff 528r–530r).

historically inaccurate, began by denying that it had ever been a doctrine or tenet of the Catholic church that the pope or a general council had the power to depose kings. In fact it was unlawful for subjects to commit acts of violence or conspire against their sovereign and government. The belief that the pope had any direct or indirect authority over the temporal powers of princes, or that he could dispense the king's subjects from their allegiance, or license people to take false oaths, cheat or injure anyone under the pretence of promoting Catholicism, was not only denied but also reprobated as abominable and sinful. Finally, Irish Catholics were bidden to be good Christian subjects of the king and charitable, honest and moral neighbours of all men.[5]

The pastoral and declaration were signed by seven bishops, one by proxy. But they were to meet stiff opposition from other bishops. Archbishop Lincoln of Dublin (1757–63) did not make use of them, but instead issued a letter to be read in his churches firmly dismissing any suggestion that Catholics took false oaths, and appealing for divine inspiration in their rulers to move them to moderation and compassion – and the mitigation of the penal laws. A further letter was even more anodyne: it again begged the congregations to pray for moderation in their rulers and trusted that they would show by their discourses their 'just abhorrence to whatsoever may give any the least offence to government'.

Lincoln took fright at the declaration, conveyed his fears to O'Reilly and was commissioned by him to write to the archbishops of Cashel and Tuam to suppress the pastoral. Thomas Burke, a Dominican ultramontane and future bishop of Ossory, who had his own axe to grind with the bishops for their hostility to the regular clergy, which had led to the Roman decree of 1751 obliging them to put an end to their novitiates in Ireland, wrote to Rome lamenting the damage done by the declaration. Archbishop Lincoln also wrote to Rome expounding the anxieties the pastoral had cost him, and the trouble it had provoked, and recounting his own part in negotiating with Archbishop O'Reilly and with his agreement inviting the archbishops of Tuam and Cashel to suppress it. Burke, who had spent several years in Rome, regarded anything that smacked of a diminution of papal authority as improper. Lincoln, though trained in Salamanca, seems to have been afraid of stirring up trouble with Rome by supporting the pastoral.

Cardinal Corsini, the prefect of the congregation of Propaganda, which had charge of Irish affairs, replied in a reasonably restrained fashion. His nuncio in Brussels had 'smelt Gallicanism'.[6] His rebuke was directed more against the imprudence of the authors of the pastoral than against its contents. They were advised to follow the wise example of Catholics in

5 Fagan, *Divided loyalties*, pp 120–3.   6 Corish, *The Catholic community in the seventeenth and eighteenth centuries*, p. 119.

Holland and Germany who lived quietly under Protestant rulers without taking oaths of allegiance to them.[7]

As the charges against the papacy and Catholics condemned in the declaration were to form the core of numerous attempts by Catholics to claim that they were being misjudged, it may be asked what possible errors were contained in them. When the seven bishops insisted that it was never a doctrine or tenet of the church that the pope could dispense subjects from their allegiance to their sovereign, or that he had direct or indirect authority over the temporal power or jurisdiction of sovereigns, they need not have used the word doctrine. Such claims could never have pertained to doctrine, with the possible exception that the pope could claim indirect power for spiritual reasons in the sense that he could condemn legislation or behaviour by a sovereign that was inherently immoral. Many bishops were just not ready to reflect on the charges Protestants made against them, and probably felt that they would have to wait for Rome to make such judgments. And the pledge of loyalty to George II may have been too much for some of those who owed their appointments to the Pretender.

Pope Pius V had excommunicated Queen Elizabeth in 1570, deposed her and released her subjects from allegiance to her. This action had had no effect on Elizabeth's sovereignty, was not welcomed even by other Catholic rulers at the time and harmed rather than helped her Catholic subjects. Since then, no pope had attempted to act in such a high-handed manner, but Pius' treatment of Elizabeth was not forgotten by British Protestants. The likelihood of a pope trying to declare a sovereign deposed was unthinkable, as the Holy See was then under attack from several European governments that had begun to expel the Jesuits. As Rome still recognized James, the Old Pretender, as the rightful king of Great Britain, the Irish bishops could have been accused of rejecting their lawful sovereign, but by 1757 only the most committed supporter of the Stuarts entertained hopes of their being restored to the throne. But as James still enjoyed the privilege of nominating the bishops of Ireland, and as it was not known how long he or his son would retain that privilege, it behoved the bishops whom he had nominated to be circumspect in their proclamations of loyalty to the Hanoverians.[8]

In the long struggle for Catholic relief, the oaths demanded of Catholics were to play a crucial and often divisive role among Catholics both in England and Ireland. The basic requirements of the governments in both countries – that oaths should include the denial of papal power to depose princes and to absolve from oaths (oaths of allegiance and loyalty to governments were

7 Fagan, *Divided loyalties*, p. 119.   8 Cardinal Corsini informed an Irish priest in 1750 that the Stuart right of nomination would cease on the king's death. The Old Pretender lived to be 77 and so he kept the right of nomination until 1766. See Fenning, *The undoing of the friars of Ireland*, p. 232.

generally intended), and that there should be a repudiation of the belief in the legitimacy of murdering heretics or not keeping faith with them – were reasonable. At times, other elements which could be regarded as offensive were added to oaths, but these central points remained.

Theologians in France or in countries influenced by Gallican thought had no hesitation in acknowledging the acceptability of such oaths. Most Irish bishops were educated in France and would not have encountered any exaltation of papal claims. But they were never Gallicans in the sense of accepting conciliar supremacy over papal authority or in not submitting disputes or difficulties to the judgment of Rome. Some of them proved to be very loyal in this respect, and thereby encountered problems with colleagues and political friends.

Officials in the Roman congregations always set great store on precedents and were always very sensitive to any ecclesiastical pronouncement that threatened to diminish papal prerogatives. When faced with queries and disputes, they were inclined to look back to see what decisions had been taken in situations that were supposed to be broadly similar. This seems to have been the explanation for much of their response to the arguments about the content of oaths. Those officials must have known that there was as much chance of a pope deposing a sovereign or releasing subjects from obedience to a ruler, as there was of his calling a crusade against Muslims or even leading an army in defence of the Papal States. But because the actions of Pius V or Gregory VII had never been formally repudiated, it was somehow thought that denying such rights of a pope would be an improper invasion of papal tradition or even a limitation of papal authority.[9] Similarly, there was no likelihood of a pope maintaining that Catholic subjects could kill heretics or break faith with them in defence of religion.

Though papal infallibility was not defined as a doctrine of the faith until 1870, and until then was not accepted as such by Gallicans, Roman theologians and officials generally upheld and defended it, and looked askance at those who denied it. Oaths in which it was repudiated were unwelcome. The denial of papal dispensing power over oaths could also have run counter to the pope's authority to release religious subjects for spiritual reasons from oaths or vows. Releasing Catholics and especially clergy and members of religious orders from the oaths involved in solemn vows was a spiritual prerogative of the pope, but this prerogative was not widely understood to refer to political questions. What concerned rulers was the pope's alleged authority to release Catholics from obedience through mental reservation in taking oaths.[10]

---

9 Gregory VII in his *Dictatus Papae* of 1075 claimed that he had the power to depose emperors.
10 Aubert, Beckmarn, Lill, *Tra rivoluzione e restaurazione*, viii, pp 1, 3–16.

Curial officials in Rome, nuncios and priests trained in Rome were much more likely than theologians and clergy in France, Austria or the German states to emphasize papal prerogatives, and to regard the diminution of such prerogatives by clergy elsewhere almost as a form of disloyalty. The attacks on the Jesuits and their expulsion from Portugal (1759), France (1764), Spain (1767), and, finally, from all other European countries except Prussia and Russia (1773), sharpened the sense of loyalty to the papacy of most Roman prelates and nuncios. The loss of influence in these countries increased the determination and efforts of Roman congregations and their officials to resist attempts, or what they perceived as attempts, to lessen the obedience of Catholics in Ireland and Britain to the Holy See.

The fear of offending the Stuart court probably motivated the archbishop of Dublin and his clergy when they refused to sign addresses of welcome to the new lord lieutenant in 1759 and to the new king, George III, in the following year.[11] The latter address was signed by some six hundred prominent Catholics and a further one was submitted by Lord Trimleston and gentry of his acquaintance. In 1760 the Catholic Association broadened its appeal by organizing an election of nine members from the Dublin parishes and renamed itself the Catholic Committee. It ceased meeting in 1763.[12] But four years later it revived in response to a business dispute, and it met irregularly after that. In 1761 Edmund Burke came to Dublin as secretary to the chief secretary, William Hamilton, who held that post for three years. Burke, an Irish-born and -educated Anglican, whose mother and close relatives were Catholics, sincerely sympathized with the plight of Catholics and was anxious to do all in his power to help them. Though he began writing his *Tract relative to the laws against popery in Ireland* in 1761 it was not completed or published until after his death. Nonetheless, it must be assumed that he tried to influence Hamilton as judiciously as he could in favour of Catholics, and presumably used on him some of the arguments found in his *Tract*. There he argued that a law against the majority of the people constituted general oppression, and noted that 'after almost a century of persecution' Ireland was 'full of penalties and full of papists'.[13]

The aspirations of Catholics for the amelioration of their condition were damaged by the agrarian disturbances of the 1760s provoked by the Whiteboys, mainly in Munster. This unrest was of social and economic origin: poorer tenants took revenge on substantial landowners and farmers who were expanding their grazing lands at the expense of tillage. Though this understanding of the agrarian troubles was generally accepted by the authorities in Dublin, Protestant landlords in the disturbed areas claimed

11 Richard Lincoln was archbishop of Dublin from 1757 to 1763. Fenning, 'The archbishops of Dublin', pp 175–214. 12 Connolly, *Divided kingdom*, p. 393–4. 13 O'Brien, *The great melody*, pp 40–8.

that Jacobites and French sympathisers were involved. Burke's patron, Hamilton, supported a slight measure that was of significance for Catholics; he moved a bill to allow Catholics to enter the military service of Portugal, a British ally, to permit them to fight for Britain. But it was defeated through anti-Catholic hostility.

In 1766 Irish Catholics were at last unburdened of their 'fatal attachment' to the Stuart family.[14] James, the Old Pretender died, and the Vatican refused to recognize his son Charles Edward as king of Great Britain and Ireland, and withdrew the Stuart right to the nomination of Irish bishops. This meant not only that Irish Catholics, gentry, merchants and prominent members of the middle class could proclaim their loyalty to the Hanoverians, but also that they did not come into conflict with the Vatican in doing so. But in the short term Catholics were possibly more endangered by this development, as the Protestant elites were scared by Catholics beginning to claim a place in the sun. The attitudes of the Protestant aristocracy and gentry in Munster to the continued activities of the Whiteboys hardened, and reached a peak with the judicial execution in Clonmel in 1766 of a priest, Nicholas Sheehy, whose life had been falsely sworn away by a clergyman obsessed with the threat of a Catholic rebellion.[15] But in that same year a new lord lieutenant, George Hervey, Lord Bristol, was appointed, and his brother, Frederick, who was named as his chaplain, was destined to play an important role in the country for many years.

Though Lord Bristol never came to Ireland, he nonetheless transferred his brother from the chaplaincy to the bishopric of Cloyne in 1767. A year later Frederick took possession of the rich bishopric of Derry, and in 1779 became by a brother's death earl of Bristol. The bishop was an eccentric and irrepressible aristocrat who, though accused of Machiavellian intent when he referred to divisions which his plans might have caused to Irish Catholics, seems nevertheless to have desired to better their political situation or at least to better the situation of those whom he regarded as trustworthy.

Contemporary churchmen questioned his commitment to Anglicanism and his taste for luxury, and accusations of personal misbehaviour strengthened their scepticism. His motives for involvement with Irish Catholics are not known. Perhaps the sympathy his mother felt for Catholicism and his experiences on the Continent influenced him. Before coming to Ireland he took advantage of his travels in France to consult French bishops and the staff of Irish seminaries in France about the details of an oath which Catholics in Ireland might take to prove their loyalty and be accepted by their rulers. He proposed an oath which differed from that of the Trimleston proclamation by including a repudiation of papal infallibility and a denial of

14 Ó Ciardha, *Ireland and the Jacobite cause, 1685–1766: a fatal attachment.*   15 McDowell, 'Colonial nationalism' in *NHI*, iv, p. 202.

the pope's supremacy over general councils. It called for allegiance to King George where the declaration had merely stated that it was unlawful to do violence against the king or government. It included the rejection of the pope's deposing power,[16] his releasing subjects from obedience and denial of claims to temporal supremacy over monarchs, as well as a pledge to 'abhor, detest and abjure … as pernicious and abominable the doctrine that faith ought not to be kept with … heretics or excommunicated princes'. The Gallican bishop of Toulouse, to whom he showed the oath, approved strongly of it. For those who took the oath Hervey held out the prospect of registered priests being recognized to practice their religion – this, in effect, was already happening – and freedom for Catholics to purchase land. Maintaining that the Protestant interest would be strengthened by division among the papists, he did not indicate how he foresaw the breakdown in numbers or how many his oath could help.[17]

Information about the oath reached the nuncio in Brussels, who acted on behalf of the congregation of Propaganda with the churches in Britain, Ireland and the United Provinces (Holland). The nuncio, Archbishop Ghilini, passed on a translation of it to Propaganda, which in turn sought an opinion from the Holy Roman and Universal Inquisition, which dealt with issues relating to faith and obedience to the teaching authority of the church. The oath was examined at a full meeting of the Holy Roman and Universal Inquisition on 17 September 1768 and a minute for a reply by the nuncio to Ireland was prepared and sent to the congregation of Propaganda. In it the nuncio was bidden to act in that very grave affair with all diligence and to keep the Holy Office informed about developments. Recalling that Hervey's oath had been proposed to Catholics in Dublin and to some bishops who were not opposed to it, the minute noted that while the archbishop of Dublin was suspected of being favourable, the archbishop of Armagh definitely was. The nuncio was invited to communicate with the prelates in a gentle way.[18]

Executing this order Ghilini sent a letter to Archbishop Fitzsimons of Dublin on 14 October 1768, which was also intended for the other archbishops. Ghilini, who was an extreme conservative, decided that the situation called for a strong response. In blunt language he alerted the four metropolitans, through Archbishop Fitzsimons, to the very grave misfortune

---

16 Constitution 3 of the Fourth Lateran Council (1215) laid down the right of the pope to depose sovereigns for reasons of heresy: 'si vero dominus temporalis, requisitus et monitus ab ecclesia, terram suam purgare neglexerit comprovinciales episcopos excommunicationis vinculo innodetur; et si satisfacere contempserit vinculo infra annum, significetur hoc summo pontifici, ut ex tunc ipse vassallos ab eius feditate denunciet absolutos et terram exponat Catholicis occupandam, qui eam exterminatis hereticis absque ulla contradictione possideant et in fide; puritate conservent, salvo iure domini principalis, dummodo super hoc ipse nullam prestet obstaculum …' 17 Walsh, *Frederick Augustus Hervey.* 18 ACDF, SO, Dubia Varia, 1766–78, N8, 14 Sept. 1768; APF, SC(Ibernia), 11, ff 437r–439r.

which was being prepared – and already had been in part carried out – for the spiritual damnation of their miserable people. He had learned from reliable witnesses that several lay persons including clerics and even bishops had not blushed to take the oath and that others were prepared to do so. If the government introduced that most pernicious novelty threatening the banishment of Catholicism, no Catholic should yield to such unreasonable violence. After all Catholics for a long time had with the greatest edification and exemplary constancy endured the penal laws, which though severe, were not entirely hostile to the profession and exercise of the Catholic religion. They were now of their own accord surrendering to a man from the flock of the pseudo-reformers to commit a reprehensible act. And so intolerable and scandalous was that act that the Holy See, the custodian of the integrity of their religion, was compelled to shackle it by a public censure.

It was intolerable for Catholic prelates to swear that faith could not be kept with heretics, or that princes excommunicated by the pope could not be deposed or killed by their subjects. That teaching had been defended and propounded by many Catholic nations and the Apostolic See had often followed it in practice. For a Catholic man it was not proper to call it 'detestable' and 'abominable'; such an assertion would be 'rash, false, scandalous and injurious to the Holy See'. As the laws of England and Ireland recognized the king as head of the church and source of all spiritual authority, the person who swore such an oath promising allegiance to the king must recognize him as head of the church and source of its spiritual authority. If that was the correct understanding of the words then the archbishop and any Catholic should realize that this was a manifest error and directly contrary to the principles of the Catholic religion which only acknowledged the pope as the head and source of spiritual authority. The oath was therefore deserving of reproach and detestable since God was called to witness and defend error.

As it was so irregular and reprehensible, understandably the pope would be greatly grieved when he heard that Catholic laity, clerics and even bishops had offered to take it, even though the government did not oblige them to do so, and without first consulting the Holy See in the spirit of filial obedience to the Vicar of Christ, their pastor, head and centre of Catholic unity to whom the noble Irish nation had always professed veneration.

Lest he be seen to be deficient in his sense of duty he felt obliged to write to the archbishop to excite his pastoral zeal, and therefore advised him to apply remedies with great efficacy and prudence to prevent further developments in this pernicious and scandalous disorder. He should recall to their duty those who had given scandal by taking an oath which was illicit and invalid and which was null and void as regards binding consciences. It was to be made known by the most opportune and efficacious means to the suffragan bishops, and by them to all the faithful, what a grave sin those who had taken it, or were prepared to take it, committed.

Catholics should all be encouraged to continue enduring the penal laws, which they had done with such constancy, rather than having recourse to an illicit and sinful oath, with such great damage to their own souls and to their religion. That religion was so threatened that it would perish in the hearts of those Catholics who instead of listening to their pastors and supreme pastor, listened rather to the false suggestions of the enemies of their holy faith.[19]

The vigorous defence of the deposition of princes by the pope and faith not being kept with heretics, and the vehement repudiation of the use of the words 'abhor', 'detest', 'abominable' and 'pernicious' as applied to them must have bewildered the Seville-educated Fitzsimons. Defence of such outmoded claims must have seemed incomprehensible to clergy living under a Protestant government in the late eighteenth century. Perhaps, the very terms used in denouncing such actions had riled the officials at the Vatican. But the difficulty about the king's headship of the established church and the confusion about allegiance possibly involving spiritual obedience to which Ghilini referred seemed ambiguous and could be understood as the denial of the pope's supremacy in the universal church. The fact that the oath was to be interpreted according to the words used by the legislators might mean that their interpretation of the king's power and authority, perhaps including the spiritual, was to be accepted. Protestant fears of the pope granting the right of 'mental reservation' were also excluded by the reference to 'the words used'.

Fitzsimons very wisely did not publicize this vehement broadside. Realizing the immense harm it would do to their chances of some relief, he passed on its contents privately. Presumably the other archbishops did the same. The letter was not publicized until 1772, four years later, when Thomas Burke, the bishop of Ossory and a strenuous opponent of oaths of that nature, included it in a new edition of his work, *Hibernia Dominicana*.[20] The archbishop of Dublin was put in a very difficult position by this letter.[21] He had had discussions with Hervey and felt that the bishop was making a serious effort to get some relief for Catholics. His experience in London and Brussels had given him an awareness of the various currents of thought in the church, helping him to see that views other than Ghilini's were deserving

19 Ghilini to Fitzsimons, 14 Oct. 1768 in Wall, *Hibernia Dominicana*, pp 925–8 and SC(Ibernia) 11, ff 437r–439v. 20 Archbishop Butler of Cashel and his suffragans were greatly angered by the inclusion of this letter by Burke, as they feared a hostile Protestant reaction to it. When prevented by Burke from meeting in his diocese to denounce it, they took out pages praising James II's and later Stuart support for Catholics from that edition. 21 Fitzsimons, born in 1695, was educated in Seville, ordained in 1720 and obtained a doctorate in divinity. He spent some time at the Spanish Embassy in London and in the nunciature in Brussels before returning to Dublin and becoming archbishop in 1763. Fenning, 'The archbishops of Dublin' in Kelly and Keogh, *History of the Catholic diocese of Dublin*, pp 175–214.

of consideration. His reply to Ghilini was conciliatory but he insisted that some kind of oath of a similar nature could be drawn up to suit the requirements of both parties.

He told Ghilini that in response to Hervey's requests he had invited the other archbishops and their suffragans to come to Dublin to see what they should do. He had discussed the oath at a meeting with some of his clergy, who concluded that with a few corrections it could be taken safely. Two bishops had been present and had agreed with the other clergy about it, but one of them subsequently backtracked on his opinion. However, as the oath had not been discussed in parliament it did not have the force of law. He wanted, however, to assure the nuncio that the king was not being recognized as the head of their church by Catholics; indeed in an appendix the primacy of the church was explicitly attributed to the Roman pontiff and refused by Catholics to the king.

Fitzsimons agreed that the right of the pontiff in the temporalities of kings had been acrimoniously defended by scholars and theologians. Irish Catholics, however, were not concerned with the temporal rights of the papacy vis-à-vis kings. Their concerns were the penal laws, and all the persecutions and loss of property they had suffered. They thought it better to make some concessions to parliament rather than to see their religion exterminated. Fitzsimons defended the Irish clergy from any charge that they upheld the Gallican articles. During their studies in France – like other graduates – they subscribed to the articles, but that was merely the practice at the time. It was part of the obedience due to the French king, and was important only because it led to disputes and strife. Finally, he noted that Hervey had been made aware of these difficulties but had insisted that the propositions in his oath had been accepted for a long time by French clergy and would soon be accepted by clergy in Spain, Portugal and other countries. He therefore asked the nuncio to supply him with plausible reasons for justifying to the government their refusal to accept articles that were accepted by ecclesiastics in other kingdoms who were in communion with the Holy See. He would have had more to write on the subject if the other archbishops and their suffragans had openly declared their opinions on it. Only the archbishop of Armagh had done so, and he had said that, if the oath were amended a little, it would not displease him – a view which the writer regarded as just and very necessary. Judging from the attitude of the other bishops it seemed they were only anxious about the advantage the oath might bring them. But he had recommended the wish of the nuncio to his own suffragans and was confident that they would not fall short in their duty.[22]

Further letters on the oath were forwarded to the nuncio from

22 Fitzsimons to Ghilini, 1768 in Moran, *Spicilegium Ossoriense*, iii, pp 315–17.

Propaganda in 1769. The prefect noted that the archbishop of Tuam and the bishop of Ossory were very opposed to it. He was not able to give a definite answer on the oath, because of the sudden death of the pope, but he trusted none of the bishops would approve the formula.[23] The nuncio was encouraged to strengthen resistance to the oath and to do so with all possible speed, and was commissioned to write two letters, one to the archbishop of Dublin and one to the other archbishops. He was provided with a minute or plan for each letter.

The minutes for both repeated much of what Ghilini had already written. In both he was told to emphasize the constancy of the Irish in the past and to state that those who took the oath were not worthy of that heroic tradition. It was pointed out that allegiance to the king meant obedience to him as head of the church, which was 'a manifest error'. The archbishop of Dublin was to be informed that the nuncio was glad to hear that no one had taken the oath since his letter of October. If the government had been threatening Catholicism with desolation, it still would not have been excusable for a Catholic to take the oath, but those who did so would have been less unworthy of compassion. To swear according to its terms was greatly sinful and religion would perish in the heart of those Catholics who listened to the false insinuations of the enemies of Catholicism. The letters to both parties were written on 3 March 1769.[24]

The archbishop of Tuam and the bishop of Ossory were not alone in opposing the oath. The archbishop of Cashel and his suffragan, John Butler, the bishop of Cork (and future Lord Dunboyne) also did so. The Catholic Committee seems not to have been involved in any negotiations with Hervey about the oath. Protestants who became aware of Ghilini's letter when it was published in 1772 in *Hibernia Dominicana* must have concluded that Catholic pledges were at the very least questionable, when the oath had been so comprehensively condemned by the nuncio. They regarded it as containing the basic denials of the papal pretensions that they felt had threatened them, and freedom from which was a condition of relief from some of the restrictions burdening the Catholics. Some of them must have concluded, like Ghilini, that Catholics should be left to the full thraldom of the penal laws.

Undaunted, Hervey persisted in his attempts to learn what Catholics would be prepared to accept in an oath of allegiance. The first chink of light in relief for Catholics had appeared in 1772 with the act which permitted them to take leases of bogland of not more than fifty acres for sixty-one years. Hervey spent that year on the Continent, where he had several audiences with Pope Clement XIV and discussed the nature of an oath for Irish Catholics. Clement, who was coming under intense pressure from

23 Pope Clement XIII died on 2 Feb. 1769 and his successor was not elected until 19 May 1769.
24 APF, *Acta* 164, ff 404r–418r, and SC(Ibernia), II ff 441r–442r, 445r–448r.

powerful countries on the Continent to abolish the Jesuit society, does not seem to have agreed even vaguely on any formula. On his way home Hervey spent time as the guest of Cardinal de la Rochefoucauld in Rouen where doubtless this strong Gallican reassured him about the propriety of taking an oath without excessive obeisance to Rome.[25] On his return to Ireland Hervey contacted Charles O'Conor and recommended that Catholics should take an oath of allegiance with a view to some relief from the penal laws. The Catholic Committee, on being informed of his demarche, agreed to produce a profession of their principles and a subcommittee was appointed to produce an oath. As a formula was being processed Archbishop John Carpenter was shown a draft which he found acceptable. The draft, however, was somewhat altered before it was submitted to Hervey.

Carpenter had become archbishop of Dublin in 1770 and attitudes to Hervey's oaths had played an important part in his promotion. John Thomas Troy, the prior of San Clemente in Rome, had submitted the names of those whom the religious orders thought should be excluded from the succession. They wanted to exclude especially Christopher Bermingham, the vicar capitular, who was the intimate counsellor of the late archbishop and the promoter of the oath proposed by the Protestant bishop of Derry, which was injurious to the Catholic faith and to the Holy See.[26] Carpenter, who had been educated at the Irish College in Lisbon, was a Gaelic scholar and as a friend of some members of the Catholic Committee had been sent on business by them to London. Viscount Taaffe supported his candidature for Dublin, as did Thomas Burke, the bishop of Ossory, who maintained that he would profess sound doctrine and would oppose illicit oaths.[27]

Robert French, the member for Roscommon, presented the heads of a bill enabling Catholics to testify their allegiance to the king. This chimed well with instructions given to the lord lieutenant from London to ease the legal position of Catholics. And French's bill, with its oath, quickly went through parliament and received the royal assent in June 1774. This oath could be taken before a judge of the king's bench in Dublin, a justice of the peace or a magistrate, and the names of Catholics who took it would be passed to the clerk of the privy council. Despite some hair-splitting comments by Charles O'Conor there was no substantial difference between the terms of the oath proposed by the Catholic Committee and that passed by parliament. The parliamentary form was longer and concluded with a promise about making the declaration without a dispensation granted by the pope or the see of

25 Walsh, *Frederick Augustus Hervey*, p. 20. Some years later Troy, as archbishop of Dublin, commented that Hervey was opposed to Catholic beliefs, especially papal supremacy, and that he was regarded as a mischief-maker (Troy to Dillon, 18 Sept. 1783, DDA). 26 Troy to Propaganda, no date, APF, CP 137, f 243rv. 27 Burke to Propaganda, 27 Jan. 1770, ibid., f 266r; MacGiolla, 'Dr John Carpenter, archbishop of Dublin (1770–86)', *Dublin Hist. Rec.*, 30:1

Rome, and without anyone thinking that the swearer could be acquitted before God or man or absolved even though the pope should dispense or annul it or declare that it was null and void from the beginning. Otherwise both contained the same promise of allegiance to George III and resistance to any conspiracies against him, the succession of George's family and renunciation of Charles Stuart.

Any claim of a pope, prince or other prelate to temporal or civil authority in the kingdom was denied, as was any claim by the pope to the power to depose princes, or, if they were deposed, that they might be murdered. And denial of any belief in the lawfulness of murdering heretics and not keeping faith with them was also pledged. O'Conor's objection that Catholics were obliged to swear that they already had no dispensation from the pope to evade the commitments of the oath had force: it was undoubtedly insulting to Catholics to suggest that they could have papal permission in advance to commit in effect a form of perjury.[28] And like various oaths tendered to Catholics subsequently, the insensitivity of the language used rather than the actual claims renounced caused them pain and led to their resistance.

The British government would have been happy to lend its support to the first modest acknowledgment of Catholic loyalty and recognize those who took the oath. With the dangers of hostilities breaking out between Britain and her American colonies, the loyalty of Irish Catholics and the possibility of recruiting soldiers from Ireland took on a new importance. Similarly the loyalty of the Catholics of Quebec for the same reasons was also sought in the Quebec Act of 1774.[29]

Though the bill became law in June 1774 no Catholic took the oath for a full year until Lord Trimleston led a group of friends to do so. That broke the ice and gradually others of the middle class followed suit. O'Conor, who had quibbled about minor details, also took it. Though the oath conferred no benefits it paved the way for further concessions. And if the oath found a foe in Archbishop Carpenter of Dublin, who opposed it without pointing out a specific article in it which violated church teaching or discipline, it also found an advocate in the far abler and much more learned archbishop of Cashel.

Carpenter, who proved to be a rigorist, wrote to the vigilant Ghilini about the oath, and Ghilini, recalling his previous condemnation of an oath in accordance with instructions from Rome submitted a copy of it to Propaganda.[30] He reported that the worthy Archbishop Carpenter as a good pastor had fulfilled his duty, but he did not believe that the prelate's zeal was sufficient to put the brake on the other bishops and priests. Only the resolutions of the congregation of Propaganda could block unworthy ways of

(1976), 2–17; Kelly, 'The impact of the penal laws' in *History of the Catholic diocese of Dublin*, pp 166–71. **28** Fagan, *Divided loyalties*, pp 138–45. **29** Bartlett, *The rise and fall of the Irish nation*, pp 80–1. **30** Ghilini to Propaganda, 18 Aug. 1775, APF, SC(Irlanda), 12, ff 63r–64r.

thinking and make those of that cast of mind recognize the poisonous doctrine in the oath. Thomas Burke of Ossory had already bypassed the nuncio in his determination to obtain a verdict from Propaganda. He sent a copy of the oath in English and explained that a letter from the nuncio did not carry sufficient weight. He argued therefore that, if Rome did not pass judgment on it, all the people of his diocese and indeed of the whole country, despite the reservations of Carpenter, that champion of the faith, and the archbishop of Tuam and other prelates, would conclude that it was lawful.[31] A formal letter to the same effect was later forwarded by the persistent and intransigent Carpenter, bearing the signatures of Burke and of the bishops of Ferns and Ardagh. They claimed that some prelates were too keen on the temporal emoluments of the country, and thought the penal laws would disappear if Catholics took the oath. They insisted, on the other hand, that Catholics would gain nothing by taking it and would lose nothing by refusing it. To prevent schism, they sought a decisive and categorical answer from Rome.[32]

II

James Butler, a descendant of Viscount Mountgarret, president of the supreme council of Catholics at Kilkenny in the 1640s, and the son of an extensive landholder in Co. Kilkenny, was born in 1743. Aged about 17, he enrolled in the seminary of St Sulpice in Paris, and after some time there moved on to the college of St Omer, where Alban Butler, the distinguished English scholar, was rector. Ordained a priest in 1771, he became a professor of rhetoric in the college at Alban Butler's suggestion, and two years later his name was put forward for the coadjutorship of the archbishopric of Cashel. In a letter of commendation to Propaganda, Alban Butler nearly ran out of superlatives in supporting James Butler's candidature. He described James as 'excellently versed in all manner of sacred learning' and paid glowing tribute to his 'unstained innocence of life, his holiness of character, his divine spirit of prayer, his zealous practice of every virtue, his wonderful modesty, humility, mortification, his tenderest charity, and effusive liberality'. Coming from the erudite Alban Butler, who had studied and written about the lives of saints, this was a powerful encomium, and doubtless helped to secure the coadjutorship for James Butler. Appointed in 1773, he remained in St Omer acting as the local vicar-general until he took possession of the see in September 1774, shortly after French's bill was passed. James Butler, as his

31 Burke to Propaganda, 3 July 1775, ibid., ff 196r–198v.   32 Carpenter and others to Propaganda, 14 Nov. 1775, ibid., f 262rv.

friend had indicated, was clever and learned, and a catechism he later wrote was widely used in English-speaking countries for many years.[33]

James Butler, whose studies had given him a wider grasp than many of his colleagues of the theological thought and attitudes to Roman discipline in the schools of several European countries, saw no reason to oppose the oath. He and his six suffragans met in Cork in July 1775 and issued a statement declaring that the oath contained nothing contrary to Catholic principles. They wrote to Rome claiming that the oath put forward by parliament was consonant with that proposed by the archbishop of Dublin and several nobles and other gentlemen at a meeting in Dublin. Many Catholics in Munster – where Catholics were coming under attack from very hostile Protestants, who threatened the closure of chapels – felt that there was a great need for an oath. In letters to Cardinal Castelli, the prefect of Propaganda, in the following year Butler set out the reasons for his actions. The king, he explained, wishing to show kindness to Catholics, and, learning that an oath hostile to the Holy See had been proposed by Protestants, deigned to have his ministers introduce a new formula which was in no way repugnant to their faith. The king and his ministers did so to close the mouths of malevolent people who were no less hostile to him than to the Catholics and who had contended that the Catholics of the kingdom, because of their devotion to the Roman pontiff, were unfaithful to the monarch. They therefore argued that it would be very imprudent to mitigate the most salutary bitterness of the laws, which were drawn up for the purpose of preventing papists from committing evil against the king or his kingdom.

The formula had been introduced at an opportune time, for in the province of Munster, peace had been disturbed by nocturnal plundering and various crimes had been perpetrated by the lower orders against those who collected tithes for the Protestant clergy. Consequently, the suspicion was spread abroad that evil was being planned by Catholics. The king's ministers thought the time was ripe for an oath of allegiance whereby Catholics could free themselves from danger and suspicion. The Catholic archbishop of Dublin and several nobles drew up an oath at a meeting in Dublin which, according to him, all Catholics could take with a safe conscience. They were not consulted about this in Munster. Parliament then passed a bill with an oath which many Catholics in Dublin took, arguing that it was similar to that which the archbishop had approved. A pamphlet then appeared seriously attacking the parliamentary oath, which hurt many Catholics in Dublin who had already sworn. They feared that this pamphlet – which was not unknown to or opposed by the archbishop – would damage the Catholic body.

33 Power, 'The Most Revd James Butler, DD', *IER*, 3:13 (Apr. 1892), 302–18, 522–38; Leighton, *Catholicism in a Protestant kingdom*, pp 145–52.

As many Dublin Catholics continued to take the oath the Calvinists in Munster, seeing that none in the province were professing allegiance to the king, began to allege that the prelates and priests there were supporters of the Stuart family and of pontifical power in temporal affairs. Among the enemies of the Catholics were some who threatened the closure of Catholic chapels, the jailing of priests and other similar vexations.

Leading Catholic laity in the province, anxious for the well-being of their co-religionists, were urging the bishops to take the oath, especially as they could, like the Dublin Catholics, do so with a clear conscience. The laymen added that the silence of the bishops gave a bad impression to the Calvinists, and that they should openly declare to the Catholic people that there was nothing contrary to the faith in the oath. The bishops of Munster were persuaded that it was not the mind of the Holy See to impose on the ill-treated Catholics of the kingdom a yoke of conscience heavier than the subjects of Catholic kings were accustomed to bear. The visits of the king's brothers to the pope had stirred the benevolence of the king and they hoped that in the next session of parliament laws would be introduced for the common good which would deter Catholics, who, for the protection of property, joined the Protestant church each year. The prelates of Munster had therefore, before conveying their views, decided to consult the theological schools of Paris and elsewhere, all of which unanimously replied that there was nothing dangerous or contrary to faith in the oath.

The archbishop of Dublin had consulted the pope and the congregation of Propaganda about the oath. He had written urgently to the archbishop to learn the tenor of the letter that had come from Rome about the oath but had received no reply even though lengthy letters had been sent to others both in Ireland and England. Fearing that the sense of the oath might not have been accurately conveyed to Rome he attached a translation of it together with the introduction to it. This preamble declared that Catholics wished to profess their loyalty to the king and their aversion to beliefs imputed to them, so that odious suspicions would be abolished, and all could testify their loyalty to the monarch in the future. The purpose of parliament in proposing this oath was to extinguish enmities which originated not from the actual doctrines of the Catholic church but from those attributed to her by malevolent people, and it was not the intention of parliament that the oath should contain anything contrary to or contemptuous of the dogmas of the faith or the authority of the church. The Protestants knew that Catholics always rejected formulas of oaths because something offensive to the faith was detected in them.[34]

34 Butler (and others) to Propaganda, 15 July 1775, 7 June 1776, 4 Oct. 1776, APF, SC(Ibernia) 12, 490r–491v, 457r–458r, 492r–494v. Moran, *Spicilegium Ossoriense*, iii, pp 341–9. Arthur O'Leary, a well-known Irish Capuchin priest and writer, stationed in London, wrote a pamphlet, 'Loyalty asserted or the new test oath vindicated', opposing the right of the Stuarts to allegiance,

In the absence of the nuncio the administrator of the nunciature had written to Rome in 1775 on receipt of the first letters and information about the oath, drawing attention to the opposing responses and presumably hoping for guidance. Seemingly no judgment was forthcoming, and so Carpenter wrote again in 1776 claiming that the majority and wiser bishops found the oath incompatible with good morals and the true doctrine of the church, and therefore dangerous. Despite not having consulted the Holy See, the bishops of Munster (Cashel, Cork and Waterford) took the oath and laity and religious bound themselves by it, thus arousing hatred against those who refused it. And they did not hesitate to attack the bishop of Ossory, a pious and learned man, a strong defender of the Catholic faith and strong opponent of the oath. Carpenter then went on to complain that Butler had written to supporters of the oath in Dublin defending his views and methods and praising Cardinal Marefoschi, the cardinal protector of Ireland. He was suspicious of any letters from Marefoschi, wondering how he could approve of what the congregation of Propaganda had condemned. As the archbishop of Cashel was so determined to win supporters it was necessary to have the whole question examined. The bishops of Ferns, Ossory, Ardagh and Elphin signed a postscript with Carpenter maintaining that those who favoured the oath claimed that Christians were not freed from its obligations even if the church were to declare it null and void.[35]

The difference of opinions between the Munster and Leinster bishops seems to have depended on the forthright views of the archbishops. The learned and confident Butler, with the approval of the University of Paris, did not hesitate to accept the oath, but the cautious and conservative Carpenter did. The administrator of the nunciature promptly forwarded Carpenter's letter to Rome with the comment that the archbishop of Dublin and others sought a solemn condemnation of the oath. They had asked him to use his offices for that purpose, but he felt that a full explanation was available to the congregation.[36]

Rome was thus presented with a hierarchy divided over the admissibility

rejecting any claim of the papacy to the power to depose or murder princes or heretics, quoting historical examples of the repudiation of these views from the scripture to the fathers of the church, and on to more modern times. Carpenter complained about the 'wild Capuchin of Cork' (Carpenter to Sweetman, 23 Nov. 1775, DDA).   35 Carpenter and others to Propaganda, 9, 12 Mar. 1776, APF, SC(Ibernia) 12, ff 348r–349r. Carpenter also accused Butler of having a pamphlet printed attacking his arguments against the oath. Fagan attributed this pamphlet to a priest from the diocese of Ossory who argued that like Catholics in Silesia or Canada, the Catholic swore allegiance not to the religion of a Protestant but to his 'personage' (Fagan, *Divided loyalties*, p. 158). Carpenter, bewailing the 'odious affair' that 'has caused such a scandalous schism amongst us', prayed that God would 'preserve the little remains of religion that exists among us' (Carpenter to Sweetman, 23 Nov. 1775, DDA).   36 Administrator of nunciature to Propaganda, 22 Mar. 1776, APF, SC(Ibernia) 12, f 359rv.

of the oath. When possible, in situations like that, the tradition of the Roman authorities is to avoid giving a black-and-white verdict which could leave one side crowing over the defeat of the other. And on this occasion Rome strove to do precisely that. The secretary of the congregation replied to Burke of Ossory. Archbishop Borgia drew attention to that part of the oath where the person taking it swore that he rejected the opinion that the pope had the power to free subjects from an oath of loyalty to their rulers, despite the fact that almost all the old theologians, many of them men of eminent learning and sanctity, and general councils had supported that teaching which was confirmed by the weightiest reasons. This implied that no one could be absolved from such an oath and that it could not be nullified by a decision of the pope. There was a danger then that men could take impious oaths which they knew to be false. Nonetheless, the congregation had decided that if the pope declared the oath inadmissible, as Paul V had done,[37] it would be dangerous and could do more harm than good. Borgia explained that in other countries – particularly Holland – forms of oath very similar to that under discussion had been prescribed, and the Holy See had neither approved of them nor condemned them. The same approach was advisable; a public declaration about the oath would arouse old hatreds and draw down the displeasure of the civil authorities on the Holy See and, in consequence, the Catholic faith would suffer greatly and, perhaps, be completely destroyed. But if the Holy See abstained from issuing a formal public decree, it did not follow that the oath was to be accepted; nor did it follow that it was not right for bishops and those in charge of the faithful to dissuade their subjects from taking such a dangerous and obnoxious oath. It was their duty to admonish the faithful privately to prevent them from substituting for their religion opinions harmful to the rights of the Holy See and damaging both to the church and truth. Should the people not listen to such advice all they could do was to pray that such new and disturbing opinions would have no effect, and that the peace of Ireland would not be affected.[38]

The recipients of this advice could certainly have been excused for being bewildered by such convoluted reasoning. If the oath was blameworthy, why should it be only discreetly declined? No serious argument was brought forward to challenge it. Its unacceptability apparently depended on former opinions of theologians and councils about the deposing power of the pope, and the idea that the rejection of the power to release subjects from their obligation to their rulers was somehow injurious to the pope. That this could lead to people taking impious oaths about false matters conducive to spiritual harm was certainly a contorted and opaque comment. But since this answer

37 Paul V had condemned the oath proposed by James I to the Catholics of England and Ireland in 1606.   38 Borgia to Burke, 6 Jan. 1776, quoted in Giblin, 'Nunciatura di Fiandra', *Coll. Hib.*, 11 (1968), 64–6.

was not published it did not cause public harm. This letter arrived before Carpenter's jeremiad about the oath and by then other bishops and several priests and many laymen were joining Butler and his friends in taking the oath.[39]

The British parliament in 1778 brought in a relief act for English Catholics, the main purpose of which was to encourage the Irish parliament to do the same. This abolished the archaic act of 1700 by which bishops, priests and schoolmasters could be imprisoned for coming to England, and allowed Catholics to inherit and buy land. To benefit from this Catholics were obliged to take an oath similar to the Irish oath of 1774.[40] The Irish act of 1778 repealed the penal law whereby a Catholic landowner had to bequeath his land by dividing it among all his sons, and which allowed the eldest son, on becoming a Protestant, to claim the estate. Catholics who took the oath of 1774 could take leases of land for 999 years or five lifetimes; this was a very beneficial corrective to the legal prohibition which prevented Catholics investing in land. It also gave a psychological boost to Catholics by removing yet another impediment to their sense of citizenship. The resistance to the oath was now crumbling and Carpenter, its main opponent, took it in 1778. Even Propaganda's hostile ambiguity about the oath softened. Archbishop Borgia wrote to say that it had neither approved nor disapproved of the oath, but noting that many bishops in England and Ireland had taken it, decided that under the prevailing circumstances acceptance of it was the best solution.[41]

III

In the latter stages of the dispute over the oath an appointment was made to the bishopric of Ossory, which was to have profound significance and importance for Irish Catholics. John Thomas Troy, a Dublin-born Dominican, aged 46 joined the hierarchy. He had spent the previous twenty-one years in Rome as a student, and later as a priest at San Clemente, the Irish Dominican house where for the last six years he had been prior. Clever and learned, able and energetic he spoke and wrote Latin and Italian fluently, and during his years in Rome had made the acquaintance of several prelates in the curia, in particular Archbishop Borgia, who was secretary of Propaganda from 1770 to 1789 and who subsequently became pro-prefect and prefect of the congregation from 1798 to 1804. Both Borgia and a later critic of Troy, the Scots

39 Walsh, *Frederick Augustus Hervey*, p. 24.   40 Bartlett, *The fall and rise of the Irish nation*, pp 82–6.   41 Troy disliked the obligation imposed by the act of 1778 on people to take the oath before they could avail of its benefits (Troy to Propaganda, 13 June 1778, APF, SC(Ibernia) 13, ff 341r–342r).

priest, Paul Macpherson, claimed that this friendship was instrumental in Troy's appointment and subsequent promotion to Dublin.[42]

The appointment (as was later to happen with Paul Cullen) was in fact a prudent practical decision by the Roman curia to have a bishop or primate in Ireland whom it knew and whose opinions and reports it could trust. It also overcame disputes within the diocese of Ossory about the oath, as the leading local candidate, Patrick Molloy, was favourable to it. And he enjoyed the strong support of the archbishop of Cashel, five suffragans of Cashel and three other bishops, who wrote to Cardinal Marefoschi with a warm eulogy of his abilities, his writings and his success in restoring religious practice in Ossory through his gifts of prudence, piety, charity and integrity.[43] The majority of the Irish bishops were educated in France, were obviously not known personally in Rome and could not have the same rapport with the Roman officials as someone like Troy, who had spent many years there. Troy repaid this Roman support by keeping the congregation of Propaganda abreast, as best he could, of the problems and difficulties facing the Irish church. He immediately became a key figure in the Irish hierarchy, as he was commissioned to settle bitter and tortuous disputes between the archbishop of Armagh and some of his clergy. He was responsible for the appointment of Richard O'Reilly as coadjutor of Armagh in 1782, and O'Reilly later as archbishop was content to play second fiddle and to allow Troy to be the acknowledged leader of the Irish church.[44]

Troy's entrée into the Irish hierarchy was not easy. Many of the bishops who had been diocesan priests, and especially Archbishop Butler, did not welcome a bishop from a religious order. Though the decree of 1751 had halved the number of friars within twenty years, opposition to them had not diminished. Added to the traditional suspicions between the religious and secular clergy was the fear that the presence of significant numbers of regulars, which their confreres as bishops were thought likely to favour, would draw down on the church the hostility of the government and of the ruling elites. The Stuarts, who were deemed to have favoured the regulars,

42 Two Dominicans, Troy and Netterville, were proposed for the appointment. Borgia described Troy as 'a subject endowed with all the best qualities'. Referring in 1799 to his confidence in Troy, Borgia reminded him that this had led to his promotion to the bishopric and later to the archbishopric (Borgia to Troy, 15 June 1799, APF, SC(Irlanda), 17, f 690rv); Peel, 'The appointment of Dr Troy to the see of Dublin', 5–16.   43 Butler and others to Marefoschi, 28 Oct. 1776 in Moran, *Spicilegium Ossoriense*, 3, pp 351–3. Six years later when the diocese of Kildare was vacant, Troy informed Rome that 'if a Gallican bishop is wanted, then Molloy would be the choice' (Troy to Propaganda, 19 Oct. 1782, DDA). Archbishop Carpenter advised Bishop Sweetman of Ferns not to support Molloy's candidature as his appointment would be 'a kind of censure' on those who opposed the oath (Carpenter to Sweetman, 8 Oct. 1776, DDA). 44 McNally, *Reform, revolution and reaction.* Keogh, 'The pattern of the flock' in Kelly and Keogh, *History of the Catholic diocese of Dublin*, pp 215–36.

no longer posed any threat to national stability, but the prejudices attached to their alleged supporters still remained. Troy could have been excused for regarding his appointment as a poisoned chalice, for he had been commissioned to settle what he later called 'unpleasant and thorny' problems in the archdiocese of Armagh, where an absentee archbishop had been at loggerheads with several clergy. He encountered opposition from some of the bishops in his efforts to pacify Armagh, and the coadjutor whom he installed to rectify the situation met with hostility and resistance from four turbulent clergy. Like his friend and fellow Dominican, Thomas Burke, who had also spent several years in Rome, Troy upheld the prerogatives of the papacy and tended to exalt the claims and privileges the Roman court attached to the pope. But confronted with political realities he gradually saw the need to play down some of these claims. In 1779 he took the oath, which by then most Irish bishops had taken, but he was less than just or accurate when he described the archbishop of Cashel and the bishops of Cloyne, Killaloe, Limerick and Meath as Gallicans, presumably because of their promptness in taking and advocating the oath.[45] And he soon won the friendship of a prominent politician, Luke Gardiner, and used such friendships as the means by which he would try to obtain improvements in the lot of Catholics. He believed that the cultivation of the powerful was more effective than confrontation.

Before Troy arrived in Ireland war had broken out between Britain and her American colonies, and the British need for increased manpower for her armies was to have crucial repercussions for Irish and British Catholics. Already proposals had been made to make use of Irish Catholics in the army but Irish Protestant hostility and fears had scuppered the prospect. Lord North, the prime minister, employed an agent to sound out the vicars apostolic in Edinburgh and London, and his Catholic agent got a warm welcome for the suggestion.[46]

The danger of invasion during the war with America led to the formation of corps of Volunteers to defend the country. The Volunteers soon passed beyond the role of defence forces and demanded reform of parliament. At a well-attended convention in Dungannon in February 1782 they called for an end to the right of the British parliament to legislate for Ireland, and an end to the power of the British privy council in effect to control bills for discussion in the Irish parliament. In a spirit of liberal goodwill they also expressed their happiness at the relaxation of the laws against their Catholic fellow countrymen. Few Catholics were welcomed among the Volunteers, and among the leaders the principal supporter of the Catholic cause was the earl-

45 Troy to Propaganda, 14 Jan. 1782, DDA.   **46** Bartlett, *The fall and rise of the Irish nation*, pp 85–7.

bishop of Derry. But his bona fides were suspected in some Catholic circles, and especially in Rome.

An undated note in the archives of Propaganda blamed him for trying to get priests to sign the four Gallican articles (which exalted local episcopal power at the expense of that of Rome) and claimed that Patrick Joseph Plunket, the bishop of Meath, assisted him in that endeavour. Plunket, as rector of the Irish College in Paris, was accused of presenting to the Sorbonne the oath that the English government had proposed to the Catholics of Ireland, and the doctors of the Sorbonne declared that Irish Catholics not only could but should take that oath, which went beyond the bounds of moderation.[47] The nuncio in Brussels also forwarded to Rome an extract from a newspaper in which Plunket lent his support to the lord lieutenant's appeal for a public fast for the success of British arms, and went on to praise the benevolent intentions of the government in proposing the oath that had been taken by the Catholics of the diocese, and who had thereby undertaken to cooperate with the liberality, the wisdom and the benevolence of their rulers.[48] Cardinal Antonelli, the prefect of Propaganda, told Troy that he was thinking of appointing Plunket coadjutor of Armagh in view of the good reports Troy had sent about him, but regarded his support for the fast as imprudent and his accompanying appeal as unworthy of the character of a bishop.[49]

Troy, still suspicious of the views of Butler and his suffragans, reported that these Munster bishops had maintained that future nominations of bishops by the pope should be restricted to three candidates chosen by the priests of the vacant diocese and the bishops of the province. He and Carpenter objected to any change of discipline without the consent of the pope and the nuncio exhorted Carpenter to oppose any innovations introduced by the government, especially in the appointments of bishops. Troy thought royal nomination would gradually ruin religion in Ireland.[50] Since the death of the Old Pretender in 1766 there was no formal arrangement for presenting to Rome the names of candidates for the episcopate. Rumours about systems of appointments had begun to circulate in parliamentary circles and the nuncio passed on to Rome what he had heard. Some politicians had proposed that the king should have the right of nomination, and some of the bishops had suggested that the pope should choose one of three candidates who would be proposed to him by the clergy of the vacant diocese

---

47 APF, SC(Ibernia), 15, f 6r. It was further remarked that the judgment of the Sorbonne had, in effect, accused popes Gregory VII and Pius V, who had ordered the deposition of sovereigns, of being heretical with the statement 'doctrina de caede et depositione Principum est haeretica materialiter et formaliter'.   48 Nuncio to Propaganda, 26 June 1781, APF, SC(Ibernia)15, f 64rv. Plunket also fell foul of the prohibition of praying for Protestants.   49 Antonelli to Troy, 28 Apr. 1781 DDA.   50 Troy to Nuncio, 5 Mar. 1782 and Nuncio to Troy, 9 Apr. 1782, DDA.

and by the provincial bishops. Carpenter informed Propaganda that some bishops objected to candidates of whom they did not approve, who had not taken the oath, being appointed as bishops, and argued that the pope should not pay attention to any external authority in promoting to the episcopate.[51]

The tide of national feeling which in parliament was leading to rearrangements of the constitutional relations between Britain and Ireland also benefited the Catholics.[52] A Catholic relief act (known as Gardiner's Act) was passed in May 1782 whereby the restriction on leases by which Catholics might hold land was abolished. A couple of months later Catholics were permitted to conduct schools, with the permission of the local Protestant bishops, and the outdated restrictions on the numbers and ministry of priests were abolished. Any priest who took the oath of the 1774 act and gave his name to the registrar of the Protestant diocese in which he resided would no longer be subject to the Banishment Act. The regular clergy were recognized on the same basis as the secular if they took the oath of 1774, but as they had to do so within six months those who were studying or stationed abroad were disadvantaged, unless they returned within that time.[53] A couple of petty regulations accompanied these relaxations: churches might not have steeples or bells and clergy were not to 'assume any ecclesiastical rank or title whatsoever'. Troy informed Rome of the general sympathy for the regulars among the Catholic laity, and though he was confident the question of the royal nomination of bishops would not be pursued, he noted that some members of parliament wanted to exclude from the episcopal ceremony of consecration the pledge to combat Protestants.[54] The words '*haereticos persequar et impugnabo*' carried a threat which, though it no longer could be brought to bear on Protestants, was distinctly abhorrent and intolerable to those who knew about it. Through his friendship with Gardiner, Troy had convinced one of those who drew up the act to exclude any threat to expel the regular clergy or to allow a royal veto on episcopal appointments.[55]

A convention of the Ulster Volunteers meeting at Dungannon in September 1783 debated the issues of parliamentary reform and relief for

---

51 Nuncio to Propaganda, 26 June 1781, APF, SC(Ibernia) 15, f 64rv and Carpenter to Propaganda, 26 Mar. 1782, ibid., f 154rv. 52 McDowell, 'Colonial nationalism, 1760–82', *NHI*, 4, 233; Connolly, *Divided kingdom*, pp 402–26. 53 Fenning, *The undoing of the friars of Ireland*, pp 381–8. The friars were feared by the Protestant elites because they were more difficult to keep track of than the diocesan clergy, and because they were deemed to be closely associated with the Old Pretender. By 1750 when the Vatican forbade them to conduct novitiates they numbered about 800, or half the clergy of the country. Their numbers dropped by about a third in the next sixteen years, and though adjustments were made to the regulations about noviciates they continued to decline, and, by 1812, numbered 250, or about 13 per cent of the clergy. 54 Troy to Propaganda, 1 June 1782, APF, SC(Ibernia), 15, ff 178r–181r. At the request of the four archbishops permission was granted to remove these words (28 July 1794, *Acta*, 164, f 559rv). 55 McNally, *Reform, revolution and reaction*, pp 11–20.

Catholics. Lord Charlemont, the president of the Ulster regiment of Volunteers, adamantly opposed the extension of the franchise to Catholics and, though his opponent for leadership at the meeting, the earl-bishop, advocated the vote for Catholics, Charlemont's view prevailed. Most of the Volunteers, representing Protestant property and stability, felt that enfranchising the Catholics was a step too far. Though the Catholic Committee made contact with the more liberal element of the delegates, the resistance of the majority, marshalled by Charlemont with the backing of the government, was too strong.

Disappointment with the attitudes of the Volunteers did not deter some of the bishops from seeking to improve relations with Protestants by gestures of loyalty to the sovereign. Carpenter refused to go along with a declaration of loyalty which Butler recommended. Troy, though approving of the sentiments of Butler and his suffragans, dissuaded him from publishing it widely for prudential reasons.[56] Two years later Troy became archbishop of Dublin and in his capacity as effective leader of the hierarchy played for the most part a cautious and prudent role in Irish politics. Embarrassed by the agrarian disturbances of the Rightboys (who were protesting against tithes, taxes, rents and financial demands made by the Catholic clergy), by the scared reactions of Protestants and by the refusal of Dublin Castle to entertain any idea of further progress, Catholics gained nothing more in the 1780s.[57]

By the end of the 1780s Catholics in Ireland had gained practical relief with the laws relating to land purchase and education. They had also successfully negotiated the problem of the oaths with Rome, but before any further developments in these areas could take place an event occurred in France which was to have profound repercussions for the whole of Europe.

56 Butler to Troy, 2 May 1784 and Troy to Butler, 23 May 1784, DDA.   57 Bartlett, *The fall and rise of the Catholic nation*, p. 120.

2

The influence of the French Revolution

I

The outbreak of the French Revolution in 1789 heightened political awareness in Ireland. Presbyterians in Antrim and Down, and particularly in Belfast, drew from the revolution inspiration for their demands for wider participation in government through parliamentary reform, and its corollary of extending the franchise to Catholics. The government at Dublin Castle, fearing the consequences of these demands, gave a more receptive ear to the aristocratic leaders of the Catholic Committee, lords Kenmare and Fingall.[1] But the influence of the aristocratic element on the Catholic Committee declined as the members grew more radical in their demands and sought the repeal of the penal laws.[2]

Patrick Plunket of Meath made his own gesture of goodwill to the government and the ruling elites when he ordered that a memorial prayer for the king should be included in every Mass in his diocese. He was delated to Rome for his pains, and defended himself by maintaining that he was following the example set by the vicar apostolic of the Western District of England, who had ordered his clergy to do so in July 1778. He argued that the discipline of the church permitted prayer for those not of the Catholic faith occasionally, a practice which had occurred in the early church, and that he had adopted it to diminish the prejudices of Protestants and serve the common cause when the revocation of part of the penal laws was being mooted. He also denied that he had given an instruction claiming that Catholics and Protestants only differed in opinions. Forwarding Plunket's defence to Rome the nuncio described him as a man of talent, to whom a benign answer should be sent, as, if he was mistaken, he was not obstinate in his opinions.[3]

The picture changed with the publication of the pamphlet 'An argument on behalf of the Catholics of Ireland' by Wolfe Tone, a radical young lawyer who was impatient with the hesitant movement for reform, and who insisted

1 Thomas Browne, Viscount Kenmare (1726–95) and Arthur Plunkett, Earl of Fingall (1739–1836) were cautious supporters of the Catholic cause. 2 Keogh, *The French disease*, p. 481. O'Flaherty, 'Irish Catholics and the French Revolution' in Gough and Dickson, *Ireland and the French Revolution*, pp 52–67. 3 Plunket to Propaganda, 16 Nov. 1784, and Nuncio to Propaganda, 7 Dec. 1784, APF, SC(Ibernia), 15, ff 560r–561r and 563r.

that any widening of the representation of the people must include granting the vote to Catholics. Tone immediately endeared himself to the more advanced reformers and to the non-gentry elements of the Catholic Committee, the richer middle-class leaders, John Keogh and Edward Byrne.[4]

John Keogh of the Catholic Committee became a member of the Society of United Irishmen, which was founded in Belfast in 1791 and advocated not only parliamentary reform but also the enfranchisement of Catholics. He and his friends pushed the Catholic Committee, which had been re-formed in 1790, in a more radical direction. The demand for total repeal of the penal laws frightened the more conservative leaders among the peers, and lords Kenmare and Fingall, resigned from it in 1791, as did some sixty others. Troy adopted the same attitude. Fingall, Troy and those who resigned suspected the motives of the members of the committee who used terminology similar to that of the French revolutionaries. The slogans used in France, however impeccable on the surface, covered up the spoliation of the church and potentially the nobles and gentry. The anti-religious excesses of the proponents of democracy in France scared the seceders, as they scared the bishops. They felt that a much more modest request to the government should be made, relying on its generosity for reform.

The seceders presented an address to the lord lieutenant, which Troy signed,[5] and which respectfully requested the government for an extension of its favours. Many of the bishops presented loyal addresses but they did not win much popular support. That support went to the Catholic Committee. Troy later reported to Rome that his situation had become more satisfactory. His moderation in his dealings with the committee had been beneficial and he was better regarded than previously. There was no further discussion about electing bishops. He felt he could temper better the violence of those who would propose 'new things'. Indifferentism to religion derived from philosophical madness was working havoc even in Ireland and the vigilance of the government was necessary to repress the independent spirit which was spreading.[6] Pressure from the government of William Pitt in London, concerned about the possible union of Catholics and Dissenters, brought about a relief bill in February 1792 which allowed Catholics to become barristers and attorneys, permitted mixed marriages, removed restrictions on foreign education and on the number of apprentices a Catholic tradesman

4 Elliott, *Wolfe Tone*, pp 111–33; Wall, 'John Keogh and the Catholic Committee' in O'Brien, *Catholic Ireland in the eighteenth century*, pp 163–70. John Keogh (1740–1817) helped organize the Catholic convention. He became prominent in Catholic affairs in 1806. Edward Byrne (1740–1804) was a wealthy distiller and merchant.   5 Troy informed Moylan that flattery and every species of intimidation had been used by the committee to prevent him from signing. Members had threatened him with the terrifying consequences of their resentment (Troy to Moylan, 23 Dec. 1791, DDA).   6 Troy to Propaganda, 8 June 1792, APF, SC(Ibernia) 28, Fondo di Vienna, ff 25r–26r.

could take and abolished the obligation for schoolmasters to seek licences from Protestant bishops.[7] Enfranchisement was not included. Keogh and his faction in the Catholic Committee were disappointed, and their appointment of Wolfe Tone as secretary was an indication of their determination to proceed more aggressively.

In March 1792 the committee appointed a subcommittee of eight members, which included Keogh and Byrne, to draw up a declaration of Catholic principles affecting politics, as the English Catholic Committee had done, and it was signed by many Catholics. The charges that excommunicated sovereigns could be deposed and murdered, that faith need not be kept with heretics and that the pope was infallible and had civil jurisdiction in the country were rejected. Catholics committed themselves to the maintenance of the land settlement, and in the event of being given the vote, an oath disapproving of any intention to alter the land settlement was to be taken.[8] Archbishop Troy signed this declaration though he had reservations about some of its clauses, especially about papal infallibility.

As the Catholic Committee swung leftwards, with enthusiasts for the French Revolution extolling revolutionary doctrines and slogans as they sought reform in Ireland, the bishops stood back, some aghast, at the crimes being committed in France under the banner of these slogans. In March 1791, Pius VI had condemned the civil constitution of the clergy which had been enacted by the French national assembly the previous year and which, in effect, tried to turn the church in France into a state church. Bishops and clergy, who were to be elected by the people, were obliged to take an oath of loyalty to the state. Not only were dioceses abolished, monasteries closed and ecclesiastical property nationalized, but violence erupted against the clergy and the Catholic people. Thousands of priests and a majority of the bishops fled France, and the French church entered a period of virtual persecution. As many of the Irish bishops had been educated in France, they felt strongly the sufferings of French Catholics.

Troy, bewailing the loss of seminaries in France and seeking a subvention for the Irish College in Paris, informed Cardinal Antonelli regretfully that the French madness was turning the heads of Catholics in Ireland. The cries of liberty and independence were being heard, and all the foresight of the government was needed to prevent the progress and dastardly consequences of that evil madness. Letting Antonelli know about his cautious approach to the political difficulties that faced him he expressed his fear that the government was being offended not only by the requests of Catholics to have the right of voting in elections but also by the manner in which those requests

---

7 Connolly, *Divided kingdom*, p. 444.   8 Rogers, *The Irish volunteers and Catholic emancipation*, pp 255–6.

were being made by the Catholic Committee. He trusted that the Catholics would not let themselves be deceived by their new-found friends, the Presbyterians, but at the same time he did not want to offend that powerful body in the north or to oppose the eagerness of Catholics to obtain their electoral rights. He concluded by reference to the tightrope on which he was compelled to walk: every Catholic was duty-bound to be loyal to the king but he, more than most, was distressed to find himself in the midst of those advocating liberty and being observed by the government, which had a good opinion of the bishops.[9] Roman officials must have been pleased by what they would have regarded as judicious and wise behaviour on the archbishop's part.

The Catholic Committee in 1792 decided to hold a convention to discuss and push its agenda for obtaining the franchise. The help of the bishops was sought in choosing the delegates, and though many of the bishops feared the direction the committee was taking they went along with its request. The convention met in Dublin in December 1792. Both Troy and Moylan of Cork attended the first and last days of its meetings, and were welcomed and applauded. This was a significant gesture on their part. They had come to realize that they had no choice but to yield to popular pressure. Troy, who had gone along with the aristocrats who had seceded from the committee, understood that resistance to the policy of the 'democrats' would have been counterproductive. Almost fifty members of the convention were also United Irishmen.[10] And the 'democrats' bypassed the authorities at Dublin Castle and had their petition for Catholic relief, which Troy had signed and lauded, presented to the king.[11]

As the situation in France deteriorated and France declared war on Britain, Troy published a lengthy letter entitled *Pastoral on the duties of Christian citizens.* Concerned to rebut the hostile arguments of prominent anti-Catholic parliamentarians and publicists, the archbishop insisted that Catholics were loyal and obedient to their sovereign. He rejected the charge that the pope was infallible and could depose kings, and maintained that the church always proclaimed the duty of obedience to proper authority. He denied the justification for violent opposition to the government of states. Though he did not quieten his most vociferous opponents, the more moderate Protestant leaders praised his comments and he won the approval of Rome for his initiative.

With the outbreak of war in 1793, Sir John Coxe-Hippisley, a self-appointed expert on Vatican affairs, who had spent time in Rome, recommended to the Holy See that it should send a representative to Britain

9 Troy to Propaganda, 15 Nov. 1792, APF, SC(Ibernia), 28, Fondo di Vienna, ff 50r–51v.
10 Whelan, 'Catholics, politicisation and the 1798 rebellion' in O'Muiri, *Irish church history today*, pp 63–80. 11 Keogh, *The French disease*, pp 57–70; O'Flaherty, 'The Catholic conven-

to keep in touch with political developments there. His suggestion was accepted and Charles Erskine, a prelate of Scottish and Italian descent was given this assignment. Erskine did not have diplomatic status but with the necessities of war creating new opportunities for contact between friendly governments, he was received at the highest levels of government with great respect. He was not a legate to the church either in Britain or Ireland, but he took on himself the responsibility of keeping the church up to the mark by encouraging the bishops to repudiate all French revolutionary demands. The English vicars apostolic came to regard him as a meddler in their affairs (an opinion which was also held by Luke Concanen, Troy's agent in Rome). Distance prevented him from having the same influence in Ireland, though he wrote encouraging letters to Troy and other bishops. Troy was advised to cooperate with Erskine, but fearing that Erskine might visit Ireland he warned Rome of the grave danger of such a visit being misunderstood and accusations being made by the extreme anti-Catholics that he would relieve Catholics of the duty of observing their oaths.[12] (It is very likely that Troy had a further motive for not wanting Erskine in Ireland. Like the English vicars apostolic he did not want a papal representative interfering in Irish affairs or trying to dictate to the bishops.)

To assist in its military engagement, the government in London was anxious both to keep Ireland quiet and to draw on Irish Catholic manpower for the army. Under pressure from London and with the sponsorship of Hobart, the chief secretary, a relief act was introduced in February 1793. On his own behalf, on that of the Catholic clergy and with the concurrence of several laymen, Troy had petitioned parliament 'to restore to the petitioners the rights and privileges of the constitution of their country'. The Irish Protestant elite was not prepared to let Catholics sit in parliament. Hobart's bill did not include this right, but it did offer them the same voting rights in the counties as others. It also opened to them civil and military offices (with restrictions at the top level), removed all restrictions on property rights and gave permission to take degrees in any college that might be founded, provided it was a member of the University of Dublin and was not founded exclusively for the education of Catholics. Debates on the bill also provoked suggestions about pensioning the clergy, with the corollary of a veto for the crown in the appointments of the bishops – something which was anathema to the bishops. Catholics were obliged to take a much-amended version of the 1774 oath to take advantage of these concessions.

The oath was said to have been drawn up by the ex-Catholic, Patrick Duigenan, who had bitterly criticized Troy's pastorals. The swearer was obliged to condemn as unchristian the principle that it was lawful to murder

tion and Anglo-Irish politics, 1791–3'. 12 Troy to Propaganda, 26 Sept. 1793, APF, SC(Ibernia) 28, ff 121r–122v.

or injure anyone on the pretence of their being a heretic, and that no unjust or immoral act could ever be justified or excused on the grounds that it was done for the good of the church or in obedience to any ecclesiastical power. He was also compelled to repudiate the belief that the pope was infallible, and to promise not to obey any order that was by its nature immoral, even though the pope or any ecclesiastical power should order it. He was also required to declare that he believed no sin could be forgiven at the mere will of any pope or priest without sincere sorrow, a firm resolution to avoid future guilt and make atonement to God, and that no absolution could be obtained without these conditions. He was also bound to promise to defend the settlement of property in the country as established by law and to solemnly disavow any intention to subvert the church establishment for the purpose of substituting a Catholic establishment, and also not to use any privilege to disturb or weaken the Protestant religion or Protestant government of the kingdom.[13]

Edmund Burke, the consistent and generous champion of Catholic rights, criticized Protestant hostility to concessions, fearing that it could be as damaging as Jacobinism: 'they cannot listen to any arguments from equity or from national or constitutional policy: the sword is at their throats; beggary and famine at their door'.[14] The oath was in fact ungracious and offensive but did not make the terrible demands on Catholics that Burke believed. They were not being forced to repudiate any doctrine, though they were being treated as untrustworthy and unreliable, and were obliged to repudiate beliefs and views that might threaten order, property and the solidarity of the state.

The first reaction of Rome to the act, though admittedly based on partial information, was generally favourable. Cardinal Antonelli informed Troy that Concanen had given him an extract of a letter detailing the advantages which Catholics were afforded by the legislation and that the pope, on hearing of them, was greatly pleased. He was happy with the permission for the establishment of colleges in Ireland though he must not have understood the condition about their connection with the University of Dublin. He asked both for a copy of the bill and for a copy of the second edition of Troy's pastoral on the duties of Christian citizens, which he was sure would have been opportune and efficacious in dissipating prejudices. What must have greatly reassured Troy, who had been afraid that parts of the oath would cause him trouble, was Antonelli's comment that he found it more tolerable than that proposed for England. Nonetheless, he had found the expressions in the last article bitter and hard, as it was the duty of every good Catholic to propagate his religion and remove, if possible, all heresy from the world, not

13 Fagan, *Divided loyalties*, p. 174.   14 McDowell (ed.), *The writings and speeches of Edmund Burke*, vol. 9, part 2, pp 640–57.

with violence, rebellion or deception but with persuasion and the charity that should move them to procure the eternal salvation of their brethren.[15]

Antonelli's mood changed when he received a copy of the act from Concanen. He was particularly concerned by the concluding clause. He reminded Troy that it was an indispensable obligation not only to weaken but also, if possible, to extinguish all false sects and religions. And while Catholics could not use illicit means such as tumults or rebellions to disturb and weaken the Protestant faith, the sense of the words in the oath was so wide that it included the licit means open to them. A good Catholic should not blush to confess that his Christian charity impelled him to use all licit means to convert those who were not in communion with that church, outside of which there was no salvation. Asking if it would be illicit to preach Catholic doctrine and work for the conversion of Protestants, he noted that these means disturbed or weakened the Protestant religion and government and maintained that Catholics could not renounce them without horror. Troy was requested to forward an opinion on the oath which might help the pope to decide on its acceptability and to let him know if it was to be taken by all Catholics or only by those assuming office.[16] Troy explained in reply that the true meaning of the pledge not to disturb and weaken the Protestant religion – and, he added, Protestant government – was to promise not to use any privileges, tumults or sedition to do so. There was no ban on preaching or working prudently for the conversion of Protestants.[17]

The congregation of Propaganda submitted the oath to the scrutiny of the office of the Holy Roman and Universal Inquisition, which dealt with doctrinal issues, and which examined it on 16 June 1794 at the same meeting at which the English and Scottish oaths were scrutinized. In the *ristretto* or account of the problem to be settled which was prepared for the cardinals, the emphasis was placed on the pledge not to weaken and disturb the Protestant religion. The oath was quoted in Latin and no other part of it was discussed, but this did not prevent the cardinals from deciding that the oath was reprehensible in many points, and that it was not licit for Catholics to take it. They felt, however, that it would be very dangerous to issue a solemn condemnation of it, and so they concluded that a letter should be sent to the archbishop of Dublin and the other bishops setting out what was censurable in the oath, and letting them know that they should ensure that Catholics would not take it; the instruction of the congregation to the bishop of Ossory in 1776 in a similar situation was quoted.[18]

The congregation of Propaganda then passed on to Troy and the other bishops the worry and unease that the oath had caused. Troy and the others

15 Propaganda to Troy, 11 May 1793, APF, LDB 264, ff 209v–212r. 16 Propaganda to Troy, 8 June 1793, ibid., ff 306r–309r. 176 Troy to Propaganda, 29 July 1793, DDA. 18 APF, *Acta* 164, ff 490r–507r.

were reminded that Propaganda had rejected the oath of 1774, had ordered himself and the pastors to direct people away from it, but had not condemned it lest by so doing more grave damage would be done to the church. This formula however was far more detestable and iniquitous and was not imposed by a magistrate but was put forward with the relaxation of the penal laws in mind to confer greater privileges. A very different oath was arranged for the relief of the English and Scots and for the sake of religion the Irish oath could not be admitted. Evil doctrines and errors abounded in it. The infallibility of the pope, though not defined as an article of faith, was held by many of the church fathers and doctors, was right and proper and at some time or other would be defined. And if Christ promised to be with his church until the end of time could the pope or a general council order immoral acts, and how could it ever be imagined that the pope or the universal church would injure a man for no other reason than that he was a heretic. The church commanded obedience to rulers irrespective of their religion. The pope and the church could not violate morals by ordering acts contrary to them, and if a person took the oath he might think the church was acting this way.

The pledge to abjure every intention of perverting the ecclesiastical constitution of the kingdom ran counter to the duty of clergy to pray that in that kingdom the form of the church ordered by God and the pure faith free from errors would again flourish with one flock under one shepherd. The true Catholic should ever keep in mind the wish to restore the Catholic foundations displaced by heresy and schism, and should never call God to witness that he did not wish to convert the present polity into a Catholic one. The pledge not to weaken and disturb the Protestant religion had been interpreted as referring to the temporal privileges of that church and the church was not to be disturbed by sedition or violence but this did not square with the sense of the words. To swear not to disturb the Protestant religion was to be hostile to the Catholic religion, which desired and ordered the weakening and destruction of what diverged from the truth, and, as St Augustine had said, to speak otherwise was a detestable form of falsehood. And it was never lawful for an individual to renounce the temporal possessions which the church enjoyed before the Anglican schism; only the pope could do so and he usually did so only for the peace and tranquillity of the church in cases of grave danger. To pray for the royal family was one thing: to swear unconditionally never to weaken and disturb the Protestant religion and establishment was another. In the hope of abrogating the penal laws the oath may have been admitted too quickly without consultation with the Apostolic See. The pope accordingly commanded that the bishops and pastors order their people not to take the oath and through warnings and private sermons not to let them be led by the hope of gain to pledge themselves to an oath which, by asserting opinions that seemed to obscure the sanctity and purity of the teaching of the pope and the church, injured or was in danger of injuring truth. But if inspired by the example and excited by the exhortations of their pastors the faithful rejected the terms of the oath as repugnant to truth, the Catholic religion would gain much credit and its opponents could not but admire the constancy of the Catholics who were not moved by temporal matters or by ambiguous words to dare to violate sacred religion. If their flocks did not listen to their exhortations, they could but ask God that their people be good citizens according to the mind of the church.[19]

This broadside from the cardinal would have placed Troy and the bishops in a very difficult and embarrassing situation had there been an order condemning the oath as immoral. It would have been very difficult to persuade an increasingly determined Catholic Committee to forego taking the oath if future concessions might depend on their doing so. The congregation certainly lambasted the oath but it stopped short of publicly repudiating it. Troy, who had already taken the oath in 1793, had been assured by Dublin Castle that what was forbidden by the words 'disturb and weaken the Protestant faith' was violence of any kind, and so took no steps to prevent people from taking the oath. Thereby he avoided angry opposition from Catholic activists. The relief act gave satisfaction to those who were expecting emancipation as they considered it an instalment, and hoped the full concession would not be long delayed.[20]

To add to the bishops' problems at this time the Defenders, 'an anti-Protestant, anti-English and anti-settler' revolutionary movement, was strengthened by the government's establishment of a militia.[21] As soldiers were recalled from Ireland to fight against the French, a militia consisting mainly of Catholic soldiers – some of whom were at first compelled to join – was established. The Defenders, who had been engaged in skirmishes with Protestants in the border counties of Ulster and Leinster, were strengthened by antagonism to the militia. When denounced by the clergy they in turn denounced priests who opposed them. Denis Maguire, the bishop of Kilmore, informed his agent in Rome for the benefit of the curia that the clergy were being accused (falsely) of being the authors of the militia. The Defenders, he claimed, then sought to punish the poor curates by not contributing to their upkeep.[22]

Charles Erskine, who proved himself a faithful guardian of Roman prerogatives, alerted by reports in the press, warned Rome about seditious meetings among lower class Catholics in Ireland (he had the Defenders in

19 Propaganda to Troy and the bishops of Ireland, 13 Dec. 1794, APF, SOCG 899, ff 133r–143r and ACDF, St-St, UU 22, N i, F.   20 Connolly, *Divided kingdom*, p. 460.   21 Bartlett quoted in O'Brien, *The great melody*, p. 498; *The fall and rise of the Irish nation*, pp 178–86.   22 James Cowan, OFM to Propaganda, 22 June 1793, APF, SC(Ibernia), Fondo di Vienna, 28, f 81rv.

mind). He quoted Lord Portarlington's view that this lower class was being misled by agitators, and referred to the information passed by the bishop of Winchester to Coxe-Hippisley about the secret plots being hatched in Ireland. Consequently, he suggested that a letter be written to the Irish bishops to let them know that the pope strongly disapproved of this conduct, ordering them to recall the seditiously minded to their duty and exhorting them to be on their guard against those who were conspiring against both themselves and the government.[23]

Alerted by Erskine to the rebellious behaviour of the lower class in Ireland, Rome, grateful for British support against the French, warned the bishops to oppose all violent movements. Propaganda, they were told, did not doubt that only a few Catholics, disobeying the voice of their pastors, were seduced by the democratic maxims which were being spread by the enemies of religion. Hence the pope and the congregation wished that the archbishops would bring those ill-advised Catholics back to their duty and warn them to be vigilant when confronted with the insidious suggestions of the evil-minded who aimed at nothing other than the subversion of altar and throne. The letter ended with a request – in effect, an order – that the archbishops keep the pope and congregation informed of what was happening in Ireland and of the decisions taken at their meetings so that the congregation could take opportune measures for the establishment of a firm and Christian peace among Catholics and for a healthy discipline among the clergy.[24] The congregation obviously held an exaggerated view of its own power and of the power of the bishops, if it thought its measures could have such a calming effect on those who were inclined to rebel.

Troy replied promptly to Propaganda, and, knowing how many of those bent on violence would disregard episcopal advice, put up the best defence he could of how the bishops had tried to dissuade their people from violent activities. And he rightly justified his not informing Rome about the situation. He explained that since the previous year some of the common people (whom he called 'Catholic *plebei*') in Co. Louth, known as Defenders, who were secretly excited by certain Protestants ill-disposed to the government, had disturbed the peace. They derived their name from their neighbours in the north who had been forced to arm themselves against the lower class of Presbyterians who had been subjecting them to rapine and outrages. The archbishop of Armagh never ceased to denounce those attacks, but then the fire spread into the dioceses of Meath and Kilmore. In the previous January

---

23 Erskine to Propaganda, ibid., n.d., but 15 Aug. 1793 written on the back of the letter by an official in Rome. 24 Propaganda to Troy and other archbishops, 17 Aug. 1793, APF, LDB 264, ff 362r–364v. Propaganda followed up this admonition with another letter on 28 Aug. complaining about seditious meetings, and a request for a translation of his *Pastoral letter on the duties of Christian citizens* and his other pastoral (ibid., ff 365v, 369v–370r).

three archbishops and two bishops had signed a short pastoral, which he had drawn up, which was published in some English and Scottish papers, and inserted as an appendix in his *Pastoral instruction on the duties of citizens*, a copy of which was sent to his agent in Rome. This admonition was effective until parliament established a domestic national militia, whereupon the fire was again rekindled and spread rapidly in the province of Tuam and in the diocese of Ferns. The malcontents among the common people maliciously put out the rumour that all who enrolled in the militia would be forced to abandon their country and sent to certain slaughter.

Among the Catholics, Troy continued, there had been some supporters of the democratic maxims of liberty and equality, but he was pleased to report that after diligent investigation both the government and parliament had done justice to the Catholic clergy and body by declaring that they had nothing to do with the recent practices of some seditious people and actually abhorred the maxims of the insurgents and their instigators. He concluded by maintaining that the newspapers, especially the English ones, and often private correspondents exaggerated such occurrences, and he had not referred the matter to the congregation for it could not have applied a remedy to a passing evil or increased the zeal of the bishops in calming the tempest.[25]

II

With the expansion of the revolution in France and the closure of seminaries and religious houses, Ireland lost its main source for the education and provision of clergy. Irish seminaries in France housed some four hundred students and their expulsion left the country with a few small seminaries in Italy, Spain and Portugal. The Irish church found itself in an extremely difficult situation. If the seminarians could not be trained in Ireland, the provision of places in Spain, Portugal and other countries would be a slow, costly and precarious exercise. An unfortunate aspect of the relief act of 1793 was an amendment by the anti-Catholic chancellor excluding the establishment of purely Catholic institutions and subjecting any future institution to the University of Dublin. However, the bishops were advised that this restriction might be circumvented by a memorial to the crown.[26] This chimed with their view that the way to success with the monarch and government was through

25 Troy to Propaganda, 24 Sept. 1793, APF, SC(Ibernia), 28, Fondo di Vienna, ff 118rv and 120rv. Troy later reported to Rome that though attacked by 'democrats' the bishops were indifferent to praise or blame. They were neither aristocrats nor democrats and spoke only as bishops (Concanen to Propaganda, 28 Jan. 1794, ibid., SOCG, 898, ff 289rv and 292r). 26 Keogh, *The French disease*, pp 71–5.

protestations of loyalty, and so they duly presented yet another address on 17 December 1793. It was signed by four archbishops and five bishops. And an address in a similar vein, recalling the wickedness of tumult and their past exhortations to their people to be obedient to established authority, was presented to the lord lieutenant.[27]

This was followed shortly by a memorial to the lord lieutenant signed by Troy on behalf of all the prelates. Pointing out the loss of their seminaries which trained students in France, they explained that they would not expose their youth to the contagion of sedition and infidelity, nor their country to the danger of thus introducing the pernicious maxims of licentious philosophy. Referring to the valuable privileges conferred during the viceroy's administration and trusting that they might appear not unworthy of the king's consideration and bounty, they maintained that Protestant fellow subjects had also expressed the opinion that Irish ecclesiastics would be better educated at home. Unable to bear the expense of education at the University of Dublin, they were prepared to establish their own houses of study but understood that the royal licence was required to enable them to secure the necessary funds legally. After a delay of almost nine months, a bleak answer was returned in January 1795, just as Lord Westmoreland was replaced by a viceroy who genuinely favoured Catholic claims.[28]

Troy had sent a copy of this petition to Propaganda, and was warmly commended for the ingenious and diplomatic approach by which the special education required for clergy distinct from that already established for lay students was laid down. The congregation was persuaded that the bishops would not support any such establishments unless they had full control of the appointments of staff and the direction of the colleges. The bishops were praised for declining any financial support for colleges in which they would have to fear the least subordination and dependence on the government.[29] This warm letter of support was not to be read merely as approval of past policy but as a warning for the future. The congregation was setting its face firmly against any interference of the state – especially from Protestant politicians or officials – in the control or conduct of seminaries. The only type of seminary that Rome would accept was one in which episcopal control was complete and unquestioned.

Troy, who was desperately seeking any help he could get to augment the declining numbers of clergy, sought financial assistance from the congregation of Propaganda, only to be told that its funds had been exhausted by grants given to the church in France. However, it was prepared to make available a few extra places for Irish seminarians in its own college in Rome; it

27 'Address to His Majesty' (London 1794), DDA.   28 Keogh, *The French disease*, pp 68–88; Corish, *Maynooth College, 1795–1995*, pp 6–12.   29 Propaganda to Troy, 5 Apr. 1794, APF, LDB 266, ff 414r–415v.

offered one student place to each of the four provinces as a special privilege.[30] In Ireland some little successes occurred, with the establishment of small seminaries at Carlow and Kilkenny.[31]

Erskine, who had successfully made contact with influential British politicians, was impressed with the return to England of English religious communities from Flanders, and especially with the financial help given to them by the state. In December 1794 Erskine met Lord Fitzwilliam, who had been appointed lord lieutenant of Ireland, and heard his views, which were favourable to the Catholics of Ireland. He therefore suggested that the pope write him a letter expressing his pleasure at this development. And, keen to uphold Roman authority in all situations, he thought that letters should be written to the bishops of Ireland and the vicars apostolic of England setting out the policies they should follow.[32]

Fitzwilliam was sworn in as viceroy on 4 January 1795 but was dismissed six weeks later on 23 February. His reputation had preceded him and Catholics in great numbers signed loyal addresses and petitions for the removal of the remaining penal laws. Henry Grattan, the Patriot orator who advocated legislative independence for the Irish parliament, introduced a Catholic relief bill to remove remaining Catholic disabilities and to open all offices except ecclesiastical (and royal) ones to Catholics, and he proposed a new oath of allegiance, but parliament rejected it. The viceroy made the mistake of moving too fast in ousting powerful conservative figures at Dublin Castle, and they conspired effectively against him. Disillusioned Catholics began to lose faith in appeals to the government and to turn towards the United Irishmen.[33]

Eighteen bishops met in February 1795 and asked Henry Grattan to appeal for a seminary for each province for the education of clergy, under their exclusive control. As negotiations continued the question of the right of the crown to nominate bishops was bruited about. But nothing had been decided when Fitzwilliam was dismissed, and though the wider emancipation of Catholics, which the cabinet in London would not tolerate, receded, the establishment and endowment of a seminary became a compensatory gesture. Faced with the war against France, the increasing disorder in Ireland and the hostility of the Irish parliament to any further major concessions to Catholics, the provision of a seminary was as far as the government would go.

Thomas Hussey, a Meath man, who was chaplain to the Spanish embassy in London and a close friend of Edmund Burke's, was commissioned by the prelates to negotiate with the leading politicians, with parliament and the

30 Ibid., 13 Sept. 1794, ff 523r–524v. 31 Troy to Propaganda, 20 Oct. 1794, SC(Ibernia) 28, Fondo di Vienna, ff 178r–179r; Concanen to Propaganda, 9 Nov. 1794, ibid., ff 186r–187v. 32 Propaganda to Erskine, 3 Jan., 6 Feb. 1795, APF, LDB 268, ff 137v–138v, 176r. 33 Curtin, *The United Irishmen*, pp 61–2, 235–6.

government about the establishment of a seminary.[34] Troy was mandated to work alongside him, and Troy's order from Rome to ensure that neither the government nor Protestant politicians interfered in the running of the seminaries was strengthened by similar advice given to Hussey by Burke. Negotiations between Hussey, Troy and Dublin Castle resulted in the production of a bill setting up and endowing a seminary. The bishops were obliged to accept on the board of trustees and visitors the four 'high judges' who were Protestants. A grant of £8,000 was provided for a new building. During the next two years £17,000 was made available for building purposes and an annual grant of £8,000 was agreed. Of the seventeen Catholic trustees six were laymen, four of whom – lords Fingall, Gormanston, Kenmare and Richard Strange – had seceded from the Catholic Committee in 1791. Of the eleven clerical trustees, all were bishops except Thomas Hussey.[35] A Catholic group of members of the old Catholic Committee had asked that Protestants should also be admitted as students, but no attention was paid to this bizarre request.

A jubilant Troy, reporting one of his greatest successes, sent an account to Cardinal Gerdil, who had succeeded Antonelli as prefect of Propaganda in February 1795, of the foundation of the college, a munificent gift from their sovereign and parliament, and of the solemn Mass of thanksgiving that had been held for the king and his government with the participation of many bishops and huge numbers of the faithful. He also explained that the senior judges had declared that they did not wish to be involved in the government of the college.[36] The answer could not have been more reassuring. Troy was informed that his letter could not have brought more comfort and consolation to the congregation. What pleased it was not only the foundation and financial grants but also the disclosure that the Protestant trustees did not intend to take any part in running the college.[37] Not every Roman official would have answered so enthusiastically. Some would have baulked at the prospect of Protestants being involved in a seminary, however modest the role assigned to them. With the establishment of Maynooth, an enormous burden was lifted off the shoulders of the bishops. Their congregations were ultimately promised a reasonable supply of priests and the state bore costs which the church could not have afforded.

The divisions between the radicals of the former Catholic Committee, some of whose leaders had joined the United Irishmen, and the more conservative wing, which was closer to the bishops, had widened. To the great

34 D. Keogh, 'Thomas Hussey, Bishop of Waterford and Lismore, 1797–1803 and the rebellion of 1798' in W. Nolan, T. Power and D. Cowman (eds), *Waterford, history and society*, pp 403–26. 35 Corish, *Maynooth College, 1795–1995*, pp 8–25. 36 Troy to Gerdil, 23 July 1795, APF, SC(Ibernia), 28, Fondo di Vienna, ff 233r–234v. 37 Propaganda to Troy, 25 Sept. 1795, APF, LDB, 268, f 319.

chagrin of the bishops these divisions were destined to widen further as the United Irishmen grew more radical and drew down on their supporters the full weight of military oppression. The failure of Grattan's relief bill to remove remaining restrictions on Catholics increased their disillusion and allowed the radicals to make further inroads at the expense of compliance with the government, which the bishops felt was the only feasible policy. And as the United Irishmen drew more Presbyterians and Catholics to their body, the Defenders and Orangemen engaged in increasingly violent conflicts. Some 4,000 Catholics were expelled from Armagh in 1795–6.[38]

In the midst of the negotiations for a seminary, Cardinal Antonelli addressed a solemn warning to the bishops of Ireland. The background to it was the gratitude Rome felt for the reception of French bishops and clergy (and the pensions granted them) by the British government on the one hand, and the reports of insurgency in Ireland on the other. The complaints about Catholic rebelliousness which Erskine had sent to Rome seemed to Roman officials to point to base ingratitude on the part of Catholics for what the British government was doing for the church. But, as the bishops were powerless to change the minds of the activists, advice or rebukes from Rome on such issues were an embarrassment. Antonelli reflected on the evils consequent on the violation and overthrow of laws, and drew out the obligations of Christians to God and society. The church exhorted its followers to be faithful to its teachings and to reject the wolves that would destroy them. Praising the beneficence and generosity of George III, the bishops were advised to persevere in obedience and to make use of the opportunities this afforded them. Antonelli summoned scripture, St Augustine and St Peter Chrysologus to his aid[39] in this encouragement to the prelates to act, in effect, as they had acted and would continue to act.

The Defenders and the United Irishmen came under fire from the bishops. The Defenders, being Catholic, were a particular embarrassment to Troy and other bishops, and Troy refused Christian burial to Defenders who refused to abjure their oaths. Several pastorals were issued denouncing them and the French revolutionaries who inspired them.[40] They in turn felt the lash of government oppression with the Insurrection Act of 1796 and the brutal measures adopted by General Lake to disarm those in Ulster who were deemed to be a danger to the state.[41]

---

38 Connolly, *Divided kingdom*, pp 454–9.   39 Propaganda to Bishops, 7 Feb. 1795, DDA. On his retirement due to ill health, Antonelli assured Troy that of all the kingdoms he had dealt with, Ireland was closest to his heart, and he flattered himself that Ireland always got justice. His regard and friendship for Troy had grown down the years (Antonelli to Troy, 5 Oct. 1795, DDA). He later became dean of the college of cardinals.   40 Keogh, *The French disease*, pp 136–41. 41 The failure of the expedition led by the French general Lazare Hoche in December 1796 was welcomed by the bishops, and in a solemn act of thanksgiving in February 1797. In a sermon, Troy lashed out at the evil principles of the French Revolution, and called for peaceful behaviour

The weakness of the bishops' position and the delicate line they were forced to tread in this dangerous situation was highlighted by the brouhaha aroused by the publication of a pastoral letter in 1797 by Thomas Hussey, the bishop of Waterford and chaplain general to the British forces in Ireland. Hussey's mistake was the robustness of the language he used in referring to past grievances as he called on his clergy to teach Catholic soldiers how contrary to the principles of their faith it was to attend Protestant places of worship.[42] His letter was vigorously condemned by government sources, several bishops were embarrassed by it and he was forced to resign from the presidency of Maynooth. The reaction to the pastoral showed that beneath the expressions of goodwill to the Catholics in government circles, a harsh strain of intolerance could be easily exposed.

Despite all the episcopal warnings, threats and appeals in several pastoral letters the movement towards rebellion gathered pace, and in May and June 1798 rebellion broke out in Leinster and Ulster. The French intervention in August, like the other uprisings, was easily crushed. Bloody battles were followed by severe repression. In the aftermath, forty Catholic churches in Leinster and in other parts of the Dublin diocese were destroyed. The number of priests involved in the rebellion has been calculated at seventy, or less than 4 per cent of the total. Many of these had very slight connections with the insurgents, and were accused on the shaky evidence of informers. Fourteen were indicted and six were executed (as were three Presbyterian ministers).[43] But because Catholics had predominated in the risings in Kildare and especially in Wexford, where Protestants had been massacred at Scullabogue, Protestant writers soon sought to turn the rebellion into a Catholic uprising. All the old charges of Catholic unreliability, disaffection and disloyalty were dredged up. This was precisely what Troy and some of his episcopal colleagues had most feared, and what they quickly attempted to correct for the benefit of Dublin Castle. They argued that those who in the name of democracy and liberty had refused to accept the bishops' lead were badly exposed by the failure of violence.

With the rebellion and the maleficent and churlish interpretation given to it by the ultra-Protestant politicians and publicists, the movement for Catholic relief suffered a setback. The mood in parliament and government circles was not conducive to sympathetic examination of Catholic grievances. However, Troy had won increasing respect and consideration from the government in the wake of the French Revolution, and the British response to it, and had proved that in any significant political developments for the

instead of violence. Bartlett, 'Defence, counter-insurgency and rebellion: Ireland 1793–1803' in Bartlett and Jeffrey, *A military history of Ireland*, p. 270. **42** Healy, *Maynooth College, its centenary history*, pp 693–6. **43** Yates, *The religious condition of Ireland, 1770–1850*, p. 39; McDowell, *Ireland in the age of imperialism and revolution*, pp 675–7.

country, the attitudes and possible reactions of the bishops would have to be taken into serious account. He had had a difficult path to follow. He had been obliged to try to steer the Catholic people away from extreme politics and encourage them to pursue their goals in a peaceful and conciliatory manner. He had been obliged to deal with Dublin Castle and seek relief in a constitutional manner when enemies accused him of not controlling seditious Catholics, whom he could never have controlled. And as he watched the resolute dechristianization of the French revolutionaries, he had striven to steer an increasingly radicalized Catholic people, including some clergy, away from the principles of a revolution long since condemned by Pope Pius VI. Some 10,000 lives had been lost in the rebellion.[44]

44 Connolly, *Divided kingdom*, p. 482.

3

The beginning of the campaign for
the relief of English Catholics

I

English Catholics gained some measure of relief, but at a lesser pace than their Irish counterparts. The difference in the progress of English and Irish Catholics was both understandable and significant. English Catholics accounted for little more than 1 per cent of the population; their number has been estimated at 80,000 in a population of 6 million in 1770.[1] Consequently, they could exercise little influence on the wider community, and were entirely dependent on parliament's goodwill and sense of fair play to obtain redress. Irish Catholics numbering 3 million and representing three-quarters of the population of Ireland and one-third of the population of the United Kingdom increasingly enjoyed the 'power' that came from the capacity to cause trouble, especially when Britain was engaged in wars with the American colonists and with France. Disturbances in Ireland could always be a painful and bothersome distraction, demanding the deployment of troops that might be needed elsewhere. Britain's wars also drew attention to another important aspect of Irish influence, as Ireland provided a pool of young men who could be drafted into British armies. The government therefore would have to deal with the demands of Irish Catholics as a political issue.

Another major difference between the Catholic communities, and in particular among the activists on their committees, was the role played by the nobles and gentry.[2] In England, Catholic peers and gentry were a much more powerful element in the church than in Ireland. Many of the Catholic priests were their chaplains and their private chapels served as local churches for the Catholics living nearby. The priest-chaplains were provided with accommodation and stipends, and some of the nobility and gentry subscribed to the incomes of the vicars apostolic and to those of priests attached to town or country churches. Since, to a large extent, the gentry paid the piper, they felt they had a right to call the tune in Catholic affairs.

1 Bossy, *The English Catholic community, 1570–1850*, p. 298. Joseph Berington (1745–1827), an able and prominent priest, and leader of the Staffordshire clergy who were accused of Gallicanism, claimed that among the Catholics there were 8 peers, 19 baronets and about 150 gentlemen of landed property. 2 Holmes, *More Roman than Rome*, pp 23–4.

In Ireland a few Catholic peers – lords Killeen, Trimleston, Kenmare, Fingall, Gormanstown, the Bellews – took an active part in the committees advocating Catholic relief. But by the 1790s they did not enjoy the dominant position of their English colleagues. Middle-class merchants, lawyers and businessmen took part in Catholic affairs from the mid eighteenth century, and as time passed became more active and less subservient to the peers in the Catholic committees. Neither the peers nor the middle-class representatives in Ireland disputed the religious element in the oaths, which they left for the most part to the bishops and clergy, but as political factors brought about measures of relief, the middle-class activists took the lead in pressing their demands at a political level.

Both sets of aristocrats and gentry were much more conservative and cautious than the thrusting Irish middle class who took control of the Catholic committees in Ireland. The English peers and committee members sought the removal of the restrictions on their professional and political life. They had no fears of the government creating any difficulties for them, should emancipation have to be won by conceding a right of veto on the appointment of bishops. Some of them, associating with their Anglican friends, might well have regarded royal intervention in episcopal appointments as a matter of little importance, a fact of ordinary political power. The Irish middle-class members feared that royal vetoes would be used for political purposes. Men could be chosen as bishops because of their political views, which were not those of the majority of their people, and they might try to combat the views of that majority.

In England the struggle for Catholic relief opened up a bitter, acrimonious conflict between the Catholic nobility and gentry, who formed the Catholic Committee, and the vicars apostolic. The committee, under the influence especially of Joseph Berington, a priest of the Midland District, put forth claims that the vicars, or at least two of them, consistently found unacceptable. Papal prerogatives and claims were under fire in several European countries, and Berington, a clever scholar whose views had led to his removal from the English College in Douay, found many of these opinions congenial in his efforts subsequently to win toleration.

In Germany, Febronius – and later, in Tuscany, Scipio de Ricci – proclaimed the supremacy of a general council over papal authority, denied the deposing and dispensing powers of the pope, emphasized the independent jurisdiction of bishops whose authority depended on the consent of the clergy, and in liturgy questioned the use of Latin. The papacy was invited to return to the simpler form it had held in the early church.[3]

Berington espoused a similar programme of reform to make the Catholic

---

3 'Gli inizi dell' evoluzione in Germania' in Jedin, *Handbuch der Kirchengeschichte*, pp 123–5.

church in England more acceptable to Protestants. He wanted less 'foreign domination' and more 'lay control of church affairs'. Declaring that he was 'no papist', he sought a church structure where each bishop was independent of Rome and its 'first ecclesiastical magistrate', the pope. He attacked the prerogatives and privileges of the papacy, and even expressed the opinion that Christ had used ambiguous language to allow greater freedom in the interpretation of doctrines. These views, which helped inspire members and supporters of the Catholic Committee, often known as the Cisalpines, drew forth vehement responses from opponents who regarded them as unorthodox.[4]

The English Catholic Committee originated from the desire of Lord North's government to gain Catholic recruits for the war against the American colonies. At the invitation of the Catholic, William Sheldon, with whom North's agent had made contact, some eighty prominent Catholics met to request the repeal of measures they regarded as oppressive. Edmund Burke lobbied hard for concessions, drawing up both an address of loyalty to the king, and with the aid of the Irish agent in London, the actual terms of a bill of relief. An act was passed 'with Irish Catholics in mind', and an Irish friend was assured by Burke that it was 'ultimately intended for you'. The government hoped that the Irish parliament would learn from this gesture.[5] Though English and Scottish mediators had been involved, the need for Irish support was far more important than achieving the goodwill of the small English community.[6] By the Catholic Relief Act of 1778 Catholics were enabled to purchase or inherit property, the penalty of life imprisonment for bishops, priests and schoolmasters was abolished, and so were the anachronistic rewards for 'informing' against them. The act was welcomed by Catholics as a gesture of recognition and an acceptance of the need to expunge from the statute book legislation that was more honoured in the breach than the observance. An oath was attached to the act, which Catholics were invited to take, and which the vicars apostolic and priests were obliged to take to enable them to avail of the act. The oath was very similar to the Irish oath of 1774. Though modest, the act of 1778 was used as an excuse by Lord George Gordon to provoke anti-Catholic riots in 1780.

William Sheldon, a Catholic lawyer who had been involved with the first committee in 1778, which had been wound up, made his house available for a meeting of Catholics in 1782 to found a new committee. It was summoned by the secretary of the previous one, the lawyer Charles Butler, who was destined to play a central part in Catholic affairs for many years.[7] Butler was

---

4 Duffy, 'Ecclesiastical democracy detected', i.   5 Bartlett, *The rise and fall of the Irish nation*, pp 83–4.   6 Ibid., p. 85.   7 Charles Butler (1750–1832), a solicitor of Lincoln's Inn, was secretary to the Catholic Committee, 1782–91, and a leading member of the Cisalpine Club. He was later called to the bar and wrote *Historical memoirs of the English, Irish and Scottish Catholics*.

a devout Catholic who worked diligently and earnestly for the Catholic cause as secretary of committees. Some twelve members of the nobility and gentry including Lord Petre, Sir John Throckmorton,[8] Sir Henry Englefield, Lord Stourton, Lord Clifford, William Fermor, Thomas Stapleton, Thomas Hornyold and John Towneley were chosen to form the committee.[9] The first matter which engaged the committee's attention and was to be a harbinger of misunderstandings to come was ecclesiastical rather than political. For almost a century the church in England had been ruled by four vicars apostolic. Though in episcopal orders these vicars were directly under Roman jurisdiction, and therefore more answerable to Rome than residential bishops. Normal episcopacy endowed church leaders with greater prestige. The committee, revealing an unwillingness to show any unnecessary subservience to Rome, claimed that the dependence of the vicars apostolic on Rome made the Catholics 'more unpopular and obnoxious to the nation', thereby inconveniencing those who would grant them religious or political relief, and, as it wished to remove any pretext for popular misconceptions, put its view of their status to the four vicars apostolic.[10] Two of the vicars agreed with the proposal; two others believed that the committee had strayed beyond its competence.[11]

John Milner, who was then stationed in Winchester and who was to become a most determined, outspoken and extreme opponent of all such lay initiatives, and indeed of nearly every initiative of Catholic committees, claimed that the request of the committee contained 'a series of assertions highly derogatory to the spiritual government of the vicars apostolic' and could only 'be excused from the intention of schism by their ignorance of theological matters'. There was, however, no intention of schism, and Milner's charge that schism was implicitly involved was to be the precursor of the baneful accusations that he would make against opponents in the years ahead.[12]

The committee stood for re-election in 1787 when its term of office ended and most of its members were again elected. In its appeal to the electors it again referred to the need for residential bishoprics, complaining that the vicars apostolic were appointed by Rome 'without any election either by the clergy or laity', and that this form of government was not only contrary to the primitive practices of the church but also opposed to the statutes of Praemunire and Provisors.[13] By expressing itself in such terms the

8 Throckmorton (1753–1819) published pamphlets calling for the nomination of bishops at the local level by both priests and laity.   9 M. Bence-Jones, *The Catholic families*, pp 31–45.   10 The restoration of the hierarchy in 1850, instead of diminishing Protestant antipathy to Catholicism, in fact brought down a torrent of abuse on the bishops and the church.   11 Bossy, *The English Catholic community, 1570–1850*, pp 330–2.   12 Ward, *Dawn of the Catholic revival*, i, pp 93–8. Milner (1752–1826) became vicar apostolic of the Midland District in 1803.   13 These statutes of the 1350s strengthened the rights of the crown against the papacy, forbade

committee was again challenging the authority Rome enjoyed over the vicars apostolic. In 1788 the committee added three clerical members to its number: James Talbot, the vicar apostolic of the London District, Charles Berington, the coadjutor to the vicar apostolic of the Midland District and Joseph Wilks, a Benedictine priest. Wilks and Charles Berington were destined to play significant roles in the future, often in opposition to the views of the vicars apostolic.[14]

Even though the other part of the committee's programme was the relatively harmless request for the establishment of a boys' school in England,[15] the aspiration of laymen to put their views forward strongly to the Catholic body in the disciplinary, and perhaps even doctrinal, practice of the church, alarmed the vicars apostolic. That alarm was greatly increased when John Throckmorton, who was elected secretary in 1787, cavalierly suggested that Catholics might take the oath of supremacy and justified his view by claiming that the denial of authority or pre-eminence to a foreign tribunal that had civil as well as ecclesiastical authority was not heretical. The committee took practical political steps in 1788 when it arranged to meet William Pitt, the prime minister, and sought a relief bill calling for the repeal of the statutes barring Catholics from serving in the navy and army, from practicing law or medicine and from having the same full rights in property as those enjoyed by Protestant Dissenters. Before Pitt made any commitments, he asked them to let him have the official views of Catholic clergy and universities regarding the existence or extent of the pope's alleged power. The committee duly requested the theology faculties of six Continental Catholic universities to answer three questions.[16] Had the pope, cardinals or any cleric any civil authority, power or jurisdiction in England? Could he absolve or dispense any British subjects from their allegiance to the king? Was there any principle by which Catholics could find justification for not keeping faith with heretics?[17] The negative answers from all the universities to these questions bolstered the Catholic case both in England and Ireland.

appeals to Rome of cases which could be held in the royal courts and restricted presentation to benefices to the king and certain lords.   **14** In *The English Catholic enlightenment*, pp viii–xi, Joseph P. Chinnci maintains that John Lingard, Joseph Berington, Charles Butler, John Kirk and John Fletcher synthesized their collective faith and the thought of the Enlightenment in church-state relations, theology, ecclesiology, history and religious practice. Lingard did not take much part in the disputes about the oaths with the vicars apostolic but the others were all involved. James Talbot (1726–90) was vicar apostolic of the London District from 1781 to 1790. Charles Berington (1748–98) was coadjutor of the Midland District from 1786 to 1795, and vicar apostolic with reduced powers from 1795 to 1798.   **15** A number of northern Catholic laymen protested against this proposal on the grounds that it would prevent young men from entering clerical life and would damage their colleges on the Continent (Ward, *Dawn of Catholic revival*, i, pp 119–21).   **16** The questions were put to the faculties of theology in the universities of Louvain, Douay, the Sorbonne, Valladolid, Alcalà and Salamanca.   **17** Hughes, *The Catholic question, 1688–1829*, p. 153.

II

In the following year Lord Stanhope, a Protestant, drew up for the Catholic Committee a statement described as a protestation (or occasionally as a declaration and protestation) repudiating doctrines falsely ascribed to Catholics, much of which was derived from the writings of the Capuchin, Arthur O'Leary.[18] This well-meaning gesture was destined to initiate distrust between the committee and the vicars apostolic. It was shown to members of the committee and to the vicars apostolic before being made public, and some alterations proposed by them were made to the text. This repeated the views of the Catholic universities denying any authority to the pope, prelates or clergy to depose or murder princes excommunicated by the pope and denying that any pope or council could absolve Catholics from their allegiance.

The opinion that Catholics could obey immoral orders, exterminate persons of a different religion, carry out an immoral act for the good of the church or acknowledge papal infallibility was also rejected. Repudiating the claim that the pope could dispense with the obligations of an oath, Catholics also negated the charge that sin could be forgiven without sincere sorrow and a firm resolution of amendment. And they also declared that the principle that no faith was to be kept with heretics was contrary to religion, morality and common honesty. They repudiated the claim that any prelates, priests or ecclesiastical power could have jurisdiction within the realm that could interfere with its constitution or sovereignty.

Some Catholics took exception to the strong language on papal infallibility, which many believed even though it was not an official doctrine, and the total exclusion of the pope's power to dispense from an oath (which could have included rash oaths taken for purely religious purposes). Some found the repudiation of claims that they had never even thought about degrading and insulting and disliked the description of the deposing power as 'unchristian-like and abominable'. However, the vicars apostolic, 240 priests and more than 1,500 lay persons signed it, though Bishop Walmesley of the Western District and Bishop Gibson of the Northern District did so reluctantly.[19]

Charles Walmesley, a scholarly Benedictine who had been educated in

---

18 Arthur O'Leary (1729–1802) wrote pamphlets in defence of Christianity and replied to John Wesley's letter on Catholicism. He moved from Cork to St Patrick's Church in London where, among other writings, he pleaded for relief for English Catholics (A clergyman of Massachusetts (ed.), *The works of Revd Arthur O'Leary, OSF*).   19 Ward, *Dawn of the Catholic revival*, i, pp 126–51. Walmesley later informed Rome that he had signed the declaration 'improvidently' and discovering on further examination that it was erroneous wished to remove his signature (Walmesley to Propaganda, 8 Dec. 1790, APF, SOCG 887, ff 147r–150r).

Douay and Paris and whose mathematical abilities had earned him fellow-
ships of the royal societies of Berlin and London,[20] challenged some of the
claims made in the protestation. So also did Matthew Gibson, who with his
brother and successor gave constant support to Walmesley's questioning of
the committee's role and work. The Talbot brothers,[21] who were in charge of
the London and Midland districts, were more reluctant to contest the
policies of the committee, partly for temperamental and political reasons and
partly because as members of an aristocratic family they were more closely
associated with the aristocrats of the committee. Divisions among the vicars
apostolic had not occurred publicly but were there below the surface from
the beginning.

In May 1789 the protestation was presented to parliament as a petition for
relief by Sir John Mitford. The committee then drew up a bill with a new
oath of allegiance based on it but the king's illness delayed its presentation in
parliament. Charles Butler, the secretary of the committee, who was closely
involved in preparing the bill, claimed that the government required more
extensive assurances than it had previously received, and that the terms used
and the longer oath were the consequence of that requirement.[22] The bill as
it emerged from discussions between members of the committee and their
friends in parliament began by reiterating restrictions on Catholic religious
orders and trusts. The foundation of any new religious order was forbidden
and 'superstitious' trusts were still not recognized as valid. All who took the
new oath, which was far stronger than the profession in the protestation,
were to be known henceforth as Protesting Catholic Dissenters, and those
who refused to do so were still to be denominated as papists. Though the
committee subsequently claimed that it did not invent the term, 'Protesting
Catholic Dissenters', it defended the use of this nomenclature. These highly
unusual distinctions were to lead to legal differences, for children of papists,
educated as such, were not to enjoy the advantages of the new bill. To add
insult to injury the name 'Protesting Catholic Dissenters' in the preamble to
the bill was explained by the committee as referring to people who protested
against beliefs erroneously attributed to them and who dissented from the
Church of England, which could have implied that they were in fact a
Protestant sect.

Those taking the oath were obliged to swear allegiance to the heirs of
Princess Sophia of Hanover, 'being Protestant'; to repudiate as 'impious and

---

20 Schofield and Skinner, *The English vicars apostolic, 1688–1850*, pp 211–15. Walmesley
(1722–97) was coadjutor 1756–70 and vicar apostolic 1790–97. Matthew Gibson (1734–90) was
vicar apostolic from 1780 to 1790.   **21** Thomas Talbot was coadjutor of the Midland District
from 1766 to 1778 and vicar apostolic from 1778 to 1795. James Talbot was coadjutor bishop in
the London District from 1759 to 1781 and vicar apostolic from 1781 to 1790.   **22** Butler,
Historical memoirs, iv, p. 26.

heretical that damnable doctrine and position that princes excommunicated by the pope' may be deposed or murdered, and the claim that the pope or general council could absolve subjects from their allegiance; to deny that any prince or prelate could have any civil jurisdiction or spiritual authority within the realm that could directly or indirectly interfere with sovereignty, constitution, the civil or ecclesiastical government of the country; to swear that no person could be absolved from sin at the pleasure of the pope or of a priest and no hostility or breach of faith could be justified on the grounds that the person hurt was a heretic; and to affirm that the pope was not infallible and could not dispense with the obligations of the oath. Finally, the person taking the oath was obliged to swear that he did so without any mental evasion.[23]

The four vicars apostolic, Walmesley, Gibson, the two Talbots and two coadjutors met on 19 October 1789 and condemned the oath as unlawful, and decided to issue a pastoral letter or encyclical telling the faithful that they should not take any new oath, or sign any declaration on doctrinal matters, without the previous approbation of their respective bishops.[24] They pronounced the 'new appellation' 'Protesting Catholic Dissenters' to be 'highly objectionable', and declared the clauses not to educate any child as a papist or the child of Protestants as a Protesting Catholic Dissenter inadmissible. They called for the suppression of the restrictions on Catholic trusts.[25]

Objections were felt by some Catholics and two of the vicars apostolic to that part of the oath that demanded allegiance to the Hanoverian line of the Princess Sophia, being Protestants.[26] Objections were also taken to the strong, if not extreme, terms by which Catholics were required to 'abhor detest and abjure' that 'damnable doctrine' that princes excommunicated by the pope could be deposed or murdered. Explanations could be given for many of the restrictions, but where opponents of the oath were on firmer ground was in their opposition to the clause that no foreign prince or prelate had any jurisdiction within the realm or any spiritual authority within the realm that could directly or indirectly interfere with the civil or ecclesiastical government thereof. Bishop Thomas Talbot said this clause could be questioned, and although its defenders and later Charles Butler claimed that the ecclesiastical government was to be interpreted as part of the civil government, it was open to the interpretation that the legitimate exercise of papal jurisdiction over Catholics was being or could be rejected. The opponents of the oath, especially Walmesley, did not spell out the precise

---

23 *First blue book*, pp 9–11. The committee published its material in three books, known because of the colour of their covers as the Blue Books.   24 MacCaffrey, *History of the Catholic church in the nineteenth century (1789–1908)*, pp 6–10.   25 Resolution of the vicars apostolic, 19 Oct. 1789, CIDA.   26 Sophia, the electress of Hanover, was a granddaughter of James I. As a Protestant she became heir to the throne in 1701 and, when she died, her son George succeeded as George I in 1714.

errors contained in it, and consequently left the committee with the serious gripe that it was not being told how and where the oath erred.

The encyclical letter which the four vicars apostolic wrote condemning the oath ended with the peremptory demand 'to these determinations, therefore, we require your submission'. Walmesley, who was the senior vicar apostolic and the most conservative of their body,[27] duly wrote to the members of the committee, who had been most closely involved in preparing the bill and oath, apprising them of his own and his colleagues' views. He further explained that the oath of 1778 was a sufficient test of their allegiance, that the term 'Protesting Catholic Dissenters' should be withdrawn, as well as the clause not to educate any child of Protestant parents a Protesting Catholic Dissenter. Both the clauses about not educating children as papists and the description of their trusts as superstitious or unlawful should be repudiated.

The members of the committee, who had an exalted view of their own dignity and importance, believed in a less hierarchical structure in church government, and felt that they should not be presented with a summons to obedience without any consultation, did not take kindly to the bishops' response to the oath. But rather than confront them, they decided their best policy was to seek a delay in the publication of the encyclical or pastoral letter. Walmesley had already published it; the Talbot brothers, as vicars apostolic of the London and Midland districts, agreed to delay publication,[28] and Bishop Gibson of the Northern District did likewise, assuming that all were so acting.

The committee replied to the bishops in November 1789 yielding nothing to the episcopal claims. The members argued that they had not encroached on the pastoral authority of the bishops and complained that they were given no indication of the improper parts of the oath, which they maintained was 'only a declaration of the innocence of our principle in social and civic concerns' and insisted that it was based on the protestation which they had all signed. Moreover, they claimed that Bishop James Talbot of London had approved of it; in fact, he had done so in a casual manner, before he had met with his colleagues. Arguing that the Catholics of England had sometimes suffered from an imprudent interference of ecclesiastical authority in civil concerns, they instanced the oath required by James I, which had left to people's consciences all its rights in matters of salvation, and only required a protestation of fidelity to the government of the state. Catholics were pleased with this arrangement until Paul V 'fulminated a condemnation of this polit-

27 Schofield and Skinner, *The English vicars apostolic, 1688–1850*, pp 213–14.   28 Walmesley informed Rome that the Talbots yielded to some of their adversaries and did not promulgate this censure. This caused great pain to Gibson and himself (Walmesley to Propaganda, 19 June 1790, APF, SOCG 886, ff 147r, 150r).

ical oath'.[29] The protestation and the oath were an addition to the oath of 1778 in response to Protestant hostility. This letter was printed and circulated to the Catholics of England, and was therefore the committee's way of appealing beyond the vicars apostolic to the people at large.[30]

Before this exchange took place Rome was informed about the contretemps. Thomas Hussey, who was then attached to the Spanish embassy, described the oath in a letter to the nuncio in Brussels as very bad, and added that it had won the approval of Thomas Talbot of the Midland District and his coadjutor Charles Berington. He himself was not prepared to take it; for good measure, he further claimed that the state of the mission in England was truly deplorable. He followed this up by letting Rome know that James Talbot's health had declined and that his intellectual faculties had notably deteriorated.[31]

The case of the committee was also presented to Rome. William Strickland, an ex-Jesuit who had been attached to the English academy at Liège, and who was then living in England, also wrote to the nuncio. An active and valuable defender of the committee, he forwarded a copy of the encyclical which, he noted, had not been published by the Talbot brothers and argued that there was discontent with the procedure of the bishops – presumably he meant especially with the other two. He predicted that, if care were not taken, there could be a schism among English Catholics (talk of schisms became a frequent ploy of controversialists in this dispute) and he expressed the hope that the bishops would explain the oath and that they would draw up one that could be taken by those with the most delicate consciences. There was a danger of scandal being given by people taking the oath, and he went on to praise the men of prudence and moderation, such as Charles Berington, who were working to prevent this. Archbishop Zondadari, the secretary of the congregation of Propaganda, who was then in the Brussels nunciature, passed on this letter to the cardinal prefect with the comment that Strickland was trustworthy.[32]

This encomium stood the committee in good stead, for Strickland soon wrote again, referring to the bishops' obstinate refusal to indicate which parts of the oath they found reprehensible and again predicting the dangers of schism. He explained that he had been using his influence with Bishop

---

29 The oath of James I of 1606 rejected any papal claim to depose him, directly or indirectly, called for allegiance to him and demanded that Catholics swear to 'abjure, as impious and heretical, this damnable doctrine and position that princes, which be excommunicated by the pope may be deposed or murdered by their subjects'. The oath was to be taken without mental reservation. It was condemned by Paul V presumably on the grounds that predecessors like Pius V, who had deposed Queen Elizabeth, were being denounced as heretics. 30 Committee to Bishops, 25 Nov. 1789, ClDA. 31 Hussey to Nuncio, 18 Sept. 1789 and 2 Oct. 1789, APF, SC(Anglia), 5, ff 95r–96v. 32 Strickland to Zondadari, 6 Nov. 1789, ibid., ff 97r–98r. Zondadari was secretary of Propaganda from 1789 to 1795.

Sharrock, the coadjutor (1780–97) and later vicar apostolic (1797–1809) of the Western District, to get him to write a paternal letter to the committee pointing out the blameworthy elements of the oath and ways of correcting them. He insisted that the government only wanted an assurance of their civil allegiance. Recalling that Protestants were obliged to take oaths of supremacy and abjuration, which were irreconcilable with Catholicism, the ministry had offered one to Catholics which it believed would conform to their principles, and would be astounded if its generous offer were rejected without any reason being given for not accepting it.[33] Walmesley, however, was not moved by the committee's defence of the oath or of the title 'Protesting Catholic Dissenters'. He insisted that his colleagues regarded the oath as inadmissible and rejected the description of 'dissenters', 'conscious that all religionists are dissenters from us'.[34] Both he and Bishop Gibson denounced the attitudes of the committee in pastoral letters, the latter referring to their 'infernal stratagems'.[35]

As a consequence of the widening of the dispute, clergy began to publish their views of the oath. While a numerous body of priests from Lancaster rejected the oath, a group of fifteen from Staffordshire in a letter to Bishop Thomas Talbot composed by Joseph Berington insisted that it demanded nothing from them other than 'a renunciation of tenets which have been falsely imputed to our church'.[36] The ecclesiastical government, which the pope's spiritual authority could not affect, was understood to be a branch of the English temporal government. This letter reflected the influence of Enlightenment thought in that circle. By prefacing it with a fulsome address they protected themselves from charges of insubordination to episcopal authority.

The committee invited the vicars apostolic to a meeting in London on 3 February 1790 to explore ways of making the oath acceptable both to Catholics and to the government. They may not then have known that it had already been condemned in Rome. James Talbot, the vicar apostolic of London, had died on 26 January and Matthew Gibson of the Northern District did not attend. Thomas Talbot, who had not signed the encyclical, and his coadjutor, Charles Berington, were present, as were Charles Walmesley of the Western District and his coadjutor, Gregory Sharrock. Talbot declared he would not object to the oath if the alteration from the protestation about the right of the pope to interfere in the temporal or ecclesiastical government of the country were restored.[37] (In the oath, unlike the

---

33 Strickland to Nuncio, 13 and 29 Dec. 1789, ibid., ff 103r–104r and 101r–102v.
34 Walmesley to the Committee, 24 Dec. 1789, CIDA.   35 Ward, *The dawn of the Catholic revival in England*, i, p. 203.   36 Fifteen priests to Talbot, 25 Jan. 1790, CIDA.   37 On 10 Mar. 1790 the original oath was condemned by Propaganda, *Catholicos viros minime decet nec Fide nec Patrum regulis est consentanium* (APF, *Acta* 164, f 331v).

protestation, a prelate had been denied spiritual authority or jurisdiction that could interfere with the laws or constitution of the kingdom.) Walmesley declared that he rejected the protestation or declaration as it seemed to him to contain the same errors, though in a less serious form, as the oath condemned by the vicars apostolic,[38] and claimed that in the absence of Bishop Gibson he was not authorized to specify the unacceptable clauses in the oath. Though reminded that he had had three months since the episcopal condemnation of the oath to point out the improper parts of it, he still insisted that he could not do so in the absence of Gibson.[39]

Charles Butler had altered the clause of the oath which denied to any prelate civil jurisdiction or spiritual authority that could directly or indirectly interfere with the civil or ecclesiastical government of the country, to make the possible interference relate only to civil jurisdiction affecting the sovereignty, laws and constitutions of the country. There was in addition a requirement that sorrow be expressed for the forgiveness of sin. Matthew Gibson, who was determined to sign no oath until he had reconciled his district to it, admitted that the amended oath was an improvement, but still took exception to 'execrable' and 'impious' as descriptions of the deposing power, and among other things to the clause about absolution from sin, which did not take account of baptism. Moreover, he insisted that it was the prerogative of the vicars apostolic to frame an oath.[40] Walmesley reported to Rome that the change in the oath was of little significance, and he complained that Gibson had not even been shown the change at the meeting on 3 February 1790.[41]

Some of the Irish bishops followed the controversy about the oath with interest. Archbishop Butler, who had had no hesitation in taking the oath of 1774 in Ireland, wrote to his friend Bishop Plunket of Meath expressing his regrets that the dispute 'must be very disedifying to all well-wishers of religion', and his surprise that any Catholic could take such an oath. The four archbishops and the bishops of his province regarded it as inadmissible and he had written to Bishop Gibson to that effect.[42]

Some two months later Butler, replying to Plunket, remarked that they were in agreement about the oath, and instanced the clause about no foreign prince or prelate having any spiritual jurisdiction within the realm:

> I think several parts of it very censurable, and the proposition of the Church's having no jurisdiction, or spiritual and ecclesiastical

---

38 Walmesley to Propaganda, 19 June 1790 (APF, SOCG 886, ff 141r, 150v).　39 Strickland to Nuncio, 5 Feb. 1790, APF, SC(Anglia), 5, ff 117r–118v. Ward, *The dawn of the Catholic revival in England*, i, pp 212–13.　40 Gibson to Walmesley, 16 Feb. 1790, CIDA.　41 Walmesley to Propaganda, 8 Dec. 1790, APF, SOCG 889, ff 148r–150r.　42 Butler to Plunket, 11 Jan. 1790 in Cogan, *The diocese of Meath, ancient and modern*, iii, pp 142–3. Butler was referring to the original oath.

authority whatsoever, that can clash with the ecclesiastical government in England, seemed to me to imply a disavowal of her spiritual power over Protestants themselves from their baptism, and the obligation she lies under of doing all she can, with prudence, to withdraw them from the Protestant religion.

The archbishop went on to say that he had been in correspondence with some of the vicars apostolic, in which he pointed out his dislike of the oath, and had a lengthy letter from Troy 'exposing his reasons against the conscientious lawfulness of taking such a test'. He also informed Plunket that his agent in Rome had assured him that it was 'highly disapproved of' there, and that he was glad that it had been 'totally reprobated' in Ireland.[43]

Both Butler and Plunket had been accused of Gallicanism by Troy, and their hostility to the oath must have disabused him of that view. Troy himself described the oath to a member of the English Catholic Committee as 'equivocal, captious, tending to schism and schismatical',[44] and complained to Cardinal Antonelli in the strongest terms about the violation of papal rights contained in it.[45] Butler also wrote to Rome, distancing the Irish bishops from the oath and adding that the protestation which proceeded it was scarcely orthodox.[46] The Irish bishops were afraid that if an 'unorthodox' oath were accepted in England a similar one would be foisted on them.

Richard O'Reilly, the archbishop of Armagh, hearing of Butler's objection to the oath, offered Troy some prudent advice for Cashel in the hope that he would confine his zeal 'within due bounds and not proceed rashly in a business that requires the greatest deliberation, and wherein one unguarded step might be attended with the most disagreeable consequences'. O'Reilly believed that, if an oath were accepted by the vicars apostolic, the Irish bishops should be slow to oppose it:

> However notwithstanding the objections we have to any oath that may be grounded on the protestation, which is certainly in several points exceptionable, yet I am of opinion that should a new oath founded in said protestation be unanimously adopted by the bishops, clergy and people of England, we should not be hasty in condemning it on this side of the water.[47]

43 Butler to Plunket, 28 Mar. 1790, ibid., pp 143–5. Walmesley referred in his notes to letters of Butler to bishops Sharrock and Gibson.   44 Troy to member of the Catholic Committee, 13 Feb. 1790, DDA.   45 Troy to Propaganda, 31 Mar. 1790, APF, SOCG 885, f 245rv. He claimed that under the appearance of allegiance to the sovereign, the oath was '*sommamente lesivo degli incontestabili diritti primaziali del Sommo Pontefice*' and the Irish prelates opposed '*tali micidiali dottrine*'. The oath damaged the primatial rights of the pope and the Irish prelates opposed such deadly doctrines.   46 Butler to Propaganda, 26 Apr. 1790, ibid., SC(Ibernia), 17, ff 89r–90r.   47 O'Reilly to Troy, 29 Mar. 1790, DDA.

Had O'Reilly's counsel about the need of Irish bishops to be careful in dealing with questions that had been decided by the vicars apostolic been taken, some of the misunderstanding and acridity which later characterized their exchanges would have been avoided.

III

The vacancy in London created by James Talbot's death was another source of contention between the committee and the vicars apostolic.[48] The committee – one of whose members, John Throckmorton, had gone on record as claiming that the laity should be permitted to elect their own bishops – now saw an opportunity for putting one of their supporters in charge of the London District. Charles Berington, the coadjutor to the vicar apostolic of the Midland District, had been elected to the committee in 1788. In that capacity Berington had signed the letters of the committee, and was regarded by its members as much nearer to their way of thinking than to that of his brethren, the vicars apostolic. Archbishop James Butler of Cashel was one of the first to enter the lists against Berington. Butler informed Propaganda that Berington had expressed his approval of a reprehensible oath in letters addressed to the vicars apostolic and to the Catholics of England, both of which contained sentiments scarcely consistent with the delicacy and respect due to the church and which the Holy See expected of a bishop. He was therefore not a suitable candidate for the most respectable diocese in England.[49] But Lord Petre, in an inurbane letter to Walmesley threatening to withdraw his support 'if the cause of Catholicity' became 'the sport of Romish punctilios and lust for power', insisted that Berington was 'the most proper person' for London and 'the only one who is likely either to be received or submitted to in a peaceable and comfortable manner'.[50]

The congregation of Propaganda, in receipt of a postulation for Berington signed by two barons, many knights and other laymen, wrote to Walmesley for his advice. Noting that the three vicars apostolic had already put forward the name of John Douglass, a priest of York, the congregation explained that against Berington's candidature was his subscribing to the oath which the four vicars apostolic had condemned and which contained bad doctrines.[51] And Rome was advised, possibly by Archbishop Zondadari, that tensions over the oath had become so heated that a delegate should be sent to England secretly to take stock of the situation and calm those who had become too inflamed by the dispute.[52]

48 Hughes, *The Catholic question, 1688–1829*, pp 163–4. 49 Butler to Propaganda, 20 May 1790, APF, SC(Anglia) 5, ff 121r–122v. 50 Petre to Walmesley, 15 May 1790, CIDA. 51 Propaganda to Walmesley, 12 June 1790, ibid., ff 127r–129v. 52 Zondadari to Propaganda,

Walmesley was most anxious to have successors both in London and in the Northern District (where Bishop Matthew Gibson had died on 17 May 1790) who would share his antipathy to the oath. Bishop Gibson's brother, William, was duly appointed to the Northern District and he and Walmesley assured Rome that Douglass and not Berington ought to be appointed to London. Berington, they insisted (wrongly), would be most unacceptable to the clergy of the London District (he had in fact obtained the majority of their votes). William Gibson also let Rome know that he himself would have preferred to go to the London District. He had lived there, he spoke French and he could deal with ambassadors. Douglass could then take the Northern vicariate. But if the London District were given to Berington, Catholicism would be ruined. The bishops of Ireland and Scotland had pointed out that the question at issue was not merely the formula of an oath but that of the whole discipline of the church and obedience to the Holy See. Gibson concluded that only the opposition of parliament would stop the committee pursuing its objective.[53]

To the intense annoyance of the committee, Douglass was appointed. It would not have known about the Irish intervention in the process, and would have assumed that its episcopal opponents in England had been responsible for defeating Berington. Consecrated on 19 December 1790, Douglass shared Walmesley's views and consistently supported his interventions. His episcopal ordination afforded Walmesley and Gibson an opportunity of discussing the oath with him, and all agreed to oppose it. They issued an encyclical or pastoral statement in January 1791 reiterating the right of the bishops alone to give guidance to the Catholic people on doctrinal issues including the oath, which had been condemned by the Holy See.[54] Thomas Talbot refused to join in any further condemnations of the oath, as he regarded such disapprobation as provocative and counterproductive. The other three recalled the pastoral of October 1789 in which all four vicars apostolic had declared that 'none of the faithful clergy or laity ought to take any new oath, or sign any new declaration in doctrinal matters, or subscribe any new instrument wherein the interests of religion are concerned without the previous approbation of their respective bishop', and they repeated their view that the committee had no right or authority to determine the lawful-ness of oaths or other doctrinal matters. And as the alteration in the oath had been of little significance, they condemned the attempt to offer it to parlia-ment without their approval, and called on Catholics to oppose it by petitions or any other suitable means. They concluded by trusting that their people

20 July 1790, ibid., ff 134r–135r.   53 Walmesley and Gibson to Propaganda, 9 Sept. 1790 and Gibson to Propaganda, 14 Sept. 1790. Ibid., ff 139r–140v and 143r. John Douglass (1743–1812) was vicar apostolic from 1790 to 1812.   54 The oath condemned by the Holy See in March 1790 was the one which first appeared in the bill, not the amended version.

would reject some of the publications which the controversy had brought forth as 'schismatical, scandalous, inflammatory and insulting to the supreme head of the church, the Vicar of Jesus Christ'. They also condemned the term 'Protesting Catholic Dissenters'.[55]

The committee responded to this pastoral by writing to Bishop Douglass. In this letter the members, in a combative mood, sought to correct the bishops' supposed misconceptions, explaining that they did not formulate the oath, which was taken from the protestation but altered by the ministers to make it conform to the style of other oaths by retaining parts of the oaths of allegiance, abjuration and supremacy which were not contrary to the Catholic faith. Nor had they 'solicited' the term 'Protesting Catholic Dissenters'. They recalled that the encyclical of October 1789 had not been published either in the London or Midland districts and that the vicar apostolic of the Western District had not pointed out any heretical passages in the oath. They noted that Thomas Talbot had only taken exception to 'the alteration from the protestation in that clause, which related to the right of the pope, or the Church, to interfere with the temporal and ecclesiastical government of the country, as by law established'. Provisos had been included in other acts for Catholic relief, and consequently it was not surprising that they were included in this one. The communication ended on a jarring and discordant note:

> It is painful for us to enter into a discussion of this nature with your lordships. At all times we have been ready to meet the apostolic vicars to inform them of our proceedings, to confer and cooperate with them for the public good. Why then, my lord, precipitate matters? Why circulate this defamatory mandate? Have the faithful been edified by it? Has it served the cause of religion? Has it recommended Catholics to the favour of the nation? To those very chapels, from the altars of which your last encyclical letter was promulgated, more than one of us have largely contributed.[56]

Despite this churlish rebuke from the pen of Charles Butler to the three vicars apostolic, the committee expressed a wish to hold a conference with Douglass. Accordingly, bishops Douglass and William Gibson and a London priest met the committee on 8 February 1791. The atmosphere was hostile and the mood of the members confrontational. The bishops were grilled about their knowledge of the oath and about the reactions of their colleagues

55 Husenbeth, *The life of Bishop Milner*, pp 30–1; encyclical letter, 19 Jan. 1791, CIDA.
56 Committee to Bishop Douglass, 2 Feb. 1791, CIDA; *Second blue book*.

in Ireland and Scotland as well as in England. Eventually Bishop Gibson called a halt to the proceedings by asking if the committee intended not to carry on with the bill without the approbation of the bishops. It replied by professing the greatest respect for episcopal authority but maintained that it could not submit to this requisition without increasing the prejudice against the faith and moral character of the Catholics, since they had been given no proof that the oath was contrary to faith or morals. The committee declared that it would appeal to all Catholic churches, and especially to the Holy See.[57]

Walmesley was outraged by the Committee's brusque treatment of his colleagues. He wrote indignantly to Gibson:

> The committee act in an open refractory and rebellious manner by the declaration of the 8th … Such ways of proceeding have been employed by heretics and schismatics in all the ages of the church, and like them the committee go on with more and more obstinacy … we ought, in my opinion, to keep stedfast [*sic*] to that point according to the tenor of our encyclical letter.

Despairing of reaching any agreement with the committee, he suggested they should write to Lord Grenville, the home secretary, or Pitt in the hope of stopping the bill and freeing the bishops 'from further vexation'.[58] A deputation from the bishops to the committee, asking if it would accept changes to make the oath acceptable, met with no success.

There then followed a furious, mordant and truculent 'protest and appeal' addressed by the committee to the three vicars apostolic, Walmesley, Gibson and Douglass. It was written by Joseph Wilks and it was more extreme in its dismissal of the bishops' case than any previous communication. Explaining that Christ only demanded submission when it was reasonable, which meant it should be preceded by instruction and reason, the bishops were told that they had pronounced the oath to be unlawful without the specification of one single objectionable clause.[59]

Recalling that the two Talbots had defended the oath, the committee argued that individual prelates and even national councils could err, and it adduced cases where judgments given by popes had been overturned. Insisting that the three bishops had been 'quite mistaken in their notions and statements of the principles of the bill', the committee accused them of having shown so many contradictions in their opinions that it was possible to call in question 'the irrefragability of your articles and determinations

---

57 Ibid., 8, 9, Feb. 1791. Strickland, the defender of the committee, complained to Rome of the vicars apostolic not giving reasons for their opposition to the oath and suggested they be told that Rome disapproved of their opposition.   58 Walmesley to Gibson (copy), 11 Feb. 1791, ClDA. 59 Chinnici, *The English Catholic Enlightment*, pp 45–8.

without incurring the guilt of heresy, schism or disobedience'. Bewailing the wrong-headed intervention of the papacy in questions of allegiance – as in the 'unwise and unjustifiable' bull of Pius V and the condemnation of the oath of James I by Paul V – the committee claimed that by the act of 1778 the encroachments of Rome had been repelled. Denying that papal infallibility was a tenet of faith, the committee accused the bishops of threatening to plunge Catholics into dishonesty by receding from the protestation, and charged them with direct responsibility for the contestation. The committee, in high-flown rhetoric, maintained that they were:

> Convinced that we have not been misled by our clergy, convinced, that we have not departed from the principles of our ancestors; convinced, that we have not violated any article of Catholic faith or communion ... [and therefore] before God, solemnly protest, and call upon God to witness our protest, against your lordships' encyclical letters of the 19th day of October 1789 and 21st day of January last, and every clause, article, determination, matter, and thing therein respectively contained; as imprudent, arbitrary, and unjust; as a total misrepresentation of the nature of the bills to which they refer, and the oaths therein respectively contained; and our conduct relating thereto respectively; – as encroaching on our natural, civil and religious rights, inculcating principles hostile to society and government and the constitution and laws of the British empire.

They therefore gave notice that they would appeal to all the Catholic churches of the world, and especially the Holy See.[60] Signed by several laymen, Bishop Berington, and Joseph Wilks, this manifesto was certainly a robust challenge to episcopal authority.

Walmesley, who was far from being intimidated by this broadside, also wrote to Cardinal Antonelli about the response of the committee to Bishop Douglass, which he denounced as insulting, arrogant and contumacious. He then referred to the manifesto and appeal signed by Charles Berington, Wilks and eight laymen protesting against everything in their encyclicals of October 1789 and February 1791, and against all that they would order in the future according to those encyclicals. Remarking that the oath they had condemned on 19 February 1791 differed in no essential point from that condemned on 19 October 1789, he added that he had suspended Wilks, and that Thomas Talbot had refused to sign their encyclical of 19 February 1791.[61]

60 Catholic Committee to three vicars apostolic, 17 Feb. 1791, CIDA; *Second blue book*.
61 Walmesley to Antonelli (copy), 14 Mar. 1791, CIDA.

Wilks and Walmesley, who both lived in Bath, held very opposing views on the issue of the bill and the oath, and both were determined and combative men. In the circumstances only one could win the struggle, and accordingly, Walmesley wrote to Wilks threatening to suspend him from ministering in the Western District and to withdraw his faculties. The suspension of his faculties was to last until Wilks made amends by repudiating the part he had played in the committee and promised to accept the policy of the vicars apostolic. Wilks replied that he could not submit without proving treacherous to a trust which had been given him and without bringing disgrace on the faith and moral character of the English Catholics. Noting that one of the four vicars apostolic had approved of their conduct, he maintained that his conscience did not charge him with transgressing Walmesley's ordinances, and he looked forward to the approbation of the present and rising generations of English Catholics.[62] Wilks' suspension further rubbed salt in the wounds of the Cisalpines, who took up his cause.

Bishop Thomas Talbot of the Midland District, a timid man caught between the militant forces of his three colleagues and the committee, backed by his coadjutor and several of his clergy, appealed to the cardinal prefect to allay the disharmony provoked by the oath.[63] William Strickland assured Rome that if Catholics were to refuse to take the oath they would justify all the odious calumnies with which Catholicism had been aspersed. The committee had repeatedly asked the vicars apostolic to point out in the oath any articles inconsistent with Catholic principles, so they could be altered. Though he knew that the oath did contain some clauses which Rome would find disagreeable, he also knew that the committee did not want to see religion persecuted, and, therefore, he recommended that the congregation should tell the vicars apostolic that their opposition to the committee did not meet with Rome's approval.[64] Whether he realized it or not Strickland was asking Rome to do what it would never do – take the side of a body of laymen against the majority of the bishops.

The bill for Catholic relief was introduced by Sir Henry Mitford in the house of commons in February 1791. Mitford listed the numerous disabilities in the statute book from which Catholics suffered or had once suffered. And referring to the favourable outcome of the relief act in Ireland in 1774 and of the act of 1778, he proposed a similar measure in England. Pitt commented favourably on it and the Whig leaders Edmund Burke and

---

62 Wilks to Walmesley, 25 Feb. 1791, ClDA; Hughes, *The Catholic question, 1688–1829*, pp 163–7.   63 Talbot to Propaganda, 10 Jan. 1791, APF, SC(Anglia), 5 f 361r.   64 Strickland to Propaganda, 18 Feb. 1791, ibid., ff 368r–369v. In a further letter on 26 Feb. 1791 (ff 275r–376v), Strickland referred to the meeting of the bishops and the committee, commenting that the committee had great respect for the bishops but could not see what was wrong with the oath. The 'moderate' committee could not abandon the protestation.

Charles James Fox called for maximum freedom for Catholics from the irksome restrictions affecting them. Gibson and Douglass wrote to Pitt, whom they regarded as sympathetic to their cause, asking for the oath of 1778 or the Irish oath of 1774. At Walmesley's request, Thomas Weld wrote to him to the same effect.[65] John Milner circulated fliers among members of parliament about the contest among the Catholics concerning the bill, denouncing the name 'Protesting Catholic Dissenters', objecting to some clauses in the oath and also proposing that the oath taken by Irish Catholics should be substituted for it. The committee was angered by Milner's intervention and challenged his authority to act for three vicars apostolic and for thousands of Catholics of England. After an acrimonious meeting with Milner the committee published a defence of its role as the publicists of the Catholic cause. It argued that Milner could not produce the names of those for whom he claimed to act other than those of three persons. And then in a display of 'democracy' which might have been drawn from the French constitution of the clergy, it contemptuously added that 'we have never heard that those three persons were ever chosen by the Catholic body to transact business in their names'. The committee could scarcely have shown more disrespect to the three bishops than it did by disputing their spiritual authority because they had not been commissioned by the Catholic body by a popular vote.

The irrepressible Milner was not cowed by such accusations; he not only did not flinch but drew strength from the hostility of a group that he believed had no claim to represent the views of the Catholic people who had taken no part in electing it. However, the three vicars apostolic began to fear that Milner's combative tactics only added to their difficulties, and he withdrew to Winchester.[66]

Milner was not alone in countering the propaganda of the committee. Charles Plowden, a former Jesuit, also bewailed the effects of the controversy, claiming that many men of rank and fortune disapproved of the committee and that a large majority of gentry, clergy and people of middle rank deprecated its proceedings. Their bishops had been reproached for their supposed ignorance of the true interests of their flock, but they knew their authority was incontrovertible and, had they entered into arguments about their motives, the altercations would have been endless. Noting that the Irish bishops also repudiated the oath, he analysed and dismissed some of the language used in it: the 'blustering' words 'impious, damnable and heretical' about murdering princes; 'the impious, damnable and heretical' aspect of the

---

65 Thomas Weld, a wealthy landowner, who had estates in Dorset and Lancashire, always refused to join the Catholic Committee and was a stern opponent of Cisalpinism. His chaplain was the ex-Jesuit, writer and controversialist, Charles Plowden. 66 Ward, *The dawn of the Catholic revival*, i, pp 262–81; Husenbeth, *The life of Bishop Milner*, pp 34–9.

deposing power; the forgiveness of sin at the 'pleasure of the pope'. He, of course, rejected the description of Catholics as 'Protesting Catholic Dissenters', and insisted that infallibility should not be foresworn, as bishops – without the pope – could not form the rule of faith.[67] This pamphlet, in which the oath itself was included, was forwarded to Rome.

As the bill was debated in the committee stage, Mitford replaced the phrase 'Protesting Catholic Dissenters' with the much more acceptable term 'Roman Catholics' and the rejection of the power of any pope or council to order an unlawful or immoral act was substituted for the denial of papal infallibility. The deposition or murder of princes and the dispensation by the pope from oaths were repudiated. Absolution from sin was made to depend on sorrow and a promise of amendment.

The changes in the oath did not diminish Walmesley's antipathy to it. In a list of objections to it found in his notes for that time, he expressed his dislike for the succession clause whereby allegiance was pledged to the successors of the Princess Sophia, being Protestants. He did not like the terms 'unchristian, impious and damnable' describing the deposing power. He completely rejected the clause declaring that 'no foreign church, prelate etc. has any jurisdiction that can directly or indirectly affect or interfere with the laws, rights, liberties, persons etc.'. He was sorry to see the word 'infidel' associated with 'heretic' in the clause about breach of faith. And he could not admit the clause 'neither pope, nor any prelate etc. can dispense with any oaths, contract, promise etc. whatsoever, made with any person whatsoever'. These thoughts, which amounted to a sweeping rejection of the oath, were committed to a draft letter presumably for a colleague.[68] Had he sent these objections to the committee there would have been a basis for discussion between both sides and, even if there was complete disagreement, the committee could not have claimed that it did not know what the offending parts of the oath were.

Walmesley and Gibson still opposed the amended oath as the bill was brought to the house of lords. In doing so, they had encouragement and, in effect, the direction of the nuncio from Brussels, who advised the vicars apostolic that Catholics should be warned against the oath.[69] Those prepared to tolerate the altered oath were encouraged by the assurance of Archbishop Troy, who explained that after a lengthy examination of it with his clergy he had concluded that it was acceptable, and regarded the words of succession, 'being Protestant', as merely narrative.[70]

Walmesley believed that the only way to get rid of the oath was to defeat

67 C. Plowden, *Observations on the oath proposed to the English Roman Catholics*, APF, SC(Anglia) 5, ff 161r–195v. William Gibson forwarded a translation of the oath on 10 Jan. 1791 (ibid., f 355r). 68 Walmesley, draft, 20 Apr. 1791, ClDA. 69 Nuncio to Propaganda, 31 May 1791, APF, SC(Anglia), 5, ff 381r–382v. 70 Gibson to Walmesley, 30 May 1791, ClDA.

the bill. He wrote to this effect both to Lord Grenville and to the archbishop of Canterbury. Milner wrote, in the same vein, to the bishops of Hereford and Salisbury. Bishop Douglass had softened his opposition to the oath and informed Walmesley that in its improved form it could be taken. Maintaining that though clauses in it were inaccurate or untheological they could still be understood in an orthodox sense. He therefore advised that they should withdraw their former prohibition so that those who would take the oath would not sin by disobedience.[71]

Douglass, at the suggestion of Joseph Berington, wrote to Samuel Horsley, the Anglican bishop of St David's, for his help in their difficulties. Horsley, a distinguished scholar, acquainted himself with the disputes and differences between the bishops and the committee about the bill.[72] Assuring his colleagues that their anxieties about papal power and the restoration of the Stuarts were without foundation, he pointed out that the majority of the Roman Catholics who found some of the terms of the oath unacceptable were prepared to swear allegiance to the king. He referred to offensive terms such as 'damnable', which had overtones of eternal damnation, and he dealt with the clause that had caused much soul-searching among Catholic clergy and some laity: the denial of the right of any prelate or priest to have any jurisdiction in the realm that could directly or indirectly interfere with the laws or constitution or with the rights, liberties, persons or properties of the people. He explained that the pope's authority would be incompatible with the recognition of the king as head of the church, and gave other examples of possible confusion. He therefore expressed regret that the oath of 1778 was not sufficient, and after some further interventions, proposed that the Irish oath of 1774 should be attached to the bill. With a few slight alterations, this was accepted. The bill was passed and received the royal assent on 10 June 1791.[73]

By the act Catholics were left free to practice their religion, with trivial restrictions such as the registration of churches and the prohibition of steeples and bells on churches, and the penalties which had been attached to religious practice were removed. The clergy were obliged to take the oath and the laity were technically bound to do likewise to obtain relief from the obligation to attend Anglican services, though few of them did so. If schoolmasters took the oath, they were free from prosecution, but Catholics were not given permission to found colleges. Barristers and attorneys were not obliged to take the oath of supremacy and the declaration against

71 Douglass to Walmesley, 12, 16 May 1791, ClDA.   72 Douglass reported to Walmesley that Horsley reproached the committee for its appeal to Rome, rightly informed, and that some of the lay lords also 'handled' the committee 'severely' (Douglass to Walmesley, 2 June 1791, ClDA). 73 Ward, *The dawn of the Catholic revival*, i, pp 288–96. The nuncio was troubled by the pledge to the successors of the Princess Sophia 'being Protestants'.

transubstantiation. The bar remained on Catholics entering parliament, or voting for parliamentary candidates or bequeathing money to charities that were designated as 'superstitious'.

The congregation of Propaganda had begun examining the bill and oath before the act was passed, but seems not to have completed its examination or reached a decision by June 1791. A long account (*ristretto*) was prepared for the meeting of the cardinals at which they would have decided if the oath, and indeed the whole bill, was acceptable. Though this *ristretto* bore the date 1791, internal evidence indicates that it was drawn up in 1790. It was a detailed and comprehensive document and, though it favoured the views of the vicars apostolic, it also included some of the claims made by the committee. The history of the dispute was traced from the foundation of the committee to Pitt, the declaration, the bill and the oath.[74] It was then noted that a species of schism had broken out between the supporters and the opponents of the oath. The judgment of Propaganda on the inadmissibility of the original oath and the courage of Walmesley in opposing it were recorded.

The cardinals were then reminded that their verdict would rest on the declaration, the oath in the bill and on any other elements of the bill which they might find worthy of judgment. The declaration and the oath were commented upon at length. The clause which excluded all foreign prelates and potentates from having any civil or spiritual jurisdiction within the kingdom that might encroach directly or indirectly on its sovereignty or constitution was discussed. It was explained that this was originally included to counteract the claims put forward by Robert Bellarmine and other theologians that the pope's spiritual supremacy could interfere with the temporal jurisdiction in states. This was a claim which concerned members of parliament. (The clause had been amended without the input of the vicars apostolic so that it was the pope's civil authority in the temporal affairs of states which was denied.) Explanations for other parts of the oath, some of which had been put forward by the committee, were added. The pope could not interfere in the established church, but this establishment was part of the government recognized by law and so he was excluded from temporal involvement in the state. Regarding the reference to the heretical doctrine of the deposition of princes it was pointed out that the word 'heretical' was often used in English merely to express a great abhorrence. Though the pope was excluded from absolving and dispensing from oaths and contracts, this did not exclude his authority over religious vows, and contracts made under threats of death would still be invalid.

It was also noted that Bishop Talbot thought the oath, if restored to the

74 This was the original oath not the one amended in 1790.

form suggested by the declaration, would be acceptable, a view which was not shared by Walmesley. And those who defended it insisted that it should simply be considered an oath of allegiance to the king, which every state had the right to demand of its citizens. Walmesley's conviction that the oath was ambiguous, that it confounded the spiritual and the temporal, with religious doctrines being mixed with political statements, and that the committee should, therefore, have accepted the judgment of the bishops, was underlined. On the other hand the claim of the committee that Catholics had suffered a lot from the consequences of the ill-fated condemnation of the oath of James I by Paul V was also put forward, though it was explained that James' oath contained much that was contrary to faith.

Understandably, the title 'Protesting Catholic Dissenters', and the distinction between those who took the oath, thereby earning this title, and the papists, who did not take it, was treated at length. The consequences both for priests and laypeople who became Protesting Catholic Dissenters and those who did not were spelt out. Protesting Catholics were those who protested against pernicious beliefs falsely ascribed to them, and Dissenters were those who dissented from the Anglican church.

Attached to this statement was an appendix which mostly concerned Charles Berington, the coadjutor to the vicar apostolic of the Midland District, who was then being put forward by the committee as its candidate to fill the vacancy left in the London District by the death of James Talbot.[75] It also included hard-hitting comments on the committee by a large group of priests, former students of the English College at Douay. They accused the members of the committee of intruding into religious affairs, insulting the Holy See and the vicars apostolic, and under the pretext of dealing with the Catholic cause, even trying to corrupt the faith.

In his discussion of Berington's candidacy for the London District, the Roman official noted that he had signed a letter claiming that Paul V had made a mistake in condemning the oath of James I and of pronouncing the oath to be innocent. The votes he had received from the London clergy were not given in the usual canonical manner but in a very tumultuous assembly. Those who thought he was unworthy of promotion drew attention to his friendship with Joseph Berington, with whom he shared a house. Joseph had published writings which were temerarious, scandalous, offensive to pious ears, blasphemous, injurious to the Holy See and to the pope and were also erroneous and heretical. Joseph did not think as a Catholic. And when the committee was composing its 'novelties', Charles Berington spent a long time helping it in London, unmindful of his duty to reside in his diocese. Not only had Bishop Matthew Gibson called into question his suitability, but

75 James Talbot, who did not have a coadjutor, died on 26 Jan. 1790.

so had Archbishop Butler of Cashel, who had predicted that the appointment of one who had defended the oath and had signed the letter of the committee to the people of England would cause scandal.

As was customary, a list of questions (*dubbi*) was attached to this account for the cardinals to answer. They were invited to formulate their judgment on the declaration, on the title 'Protesting Catholic Dissenters', and on other possibly reprehensible contents of the bill. They were also called upon to decide whether the censure of the oath by the four vicars apostolic should be published in all the English provinces, and whether to write to Bishop Thomas Talbot, who did not have the courage to publish it in his district and rebuke him for declaring that he would accept the oath, if it were the same as the declaration. And likewise they were to decide whether to rebuke the vicars apostolic for signing the declaration. They were asked to consider whether to write to Charles Berington and Joseph Wilks about signing the letters of the committee to the English people and to the vicars apostolic, and to consider what to do about Joseph Berington and how to get the committee to desist from pursuing the bill in parliament. They were also to weigh up the possibilities of proposing other means whereby the Catholics might obtain the desired relief, perhaps even begging the pope to open a correspondence with the king. The final queries related to the vacancies in the Northern and London districts, and to the complaint of the committee about their form of ecclesiastical government.[76]

Fortunately the full congregation of Propaganda did not pursue this question in 1790 or early in 1791. Had it done so, there is little doubt that it would have issued condemnations of several elements of the bill and of the part played by the Beringtons, and possibly also by Thomas Talbot. The original oath would most likely have been condemned. The whole tenor of the queries pointed towards unfavourable verdicts. And had such verdicts been published or even conveyed privately to the committee, a further rift would have been opened up between it, Walmesley, Douglass and William Gibson. If the committee had been told to desist from pursuing the bill, its reaction would have been hostile and a split could have occurred in the Catholic community. News of further developments, perhaps of the alteration to the oath, may have suggested the postponement of an examination, and by the time the bill became law, all the worst features of it – from a Roman viewpoint – had been changed.

---

76 APF, *Acta* 164, ff 326r–400r. The act of 1791 did not apply to Scotland. A case of disputed succession to a Catholic estate, where Protestant relatives wanted to claim it on the basis of a penal law, led to a petition to parliament and then to a bill relieving Scottish Catholics of several penal laws in 1793. They were required to take the same oath as that of 1791 (Johnson, *Developments in the Roman Catholic Church in Scotland, 1789–1829*, pp 29–32).

4

The vicars apostolic and the Catholic Committee at loggerheads

I

The hopes of those who looked forward to a calm acceptance of the modest improvements afforded by the act, without reproaches or recriminations, were not realized. The activists on the committee, still angry with the encyclicals attacking the oaths, showed their resentment at the first meeting after the bill had passed the house of lords but before the royal assent was given to it. They succeeded by a fairly small margin in passing a resolution that Catholics should repeat their adherence to the protestation. The atmosphere was very hostile to the vicars apostolic. A further resolution expressed thanks to the nobles and gentry of the committee for obtaining the desired relief for the Catholic community. But when the vicar general of the London District and Milner proposed an amendment thanking the vicars apostolic for their part in obtaining an orthodox oath, they were shouted down and no vote was taken. A vote of thanks was passed to Bishop Douglass but the committee was unwilling to thank Walmesley, who had suspended Joseph Wilks.

Asked why Wilks was suspended, Walmesley's representative at the meeting explained that he had been so punished because he had 'rebelled and protested against the divine established government of the church by bishops and their authority'.[1] Walmesley's action looked like vindictiveness as Wilks, however contrary he may have been, had not violated any doctrinal principles and had done little different from Bishop Charles Berington, whose role in the agitation of the committee was not publicly challenged. The committee interpreted Walmesley's censure of Wilks as an attack on itself, and, though decidedly hostile to the bishop, begged him to restore Wilks to his missionary duties. Wilks himself was prepared to apologize but not in terms which Walmesley would accept: he was ready to disclaim his protest on the grounds that it was of a civil not a spiritual nature.

Several intermediaries appealed to Walmesley to restore Wilks to his ministry. Strickland let Rome know that Walmesley's persistence was causing

---

1 General meeting of English Catholics, 9 June 1791, CIDA.

division, and maintained that some people believed he acted for temporal and personal reasons.[2] When it seemed that an agreement was within reach, the committee stiffened Wilks' resistance. The Staffordshire clergy, under the leadership of Joseph Berington, who was always inclined to minimize ecclesiastical authority, took up the cudgels on behalf of Wilks.[3] Walmesley held out, involved Wilks' Benedictine superior in the dispute and, though he withdrew the censure, he did not restore his faculties so that Wilks could minister in the Western District. A group of laymen accompanied Wilks to a meeting with Walmesley, and having submitted a document supporting Wilks, they announced their refusal to contribute to the mission at Bath. The bishop replied by excommunicating them.

Walmesley, Gibson and Douglass, anxious to vindicate their response to the 'manifesto and appeal', employed Charles Plowden to advocate their cause, which he did in a pamphlet. They could not have made a worse choice. His extreme comments on the committee infuriated its members, and even Milner, the master of intemperate language, believed that Plowden's strictures on the committee were too harsh and insensitive. Plowden dragged up the old quarrels about the declaration, the Protesting Catholic Dissenters and the unacceptable language of the oath. He insisted that only the bishops had the authority to decide on the lawfulness of oaths and regretted the misfortune of the committee in being ill-advised. Many of its members, he maintained, were not competent to pass judgment on the various subjects discussed, and were misled by their advisers. He called into question their motives, charging that the members were prepared to insult and betray the English Catholics,[4] and claimed that to resist bishops in the discharge of their functions was to rebel against God.

The already strained relations between the three vicars apostolic and four other members of the committee were brought to breaking point by this intervention. Lord Petre complained to Walmesley that it contained many imputations on their moral character as well as many erroneous statements. And they did not hesitate to point out that they were charged with crimes of a very serious nature.[5] When questioned about their role in the authorship of Plowden's writings, the bishops, foregoing the opportunity to soften the anger of the committee by some apology for the bellicose sentiments that so incensed them, refused to make any comment on Plowden's pamphlet. Thomas Talbot, the fourth vicar apostolic, in his response, proclaimed the benefits of peace and reconciliation.[6]

2 Strickland to Propaganda, 10 June 1791 APF, SC(Anglia) 5, f 387rv.   3 Walmesley subsequently opined that several of the propositions of the condemned Synod of Pistoia were 'more or less analagous to the Throckmorton and Staffordshire clergy's doctrine' (Walmesley to Douglass, 2 May 1795, WDA).   4 Plowden, 'An answer to the *Second blue book*'. APF, SC(Anglia) 5, ff 200r–285r.   5 Petre and others to Walmesley, 2 Feb. 1792, ClDA.   6 Ward,

Bishop Douglass was alarmed by the political views of the committee, as well as its religious views, and in particular by Throckmorton's latest pamphlet calling for the election of bishops. Charles Plowden sought Pitt's judgment on 'the principles of these democratic gentlemen'. And Pitt expressed support for opposition to the 'democratic principles' of the opponents of the vicars apostolic and vowed always to 'sett [*sic*] his face against such persons, as encourage the levelling spirit which has gone abroad'. (Pitt, who detested the principles of the French Revolution, was naturally opposed to anything that smacked of those principles in England.) Accordingly, Douglass passed on Plowden's suggestion that Walmesley should send as many representatives as he could to the meeting of the committee in May 1792 'to oppose any obnoxious motion that may be made by the friends of the committee'.[7]

The discord and the rupture of relations between the bishops and the committee had become so notorious that three prominent Catholic laymen came forward to try, through their mediation to restore harmony.[8] In advance of their May meeting, the committee published a letter to the Catholics of England. Professing loyalty to the church and its system of government, the members argued that the vicars apostolic had erred in matters of fact, misunderstanding the aims and work of the committee on behalf of the English Catholics. They defended their refusal to submit to the request of bishops Douglass and Gibson to yield to the bishops' judgment on the oath contained in the bill. Contemptuously dismissing Plowden's pamphlet, they noted that he claimed to write at the request of three vicars apostolic. With this letter the two clerical and eight lay members of the committee ended their communication with the Catholic laity, conscious of 'having on every occasion endeavoured to discharge' their trust.

Invited by the mediators to submit a list of their grievances, the committee mentioned Wilks being deprived of his faculties and Plowden's pamphlet. The restoration of normal episcopal rule was also put forward. The bishops did not submit a list of their complaints but suggested a form of submission for Wilks to sign, and on this being rejected by the committee, suggested to Walmesley that he should try to get Wilks admitted to some other vicariate. Though Walmesley complained of Wilks' refusal to cooperate, he offered to raise no objections if his religious superior should arrange to have him admitted into some other district.

The vicars apostolic also softened the response they had given about Plowden, admitting that, though they had commissioned him to answer complaints or charges made by the committee, they did not stand over

The dawn of the Catholic revival, i, pp 333–7. 7 Douglass to Walmesley, 21 Apr. 1792, CIDA. 8 The mediators published their report and the letters submitted to them in a pamphlet known as *The Buff Book*.

language which demeaned the reputations or characters of the members of the committee. They stalled on the issue of replacing their system of church government with bishops and parish priests, promising to study it, though expressing their fears that it was not a practical alternative.

The committee accepted the bishops' disclaimer on Plowden's writings, but they were far from mollified by Walmesley's offer to permit the reinstatement of Wilks in another jurisdiction. They insisted that the vicar apostolic had suspended Wilks to show his disapproval of their part in the arguments about the bill, and, though they claimed not to deny his canonical rights, they certainly implied that he had abused them to the detriment of justice. They peremptorily demanded that the other bishops vindicate Wilks' moral character and declare their disapprobation of Walmesley's censures, which would have involved an improper intervention on their part in the affairs of another's jurisdiction. Failing this it stood prepared 'to support an injured and oppressed man'.

Despite this forward and defiant answer, the mediators thought they had settled the points in dispute, apart from Wilks' case. But when they sent out their report, the committee claimed that it did not give a proper account of the negotiations with the vicars apostolic about the bill and about Wilks. And when the members met the mediators they expressed their demands, especially about Wilks, in such a bellicose fashion that the mediators broke off contact with them, but not before they invited the bishops to write to the committee in the hope of healing the wounds that had been opened up.

Instead of an anodyne expression of good wishes the bishops, still smarting from the 'protest and appeal', undiplomatically raised that issue with the mediators hoping that the committee would 'recall' it, 'as far as regarded the spirit and language of it'. By so doing, they raised the hackles of the members of the committee. It responded that it could not withdraw the 'protest and appeal' as the bishops' encyclicals had not been withdrawn. And it accused the bishops of demanding its submission on the legitimacy of oath-taking and of claiming a right to condemn an oath on allegedly spiritual grounds without specifying the particular objections to it, and of insisting that an oath which was doctrinally orthodox could not be taken without episcopal approval. The mediators begged the members of the committee to tone down their answer, but without success. In fact, they demanded that their last letter – with every paper written to the mediators by the vicars apostolic and by the mediators – be published.[9]

With this resentful retort the exchange ended, though the mediators adjusted their report in accordance with the requests of the committee.

9 Douglass to Walmesley, 28 June 1792, CIDA. Gibson, Douglass and Walmesley warned their people in a pastoral against the 'pernicious, schismatical doctrines' in John Throckmorton's pamphlets and in the Blue Books.

Instead of all the clergy and laity coming together to celebrate the first act of parliament that removed the stigma of the penal laws and granted them a little relief, suspicions, misunderstandings and personal antagonisms kept them apart in the hour of their triumph. Perhaps the peers and gentry who led the committee only represented one or two hundred of their body, but they were a very powerful and influential group, not least in terms of financial resources, which they threatened at times to withhold from the clergy.[10]

The distrust between the parties was carried through to small matters as well. In response to a query from Rome about establishing a seminary in England in 1793, Bishop Gibson answered that it would be difficult to do so because of the contentions and divisions between the vicars apostolic and the members of the Catholic Committee (though the committee had by then been dissolved). Rather than seek funds from former members, he begged Rome for a subsidy.[11] When Joseph Berington sought permission from Bishop Douglass to minister in his district, as chaplain to the Throckmortons, Gibson advised Douglass to refuse.[12] (Berington eventually moved into the Throckmorton household without permission.) And when Berington, in a book on the memoirs of Gregorio Panzani (a papal legate who came to England in the seventeenth century), took issue with Roman treatment of the English church, Walmesley, Gibson and Douglass were offended by comments about themselves in the preface. Walmesley objected particularly to Berington's 'arrogant and scandalous assertion' that 'the men they despise whom they call *heretics* and *schismatics* believe what on the authority of revelation, is proposed to be believed, and neglecting the traditions of man, emulate better gifts'.[13] He called on Talbot to 'repress the scandalous audacity of the author'.

Though the English committee did not meet after the act was passed, it formed itself into the Cisalpine Club in 1792. The title implied a certain distancing of the members from Rome, and its vicars in England or as Douglass claimed, 'a setting of their faces against the see of Rome'.[14] It stood out in opposition to ultramontanism, which implied a readiness to defend papal rights and claims. The name 'Cisalpine' was regarded in Rome as indicating hostility to Roman authority, and Milner later referred to its members as 'anti-papal'. The timing of the club's foundation (1792) was unfortunate, as Britain grew more hostile to the claims of the revolutionaries in France, and welcomed the French bishops and clergy who had sought exile from their encroachments. Collections were taken up for these exiles, accommodation was provided for them and the government gave bishops a monthly pension of £10 and clergy of £2.

---

10 Ward, *The dawn of the Catholic revival*, i, pp 339–56.   11 Gibson to Propaganda, 2 Sept. 1793, APF, SC(Ibernia), 28, Fondo di Vienna, ff 60r–61v.   12 Gibson to Walmesley, 8 May 1793, ClDA.   13 Walmesley to Talbot (copy), 19 July 1793, ClDA.   14 Douglass to Walmesley, 21 Apr. 1792, ClDA.

Though the bill was passed in June 1791, it was not formally discussed at Propaganda until three years later, and that discussion was brought on by the oath included in the act for Ireland in 1793. The account (*ristretto*) of the background to the English oath was short but gloomy: reference was made at the beginning of it to the committee assuming authority without the necessary prudence to deal with that delicate and important matter. Hence there arose very serious disturbances and disorders among the Catholics. The flame of a most doleful schism was almost lit.

A brief narrative of the action of the committee in consulting Pitt and drawing up a declaration repudiating false accusations against Catholics and its concession with a bill was then given. To the condemnation of the oath by the vicars apostolic the committee returned an insolent and injurious reply. The oath in its original form, its condemnation by the Holy See, and its amended form was given. The further meetings with the committee and the acceptance by parliament of the Irish oath of 1774 were outlined. And the amendment by which persons taking the oath were obliged to promise acceptance of the succession to the heirs of the Princess Sophia, being Protestant, was given.

The examination by Propaganda took place on 16 June 1794, and the same verdict was given as had been given on the Irish oath in 1776: it could be tolerated but it was neither to be approved nor condemned. This amounted to a request that no public comment about the attitude of Rome should be made about it. No opposition had been raised against it since the act was passed and as the three vicars apostolic, who had been most concerned about the original oaths, had accepted it, there was no likelihood of objections being raised against it. Rome did not like some of its terms which it regarded as discourteous but was prepared to permit it.[15]

II

The wounds caused by the controversy between the committee and the vicars apostolic were given little time to heal before they were again reopened. Thomas Talbot, the vicar apostolic of the Midland District, died in 1795. Under normal circumstances his coadjutor, Charles Berington, would have succeeded to the see; Rome, on hearing of the bishop's death, would have conferred full or 'extraordinary' faculties on his coadjutor. But in this case the faculties were withheld and Berington was left with the 'ordinary' faculties which allowed him to exercise his orders in some ways,

---

15 APF, *Acta* 164, ff 474r–507r. Walmesley was relieved by Cardinal Antonelli's comment 'valde gavisus sum, tantam ac tam acriter agitatam quaestionem hunc felicem exitum habere' – the bitter dispute had a happy ending (Walmesley to Gibson, 25 Aug. 1791, ClDA).

such as conferring confirmation or ordaining priests who were members of religious orders (but not secular clergy). In the eyes of the other vicars apostolic and of most clergy this restricted authority placed him in a rather helpless and embarrassing position.[16]

Even before Talbot died, the congregation of Propaganda, in response to information supplied by Walmesley, Gibson and Douglass, had discussed Berington's situation at a plenary meeting, and with the authorization of the pope had decided to take action. Accordingly, it wrote to Charles Erskine in England, pointing out (with more exaggeration than accuracy) that Berington had been the head of a committee seeking to obtain legislation to remove penal laws, which drew up an oath full of Protestant propositions damaging to the authority of the Holy See and thrice condemned by the vicars apostolic. Though heretical, schismatical and full of erroneous material, he had supported it, and had written letters in its defence. Berington was a member of the committee which had strenuously resisted Gibson, Douglass and himself, had wished to impose on them an oath that was inadmissible and had published books repugnant to Catholic doctrine,[17] one of which – authored by thirteen priests in his district – was schismatical and heretical. The pope had decided that such a situation could not be ignored, and that Berington should publish a retraction of his views.

Erskine was invited to acquaint himself fully with the role played by Berington, and, if he really had signed the papers ascribed to him, to get him to retract his views.[18] Erskine's discussion with Berington was not satisfactory, so he requested that Berington set down his response on paper. Berington duly recounted some details about the protest and the part he and Wilks had played in trying to get inserted into the protestation the changes which the vicars apostolic wanted. It was then signed by them and by many clergy and laity. In rejecting false beliefs ascribed to them the protestation played an important part in promoting the hospitality which the English people showed to the exiled French clergy. The protestation, having been drawn up by Protestants, did not have the exactness and the clarity he would have liked. But the oath was not condemned by Rome, and though rejected by the vicars apostolic the ministry did not wish to change it until a Protestant bishop succeeded in doing so in the house of lords. He went on to claim that his fellow members of the committee were committed Catholics who would have given up any temporal advantage rather than violate the integrity of the faith, and that he shared those sentiments.[19]

16 Husenbeth, *The life of Bishop Milner*, pp 57–8; Schofield and Skinner, *The English vicars apostolic, 1688–1850*, p. 111.   **17** Rome confused the two Beringtons. Joseph had written the books that it complained about.   **18** Propaganda to Erskine, 5 July 1794, APF, *Acta* 164, ff 214r–216r and 741r–745r.   **19** Erskine to Propaganda (with enclosed note), 5 Sept. 1794, ibid., ff 746r–749v.

The picture changed with Talbot's death on 24 April 1795. Not long afterwards Walmesley wrote to Propaganda, firmly reminding the congregation that Berington was not worthy to succeed.[20] Gibson promptly endorsed this view, adding that Berington had signed the protestation and expressing his fear that Berington's appointment would be the cause of scandal to Catholics not only in England but also in Ireland and Scotland.[21] Erskine later assured Propaganda that, even if Berington gave ample satisfaction for his past conduct, he could not be the vicar apostolic of the Midland District which was the seat of turbulent ecclesiastics.[22] Despite the limitations originally placed on his mission, the congregation of Propaganda used Erskine as its intermediary with Berington for the next two years, and trusted him to put Berington 'on the right road' rather than have Rome obliged to make a substitution.[23] Troy had been assured by Cardinal Antonelli that Erskine had been sent in 1793 to thank the king and parliament for the protection and favour shown to Catholic subjects,[24] but he remained until 1801 and enjoyed the status of an unofficial delegate with the government.

Erskine, who took a firm Roman line, was not confident of success. In his next encounter with Berington he did not find him disposed to make amends for his past conduct. Regretting that he was associated with some of the disruptive and refractory priests who published the worst books, Erskine explained that three or four leaders of those priests disseminated perverse doctrines and fomented disharmony. They could not be prevented from publishing material because they would complain in public that their constitutional rights were being violated. He then put forward Bishop Douglass' solution which was to suspend those priests and get them to retract improper propositions from these books (or more likely pamphlets).[25]

Erskine was given a letter for Berington explaining what the congregation of Propaganda required from him and he duly reported a two hour conversation with him in which he tried all means to entice him to sign an agreement that he would submit to the Holy See until it pronounced judgment on the books bearing his signature. Erskine told him that it was necessary that he make such a declaration, that he would thereby give edification by his example in removing some of the independence lately manifested by some Catholics and bring about security by ending the disputes and dissensions that divided them. Submission would bring consolation to the pontiff, but his soul would be filled with bitterness if he were forced to remove the bishop from office. To Berington's proposal that he

20 Walmesley to Propaganda, 27 Apr. 1795, APF, SC(Anglia), 5, f 452rv. 21 Gibson to Propaganda, 6 May 1795, ibid., ff 460r–461v. 22 Erskine to Propaganda, 8 May 1795, ibid., ff 462r–463v. 23 Propaganda to Erskine (minute), May or June 1795, ibid., ff 468r–469r. 24 Propaganda to Troy, 5 Dec. 1793, DDA. 25 Erskine to Propaganda, 7 July 1795, APF, SC(Anglia) 5, ff 476r–479v.

would wait to see what propositions were condemned before signing, Erskine replied that by so acting he would be making himself a judge of the Holy See. And given his dispositions, translation to another vicariate would not be feasible, Erskine concluded.[26]

Berington then wrote to Propaganda that the declaration had been signed by the four vicars apostolic and nearly all Catholics.[27] Controversy had later arisen with the condemnation of the oath by the four vicars apostolic but that condemnation had not been published by two of them, including the one in charge of the district to which he belonged. If anything in the Blue Books or in the formula of the oath contained any 'seeds of evil opinions', he revoked and repudiated them, and submitted to the Holy See promising filial obedience.[28]

This submission did not satisfy Walmesley and Douglass. Walmesley thought the retraction, of which he had a copy, was conditional and therefore useless since Berington contended that he had signed no evil doctrines. Walmesley called for a full retraction from both Berington and Wilks, and Douglass felt that a full public retraction from the bishop was necessary to overcome the scandal they faced.[29]

Like the other three vicars apostolic some officials at Propaganda believed that many errors were contained in the Blue Books. One official drew up a list of eight 'heretical propositions' from the writings of the committee, indicating an extremely anachronistic view of papal prerogatives. These included the obligation to swear that princes excommunicated or deposed by the pope could not be deprived or killed by their subjects, that no pope or council could absolve subjects from the oath of fidelity to the king, that no pope could absolve anyone from the obligations of the English oath and that no prince or government agency had spiritual authority which could directly or indirectly affect the laws or constitution of the kingdom.

The last four propositions that were deemed improper were the hostile and critical comments on the bulls of Pius V, which allegedly provoked national odium and caused dark crimes, the bull of Paul V which had declared that the oath of fidelity proposed by James I was not in agreement with articles of the faith, and that of Sixtus V, which was said to have been the cause of calamities.[30] Though dubbed 'heretical', these propositions were mostly disciplinary responses dictated by circumstances at different times, and there was no justification for holding them up as permanent principles by which oaths in the late eighteenth century would have had to be judged.

---

26 Erskine to Propaganda, 11 Aug. 1795, ibid., ff 486r–491r. 27 This latter claim was a great exaggeration; some 1,500 Catholics were said to have signed it. 28 Berington to Propaganda, 8 Sept. 1795, ibid., ff 492r–493r. *'Pravarum sententiarum semina'* was the phrase used by Propaganda. 29 Walmesley to Propaganda, no date, ibid., ff 500r–501r and Douglass to Propaganda, 9 Oct. 1795, ibid., f 507r. 30 Ibid., ff 496r–497v.

Had the congregation adhered rigidly to a policy of judging politico-religious situations in Britain and Ireland by these standards, Catholics would never have been allowed to swear oaths of allegiance to the monarch.

Rome persisted in encouraging Erskine, Walmesley and Douglass to persuade Berington to make a full retraction of all improper writings. He was expected to profess full obedience to the Holy See, to renew his profession of faith and the revocation of his subscription to material contrary to the authority and dignity of the pope and unite himself in mind and will with his episcopal colleagues.[31] Erskine, much to the chagrin of Walmesley continued to communicate with Rome about Berington and was warmly thanked by Cardinal Gerdil, the prefect of the congregation of Propaganda. Walmesley resented this, reminded the cardinal that Erskine had no authority in that area, that he had divulged material from Rome about Berington and asked that the congregation deal exclusively with the vicars apostolic.[32]

From Winchester, where he was in charge of the mission, Milner, who did not want to miss the fray, launched a broadside against Berington. He argued that, if Berington were confirmed as vicar apostolic without public restitution of the spiritual damage he had caused, a horrible scandal and great harm to the church would result. Bemoaning the excessive democracy of the Staffordshire clergy, Throckmorton and the Cisalpine Club, he maintained that, if Berington had been given the appointment that he had sought in the London District, they would all have become 'Protestant Catholics' instead of Roman Catholics.[33]

The Holy See widened its demands, insisting that Wilks, the Staffordshire clergy and especially Joseph Berington, all retract their disputed writings. Joseph Berington was to be threatened with the removal of his faculties. Not only were the prominent members of the Catholic Committee concerned about this contention but so was the duke of Portland, the minister of home affairs, a prominent Whig who had been sympathetic to the relief of Irish Catholics. Lord Petre, who contacted Erskine, had discussed the problem with Portland, who in turn called on Douglass. Portland was worried about possible dissensions and disturbances if the affair became public. Petre reminded Erskine of the sacrifices his colleagues had made for religion, in terms of financial support for churches and clergy, but Erskine insisted that Berington's confirmation or rejection depended entirely on his submission to the orders of the Holy See.[34]

Lord Stourton, another influential member of the former committee, and Petre then informed Erskine that the censure of Berington indirectly

---

31 Propaganda to Douglass, no date but 1796, ibid., ff 535r–539v.   32 Walmesley to Propaganda, 25 Jan. 1796, ibid., f 543rv. Gerdil was prefect of the congregation from 1795 to 1802.   33 Milner to Propaganda, 7 Feb. 1796, ibid., ff 546r–547v.   34 Erskine to Propaganda, 12 Feb. 1796 and 15 Apr. 1796, ibid., ff 549r–552r and ff 564r–569v.

affected those who supported the committee, and that they could not suffer in silence the stain which was being placed upon them. They believed their case had been badly represented or misinterpreted in Rome, and so they intended to appeal to the pope. Erskine duly forwarded their appeal, and their request that Berington be told precisely what proposition was specifically censured so that he could retract it without their enemies being able to use a general condemnation to discredit them before the nation. Erskine replied that a retraction in general terms was the mildest and most proper way to end the affair without further noise.[35]

In another letter, six prominent members of the Catholic Committee, including Petre, Stourton and Throckmorton, claimed that any censure on Berington's conduct applied to theirs, and maintained that they had fought only for the freedom of religion and the education of their youth, and that by their long and diligent labour they had won nothing for themselves but something for the clergy and religion. Their intentions had never been wanting in respect for the Holy See, and they had never wished to separate themselves from the church for adherence to which they continued to suffer the deprivation of all their civil rights. They dreaded the dissensions which such a censure would perpetrate.[36]

Berington continued to insist that he could not sign a retraction because of the variety of publications with which he had been associated. As Catholics in England were accused of total dependence on Rome even in temporal concerns, propositions regarding their civil as well as their spiritual responsibilities had been put out by the committee. There was therefore a danger that their enemies would believe that a general retraction on his part would apply to civil as well as to religious principles. He therefore requested that the congregation of Propaganda be satisfied with his submission to dogmatic decisions and formal renunciation of 'seeds of evil opinions' that they might have discovered in the Blue Books, or that those opinions be specified so that he could explain what he intended to do by supporting such tenets, and so let the pope know that he never meant to depart from the centre of catholicity and the doctrines of the church.[37]

Cardinal Gerdil, the prefect of the congregation, passed on Berington's letter to his predecessor, Cardinal Antonelli, who had already dealt with the question of Catholic relief. Antonelli was not prepared to agree to Berington's request that the 'seeds of evil opinions' be selected from his writings so that he could withdraw them. He maintained that by asking for this Berington was doubting the rectitude of the judgment of the congregation and wanted a contest with it. It required a simple, authentic retraction

35 Ibid., 19 and 26 Apr. 1796, ibid., ff 574r–577v.   36 Ibid., ff 578r–582r.   37 Berington to Erskine, 3 May 1796, ibid., ff 604r–605r. Berington used the phrase '*pravarum sententiarum semina*'.

which would satisfy the pope, along the lines of the formula already made available to him. No one had pretended that his retraction extended to all that was in the Blue Books, but in his writings there were points of religion, maxims of faith, of the oath, of ecclesiastical jurisdiction and of Roman communion, which had all been examined by theologians, and the fact that these represented not only his opinions but also those of the committee did not excuse him. Indeed, having many companions in suspect doctrine did not exempt him from responsibility, and he himself admitted that there were 'seeds of evil opinions' in his writings.[38]

Erskine recommended that Berington be asked to express his views on each of the propositions which had been already sent to him. But he was losing his patience and threatened to end the 'scandalous tergiversation' if Berington did not comply with the requests from Rome. The congregation had reached the same conclusion.[39] But it hesitated about taking a final painful decision and continued to urge the other vicars apostolic to persuade him to sign the formula of rejection without restrictive clauses. William Gibson in response to Rome claimed that he wrote in the friendliest terms to Berington but could not effect any change. Gibson insisted that if Berington's excuse that he never wrote anything against any dogmatic decree were admitted, Catholics would continue to be scandalized, and both the vicars apostolic and the congregation of Propaganda would suffer in consequence.[40] Walmesley, the most persistent of the vicars apostolic, maintained that any priests whose names had appeared with the members of the committee would have to make a public retraction before they would be allowed to minister in his district. He informed Rome that Berington refused to retract his disputed views, allegedly on the advice of his lay friends, some of whom were not orthodox and who to cover their own infamy told him that to remove his signature would give offence to Protestants.[41]

Bishop Douglass, adopting a more emollient approach than Walmesley, asked James Archer, one of his priests, to contact Berington and persuade him to withdraw his name from the Blue Books, as required by the congregation of Propaganda. Archer had almost succeeded until Berington consulted Lord Petre and Sir John Throckmorton, and all Archer's and Douglass' efforts were of no avail. Berington proved willing to renounce the 'doctrinal points' that Rome had mentioned but maintained that withdrawing his signature from the Blue Books would 'appear in the eyes of their Protestant friends a renouncing of *everything* contained in those books, even of their civil allegiance'.[42]

38 Gerdil to Erskine, sending Antonelli's observations, ibid., ff 621r–623r.   39 Erskine to Propaganda, 23 Sept. 1796, and Propaganda to Erskine, 8 Oct. 1796, ibid., ff 634r–637r.
40 Gibson to Propaganda, 17 Oct. 1796, ibid., ff 638r–639r.   41 Walmesley to Propaganda (copy), 18 May 1797, ClDA.   42 Douglass to Walmesley, 13 May 1797, ibid.

Eventually Berington yielded and signed the formula demanded by Rome, withdrawing his name from the Blue Books. The 'extraordinary' faculties which had been withheld were then forwarded to Bishop Douglass to be transmitted to Berington, but he died suddenly in June 1798, before he could receive them.[43] Walmesley died in November 1797 shortly after Berington had made his submission but before Rome had had time to respond to it. Wilks, who had never fully made peace with Walmesley, also withdrew his name from the *Third blue book* by assuring Bishop Sharrock, who succeeded Walmesley, that he accepted that the church had 'a right to make laws for all the faithful, and to enforce obedience by external judgments and salutary punishments'. He also declared that since September 1791 he had repudiated the 'protest and appeal' of the Catholic Committee, which he judged to have contained 'some irregularities and informalities' and to have been extended 'to more objects than were necessary'.[44]

With the death of Berington and the reconciliation of Wilks with Bishop Sharrock the public discord and antagonism between the Catholic Committee and the vicars apostolic ceased. The ruffled feathers remained, especially on the part of the committee. Bishops Douglass and Sharrock wanted reconciliation rather than conflict, and occasions for public disagreement on political issues did not arise until the end of the first decade of the nineteenth century. John Milner, who had entered the contest against the committee, formed an abiding distrust of its members and of their religious attitudes. The title of the club which they formed – the Cisalpine Club – summed up everything he disliked about them. He accused them of being anti-hierarchical, anti-Roman and anticlerical.

Walmesley, before Berington died, had been despairing of his accepting the conditions laid down by Rome for his confirmation as vicar apostolic, and had suggested Milner's name to the secretary of the congregation of Propaganda.[45] When the vacancy occurred, Walmesley was already dead, and Douglass was having second thoughts about Milner's suitability in 'the *present* circumstances', and with 'the members of the Midland District'. Determined to pray for guidance he opined:

> The circumstances of the times and of the Middle [*sic*] District in particular call for all the lenity and forbearance of St Francis of

43 Husenbeth, *The life of Bishop Milner*, p. 59. Troy in correspondence with Bishop Sharrock maintained that the writings of Joseph Berington were 'unquestionably heterodox' and 'schismatical in many instances'. He advised that the vicars apostolic should devise a formula of retraction for him to sign (Troy to Sharrock, ClDA, 3 Aug. 1798). Replying to a rebuke of Bishop Douglass about a pamphlet on miraculous cures in Italy, Joseph Berington told Douglass that his behaviour had been 'uncanonical, unmerited and cruel' (Berington to Douglass, 12 Dec. 1796), WDA).   44 Declaration of Joseph Wilks, 13 July 1798, ClDA. A few days later Sharrock asked Troy to find a form of retraction for Wilks and sent it to Cardinal Gerdil (Sharrock to Troy, 18 July 1798, DDA).   45 Walmesley to Propaganda (copy), 18 May 1797, ClDA.

Sales, united to the fortitude and perseverance of St Charles Borromeo. May our Lord Jesus Christ grant us to make choice of such a character.[46]

During the vacancy a dispute arose between Bishop Gibson and John Bew, the vicar general, about jurisdiction in the vicariate. Gibson argued that Bew's appointment was invalid as Berington's faculties did not authorize him to make such appointments. There were echoes of the dispute between the vicars apostolic and the committee in this contretemps, as Bew had been a supporter of the committee and had come under the suspicion of the vicars apostolic.

After an interregnum of nearly two and a half years Gregory Stapleton, the president of St Edmund's College, Old Hall Green, was appointed, but his episcopate was cut short by death after little more than a year in office. Milner's time had come. In 1803 he was consecrated bishop and vicar apostolic of the Midland District. He was destined to play an important – and to some Catholics, sinister – role in controversies which would break out several years later. But he came to office at a time of calm and peace in the Catholic community.

As no further attempts were made by parliament to grant relief to Catholics until after the Act of Union of 1800, opportunities for disputes about oaths and declarations of allegiance did not arise for some time. Questions were raised again about oaths in the bills of 1813 and 1821 when they were linked to the desire of the government to have some measure of control over the appointment of bishops. Disputes arose about the kind and degree of allegiance to be sworn to the state about the intervention of the sovereign in Catholic ecclesiastical organization.

III

The first modest attempt by English Catholics to obtain some relief from the penal laws had, to the regret of many of them, led to bitter and acrimonious infighting, pitting three of the vicars apostolic against the committee, and clergy against laity. Like many quarrels it developed from simple beginnings and gathered pace as it progressed. Neither side felt that it could back down without surrendering its rights. The bishops, or at least three of them, firmly insisted that they were in conscience-bound to reject oaths and declarations of faith which they regarded as heterodox. The committee, or some of its leading members, proud, self-confident men, imbued with Enlightenment

46 Douglass to Sharrock, 20 June 1798, ClDA.

thought, felt entitled to claim that oaths should not be condemned by the bishops unless they specified where Catholic truth was violated in them. They were not prepared to submit to what they regarded as the dictates of the bishops and demanded that the prelates justify their every action. Three of the vicars apostolic upheld their authority to pronounce on Catholic beliefs and practice; the committee demanded clear proof that it had diverged from this practice. It was ironical that it took the intervention of an Anglican bishop in the house of lords to produce a solution which led to the passing of an act that both sides could accept.

One lasting and astringent personal antagonism that emerged from the disputes between the bishops and the committee was that of John Milner for Charles Butler. Milner resented and opposed what he regarded as the pretensions of the peers and gentry of the Cisalpine Club to represent the Catholics of England, and for the rest of his life maintained his hostility to the leadership of the rich and titled. He believed that only the vicars apostolic had the right to give guidance to the Catholic people on any moral or spiritual issue, and that when others tried to do so they strayed beyond their duties and created divisions and confusion.[47] As secretary of the committee Charles Butler wrote some of its exchanges with the bishops, a few of which were tart and truculent. Though Butler himself was a sincere and committed Catholic, his initial advocacy of the committee's case damned him in Milner's eyes, and ever afterwards Milner was obsessed with Butler's alleged perfidy.

The congregation of Propaganda, though it condemned the first version of the oath, did not pass a formal judgment on the dispute until it had ended with the act of 1791. Had it done so before the bill reached its final stages in parliament, there is little doubt that its verdict would have been hostile and would have produced further conflict. The comments made in the *ristretto* about the oaths and the attitudes of the committee to the bishops were mostly adverse. Roman officials always defended papal rights and prerogatives much more strongly than the theological faculties of the northern European universities would have done. The committee could not have got from Rome the benign answers to the questions which on Pitt's insistence it had posed to the French and Spanish universities. The congregation usually felt bound to steer churches away from concessions which might derogate from papal jurisdiction.

When calls for Catholic relief were first made in parliament after 1800 they were made by Irish members with Irish Catholics in mind. English Catholics did not play a role of any significance until 1810 when the peers and gentry were again prepared, if necessary, to show their independence of

47 Leighton, 'John Milner, history and ultramontanism', *Arch. Hib.*, 63 (2010), 346–74.

the vicars apostolic. The passions of the 1790s had by then cooled, and at least two of the vicars apostolic, led by Bishop Poynter, aligned themselves with the nobles and gentry against the Irish bishops. Archbishop Troy had by then succeeded to the role of Bishop Walmesley.

5

Towards the Act of Union

The Act of Union, which had profound consequences for Britain and Ireland, took effect on 1 January 1801. As far as those who wished to see Catholics being made eligible for seats in parliament and the higher offices of state were concerned, the question they asked was whether their hopes and aspirations would be realized. In 1785, not long after his appointment as prime minister, Pitt had brought forward commercial proposals to aid the Irish economy. Though his plans fell through, their failure turned his mind to the possibility of closer union between Britain and Ireland. He thought that, if an arrangement could be made in trade and financial obligations, the two parliaments could continue to legislate without clashing with each other.[1] He did not develop these thoughts further, but the changed political circumstances of the 1790s moved him to think of fuller union between the countries. The Irish parliament and the leading officials of Dublin Castle had resisted the major concession of allowing Catholics to become members of parliament. What had not been possible in the Irish context might now become possible, as Catholic members in Westminster would be a small minority and could pose no great difficulty to a Protestant kingdom.

In June 1798 the government in London, realizing that more than the torture and executions carried out by General Lake was required to deal with the Irish situation, replaced him with Earl Cornwallis as commander and lord lieutenant. Cornwallis, the defeated general of the American Revolution, was known to be sympathetic to the Catholic cause and had already refused the viceroyalty because he had not been given any assurances about the enfranchisement of Catholics.[2] Pitt consulted the outgoing viceroy, Earl Camden, and his foreign secretary, William Grenville, both of whom favoured Catholic emancipation. But Pitt soon encountered an immovable obstacle in the attitude of George III, who insisted that 'no country can be governed where there is more than one established religion'.[3]

A large majority of the members of parliament in Dublin were bitterly opposed to union. The leaders of the Catholic laity, who had no great reason to be grateful to the parliament which had opposed emancipation, did not regret its demise. Lord Clare, the chancellor, who feared, like many of his

---

1 Ehrman, *The younger Pitt*, p. 171.   2 Bartlett, *The fall and rise of the Irish nation*, p. 234.
3 Ehrman, *The younger Pitt*, p. 176.

parliamentary colleagues, that the union would be coupled with emancipation, travelled to London to dissuade the government from this policy.[4]

The insurrectionists in Antrim and Down had nearly all been Presbyterians, but those in Kildare and Wexford, and those from the west who had joined the French forces of General Humbert, had been overwhelmingly Catholic. When rebellion first broke out Archbishop Troy denounced it in the most uncompromising terms. He claimed that every good Christian viewed 'with grief and horror the desperate and wicked endeavours of irreligious and rebellious agitators to overturn and destroy the constitution and reminded his people of the heinousness of violating the laws of our country and of attempting, by insurrection and murder to subvert the government of our gracious king'. Lamenting the fatal consequences of the anti-Catholic conspiracy he begged Catholics to surrender their arms without delay.[5] Bishop Edward Dillon of Kilmacduagh, before the arrival of Humbert's French force, warned his people about the atrocities which had marked the behaviour of the French, 'in every country into which they have intruded themselves'. Like several of his colleagues he drew attention to their profanation of Catholic churches and properties and their maltreatment of the pope.[6] Despite the participation of the northern Presbyterians, and the vigorous condemnation of the rebellion by Archbishop Troy of Dublin and several other bishops, whose people were involved, Catholics were made to bear the brunt of the blame. Bishop Caulfield of Ferns excoriated the rebels in Wexford, especially his priests who had been involved, and Troy assured Dublin Castle that 'the guilty cannot be too severely punished'.[7] Troy regretfully complained that 'the monstrous prevarication of some few profligate and ignorant priests who abetted the rebellion afforded a pretext to prejudiced persons to calumniate our holy religion and cry out a popish plot'.[8]

Despite the sincere efforts of these and other bishops to deter their people from participation in what they regarded as a madcap adventure, several pamphleteers and Sir Richard Musgrave, in his *Memoirs of the different rebellions in Ireland*, accused the bishops of maliciously concealing their knowledge of the conspiracy from the government. Bishop Caulfield, who sternly condemned the involvement of priests with the rebels in Wexford, was condemned for not preventing the slaughter of Protestants in Wexford town. The bishops, who detested the outrages committed in France and the contagion of French slogans in Ireland were blamed by Protestant publicists for tolerating the revolutionary activities of priests, which were totally opposed to their directives.

4 Geoghegan, *The Irish Act of Union*, pp 1–24.   5 Pastoral Letter, 27 May 1798, Cast. Corr., i, 209–11.   6 Address of Dillon, 6 Apr. 1798, ibid., 172–6.   7 Troy to R. Marshall, 12 Oct. 1799, ibid., ii, 418–22.   8 Troy to Bishop Sharrock, 3 Aug. 1798, ClDA.

By December 1798 the cabinet had approved of the principle of union and the king accepted its recommendation. George's speech welcoming union was read in the Irish parliament on 22 January 1799 and at Westminster the following day. A single vote was the margin of victory against an anti-union motion that month in the Irish house of commons, and consequently Cornwallis and the chief secretary, Lord Castlereagh, engaged in an elaborate plan to win over the hostile members by bribery for the loss of boroughs, and by conferring patronage, pensions and peerages.[9] To ensure a quiet and tolerant response from the Catholic community, Cornwallis and Castlereagh consulted the leading Catholic peers, lords Kenmare and Fingall, neither of whom offered resistance, and the Catholic bishops, especially Archbishop Troy. The bishops believed that direct rule from London would be less sectarian and more beneficial to Catholics than rule through the Irish parliament. It was from the government in London that they had obtained encouragement for their seminary at Maynooth. Bishop Dillon expressed the hope that it would overcome the tensions in Irish society and 'restore harmony and happiness to our unhappy country'.[10] In accordance with Castlereagh's wishes they abstained from embarrassing the government by passing any resolution referring to the union. But several of them signed resolutions organized by Catholic groups in its favour.[11] Castlereagh, later commenting on the views prevailing in the Irish parliament and among Protestants in late 1799, opined that 'the measure could not be carried, if the Catholics were embarked in an active opposition to it'.[12] After the bill for the union had been passed, Bishop Moylan of Cork not only sang Castlereagh's praises for his 'highly honourable' conduct in steering the measure successfully through parliament but begged God to grant him 'health and length of days to consolidate this good work'.[13]

The bishops, who had long thrown off the yoke of attachment to the exiled Stuarts were anxious to win the favour of the government by demonstrating their loyalty to it. Details of the meetings of Troy with Cornwallis and Castlereagh have not survived, but it is clear that in secret negotiations the bishops were promised financial support for the clergy in return for some guarantee of their loyalty to the state, which the government demanded as part of a future deal for emancipation. But Castlereagh was not prepared to bid in public for Catholic support, and in fact was reassuring Protestants that their ascendancy could only be guaranteed by a union.[14]

9 Bishop Young of Limerick wrote privately that he was satisfied with the constitution of the country, and would accept no bribe to acquiesce in its annihilation (Young to Bray, 28 Dec. 1798, CaDA). 10 Dillon to Troy, 1 Sept. 1799, Cast. Corr., ii, 387. 11 D. Keogh, 'Catholic responses to the Act of Union' in Keogh and Whelan, *Acts of Union*, pp 159–70. 12 Castlereagh to Pitt, 1 Jan. 1801, iv, 8–9; Castlereagh to Pitt, 1 Jan. 1801, iv, 8. 13 Moylan to R. Marshall, 26 July 1800, Cast. Corr., iii, 364–5. 14 Bartlett, *The fall and rise of the Irish nation*, p. 252.

The bishops did not comment on the union of the parliaments in their letters to Rome. The purely political aspect of the union did not concern the Vatican but the religious consequences, which included a possible veto on the appointment of the bishops and the payment of the clergy, certainly did. Both these policies had been suggested as early as 1782. Thomas Lewis O'Beirne, a former Catholic who had become an Anglican and (later) bishop of Meath, and who was private secretary to the viceroy, had put this proposal to him. Ten years later reports of a similar démarche scared the bishops, and Troy feared that pensions would lead to an unholy competition for places and patronage. The threat of a royal intervention in episcopal appointments caused even greater anxiety.[15] The resistance of the bishops prevented this plan from going any further.

When rumours were again raised in 1794 about a possible veto and provision for the clergy, Troy let Rome know of the dangers posed to the Irish church by these proposals. But as there were no specific arrangements put forward he did not receive any ruling from the congregation of Propaganda.[16] At a meeting with Pelham, the chief secretary in 1797, Troy was reminded that the kings of France and other Catholic rulers had appointed bishops. He admitted that the pope gave the privilege of nominating bishops to rulers in countries where they enjoyed estates or revenues. When Pelham suggested that the state might grant an annual revenue to every bishop and priest, Troy 'deprecated the measure as impolitic and inexpedient', because their 'exertions to promote subordination and peace would be ascribed to self-interest'. He later explained to Bishop Plunket that if that measure were ever adopted it would be followed by the decline and perhaps the final destruction of their religion.[17]

The rebellion weakened the hand of the bishops enormously. The few priests and the Catholic people who took part in it allowed the castle to point to the need for some measure to bind the priests and, in consequence, the people to the state. Proposals about stipends to diminish the dependence of the clergy on poor people, and its corollary – royal intervention in episcopal appointments – could not be brushed off. Troy, who had opposed royal intervention in appointments, must have concluded that as a result of the rebellion and the involvement of a few priests he could not resist the proposals.

In January 1799 the episcopal trustees of Maynooth, meeting on college business, devoted three days to a discussion of the quid pro quo the govern-

---

15 Troy to Bray, 9, 27 Apr. 1793, CaDA.   16 Troy to Concanen and Propaganda, 25 Sept. 1794, APF, SC(Fondo di Vienna), 28, f 187rv and 10 Jan. 1795, SOCG 900, f 217rv. Troy also warned Rome about the danger of the religious settlement the British government imposed in Corsica (Troy to Propaganda, 9 Nov. SC(Irlanda), 28, ff 186r-187v).   17 Troy to Plunket, 23 May 1797 in Cogan, *The diocese of Meath, ancient and modern*, iii, pp 211–15.

ment was requesting in return for emancipation. The length of time they spent discussing the proposals indicates their awareness of the gravity of the decision they were taking, and the hesitations and, perhaps, opposition some of them must have felt to the government's novel requests. Four archbishops and six bishops, including Moylan of Cork and Plunket of Meath, who were among the most prominent members of the hierarchy, were present. They decided that 'a provision through government for the Roman Catholic clergy competent and secured, ought to be thankfully "accepted"', and that in the appointment of prelates to vacant sees 'such interference of government as may enable it to be satisfied of the loyalty of the persons to be appointed is just and ought to be agreed to'.

The ten prelates then detailed the practical arrangements for the election of bishops: when a vacancy occurred in a diocese, the clergy would recommend a candidate to the bishops of the ecclesiastical province, who by a majority would then elect him or someone else, and in the case of a tie, the archbishop could have a casting vote. In the case of a metropolitan or archbishop, if the prelates of the province did not agree with the choice within two months of the election, the senior bishop would then invite the other archbishops to vote, and in the case of a tie the senior metropolitan would have the casting vote. The presiding archbishop or bishop would then present the name of the person chosen to the government and, if it had no objection, would within a month of the presentation submit the name to the Holy See or would return the name to the presiding prelate who would submit it. If the government objected to the candidate chosen it would inform the presiding prelate within a month and he would then proceed to the election of another candidate. The bishops emphasized that these proposals could not take effect without the approval of the Holy See. They also agreed to inform the government of the selection of parish priests, who would already have taken the oath of allegiance.[18]

Monsignor Charles Erskine, who had always taken a strong ultramontane line in his reports to Rome, got wind of some of the proposed arrangements immediately after the bishops met. He informed the nuncio at Florence that someone had advised the government to provide stipends to the bishops and parish priests, a recommendation that he regarded as 'ill-considered and pernicious'. The lower classes, he thought, would believe that their pastors might be sold to the government, and so the clergy would lose their credit with their flocks to the great detriment of religion. He had had lengthy conferences with Castlereagh and the chancellor on the issue and had used other arguments against the project. He was not sure that he had persuaded Castlereagh but the chancellor agreed with him.[19] Erskine may not have

18 MacCaffrey, *History of the Catholic church in the nineteenth century*, ii, pp 146–8.   19 Erskine to Nunzio of Florence, 23 Jan. 1799, APF, SC(Irlanda) 17, f 529rv.

known that the anti-Catholic chancellor, Lord Clare, would have disapproved of any scheme that would benefit Catholics.

A couple of months later, Erskine writing officially to Cardinal Borgia in Rome, elaborated on his contacts with Castlereagh. The chief secretary had complained about the dependence of the Irish clergy on their people for their maintenance. Consequently, they could not correct or admonish them, often turned a blind eye and sometimes joined them in rebellions. Erskine replied that this remedy would have increased the evil, as the leaders of the rebellion had endeavoured to discredit the bishops and clergy by saying that they were paid by the government. And so the bishops in their pastorals had expressly declared that they had received nothing from the government. He suggested that any financial help should be deferred until a time when minds were calmer and should be placed in a fund so that the clergy would not have to go to the government for their stipends. He stressed, however, that everything depended on the pope. He had learned from Troy what he had always suspected: that the government wished to be involved in the selection of bishops, and that Troy hoped the project would never materialize. The bishops had agreed to it under pressure and Castlereagh was pleased that it should remain in suspense when the ministers were engaged in discussions about the union of the parliaments. The prelates wished to keep the matter secret but Troy had sent him the details so that they could receive instructions from the pope. He begged the cardinal to forward his official answer to the Irish bishops.[20]

Since the French occupation of Rome the pope had been detained in Florence and his advisers were scattered to various cities in the north of Italy. Cardinal Borgia, the pro-prefect of the congregation of Propaganda, took up residence in Padua. In March 1799 the pope was moved to Turin and thence to Valence in France where he arrived on 13 July 1799 and where he died six weeks later. There was little if any possibility of making contact with him or of his devoting time to this Irish matter in the midst of his other problems and difficulties.

The plan accepted by the bishops was, in fact, very vague. It was not clear whether all the priests of a diocese or only the parish priests would be summoned to recommend a candidate to the bishops of the province. The bishops were empowered to disregard the name submitted to them and select someone else and in neither case was any indication given as to whether the person chosen should be serving in the vacant diocese or not. No provision was made for further recommendations, if the government rejected a second candidate put forward by the clergy and bishops. And the bishops did not state whether or not they would pass on to the government any alterations in

20 Erskine to Propaganda, 3 Apr. 1799, ibid., ff 536r–539v.

the system which the Holy See might demand. The method by which the clergy were to be paid or the amount they would receive were not arranged. Though they would all have known that payment was made to the clergy in Catholic countries on the Continent, they were well aware that the purpose of the plan was to attach them more firmly to the state. John Young, the bishop of Limerick, was not alone in fearing that the government wanted to diminish their independence.[21]

When Cardinal Borgia heard from Erskine about the bishops' response to Castlereagh's proposals, he wrote to Troy from Padua admitting that the details he had been given were vague and he hoped false. He argued that as the plan would tend to the overthrow of the old system and the deprivation of the rights of the Holy See, and, as Troy had taken the principal part in it, he begged him not to deviate from the path he had hitherto so successfully followed.[22] The Holy See was always very cautious in dealing with a Protestant government about ecclesiastical matters, and in the midst of its many difficulties with France it did not have the time or the full information or opportunity to negotiate with Britain.

Troy assured his 'constant patron and friend' Cardinal Borgia that in the wake of the rebellion in which several priests were involved the king wanted to attach bishops and priests to himself, giving them a suitable stipend and relieving them of dependence on the people whom they had recently embraced in the popular delirium. In that case the king should have the privilege of presenting to the pope the candidates whom he deemed suitable for the episcopate, as in Canada. To Troy's objections – that the clergy would be made to appear mercenary and so lose the respect of the people, that an immense sum of money would be required and that only the pope could alter the present discipline – Castlereagh had replied that the government did not wish to attack the jurisdiction of the pope. Enclosing the details of the concessions made to the government, Troy added that the bishops who signed them had wished to avoid them, but insisted on upholding the rights of the Holy See and their own.[23]

21 Young, on hearing of this suggestion, told Archbishop Bray of Cashel that it would be dangerous to the interests of religion, that the clergy could lose the confidence of their people, and that, being regarded as state pensioners, they would not receive any support from their congregations (Young to Bray, 17 Nov. 1798, CaDA). 22 Borgia to Troy, 15 June 1799, ibid., f 690rv. Borgia, recalling his role in promoting Troy to the bishopric and archbishopric, begged him to write as soon as possible and to ensure that spiritual matters belonged to the church and its head, to whom no further affliction should be offered at that time. 23 Troy to Propaganda, 17 Aug. 1799, APF, SC(Irlanda) 17, ff 692r–694v. In a letter to Concanen Troy explained that 'if the prelates had refused to consider the proposal, they would be accused of a design to exercise an influence over the people independent of government for seditious purposes. Nothing but the well grounded apprehension of such a charge, tho' groundless in itself, would have induced the prelates to consider the proposal in any manner' (Troy to Concanen, [day unknown] April 1800, ibid., ff 429r–430r).

Troy's agent in Rome, his fellow Dominican, Luke Concanen, who was attached to the Dominican theologate, had done some research on methods of appointing bishops and informed Troy that 'it would be fatal to religion were government to adopt at any time the mode of appointment of prelates that the Prussian Majesty exerts'. The Prussian minister in Rome had told him that 'thro regard and consideration of his indulgence to his R. Cath. subjects, the H. See promotes to bishopricks the very person he nominates to the vacant sees'. Asked if the chapters recommended candidates to the king, the minister replied that they did, so that the king knew the merits of the candidates.[24] Borgia, he later opined, disapproved of 'every sort of innovation' as emerged from the government's plans but 'his connection with Sir John H ... y whose interest he courts and with whom he corresponds, renders him cautious to speak out his mind'.[25] The congregation of Propaganda was later to let the Irish bishops know that it did not allow Protestant rulers to nominate bishops. In fact Roman practices were more pragmatic. For example, the bishop of Quebec obtained the approval of the governor for his choice of coadjutor before applying to Rome for the appointment. Roman officials invariably ruled out the right of Protestant governments to examine communications from Rome to their churches, but they were later to show that even on this point they could be pragmatic.

Bishop Moylan of Cork crossed to London in the summer of 1799, met some leading politicians and discussed the bishops' decisions with Erskine. Erskine, unlike Moylan, was sceptical about the goodwill of the government. His contacts with the leading politicians for several years had not softened his view of their sturdy Protestantism and disrespect for Catholicism. And as the channel of the Vatican to the government he claimed the right to intervene when political issues were involved. Moylan had found evidence of goodwill in the government's willingness to pay for the rebuilding of the Catholic churches which had been wrecked during the rebellion,[26] but Erskine, refusing to believe that the government was sympathetic to the Catholic religion, took the view that it was moved by the need to keep the population, which was mainly Catholic, quiet. Moylan had assured him that pending the approval of the pope nothing had been decided. But Erskine replied that they might have compromised the Holy See, which would have to bear the brunt of the hostility if some of the articles were not approved, and consequently he should have been contacted when the government first made its

24 Concanen to Troy, 10 May 1800, DDA.   25 Ibid., 10 Oct. 1800. The reference was to Sir John Coxe-Hippisley, whose sister lived in Rome and who spent time there since 1794. He had got to know several prelates and he regarded himself as an unofficial British envoy at the Vatican. 26 Bishop Caulfield of Ferns informed Troy that twenty-four chapels in his diocese had been burned (Caulfield to Troy, 1 June and 10 Sept. 1799, DDA). Troy noted that, in all, forty-three chapels had been damaged or ruined (Troy to Fr Dunne, 13 July 1799, DDA).

proposals. He further counselled Moylan to consult his colleagues about finding a way out of their commitment by letting it be known on a suitable occasion that they had taken too much responsibility on themselves and that their conduct would not be approved by the Holy See.[27]

With the death of Pius VI in August 1799 and the disruption of the Roman machinery of government no decision was taken on the matter. The new pope, Pius VII, was not elected until 14 March 1800, and normal business did not resume until he reached Rome the following July. He was soon faced with the question of a Protestant government intervening in a mild way in ecclesiastical affairs, for as an encouragement to the Irish clergy, the Scottish clergy were given stipends. Concanen relayed his surprise to Troy when no complaint was made about the Scottish clergy receiving stipends (Borgia had enjoined Bishop Moylan to thank Sir John Coxe-Hippisley for 'procuring an assignment').[28] Archbishop Brancadoro, the secretary of the congregation of Propaganda, had told him that the Scots were excused because they had no means of support while the Irish were maintained by the faithful. Concanen sought to exculpate Troy from taking a leading part in making arrangements with the state but was told by Brancadoro that he should have opposed the scheme. He regarded Coxe-Hippisley, who tried to interfere on the Castlereagh side in Rome, as a troublesome 'meddler' and predicted that he 'will not stop till he vests government with the nomination of C. Bishops'.[29] Borgia disliked the pension plan much more heartily than the plans for the nomination of the bishops. He wanted the former 'entirely forgotten and drop'd', even if the latter were left with the status quo.[30]

Troy heard nothing further from Castlereagh about clerical stipends for nearly two years after submitting the resolutions of January 1799. The bishops hoped the government had abandoned its plan but then in October 1800 Castlereagh asked for information about clerical appointments and incomes, and the canons or laws regulating their churches, and explained that this was a preliminary to the payment of the clergy. This placed the bishops in an awkward situation. They could not easily refuse Castlereagh's request and yet they knew that Rome did not approve of his scheme. The bishops,

---

27 Erskine to Propaganda, 7 and 8 Aug. 1799, APF, SC(Irlanda) 17, ff 550r–553r. Erskine feared that Moylan was succumbing to the flattery of the government, though he admitted that he was cooperating with it for the good of religion. A copy of Erskine's draft of this letter was sent to Troy. In it he reported that Troy had told him that he and the Irish bishops would have been better pleased if the government had not made the proposals about episcopal appointments and clergy stipends. DDA, 8 Aug. 1799.   28 The Scottish vicars apostolic were granted £100 yearly and their coadjutors £50. Each priest was assigned £20 and each college £50 in addition to £600 to defray the debts incurred in their erection. The bishops thanked Coxe-Hippisley profusely for his part in procuring this help (Scottish bishops to Coxe-Hippisley, 19 June 1799 in Cast. Corr., ii, 332–3).   29 Concanen to Troy, 10 Oct. 1800, DDA.   30 Ibid., 25 Oct. 1800.

thirteen of whom came to Dublin for a meeting, complied with this request, and Troy, the archbishop of Armagh and bishop of Meath were delegated to negotiate with the government, to ensure the maintenance of the rights of the Holy See and the freedom of episcopal elections.[31]

Concanen, invited by the congregation of Propaganda to submit reflections on the plan of pensioning the clergy, dismissed it completely. He denounced it as insidious and suspect in its origins, injurious to the religion and discipline of the clergy, damaging to the Catholic faith of the country, and tending to dissensions and disharmony in the hierarchy. He pointed out that the bishops had vigorously condemned the rebellion and that very few priests had been involved in it. Made independent of their bishops the clergy could even teach the errors of the Anglican church without losing their stipend. And if the government had the right of vetoing the appointments of bishops and pastors it could exclude candidates until it could find an acceptable semi-Catholic. As clergy became more dependent on the British court than the Holy See, disputes leading to appeals to the government would arise about the choice of bishops and the destination of parish priests. Consequently, he advised the cardinal to write a strong letter to the archbishops to get them to oppose as energetically as they could these dangerous innovations.[32] His views were to find many echoes in the years to come.

In response to this advice the secretary of Propaganda informed the pope of the government's plan and was authorized by him to thank it in his name for its generous liberality and for its support for the Catholics of its dominions. The pope, however, believing that the loyalty of the Catholic clergy to their sovereign derived from their faith, desired that the government be assured that the bishops and clergy would recognize their obligation to it. But he opposed acceptance of the plan:

> The Holy Father most earnestly wishes the said clergy to pursue the fair system they have hitherto observed, scrupulously abstaining from aiming at their own temporal advantage and always evincing by words and deeds their sincere attachment, acknowledgment of and submission to the British government and manifest the reality of that gratitude for the generous benefits recently offered by declining to accept them. By so doing they would give an acceptable proof of constant disinterestedness conformable to the apostolic zeal of ministers of the sanctuary ... and render themselves more venerable and dear to the faithful committed to their spiritual care.[33]

31 Troy to Propaganda, 22 Dec. 1800, APF, SC(Irlanda), 17, ff 703r–704r.   32 Concanen to Propaganda, 17 Mar. 1801, ibid., 755r–756v.   33 Propaganda to Concanen, 7 Aug. 1801, DDA.

To this formal command of the pope himself, Troy replied that the bishops would not adopt any plan that was not conformable to the unalterable principles of their religion and to the rights of the Holy See, considering any plan not authorized by it as invalid. There would be no further talk of the proposed plan before the publication of the concordat between the Holy See and the French government, according to which some articles of agreement might be regulated by the government here. In the meantime the bishops hoped to have the guidance of the pontiff in that difficult question and in the regulation of their conduct in the present difficult circumstances.[34] They were now enabled to use the cloak of papal intransigence in their dealings with Castlereagh.

The replies by the bishops on their incomes were filed by Castlereagh and were subsequently printed by his brother in 1848 in one of the volumes of his memoirs and correspondence. Apart from listing the numbers of parishes and some general disciplinary regulations the returns showed that the 1,026 parishes of Ireland were served by 1,800 priests of whom 800 were curates and 400 were members of religious orders. The average income of a parish priest, excluding the £10 of a curate, was £65 and that of a bishop was £300. The annual incomes of bishops varied from the £550 enjoyed by the bishop of Cork to £100, which the bishop of Kilfenora and Kilmacduagh received. Some dioceses reported at greater length than others on the stipends of the clergy in every parish. In the diocese of Raphoe the average was £55 and in Armagh a few priests had £40. Those who had curates provided them with accommodation, the upkeep of a horse and £10 per annum.

Castlereagh prepared the draft of a bill 'to make a competent and independent provision' for the Catholic clergy, which took account of the bishops' replies. It was explained that the spiritual duties discharged by the clergy were 'extensive and laborious and the remuneration received by them is precarious, and in a great degree derived from the poorer classes ... and such remuneration being oppressive to the contributor and unsuitable to the receiver, it is just and expedient that a competent and independent provision be made for the clergy'. Details of how the money was to be found and how the elections of bishops were to take place were then given. When an archbishop died the senior suffragans were required within a period of time to convene the suffragans, who would elect three of their number and submit the names to the chief secretary or undersecretary to be forwarded to the lord lieutenant, who within a certain period of time would recommend one of the three so chosen to the Holy See. In the case of a suffragan, the dean or senior parish priest would convene the parish priests, who would elect three of their

34 Troy to Propaganda, 19 Nov. 1801, APF, SC(Irlanda), 18, ff 13r–14v. The concordat between the Holy See and France was concluded in July 1801 but did not become law until April 1802.

number and transmit the names to the primate or, in his absence, to the senior archbishop, to be submitted to all the Irish bishops. If they or the majority approved, the three names would be ultimately passed on to the lord lieutenant, who would recommend one of them to the Holy See. If the majority of the bishops did not approve the choice of the clergy, the parish priests would be again convened to elect one or more of their number to replace the one or more than one who had not won the approval of the bishops. This process, if necessary, would be repeated until the majority of the bishops approved of the choice. Should the dean or presiding parish priest not proceed to an election, the body of bishops could elect any three ecclesiastics from the diocese and submit the names to the chief secretary. Arrangements were made for casting votes in case of a tie or in case the dean or senior parish priest did not organize an election.

The bishops were also required to submit the names of three priests to succeed in a vacancy caused by the death of a dean or parish priest to the lord lieutenant, who would recommend one of them for appointment. The bishops were free to appoint curates but were obliged to let the lord lieutenant have a certificate proving that they had taken the oaths of allegiance. Only a bishop or priest who had taken the appropriate oath would qualify for appointment to any ecclesiastical office.

The existing dioceses were to be replaced by new dioceses corresponding to the thirty-two counties. Each province would be headed by an archbishop and the old ecclesiastical sees were to be replaced by an archbishopric of Leinster, based in Dublin, to which the primacy was attached, an archbishopric of Munster in Cork, an archbishopric of Connaught in Galway and an archbishopric of Ulster in Donegal. Their incomes were to vary from £2,000 for the primate to £1,200 for the archbishop of Ulster. Of the bishops, three were to receive £900, four £800, four £700, six £600, and the remaining eleven £500. The incomes of the deans were to vary from £750 for Dublin to £250 for the eleven lowest paid. The parish priests were to be divided into three classes with 500 in each, earning £120, £100 and £80, and 1,000 curates were each to be allotted £50. These were very generous stipends and would have ensured that every bishop and all but a very small number of priests would have been much more comfortably remunerated than they had been without state assistance. The financial part of the proposed agreement was not made public until Castlereagh's memoirs and correspondence were published almost fifty years later.[35]

No mention was made at this stage of another element in the veto package that later caused annoyance – the concession to the government of the right to examine official correspondence from Rome to the bishops. But Coxe-

---

35 Charles Vane (ed.), *Memoirs and correspondence of Viscount Castlereagh*, iv, pp 97–151, 425–33.

Hippisley, the self-appointed expert on Vatican affairs, who gave advice to both government ministers and bishops, raised this issue at an early stage in the discussions about the payment of the clergy. He suggested to Lord Hobart, a former chief secretary, that 'an essential line of conduct would be that the government should not ever blink, but fairly face the whole Catholic subject, not tacitly allow, as they do, the introduction of *bulls, briefs* and *rescripts* without availing itself of those safeguards which almost every Catholic as well as Protestant country on the Continent had wisely instituted'. Castlereagh did not take up this suggestion,[36] but later, in a memorandum in 1813, pointed out that 'the pope often sends secret orders to his bishops etc. but they are of no political nature, and it is against this kind of secrecy we complain'.[37]

Castlereagh and his advisers had obviously studied the Irish clerical scene seriously and made a reasonable plan for a deal with the church. At that point he must have been fairly confident that the government could pass a bill for emancipation, and that the approval which the bishops had given to proposals about appointments and payment would be carried through. Throughout these negotiations about the union, Cornwallis and Castlereagh had never given the Catholics any guarantee or even a firm promise that emancipation or the right to sit in parliament would follow. What their leaders had been given was a kind of gentleman's 'understanding' that this would be so, and the bishops and Catholic peers, realizing the delicacy of the situation, did not seek any precise commitment. Troy later explained that while Castlereagh 'made no explicit promise of emancipation, he distinctly said the union would facilitate it'.[38]

With the union taking effect on 1 January 1801, the cabinet soon had to decide whether and how to put into effect the 'understanding' Cornwallis and Castlereagh had adumbrated to the Irish Catholic leaders.[39] Towards the end of January, Pitt and his senior ministers expressed opinions sympathetic to emancipation, but before they could formally bring the matter to the king, he approached the home secretary at a levee and, in an agitated manner referring to Castlereagh's support for emancipation, declared that 'I shall look on every man as my personal enemy, who proposed that question to me ... I hope all my friends will not desert me'. The king's reaction was overheard and instantly became notorious. Pitt summoned a cabinet to discuss the question formally and let it be known that he would have to resign if prevented from carrying emancipation. He then composed a paper for the king pointing out that emancipation would pose no threat to the established

36 Coxe-Hippisley to Lord Hobart, 12 Jan. 1799, Cast. Corr., iii, 86–93.   37 Cast. Corr., iv, 250.
38 Troy to Scully, 8 June 1813 in MacDermot, *The Catholic question in Ireland and England, 1798–1822*, p. 463.   39 Whelan, 'The other within: Ireland, Britain and the Act of Union' in Keogh and Whelan, *Acts of Union*, pp 13–33.

church or Protestant interest, that any political dangers the Catholics might pose had been declining, that an oath on admission to parliament would ensure that they presented no danger and, in fact, that the clergy would be brought into closer union with the state, which its financial support for them would further strengthen. Pitt then told the king that, if his objections to the measure could not be removed or diminished to the extent that the measure could be brought forward, he would have to be released from an office, which he could not fill 'but with the greatest disadvantage'.[40] Far from being moved by this appeal George insisted in reply that 'those who hold employments in the state' must be members of the established church, and maintained that he was therefore prevented 'from discussing any proposition tending to destroy this ground'. Pitt formally resigned on 3 February 1801. His successor had already been chosen.[41] With Pitt's resignation Castlereagh's plans for pensioning the clergy and intervening in episcopal appointments lapsed. He became president of the Board of Control in 1802, secretary for war in 1807 and foreign secretary in 1812, when he again became involved in discussions about episcopal appointments.

Though Pitt's motives in resigning may not have been exclusively dependent on Catholic emancipation, that was the issue which concerned Cornwallis and Castlereagh. Both had been keen advocates of the policy and so had to cope with Catholic reaction and disappointment. As opposition had mounted in the cabinet before the final denouement Castlereagh had reminded Pitt of how, by 'flattering the hopes of the Catholics', a favourable impression had been created among them in Cork, Tipperary and Galway.[42] He had given Cornwallis to understand that, as the cabinet favoured the policy, he could encourage the Catholics to support the union without giving them any direct assurance about their future status. Consequently, Cornwallis would be pained by the abandonment of a measure which he thought essential for the future interests of the empire.[43] Cornwallis was not only despondent at the collapse of his hopes but also fearful of the Catholic reaction. He predicted that the peaceful situation they were then enjoying could not last 'if the evil genius of Britain should induce the cabinet to continue the proscription of the Catholics'.[44] To add to his difficulties Castlereagh informed him that it was Pitt's wish that he should let the Catholics know that an obstacle which the retiring ministers could not surmount precluded them from bringing forward the question of emancipa-

---

40 Geoghegan, *The Irish Act of Union*, pp 156–91.   41 Ehrmann, *The younger Pitt*, pp 496–513.
42 At a meeting of the Catholics of Leinster and Dublin a letter from the bishops advising them to wait patiently for relief was read out and at the end of a debate the advice was accepted by a large majority (quoted in Bartlett, *The fall and rise of the Irish nation*, p. 255).   43 Castlereagh to Pitt, 1 Jan. 1801, Cast. Corr., iv, 8–12.   44 Cornwallis to Castlereagh, 2 Jan. 1801, ibid., 13; Castlereagh to Cornwallis, 9 Feb. 1801, ibid., 88–9.

tion. He was advised not to mention the king's name, although how the Catholics were expected to accept the interposition of some mysterious obstacle to block their hopes was not made clear. The cabinet's resignation was to be portrayed as the means most likely to achieve the desired goal, and in the meantime the Catholics were to strengthen their cause by good conduct.[45] Barring the outright refusal even to consider emancipation this counsel was about as bleak and unconvincing as could be imagined. But if membership of parliament was withheld, the bishops were spared tricky dealings with the government about appointments and pensions.

Before his departure from Ireland Cornwallis obeyed Castlereagh's injunction and gave to Troy and Fingall statements to be discreetly communicated to the bishops and principal Catholics but not to be published in the newspapers. The Catholics were to be informed that the retirement of the ministers was the line of conduct most likely to contribute to the ultimate success of concessions to their body (though how precisely was not explained) and were advised to see how much their future hopes depended upon strengthening their cause by good conduct, avoiding any association 'with men of Jacobinical principles', and taking 'the most loyal, dutiful and patient line of conduct'. They were encouraged to rely with confidence on those who were retiring and on many remaining in office, and were assured that Pitt would do his utmost to establish their cause in the public favour and 'prepare the way for their finally attaining their objects'.[46] Troy dutifully transmitted copies of these 'sentiments of a sincere friend to the Catholic claims' to his colleagues, and presumably Fingall did likewise.[47] The leading Catholic leaders observed this advice and did not start any agitation for the next three years.

The failure to grant emancipation and remove some of the barriers to equality ensured that the union began under very unfavourable circumstances. The Catholics who had relied on the 'understanding' their leaders had received and gratefully accepted from Cornwallis and Castlereagh felt abandoned, disheartened and deceived. Castlereagh and his friends felt that emancipation might be dead for many years. Yet he believed that apart from the king and the Anglican bishops there was no strong feeling in England against it.[48] With emancipation rejected or postponed until a distant future the likelihood of other adjustments, such as the payment of tithes to the clergy of a different and minority denomination seemed remote. Some Catholics felt that their cooperation in the negotiations had been ungratefully rejected and, consequently, their trust in the honesty and sincerity of the government was diminished. Some became firm opponents of the union.

45 Troy to Moylan, 29 May 1802, CRDA.   46 Cornwallis, 'Memoranda to the Catholics', Mar. 1801, Corn. Corr., iii, 347–8.   47 Troy to Moylan, 29 May 1802, CRDA.   48 Bew, *Castlereagh: Enlightenment, war and tyranny*, pp 169–71.

The painful consequences, however of the failed appeal to violence in 1798 at least discouraged any serious thought among the majority of trying to remedy grievances by that method.

The firm rejection by Rome of the attempt to meet the demand of Castlereagh and the government for pensioning the clergy and its reluctance to agree to the intervention of a Protestant government in the process of appointing bishops left the hierarchy in no doubt that emancipation would not be easily achieved. Castlereagh had let it be known that the government wanted some of the rights or privileges enjoyed by other sovereigns as a quid pro quo for emancipation, and that was a claim beyond the prelates' power to concede. The need for 'securities' from the Catholics became a constant refrain in subsequent discussions about emancipation. Not only were Irish Catholics disappointed by the failure of their hopes from the union but they were further disillusioned by the efforts of evangelical societies to convert them to Protestantism, mainly through the medium of education.

Before the Act of Union the term 'Catholic emancipation' had come into use, and thereafter it became common currency. After the union as Ireland came under the jurisdiction of the same parliament as England, no distinction could be made in the treatment of the Catholics in the two countries. Each community would benefit from the agitation of the other, and Irish Catholics being more numerous and being able to play a more determined role in Ireland were in a position to agitate more effectively than English Catholics. As John Power, the bishop of Waterford, was later to remark, the Catholics in Ireland had more weight with the men in power, because of the weight of their numbers, than their co-religionists in England.[49] And as agitation for emancipation began at Westminster, Rome had to deal with a tricky problem in the vicariate of the London District.

From a Roman point of view the destinies of the two communities were inextricably linked. Both sets of bishops raised the same queries in Rome about state interference in episcopal appointments and oaths. And to a lesser extent their misunderstandings came under Roman surveillance. The Vatican had to pay attention to the demands of the British government and to the responses they provoked among the bishops and the members of parliament.

---

49 Power to Bray, 14 Feb. 1810, CaDA.

6

A failed manoeuvre in the London District

I

In the last years before the Act of Union, Archbishop Troy had easy means of communication with Dublin Castle. He could engage in discussions on matters relating to church and state with the chief secretary and his senior officials and assistants. Both parties found these contacts agreeable and beneficial. With the union and the transfer of power to London, Troy realized that he could no longer enjoy that kind of convenient relationship with leading politicians. Visits to London would be costly and any money that he had was needed for the upkeep and expansion of the pastoral work of his diocese. Irish dioceses did not have any central funds, as each parish provided for its own needs, and the expenses of frequent travel to London would have taxed the archbishop's personal resources.

The archbishop had been impressed by the part played by John Milner in the disputes between the vicars apostolic and the Catholic Committee in 1790–1 and by his opposition to the oath in the bill for Catholic relief. He had doubtless heard of Milner's circularizing the members of parliament against the bill. He concluded that Milner was suited to the role of intermediary for the Irish church at Westminster. It is likely that Milner, who in 1803 had become vicar apostolic of the Midland District, had hinted to Troy that he might play the role of intermediary for the Irish church in political circles in London. He certainly had a taste for political activities but he also realized that at Wolverhampton he was far removed from the centre of political action. His responsibilities for an extensive vicariate much larger than any Irish diocese would have made frequent visits to London difficult, and would not have permitted him to spend time there to get to know politicians.

The solution was to have Milner transferred to London, but it was a solution bristling with difficulties. John Douglass, the vicar apostolic, was 62 in 1805, and his coadjutor, William Poynter, was 43.[1] There was no likelihood of an immediate vacancy. For Troy to intervene in the English church to displace Douglass or Poynter to make way for Milner was both audacious and temerarious. But this is what he proceeded to do, and, not surprisingly, his interference was deeply resented by those whom he sought to dislodge. And it brought him their lasting distrust.

1 Douglass was vicar apostolic of the London District from 1790 to 1812.

A few months after the presentation of a petition for emancipation in May 1805,[2] Troy, presumably after consultation with Milner, wrote to Rome pointing out the importance of having an active, learned and zealous agent in London who could negotiate with ministers and members of parliament about the interests of the Catholic church.[3] Praising Milner's recent contribution in that sphere and his publication of an excellent booklet on that subject and drawing attention to the difficulty caused by the distance from Dublin to London, he asked if Milner could exchange places with Douglass or else with Douglass' coadjutor. Remarking that both the friends and indeed enemies of the Catholic cause had a high regard for Milner's erudition and talents, he explained that they had a very different view of Douglass.[4]

Troy's initiative must have been sweet music to the ambitious Milner, who was most anxious to be stationed in London to be able to pursue his political agenda there.[5] It was almost certainly on Troy's advice that Milner appointed Luke Concanen as his Roman agent. Writing to Concanen in June 1805, shortly after the failure of the petition to parliament, Milner explained that he had written a pamphlet at Troy's request in defence of Catholicism. Enthusing about the support for emancipation in parliament, he claimed that pensions for the clergy would accompany it, but expressed strong reservations and anxiety about the plans being made to interfere in their ecclesiastical discipline in any way that could weaken the influence of the Holy See and strengthen that of the crown.

Some supporters of their cause, he explained to Concanen, had proposed that all communication of their bishops with the Vatican should be subject to examination by the king's ministers. All sides spoke of the need for the civil power to have influence in the appointment of bishops: one party would be satisfied with the king being able to exclude a candidate who was unacceptable; the other party wanted a positive right of appointment from among a class of clergy previously examined and approved by the bench of bishops. Some of their peers and gentry were unhappy with the condition of the vicars apostolic as being too dependent on Rome, and at the same time at the behest of Protestant bishops, they condemned the names and titles of the bishops of Ireland. Milner wanted to know to what extent the Holy See would be prepared to make concessions, especially as the strong party associated with the Cisalpine Club headed by Sir John Throckmorton was ever

---

2 See Chapter 7.   3 On hearing of Milner's appointment to the Midland District, Troy had assured Cardinal Borgia that it was regarded by all the bishops and zealous Catholics of Ireland as most advantageous at a time when learned and vigilant pastors were never more needed (Troy to Propaganda, 26 Feb. 1803, APF, SC(Irlanda), 18, ff 81r–82r). And Bishop Moylan told Archbishop Bray that he was happy to think that letters of their prelates had 'contributed to make known at Rome the merits and real character of that most worthy ecclesiastic' (Moylan to Bray, 4 May 1802, CaDA).   4 Troy to Propaganda, 2 Nov. 1805, APF, SC(Irlanda), 18, f 342rv, 2 Nov. 1805, f 342rv.

ready to restrict the authority of the pope and humiliate the clergy. He had already had some success in obtaining greater liberty for Catholic soldiers in the exercise of their religion and disposing the minds of Protestant bishops and the king's ministers and legal advisers to legalize marriages contracted before a Catholic priest.[6]

Milner's letter was well received at the congregation of Propaganda, which sent a lengthy reply to Concanen. It advised the vicars apostolic and the bishops of Ireland to eschew all advantages in their dealings with a Protestant government whose proposals were not to be trusted. Recalling the letter of Pius VII in August 1801 to Archbishop Troy and the reply of the Irish archbishops willingly renouncing all temporal advantages to preserve the Catholic religion unstained, the congregation decided to send a copy of the pope's letter to Milner. The participation of a Protestant sovereign in the appointment of bishops was rejected and the letter of Benedict XIV to the bishop of Breslau in 1748 to that effect was quoted.[7] Though the proposal of excluding candidates was more limited it could lead indirectly to appointments. Moreover, the Holy See always took great care to exclude candidates who were not acceptable to governments. Rome, it continued, would have no difficulty in having bishops instead of vicars apostolic in England, but care would have to be taken with the motivations of the Cisalpine Club in furthering such a proposal. The congregation ruled out completely any suggestion of a Protestant government examining communications with the Holy See. Finally Milner was commended for his efforts to establish the ecclesiastical rights of Catholic soldiers and the validity of Catholic marriages.[8]

Emboldened by this encouragement, Milner further developed his comments about the parties favourable to Catholic emancipation, and drew attention to the less than honest practices for which English Catholics had fallen: for example, Lord Redesdale, who had sponsored an oath allegedly to facilitate English Catholics, later showed himself as chancellor in Ireland to favour anti-Catholic behaviour. The key passage in this communication to Rome was a barely concealed attempt to promote himself as a political agent of the Catholics in London. He wondered if Rome would share the view of the Irish bishops that someone noted for orthodoxy, literature, zeal, prudence and experience should reside in London ready to respond to the calumnies and sophisms of such as Lord Redesdale and to make use of the goodwill of those who favoured Catholic soldiers and Catholic marriages. He referred to

5 Milner later admitted to Troy, 'I own I am not partial to the country I now inhabit' (Milner to Troy, 22 Apr. 1806, DDA).   6 Milner to Concanen, 21 June 1805, APF, SC(Anglia) 6, ff 203r–204v.   7 In 1742 Silesia, a mainly Catholic territory, was ceded by the Empress Maria Theresa of Austria to the Protestant King Frederick the Great of Prussia.   8 Propaganda to Concanen for Milner, 7 Sept. 1805, ibid., ff 217r–223v.

published correspondence between Lord Fingall and Lord Redesdale in which the latter had insisted that Catholics, by not recognizing Protestants as fellow Christians, were contributing to the divisions and dissensions which had led to rebellion, violence and deaths, and could never be loyal and dutiful subjects of the king. The whole priesthood of Ireland acknowledged obedience to one who was the vassal of France.[9] He hoped that the suggestion about an agent in London, which came from the wise Irish bishops, would lose none of its weight because of their partiality for him and their belief that he was the one most suited to that position. He expressed his readiness to accept any commission, however unsuited to his rank or income, in which the Apostolic See might judge him capable of doing good, even though he was persuaded that there were many others more qualified than he to carry out that duty with dignity.[10] He prudently abstained from naming these highly qualified agents.

For more than a year Troy, aided by his Roman agent, Concanen, and encouraged at every step by Milner himself, fought at Rome to have Milner transferred to London. He also enlisted the aid of other Irish bishops, notably Moylan, whose letter to Concanen was translated and passed on to Propaganda. Moylan predicted that emancipation would take effect in the next session of parliament but no final accommodation would be made without 'the disposition of our hierarchy'. It was therefore very important for them to have a capable person resident in London to deal with the government. Bishop Douglass was not suited to that role. He possessed neither the ability nor the necessary influence to manage such an affair, and this view of him was also shared by Cardinal Erskine.[11]

On the other hand Milner possessed the necessary ability and learning, had worked hard for the cause of religion on all occasions, was attached to the Holy See and enjoyed the esteem of MPs and the government. It was due to his labours and influence with the principal members of the legislature that the Catholics of England in 1791 owed their preservation from the perils that threatened them from a committee composed for the most part of deists and Jansenists that proposed an oath to parliament tending to the ruin of religion. A prelate of zeal and ability was required to deal with the affairs of the Catholic body in London and prevent any measure that could weaken

9 *Correspondence between the Right Hon. Lord Redesdale, lord high chancellor of Ireland, and the Right Hon. the Earl of Fingall* (Dublin, 1804). In 1804 Napoleon forced the pope and several cardinals to travel to France for his coronation as emperor. English opponents of Catholic emancipation often depicted the pope as the chamberlain of Napoleon, their national enemy, and therefore not to be trusted in his dealings with British or Irish Catholics.   10 Milner to Propaganda, 31 Oct. 1805, ibid., ff 213r–216r. He referred in this letter to his agency for the Irish bishops to which he had been appointed for a second time.   11 Erskine had returned to Rome from London in 1801 and was created a cardinal *in pectore*. His appointment was announced in 1803.

their union with the Holy See. If his suggestions would receive the consideration of Propaganda, he would recommend that Douglass be removed to the Midland District, to be replaced by Milner, or that Poynter, his coadjutor, be appointed to the Midland District, and Milner became coadjutor to Douglass.[12]

Troy, keeping up the pressure on Rome, explained to Cardinal di Pietro, the prefect of Propaganda, that after the union of the two countries Irish Catholics would have to deal with public affairs in England, and in making common cause with the vicars apostolic of England and Scotland, they required an agent in London. No one was more suited to that post than Milner, 'a prelate of great knowledge, of equal zeal and activity, well regarded and esteemed by various gentlemen and particularly by the king's present ministers'. The bishops of Ireland had commissioned him to beg Propaganda to change Poynter, the coadjutor of the London District, to the Midland District so that Milner could succeed him as coadjutor to Bishop Douglass in London. He claimed that there were precedents in the English church for such a move and that the good of religion required it, as Cardinal Erskine, who was well aware of the distinguished qualities of Milner well knew.[13]

Milner's initial confidence that Douglass would cheerfully comply with an order from Rome to agree to the switch, and that Poynter would 'be glad of an exchange which would remove him from a very perplexing situation to another of superior quiet, rank and emolument' could not have been more mistaken.[14] Once Douglass and Poynter heard of the proposal they wasted little time in letting Rome know that they fully disagreed with it. In response to a notification from Propaganda about the request of the Irish prelates, which, they noted, was made against their will, they jointly paid tribute to Milner's services to the Catholic cause in the previous year, but argued that his transfer to London as coadjutor would, in the eyes of both clerical and lay Catholics, be an obstacle to the tranquillity and happiness of the district. They feared that such a transfer by the Holy See against their will would provoke hostility both from the Catholic gentry and from prominent Protestants. And, though admitting that Milner was adorned by many virtues, they pointed out there were strong prejudices against him and he could not operate in the London District without causing very grave offence to many.[15]

12 Moylan to Concanen, 29 Jan. 1806, APF, SC(Irlanda) 18, ff 356r–357r. William Poynter, a former student and professor at the English College, Douay, became coadjutor of the London District in 1803. When the college was transferred to the school at Old Hall Green in Hertfordshire, Poynter became vice president and later president, a position he held until he succeeded Bishop Douglass in 1812. He died in 1827. 13 Troy to Propaganda, 3 Mar. 1806 (copy), DDA. Di Pietro was prefect of the congregation from 1805 to 1814. 14 Milner to Troy, 17 Feb. 1806, DDA. 15 Douglass and Poynter to Propaganda, 24 Mar. 1806, APF, SC(Anglia),

Milner had got wind of Douglass' opposition before this letter was written and accordingly informed Troy that he proposed asking Rome whether he might be given some limited jurisdiction in London, if he were to live there, or, as Cardinal Erskine had envisaged, that he and Douglass should exchange vicariates. He was confident that Bishop Sharrock of the Western District wanted him to live in London and expected Bishop Gibson of the Northern District to hold the same view.[16] Thanking Troy for his promotion of the scheme, he later informed him that Sharrock approved of his residence in London as Douglass had 'no weight or consideration whatever with the men of talents and power', but that Gibson opposed the appointment of an agent in London for the English bishops. In fact, Sharrock had constituted him as his agent in any business that was to be transacted with the government but also recommended that he should keep to his own district and not offend Douglass by proposing an exchange with his coadjutor.[17]

In his enthusiasm and ambition to move to London, Milner soon found that he had misunderstood not only Douglass' attitude but also Cardinal Erskine's. Concanen let Troy know that while the secretary of Propaganda was willing to comply with the archbishop's wish, Erskine not only 'decidedly opposed the permutation of the coadjutorship but even any official appointment of Dr Milner in quality of agent' and he termed him 'a hot and intriguing man'. Erskine took the view that the Irish bishops could depute one of themselves to conduct their business in London. A disappointed Concanen advised Troy to get the Irish bishops to give Milner a formal commission to transact their business with the government and handle all Catholic matters.[18]

As the optimism with which Milner interpreted the answer of Cardinal di Pietro to the formal request of the Irish hierarchy for the exchange of Milner and Poynter,[19] which merely stated that the congregation was investigating the request,[20] diminished, Milner had to think of some other plan. His solution was to sweeten the pill for Douglass by the offer of an expanded Midland District, which would include Hertfordshire, where Poynter's college of Old Hall was situated, and to which Douglass was greatly attached, and to create a new status for him as arch-vicar, with the injunction to hold annual synods and transmit the results of their deliberations to Rome. He concluded hopefully that Douglass 'wd [*sic*] have no objection to

6, f 243rv.   16 Milner to Troy, 13 Mar. 1806, DDA. William Gregory Sharrock, OSB was coadjutor of the Western District from 1780 to 1797 and vicar apostolic from 1797 to 1809. William Gibson was vicar apostolic of the Northern District from 1790 to 1821. Thomas Smith, his coadjutor from 1810 to 1821, succeeded him and died in 1831.   17 Ibid., 22 Apr. 1806. 18 Concanen to Troy, 7 June 1806, DDA. Bishop Moylan, who visited England on several occasions and met the vicars apostolic, would probably have been happy to fill this role suggested by Erskine.   19 Troy to Propaganda (copy), 3 Mar. 1806, DDA.   20 Propaganda to Troy, 26 Apr. 1806, ibid.

exchange a poorer for a more opulent situation, at the same time keeping his coadjutor'. His obsession with the imagined hostile intrigues of Charles Butler found expression in his belief that Rome had been influenced by them: 'I find that the history of the persecution I have so long suffered from an unprincipled Catholic, for refusing to take part in his violations of every law, human and divine, had been maliciously represented to Rome.'[21]

Faced with conflicting views, the congregation of Propaganda hesitated about taking a final decision. In the meantime the secretary informed Concanen that the proposed changes would cause bitterness among prelates, and though he admitted that it would be difficult to find someone to represent the Catholics, should the question of emancipation arise, he believed – in accordance with Milner's own information – that such an eventuality was not likely.[22] Disappointed and depressed, Concanen, who had been greatly influenced by Troy's inflated assessment of Milner, duly notified the archbishop of the way the wind was blowing at Propaganda, and how it had blown away Milner's plans and aspirations. He regretted that 'the humiliating disregard shewn by Propaganda to his merits and labours and to the petition of the Irish prelates have eventually discouraged and disgusted that great man', and begged Troy to dissuade him from his threat 'of leaving off all future publications and of renouncing his station'. Claiming that the cardinal prefect (di Pietro) was wholly incompetent and that the secretary (Archbishop Coppola), though 'exemplary and well informed' was distracted by 'unnecessary avocations ... rather too scrupulous and diffident and suspicious like all Neapolitans', he advised the archbishop to write to Coppola 'in a respectful, but forcible style ... to insist on the permutation between Dr Milner and Pointer [*sic*]'. Suggesting to Troy to contact the influential Cardinal Antonelli, and to obtain the support of influential persons like Sir John Coxe-Hippisley, Bishop Cameron of Edinburgh and Cardinal Casoni, the secretary of state, he bewailed the danger that 'the great Docr. Milner will retire disgusted' after seeing 'himself slighted, lest an unreasonable and ill conceived displeasure might be given to an indolent, inert and weak prelate, who was not even to be touched in his own dignity or interests'.[23]

Milner certainly felt disgust when he received a letter from Cardinal di Pietro, the prefect of the congregation of Propaganda, in September. Di Pietro admitted that an exchange was possible but could not take place without complaints, and then proceeded to avoid the issue by maintaining that emancipation was 'put off – that in the opinion of some well informed persons (viz. Cl. Erskine) no favour whatever is to be expected from government'. Revealing his ignorance of the political situation in Ireland and

21 Milner to Troy, 20 June 1806, ibid.   22 Propaganda to Concanen, 9 Aug. 1806, DDA.
23 Concanen to Troy, 13 Aug. 1806, ibid. Antonelli, a former prefect of the congregation of Propaganda, was then dean of the college of cardinals.

England, he opined that 'the evils to be expected from such a measure ought to deter all good Caths and particularly prelates from promoting it' and furthermore that Milner's residing in London might 'induce interested persons to urge this business'. Should any new development occur, Milner should then go up to London to see that Catholic interests did not suffer.

Di Pietro's great fear was that emancipation would be accompanied by 'a concordatum with the civil power, pensions to the clergy etc.'. There was 'a plan on foot for buying off our bishops and clergy', to which he objected though he saw no reason to oppose a grant for an English seminary like Maynooth. Accordingly, Milner advised Troy to let Rome know that the Irish bishops had not even been consulted about the petition for emancipation. He also told Troy that Concanen would let him know about the suggestion he himself had made to Rome about appointing Douglass as arch-vicar.[24]

Troy took Concanen's advice and contacted Coppola, the secretary of the congregation. Dismissing opposition to Milner from opponents and from those who were little interested in the advantages his move to London would bring to religion and the Holy See, he insisted that emancipation was a political issue pushed by Catholic laity and, though no one would place an obstacle in its way, the Catholic clergy were taking no part in it. Should the innovations which the congregation abhorred – such as the intervention of the government in the hierarchy or in ecclesiastical power – be part of it, they would have nothing to do with it, much as they desired the temporal well-being of their people. But, if they were requested by the agents of the Catholic laity to sign a petition to the government or parliament requesting unlimited emancipation, they could not oppose that request without losing the trust and financial support of their people. And if the sacred congregation were suspected of opposing unlimited emancipation, the Holy See would be blamed, if not despised, as the enemy of the Catholics. Milner's move to London was sought by the vicars apostolic of Scotland and two vicars apostolic in England as well as by most intelligent Catholics and well-disposed Protestants. Recalling Milner's scholarly work and resistance to the schism provoked by the Cisalpine Club, Troy emphasized that their aim was the defence and promotion of the interests of religion and not a desire to raise political issues with the government by pushing emancipation.[25]

A month later Concanen was still angry at the 'contemptuous manner' with which Propaganda had rejected 'the petition of the Catholic body' to avoid giving 'an unreasonable displeasure to a weak but obstinate vicr apostolic'. Archbishop Coppola had no answer to the comment that 'it was mere jealousy or obstinacy that caused Dr DS to oppose the exchange of his

24 Milner to Troy, 14 Sept. 1806, DDA. 25 Troy to Propaganda, 3 Oct. 1806, APF, SC(Irlanda), 18, ff 389r–390v. At most only one vicar apostolic in England would have approved of Milner's move. Bishop Gibson, a friend of Poynter, did not want this reshuffle.

coadjutor, whereas by such an expedient his Lordshp lost nothing in his dignity, jurisdiction or income'. Coppola admitted that their chief opponent was Cardinal Erskine, and he suggested to Troy that the best plan was to give up the idea of Douglass moving to the Midland District and concentrate on the exchange between Milner and Poynter. He advised Troy to write to the influential Cardinal Antonelli seeking his support, and to mention the fact that a cardinal for some reason opposed the move.[26] However, neither Milner nor Troy gave up the fight. Milner encouraged Troy to pursue the project of transferring Douglass to the Midland District with the sweetener of Hertfordshire and the title of arch-vicar, which Troy duly did, though he also put forward the exchange of Milner and Poynter.[27]

As all parties awaited the formal examination of the case at a full meeting of the cardinals attached to the congregation of Propaganda, Milner was prepared to grasp at any straw in his ambition to establish himself in London. He assured Troy that the cardinal prefect and secretary of the congregation wanted Douglass and himself to settle the question between them, not realizing that this was merely their way of avoiding having to give an answer before a full meeting of the cardinals, knowing as they did that Douglass would not agree to any exchange. He, therefore, requested Troy's assistance in persuading Douglass to reach an agreement, since he felt that the vicar apostolic of London distrusted and disliked him:

> I am of opinion, however (if I must speak plain) that he has now and had even whilst I was his subject a sort of jealousy of me, which will always induce him to keep me as far as possible from the scene of action. Amongst other things he fears that if I were in London, I shd. be for reforming many things, which he thinks it best to overlook, and I must own he is not deceived in his conjectures. For really the state of things there with respect to doctrine as well as discipline, is almost like that of the Israelites, when the latter were without a judge and every one did what seemed good in his own eyes. I cd. draw such a picture of my good but weak brother, as wd amaze Yr Grace and every other well informed beholder.

He went on to claim that Bishop Gibson's opposition arose from 'mere wrong headedness' as a consequence of Douglass' representations, and

---

26 Concanen to Troy, 13 Sept. 1806, DDA.   27 Milner to Troy, 30 Sept. 1806, ibid.; Troy to Propaganda (copy), 3 Oct. 1806, ibid.; Troy to Cardinal Antonelli, 28 Oct. 1806, APF, SC(Irlanda) 18, f 394rv. Milner alerted Rome to the danger that Erskine had spread the rumour that the Irish were keen on receiving state pensions. Troy asked his agent to deny this claim (Milner to Troy, 30 Sept. 1806 and Troy to Concanen (copy) 3 Oct. 1806, DDA).

though Sharrock had made him his agent, he too was afraid of giving offence to his colleagues by pushing for change in their ecclesiastical arrangements.[28]

Concanen, whose antennae were more closely trained on the decision-makers in Rome, had given up hope of Milner's transfer to London before the full meeting of the congregation. Realizing that it would be difficult to obtain an exchange of vicariates he passed on his conclusion that 'it would be better for that shining man' to accept a dispensation from residence in his own vicariate and to act in London as agent for the bishops and commissary of the congregation of Propaganda rather than be exposed to conflicts with Douglass. He rightly detected that the chief difficulty would rest with Cardinal Erskine,[29] and he was correct.

The full meeting of the congregation took place on 15 December. Cardinal Antonelli, on whom Concanen had pinned his hopes was absent and, consequently, 'the Scotch gentleman [Erskine] had an open field and easily led the other members (too little versed in our affairs) over to his side'. Erskine described Milner as 'a hot and violent man' with too many enemies in the government, who was responsible for bringing hostility on the Catholic church by his writings, and the congregation went along with that characterization and decided that it was not expedient to make any alterations in the governance of the church or even to give Milner a dispensation from residence in his own vicariate. A despondent Concanen could hold out only a little hope that Cardinal Antonelli might obtain another examination of the issue but he was doubtful that this would happen.[30]

Apart from the exchange of vicariates and the coadjutorship Concanen had also suggested a third possibility, that of Milner spending most of the year as agent in London for the Irish and Scottish bishops and as commissary for the congregation of Propaganda for the British missions.[31] But the congregation's official response to Troy was that all the combinations had been examined twice, and all had been found impossible to execute. Milner's vicariate would suffer serious harm if he were absent from it for nine months each year. There was then no important issue for Irish Catholics requiring negotiations with the government. When one did arise, an Irish cleric could deal with it. If Milner's participation were necessary, he could seek from the pope a temporary dispensation from residence in his vicariate.[32]

Reaching for an explanation for the Roman decision, Milner decided that the Holy See was afraid of too close a relationship between the Irish bishops and the government, which might lead to the prelates being bribed to enter into a concordat and other innovations. He also expressed the strange view, without offering any evidence for it, that the Vatican was probably expecting

28 Milner to Troy, 8 Nov. 1806, DDA.   29 Concanen to Troy, 26 Nov. 1806, ibid. 30 Concanen to Troy, 30 Dec. 1806, ibid.   31 Pro-memoria (1807), APF, SC(Irlanda) 18, f 426rv.   32 Propaganda to Troy, 18 Apr. 1807, DDA.

the two islands to go their separate ways rather than remain in the same empire. He advised Troy to assure Rome that only the heads of the Cisalpine Club held such views and that it was to oppose them and 'chiefly for the purpose of guarding against innovations and defending the cause of religion and the H. See by the pen as well as by word of mouth' that the archbishop had recommended his transfer to London.[33] Strangely, he seems to have overlooked the most obvious reason that Rome would not juggle vicariates without some grave reason concerning orthodoxy or morality: the victims of transfers would be publicly hurt.

Milner, in his complaints about Douglass, bewailed 'the crying injustices and gross neglects of which he is guilty of with respect to his brethren' and singled out for condemnation the London vicar's habit of not answering letters.[34] When informed by Troy that Erskine had also opposed their plan, Milner was deeply dismayed and angered. Recalling Erskine's support while in England and his promise to help in removing the evils in the church, he could only conclude that Sir John Throckmorton had influenced him or that he might have intended to return to London and did not want someone of Milner's stature to be in the same city.[35] Milner, with good and virtuous motives, would like to reside in or near London, and to do so he would be prepared, if necessary, to sacrifice all rank, jurisdiction and emoluments, but, if it was God's will that he continue to bear his present cross, he would either apply for a coadjutor, who would take care of the northern part of the district, leaving him free to be closer to London, or he would resign his episcopate completely and live on his own means.

He then listed the evils to which, in his report to Rome, he had drawn the attention of the congregation of Propaganda: 'the frequent and notorious publication of heterodox and schismatical doctrine' in London; 'the diversity of discipline and practice that prevails amongst the clergy'; 'the constant and systematic opposition of B. Douglass to the holding of any synod or other meeting of his episcopal brethren for remedying these and other evils'; Douglass' 'arbitrary proceedings in seizing upon all the most able and virtuous priests and sending into my district the lame, the drunken, and the slothful'; 'the same tyranny with respect to our colleges of Lisbon and Valladolid in consequence of which all the superiors and all the students in these establishments except four boys who belong to me and one to B. Sharrock are divided between London and the north'; Douglass' 'seizing and keeping several sums of money to a great amt. belonging to the Middle District as appears by his own letters in my hands concerning which he refuses to enter into any explanation with me'. And, he continued:

---

33 Milner to Troy, 10 Jan. 1807, DDA.   34 Ibid., 4 Apr. 1807.   35 Throckmorton's views on papal prerogatives and episcopal jurisdiction were diametrically opposed to those of Erskine.

his general refusal of communicating with me and his other brethren concerning the common concerns of religion, as was lately exemplified when he disdained to answer either of the letters which I wrote to him concerning the newly proposed oath and our English oath of 1791 notwithstanding that B. Gibson, B. Sharrock and Yr Grace were no less solicitous on the subject than I was ... [and] lastly his inattention to the passing occurrences of the times in consequence of which many opportunities of serving religion in its most essential interests are lost.

To deal with these problems, a formal visitation was required by 'one or more of the enlightened and illustrious prelates of yr islands', who would send an official report to Rome. Such a list of complaints against the bishop he was proposing to assist raises the question of how they could ever have cooperated.

Interestingly, Milner admitted that the majority of the clergy in the London District, to which he had once belonged, were 'up in arms' against him. They had been annoyed by the rumour that he was aiming at 'archiepiscopal honors etc.' but, when informed that his proposed work was dictated by the offer of becoming agent for the Irish bishops, they accepted this explanation but still 'expressed the most decided opposition to the proposed exchange with Dr Poynter'. He attributed this opposition to their supposing that he had been the principal promoter of the prohibition of clergy attending the public theatres.[36] It is much more likely that he could not appreciate or was not prepared to admit that there were other reasons for the hostility of the London clergy. They, with many other clergy and at least a couple of the vicars apostolic, regarded him as a dangerous firebrand who could make use of any occasion to cause trouble.

Still reeling from the shock and disappointment of the Roman rejection of his move to London, Milner conveyed to Propaganda his sorrow at the failure of the Irish to achieve their aims. He bemoaned the humiliation of the Irish hierarchy and wondered how the Holy See could refuse it the means which it judged best for its own defence and that of the Holy See. Again drawing attention to the Cisalpine Club, 'whose professed object is to curb the alledged [sic] tyranny and usurpations of the pope' he remarked that some of its members were London priests, the most bitter of all his enemies. To emphasize the affront to the Irish prelates and the slight to himself, he recalled that his predecessor, Bishop Stapleton, had been offered the coadjutorship of the London District, and little or no account was taken of Bishop Douglass' wishes. Bishop Thomas Hussey, as chaplain general to the army,

36 Milner to Troy, 25 Apr. 1807, DDA.

had been given a special commission to live in London. His opponents were Bishop Douglass, who gave a 'pernicious example of soliciting subscriptions' from clergy and laity for his own objects; Bishop Gibson of the Northern District, 'possessed of an unaccountable jealousy of my getting credit superior to his own in the transaction of public business'; Sir John Throckmorton, Charles Butler and other heads of the 'Cisalpine or antipapal association'; some leading London priests who were annoyed by regulations published by him and the other vicars apostolic against clergy 'frequenting the playhouses'; and Robert Smelt, the agent in Rome of the other vicars apostolic, who had been playing a double game, contrary to instructions. Commenting on Cardinal Erskine's repeated assurances and promises, he referred to pledges of assistance from his letters, and promises to redress 'the evils of their ecclesiastical concerns'. Taking a further swipe at Douglass, Milner claimed that false and schismatical doctrine was being openly professed in London and that the catechisms printed there often contained inaccurate and erroneous material. And before the vicars apostolic could hold a meeting about petitioning for an end to abstinence from meat on Saturdays, Douglass had encouraged some of his clergy to discuss and decide the point.[37]

Troy and his friends were not only disappointed by the Roman decision on Milner's move to London, but believed that they had been calumniated, presumably in England, for their demarche, and so the four archbishops sent a joint letter to Rome to vindicate their soliciting Milner's move to London. They drew attention to the pernicious doctrines of the Cisalpine Club, which circulated even among the clergy and were destructive of church discipline and papal rights and according to which the pope – in the style of the Febronians – was a mere *primus inter pares*.[38] To resist these attacks, which were reflected in the sermons of some priests and in the poisonous tracts of Protestants, they required the help of the orthodox, learned and valorous Milner in London, where he would have access to public and private libraries. Justifying their action by reminding the congregation of Propaganda that it had appointed Milner's predecessor to the coadjutorship of London,[39] they referred to a delicate forthcoming discussion in parliament about an oath to the sovereign in his capacity as a Protestant and the consequent need felt by three vicars apostolic in England and their brethren in Scotland to have Milner in London to obtain some clarification of that clause or to have it revoked. Referring to Douglass' general incapacity and refusal to hold meetings and work harmoniously with his colleagues, and the

37 Ibid., [day unclear] June 1807. Milner often detected the hand of Joseph Berington behind Throckmorton's writings.   38 The Febronians held that the pope should be the mere executive of all the bishops as the legislators for the whole church.   39 They were mistaken. Stapelton had never actually been appointed coadjutor.

difficulty and cost of keeping an Irishman as agent in London, they explained that Milner, who had recently paid a successful visit to Ireland, could carry out the work of the agency easily and conveniently. Admitting that they knew he was described as ambitious, violent and an intriguer, they insisted that it was his enemies in the Cisalpine Club who so characterized him.[40] The congregation, however, was not moved to overturn its previous decision.

A formal request for Milner to be permitted to reside temporarily in London when engaged on political and theological matters was then made by the archbishops and bishops of Ireland. Recalling the answer given to them in April 1807, they requested the dispensation for him for as long as he was dealing with the good of religion, and referred to his need to be there to have his books and tracts printed. The pope gave his consent to their request in January 1808,[41] and both they and Milner had to be satisfied.

This temporary permission for Milner to reside in London ended one of the most remarkable and unfortunate interventions of Irish bishops in the affairs of the English church. Understandably both Bishop Douglass and Bishop Poynter regarded it as improper and unjustifiable. There had been no tradition of the bishops of either country intervening in the ecclesiastical affairs of the other. Few of them ever met. Rome did not normally consult either party about appointments to episcopal office in the other country. From his long years in Rome, Troy must have known the ecclesiastical protocol, which forbade bishops from interfering in the affairs of neighbouring dioceses, except in rare cases of misgovernment or heresy when metropolitans and senior suffragans were permitted to interfere. But, impressed by what he knew of Milner's role in the English church, he believed that this vicar apostolic could make a valuable and necessary contribution to religion among influential people in London. Had there been a vacancy in the London vicariate either for a vicar apostolic or a coadjutor, a private letter from Troy to Rome pointing out the suitability of a particular candidate in view of the special political situation might have seemed reasonable to the Roman authorities. But there were few precedents even in the universal church for prelates exchanging dioceses and as there was no serious accusation of any form of inappropriate behaviour against Douglass or Poynter, a forced transfer of either against his will would have been unjust both to the bishop involved and to his reputation in the eyes of the public.

Once news of Milner's proposed transfer became known there was bound

---

40 Archbishops to Propaganda, 28 July 1807, APF, SC(Irlanda), 18, ff 414r–415r.   41 Bishops' appeal to the pope, and reply, 17 Jan. 1808, ibid., 438r–440v and Propaganda to Troy, 23 Jan. 1808, DDA. Milner was told to return to his district once his business was completed, to ensure that he did not provoke party hostility and to be prudent in his political discussions. Concanen later obtained an extension of this permission (Concanen to Troy, 21 May, 8 Oct. 1808, DDA).

to be a strong public reaction, and his enemies were sure to publicize their hostility to it widely. Both Douglass and Poynter were humiliated by the proposal. They were being portrayed as inefficient, incapable and unsuited to their positions. The indignation this misconceived intervention provoked in Poynter led to mistrust and friction between himself and Troy which lasted to the ends of their episcopates.

7

The campaign for Catholic emancipation begins

T hough Archbishop Troy and the episcopal trustees of Maynooth had been led to believe, or at least given the impression, that emancipation would follow the Act of Union, they did not start campaigning for it either in public or private after the act had taken effect. The admonitory counsels of the pope and Cardinal Borgia had given them pause. The Catholic laity, especially the gentry and the middle classes of professional and business people, had no such restraint. To them emancipation meant not only the right to sit in parliament but also the opening of professional and political appointments and opportunities.

Lord Cornwallis, the lord lieutenant who had left office in the wake of Pitt's resignation, had sought to reassure Catholics that all was not lost and had advised them to be patient. Patience suited both Fingall and the gentry on the one hand, who were naturally deferential to the government and Troy, and his colleagues on the other, who were somewhat frightened of the embarrassment they could be plunged into by demands from the government for 'concessions'. The administration in Dublin Castle made no attempt to win Catholic favour in the wake of the union. Robert Emmet's rebellion, though led by Protestants, and a pathetic failure, was blamed by leaders of both church and state on the Catholics. Troy's pastoral letter condemning the rebellion outright and committing the church to loyalty to the king was dismissed by Lord Hardwicke, the lord lieutenant, as 'the greatest piece of craft, dissimulation and hypocrisy' that he had ever read, and he poured scorn on the archbishop's alleged ignorance of the conspiracy.[1] This outrageous accusation against the most loyal of churchmen illustrated the gap between the administration and the Catholics.

Meanwhile the English Catholic Committee, which had been re-formed, had decided to campaign for some of the privileges which Irish Catholics had enjoyed since 1793. Sir John Throckmorton and Charles Butler approached the Whig leader Charles James Fox about obtaining his support for their demands, and Fox was sympathetic to their case. But Lord Fingall, the leading Catholic peer in Ireland, was reluctant to push for a combined effort of the Catholics of both countries. However, the upwardly mobile Catholic

---

1 Connolly, 'The Catholic question, 1801–12', in *NHI*, v, 25. Disturbances in the first decade of the century were generally agrarian in origin. The Ribbonmen in the second decade had more revolutionary and nationalist motives.

professionals, merchants, lawyers and businessmen were keen to be free of religious restrictions so that they could obtain the positions in life that they thought were their due.

In October 1804 James Ryan, a Dublin merchant, invited some thirty-five Catholic merchants, professional men and landowners to his house to discuss the presentation of a petition for emancipation. Among those present was Daniel O'Connell, an up-and-coming lawyer who was determined to keep pressing for relief and was destined to bring the issue to a successful conclusion. After a series of meetings, a petition was drawn up by the lawyer Denys Scully,[2] and the decision was taken to organize a deputation to London to ask Pitt, who had returned to power a few months earlier, to present it. Despite their trust in Pitt, the likelihood of his obliging them was remote. He had returned to power and pledged not to annoy the king by raising the question of emancipation. Though some Catholics were keen not to embarrass him, he was duly asked and understandably refused.[3]

The signatures on the petition were headed by the earl of Shrewsbury, Waterford and Wexford, who, despite the Irish titles, lived in England.[4] Lords Fingall, Kenmare, Gormanston, Southwell and Trimleston also signed, but the rest of the signatures were from the professional and mercantile classes, to whom the real power of the Catholics was passing. Bishop Moylan of Cork doubtless represented the views of most of the bishops when he wrote that unless those who sought relief had received encouragement from the ministry in London, he thought the time for such petitioning was unsuitable.[5] Lord Grenville, a former colleague (and cousin) of Pitt's, who had passed over to the Foxite Whigs, presented the petition in the house of lords and Grattan, who through Fox's influence had been returned for an English constituency, presented it in the commons. The petition professed profound loyalty to the king, repudiated allegiance to any other sovereign, and rejected as unchristian the belief that it was lawful to injure anyone as a heretic or that no faith was to be kept with heretics. It abjured the opinion that princes excommunicated by the pope could be deposed or murdered, and rejected the view that the pope or any foreign prince had temporal or civil jurisdiction. It also rejected the infallibility of the pope and the forgiveness of sin without sincere sorrow and resolution to avoid further guilt, and it gave a pledge to defend the arrangement of property and not to subvert the established church.

2 Denys Scully (1773–1830), son of a well-to-do grazier in Co. Tipperary, became a barrister and played an important part in Catholic committees until 1817. He wrote an account of the penal laws, and helped prepare the petition of 1810.   3 MacDonagh, *The hereditary bondsman*, pp 95–7.   4 Bishop Moylan, later questioned by the lord lieutenant as to why the bishops had not signed the petition, explained that the members of the committee had not called on them to do so as it treated only of civil and political rights (Moylan to Bray, 8 July 1805, CaDA).   5 Moylan to Bray, 20 Nov. 1804, CaDA.

The core of the petition consisted of the central elements of the oath which had been drawn up for Irish Catholics in 1793. The petition went on to maintain that the exclusion of Catholics from civil offices and honours and from advancement in the army and navy impaired the resources of the empire. Their sole object, they insisted, was 'an equal participation upon equal terms with their fellow subjects, of the full benefits of the British laws and constitution'.

The archbishop of Canterbury, expressing the views of many opponents of emancipation, pointed out that the request for equal partnership and the full benefits of British laws and the constitution was a request for admission to places of power and trust – without a corresponding promise to give due security. The Roman Catholics wanted to legislate for a Protestant country, dispense laws, command armies and share in the executive councils of a Protestant kingdom – a request that struck at the justice and policy of the Act of Settlement.[6]

The petition was overwhelmingly defeated by the margin of 178 to 49 in the lords, and by 336 to 124 in the commons. Defeats, though not so extensive, were to become the pattern for several years. English Protestant prejudice, drawing on atavistic fears of the power and malice of Rome and the unquestioning acceptance by Catholics of its dictates, were to prove very difficult to overcome, especially in the house of lords. Despite the assurances of allegiance in the oaths and petitions, and the rejection of the far-fetched fantasies of papal claims and ambitions, the antipathy to Catholicism was so deep-rooted as almost to stifle rational thought on emancipation. In the lords, the bishops of the established church consistently opposed Catholic relief, with the exception of Henry Bathurst of Norwich (1805–37), Samuel Horsley of St David's (1788–93) and later Rochester and St Asaph (1793–1806). Like the archbishop of Canterbury the overwhelming majority of Protestants believed that Britain (and Ireland) were or ought to be Protestant, and that the participation of Catholics in legislating for a Protestant country was anomalous and abnormal. They felt that any alteration in the settlement of 1688 would be harmful to both church and state.

Lord Grenville, in the house of lords, had defended the bishops from the accusations which had been made against them: that they had not signed the petition because they were not willing 'to subscribe to the sentiments of loyalty' in it and because they regarded the clergy of the established church as unrightful possessors of their property. Grenville's brother, the marquis of Buckingham (whose wife was a Catholic), suggested to Milner that the bishops should let Grenville know that they were grateful for his support. Milner passed on this suggestion to Troy, and the four archbishops and

6 *Hansard 1*, iv, 775–8, 25 Mar. 1805.

twenty-two bishops duly sent him a letter of thanks. They assured him that they accepted the principle of the petition which they had often pronounced in their oaths, and they repudiated any intention of disturbing the security or privileges of the established church.[7] They may have felt that the time for their intervention was not propitious, but they were doubtless happy to quash false rumours.

Writing after the defeat of the petition to his agent in Rome for the benefit of Propaganda, Milner forecast optimistically that emancipation and pensions for the clergy were certain to be soon granted. Consequently, several of their most illustrious legislators were devising plans to adapt Catholic discipline to a future situation – plans which were very dangerous for the purity and stability of their religion, and which were designed to weaken the influence of the Holy See in their affairs. He passed on to Concanen reports that he had heard about the appointments of bishops: one suggestion was that the king could veto a particular candidate and the other was that he might choose from a corps of 'grand vicars', of which each diocese would have two. He feared that his bête noire, the Cisalpine Club, was seeking to have the vicars apostolic in England replaced by bishops and thereby weaken the influence of the Holy See.[8] Concanen requested Propaganda to give Milner suitable instructions for his future guidance.

The secretary of Propaganda replied to Concanen pessimistically, bemoaning the dangers facing the church in Britain and Ireland from the plans of the politicians. He recalled that the pope had written to Archbishop Troy on that subject in 1801 and had been assured that the Irish bishops were willingly renouncing any temporal advantage in that field to preserve their religion unsullied. When the civil constitution of the clergy offered a pension to the priests in France in 1791, the pope rejected the offer. He used even stronger language on the question of episcopal appointments, recalling that Pope Benedict XIV had refused absolutely to grant the right of appointments to a Protestant sovereign. Reflecting on the possibility of a royal choice among grand vicars, and the fear that such a plan might stimulate ambition in those chosen for that position, he indicated that the right of exclusion presented lesser inconveniences provided it was limited, as otherwise it could turn into a nomination. And he noted that the Holy See always strove to promote to the bishopric candidates who were not only not unwelcome to governments but who were acceptable to them. Regarding the suggestion of the government examining Roman documents, he pointed out that such a

---

7 Milner to Troy, 17 May 1805, and bishops to Grenville, 5 July 1805 in MacDermot, *The Irish Catholic petition of 1805*, pp 118, 124–5. 8 Milner to Concanen, 21 June 1805, APF, SC(Anglia), 6, ff 203r–204v. Milner also advised that any innovation in the ecclesiastical system of vicars apostolic should be avoided to prevent the Cisalpine Club from gaining any advantages by such a change.

privilege was never granted to a Catholic prince, let alone a Protestant one.[9] Propaganda was rejecting for Ireland what several English politicians were frequently to claim was permitted in other countries, both Catholic and Protestant. And whatever about the constitution of the clergy, the pope had since agreed to a concordat with Napoleon whereby the clergy received stipends. Catholic rulers had often insisted on examining papal documents and Napoleon had recently claimed this right in the Organic Articles.

Milner had not made clear whether the sources from whom he had received the accounts of pensioning the clergy and giving a veto on the appointments of the bishops were in any way reliable. In the wake of the defeat of the petition, there did not seem to be much interest in such a move. Troy told his agent in Rome that the bishops were opposed to any changes on these matters, and felt that while the war with France lasted, no such changes would be introduced.[10]

Concanen reassured Rome that if the bishops of Ireland and the vicars apostolic rejected all pensions or financial support, the ministers and politicians would not pursue their plans to interfere in the nomination of the prelates or seek a concordat. The peace and security of the kingdom required emancipation but no political principle necessitated the payment of the clergy. Not only would payment of the clergy cause the loss of their people's confidence in them, but a huge sum, £100,000, would be needed, which would be better 'spent in giving relief to the poor'. Apart from the nomination of bishops, which the Holy See could not give to a Protestant sovereign, there was no reason for a concordat. The Holy See could not submit documents for scrutiny by the state, especially when they referred to such strictly private matters as marriage dispensations. As the king's coronation oath was brought forward against changes in the law, and parliament would repeat its response to appeals for relief, Milner should be given advice by the congregation on how to handle the attacks and pretensions of those who wanted to introduce these changes.[11]

A note in the archives, which was probably a summary of a letter to Milner, bade him oppose the plan for a concordat, and convince both the ministers and the Catholic priests of the grave inconveniences of pensioning the clergy. As Concanen had suggested, he was advised to recommend that the money be used for the relief of the poor who were burdened with tithes.[12]

With the death of Pitt in 1806, a new government under Grenville and

---

9 Propaganda to Concanen, 7 Sept. 1805, ibid., ff 217r–223v. Concanen sent a copy of this letter to Troy for himself and the other archbishops, and in accordance with the suggestion of Propaganda asked him to send to Milner a copy of its letter of 7 Aug. 1801 (Concanen to Troy, 25 Sept. 1801, DDA).   10 Troy to Concanen, 2 Nov. 1805, APF, SC(Irlanda) 18, f 342rv. 11 Reflections of Concanen, no date, ibid., ff 384r–385v.   12 Note dated Aug. 1806, ibid., ff 382r–383r.

Fox came to power, known as the 'Ministry of All the Talents'. Both were genuine supporters of emancipation, but confined by the limitations of office, called for time and prudence from their friends who sought relief. Both intimated that they would deal with the issue at the appropriate time, and Fox advised the Irish to postpone the presentation of a petition. The new committee in Dublin took this advice, and Fox rewarded it by removing from office the bitterly anti-Catholic chancellor Redesdale and John Foster, the former opponent of the union, who had used his new power under the union to protect Orangemen and yeomen, the traditional foes of the Catholics. George Ponsonby,[13] who was sympathetic to the Catholic cause, became chancellor and Lord Donoughmore,[14] who favoured emancipation, was also offered an appointment. Grenville toyed with the idea of establishing regiments of Catholic soldiers under Catholic officers of all ranks, but could not get further than extending to English Catholics permission given to the Irish in 1793 to become junior ranking officers. George III had baulked at the prospect of Catholics being appointed to the higher ranks, and his demand that the Catholic question should be permanently set aside spelt the end of the Grenville-Fox government.[15] It was succeeded by the no-nonsense Protestant government of the duke of Portland, which won the election of 1807 on that basis.[16]

In Dublin, opposition had arisen to James Ryan's holding meetings of concerned Catholics in his house, and a new Catholic Committee had been formed in 1806. Lord Fingall and Sir Edward Bellew had joined it, and, though some had wished it to become more representative by a process of election, the lord lieutenant would not acknowledge any body chosen against the terms of the convention act, which forbade representative assemblies. At a public meeting of Catholics in 1807, O'Connell spoke forcefully in favour of a petition and the decision was taken to present one but was later rescinded. However, in January 1808 it was decided to proceed.

Milner's role in this petition became controversial and the accounts he gave of his activities were not consistent. He visited Ireland in 1807 and met some of the bishops. He subsequently claimed that he understood them to accept the view that no one would be chosen as bishop who was unacceptable to the government but the government would not do the choosing.[17] That

---

13 Ponsonby (1755–1817) had supported the enfranchisement of Catholics in 1793 and had become attorney general in the Fitzwilliam administration in 1795. He became leader of the Whigs at Westminster after the collapse of the Fox-Grenville ministry.   14 Lord Donoughmore (1756–1825) was a consistent supporter of Catholic relief in both the Irish and British parliaments. He presented several petitions for the Catholic committees in Westminster.   15 The government had agreed to increase the Maynooth grant from £8,000 to £13,000 but went out of office before this could take effect. Its successor set the grant at £9,250 (Corish, *Maynooth College, 1795–1995*, p. 34).   16 Bartlett, *The fall and rise of the Irish nation*, pp 284–9.   17 Milner, *Supplementary memoirs*, p. 121.

committed them to do nothing more than they already did. But Milner also claimed that he had been given the impression that the crown might be granted some power of excluding candidates. He was present at a meeting of the bishops who were trustees of Maynooth, but the question of a royal veto does not seem to have been formally discussed at it.[18] And some of the bishops who were known to be most opposed to a veto were not trustees of the college.

On 23 May 1808, Grattan presented the Catholic petition. Claiming that in the answers of the six foreign universities of 1791 Catholics did not refuse allegiance to a Protestant prince, he went on to say that he was authorized to state that in future the king could exercise his royal prerogative to ensure that no bishop would be appointed without his entire approbation. Not only would this arrangement prevent Napoleon, who then held the pope in virtual imprisonment, from having control of the clergy and laity and therefore of a large proportion of the British army and navy, but it would have the beneficial result that 'the two churches will be one, and the king at the head'. George Ponsonby gave a more detailed account of how he claimed the Catholics would make their superior clergy subject to the crown. On the death of a bishop, his former colleagues of that ecclesiastical province would select three candidates whom they deemed worthy to succeed him and send their names to the pope. When the three names were returned from Rome they would be forwarded to the lord lieutenant. If he objected to all three, another three would be chosen, until the king's approbation of one of them was obtained, and then his name would be sent to Rome for papal approval. Ponsonby concluded that such a scheme giving 'the real and effectual nomination to the crown' was the best possible proof of Catholic loyalty. Challenged as to the authority on which he based this claim, Ponsonby attributed the plan to Milner, who had been authorized by the Catholic bishops of Ireland to put it forward, should Catholic emancipation be conceded. Though not in his parliamentary speech, he was also quoted as saying that the Catholic bishops would have no objections to making the king virtually head of their church.[19] The conclusions that Grattan and Ponsonby had made about the king's possible headship of the Catholic church were ludicrous, and no bishop could have suggested them.

The right to repeated rejection of candidates as described by Ponsonby amounted in effect to the right of nomination by the crown. This was exactly what the congregation of Propaganda, with papal approval, had specifically

---

18 Milner to Troy, O'Reilly and Bray, 2 Nov. 1811, DDA.   19 Cobbett's Parliamentary Debates, 1st series, vol. xi, pp 489–619. Castlereagh denied that any pledge or promise of emancipation was ever given by Pitt or himself (pp 589–91). Butler in *Historical memoirs*, p. 74, quoted Elliot, the chief secretary, as saying on 25 Mar. 1808 that something like promises had been held out to Catholics.

ruled out in its letter to Concanen for Milner in September 1805, which had been copied to Troy. Propaganda had clearly and vigorously repudiated any suggestion of payment for the clergy, or any right of the state to interfere in its communications with the bishops and was only reluctantly prepared to tolerate the intervention of a Protestant king on the grounds of the possible disloyalty of a candidate for the episcopate. Milner claimed that he would not have encouraged the veto had he 'not conceived that the prelates assembled at Maynooth July 1, 1807, when I foretold them of the approaching storm, were prepared to admit of it to a certain degree'.[20]

Milner, in fact, had met Ponsonby four days before the debate on the Catholic question, and on being asked as agent for the Irish bishops what concessions they would make to the crown in future nominations to vacant sees, had replied:

> they never could grant to an uncatholic government a positive power in this religious concern; but that I had no doubt of their yielding to it such kind of negative interference as would satisfy it with respect to the loyalty of future candidates. I added, however, and repeated with emphasis that I had no instructions on the subject and, therefore, could give no pledge on the part of my constituents.

He further explained that this concession merely granted the power of excluding a disloyal candidate, should such a one be proposed. Ponsonby, on reading this, published the note which Milner sent him after their conversation. In it, Milner had stated that the bishops in Ireland would transmit the name of the selected candidate to the government and, if it objected, would transmit 'another and another' and the process would continue until both the government and the pope agreed on a candidate. Though in his note no limitation as to the number of single names which might be negatived was given, it was understood that the negative was to be confined to a reasonable number of times. As put forward it seemed to be unlimited and was therefore equivalent to a positive nomination. Ponsonby admitted that Milner had not authorized him to say that, if their petition were granted, the Irish bishops would have no objection to making the king head of their church, and explained that he was arguing from the premises as he thought proper.

Milner did admit that he had said to Ponsonby that the Irish bishops were 'disposed to attribute a negative power' to the king, but he also argued that he had assured Catholics at the time that he did not advocate any change in the discipline of the church. He contemptuously dismissed Ponsonby's claim

20 Milner to Troy, O'Reilly and Bray, 2 Nov. 1811, DDA.

about the king's virtual headship of the Irish Catholic church, maintaining that he had never been 'accused of uttering so much inconsistency, heterodoxy and schism'.[21] But bestowing upon the king a negative was a change in the discipline then prevailing. Moreover the method of using that negative and the frequency with which it could be used, as allegedly explained in the note to Ponsonby, were very serious and disputed matters.

Troy, despite the warning signals he had received from Rome, assured Milner that all the Irish prelates would fully approve of his negotiation with Grattan and Ponsonby, and predicted that the prelates would ratify the royal veto on one candidate at a time but not on two or three candidates recommended by the prelates.[22] The archbishop had no authority from all the bishops for his claim about a royal veto, and he soon discovered how unpopular it would be. The reaction to the proposals in parliament and to the concessions made by the ten bishops in 1799, which now became public for the first time, was one of almost disbelief and general fury, except on the part of a few peers and two or three bishops. Anger at what was perceived to be a surrender of sacred rights was visceral and widespread. Irish opponents of royal intervention feared that the concept of loyalty would be so broadly applied that they would be left with spineless bishops who would do the government's bidding in every dispute or contretemps, and that their prelates would be turned into a kind of auxiliary police. O'Connell led the charge against the veto, which he maintained would copper-fasten the power of the Protestant and British ascendancy, and succeeded in whipping up the press against Milner and the concept of a veto.[23]

Milner, who visited Ireland in 1808, was taken aback by the violent response of Irish Catholics to his initiative. He received sharply critical letters from bishops about the role he had played, and to defend himself he wrote and printed *Letter to a parish priest*, which he forwarded to the bishops of both Britain and Ireland. Referring to the resolutions of 1799, he claimed they were regarded as binding both by the government and the opposition, and (quite wrongly) that they enjoyed the consent of Propaganda. Maintaining that the sovereigns of Prussia and Russia exercised a much more effective power than that which the Irish bishops had offered,[24] he explained that the king already enjoyed similar power in Canada, as the bishop of Quebec was not allowed to choose a coadjutor until he had been approved by

21 Milner, *Supplementary memoirs*, 122–9; the *Statesman*, 29, 30 May 1810.   22 Troy to Milner, 2 June 1808, DDA.   23 MacDonagh, *The hereditary bondsman*, p. 99.   24 The king of Prussia chose the candidate whom he wanted to succeed to a bishopric, forwarded the name to Rome, and if Rome accepted his choice, the name was then forwarded to the diocesan chapter, which elected him. The sovereign's intervention was not mentioned. A similar system operated in Catholic territories under Russian control. In Canada the bishop of Quebec submitted the name of his future coadjutor to the government for approval before the appointment took place.

the governor. He then proposed a limit of three rejections by the crown for each vacancy. Encouraging the Irish bishops to hold fast to their earlier commitment, he offered to resign his agency, if, presumably, his views were not acceptable to them. And he also defended himself in public by letters of similar content to the newspapers,[25] but was overwhelmed by the virulence with which Catholics in the press denounced him.

During Milner's visit to Ireland in 1807 it would seem that a few bishops who were 'soft' on the issue of the veto – Troy, O'Reilly, Moylan – may have discussed it in general terms with him, and given him the impression that they would not object to the royal veto on one or two candidates. It is most unlikely that the issue was seriously discussed at a formal meeting and a vote taken. Milner seems to have gone beyond this in his discussions with Ponsonby, who in turn was far from precise in his comments, and committed himself to suggestions which on such a serious issue he had no right to make. The bishops as a body blamed Grattan and Ponsonby rather than Milner.

Faced with the hostile reaction of their people, the Irish bishops held a meeting to discuss the problem on 14 and 15 September 1808. They passed a resolution by a huge majority declaring that it was 'inexpedient to introduce any alteration in the canonical mode hitherto observed in the nomination of Irish Roman Catholic bishops, which mode by experience has proved to be unexceptionably wise and salutary'. Pledging themselves to recommend to the pope for episcopal office only men of 'unimpeachable loyalty and peaceable conduct', they expressed regret for the gross misrepresentation Milner had suffered and offered him their warmest thanks for his 'powerful and unwearied exertions' in the Catholic cause. He was then honoured by being requested to act as the official agent of the Irish clergy at the seat of government in accordance with the instructions he might occasionally receive from the archbishops in concurrence with their suffragans.[26]

The word 'inexpedient' was a compromise. Troy wanted to keep his options open should more acceptable terms and conditions be offered to the bishops, and perhaps, one or two of his colleagues who also wavered on the veto supported him. He admitted to Archbishop Bray of Cashel that he regretted that the words 'now' or 'in present circumstances' were not attached to the word 'inexpedient'.[27] The majority opposed him on the issue. John Power of Waterford did not regret the absence of 'now' and doubted if

25 *Letter to a parish priest*, 1 Aug. 1808, quoted in Ward, *The eve of Catholic emancipation*, i, pp 68–71 and *Dublin Evening Herald*, 8 Sept. 1808. Milner in private bewailed the violence of the 'democratic party' in Ireland and regretted the 'imprudence' of the bishops in surrendering to it. **26** Troy to Propaganda, 28 Nov. 1808, APF, SC (Irlanda) 18, ff 480rv, 489rv. Troy explained that Catholic nobles and rich Catholics were displeased by their resolutions as they thought that emancipation would follow concessions to the king. He thought a more favourable government might propose emancipation with the request for a royal veto, and wondered if the Holy See would concede a veto, and if so under what conditions. **27** Troy to Bray, 24 Oct. 1808, CaDA.

it could 'be ever considered expedient unless a mutual change should take place in the spirit that generally actuates the British government with regard to the Catholic religion'.[28] James O'Shaughnessy of Killaloe was pleased that the resolutions were so strongly and firmly framed as to leave no hope for innovation in their discipline.[29] John Young of Limerick, unimpressed by Troy's regret, argued that the prefix 'now' 'would be laying a snare for involving ourselves or posterity in the perplexing circumstances we so happily got over; and I hope the question of the veto is put down forever and believe from the unanimity with which it was carried that the H. Ghost suggested the resolution'.[30] The majority of the bishops were as hostile to the veto as O'Connell and his supporters in the press.

Those who were suspicious of the use of the word 'inexpedient' in the formal statement subsequently felt vindicated by explanations from the archbishops of Armagh and Dublin. Archbishop O'Reilly of Armagh assured Viscount Southwell and Sir Edward Bellew,[31] who wanted to know if the resolution 'determined against the admissibility of the negative in question under *any circumstance whatever*', that he was certain that:

> the prelates did not mean to decide that the admission of a veto, or negative, on the part of the crown, with the consent of the Holy See, in the election of Roman Catholic bishops, would be contrary to the doctrine of the Roman Catholic Church or to any practice or usage essentially and indispensably connected with the Roman Catholic religion.

He went on to indicate that the prelates feared that dangerous consequences might have ensued from that concession, but, he insisted that in his mind and in that of several other bishops, such danger was of a temporary nature, 'resulting from existing circumstances though many persons suppose it to arise from the nature of the measure, thus giving to the resolutions of the bishops a meaning it [*sic*] does not deserve'.[32]

Though Troy, O'Reilly, Moylan and one or two other bishops may have remained open to the possibility of some kind of veto, the determined resistance of the majority of their colleagues ruled out any episcopal concession of it for the future. In 1799 clerical stipends and the veto had been proposed by the government. By 1808 the government in London showed no interest in

28 Power to Bray, 4 Nov. 1808, ibid., Coppinger of Cloyne and Delany of Ossory were also strongly opposed to any innovation in the system of appointments.   29 O'Shaughnessy to Bray, 9 Nov. 1808, ibid.   30 Young to Bray, 9 Nov. 1808, ibid.   31 Edward Bellew (1758–1837) was an active campaigner for Catholic emancipation and a member of the Catholic Board, who represented the aristocratic side, and later seceded from the board because of its style under O'Connell.   32 O'Reilly to Southwell and Bellew, 29 Oct. 1808 in APF, SC(Irlanda) 18, f 554r.

pursuing emancipation and the concessions were offered by members of parliament on behalf of Catholic petitioners. However well-intentioned they were, their proposals carried much less weight than Castlereagh's.

Troy later defended the caveats that the bishops included in their use of the word 'inexpedient'. Writing to Charles O'Conor, an Irish priest stationed in England whose writings had caused deep concern to the Irish and English bishops,[33] Troy explained that expediency or inexpediency depended on circumstances and not on unalterable principles. Consequently, he found it strange that the bishops' resolution should be 'so generally conceived to reject the veto as inadmissible and to preclude any future discussion about it'. Many prelates, including himself, did not adopt the word in that sense, but decided that it was inexpedient to tolerate any alteration in their discipline under a government that was avowedly hostile to Catholic claims and would not acquiesce in them, even if they renounced articles of faith, as long as they maintained papal supremacy. He pointed out further that the circumstances in 1799 had been very different from those in 1808. In 1799, 'an administration supposed friendly' held out the prospect, if not an implied promise, of considering a veto as a condition of emancipation: in 1808 a 'no-popery administration' had made it clear in both houses of parliament that no such scheme was on offer.[34]

Provoked by a letter by Milner to the *Morning Chronicle*, Patrick Ryan, the coadjutor bishop of Ferns, unburdened himself to the vicar general of Dublin about his anger at the outcome of the bishops' meeting. He claimed that the great majority of the prelates had made up their minds long before it took place to reject the intervention of the crown in their appointments, and quoted with approval the view of Bishop Caulfield of Ferns regretting that the resolutions of 1799 had not been rescinded and the bishop of Clogher's indignation at the part played by Archbishop O'Reilly of Armagh. Ryan had told Milner that the vote of thanks to him would not have been passed, had Troy and Moylan not assured the bishops that he would not in future write or speak in favour of the veto. Ryan was annoyed by Milner's reply, in which he was accused of making a long speech that determined the votes of the bishops, and was somewhat puzzled by his claim that 'great personages will exhibit documents to prove that they had *authority* to state at least as much as they did'. He could only suspect that this referred to letters from Troy, Moylan and Archbishop Dillon of Tuam to Lord Grenville, and concluded that, if that were the case, it would be 'sad work indeed'.[35]

33 In a book entitled *Columbanus ad Hibernos*, about the system of appointing bishops in Ireland, published in 1810, O'Conor caused great annoyance to the Irish bishops by calling for free elections of the bishops by all the diocesan clergy.   34 Troy to O'Conor, 11 Nov. 1808, quoted in Ward, *The eve of Catholic emancipation*, i, p. 81.   35 Ryan to Hamill, Dec. 1808 [day not given], DDA.

Bishop Ryan was convinced that Milner, Troy and O'Reilly of Armagh would persist with the plan of making some arrangement with the government about episcopal appointments. And he distrusted their motives: 'the first has some courtly object in view and the two latter appear to me of late more occupied with the idea of their dignity and importance than with any veneration for the hierarchy which they will allow to fall if they themselves as individuals can rise'.[36]

Reflecting on the bishops' resolution two months later, Coppinger of Cloyne concluded that the veto would destroy their religion. The very qualities that Catholic electors would look for in candidates would be sufficient grounds for their rejection by the king's advisers. The executive would continue rejecting candidates until they got 'their immoral blockhead; their drunken infidel; their cringing tale bearing sycophant' appointed. Coppinger was also 'highly critical' of the response of the Catholic aristocracy to the bishops' resolution arguing that the gentry were more interested in their individual aggrandizement than they were in the welfare or perhaps in the existence of Catholicity.[37] The reactions of men like Ryan, Coppinger and O'Shaughnessy showed that from the first public airing of the veto there was a solid bloc of prelates who would resist all such concessions to the state.

Three of the English vicars apostolic – John Douglass of the London District, William Gibson of the Northern District and Gregory Sharrock of the Western District – knew nothing about the veto until they saw the parliamentary reports in the newspapers and, subsequently, received Milner's letters. They were taken aback by the claims of Grattan and Ponsonby but did not make any public comments. The members of the English Catholic Board, headed by nobles and gentry, had always been much more willing to compromise with the government to gain their civil rights than the vicars apostolic, and consequently had been encouraged by the resolutions of the Irish bishops of 1799. Milner, depressed by the failure of the Irish bishops to support his stance and hurt by the abuse he had received in the Irish newspapers, announced in a pamphlet that he was taking leave of the Irish Catholics.[38] But the issue was too pivotal and compelling for someone who prided himself on his orthodoxy and devotion to duty to neglect and he bounced back with renewed energy and determination.

Thereafter he became and remained for the rest of his life a most resolute and implacable opponent of the veto. His flirtation with it in 1808 continued to embarrass him. And in reply to Butler's reference to it in his *Historical*

---

36 Ryan to J.B. Clinch, 23 Oct. 1809, DDA. Ryan also remarked that he had rebuked Milner for 'the impropriety of his agitating the question' (of the veto) and received 'an answer of great length filled with chicanery, falsehood and contradiction'. Milner's colleagues in England were later to make similar accusations against him.   37 Coppinger to Moylan, 11 Nov. 1808, CRDA. 38 Ward, *The eve of Catholic emancipation*, i, pp 80–1.

memoirs, he tried to excuse himself by describing his *Letter to a parish priest* as a 'mooting essay' or a kind of argument in a debate. But Butler rightly repudiated this spurious justification.[39] At the time, Butler regarded 'the bishops' disavowal' of Milner's offer of the veto as 'a wayward circumstance', which was of no significance even though their enemies would reproach them with it.[40]

39 Butler, *Historical memoirs*, iv, pp 155–60.   40 Butler to Scully, 12 Dec. 1808 in MacDermot, *The Catholic question in Ireland and England, 1798–1822*, pp 178–9.

8

The English board and the fifth resolution

I

A s the Irish Catholics continued to hold meetings pleading for emancipation and prepared to make further petitions, a request from Bishop Gibson and the Catholics of the northern vicariate spurred the reconstituted English Catholic Board into action in 1809. Too late for the parliamentary session of that year, it decided to make its submission in early 1810. In anticipation of an Irish petition, Lord Fingall sought the support of Lord Grenville, a former prime minister, who had presented the previous one in the house of lords and who had been formally thanked by the bishops for his advocacy of it. Grenville replied in a public letter to ensure as wide an understanding as possible of what he thought the concession of emancipation by the government would require from the Catholic side. He hoped thereby to prevent a recurrence of the embarrassment which had accompanied the last failure. Noting that 'all due provision' would have to be made 'for the inviolable maintenance of the religious and civil establishments of the United Kingdom', he singled out the need for 'vesting in the crown an effectual negative' in the appointment of the bishops. Remarking that he had regretted the reaction in Ireland to his reference to that proposal on the previous occasion, he referred to 'adequate arrangements; consistent with adherence to the strictest religious tenets being made' and to 'the acquiescence of your church to similar arrangements with other governments, by the sentiments which many of yourselves still entertain as to the proposal suggested in 1808, and, most of all, by the express consent formerly given to that proposal in a declaration signed by the most considerable of your own bishops'.[1]

Even before Grenville's letter was published, rumours of other plans involving a veto, including one by Sir John Coxe-Hippisley, had caused alarm in Ireland.[2] Edward Jerningham, the secretary of the English Catholic Board,

---

1 Grenville to Fingall, 22 Jan. 1810 in *DEP*, 30 Jan. 1810. 2 The *DEP* on 18 Jan. 1810, referring to a rumour that the English Catholics had agreed to an arrangement by which any objectionable name would be struck out of the list of candidates for episcopal orders by the king, remarked that Irish Catholics would never accept emancipation on terms 'so humiliating and disgraceful'. They had suffered persecution for conscience sake and would not make 'an inglorious sacrifice' of their consciences.

assured his counterpart in Ireland that no such arrangement had been made.[3] When he and three colleagues – including Charles Butler and the indefatigable lawyer Sir John Throckmorton, of Cisalpine Club fame – met Lord Grey and William Windham,[4] who had agreed to pilot their petition through parliament, they specified that they would make no commitment without the consent of the Irish and that they should 'do on their part those things which, while they were conformable to their religion, might at the same time give mutual satisfaction and security to government and the Catholics'. This replaced the resolution which had seemed closer to a veto by referring to an assurance being given of 'the loyalty of those who were to be proposed to episcopal order and dignity'.

On 31 January 1810 a few Catholic nobles and gentlemen, including Butler and Throckmorton, met Grey, Grenville and Windham and agreed to a resolution to be brought forward the next day at a meeting of Catholics at St Alban's Tavern in London. This was the famous 'fifth resolution' of the series to be presented to the Catholic meeting, which became the subject of a heated, bitter and prolonged debate. It declared that English Catholics were actuated less by a sense of the hardships and disabilities under which they laboured than by a desire to secure the peace and harmony of the empire, so as to obtain opportunities of manifesting their zeal in the common cause in which their country was engaged. It concluded that they were:

> firmly persuaded that adequate provision for the maintenance of the civil and religious establishments of this kingdom, may be made, consistently with the strictest adherence on their part to the tenets and discipline of the Roman Catholic religion: and that any arrangement founded on this basis of mutual satisfaction and security, and extending to them the full enjoyment of the civil constitution of their country will meet with their grateful concurrence.[5]

There was no specific reference to a veto or negative in this formula, though the wording of the resolution was adapted from Grenville's public letter to Fingall, which went on to include – among the necessary measures for the maintenance of the religious and civil establishments – 'vesting in the crown an effectual negative in the appointment of your bishops'. Opponents of the

---

3 *DEP*, 27 Jan. 1810. Jerningham said English Catholics were anxious to remain united with their friends throughout the empire. Butler assured Scully that English Catholics wished to cooperate fully with the Catholics of Ireland (Butler to Scully, 4 Feb. 1809, MacDermot, *The Catholic question in Ireland and England 1798–1822*, p. 188). 4 Charles Grey (1764–1845), a Whig leader, supported Catholic emancipation. As prime minister, he carried the Reform Act of 1832. William Windham (1730–1810), a friend of Edmund Burke, was a member of Grenville's ministry of 1806–7. 5 *DEP*, 6 Feb. 1810.

veto, and especially Milner, immediately detected the danger of the veto lurking beneath the demand for 'adequate provision'.

Since 1808 Milner had undergone a complete volte-face and had become a most violent opponent of any governmental interference in the nomination of bishops. From being prepared to allow the government to reject candidates who were not acceptable, he was, a few months later, ready to savage any member of the English Catholic Board or vicar apostolic who would even countenance such a proposal. The meeting of Catholics was held in the St Alban's Tavern on 1 February 1810 to convert the resolutions into a petition and obtain signatures in its support.

The vicars apostolic of the London and Western districts and the coadjutor of the London District, William Poynter, had met on 31 January, and had agreed not to sign the resolutions until all four vicars could discuss them together. Before the fifth resolution was put to the meeting on 1 February, Milner, acting as agent for the Irish bishops and not wanting to repeat the misunderstandings of 1808, begged for a delay until he could consult them. The chairman explained that the resolutions only bound them to 'a general disposition to treat with government' and that 'it was possible to give satisfaction and security to government by means not inconsistent with the principles of their Catholic religion'. The vicar apostolic of the Western District, Peter Collingridge,[6] and Bishop Poynter came under pressure to sign, and did so in consequence of the chairman's claim and the sway exerted by the gentry present. Bishop Gibson of the Northern District and his coadjutor-elect arrived two weeks after the meeting, and, on being assured by Lord Grey that there was no allusion to a veto in the fifth resolution, signed it.[7]

Milner was the only vicar apostolic who had not signed the resolutions and he promptly printed a defence of his conduct in *Letter to an English Catholic peer.*[8] It was circulated among those who had been present at the meeting, as well as among some clergy and laity, and was also sent to a couple of the bishops in Ireland. On 31 January, Milner had dined at their invitation with some prominent Catholics, and had refused their request to sign the fifth resolution. When Lord Clifford had asked him if he might sign it, Milner had replied, 'You may sign it if you will,' and this answer subsequently led to controversy. Milner later explained that he intended to say that Clifford could follow his own conscience, but his opponents suggested that the bishop was deliberately giving Clifford the green light to sign. But the bishop insisted that he would rather mount the scaffold than submit to the

6 Peter Bernardine Collingridge (1757–1829) was coadjutor to Walmesley 1807–9 and vicar apostolic 1809–29 (Dockery, *Collingridge: a Franciscan contribution to Catholic emancipation*, pp 6–20). He was a confidant and supporter of Poynter.   7 Ward, *The eve of Catholic emancipation*, i, pp 114–23.   8 5 Feb. 1810, DDA.

terms of a resolution that was 'couched in vague and ambiguous terms for the express purpose of amusing one party, and of being interpreted by the other as circumstances might point out'. He was convinced that nothing would satisfy their parliamentary friends but 'a complete shackling and fettering of us churchmen' by acquiring an 'effectual negative' on the election of the bishops, 'a veto absolutely efficient and unrestrained'. Moreover he could not pledge his consent to the making of adequate provisions 'for the maintenance of the (Protestant) religious establishment'. Seeing the signatures of two vicars apostolic to the resolution, he thought at first they were forgeries, as both men had agreed with him not to sign and had arranged a meeting for the next day at Bishop Douglass' house, since it was deemed necessary for the four vicars apostolic to make a decision together. He concluded that the two bishops were pressurized into signing.[9]

Bishop Poynter, feeling that his character was injured by Milner's account of his conduct, replied in a public letter. He insisted that the chairman had assured him at the meeting that the 'resolutions contained no specific engagement but only expressed a general disposition to treat with government on the great subject of Catholic emancipation'. Though he had declared that all four vicars apostolic should deliberate on the resolution, he was assured by a lord that Milner would only act as agent for the Irish bishops and not as vicar apostolic. Knowing that Milner had said he would not disapprove of any priest in his district signing, he and Collingridge went ahead and signed. But when Poynter asked Milner if he would sign, he said no, because he had been burnt in effigy once and feared he would be burnt again for signing. The coadjutor of the London District wondered if this was a theological reason for his decision. Finally, Poynter denied that he actually said it was necessary for the four vicars to meet to discuss the matter before signing.[10]

Milner, never one to surrender without a fight, replied at length to Poynter. He charged Poynter with being 'blameable' in his public conduct on two important occasions: in a want of firmness in supporting the decisions of his own upright mind, and in a want of cooperation with the other vicars apostolic, especially himself. He then asked why he had not been invited to Bishop Douglass' house, where a discussion on the resolution had taken place. He asked why Poynter had relied on the word of a lord about his decision to act as the agent of the Irish bishops and not as a vicar apostolic, when Poynter could easily have made that inquiry to himself. Quoting some of those present that they 'over-persuaded' the two bishops to sign, he denied Poynter's claim that the tenets of their religion were protected by the

9 Butler, *Historical memoirs*, iv, pp 166–7; Milner, *Supplementary memoirs*, pp 145–55.
10 Poynter to Milner, 14 Feb. 1810, DDA.

resolution, since it called for a pledge to support 'the maintenance of the established religion of the country'.[11]

This was the first controversy provoked by the fifth resolution. Poynter declared himself injured by it, but Milner, who seemed to relish such jousts, was certainly not deterred from entering the lists again. Apart from the hostile public reaction in Ireland, the resolution led to conflicts between Jerningham, the secretary of the English board, and Troy and Moylan, and, more seriously and painfully, between Troy and Poynter. Though unity and harmony among the church leaders would probably not have hastened emancipation one whit, disharmony discouraged those who were prepared to try to obtain relief for Catholics. And in the long struggle for emancipation, the absence of unity and cooperation was frustrating for the friends of the Catholic body.

On the day after the meeting, Jerningham did not endorse a veto. He explained that he had waited on lords Grenville and Grey after the publication of Grenville's 'very rash and ill-judged' letter and to their admission that they expected the English petition to be open to the concession of the veto, had replied that because of their cooperation with the Catholics of Ireland 'any negotiation upon this subject' was impracticable. Grey and Grenville stated 'as a *sine qua non* of presenting their petition that it should be accompanied by willingness ... to acquiesce in any arrangements consistent with our religious principles and the discipline of the Roman Catholic Church', and they felt it impossible to object to a declaration 'so vague and general'. Jerningham predicted that if such a declaration could be inserted into an Irish petition, the question of a veto would be removed. Grenville had in fact drawn up the fifth resolution and Grey had approved of it, and by excluding mention of a veto they hoped that the incorporation of that declaration 'might prove the medium of general conciliation'.[12]

Troy, however, had he tried, would have been unable to persuade his colleagues to take such a benign interpretation of the fifth resolution. Bishop O'Shaughnessy of Killaloe represented the strength of feelings of the great majority of them when he wrote:

> Let Dr Troy and his adherents, if any he has, put it out of their heads! May the hand be paralyzed that will ever sign for a veto in

---

11 Milner to Poynter, 19 Feb. 1810, ibid. Power of Waterford remarked that Milner was 'rather warm' in the controversy. He hoped the manoeuvre of the English Catholics or Grattan would not alter the methods used by the Irish. The English, he claimed, are 'a weight on us. Our success will be owing not to the respectability so boasted of in England, but to the physical strength and numbers of the Irish Caths.' (Power to Bray, 26 Apr. 1810, CaDA). 12 Jerningham to Troy, 2 Feb. 1810, ibid. Jerningham (1774–1822), a barrister, became secretary of the English board in 1808.

any shape or form. The Catholics of this county proposed to me that if I called a meeting, they are ready and willing, in the most unqualified manner to express their total disapprobation of this fatal measure.[13]

Coppinger of Cloyne and Power of Waterford were not prepared to attend the meeting called by Troy to discuss the problem. Coppinger authorized Bray to sign for him against the fifth resolution and the 'infamous veto', and Power expressed similar opposition to 'the veto and state provision'.[14] Even had there not been a strong public reaction in Ireland to the supposed concession of a veto, the strength of episcopal reaction would have called forth a firm rejection of it.

The Irish bishops, at their meeting three weeks later (on 26 February 1810), combining their hostile views with those articulated by Catholic activists, renewed the rejection made in 1808 of any innovation in the system of episcopal appointments. Noting that their oath of allegiance was sufficient to exclude all foreign intervention, both spiritual and temporal, in civil establishments, they explained that their religion insisted on obedience to the laws, to the king and to lawful authority. They emphasized that:

> any change, at present, in our ecclesiastical appointments, expressly innovating upon our religious discipline, on the ground of its being perilous to the state, because Roman Catholic, and this without a single instance of danger incurred, must at once degrade our church in the estimation of Europe ... and must prejudice at home the interests of the public cause by disabling our authority, which is and has been, and will ever be, exerted in that cause.

They ruled out domestic nomination of bishops by declaring that 'the idea of making the elections of bishops entirely national, by confining said elections to chapters alone, or to chapters and metropolitans ... is, moreover, not within our competence'.[15] In their sixteenth resolution, the bishops also declared that their duty forbade them to pass judgment on arrangements which were said to accompany a proposal for emancipation, but that they were always prepared for conciliation and sought nothing 'beyond the mere integrity and safety of the Roman Catholic religion'.[16]

---

13 O'Shaughnessy to Bray, CaDA, 1810, quoted in Murphy, *The diocese of Killaloe, 1800–1850*, p. 25. 14 Coppinger to Bray, 17 Feb. 1810, CaDA and Power to Bray, 14 Feb. 1810, ibid. 15 Domestic nomination here means the right of chapters or clergy to elect the bishop, reserving to the pope only the right of canonical institution. The bishops objected to the idea of placing such extensive power in the hands of the lower clergy, and to the limitation of the pope's power. 16 *Address of the Roman Catholic prelates ... to the clergy and laity ...*, 26 Feb. 2010, DDA. At a

The English petition was presented in the house of lords by Lord Grey. An Irish equivalent was introduced by Lord Donoughmore and Grattan on 27 February. And despite the brouhaha raised by the fifth resolution, Grattan, presumably with the danger of Napoleon's control of the pope in mind, argued that some protection against foreign interference in the appointments of the bishops was necessary, and proposed that their nominations be purely and exclusively domestic. This suggestion, though condemned by the bishops in their public statement, had been put forward by the Catholic Committee at its weekly meeting in Dublin on 2 March as a compromise and way out of the impasse.[17] During the further discussion in parliament in May, Ponsonby and Coxe-Hippisley adhered to the view that some governmental input into the appointments of the prelates was essential. Grattan's motion in the house of commons was defeated by over a hundred votes and Donoughmore's in the house of lords by ninety-six.[18]

Troy informed Rome that their petition for emancipation was rejected on the pretext of their refusing a veto to the king in the appointment of bishops. The fear of French influence over such appointments had been widespread among Protestants. Since the bishops could not agree to a policy of domestic nomination which would exclude the pope from the process of appointment, he proposed that the pontiff should make a concordat with the prelates which would limit appointments to those recommended by the bishops of the province and by the chapters, to whom the pope would then give canonical institution.[19] He thus advocated a form of domestic nomination, in which due allowance was made for papal authority, and which differed from the proposal of the Catholic Committee. He probably had in mind a larger role for the pope than that of merely refusing to institute unworthy candidates.

The Irish bishops at their meeting on 26 February had also passed a

meeting of the Catholic Committee on 7 May, the resolution of 2 March, rejecting any control by the crown over the appointment of their bishops, was reaffirmed, but it was then resolved that the privilege of exclusively appointing bishops did not form part of the primitive rights of the Holy See. Consequently, the Irish bishops were requested to put into effect a plan for the election of bishops which would remove the apprehensions of the government about foreign or hostile influence. The bishops ruled out purely domestic nomination which would only have allowed the Holy See the right of canonical institution of the person chosen.   17 Milner complained that Grattan's proposed motion for 16 May 'setting aside the essential jurisdiction of our Holy Father and substituting that of King George' would not have been made without the fifth resolution. He warned Grattan of the sad consequences for his reputation in Ireland of this design (Milner to Bray, 16 Apr. 1810, CDA).   18 Castlereagh, who praised the 'judicious and temperate manner' in which Grattan always argued his case, maintained that the uncompromising tone of the advocates of emancipation antagonized parliament (Bew, *Castlereagh: enlightenment, war and tyranny*, pp 294–5).   19 Troy to Propaganda, 13 June 1810, APF, SC(Irlanda) 18, ff 563r–564r. Concordats were agreements between the Holy See and governments. Troy had in mind some kind of arrangement between the pope and the hierarchy.

seventeenth resolution, which was not published widely with the other sixteen, but was communicated to Milner. In forceful language which represented the views of the more intransigent among them they expressed:

> their thanks for his faithful discharge of his duty, as agent ... and more particularly for his apostolical firmness in dissenting from and opposing a general vague and indefinite declaration or resolution pledging the R. Catholics to an eventual acquiescence in arrangements, possibly prejudicial to the integrity and safety of our Church discipline.[20]

This encomium on Milner was ill-advised and uncircumspect. The other vicars apostolic now found themselves in effect excoriated by a neighbouring hierarchy for possibly endangering the integrity and safety of church discipline. The clear implication of the seventeenth resolution was that Milner was the only vicar apostolic who maintained a fully safe and orthodox line. Had the bishops addressed the issue in a more oblique way, by simply stating that they continued to adhere to the opinions already expressed, and as always would take their guidance from Rome, English Catholics could not have found fault, and Irish Catholics would have been reassured. But the singling out of Milner, who had already antagonized his colleagues with churlish tactics, caused great offence, and led to an exchange of correspondence between English and Irish prelates which gradually became more ungracious and inurbane.

Milner had made it known that he was not authorized by the Irish bishops to transact any business relating to the veto or 'any other ecclesiastical or political business whatsoever', and consequently, Jerningham, the secretary of the English board, wanted to know what Milner's role was and whether the vote of thanks was authentic. Congratulating Troy on 'the final close in Ireland of the late unfortunate question of the veto', he commented favourably on the unanimity of sentiment which seemed to prevail among the Catholics of both countries.[21]

Troy, in reply, explained that Milner, as their agent, had indeed been thanked, and though he had had no specific instructions from them on the veto, he had been entitled to appear in that capacity at the English meeting. The fifth resolution, to which he had objected, seemed to both the bishops and Catholics of Ireland 'to imply a pledge to sanction future arrangements for the maintenance of the Protestant religion which might prove inconsistent with the integrity and safety of the Catholic faith and discipline'.[22]

20 Ward, *The eve of Catholic emancipation*, i, p. 144. **21** Jerningham to Troy, 17 Mar. 1810, DDA. **22** Troy to Jerningham, 26 Mar. 1810, ibid.

Jerningham next conveyed the hurt feelings of his colleagues to Bishop Moylan of Cork. Interpreting the vote of thanks to Milner as a 'direct implied censure upon the collective body of their brethren in England', he asked the bishop of Cork if there was any substantial difference between what the English had stated, and what the Irish had previously sworn – that they would not subvert the Protestant church establishment. On a very pessimistic note, he suggested that 'the very demon of discord must have been at work, to have raised such scandal and division upon grounds like these'. He feared that the many Irish residents in England would be distracted 'by the knowledge of such unaccountable, and such senseless divisions'.[23]

Moylan reminded Jerningham that Grey – who with Grenville had penned the fifth resolution – had declared, when presenting the petition in the house of lords, that 'to every reason, to every sentiment, and to every word of Lord Grenville's letter, he most entirely subscribed'. He was therefore proclaiming 'the necessity of the effectual veto as the *sine qua non* of Catholic emancipation'. He also denied that the Irish bishops had strayed outside their jurisdiction by applauding Milner for refusing to sign the resolution: all they had performed was 'a mere exercise of judgment', and their object in refusing 'effectual control' was only 'to protect and preserve their own church against the inroads of infatuated bigotry'.[24] He could have taken the opportunity of expressing regret if, in any way, the Irish bishops had misinterpreted the sentiments of their English brethren, but he did not do so.

Before waiting for Moylan's reply, Jerningham responded to Troy's admission of responsibility for the vote of thanks passed to Milner by designating it 'a censure upon the Catholic prelates, clergy and laity of England'. And he went on to regret that this had changed what in the past had been a misunderstanding into a serious disappointment at the loss of conciliation and union, and to deplore the 'disgusting and false assertions' of the Irish press about 'an imaginary concession of the veto'.[25] The comments of the Irish bishops had certainly touched a raw nerve in the members of the English board, who had already been reeling from Milner's public hostility to its resolutions, as the increasingly acrimonious correspondence revealed.

Jerningham, who professed respect for Milner, also let him know that the members of the English Catholic Board resented the role he claimed to have played at their meeting as the agent of the Irish bishops, and were nettled by the 'foreign synodical censure' on the vicars apostolic and Catholic laity.

---

23 Jerningham to Moylan, 28 Mar. 1810, ibid.   24 Moylan to Jerningham, 3 Apr. 1810, ibid. Moylan believed that the 'leaders in London' were the Cisalpines who had invented the name Protesting Catholic Dissenters (Moylan to Bray, 4 May 1810, CaDA).   25 Jerningham to Troy, 7 Apr. 1810, DDA.

Instead of furthering the cause of conciliation and peace and preventing misconceptions, he had done the opposite. Hoping that the sixteenth resolution of the Irish bishops and the fifth of the English would no longer be considered as substantially different, he quoted a resolution passed by the Catholics of Tipperary which described the sixteenth resolution as evincing 'a becoming patriotic spirit of conciliation towards suitable arrangements, regarding the Catholic church and said to be intended to accompany Catholic emancipation'.[26] Not mollified by Moylan's replies, Jerningham charged him with telling the English Catholics that their bishops were 'incompetent to be the interpreters of their *own* intentions, or judges of a resolution in their *own* language', and that no explanation offered by them would be accepted in Ireland, unless it enjoyed Milner's approval.[27] Charles Butler greatly regretted that the breach between the hierarchies paralysed their general efforts to redress grievances, and occasioned 'infinite scandal'.[28]

However stung the secretary of the English Catholic Board was by the Irish bishops' resolutions, his pain was mild compared to that suffered by the vicars apostolic, and especially by Poynter. Milner's colleagues had long winced at the immoderate and bellicose language he used against those with whom he disagreed in politics or in ecclesiastical affairs. His agency for the Irish bishops, being somewhat indefinite and imprecise, meant that he could use them as a cover for some of his most vituperative and unscrupulous attacks against the other vicars apostolic, if it so suited him. And with his new-found antipathy to any mention of a veto on episcopal appointments, he was able, in his double capacity of vicar apostolic and agent, to attack his colleagues' alleged softness in their attitudes to a deal which might involve a veto. The more Milner, in the press, belaboured the other English bishops for their weakness and contrasted their cooperation with the gentry and the politicians angling for a veto with the manly and formidable rejection of any such policy by the Irish bishops, the more hurt and angered the vicars apostolic became, especially Poynter. They felt they were being unjustly depicted and condemned for forwarding a policy that they did not in fact espouse, and this provoked tension with Troy and led to acrimonious exchanges.

Poynter was an able, scholarly and sensitive man, who found Milner's style abrasive and hurtful. Fluent in French, he also wrote competently in Latin and Italian, and was keen to cooperate with Charles Butler and other

---

26 Jerningham to Milner, 17 Apr. 1810, ibid.   27 Jerningham to Moylan, 24 Apr. 1810, ibid. Milner claimed that Jerningham's letters were 'really written by that old rat of the Catholic cause, Charles Butler' (Milner to Bray, 16 Apr. 1810, CaDA). Milner often repeated this image and, for good measure, called Jerningham his 'ape and secretary' (Milner to Scully, 20 Dec. 1810, MacDermot, *The Catholic question in Ireland and England, 1798–1822*, p. 258).   28 Ibid., 20 Dec. 1810, p. 258.

professional men in presenting a favourable image of the church as it sought emancipation. Perhaps he was too deferential at times to the gentry of the Catholic Board, and too persistent and tenacious in pursuing his case when, in the interests of peace and harmony, he would have been better advised to let sleeping dogs lie.[29]

After Milner's publication of the pamphlet 'Elucidation of the veto', Poynter wrote to him denying that the other vicars apostolic had had anything to do with a veto.[30] And on behalf of the other bishops and their coadjutors, and on his own behalf, he took Milner severely to task for damaging their good name and injuring their characters with his spurious charges against them. Their patience, he complained, was exhausted with his accusations that they had pledged themselves to agreements incompatible with the safety and integrity of their faith. (What probably antagonized them most was that they had heard that these allegations had been sent to Rome.) The vicars apostolic furthermore maintained that they were hurt by his lament about their disunity, which they indignantly attributed to him, as they were not prepared to follow him into 'every hasty measure' or approve of 'his harsh and overbearing language'. As a result of his calumnies, they were denounced in Ireland for abandoning their faith. Consequently, they called on him to do justice to their characters with repairing the harm he had done with his false representations.[31]

Milner was not moved by these charges. Nor was he moved when, at a meeting, Poynter told him that the other vicars apostolic had not made any commitment other than a general expression of their willingness to treat with the government on terms of mutual satisfaction and security. It was he who had 'implicated himself in the veto business', was ashamed of himself and was then 'unfairly and unjustly throwing the odium of it on the other bishops'. Bishops Douglass and Poynter reminded him that he had once proposed an unlimited veto to Ponsonby, and that on the day before the meeting in St Alban's Tavern he had told Lord Clifford that he might sign the fifth resolution.[32]

29 Distressed by the fear that the faithful would be scandalized by the disunion among the vicars apostolic that Milner's 'imprudent publications' were causing, and by 'the most incompetent, unprovoked and uncanonical censures from the Irish bishops', Bishop Collingridge suggested to Douglass that the other vicars apostolic should publicly state that they were not responsible for any of his opinions. Milner, however, insisted that he always tried to work in concert with his brethren, and hence kept calling for them to hold synods (Milner to Douglass, 21 June 1810, WDA).   30 Poynter to Milner (draft), 15 July 1810, WDA.   31 Poynter on behalf of Bishops Gibson, Douglass, Collingridge and Smith, 18 July 1810, WDA (copy)   32 Poynter to Bishops Gibson and Collingridge (copy), 24 July 1810, ibid. Milner in a very hard-hitting letter to Douglass repudiated the accusations of his colleagues, and in turn charged Douglass with countenancing violent denunciations of him, which had been made by priests of the London District. He had opposed a plan which would have laid their church 'bound and gagged under

Poynter also took issue with Troy and the Irish bishops. On behalf of himself and four others, he complained bitterly to Troy that their feelings had been hurt, their sacred and public characters as bishops and guardians of the faith had been injured and their rights had been violated by the imputations unjustly cast upon them by the Irish bishops, and particularly by a libellous sermon preached in Cork by a Dominican on St Patrick's Day. The seventeenth resolution praising Milner, which was widely understood to condemn them, had been reprinted and circulated ad nauseam. The resolution, described by the Irish bishops as vague and indefinite was, in fact, fixed and defined by the terms of what was consistent with the tenets of the faith. The vicars apostolic therefore reprobated the sentence pronounced against them by a tribunal that had no jurisdiction over them, and its frequent repetition as a public insult to their characters. The veto had been accepted by a group of Irish bishops in 1799 and their agent had supported it in 1808; they, on the other hand, had condemned and rejected it. In conclusion, Poynter put a very difficult question to Troy, asking if the other vicars apostolic were to assume that all that was said or done by the Irish agent enjoyed the bishops' sanction.[33]

In reply, Troy expressed his regret that there should be even a suspicion that the character or rights of their brethren in England had been violated by the Irish bishops and went on to explain that in publishing their disapprobation of the fifth resolution they had done so

> within their own sphere and competency, on a public measure of material import affecting the Catholics of Ireland, and conceived themselves conscientiously obliged, to express their apprehension of eventual danger to religion, lest their respective flocks should be induced to follow the example of the hundred Catholics assembled at the St Alban's Tavern.

The Catholics of Ireland, the archbishop continued, had concluded from Grenville's letter to Fingall that arrangements for the security of the

---

the feet of an hypocritical Protestant establishment' as he had opposed Douglass' weakness in assenting to arrangements made by laypeople in the past (Milner to Douglass, 23 Aug. 1810, ibid.). **33** Poynter to Troy, 9 Aug. 1810, DDA. Poynter declared that Milner had branded his English colleagues *'fautores schismatis incipientis'*, promoters of an impending schism. Troy disclaimed any knowledge of this but Poynter later repeated it. He quoted John Ryan OP as saying 'the treacherous bargain (the veto) has been held out to our brethren of a neighbouring country. They have received the advances of the seducer with servile complacency. A single pillar of this little church stands alone to uphold the tottering fabric. And the name of Milner has become identified with whatever of honour or of safety may yet remain to the Catholic faith in his country.' Whatever about the views of the bishops, Troy could not have been held responsible for those of every maverick priest.

Protestant establishment, which might endanger the safety and security of their discipline, were being contemplated, and as the fifth resolution had been written by Grenville and Grey, 'it was in like manner apprehended that it implied something of a veto'. Exculpating the episcopate from responsibility for the slanderous attacks of anonymous writers in the newspapers and for the sermon in Cork, he pointed out that they only sanctioned what Milner did as their agent and under their instructions. And they were not so ignorant or vain as to attempt to exercise jurisdiction over the vicars apostolic.[34]

Far from being contrite or apologetic Milner remained obstinate and defiant. He told Troy that he had quoted in reply the claim of the vicars apostolic that they had nothing to do with the veto but 'to condemn and reject it', and commented sarcastically that he scarcely thought Jerningham and Butler would have allowed them to repeat that denial in public. He reiterated his strongly held view that the vicars apostolic should act independently of the laity, and adverting to a plan by which some laymen were prepared to raise £500 each for bishops Douglass and Collingridge, he declared that not for ten times that sum would he countenance arrangements calculated to '*lay our church bound and gagged* under the feet of the Prot establishment'.[35]

Had Poynter and Troy called a halt to their exchange after the first letters, neither would have lost face and both would have made their points. But Poynter was so obviously hurt by what he believed was the injury to the characters of the vicars apostolic that he wrote again repeating many of his accusations, and denied that anything pertaining to a veto was implied in their fifth resolution. He insisted that if Grey and Grenville 'had any arrangements in view relative to a veto' or to any measures inconsistent with the integrity and safety of the Catholic religion, such arrangements were 'foreign to the obvious and natural meaning of the resolution' the vicars apostolic had signed and had never been proposed to them. Explaining that the late coadjutor of the bishop of Cork had sent a letter maintaining that the sermon preached in that city represented the opinions of the majority of the Catholics of Ireland, he admitted that the plan to print it in London had been abandoned.[36] He concluded by calling on the Irish bishops to admit that their resolution charging the English vicars apostolic with having pledged themselves 'to an eventual acquiescence in arrangements possibly prejudicial to the integrity and safety' of their church discipline was grounded in an

34 Troy to Poynter (copy), 18 Aug. 1810, DDA.   35 Poynter to Milner (copy) and Milner to Troy, 27 Aug. 1810, ibid.   36 Bishop Moylan assured Poynter that he had 'never sanctioned or given the least encouragement to that libellous denunciation or to any other'. He explained that the Irish bishops thought the resolution 'might eventually tend to countenance an arrangement prejudicial to our holy religion', as Lord Grey, in presenting the English petition, had committed himself to every sentiment and word of Grenville's letter (Moylan to Poynter, 16 Aug. 1810, WDA).

error of fact and trusted that they would do their English brethren the justice they had the right to expect.[37]

Troy was taken aback by Poynter's persistence, as he had hoped to clear up all misunderstandings with his previous letter. In a short answer, he described Poynter's latest letter as mainly a repetition of his first, referred him to the answer already given and challenged the denial that the fifth resolution was vague and indeterminate. Claiming that it was purposely drawn up in vague terms as a merely speculative abstract proposition, he argued that it should have been 'maturely weighted in the scales of the sanctuary by the prelates of England assembled together in council without lay-dictation or interference', and with particular attention to the views of those who had framed it. He expressed amazement at their being censured for passing judgment on their English brethren, and again disclaimed any entitlement on their part to do so.[38]

Troy undoubtedly hoped that Poynter would not pursue the issue any further. Poynter, on behalf of his episcopal colleagues, again complained of Troy's not assuaging their wounded characters and accused him of applying the adjective 'false' to the terms 'vague and indeterminate'. They were not prepared to admit that the fifth resolution was vague in the sense that it could include anything inconsistent with the integrity and safety of their religion.

Troy replied at great length that Grenville's letter to Fingall manifested 'an unalterable hostility' to the known views of the Irish bishops on the veto (and, he might have added, those of the great majority of the laity) and had insisted on the admission of the veto together with other arrangements or changes in ecclesiastical discipline as essential to the security of the Protestant establishments. The English bishops, had given 'the weight and authority of their names to a resolution contrived and modelled for the purpose by Lord Grenville himself' and prescribed by an assembly of laymen who 'were disqualified from judging in a question merely ecclesiastical'. Milner's advice to communicate with the Irish bishops or even to confer together had been disregarded. Though the word 'veto' was not mentioned, the resolution should be understood 'conformably to the known sense and intention of its author'. And the sole object of Grenville in framing it, he added – without any evidence – was to contravene the rejection of the veto by the Irish bishops. In alluding to the fifth resolution in their vote of thanks to Milner, they had 'endeavoured to cast a veil over its visible and flaring omission of the veto', and had selected 'the most guarded and gentle terms which a respect for the episcopal character of their brethren' could suggest. To break the stalemate their correspondence had reached, and in the interests of charity and harmony, Troy suggested that the vicars apostolic

37 Poynter to Troy, 29 Aug. 1810, DDA.   38 Troy to Poynter (copy), 19 Sept. 1810, ibid.

should publicly and authentically declare what they had privately and confi-
dentially averred – that nothing was further from their minds than allowing
the veto – and then the Irish prelates would meet this action 'with corresponding advances' that would indicate a desire of resuming cooperation.[39]

This solution would have put an end to a controversy that had been
unnecessarily prolonged and had become rather heated. At once, the English
bishops would have let the public, both Catholic and Protestant, know that
they were not prepared to seek emancipation by paying what they regarded
as an impossible price – the acceptance of a royal veto in their appointments.
Whether they were afraid of antagonizing their laity, who were more aggressively led by nobles and gentry than was the case in Ireland, or whether they
did not want to stir up a public controversy or hand a victory to Milner
cannot be known. They did not take up Troy's proposal. The tenacious and
pugnacious Poynter asked the Irish bishops in the course of a further controversy if their sending a synodical resolution in February 1810 condemning
the conduct of the English bishops was 'any thing else than an assumed act
of jurisdiction in this country?'[40]

Poynter had already been pained by Troy's attempt to have Milner
appointed to London either as vicar apostolic or coadjutor. This would have
involved his transfer or his remaining as Milner's assistant, and understandably both these options riled him. The condemnation of the fifth resolution
by the Irish bishops and their encomium on Milner added a further layer of
irritation. The Irish bishops who were most opposed to the veto doubtless
thought that the fifth resolution, linked as it was to Grenville's letter to
Fingall, a long time advocate of Catholic relief in Ireland, was putting
forward a policy they could not accept. But more nuanced language in the
exchanges about the possibilities opened up by the fifth resolution would
have led to less hurt and annoyance.

It was ironical that Troy should have engaged in the controversy as the
Irish champion of diehard opposition to the fifth resolution. He was in fact
far from being the extremely rigid opponent of the veto that this exchange
with Poynter suggested, but probably felt obliged to put forward the
obdurate and inflexible views of many of his colleagues. In fact, some of his
colleagues did not trust him to oppose the veto forcefully and effectively.
Poynter, however, regarded him not as a representative of others' opinions,
but as an obstinate and pertinacious antagonist. This contention led to a
further unnecessary and unfortunate deterioration in the relationship
between the two prelates.

The trouble with the fifth resolution was its ambiguity and imprecision.
Both Milner's and Poynter's interpretations were feasible, especially when

39 Troy to Poynter (copy), 16 Nov. 1810, DDA.   40 Poynter to Troy, 17 Oct. 1811, ibid.

the wider context of Grenville's letter was taken into consideration. Grenville left no doubt that an 'effectual negative' for the crown in the appointments of bishops was an essential requirement for the granting of emancipation by the government. The use of the words 'arrangement ... founded on security' had an ominous ring to those who feared that a veto was lurking in the letter to Fingall. Charles Butler told his friend, Denys Scully, that he was amazed that the fifth resolution could even have been thought to refer to the veto, and given the contradictions of those accused of using it in that way, he wondered if it was 'fair, just or congruous to persist in that charge'.[41] Poynter was right to stress that the vicars apostolic had given no pledge to accept any kind of veto, and therefore could rightly deny that they had committed themselves 'to an eventual acquiescence in arrangements possibly prejudicial to the integrity and safety of our church discipline'. His rebuttal of the charge that the resolution was vague and indefinite in the sense that it could include 'whatever may be consistent or inconsistent with the integrity and safety of religion' but was rather '*fixed* and *defined* by the terms of what is consistent, on our past, with tenets and discipline of the Roman Catholic religion' was fair and reasonable.[42]

The openness of the resolution in its wider context to differing interpretations meant that it could be used by Milner both in England and in Rome to accuse Poynter of being a vetoist. And it was more difficult for Poynter to answer Milner's charges in Rome since a defence of his position involved an explanation of the way the resolution came to be signed. By frequently referring to the place of meeting as a tavern, Milner was able to give the impression in Rome that the location and circumstances in which the vicars apostolic met with the lay committee were vulgar and unwholesome. In his frequent onslaughts against Poynter in Rome, Milner invariably produced the fifth resolution as his trump card.

II

If the dispute about the fifth resolution were not enough to occupy the minds of the English and Irish bishops, a further one involving French churchmen broke out. It led to bitter exchanges not only between Milner and his episcopal colleagues, but also between Troy and Poynter. The old sores created by the fifth resolution were reopened and new bruises were sustained. It caused a further deterioration in the relations between Poynter and Troy, and the vicars apostolic of the Northern and Western districts

41 Butler to Scully, 28 Dec. 1811, MacDermot, *The Catholic question in Ireland and England, 1798–1822*, p. 316. 42 Poynter to Troy, 29 Aug. 1810, DDA.

resented and rejected the interventions of Milner, Troy and the Irish bishops.

Milner's intervention, however unnecessarily meddlesome, was understandable within his overarching view of his responsibilities to the Catholics of England. Troy's intervention could only have been based on the general clerical obligation of supporting a pope who had restored the church after the disruption of the French Revolution. His defence that he was protecting the Catholics of Ireland was weak and far-fetched, as only a tiny minority of priests and even fewer laypeople would have read, or, perhaps, even heard of the books at the centre of the altercation. The author of the books did try to bring the Irish bishops on to his side, but they could easily have ignored him.

This dispute was provoked by Paul Blanchard, a French priest resident in London, an irreconcilable Gallican who objected strongly to the concordat which Pius VII had made with Napoleon. By the terms of that concordat, the number of dioceses in France was greatly reduced and new bishops were appointed, including some of those who had been part of the constitutional church. They and priests who had also accepted that church were reconciled on the basis of a public oath acknowledging the new arrangements. Those who rejected the concordat formed *la petite église* in London and in Continental countries but were refused recognition by the host churches there.

Blanchard in 1805–6 published pamphlets attacking the action of Pius VII in forcing the resignation of bishops as an improper usurpation of the rights of the Gallican church. Milner in 1808 took issue with him, and – before Douglass, in whose district the majority of the French bishops and clergy lived, could take action – denounced Blanchard's scandalous and schismatical doctrines. One of Blanchard's supporters, Abbé Gaschet, went further than Blanchard, accusing Pius VII of committing blasphemy and schism. Douglass was then provoked into action and eventually censured Blanchard, Gaschet and five others who had backed them, by removing their faculties. Blanchard retorted with a book entitled *Abus sans exemple de l'autorité écclesiastique*. The bishop of Angoulême appealed to Douglass to remove the censure on one of Blanchard's followers, Jean de Trevaux, on the grounds that he had not intended to commit himself to the extreme position represented by Blanchard.[43]

Douglass, who favoured conciliation over confrontation, responded to the request of the bishop of Angoulême by reinstating de Trevaux. The erring

---

43 Blanchard then appealed to the Irish bishops, telling them that he would consider their silence as an approbation of his doctrines. Troy and his suffragans promptly censured several propositions extracted from *Abus sans exemple de l'autorité écclesiastique*, and several other prelates to whom the book was submitted added their signatures (Cogan, *The diocese of Meath*, iii, pp 384–5 (17 July 1809)).

Frenchman, however, did not make, and was not called upon to make, a public statement or retraction of his views, as was normally required of anyone who had been censured for holding schismatical or heretical opinions. What further aggravated the situation was the use made by Blanchard of de Trevaux's reinstatement: he published a work entitled *La vérité proclamée par ses agresseurs*, in which he claimed that Douglass had retreated from his previous stand and rejoiced that censure had been withdrawn.

Milner took exception to this quiet restoration of faculties to de Trevaux, and published a remonstrance against it addressed to Bishop Douglass on 29 June 1811. He insisted that, since de Trevaux had made a public parade of his support for a schismatical work, he should be compelled to make an equally public disavowal of it. The issue was not one between Bishop Douglass and de Trevaux but between de Trevaux and the universal church. And this was to be the crux of the whole dispute. Poynter and his friends maintained that Douglass had the authority to reinstate de Trevaux without a public retraction of his views; Milner, Troy and other opponents of de Trevaux maintained that a formal retraction was demanded by canon law. Bishop Collingridge interpreted Milner's intervention as 'tending to render the episcopal duties quite odious and insupportable by making a Bishop responsible to every neighbouring or even distant prelate who might conceive himself entitled to call for a public explanation of any *act whatever* for his administration'.[44]

At this point Troy, claiming to write also on behalf of the prelates of Ireland, entered the fray with a peremptory and truculent call to Douglass to explain his action. Quoting from a pamphlet by Blanchard that said his schismatical system was admitted by Douglass 'in opposition to a *violent and obstinate combination of so many prelates to deny the truth*', he asked Douglass 'to state distinctly' whether spiritual faculties had been restored to de Trevaux so that the bishops of Ireland could 'determine conformably to the practice of the church whether we continue in Catholic communion with Your Lordship' and silently acquiesce in Blanchard's schismatical doctrines.[45] Douglass was doubtless shocked by this clamant intervention in his spiritual responsibilities and frightened that Troy might bring his dire threat to the attention of Rome. However, true to character, he begged Poynter to write to Troy in his name 'with more than your usual mildness, *a soft answer*'.[46]

---

44 Collingridge to Poynter, [probably 24] July 1811, WDA; Ward, *The eve of Catholic emancipation*, i, pp 82–97.   45 Ibid., i, pp 159–65. Troy to Douglass, 30 July 1811, WDA. Coppinger of Cloyne objected to any intervention by Troy in Blanchard's case. He believed the Irish should have been left in ignorance of Blanchard's 'foul language' and asked 'is it not better that Troy instead of irritating this most dangerous man by a publick censure should write him a charitable private letter expressive of regret and disapprobation and try to gain him over by mild expostulation?' (Coppinger to Bray, 4 May 1809, CaDA).   46 Douglass to Poynter, 6 Aug. 1811, WDA.

Poynter, however, was in no mood to take what he regarded as dictation from Troy and the Irish bishops. Claiming that Milner had not fairly represented de Trevaux's limited approval of Blanchard, which instead of referring to all his views referred only to 'the divine rights of the episcopacy and the natural duties of subjects to their sovereigns', and that Douglass had received a satisfactory answer from de Trevaux, he reminded Troy that neither Milner nor the Irish bishops had any jurisdiction over Douglass nor any right to call on him to explain his conduct. Moreover Troy's 'requisition' was made in a tone of authority that they did not acknowledge. He asked rhetorically what would be thought of the English vicars apostolic if they were to demand an account from the Irish bishops of their conduct and threaten them with a breach of communion? And returning to their former quarrel he referred to 'the slanderous imputations cast upon us even from the pulpit in Ireland last year'.[47]

Exasperated and perhaps inflamed by Troy's and Milner's strictures on the fifth resolution and the case of de Trevaux, Poynter went off to visit Bishop Collingridge and then they both travelled to Durham, where they held a three-day meeting, 29–31 August 1811, with Bishop Gibson of the Northern District and his coadjutor. The series of resolutions which they passed but did not publish were a hard-hitting attack on Troy and Milner. They repeated in trenchant terms the repudiation of the interpretation of the fifth resolution as a pledge to acquiesce in arrangements fatal to religion, and excoriated the Irish prelates and their meddlesome agent for their assumption of authority in matters and places where they had no right whatever to pass judgment. The language of these resolutions was sharp and caustic, and it may have been that they then decided, on reflection, that relations would only have been further soured by their publication.[48] However, they sent a milder version to the archbishops of Armagh and Cashel in the hope that 'all ideas of a breach of Catholic communion will be laid aside'.[49]

Troy, in a further communication, denied that his colleagues had made 'even an insinuation or innuendo of jurisdiction or authority', and insisted that de Trevaux had publicly approved of Blanchard's whole book, *Défense du clergé Français*, and not merely of a couple of uncontroversial points in it. Since that book had been condemned by Douglass as scandalous and derogatory to the respect due to Pius VII, he should publicly and officially retract those views before having his spiritual faculties restored. He explained

---

47 Poynter to Troy, 6 Aug. 1811, DDA.   48 Ward, *The eve of Catholic emancipation*, i, pp 256–61.   49 Gibson, Collingridge, Poynter, Smith to Richard O'Reilly (copy), 29 Aug. 1811, WDA. Poynter explained that the offensive title *Approbation de l'ouvrage condamné par Monsig' Douglass* was not prefixed to the paper which de Trevaux signed or at least by an artifice it was concealed from him.

further that the offending sermon of the previous year by a Dominican was preached without his knowledge and in another diocese, and that he could not subsequently refuse the preacher faculties 'without indisposing the Catholic population of Ireland against me, disappointed and irritated as it was, at the precipitate resolution of the Board of English Catholics last year, in defiance of their pledges to act in concert with their Irish brethren'.[50]

The touchy and sensitive Poynter was not prepared to let Troy off the hook, and in his frustration listed examples of Irish interference, including the resolutions of 1810 and the attempt to have Milner installed as coadjutor in London. Denying that de Trevaux had made the extensive claims Troy attributed to him, and arguing that Troy had written to Douglass as if he possessed authority over him, he accused the archbishop of 'going to extremities' by the threat of a breach of communion, a threat which had hurt the vicars apostolic 'exceedingly'. However, he noted that Troy's letter, though purporting to come from all the bishops, bore only one signature, so he concluded that it merely expressed Troy's views or, at most, those of only a few of the prelates.[51] Consequently, he conveyed his hope that the seventeenth resolution of 26 February 1810, which had praised Milner and was not signed by all the prelates, did not represent the judgment of the Irish episcopate as a whole.[52]

The archbishops of Armagh and Cashel, to whom the letter from Durham had been addressed, met Troy and four other bishops on 16 October, and forwarded a joint reply to the English bishops. Somewhat more diplomatic than Troy's solo efforts, it still noted that de Trevaux was guilty of an act of schism by publicly approving Blanchard's schismatical production. Accordingly, the bishops trusted that they would not give offence by requesting that Douglass would either dismiss him from the ministry or oblige him formally and publicly to retract his approbation of Blanchard.[53]

A few days later, Troy replied to Poynter's last communication, repeating much of what had been said by himself and his colleagues. Claiming that Douglass had doubtless unintentionally countenanced de Trevaux's approbation of Blanchard's schismatical doctrines, he asked whether they were in

---

50 Troy to Poynter, 26 Sept. 1811, ibid. Archbishop O'Reilly of Armagh, who was more conciliatory than Troy, maintaining that he was unsure about de Trevaux, as the English bishops denied he was schismatical, declared that he did not want 'to implicate himself in controversies' with the English bishops (O'Reilly to Bray, 14 Sept. 1811, CaDA).   51 Dominic Bellew, the bishop of Killala, who had been a disputatious priest in the archdiocese of Armagh against whom Troy had written an unfavourable report to Rome, had informed Poynter that 'I should hesitate to pledge myself that the good doctor in question has not consulted a third nor even a tenth part of our bishops in the present precipitate and ill timed business', a liberty he took on occasions and he added that the archbishop was wont to take this liberty (Bellew to Poynter, 15 Sept. 1811, WDA).   52 Poynter to Troy, 17 Oct. 1811, DDA.   53 O'Reilly and Bray to vicars apostolic (copy), 21 Oct. 1811, WDA.

communion with Douglass or with Blanchard and de Trevaux. And that question was put not to break communion but to find out whether de Trevaux had publicly retracted or not. Then, averting to a complaint Poynter had made about the Irish prelates' attempts to have Milner transferred to the coadjutorship of the London District, he gave the astonishing answer that all they had sought from Rome was permission for Milner to be allowed to spend more time in London to enable him to carry out his work on their behalf. If their agent in Rome had suggested a transfer, he had done so without their instructions or authorization. Troy either had a very weak memory or he was being economical with the truth.[54]

As Poynter continued to complain about the interference of the Irish bishops and the injuries they had done to the character of the vicars apostolic, he introduced a very serious charge to illustrate the interference: that he had instructed 'the agent of the Irish prelates in England to treat with ministers, parliament and others on *all business* respecting religion *in England*, as well as in Ireland, *independently of the English apostolical vicars*'.[55] That certainly would have been a very grave violation of the canonical responsibilities of the vicars apostolic, and Poynter must have been in a very aggressive mood to suggest such irresponsible meddling on Troy's part. Troy replied that Milner in 1808 was commissioned 'to act agreeably to occasional instructions ... but was never instructed to treat with ministers and parliament *independently* of the English *apostolical vicars* in matters *purely religious*'.[56] The obvious explanation that Milner was requested to act on the political issue of emancipation did not satisfy Poynter, but with his experience of Milner's ability to drag all kinds of questions into his writings, his reaction was understandable. Poynter was not convinced by Troy's denial. He maintained that when the vicars apostolic saw the Irish agent 'instructed, *as* such, to treat on *our religious* concerns' they believed it was their duty to protest against and resist the 'interference of the principals and of their agent'. He asked indignantly if it was then 'in our concern of a *mixed nature*, partly religious and partly civil, that he was instructed to treat independently of us', and went on to claim that such a mandate made the interference of the Irish bishops 'still more unjustifiable'.[57]

Though Troy did not make personal criticisms of his opponents, Milner and Poynter could not resist doing so. Referring to one of Poynter's letters, a copy of which Troy had sent him, Milner commented 'how despicable is its

54 Troy to Poynter, 24 Oct. 1811, WDA. Troy had written several letters to Rome requesting the transfer of Milner to the coadjutorship of London. In writing to Concanen on 2 Nov. 1805 he argued that this proposal had the support of all the friends of the Catholic cause and even of many enemies in England who had a high regard for Milner's erudition and talents (APF, SC (Irlanda) 18, f 342rv).   55 Poynter to Troy, 17 Oct. 1811, DDA.   56 Troy to Poynter, 24 Oct. 1811, WDA.   57 Poynter to Troy, 7 Nov. 1811, DDA.

chicanery, prompted, I am convinced for the most part by a professional master of that art, Chs Butler'.[58] Poynter, anxious to disabuse Archbishop Carroll of Baltimore and his suffragans of any appreciation of Milner as 'the champion of the Catholic cause', wrote to him, referring to his misrepresentations, and explained:

> To those who are at a distance and who are otherwise unacquainted with the facts and circumstances he relates, he must appear in the character of Apostolical zeal, vigilance and firmness but it is not difficult to shew that his zeal is not always *secundum scientiam*; that his vigilance is, in several instances an officious and uncanonical interference in the concerns of other bishops and that his firmness, which is celebrated, might rather be qualified by other epithets than that of apostolical ... We do not pretend that he has wilfully and intentionally injured truth; but that he is often hurried by an impetuous and blind zeal into misconceptions and misstatements, which are very injurious, is too well known here and felt.[59]

Milner published a booklet in 1812 entitled *An explanation with the Rt Rev Dr Poynter, coadjutor LD*, and sent it to bishops in England, Ireland, Portugal, Spain, Sicily and America.[60] It recapitulated his charges against all his colleagues but especially Douglass and Poynter, and provoked three vicars apostolic and a coadjutor to defend themselves in a communication to Rome and to other bishops. They set out to rebut his two principal criticisms of them: their signing the resolution which he claimed was contrary to the faith and discipline of the church, and Douglass' restoration of faculties to de Trevaux. Repeating the arguments which Poynter had often used, they added that the Irish bishops had been deceived by Milner's claims and had themselves signed a resolution of similar import. Confident that the pope would approve of Douglass' handling of the de Trevaux case, they rejected the right of either Milner or the Irish prelates to interfere in the jurisdiction of another bishop. And they noted that Milner, since he failed in his attempt to switch places with Poynter to become coadjutor in the London District, had found fault with everything Poynter did.[61]

Milner passed on his complaints about his colleagues to Rome. He reminded the congregation of Propaganda that English Catholic nobles and

---

58 Milner to Troy, 11 Nov. 1811, ibid.   59 Poynter and four bishops to Carroll (copy), 27 Nov. 1811, WDA.   60 Bishop Collingridge subsequently advised Poynter to publish all the correspondence, and also suggested that their dispute should be submitted to arbitration by the Scottish vicars apostolic (Collingridge to Poynter, 10 Jan. 1812, WDA).   61 Gibson, Collingridge, Poynter and Smith, 7 May 1812, APF SC (Anglia) 6, ff 302r–303r. In a postscript it was stated that Douglass died as the letter was being prepared.

lawyers had not hesitated to call themselves Protesting Catholic Dissenters, were prepared to take a heterodox oath to the government which was condemned by the Holy See and were only saved from doing so by the vigilance of the vicars apostolic and the Holy See. Explaining the danger of the negative power which was being sought for the king in the nomination of bishops, he admitted that he had first been mistaken but had then changed his mind. The other three vicars apostolic however had signed a resolution which was dangerous to the faith and discipline of the church. The laity sponsoring this affair then assigned pensions to the other vicars apostolic. He quoted Blanchard's statement that the pope favoured heresy and gave a detailed account of the de Trevaux affair. Two major issues confronted them: a petition to parliament which ran counter to the discipline of the church and the authority of the pope; as well as the Blanchard schism and the need to make de Trevaux retract his support for the schism or lose his faculties. The authority of the Holy See was required to deal with their difficulties.[62]

With the death of Bishop Douglass on 8 May 1812, Poynter became vicar apostolic and assumed full authority to deal with the de Trevaux case.[63] To assure himself of de Trevaux's denial of support for the extreme views of Blanchard, he obtained from the bishop of Angoulême a statement that de Trevaux had repudiated any schismatical or anti-papal beliefs. Though he refused to let anyone see this statement, he insisted that it closed the case against his French subject.[64]

A couple of months after Douglass' death, Bishop Moylan paid a visit to England and invited the vicars apostolic to meet in Durham (Bishop Gibson was not able to travel) to discuss the differences between the Irish and English bishops about state intervention in episcopal appointments and the de Trevaux case. Though they did not agree to pass resolutions, Poynter gave Moylan a letter to be shown to Troy and he sent a copy to O'Reilly of Armagh. In it, he renewed their determination 'not to innovate on the established mode of appointing Catholic bishops' without papal consent, and not to allow any person suspected of claiming that Pius VII was a heretic to exercise sacerdotal functions.

The Irish bishops delivered their final comments on this unnecessary and infortunate dispute at their annual meeting in November 1812. Moylan had informed them that Poynter had de Trevaux's retraction in his possession. They requested the vicars apostolic of the London District to let them have

62 Milner to Propaganda, 29 June 1812, APF, SC(Anglia) 6, ff 300r–301v. A further letter dated 23 Sept. 1812 reinforced these arguments, ibid., ff 345r–346v.   63 In his last letter to Troy he had paid warm compliments to the archbishop's 'long service to the cause of Christ and his Church'. Troy rather ungraciously suggested that these were intended 'to soften and smooth the harshness and asperity of other dictatorial passages in the letter' (Troy to Poynter, 30 Nov. 1811, WDA).   64 Ward, *The eve of Catholic emancipation*, ii, p. 5.

the documents testifying to the formal retraction of de Trevaux, so that they might 'communicate it to our respective clergy for their edification and inclination'.[65] Poynter, in a printed reply, regretted that they had revived that subject after all the explanations they had already been given, and very reasonably remarked that he could not understand why the production of such documents was necessary for the edification of their clergy. Nonetheless, he repeated that Bishop Douglass had restored faculties to de Trevaux after an oral assurance of his submission to his ecclesiastical superiors, just as Pope Pius VII had admitted some of the constitutional and schismatical clergy of France to full communion in the church without a formal and public retraction of their errors and schisms.[66]

For two and a half years, fervent and overwrought communications had passed between the Irish bishops and the three vicars apostolic, or more precisely between their representatives, Troy and Poynter. In the dispute over the fifth resolution both sides could legitimately claim to have had some truth on their sides. But the prolongation of the argument about the resolution once the petition had been defeated in parliament was futile and superfluous, and destructive of the good relations which should have existed between the two sets of bishops in their campaign for Catholic emancipation.

The issue of Blanchardism and de Trevaux only added a further irritant to the relations of the episcopates. The intervention of the Irish bishops is difficult to justify. Very few Irish priests would have been troubled by the dispute and the great majority of the Irish people would never have heard of it. And, as Poynter kept reminding the Irish bishops, they had no jurisdiction whatever in the London District and no authority to pursue Douglass' handling of a theological matter once he had given them an assurance that de Trevaux had submitted to lawful authority. The annoyance and exasperation of the three vicars apostolic at the persistence of Troy in pursuing the issue, especially as the Irish prelates' views were diffused and exploited by Milner, were understandable and only conducive to disharmony.

Milner undoubtedly played a major and malign role in these disagreements. His three English colleagues could not understand how someone who advocated a veto in 1808 could oppose even the shadow or possibility of one two years later. Poynter accused him of personal hostility since his failure to obtain the coadjutorship of London, and he suspected that his attitude to the fifth resolution and to the disputes with the French clergy were coloured by disappointment and jealousy. The other three vicars apostolic were undoubtedly right in thinking that Milner influenced the Irish clergy to the detriment of their better judgment. To those prepared to believe him and accept his

---

65 Address of the Roman Catholic prelates, 18 Nov. 1812, DDA.   66 Poynter to Irish bishops, 18 Jan. 1813, WDA.

case, he could present plausible arguments, and his shorter writings found a
welcome in his extensive vicariate especially among the middle classes and
the educated workers who appreciated his pastoral commitment. A too
unquestioning acceptance of his views led the Irish bishops, and especially
Troy, into further divergence from the other English vicars apostolic than
might otherwise have been the case.

When the other three vicars apostolic and Milner presented their cases at
Rome in 1812 the congregation of Propaganda was understaffed. The pope
and his closest advisers were still detained in France, and the congregation
was under the care of Monsignor Quarantotti. Though disturbed by any
mention of prelates not quashing dangerous or heretical opinions, the issue
had not been recounted or explained sufficiently to enable or compel him to
take action. He may have assumed that another congregation would later
investigate the charges brought against the French clergy. Poynter duly
briefed his agent about the role played by Troy and the Irish bishops in the
dispute, and the agent was able to make use of it later to help convince the
vice prefect of Propaganda that the archbishop of Dublin had been interfering without any justification in English ecclesiastical affairs.

Apart from the personal animus between Milner and Poynter, there was
the additional difference of attitudes to the role of the nobility and gentry in
the church. Milner, in defending his own outlook and attitudes to Douglass
once deplored 'yr coadjutor's over-strained politeness to persons of rank and
wealth and his unbounded jealousy of and antipathy to me',[67] and thereby he
drew attention to a major difference between them. Milner resented and
opposed the power and influence of the nobility and gentry in the English
church and regarded it as deleterious to their mission. He believed that only
the bishops and clergy, in full obedience to Rome, should determine the
discipline and policy of the church, and had fought for years against the role
played in it by prominent laymen, and especially by lawyers like Charles
Butler, in deciding what degree of loyalty or subservience Catholics should
show to the government. In contrast, Poynter respected and accepted the
role traditionally played by the gentry and wished to cooperate with them as
fully as possible.

As the campaign for emancipation went on, all these tensions and interests added complications to the political difficulties of the struggle, and the
Catholic laity in England who followed the public exchanges must have been
disconcerted and distressed by them.

---

67 Milner to Douglass, 23 Aug. 1810, WDA.

9

Grattan's bill, 1813

After his election to parliament for an English constituency, Henry Grattan took an active and sympathetic interest in the Catholics' quest for relief. In 1808 he had presented a petition on their behalf, which failed in parliament and led to controversy in Ireland. From his contacts with English colleagues, he came to believe that the Catholics would have to make concessions about the appointments of their bishops. He understood from his colleagues in parliament that Protestant hostility to emancipation would ensure that no such measure could be passed without Protestants feeling that Catholics had given them 'securities'. He had attached 'securities' to his petition in 1808, and he was to do the same in 1813.[1]

On 2 February 1808, French troops entered Rome and proceeded to annex part of the Papal States. In the following year, the French would take over all the papal territories and Pope Pius would be brought to Savona, where, with some of his cardinals, he would be held under house arrest for three years. Before his threatened expulsion from Rome, Pope Pius VII entrusted Cardinal di Pietro with full faculties to administer the affairs of the congregation of Propaganda and to delegate to others, if it was not possible to seek the pope's own judgment. A year later di Pietro delegated his authority to Monsignor Giovanni Quarantotti, the secretary of the congregation, whom he designated vice prefect, with full powers to conduct its affairs in his absence.[2] Contact between Rome and Savona was often difficult and haphazard, and consequently, some decisions that would normally have been submitted to the pope for confirmation were sent out on the authority of the congregation alone.

After the appointment of Luke Concanen, his able and active agent in Rome, to the bishopric of New York in 1808, Troy had to rely on the services of John Joseph Argenti, an official in the congregation of Propaganda who was not a priest. Unlike Concanen, Argenti was unable to present Troy's arguments effectively to the high officials of Propaganda, as Poynter's agents, especially the rector of the English College, were later able to do. He did not understand the Irish background and did little more than pass on mail. Milner had also used Concanen's services, as he was loath to use the same channels as his colleagues.

---

1 McDowell, *Grattan: a life*, pp 207–14. 2 Note, 17 July 1808, APF, *Acta* 177, f 15r.

A new and important player in the struggle for emancipation and in the antagonisms and disputes between the Irish bishops, Milner and the other vicars apostolic entered the stage in November 1812. Paul Macpherson, a native of Glenlivet and a former student of the Scots College in Rome, had been agent there for the Scottish vicars apostolic from 1793 until he had been expelled by the French authorities in 1798. He had returned in 1800 to take charge of the college, and, in the following year, had been appointed its rector. Expelled again in 1811, he returned to Scotland but went back to Rome the following year when requested by Poynter to act as agent for the English as well as the Scottish vicars apostolic.[3] Coxe-Hippisley, whom he had known in Rome, also invited him to act, in effect, as a secret agent for the British government, and to contact the pope at Savona and acquaint him with the plan of the British navy to rescue him from his French captors. This did not materialize, as the French, on hearing of the plan, moved the pope to Fontainebleau.[4]

The historian of the Scots College described Macpherson as 'a born diplomat', and quoted another historian's description of him as 'endowed with courage and intellectual gifts of a very high order'.[5] His possession of these gifts is rather questionable. He was a very loyal and active agent for Poynter,[6] but his diplomatic skills were far from evident in most of his work. Though only 56 in 1812, his handwriting was very shaky and he was guilty of occasional grammatical lapses. However, he made the acquaintance of Monsignor Quarantotti, the vice prefect or acting superior of Propaganda, and persuasively relayed to him Poynter's arguments and queries. He also successfully cultivated Michele Galeassi, Quarantotti's chief aide or 'substitute'. En route from Scotland to Rome, he had stopped in London, where he had held long conversations with Poynter, and learned all about the complaints that vicar apostolic had against Troy and Milner. Arriving in Rome, he was ready and willing to pass these on to any official at the congregation of Propaganda who was prepared to listen to him. Milner complained to Troy of the advantage that Poynter had gained over them 'in possessing a keen and experienced agent actually on the principal scene of action'.[7] And later both Milner and Cardinal Litta deprecated the influence Macpherson obtained over the ageing vice prefect, Quarantotti.[8]

---

3 Poynter paved the way for Macpherson's work in Rome by informing the congregation of Propaganda about the pain Milner had caused him and his predecessor by his interference in the London District (Poynter to Propaganda, 2 Nov. 1812, APF, SC(Anglia), 6, ff 347r–348r). He also gave Macpherson copies of his correspondence with Troy. 4 McRoberts, *Abbé Paul Macpherson, 1756–1846*, p. 12. 5 McCluskey, *The Scots College Rome, 1600–2000*, pp 59–67. 6 Strangely, Poynter's vicar general, Joseph Hodgson, expressed anxiety on hearing of Macpherson's return to Rome. He claimed that Macpherson had said he was going to negotiate the veto without consulting the clergy in England, and mistakenly thought he was in cahoots with Milner (Hodgson to Poynter, 14 Sept. 1812, WDA). 7 Milner to Troy, 25 Jan. 1814, DDA. 8 Quarantotti (1733–1820), a career bureaucrat, had become secretary of the congregation of

Milner feared that the Scotsman would misrepresent Troy and himself on behalf of Poynter and Coxe-Hippisley. Despondent about their situation, he quite unrealistically harked back to the solution that had already been rejected more than six years previously. He confided to Troy that 'there appears to me but one practicable remedy for the dreadful divisions and schisms which exist amongst us and that is for the Holy See to invest me with some sort of jurisdiction in the London Dist.'. If this was meant to be an appeal to the archbishop of Dublin to raise this possibility with Rome again, it was of no avail. Troy realized that the Roman authorities would not find any reason to overturn a decision which had been reached after serious investigation. But Milner, doubting the abilities and bona fides of both Poynter and Collingridge, the vicar apostolic of the Western District, to deal with their domestic enemies – the Cisalpine Club and the refractory French bishops – claimed that if the congregation of Propaganda had understood the situation, it would not have given faculties to Poynter, the '*fautor* [promoter] of schism'.[9]

His fear of Macpherson bringing his influence to bear on behalf of Poynter proved to be well-founded. The Scotsman quickly informed the congregation about Milner's intervening in the jurisdictions of others, and followed this up with a hostile report on the similar activity of the Irish bishops, and especially of Troy. He claimed that the able and capable Troy, who as prior of San Clemente in Rome and as agent for the Irish bishops, had got to know various officials of the congregation, especially Cardinal Borgia, whom he had sedulously cultivated and through whose patronage and against the normal rules, he had become bishop of Ossory and later archbishop of Dublin. He had then became a little pope in Ireland, regulating the ecclesiastical affairs of the country. Then, greedy for more power, he had started to interfere in the affairs of England. And so he had strongly recommended Milner for episcopal office, and had later constituted him agent, not only for Ireland, but also for England and Scotland, without consulting the bishops of those countries. He then tried to have Milner appointed an archbishop or general visitator but then Cardinal Borgia had died and the plan had miscarried. Troy nonetheless protected Milner in all his extravagant statements as if they were decrees of the Holy See. Having scandalized both Catholics and Protestants by supporting Milner's rejection of the fifth resolution, he threatened Bishop Douglass with excommunication, if a sufficient reason were not given for restoring faculties to a French priest, de Trevaux – an action he defended by claiming that every bishop

Propaganda in 1808. 9 Milner to Troy, 2 Jan. 1813, DDA. Milner forwarded to Troy a letter from Cardinal della Somaglia to a friend of his in France in which Milner's pamphlet dealing with the fifth resolution, the part played by the Irish bishops and the condemnations of Blanchard and de Trevaux were praised.

should vigilantly guard the purity of the faith. This, Macpherson maintained, was a dangerous, scandalous and erroneous proposition. In fact, the French priest had sought pardon and given proof of his innocence. If Douglass had done what Troy did, the archbishop of Dublin would not only have excommunicated him but would have had him burned, if possible. Had the English bishops wished to fish in the dark waters of Irish dioceses, they would have found a great catch, but they were too learned in canon law to do so. He therefore asked the congregation to use its authority to prevent such intrusion in the future.[10]

On the same day as Macpherson made this submission to Propaganda, Troy's agent told him in a letter that both Macpherson and John Connolly, an Irish Dominican, had taken part in a meeting at the congregation with Monsignor Quarantotti. Macpherson seems to have made a submission in writing but there is no evidence of Connolly having done so. Whether by the written or spoken word, Macpherson used every opportunity to draw attention to Troy's alleged transgressions. Propaganda then informed Troy that it had not reached any decision about the complaints made to it against Milner and some Irish bishops, but it felt bound to warn Milner not to interfere in the affairs of the other vicars apostolic and to chide Troy for rebuking the vicar apostolic of London for restoring faculties to de Trevaux, which was none of his business. Reference was also made to the condemnation of the views of the vicars apostolic in Dublin in February 1810, to Milner's subsequent publication of it and to various other improper interventions. Quarantotti concluded his observations by reminding Troy that controversies among bishops should be referred to the Holy See, and begged him not to meddle in matters which did not concern him.[11] Troy subsequently responded to these accusations, and the whole hierarchy wrote and signed a letter defending their agent's role in the various controversies about the fifth resolution, the Blanchard schismatical writings and the dispute about de Trevaux.[12]

However, a matter which concerned both the vicars apostolic and the Irish bishops soon engaged Milner's and Troy's attention: Grattan's bill for

10 Macpherson to Propaganda (copy), 20 Feb. 1813, WDA. Troy did not propose Milner for an archbishopric. Borgia died before Troy proposed Milner's transfer to London. On 1 Jan. 1814 Poynter complained forcefully to Quarantotti about the persecution he was suffering from Milner in various writings and in the *Orthodox Journal* (APF, SC(Anglia), 6, ff 417r–418r). 11 Propaganda to Troy, 20 Feb. 1813, DDA. Daniel Murray, the coadjutor archbishop of Dublin, at the same time, in a characteristically conciliatory letter to Poynter, tried to mend fences with him by explaining that the Irish bishops only wanted evidence of de Trevaux's retraction to end the scandal (Murray to Poynter (copy), 17 Feb. 1813, WDA).   12 Bishops to Cardinal di Pietro, 12 Nov. 1813, APF, SC(Anglia) 6, ff 393r–394r. Milner covered much of the same ground in a letter to Mgr Caleppi, the nuncio in Brazil, who passed it on to Rome (9 Jan. 1814, ibid., ff 408r–410r) and to Quarantotti (18 Feb. 1814, ibid., f 544v).

Catholic relief. Milner distrusted intensely the alleged friends of emancipation – Coxe-Hippisley, Grattan, Ponsonby, Castlereagh, Grey and Grenville
– as vetoists, and he suspected that Coxe-Hippisley desired the establishment
of a ministry of religious affairs on the French model, with himself as
minister. Writing to Troy he reserved his worst scorn for Poynter, whom he
accused of weakness in dealing with these politicians. He explained that he
had recently left London 'chiefly to avoid being called upon to act or give my
opinion with such a poor pliable creature as Dr Poynter', with whom, nevertheless, he would be reconciled but for the need to preserve the doctrine and
unity of the church. Maintaining that Poynter's was 'a soul of artifice
entrenched in sophistry', he hoped to get a passport to travel to Rome as
'some precaution against the weak cringing disposition of Dr Poynter'
seemed necessary.[13]

Petitions for Catholic relief (and numerous counter-petitions) had been
presented in 1811 and 1812, and the English and Irish Catholic boards each
planned to present one in 1813. As the English board prepared to draw up its
petition, Poynter requested that it be unambiguous and that matters of
religion be left to the guidance of the vicars apostolic. Collingridge, on
hearing of the terms of the petition, feared that it would 'egregiously
exasperate the Irish and commit us with them in the most hostile and decided
manner', as it would unnecessarily remind them of the Grey-Grenville intervention.[14] He was pleased to find the members accommodating. Grattan, in
anticipation of submitting a bill with the support of George Ponsonby and
William Elliott, had commissioned Charles Butler to draft one, with the
restriction that the rights of the Protestant church and Protestant succession
be guaranteed.[15] Butler informed Edward Hay, the secretary of the Irish
Catholic Board, that he had been requested by a parliamentary friend to
provide a 'sketch' of a bill for the repeal of all laws in force against Catholics.
He forwarded a 'sketch' to Denys Scully, an Irish lawyer and member of the
Catholic Committee, who declined 'any particular consideration' of it, but
submitted some 'observations' to which Butler attended. During this time,
Butler had a conversation with Lord Castlereagh, who complained of the
intemperance of the speeches at the Irish board, and of the Irish insistence
'upon having everything without any qualification whatsoever'. The government, in consequence, could not attend to those excessive demands.[16]

The bishop of Waterford, John Power, was alerted to the rumours about
the contents of the bill by his friend, the Whig Sir John Newport, who was
the MP for Waterford city. Newport expressed the hope that the Irish

13 Milner to Troy, 5, 25 Mar. 1813, DDA.   14 Collingridge to Poynter, 2 Feb. 1813, WDA.
15 Grattan's successful motion that the house should go into committee to consider the laws
relating to Catholics was 'his greatest parliamentary victory since 1782' (McDowell, *Grattan: a
life*, p. 208).   16 Butler to Hay, 29 Mar. 1813, in *DEP*, 29 June 1813.

bishops would propose an arrangement, which, while not infringing on doctrine or discipline, would ward off the danger of foreign influence, either through a negative exercised by a commission of bishops with perhaps a layman appointed by the crown, or by domestic nomination with reservation in extreme cases to the pope. Power feared that if the pope rejected a plan proposed by the bishops, the consequences would be very bad.[17] Troy did not approve of either of Newport's arrangements, though he thought domestic nomination might be conceded if the canonical institution were reserved to the pope. He thought a general meeting should be called to discuss Grattan's proposals.[18]

Catholics mostly welcomed Grattan's bill, which was presented on 30 April 1813 as it was not burdened with the kinds of restrictions they disliked. British Catholics were to be given the franchise (Irish Catholics had enjoyed it since 1793), and all Catholics were to have the right to sit in and vote in parliament, and to hold all offices in the army, navy and corporations; they were only excluded from the offices of lord lieutenant and lord chancellor, and from appointing clergy to livings in the established church. They were obliged to take an oath which imposed nothing much beyond what was contained in the Irish oath of 1793. They were obliged to defend the succession to the crown as limited to the heirs of Princess Sophia, being Protestants, to declare that they did not believe in papal infallibility and to deny that sin could be forgiven by any pope or priest without sincere sorrow. The usual repudiations of the pope's temporal and deposing powers were also included. The clergy were obliged to swear that they would not be responsible for the appointment of bishops, deans or vicars apostolic who were not men of 'unimpeachable loyalty and peaceable conduct', and would not correspond with Rome except on purely spiritual and ecclesiastical business, and not on any matter leading directly or indirectly to the overthrow of the Protestant government or Protestant church. No foreign priest was to become a bishop in Britain or Ireland, and none who had not been resident there for the previous five years.

The demand for safeguards and securities soon arose. The more politicians emphasized securities, the stronger and more political became the resistance of the Irish Catholics to the bill.[19] Already, Castlereagh, in the debates about the preliminary motion, had drawn attention to the need for safeguards when the pope was 'being detained by our most inveterate enemy, [and] may be compelled to become the instrument of his perfidious and ambitious views'.[20] Lord Liverpool, the prime minister, who wanted no

17 Power to Bray, 20 Mar. 1813, CaDA.   18 Troy to Bray, 27 Mar. 1813, ibid.   19 Leighton, CDA, 'Gallicanism and the veto controversy: church, state and Catholic community in early nineteenth century Ireland' in R.V. Comerford, M. Cullen, J.R. Hill and C. Lennon (eds), *Religion, conflict and coexistence in Ireland*, pp 145–9.   20 *Hansard*, xxiv, 1018–28, 2 Mar. 1813.

change in the principle of 1688 of a Protestant king and a Protestant state, opposed the bill.[21] George Canning, a supporter of Catholic emancipation, who maintained that he was very anxious to carry the bill, introduced amendments to disarm its critics.[22] The securities which he introduced were to embrace both the veto and the *exequatur*. His plan was to form two commissions (one for England and one for Ireland) consisting of Catholic peers or prominent commoners to advise the king on the election of bishops and deans, and to inspect bulls and dispensations from Rome. These commissions were to testify to the loyalty of the candidate for episcopal office without which he could not exercise his functions. Priests electing candidates for episcopal office were obliged to swear that they were loyal to the throne. The pope would give canonical institution to the candidate accepted by the king, and would give assurances that no political matter would be included in the material from Rome. If a bishop received an official document from Rome and swore that it referred only to spiritual matters, it would not be examined by the commissioners.

This was the first occasion on which the *exequatur* was mentioned in Parliament. It was a right which Catholic rulers often arrogated to themselves, and which Napoleon had claimed in the Organic Articles. The Holy See was forced to submit to it, often under duress, but objected strongly. Still, pragmatism could prevail, and although strong opposition was expressed to a Protestant government exercising that right, it seems likely that, if forced, the Holy See would have tolerated it, or if it were later added to a concordat or agreement as had been done by Napoleon, the Vatican would not have pulled out of the whole agreement because of it.

Robert Peel, who six months previously had become chief secretary for Ireland, and who was to be a persistent opponent of Catholic emancipation, explained his thinking to the lord lieutenant:

> at no time and under no circumstances, so long as the Catholic admits the supremacy in spirituals of a foreign earthly potentate, and will not tell us what supremacy in spirituals means – so long as he will not give us voluntarily that security which every despotic sovereign in Europe has by the concession of the pope himself – will I consent to admit them. They are excluded from privileges for which they will not pay the price that all other subjects pay, and that all other Catholics in Europe feel themselves bound to pay.[23]

Castlereagh claimed that the veto was not proposed by himself or his colleagues but was 'formally and explicitly proposed to His Majesty's ministers by the Roman Catholics themselves'. 21 Gash, *Lord Liverpool*, p. 106.   22 W. Hinde, *George Canning*, pp 263–4.   23 Peel to the duke of Richmond, 2 Mar. 1813, in Parker, *Sir Robert Peel from his private papers*, i, p. 76.

A little later, he expressed his support for Castlereagh's views, which he took to be:

> that the crown should have a direct influence, in its nature somewhat resembling the veto in the appointment of Catholic bishops. And that a provision should be made from the public funds for the maintenance of their clergy, similar to that which is granted annually to the seceding ministers in Ireland. It is not very probable that the Catholics will accede to these terms.[24]

Canning had been in touch with Troy about the commissions. And as the archbishop later explained in a public letter to Daniel O'Connell, he had been given a copy of the heads of the bill on 2 April by Lord Donoughmore. In his reply, he had 'deprecated any lay interference, not authorized by the church' in the appointment of bishops and 'particularly objected to the proposed inquisitorial, close, absolute and summary commissions or boards of five lay persons ... as a kind of lay eldership unknown in our church government'. He had also made known to Lord Fingall that the exclusion of bishops from the commissions was insulting to their clergy and held out a suspicion of disloyalty. Troy then received a note from Canning explaining that the two commissions had been altered to admit four new commissioners – the lord chancellor, the chief secretary and two archbishops – and proposing that one of the three composing a quorum should be a Protestant. Troy replied that the commission should consist of a majority of prelates or at least of an equal number of peers and prelates, and pointed out that no change in the appointment of bishops could take place without the sanction of the pope.

Writing to Bishop Moylan, Troy mentioned his fear that some of the peers on the commissions might be nominal Catholics, but in reality deists. And he ruled out the transmission of correspondence with the Holy See through the commissions. He also feared that an effectual negative might in time become a positive.[25] Canning was not disposed to accept these suggestions. In a subsequent communication with Lord Donoughmore, he expressed the hope that the bill would be free from all 'revolting provisos' and the complex machinery of securities would be simplified.[26]

By agreement in the house of commons, the bill was reprinted to incorporate the clauses about the commissions which had been revised. In the new

---

24 Ibid., 12 May 1813, p. 84. Peel, worried about the problem of maintaining Protestant ascendancy in a country with 4 million Catholics and only 800,000 Protestants, believed that they should crush the Catholic Board, and 'destroy the seeds of future boards, committees and conventions'. He got his way in 1814 (Gash, *Mr Secretary Peel*, pp 156–8).   25 Troy to Moylan, 8 Apr. 1813, CaDA.   26 Troy to O'Connell, 4 June 1813, in *DEP*, 8 June 1813.

version, in each commission there would be five Catholic peers or prominent commoners, one or more Protestant privy councillors, the archbishops of Armagh and Dublin for the Irish commission, and the vicar apostolic of the London District for the English commission. The archbishop or senior prelate was obliged to let the commission know the name of the candidate proposed for a bishopric, and the commissioners within six weeks would pass on to the king or lord lieutenant their views on his loyalty. Within ten days the king or lord lieutenant would approve or disapprove of the nomination. If the candidate were rejected the procedure would be repeated. But if a candidate took up office without approval he would be subject to exile from the country. An ecclesiastic receiving a document from Rome could swear that in conscience it concerned personal, spiritual matters and the communication would not then be submitted to the commission.

The terms of the bill did not make clear how many times the commission could reject a candidate proposed for a bishopric. If no limit were placed to its powers of blackballing candidates, the negative power would become a positive power of appointing someone who was deemed to be *persona grata* to the government. Though the *exequatur* or investigation of documents was limited, it was by its very nature an unwelcome intrusion into confidential communications between the bishops and Rome.

As the bill was being debated, some of the Irish bishops became more anxious about its contents. Moylan told Troy that Canning's additions would have to be 'reprobated',[27] and O'Shaughnessy of Killaloe, detecting the government's veto not in disguise but in a more public form, complained that it was usurping their rights. He demanded a meeting to protest against the innovations.[28] Young of Limerick deplored 'the shackling conditions they were to be laid under by the restrictions agreed to'.[29] In response to these demands and also to a complaint from Milner about his silence,[30] Troy summoned the bishops to a general meeting.

Before a vote was taken in the house of commons the Irish bishops met, and after expressing their gratitude to parliament declared that they could not assent to 'certain arrangements respecting our ecclesiastical discipline' without incurring the guilt of schism as those arrangements would have invaded papal jurisdiction. They objected to commissioners recommending or rejecting candidates and examining documents from Rome. They drew up resolutions to this effect and went on to pledge their willingness never to consent to the appointment of any bishop whom they judged not to be 'of unimpeachable loyalty and peaceable conduct', and their willingness not to enter into any communication with the pope or a representative of his to

---

27 Moylan to Troy, 8 May 1813, CaDA. 28 O'Shaughnessy to Bray, 8 May 1813, ibid.
29 Young to Bray, 16 May 1813, ibid. 30 Bray to Moylan, 15 May 1813, CRDA.

overthrow or disturb the Protestant government or the established church or the Church of Scotland.[31] They also expressed their confidence in their 'vigilant incorruptible agent' Milner. Milner, as was to be expected, took great exception to the proposals about the commissions, claiming that no Catholic could be a member without committing schism. Poynter, meanwhile, had agreed substantially with the Irish bishops and was strongly opposed to giving his concurrence to the clauses about securities, but distinguished between concurrence and submission, if the securities were imposed.[32] He hoped, in line with Troy's thinking, that the commissions would be altered to ensure that half their members would be bishops. But he feared that popular Irish rejection of the bill would have a very deleterious effect in the long term. He told Macpherson that 'the violence, which the Irish have showed, has injured the cause of emancipation so much that the general opinion is that we are further from complete emancipation than we were last year'.[33]

Milner hastened to London and quickly circulated a 'brief memorial' denouncing the bill to members of the house of commons.[34] Describing the commission as 'more secret and arbitrary in its forms than the Star Chamber or the Inquisition', he maintained that the prelates who joined it would be undeservedly degraded in their civil characters, in their own body and in the public at large. It was incompatible with the characters and duties of bishops and priests to submit their correspondence with Rome to the opinion of laypeople. In a postscript he added that 'the pure, undisguised and unrestricted veto is added to the oppressive, unconstitutional clauses against the Catholic clergy', and declared that such measures could 'never have been countenanced by any of the members of the legislature had they not been suggested by certain false brethren of the Catholic body'.[35]

The English Catholic Board, some of whose members were very keen to take seats in parliament and who did not want to see their ambitions frustrated by what they regarded as ecclesiastical prejudices, resumed its uninhibited stance of the 1790s. It replied to this broadside and encouraged the legislature, in language reminiscent of previous jousts with the vicars apostolic, to proceed 'regardless of the interference of unaccredited individuals'. Milner attended a meeting of the board called to discuss the bill, and then in the presence of Poynter and Collingridge insisted that no Catholic

31 *DEP*, 29 May 1813. O'Connell read the bishops' address at the Catholic Board on 29 May and his comments on the membership of the commission could not have been more scathing, lambasting possible members such as Saurin, the anti-Catholic attorney general and Peel. It was on this occasion that he described Peel as 'a raw youth, squeezed out of the workings of I know not what cotton factory in England ... and was sent over here before he had got rid of the foppery of perfumed handkerchiefs and thin shoes ...' (*DEP*, 1 June 1813).   32 Ward, *The eve of Catholic emancipation*, i, pp 39–40.   33 Poynter to Macpherson, 6 Dec. 1813, AVEC, 55.1.7.   34 A brief memorial on the Catholic bill, *DEP*, 29 May 1813.   35 *DEP*, 29 May 1813.

bishop or layman could become a member of the commission or take the oath required to do so without committing schism. When the house went into committee, the speaker proposed that the clause in the bill giving Catholics the right to sit and vote in parliament should be rejected. By a majority of four votes this proposal was carried, and so the bill collapsed.[36]

The majority of the English Catholic Board was angered by Milner's role in helping to destroy the bill, and decided to take revenge by expelling him from the board. He was invited to attend a meeting, and when challenged about his reference to 'false brethren' in the 'brief memorial', he admitted that he had had Charles Butler in mind. A resolution was then passed praising Butler and another dismissing Milner. The vicar apostolic of the Midland District, however hurt he may have been by this action, must have drawn comfort from the compliments paid to him by the Irish bishops, who resolved at their meeting that he continued to possess their esteem, confidence and gratitude.[37] And Bishop Smith, the coadjutor of the Northern District, greatly regretted the action of the board.[38]

A few weeks later, a friend of Milner's founded 'the *Orthodox Journal or Catholic Monthly Intelligencer*', and he was free to use its pages to expound his views on religious questions and to lambaste his opponents, both clerical and lay. He did so in characteristically robust language. He denounced Grattan's bill as 'cruel and most insulting' and wondered if there was ever 'a more shameful or more unblushing attack on the Catholic clergy'.[39] The *Orthodox Journal* disgusted the other vicars apostolic and the grandees of the Catholic Board by its vehement and immoderate criticism of anything approaching a concession on a royal veto, but it won support among the middle and lower middle classes in the towns and cities. Many of these readers supported Milner and resented the role taken by the grandees in the church.

Troy wrote to Propaganda explaining that Poynter and two other vicars apostolic, though disapproving of the conditions in the bill, expressed a willingness to submit to it to obtain emancipation, thereby enslaving themselves to free the Catholic laity. Recalling the votes of thanks passed at public meetings in Ireland to the bishops and to the intrepid Milner for his manly and just opposition to the bill, Troy concluded by pointing out that Poynter and the other vicars apostolic, when asked by Milner to give their public assent to the pastoral of the Irish bishops, remained silent for fear of offending the English Catholic nobility.[40]

36 Castlereagh's biographer claims that he would 'not have considered pushing the measure had he not believed victory was possible' (Bew, *Castlereagh, enlightment, war and tyranny*, p. 308). 37 Husenbeth, *Life of Bishop Milner*, pp 230–42. Milner and Butler had been 'reconciled' at a private meeting on 19 Feb. 1813, but Milner had soon rejected a statement put out by the mediators which had been designed to settle their differences.   38 Smith to Collingridge, 9 July 1813, CIDA.   39 *OJ*, June 1813.   40 Troy to Quarantotti, 3 Aug. 1813, APF, *Acta* 177, ff 43r–45v.

Butler came in for criticism at the Irish board partly as a result of Milner's excoriation of him, and partly from the publication of his letters to Edward Hay, the board's secretary. Nicholas O'Gorman, a friend of O'Connell's, criticized Butler for a lack of commitment to the purity of his religion, improper conduct towards bishops and unauthorized interference with the concerns of Irish Catholics.[41]

Milner was profoundly grateful for the thanks of the Irish bishops and the Irish board. Remarking that his 'poor mercenary brethren Poynter and Collingridge' would have 'submitted' to the terms of the bill, he declared that he could not refrain from denouncing them to Troy as '*fautors of a twofold schism*, that of Blanchard and that of Charles Butler'.[42]

Milner's comments on Poynter grew more extreme and abusive as he reflected on the events surrounding the bill. He commented on Poynter's '*doublefaced, doubletongued* conduct and language', and referring to a rumour that Poynter might be raised 'to a superior authority in our mission' he declared that, if so, he would 'seriously and earnestly solicit my discharge from my post and from the mission, being unwilling to see that ruin of religion, which I know to be the consequence of the present system'.[43]

Poynter, who was wounded by the 'libellous pamphlets' that Milner circulated against him in London and elsewhere, was also annoyed by Milner's Irish supporters. But he maintained that the English Catholics would not be influenced by their 'violent temper' and he queried the motives of the Irish Catholics:

> Those amongst the Irish who are the loudest in their cries for emancipation, would many of them be the most unwilling to see it granted and the Irish bishops must be most perplexed to determine what is most *expedient* to be done in the circumstances.[44]

Faced with the difficulty of not knowing what, if any, concessions might be made to the government in connection with episcopal appointments, should another similar bill be brought in, the vicars apostolic of England and Scotland met in Durham on 25 October 1813. They had been urged to do so by the 'noblemen and gentlemen' of the Catholic Board, who were anxious to find out what might 'be conscientiously admitted or submitted to', and who were prepared to defray the participants' expenses. Poynter was loath to invite Milner, in case 'he would communicate everything to the Irish bishops

---

41 *DEP*, 8 July 1813. 42 Milner to Troy, 19 June 1813, DDA. Milner wrote that he deeply felt 'the superabundant recompense which the Catholics of Ireland have made to me for the affronts put upon me by my half-Catholic brethren of this island' (Milner to Scully, 17 June 1813, in MacDermot, *The Catholic question in Ireland and England, 1798–1822*, p. 465). 43 Milner to Troy, 10, 19 Dec. 1813, DDA. 44 Poynter to Gibson, 21 July 1813, LDA.

and even to the public in some pamphlet or other'. His hope was that they could obtain an answer from Rome 'to settle the minds of the Catholics'. He consulted his other two colleagues in England and the vicars apostolic of Scotland, some of whom agreed about the danger of Milner's presence.[45] Milner was not invited.

The bishops' deliberations lasted ten days. Their pastoral letter, signed by the vicar apostolic of the Northern District and his coadjutor and then by the other vicars apostolic for their districts, was read throughout Britain, except in Milner's district. It certainly seemed to exclude any acceptance of conditions or restrictions which would have limited the pope's freedom in making episcopal appointments, but references to their willingness to accept the terms of the fifth resolution renewed that searing dispute and enabled opponents to accuse the bishops of being willing to surrender their ecclesiastical freedom to obtain emancipation.

Having praised their people for their fidelity and loyalty to king and country, they assured them that amid any changes which might ameliorate their condition in the state 'no change whatever may be admitted inconsistent with the faith or discipline of the Roman Catholic Church'. The bishops were resolved 'to the utmost of their power to remove any obstacle or difficulty which might interfere' with the attainment of emancipation. Harking back to the contentious fifth resolution, they noted that while they expressed their conviction 'that adequate provision for the maintenance of the civil and religious establishments of this kingdom might be made ... consistently with the strictest adherence on their part to the tenets and discipline of the Roman Catholic religion', they were bound to guard against pledging themselves to 'any measures that might not be perfectly consistent with the integrity and safety of their religion and thus to declare that any arrangement, founded on the basis of mutual satisfaction and security and extending to them the civil constitution of the country, will meet with their grateful concurrence'. But such arrangements 'founded on this basis of *mutual satisfaction and security* must preclude, on their part, the idea of any concurrence in, or approbation of, any restriction or condition that might possibly prejudice the integrity or safety of the Catholic religion'. Catholics were praised for their determination not to surrender any point of their religion for the advantages of emancipation, and for their readiness to refer any terms of emancipation 'to the judgment and decision of their pastors'. The free appointment of those pastors was required not by any spirit of independence from the state, but to ensure that they were faithful ministers of salvation.

Expressing confidence that the British legislature would not propose any restrictions on the Catholic clergy that were painful or humiliating, the

---

45 Poynter to Collingridge, 3 July 1813, CIDA.

bishops declared that they could not consent to any restrictions on the pope's power in spiritual matters, in the appointment of vicars apostolic or in his communication with the members of the church on spiritual concerns. Catholics, in their oaths, had always made a clear distinction between the submission they owed to the pope and that which they owed to the king, and had disclaimed all rights or pretensions of foreign princes or prelates to any civil authority or jurisdiction in the realm. Being loyal subjects, they hoped that no unmerited or degrading restrictions would be imposed on the British Catholic clergy. Some of the clauses in the last bill contained such restrictions, which those who framed it were compelled by 'groundless prejudices' to include. Catholics who enjoyed any influence were encouraged to use it legally, mildly and peaceably 'to prevent a repetition' of unacceptable clauses in a future bill, and to ensure that their clergy were 'free in the exercise of their spiritual functions'.[46]

This pastoral, drafted by Poynter, apart from the reference to the fifth resolution, was skilfully crafted, clearly expressed and balanced. Had members of parliament who were not ill-disposed to Catholics read it, they would surely have seen the 'reasonableness of the Catholic case'. Poynter, for some time, had been coming under pressure from the aristocracy and gentry of the Catholic Board to conciliate the members of parliament who were favourable to emancipation but believed that unless concessions were made about the appointment of bishops, their opponents would defeat any bills for Catholic relief. This may explain his use of the language of the fifth resolution which had already caused so much controversy, and which was bound to give a hostage to fortune.

And this was one of the elements of the pastoral that Troy singled out for criticism. Bishop Gibson sent him a copy, and in a hard-hitting and discourteous reply, revealing the influence of Milner's animus against his colleagues, Troy listed his objections to it. Expressing himself pleased with its disapproval of restrictions on the pope's power in appointing bishops or in communicating with the church, he regretted that it did not condemn other restrictions in the recent bill as inadmissible, rather than disapproving of them as painful to their feelings. He then turned to the fifth resolution and, in what must have struck Gibson and those to whom he showed the letter as an unjustified intervention, he commented on the exclusion of Milner from the meeting:

> Above all I regret, that by the uncanonical and indecorous exclusion of Doctor Milner from the late meeting at Durham, so long previously announced in the public prints, Your Lordship and

46 Pastoral of Bishop Gibson, 27 Oct. 1813, DDA.

confrères have in a great degree identified yourselves with and followed the unbecoming example of those lay persons, however otherwise respectable who ignominiously to themselves expelled him from their board for advocating with the incorruptible firmness that has long distinguished him the integrity of our church discipline ... [47]

Gibson was then 75 years of age, ill and partially incapacitated. This bombshell from Troy would certainly not have helped him in his weak condition. Whatever else the exclusion of Milner from the meeting was, it was certainly not uncanonical. Meetings of bishops both in Ireland and Britain were not held in a synodical manner and therefore the refusal to invite anyone to them was a matter for the others to decide. Milner had no canonical right to participate, and it was certainly not Troy's place to rebuke Gibson or the other vicars apostolic for not inviting him. The whole Catholic community was congratulated on its determination not 'to surrender one point of their religion for all the advantages of their civil emancipation'. But as Gibson himself had been firm in opposing any change in the way bishops were appointed or in giving the state any right to check documents from Rome, perhaps he would not have felt so strongly against Troy as the other two must have done when they heard about his letter.

Milner, who was determined to go to France or Italy to put his case to Roman officials as soon as he could wangle permission and a passport,[48] was outraged by the reference to the fifth resolution in the pastoral. He told Troy that Jerningham, the secretary of the English board, had claimed that 'the English would steer a quite opposite course to the Irish, as they would *conciliate, not bully* etc.'. He believed therefore that Jerningham and his board, and 'Dr Poynter with his bench' had placed 'the affairs of the British Caths. exactly in the situation they were in after the meeting at the St Alban's Tavern'. 'The laity,' he continued, 'surrender their religion at the discretion of Protestants ... and the bishops with a few cold and unmeaning salvos promise to go along with them in the measure being prepared to excuse themselves when the schism is irretrievable [*sic*] (as I found them disposed to do in last May) by saying *who could have thought it? And who could help it?*' The laity, he maintained, and the vicars apostolic had renewed the war against the laity and prelates of Ireland.[49]

Poynter's private sentiments about Milner were no less robust. He told a Roman friend that Milner had lost his character for veracity with both Catholics and Protestants. It was an absolute disgrace to the Catholic name

47 Troy to Gibson (copy), 20 Dec. 1813, ibid. 48 Milner to Troy, 10 Dec. 1813, ibid.
49 Ibid., 19 Dec. 1813.

and episcopal character that he should so publicly violate the truth. He explained that 'some to excuse him from moral guilt say that he must be deranged in his mind', and deplored the trust the Irish bishops who had joined with the 'violent democrats' placed in him.[50]

Shortly after the conference at Durham, the Irish bishops came to Milner's defence by writing to Cardinal di Pietro in France. Di Pietro was prefect of the congregation of Propaganda, but in his absence from Rome, Quarantotti had taken it upon himself to charge Milner with inappropriate interventions in other vicariates and with condemnations of the decisions made there. The bishops, in a lengthy Latin letter, defended their agent and the commendable part he had played in several crises, recalling the controversies about the veto in 1808, the fifth resolution in 1810, the schismatical clauses of the recent bill, the disputes about Blanchard's schism, the restoration of faculties to de Trevaux without his making a public retraction and the wish of many members of parliament to diminish episcopal authority. And they claimed that many Catholic nobles were prepared to exchange the liberty of the church for their own privileges and advantages. The letter concluded with the offensive slur that Milner had publicized against Poynter, namely, that these Catholic nobles had created a fund for Poynter after he had signed the fifth resolution.[51]

Macpherson got hold of this letter at the congregation of Propaganda, and, blaming it on Troy, described it as 'abominable', and let Poynter know some of the charges that were in it. Poynter, consulting Collingridge, wondered whether he should let their nobility know about the charges against them, but thought it more advisable to hold back. Macpherson, however, had some good news for him. Quarantotti had assembled 'a dozen of the first canonists at Rome' to examine the ecclesiastical clauses of Grattan's bill.[52] In the campaign for emancipation another thorny and perplexing phase was about to begin. The bill, which like some of the failed petitions, might have been quickly forgotten, was destined, as a result of Quarantotti's decision, to lead to controversial proposals and acrimonious disputes. Quarantotti, because of O'Connell's vigorous denunciation of him, and the reverberations of that hostility in Rome, was to acquire a fame far beyond his station as a Roman bureaucrat.

50 Poynter to Loreto Coradius, 7 Mar. 1814, AVEC, 55/2/11.   51 Troy and other bishops to Cardinal di Pietro (copy), 12 Nov. 1813, DDA.   52 Poynter to Collingridge, 25 Mar. 1814, CIDA. The verdict had been given before this letter was written but Poynter had not received it.

10

The Quarantotti rescript

I

A fter the defeat of Grattan's bill, Poynter forwarded it in full, together with a summary, to Macpherson, but his letter with the full text went astray. He believed that a similar bill would be brought forward in the following year and he wanted to know what Rome would permit the vicars apostolic to accept and whether they could submit to certain terms which they might dislike, if emancipation were part of the package. A verdict from Rome would both relieve his own conscience and allow him to give to the Catholic Committee a definitive judgment on the acceptability of all or part of the bill. Whether the committee agreed to the Roman decision or not the vicars apostolic would not have to engage in a running argument about it as had happened in 1789–90. The blame could be put on Rome if the terms of the bill were substantially rejected.

Accordingly, Poynter sought guidance especially on parts of the bill which he thought were dubious and too vague. He explained that he had told one of the framers of the bill that a priest would be embarrassed if his testimony of loyalty or approbation by the king were refused after his appointment by Rome. But he had been assured that the bishops or pope could provide against that by procuring a testament of loyalty before matters reached that stage. When he had objected that the words 'peaceable conduct' were 'too wide and undefined', he had been informed that Milner had suggested them. The members of parliament were so instructed by Coxe-Hippisley about the arrangements for episcopal appointments in Europe that they would not let a disloyal man or one who was not of peaceable conduct exercise an office of such influence in England or Ireland. One of those who composed the bill had told Poynter that cases might arise when the government would suspect something treasonable might be contained in letters from Rome, and hence would have to have them examined, though letters containing matters of conscience would be excluded.

Poynter remarked that certain clauses were not admissible without the approval of the Holy See and confessed that, on further reflection, he was glad the bill had been rejected. He felt however that there was nothing objectionable in the oath, as it contained nothing which had not been tolerated by the Holy See and been taken in Britain and Ireland for twenty years. That part of the oath where the person was to swear not to overthrow or disturb the Protestant church caused no problems, if it were understood to be by force. It did not imply that Catholics could not propagate their faith. The clause by which no candidate could be appointed to a bishopric who was not born of British or Irish parents and who had not been domiciled in either country for five years, could not be accepted without the approval of the Holy See.[1] Poynter complained that Catholics' oaths were not accepted as others' were, and that they were placed under the scrutiny of a tribunal. For two hundred years, even in the midst of persecutions, Catholics had never been disloyal, and their catechisms and books of moral theology stressed loyalty to sovereigns. He therefore asked for guidance on those points that required the approval of the Holy See. Noting that the penalty for bishops exercising their ministry without authorization from the king was exile, he wondered if the vicars apostolic should say to Catholics that rather than consent to certain clauses, if the bill were again introduced, they should 'go with their bishops into exile and leave Britain without a single Catholic'.

Commenting on Milner and the Irish bishops, Poynter reported to Rome their views that it would be an act of schism to abide by clauses in the bill which authorized a commission to attest to the loyalty of Catholic bishops. But the Irish bishops did not say that no Catholic could submit to them. Irish Catholics, he regretted to say, were obstructive and desirous of independence:

> The Irish people are in many places very violent. There are powerful parties amongst them; there is one faction loud for emancipation, but which does not wish for it, because if it were granted it would defeat their views who wish only to separate Ireland from England. Because the English Catholics are more quiet and conciliatory, we are considered as a people ready to abandon our religion for the sake of getting a few peers into parliament.[2]

Poynter's remark about Catholics going into exile was a rhetorical exaggeration but was later misunderstood in Rome. He could not possibly have meant that English Catholics could lead an exodus from England, presumably followed by Irish Catholics. He was undoubtedly right that English Catholics were more moderate and placatory than Irish Catholics, as befitted a tiny minority with no political clout, but while O'Connell and his

---

1 Had a bill with this clause passed, two of the most influential prelates in the English and Irish churches – the future cardinals Wiseman and Cullen – could not have been appointed.
2 Poynter to Macpherson, 21 June, 28 June 1813 (copies), WDA and APF, *Acta* 177, ff 27r–40v. He later claimed that he and his colleagues were opposed to almost every clause of the bill (ibid., 6 Sept. 1814, APF, CP 146, f 364r).

friends were much more robust in their language, they were certainly not separatists, and to label them as such was both inaccurate and unjust. English critics and newspapers accused them of violence on the basis of their forceful contentions.

Armed with Poynter's letters seeking a judgment from Rome on disputed elements of the bill, Macpherson went to work on Quarantotti to have the issue examined in the full and formal manner which the congregation used under normal circumstances. But the circumstances were far from normal, and with no cardinals in Rome to constitute a full, plenary meeting of the congregation, Quarantotti – as cardinals Pacca and Consalvi later complained – should have confined himself to giving advice until such a serious issue could be examined at the highest level. Macpherson seems to have convinced him of the need to give a definite decision in case, as Poynter had said, the bill or one very similar to it was presented in 1814. The Scotsman gathered together the documents that would be further studied by consultors, whose advice would guide Quarantotti in making his decision. He was able to inform Poynter's friend, Hodgson, that he had put in evidence for the congregation Poynter's narrative (presumably of the late bill), the resolutions of the Irish bishops in 1799, 1808 and 1810, Moylan's letter, Quarantotti's letters to himself and part of a letter from Troy.

For some time, Macpherson explained to Poynter, he had had difficulty in persuading Quarantotti to take 'the question into consideration', but he persuaded his assistant 'to embrace my side of the question'. Then, 'on perusal' of notes which Macpherson had prepared, 'the good old man changed his mind and is now as eager to have the whole matter fully discussed without delay as I am'. He then named 'a whole dozen of the first divines and canonists in the city to sit with him and his substitute on the question' and Macpherson busied himself in drawing up more material for their consideration. He complained of the difficulty in doing so 'as no archive now exists', which was a consequence of the French invasions and the ensuing disruption.[3] Macpherson seems to have cultivated both Quarantotti and Galeassi and won them over to his side.

Apart from collecting material for the examination of the issue, Macpherson realized that he should counteract Troy's submissions, and he did so with zest and virulence. Troy had written an account of the opposition of the Irish bishops to the veto, praising the 'intrepid' Milner for his rejection of it and complaining that Poynter and the other vicars apostolic had been willing to accept a veto insidiously embodied in the fifth resolution and in the arrangements for commissions in the bill of 1813. Macpherson

---

3 The French carted off some of the archives of Propaganda to Paris. Others were left in a disturbed state.

commented at length on many of Troy's arguments. He referred sardonically to Troy's account of the meeting at the St Alban's Tavern – where the fifth resolution was discussed amid clamour and noise – and explained that the meeting took place in a large room at an inn, not amid the clinking of glasses, and repeated the charges against Milner's role on that occasion. He rehashed the controversy about Blanchard and de Trevaux, recalled the acceptance of a veto by the Irish bishops in 1799 and denounced the interference of the Irish bishops in the affairs of the English church. He claimed without evidence that the Irish bishops had tried to have Milner elevated to the position of metropolitan of Britain,[4] and he remarked sarcastically that they should find a large field for their zeal in their own dioceses. And he contemptuously dismissed Troy's accusation, which he had borrowed from Milner, that Poynter and Collingridge had 'sacrificed conscience and religion for money', and commented that perhaps he formed 'a judgment on the bishops of England from the conduct of the bishops of Ireland'.[5]

Having been persuaded that Poynter and his colleagues needed a formal answer about the acceptability of the bill, Quarantotti and his chief assistant, Galeassi, followed the usual pattern of the congregation when examining a serious issue.[6] They began by inviting a number of consultors or experts to study the question in depth and submit *vota* or opinions which would help the judges (normally cardinals) to reach a decision on it. Quarantotti chose five experienced consultors for this purpose: archbishops Devoti and Tassoni, both of whom were distinguished canonists; Fr Giacomo Belli and Fr Arcangelo dell'Assunta, consultors of the Holy Office, which dealt with doctrinal matters; and Fr Carlo Maria Quarantotti, a consultor of the congregation of Rites, who was his brother. The consultors were given copies of the letters – which Quarantotti and Galeassi had collected, with the assistance and impulsion of Macpherson – and were asked to study them. There were eleven documents in all: three letters from Poynter to Macpherson in 1813; the Irish bishops' pastoral of 1813, their resolutions of 1799 and one of 1810; Troy's letters to Quarantotti and to his agent, Argenti

---

4 Poynter, later complaining about the likely failure of their struggle for emancipation, blamed the Irish for having 'completely disgusted' their parliamentary friends, and remarked that Milner felt that he alone could guide the church as metropolitan (Poynter to Cameron, 24 Mar. 1814, SCA). Milner had suggested in 1806 that Douglass could have been compensated for removal from London by being given an enlarged vicariate as an arch-vicar. This may have caused the confusion about the status of metropolitans.   5 Macpherson to Hodgson (copies), 13, 31 Dec. 1813, WDA. Troy to Quarantotti, 3 Aug, and to Argenti, 11 Oct. 1813, ASV, AES, Pos 9, fasc 2, ff 20r–22v and ff 22v–23v.   6 The *ponenza* or examination of the bill by Quarantotti and his team is included in the archives in a larger examination of the whole question, which was ordered by the pope on his return to Rome. The full meeting of the cardinals or *plena congregatio* to deal with the case may have been postponed by Napoleon's return to France, but the congregation for Extraordinary Ecclesiastical Affairs made use of it in 1815 (APF, *Acta* 177, ff 3r–13r).

in 1812 and 1813; and two letters from Milner in 1808. Having investigated the issue at length, the five consultors were asked to respond to ten questions. They all responded positively to the first which sought to know if Quarantotti, endowed with unlimited faculties as he was, should offer a solution in view of the danger of delay. One of them feared the threat of exile to all Catholics if the conditions in the bill were not accepted.[7] To the question of whether it was lawful to take the oath that committed clergy not to subvert the church establishment or use any privilege, power or influence to overthrow or disturb the church establishment, and if this were difficult, what modifications were required, the consultors agreed that it could be taken with the understanding that the disturbance referred to was by force. And one wanted this phrase added.[8] They all agreed that the commissions to examine the loyalty of the candidates for episcopal office and correspondence from Rome could be tolerated. One referred to the role played by the governor of Quebec in the appointment of bishops and another referred to that role as well as to the parts played by the rulers of Prussia and Russia. Since purely spiritual matters in Roman documents were not to come under the surveillance of the commissions, they did not object to other correspondence being examined.

Regarding the restriction on those not born of British or Irish parents or domiciled for five years in Britain or Ireland, three saw no problem, one asked that an exception be included in the law for those born by accident abroad and one agreed that the practice was admissible until the pope determined otherwise. Asked if the king should have the power to approve or exclude subjects for the offices of bishop or dean, one mentioned the right of exclusion that some countries enjoyed in the election of popes, another mentioned the Canadian arrangement, and all accorded the king that right. Questioned as to what method should be adopted for electing bishops in Britain for presentation to the Holy See or whether the method proposed by the bishops of Ireland and Milner be adopted,[9] three approved of the Irish proposal, one wanted no change and one thought that the candidate should be presented to Rome after having received the royal approval. In sending briefs and decrees, the consultors were asked if mention of the royal assent

---

7 Exile in the bill was only a threat to bishops who took up office after having been vetoed by the king. This was a serious misunderstanding of the terms of the bill.   8 In the archives of the Secretariat of State there is an unsigned *votum* or opinion on the licitness of the oath. Expressing extreme views, the official or consultor quoted the theologian Suarez that it was sinful to profess by oath the false, temerarious and erroneous assertion that the pope did not have the power to depose a delinquent sovereign, and did not have indirect power over the temporals of princes. The denial of the infallibility of the pope was close to heresy. The pledge not to convert or overthrow in the proper manner the Church of England was contrary to justice. And the pope could dispense from oaths (ASV, AES, 1814, Pos. 9, fasc. 3).   9 This was the method to which the ten Irish bishops had agreed in 1799.

should be made: two suggested that the same pattern be followed as in Prussia and the others thought the royal assent should not be named. All agreed that no notice should be taken of the fifth resolution. Finally the consultors were asked what should be done if the conditions proposed in the bill could not be approved and if the government would not admit any modification. One consultor expressed the ludicrous view that all Catholics might be exiled if they did not consent to the terms of the bill and the equally ludicrous one that there would be a large conversion of Protestants to Catholicism if they did. One called for some change in the oath and in the personnel of the commission and one hoped for favourable changes. Three others thought they should take any improvements they would get, hoping for them in the oath and in the personnel of the commissions.

The normal practice of the congregation when asked to pass judgment on a serious issue was to appoint a cardinal to prepare all the material for the ten or twelve cardinals who would decide the issue. Their decision was then passed to the pope and it took effect if the pope approved. The *ponenza* or case, which the cardinal or his secretary prepared with the assistance of officials of the congregation, consisted of a *ristretto* or account of the disputed issue and a *sommario* or collection of documents, which consisted of the letters or presentations of the parties and the opinions of the consultors. As there were no cardinals in Rome, Quarantotti assembled a smaller or 'particular' congregation, which comprised the five consultors who had already submitted their views, along with Galeassi and himself. Presumably Galeassi, perhaps with the help of Quarantotti, drew up the *ristretto* or account of the case and the *dubbi* or queries on which the decision was to be reached. Another unusual aspect of this procedure was that the *dubbi* were exactly the same as those that had been given to the consultors.

The *ristretto* or account of the case opened with the fantastic statement that Quarantotti believed it was his duty to deliberate over the situation and thereby prevent the exposure of thirty-seven bishops, a very flourishing clergy and nearly 5 million Catholics to the danger of banishment from the kingdoms of Britain and Ireland.[10] The bill would be brought forward again in the next session of parliament and, if approved, would become law. If the Catholics accepted it, they would be admitted to all honours and rights on the same terms as Protestants but if they did not, they would be condemned to perpetual exile. The English Catholic nobles had declared that they would not accept a bill that was detrimental to the Catholic religion or did not have the approval of the Holy See, but they hoped the Vatican would be generous

10 When another *ristretto* was later drawn up, it was explained that Quarantotti and his consultors did not have a copy of the bill when their examination took place. Poynter, however, had explained that the threat of exile only applied to bishops who took office after they had been vetoed by the king.

in its disciplinary requirements. They argued that the Irish, though not united with them in their demands, were also persuaded that the bill contained nothing to which the Holy See would object. But if, for political reasons, the Irish held back, that should not harm the British Catholics. In fact, the formula of an oath for the clergy proposed by the Irish bishops gave the government what it wanted. The fifth resolution was referred to in different terms by Troy and by the vicars apostolic, but the substance was the same. Though Troy and Milner condemned the vicars apostolic for signing the fifth resolution on the grounds that the veto of the king was tacitly embedded in it, the vicars apostolic, who regarded Milner as capricious, ambitious and turbulent, never understood the fifth resolution as attributing a veto to the king. What induced them to sign it was the protestation of members of parliament that emancipation would never have been conferred without their signatures.

Both the English bishops and the Irish bishops agreed that without papal approval they would not accept any restrictions on the pope's power. They also agreed that there was nothing in the bill which the Holy See could not easily concede, and which it had not already conceded to other kingdoms. The example of Prussia in the appointment of bishops was explained:

> There the king through his agent presented his choice to the Holy See and it committed the process to a Catholic bishop. The bulls of appointment were then transmitted to the candidate without mentioning the royal nomination. Where a chapter had a right of election it elected the subject nominated by the king who was then presented to the pope for canonical institution.

Among the documents included in the *sommario* was a letter from the chapter of the diocese of Gnesen in 1805 to the pope, seeking the appointment of the candidate put forward by the king of Prussia.

The conversion of a large number of Protestants, especially from the nobility, was predicted if the bill were passed. The ease with which Catholics, as future members of parliament, could abolish or mitigate clauses they found burdensome was also foreseen. Keeping in mind the circumstances in which England could bring its influence to bear on the pope and on the temporal affairs of the church, it was to be hoped that cooperating with the government would render it more supportive.

The meeting of the 'particular congregation' of Quarantotti and the five consultors, with Galeassi as secretary, took place on 15 February 1814. As the consultors had already examined the letters and probably also the introduction or *ristretto*, which Galeassi had drawn up, all that remained was to check all their responses and, if possible, coordinate them. In fact those responses had all been favourable to the bill, and the only hesitation raised about them related to the oath, where the consultors had expressed the need for the pledge not to overthrow or disturb the Protestant church to be explained or understood in the bill as referring only to physical force. The regulation that no one who was not born of British or Irish parents or domiciled in Britain or Ireland for five years should be appointed a bishop or dean was accepted unless the pope decided otherwise. In sending decrees or briefs, the Prussian practice of not mentioning the royal assent to the nomination was to be followed. The method of electing bishops suggested by the Irish bishops in 1799 was also to be followed. Otherwise positive answers were given to the queries, including the last one, which asked if it were expedient and opportune for Poynter to recommend the temporal affairs of the pope to the British court.[11] The decision of this 'particular congregation' could scarcely have been more favourable. As the papal approval of this judgment could not be given because of the pope's 'house arrest' in France, Quarantotti assumed the right to confirm it and forward it to the bishops in England and Ireland.

The official letter to Poynter conveying the verdict of Quarantotti and his team was drawn up by Galeassi, dated 16 February 1814 and addressed to Poynter. Both its style and its contents must have cheered the hearts of the English Catholic Board. Having referred to the great pleasure with which the signatories, Quarantotti and Galeassi, had learned of the bill for the emancipation of Catholics in the flourishing kingdom of Britain, and to their ardent wish that the bill should at length be passed, mention was then made of the 'most beneficent sovereign' and 'that illustrious nation which on former occasions, and especially in these latter times, has acquired so much glory in the estimation of the whole world for its equity, prudence and other virtues'. Poynter was then told that Quarantotti, 'invested with full pontifical powers', had thought it incumbent on himself to remove every ambiguity which might impede conciliation, and so, with the help of learned divines, had examined the letters sent by him and by Troy, and having discussed the matter in a special congregation, decreed:

> that the Catholics may, with satisfaction and gratitude, accept and embrace the bill, which was last year presented for their emancipation, in the form in which Your Lordship has laid it before us. One point only requires some explanation – and that is the second part of the oath by which the clergy is so restrained, as not to be permitted to hold any correspondence with the sovereign pontiff and his ministers, which may, directly or indirectly subvert, or in any way, disturb the Protestant government or church ... now

11 APF, *Acta* 177, ff 18r–79v.

should a Catholic convert any Protestant to the orthodox religion, he might be deemed guilty of perjury, as, by such conversion, he might seem, in some sort, to disturb the Protestant church. Understood in this sense, the oath cannot lawfully be taken, as being repugnant to the Catholic faith. If, on the other hand, this be the meaning of the Legislators – that the ministers of the Catholic church are not forbidden to preach, instruct, and give counsel; but are only prohibited from disturbing the Protestant church or government by violence and arms, or evil artifices of whatever kind – this is just and entirely consonant to our principles.

Poynter was therefore asked to beg parliament to obtain this modification. If the bill had been passed containing those words, clergy who took it were to declare that did so only in the sense of not using physical force.

The desire of the king to have candidates scrutinized and to require that foreigners and those who had not resided for five years in the kingdom be excluded from dignities could be tolerated. When the clergy had chosen those candidates whom they deemed worthy of promotion the metropolitan of the province in Ireland and the senior vicars apostolic in England and Scotland should submit the names to the commission for royal approbation or dissent.

If the candidates be rejected, others shall be proposed who may be pleasing to His Majesty: but, if approved, the metropolitan or apostolical vicar, as above shall send the act of their election to this sacred congregation, which having weighed with care the merits of each individual, shall apply to the sovereign pontiff for canonical institution.

Noting that the commission was authorized to examine letters from 'the ecclesiastical authority' and to inquire if they contained anything 'obnoxious to the government, or in any way disturb the public tranquillity', Quarantotti maintained that this inspection, as it regarded 'only matters of civil policy ... ought to be acquiesced in'. The bill made adequate provision for keeping secret those matters 'which affect the internal tribunal of conscience'.

Having dealt with the details that were in dispute, Galeassi, who had written the letter on behalf of Quarantotti in the portentous mode he thought the occasion required, then pronounced that nothing could be:

more gratifying and delightful to the Apostolic See, than that between the government and its Catholic subjects there should exist an entire concord and a mutual confidence; that the Ministers of the state should never be able to doubt their loyalty, obedience, and attachment; and that the Catholics themselves should be devoted to their country with every effort of zeal, candour and alacrity.

He exhorted all, especially the bishops, to lay aside contention and if the bill were passed to 'not only embrace it with entire satisfaction, as has already been said, but express the strongest sentiments of gratitude to His Majesty, and his most august counsel, for so great a benefit; and, by their conduct prove themselves worthy of it'. In a separate letter, Poynter was exhorted to use his good offices at the British court to plead for the full restitution of the pope's rights and states.[12]

Two elements in the rescript, or official answer, ran counter to assertions often made by the congregation of Propaganda: that permission would not be given to a Protestant ruler to dictate the nomination of bishops, and that the *exequatur*, or right to scrutinize letters from Rome to local bishops, would be denied to Protestant rulers. Both the canonists, Devoti and Tassoni, were prepared to make these concessions. In fact, the Holy See could be pragmatic about such matters. In Quebec and Prussia, Protestant rulers were, in effect, granted the freedom to influence the choice of bishops. Though the *exequatur* was never willingly conceded, Consalvi expressed surprise that Bishop Moylan of Cork had been astonished to learn that it was common both in Catholic and non-Catholic states despite the complaints of the Holy See.[13] He had quoted without disapprobation the view of an English parliamentarian that it was up to the government to insist on the *exequatur* and the Holy See could then tolerate it while complaining about it.[14]

One of the most important aspects of the rescript was what it omitted: the number of candidates the king or government could reject. By being given no number the government could, by a process of elimination, choose its own candidate, and no provision was made for the church to limit the royal choice. Consequently, Quarantotti's letter or rescript was a wonderful bonanza in England for the vetoists of the Catholic Board, and in Ireland for the small minority of aristocrats or gentry – lords Fingall, Kenmare, the Bellews – who must have thought the doors of parliament would quickly burst open to them when their friends in both houses satisfied their opponents with proof that emancipation could hold no terrors for them. The obstacles that Milner and the Irish bishops had put in the way of the bill in 1813 had all been removed. Macpherson's cultivation of Quarantotti and

12 Quarantotti to Poynter, 16 Feb. 1814, APF, SC(Anglia), 6, ff 380r–383r.   13 Roveri, *La missione Consalvi e il Congresso di Vienna*, i, 264.   14 Ibid., i, 272.

Galeassi had paid dividends and it was little wonder that he immediately offered to bring the rescript to London to share his victory with Poynter. But the rescript was not to enjoy the undiluted success that its supporters hoped for, and the lay members of the Irish board and several of the Irish bishops were not alone in refusing to offer their 'strongest sentiments of gratitude to His Majesty'.

II

Quarantotti sent Troy a brief note informing him of their verdict on the bill, together with a copy of the rescript. Poynter was commissioned to send copies of it to all the bishops in Ireland and Britain.[15] As soon as Troy received his copy of the rescript, he wrote to Archbishop Bray of Cashel: '*rescripta Roma venerunt causa finita est*', the rescripts have come from Rome, the cause is finished. Enclosing a copy for Bray he declared 'whatever be our sentiments on the subject, it is our duty to acquiesce with the decision of such authority and set the example of submission to it'.[16] Far from complaining about the verdict of Rome, Troy's comments imply that he was satisfied, perhaps even pleased with it. His opposition to the veto had been 'expedient' rather than strictly principled, and he was probably relieved that Rome had taken the burden of decision-making from his shoulders. He could no longer be compelled to defend a position which he did not fully accept.

The prompt and hostile response of John Power, one of Bray's suffragans, to Quarantotti's letter was a better indicator of episcopal attitudes to the rescript than Troy's. Power complained of the great 'embarrassment and difficulty' into which Quarantotti's 'extraordinary' letter had plunged them. He apprehended 'much mischief from the fatal document' calculated as it was 'to weaken the attachment of the Irish to the H. See more than anything that has perhaps ever occurred, should his Holiness require us to submit to it'.[17] His reaction represented that of the great majority of the Irish bishops.

Poynter conveyed his appreciation of the rescript to Quarantotti on 14 May. Macpherson had brought it to him on 28 April and, he added, when it was published in the newspapers, it was gratefully received by both Catholics and Protestants, including the prince regent, and by the English nobles and members of parliament. He trusted it would be of great benefit, and he was obviously very pleased to repeat what Troy had also written to him – '*causa finita est*'. He then went on to inform Quarantotti that he was carrying out his commission to write to the government to defend the rights of the Holy

---

15 Quarantotti to Troy, 17 Feb. 1814, DDA; Poynter to Troy, 30 Aug. 1814, ibid. 16 Troy to Bray, 5 May 1814, CaDA. 17 Power to Bray, 16 May 1814, ibid.

See.[18] Lord Bathurst, the secretary for war, had told him that in the recent negotiations among the powers, the rights of the pope to his territories had been dealt with just as much as those of other rulers. The pope was advised to send a legate to Paris without delay to treat of his rights at the peace conference. Poynter did not discuss Troy's reaction, which he must have found as astonishing as it was welcome, and he would not have known the balance of opinion among the Irish prelates.

Shortly after getting the cheerful news, Poynter went off to Paris to visit Castlereagh, the foreign secretary, to win his support for the restoration of the Papal States. Accompanied by Bramston, his vicar general, Poynter called at Castlereagh's house and showed him the rescript. The minister read it with great pleasure. He wanted to know if it was authentic, and then suggested that to avoid equivocation something should be included in it to indicate that it enjoyed papal authority. He invited Poynter and Bramston to a further discussion about the restoration of the pope's territories, and knowing that Milner was on his way to Rome, inquired if the vicar apostolic of the Midland District was going there to cause trouble as he did in Britain, and stir up the pope and cardinals. Poynter and Bramston met Castlereagh by appointment two days later and were again told that at the peace congress in Vienna, he would use his authority in favour of the papal claims. In a footnote to his letter, Poynter let Quarantotti know that he had passed on the rescript to all the bishops and had written a few words to say that nothing was closer to his heart than Quarantotti's exhortation that all contention should be set aside, and he asked each of the bishops to believe that he earnestly hoped for the most perfect trust and concord between them all.[19]

A few days, later Poynter wrote to the pope, expressing his joy at the pontiff's release consequent on Napoleon's abdication, and repeating much of what he had told Quarantotti about Castlereagh and the restoration of papal territories. He also let the pope know about the joy caused by Quarantotti's letter, and their hope of concord and trust being established between the British government and the Catholics. He also passed on Castlereagh's view that it should be made known that the contents of the rescript were in accordance with the mind of the pope and were approved by him. The minister had also indicated that much could be done to quieten things in Ireland and sustain and enhance the authority and dignity of the pontiff, if Pius were to order that all matters and issues relating to the status of the Catholic church in Britain and especially in Ireland, were to be examined by the sacred congregation. Then, if the pope were by his authority to sanction whatever would put an end to all complaints and bring

18 Napoleon had abdicated on 11 April, and so the danger of an enemy influencing the papacy in a way detrimental to British interests no longer existed.   19 Poynter to Quarantotti, 14, 16 May 1814, ASV, Segr. Stato, Inghilterra 1814–1856, 29, ff 42r–43v.

about order and mutual trust between the church and the British government, there could be perfect confidence and concord between them.

Poynter gave the pope little time to deal with major international issues before returning to his obsession with Milner. Referring to the injuries he and his colleagues had received from Milner in the press, he explained that they had preferred to suffer in silence rather than engage in public quarrels. And as they did not have to give an account of their actions to Milner or to the Irish bishops they had brought their case to Rome. Many documents relating to their cause had been passed on to Quarantotti, and Poynter had also communicated in person with Monsignor de Gregorio, and was ready to explain himself to the pope and even, if the pope requested it, to make the journey to Rome. Poynter informed the pope that the vicars apostolic of England and Scotland (excluding Milner) had met at Durham the previous October and had published pastorals in which they had declared that they would not give their approbation or consent to the commissions concerning the appointment of bishops or communications with the Holy See without papal approval nor would they wish to diminish the rights of the Holy See nor usurp its authority.[20]

Poynter's colleague, Bishop Collingridge of the Western District, had personal and national reasons for welcoming the rescript. He was pleased that it would free the vicars apostolic from the dictates of the Irish bishops and Milner. In a jubilant mood, he exulted to Poynter that the Gordian knot had been cut, and that the Irish bishops and their agent were thrown on their backs, and he expressed the hope that they would hear no more of Irish domination or of the interference of the Irish agency in their affairs.[21]

The English Catholic Board wrote a formal letter of thanks to the pope. Its members, seeing their relationships both with the Holy See and with their own government vindicated, promised their full adherence to the rescript, which they had received with unspeakable joy. They also did not miss the opportunity of having a crack at Milner and his friends, who had levelled accusations against them, which the rescript had shown were false. Milner, in turn, gave as good as he got, by referring to information he had received from Troy that the rescript had caused 'the universal dissatisfaction among the Catholics of Ireland'. He entered his own protest against the response of the Catholic Board, assuring Cardinal Litta, the new prefect of Propaganda, that the vast majority of Catholics fully rejected the idea of exchanging the influence of Rome for that of men who were in the habit of swearing that the Holy See was idolatrous.[22]

If Poynter thought his problems with the Irish bishops had ended with

20 Poynter to Pius VII, 21 May 1814, ibid., ff 40r–41r. 21 Collingridge to Poynter, 5 May 1814, WDA. 22 Milner to Litta, 20 Aug. 1814, APF, CP 146, ff 570–571r.

Troy's '*causa finita est*', he was to be bitterly disappointed. Though Troy had led the charge against the veto in 1808 and against its supposed inclusion in the fifth resolution in 1810, he was never the unbending anti-vetoist which the vicars apostolic imagined. He had led his nine colleagues in support of a veto in 1799, and his withdrawal of that support in 1808 and hostility to the resolution of 1810 reflected the determined disapprobation of his colleagues much more than his own. He had been forced to bow to their wills, but assumed that Quarantotti's rescript would put an end to acrimonious disputes about the veto. He could not have been more wrong.

William Coppinger of Cloyne immediately pronounced the rescript to be 'a very mischievous document', which he had read 'with feelings of disgust and indignation'.[23] Edmund Derry of Dromore likewise described it as 'absolutely unnecessary and mischievous in its consequences', and, remarking that the veto was called forth by the government's silly fears of Napoleon's influence over the pope, he felt that with Napoleon's defeat there was no need for such precaution.[24] James O'Shaughnessy of Killaloe informed Poynter that, if carried into effect, that 'pernicious measure' would be fatal to the Catholic religion, and therefore he protested against it, and insisted that even though he should stand alone, he would do so while he had breath in his body.[25] John Power of Waterford argued that 'the fatal document' was most 'unfortunately calculated to weaken the attachment of the Irish to the H. See', and feared a schism should the pope order them to submit to it.[26]

Despite the hostility of some Irish bishops to the rescript, Poynter must have been pleased with Troy's attempt to bury the hatchet that had hung over their relationships for some years. In acknowledging Quarantotti's letter, he expressed his willingness to put into effect the exhortation to them to 'lay aside contention':

> It is equally near my heart to attend to the exhortation therein of maintaining the best understanding and the most perfect harmony with Your Lordship, and every other prelate of the United Kingdom; and I hope that whatever may have appeared to inter-rupt it latterly has not been ascribed to party feelings, or to undue influence of any individual in the minds of the Irish prelates. Be assured, My Lord, of the contrary; and that their opposition to the miscalled *relief bill*, and difference in opinion from their English brethren on other subjects, originated entirely from a desire to

23 Coppinger to Poynter (copy), 9 May 1814, DDA.   24 Derry to Poynter (copy), 14 May 1814, ibid.   25 O'Shaughnessy to Poynter (copy), 9 May 1814, ibid.   26 Power to Bray, 16 May 1814, CaDA.

preserve the integrity of discipline, and the independence of our ministry.

He then went on to suggest that modifications apart from Quarantotti's might occur to Poynter, and that the veto should be restricted to two occasions.[27]

Groups of priests in Ireland soon met to protest against the rescript. A number of Dublin clergy, discussing the rescript as 'non-obligatory' since it lacked the 'authoritative marks whereby mandates of the Holy See are known and recognized and especially the signature of the pope', resolved that the granting of a veto to a Protestant government would be not only 'inexpedient but highly detrimental to the best and dearest interests of religion and pregnant with incalculable mischief to the cause of Catholicism in Ireland'. They maintained that such arrangements for domestic nomination of the clergy as would preclude foreign interference and destructive securities could be made. They therefore begged Troy and the other prelates to remonstrate against the document, and to convey to the pope the tremendous evils which would flow from the adoption of its principles.[28] The Cork clergy, repudiating the interference of the government in the appointment of their prelates, which would lead 'to the serious injury and probable destruction' of their religion, resolved that Quarantotti's rescript would 'be productive of incalculable mischief, if not of utter ruin to the Roman Catholic religion in Ireland'.[29] Similar protests were made by the clergy of several dioceses.

Those of Ossory, like their colleagues in Dublin, emphasized an alternative to the proposals contained in the bill of 1813. They argued for domestic nomination of bishops by deans and chapters, and claimed that that method should satisfy British demands for the exclusion of non-British candidates from episcopal office. As they would already have taken an oath of allegiance, their loyalty was guaranteed, and apart from investigating documents from Rome, the requirements of the government would have been met. The Ossory clergy protested against the rescript and the veto and rejected the interference of the king as uncanonical, just as they rejected, as citizens, the unconstitutional interference of the pope.[30] Domestic nomination, whereby the candidate would be chosen by the chapters and priests in Ireland, and presented to the pope for canonical institution, was put forward as a way out of the impasse created by the rescript.[31] But it had different meanings for different groups, and, as the bishops later recommended, it made provision for their role and a greater role for the pope than that suggested by some of the laity.

27 Troy to Poynter, 4 May 1814, WDA. 28 *FJ*, 18 May 1814. 29 Ibid., 30 May 1814. 30 Ibid., 24 May 1814. 31 C.D.A. Leighton, 'Gallicanism and the veto controversy' in R.V. Comerford, M. Cullen, J. Hill and C. Lennon (eds), *Religion, conflict and coexistence in Ireland*, pp 156–8.

Distrust of the motives of the government in seeking to interfere in episcopal appointments was widespread among Catholics. They could not understand the need for security that lay behind such interference, as no bishop in the previous fifty years could have been accused of the least element of disloyalty. They suspected that these powers would be used for nefarious purposes: to promote candidates who were unreliable, either spiritually or politically. The more politically minded laity saw in the power given to the government in the appointment of bishops a means of controlling the church for political ends, of putting into key ecclesiastical positions those who would forward the attitudes and policies of the government. Episcopal office in the established church had been used in that way, and the fear was that after a long struggle for equality, Catholics could see their religious leaders corralled into a state camp, from which they might try to dictate unwelcome guidance to their people. The fruits of Catholic emancipation would be tainted at a vital source.

Lay Catholics did not wait for a statement from the bishops before showing their determination to oppose Quarantotti by pouring scorn and abuse on both the rescript and its author. In the *Dublin Evening Post*, Quarantotti was denounced as 'a barefaced and swaggering *mozzorecchi* [trickster]', 'an understrapper of Propaganda', a person of 'intolerable audacity', the son of a man who had no name and 'a consummate blockhead', and his document was described as 'a scroll of stupidity'.[32] In vain did the *Freeman's Journal* protest that 'a good and honest man' was being treated as 'the vilest ruffian'. Daniel O'Connell galvanized both lay and clerical opposition to the rescript with his famous comment: 'I would as soon receive my politics from Constantinople as from Rome'. Praising the Dublin clergy for their spirited response to Quarantotti, he pronounced in very unbecoming and intemperate language his disrespect for Roman officials:

> From the retreat of their virtues, they had come forward on the present occasion, to save us from the degradation prepared for us by the vandals of Rome – from the effects of that corruption, which the learned gentleman feared had found its way even into the holy places, they came forward and proclaimed, that the rescript from Rome was not mandatory, and that its effect, if admitted would be to overturn the Catholic religion.[33]

A general meeting of Catholics was held on 19 May in Dublin, and strong resolutions were passed against the rescript. The second resolution rejected the political interference which they detected in Quarantotti's letter:

32 Quoted in *FJ*, 10 May 1814.   33 Ibid., 14 May 1814.

> That we deem it a duty to ourselves and to our country, solemnly
> and distinctly to declare that any *decree, mandate, rescript or decision*
> whatsoever, of any foreign power or authority, religious or civil,
> ought not and cannot of right assume any dominion or control over
> the political concerns of the Catholics of Ireland.

They praised the clergy of Dublin for consoling the people of Ireland by the
public declaration of their sentiments respecting the '*mischievous document
signed* [by] *Quarantotti*' and respectfully invited the bishops to take into
consideration at their synod 'the propriety of forever precluding any possible
danger either of ministerial or foreign influence' in the appointment of their
prelates.[34]

Significantly the laity feared the political consequences of the rescript
foreseeing the danger of the government using it to interfere in their political goals in the future. This weighed more heavily on them than the purely
religious effects that would flow from it, and they were keen to resist any
possible invasion of their civil rights. Equally strong resolutions were passed
at meetings of clergy and laity in several dioceses.

Discontent among English Catholics outside of London with the behaviour of the Catholic Board was expressed at a meeting in Liverpool. Their
exclusion from decisions which were deemed to apply to the whole country
riled them. They resolved:

> we cannot express our feelings of indignation and horror at the
> unwarrantable dominion which these persons, stiling [*sic*]
> themselves the Catholic Board of England, have dared to assume
> over our political rights and spiritual interests.[35]

When the vicar apostolic of the Midland District, claimed he was speaking
for many outside the narrow circle of aristocrats and gentry, he could point
to groups like the one in Liverpool and in other towns and cities.

The Irish bishops met on 27 May to issue a public response to the rescript.
Having first planned to write to congratulate Pope Pius VII, who, three days
previously, had returned to Rome from French captivity, they declared that
Quarantotti's rescript was not mandatory. They resolved to send two of their
number to Rome 'to convey our unanimous and well-known sentiments to
the chief pastor, from whose wisdom, zeal and tried magnanimity we have
reason to expect such a decision as will give general satisfaction'. And
Donoughmore and Grattan were requested to endeavour to exclude from any
future bill those clauses which they had already denounced as injurious.[36]

---

34 Ibid., 26 May 1814.   35 *FJ*, 7 June 1814.   36 Ibid., 28 May 1814.

In the three weeks that had now elapsed since Troy had acknowledged the rescript as ending all discussion about the veto, he had been forced by the pressure of episcopal, clerical and general Catholic opinion to back down. He and the few who thought like him had been compelled to go along with the majority.

III

The rescript had revealed most clearly the divergent attitudes and aspirations of the Catholic committees in England and Ireland. The English committee represented the peers and gentry, with a background of pushing their own views irrespective of those of the vicars apostolic, who were keen to share in the privileges of their class and take their places in parliament and in the higher echelons of power. The Irish committee represented the active middle classes (it could happily dispense with its aristocrats and gentry). They were suspicious of the intentions of the government, and did not want to see bishops manipulated or used in any way contrary to national interests. In Ireland, the committee had widespread support for its views; in England, increasing numbers of the middle classes were growing tired of the dominance of the aristocrats and gentry – although they could not oust them from their positions.

Fiercely opposed to the rescript, Milner set off for Rome, authorized jointly with Daniel Murray, the coadjutor archbishop of Dublin, to represent the Irish bishops. He passed through Paris when both Castlereagh and Consalvi were there, and the foreign minister expressed his anxieties to the cardinal that he might succeed in overturning Quarantotti's decision. Arriving in in Rome in late May 1814, Milner promptly began to lobby any cardinal or official he could contact. He certainly played his part in the reopening of the whole question of the bill and the veto, as Troy's agent, Argenti, maintained.[37]

The pope, in response to advice from cardinals who had heard of the hostile reception of the rescript in Ireland and who believed that Quarantotti had acted ultra vires, ordered that the whole issue be studied afresh. Cardinal Litta, the prefect of the congregation of Propaganda, and possibly also Cardinal Pacca, the acting head of the congregation for Extraordinary Ecclesiastical Affairs, may well have suggested this step. Several considerations, given the commitment and heat of the two parties, delayed the investigation by the congregation. Nonetheless, the pope continued to interest himself directly in the issue, hoping to put an end to the disputes, to

---

37 Argenti to Troy, 25 June 1814, DDA.

satisfy both parties. Litta advised Troy to remain calm and trust to the well-known prudence of the pope.[38] Milner not only held various discussions with Litta, but also presented him with copies of his writings, and the steady support which he had given in these to the Holy See stood him in good stead. Litta, unlike several of his colleagues, knew English, and could appreciate Milner's writings. Galeassi complained to Macpherson that Litta was well disposed to Milner.[39]

A new study of the bill was eventually prepared at the congregation of Propaganda. The *ristretto* made use of the memorials submitted by Milner and Murray against the rescript. Milner was quoted in reference to the petitions for relief in 1805, 1808 and 1810, as well as to the bill of 1813, which he zestfully belaboured, describing it as illicit, injurious to the authority of the Holy See, contrary to the wisdom of the Catholic religion and schismatical in its consequences. He had argued that the retention of a negative power by the king was designed to strengthen Protestantism and weaken Catholicism. The government was empowered to ensure the admittance of tepid ecclesiastics tolerant of heresy, and perhaps even Protestants, to high office. The object of the bill was not the good of religion but rather damage to it, and it was supported by the few Catholics and Protestants, working for their own interests rather than the government, who sought emancipation.

The negative power assigned to the king could become a positive power as he could exclude all others except the one he wanted. Should the Holy See grant that power, there might be in Ireland schismatical tumults, as had occurred after the publication of the rescript. If the bill were allowed, the government would acquire despotic powers in ecclesiastical affairs, such as the right to exile bishops and other Catholics without proof or public examination. The publications of documents from the Holy See would give rise to calumnies, and apostolic dispensations relating to monks, nuns and marriage cases, which might be contrary to English law, could not be admitted by the commissions as being contrary to the laws of parliament. A bishop, as a member of the committee, was bound to observe both its secrets and the secrets of the Holy See, and if asked by the pope why a candidate was excluded from the episcopate he could not answer. Milner also remarked that the experience of previous acts of relief was that instead of causing conversions to Catholicism, they were met with great tepidity among the Catholics, and even the apostasy of some. To satisfy the demands of Protestants for some assurance about episcopal appointments, the bishops and vicars apostolic, before transmitting the names to the Holy See, should ask the

38 Litta to Troy, 11 Oct. 1814, DDA. Litta, a former nuncio in Poland, was prefect of the congregation of Propaganda from 1814 to 1818. A strict ultramontane, he had been ordered to France in 1809 and was angered by the treatment given to Pius VII by Napoleon. 39 Macpherson to Poynter, 15 June 1814, WDA.

government if it knew of any disloyalty to the king, sedition or other social crime from which the candidates could not free themselves.[40]

Milner not only denied that he had ever interfered in other prelates' jurisdictions, but accused Poynter of invading his jurisdiction, trampling on his rights, retaining his money and having favoured the errors of Charles O'Conor,[41] Charles Butler and Joseph Berington. He blamed Poynter and Collingridge for conniving at the recent bill, which contained schismatical clauses. Presenting himself as the champion of the Holy See, he claimed that he only wrote publicly to counteract the Cisalpines, and was never the cause of dissent. The fifth resolution was the fount and seedbed of all the irreligious oaths of the late bill.[42]

Murray, in a lengthy submission, which was summarized in part for the *ristretto*, repeated much of what Milner had already put forward. He pointed out that the members of the commissions would be under the control of the king's ministers, who would appoint and could dismiss them. One bishop on a commission could have little influence against a majority and, in fact, could be perverted or corrupted. A candidate who promoted the doctrines of the church or corrected immorality might be regarded by the Protestant members of the commission as a turbulent spirit, not of peaceable conduct, and his very merits might become a bar to his promotion. Contrary to the view of the rescript which seemed to hold that the British government wanted Catholics to remain attached to their religion, the reverse was the case. Immense sums of money were voted by parliament every year to educate Catholic children in the Protestant religion, and occasional grants were given to an association to distribute 'perverted translations of the Holy Scriptures' freely.[43]

The hostile spirit of the government was to be presumed from the fact that comparatively few Catholics had been admitted to places of trust or emolument. Admission to parliament depended on swearing that the Mass and the invocation of the saints were superstitious and idolatrous. When the rescript became known in Ireland, the great body of the people, and above all

---

40 APF, *Acta* 177, ff 6v–9r.   41 Charles O'Conor (1764–1828), whose brother became the O'Conor Don, was a priest of Elphin diocese. He spent most of his life as librarian to the marquis of Buckingham. His writings on ecclesiastical matters were considered to be Gallican and for many years he was forbidden to celebrate Mass in London and Dublin. Far from favouring O'Conor Poynter had censored him. Butler did not write on theological matters and Berington's controversial works had been published before Poynter became a vicar apostolic.   42 Milner, Memorial to Litta, 23 Sept. 1814, APF, CP 146, ff 640r–642v.   43 The Association for Discountenancing Vice and Promoting the Knowledge and Practice of the Christian Religion received parliamentary grants for its schools. It in turn aided the London Hibernian Society, which also used the authorized version of the Bible and Protestant prayer books in its schools. The Kildare Place Society, which also educated Catholic children, used the Bible without note or comment, but it did not receive grants until 1816 (Akenson, *The Irish education experiment*, pp 80–8).

the most virtuous, were 'overwhelmed with bitterness' and some threatened to have nothing to do with bishops appointed under that system. The prelates believed that if the new mode of appointing bishops were approved, religion would suffer more by such concessions than by all the penal laws, which still oppressed the Catholic body.

Murray recalled that fifteen years previously, ten prelates 'seduced by the fallacious promises of the Irish secretary' were led to believe that some control over the appointment of bishops might be conceded, but having conferred with their brethren, and having heard 'the loud and almost universal clamour of the nation' had the 'truly Christian fortitude to acknowledge their momentary delusion'. To counteract the fear of the government that the pope under the power of some Continental government might appoint bishops who would incite their priests to disavow their allegiance, he suggested that if the pope made it known that he would only appoint mature men at the representation of the Irish bishops or clergy, the fear of foreign influence would disappear. The clergy would then bind themselves by oath not to recommend any candidate for the episcopate of whose loyal principles and peaceable conduct they were not convinced. Should this be done, the Irish bishops felt sure that the British legislature would not attempt to force upon them 'the odious restrictions' of the late bill.[44]

The prelate who introduced this *ristretto* or narrative for his colleagues' decision noted that an answer would be badly received by either the Irish or English bishops, and, if the rescript were revoked, the government might be offended. Consequently, the cardinals were asked to consider whether it would be more expedient to defer the announcement of their decision for some time. They were given seven queries or *dubbi* to answer. The first two or three posed little difficulty, as they concerned Quarantotti's authorization to take the action he had, and, assuming his resolutions were rejected, what recommendation should be made to the pope. Other queries related to the adoption of the proposals of Milner and Murray, and to the oaths, which had not been considered but were included in the documents. The last two concerned the bishops of Ireland and the vicars apostolic: should a letter be written to the Irish archbishops to diminish the effects of the rescript and confirm their attachment to the Holy See, and what should be done to re-establish harmony and concord between the vicars apostolic of England and the bishops of Ireland.[45]

At this point the normal procedure of the congregation was not completed. Macpherson, Poynter's agent, later informed his friend that the

44 Murray to Propaganda, ibid., 9r–10v and ASV, AES, Inghilterra 1814, Pos. 9, fasc 4, ff 73r–77r (undated).   45 APF, *Acta* 177, ff 11v–13r.

pope told him that Cardinal Litta had got the question transferred to another congregation. This could only have been the congregation for Extraordinary Ecclesiastical Affairs under Cardinal Pacca, which was then dealing with issues of a political nature.[46] In that congregation, all the material dealing with Quarantotti's examination of the bill and his verdict were again submitted to a consultor. He decided that Quarantotti's rescript was censurable. It should be declared null and a new and accurate instruction should be provided, subject to papal approval. Quarantotti and his counsellors, he maintained, had made a great mistake in dealing with such an issue of discipline, in which any change was illicit without papal approval. His faculties did not extend to doctrinal matters or to the private rights of the Holy See, immunity, ecclesiastical liberty or the discipline of the universal church. Quarantotti had approved an oath that was ambiguous and would have been illicit had the government not clarified it. The innovation of a mixed committee of Catholics and Protestants examining all documents apart from those from the penitentiary was to be avoided. Rather than concur in undignified practices and sanction them by oaths, the bishops and Catholics should renounce emancipation and continue to suffer patiently the penal laws, as it was doubtful if they would get emancipation even by surrendering to pernicious innovations. The consultor then added (mistakenly) that the Irish had been promised emancipation, took an oath against the express mind of the Holy See, and never got what was promised.

The consultor also called for the removal of the term of five years' residence in Britain or Ireland before any priest could be appointed a bishop. Moreover, he found it unjust to the Holy See to suggest that it would appoint persons who were disaffected to the government. The proposed role of the committee in selecting vicars apostolic was unacceptable, and there should be no change. The clergy of Britain should always guard against insidious attacks by the enemies of the Catholic faith and stay united to avoid the danger of schism. If the government permitted no changes in the bill, it should be rejected.

The consultor suggested that two instructions should be issued, with the pope's authority. One should be directed to the public, regretting that the pope could not approve of the conditions and clauses of the bill, but exhorting Catholics to be loyal to the government. The other, directed to the bishops, should state that the pope, in accordance with the sentiments of the cardinals, declared the rescript to be null and void, and wished that it had

46 In Consalvi's absence, Cardinal Pacca had charge of this congregation. Pacca's policies were diametrically opposed to Consalvi's. He was very much the *zelante* determined to uphold traditional papal and curial rights. Consalvi, the *politicante*, believed that many of the reforms of the French in the Papal States should be maintained and that new relationships should be established with the states that emerged from the Napoleonic upheaval.

never been issued. The most bitter opponents of the rescript could not have wished for a more damning verdict on it.[47] The consultor, whose name was not attached to his *votum*, offered the Catholics of England and Ireland a rather bleak prospect. According to his views, scarcely any concession should be made to obtain emancipation. It seems that no particular attention was paid to his advice.

As the weeks passed, Milner grew disheartened by the slowness of the Holy See in reaching a decision on the disputes between the Irish bishops and himself on one side, and the other vicars apostolic on the other, which had 'convulsed the religion of our two islands for the last four years past'. Disappointed, he threatened to leave Rome, confessing that though he had received private approbation from Litta 'that will not avail to *vindicate his character before the public* much less to *strengthen his hands in pursuing his former conduct*'. Without some public proof of support from Rome '*the little but powerful Cisalpine party will triumph* beyond measure and the friends of the Holy See, who are by far the most numerous party, will hang their heads with shame'. He feared that if his appeal to Rome failed, he could not publish his views, act as the agent of the Irish bishops or go to London to oppose new oaths or new bills.[48] Litta, though generally sympathetic, had received warnings about Milner's contentiousness. Quarantotti had let him know that Milner was 'turbulent, factious and always opposed to the other vicars apostolic'. He further complained that Milner, who had never fulfilled his obligations to reside in his vicariate, had travelled to Rome without the permission of the congregation.[49] Litta complained to Milner about his controversial writings, but the vicar apostolic replied robustly and declared himself ready to meet his opponent (Poynter) in Rome.[50]

Macpherson, having delivered the rescript, was anxious to return from London to Rome lest Milner succeed in altering the minds of the pope and prelates, who had arrived there in his absence. On his journey, he assured Poynter from Paris that Quarantotti's rescript would be confirmed, given the influence and activity of Galeassi. Milner, he added, was not held in much esteem in Rome and was already found to be no slave to the truth.[51] But a mere three weeks later, when he arrived in Rome, he contradicted his assessment of Milner's influence. This reversal of his claims – taken together with his prediction about the rescript, which had already been proved wrong – demonstrates that he knew far less about curial politics than he thought he

---

47 AA EE SS, Inghilterra, Pos 9, fasc 5, ff 52r–68v.   48 Milner to Litta, 3 Aug. 1814, APF, CP 146, ff 566r–567v.   49 Quarantotti to Litta, 11 June 1814, APF, CP(Anglia), 146, f 545rv. Coxe-Hippisley later weighed in against Milner and the Irish bishops, whose conduct was 'a tissue of inconsistency', as contrasted with the consistency of the English vicars apostolic (Coxe-Hippisley to Litta, 30 Aug. 1814, ibid., ff 707r–740v).   50 Milner to Propaganda, 25 Aug. 1814, ibid., ff 579r–581v.   51 Macpherson to Poynter, 20 July 1814, WDA.

did. As Milner, he regretted to say, was enjoying 'very considerable credit and even influence' at the Roman court, Macpherson begged Poynter to hurry to Rome.[52] Meanwhile, he set about challenging the case put forward by Milner and the Irish bishops against the rescript. He found this difficult, as, by his own admission, in the altered circumstances in Rome, Milner had met with more success than he would have wished.

IV

The situation at the congregation of Propaganda and in the curia generally had greatly changed since Macpherson's departure in February. The aged Quarantotti, whom he had successfully influenced, had lost power.[53] Cardinal Littta was firmly in charge of the congregation and, though Quarantotti was allowed to remain as vice prefect, Archbishop Pedicini as the *sostituto* took effective control of that position. At first, Macpherson would not have known how many influential figures, including the pope himself, disapproved of the rescript, and he assumed that Milner had poisoned the minds of cardinals and senior officials against it and against the other vicars apostolic. He therefore arranged several meetings with Cardinal Litta to counteract Milner's machinations and to convince the cardinal that the rescript had been deservedly welcomed in England. He found Litta austere, forbidding and unwelcoming, but instead of responding patiently and gently to the cardinal's remarks seems to have done so in a blunt, ungracious and undiplomatic manner. Some of Litta's comments may have seemed harsh, but if Macpherson accused the cardinal of ignorance of English affairs, as he claimed to have done, he behaved in a most impolitic manner and could have done his cause nothing but harm.[54]

Litta, doubtless influenced by one of Milner's favourite charges, began by telling Macpherson that the English bishops had sacrificed the discipline of the church to curry favour with the rich laity. Then, blaming Macpherson for the part he had played in obtaining the rescript, he complained that 'you in particular should not have used such arts and industry to wrench that infamous paper from the old man's hands'. Macpherson countered that Litta 'was ill-informed and egregiously deceived in every possible point he had mentioned', and offered to resume discussion when the cardinal was in a

---

52 Ibid., 10 Aug. 1814.   53 Quarantotti was 81 when he approved of the rescript. Both Litta and Macpherson implied that his age was a factor in his readiness to respond to Macpherson's arguments.   54 Consalvi referred to *'una certa severità'* in Litta's character when he suggested to Pacca that Litta would not be suited to attempting reconciliation between Poynter's and Milner's views on politico-ecclesiastical issues (Consalvi to Pacca, 11 Mar. 1815, Roveri, Fatica e Cantù (ed.), *La missione Consalvi e il congresso di Vienna*, iii, p. 268).

calmer mood. But, in a less-than-calm mood, Litta told him, 'You think then that Quarantotti can define even in matters of faith – these are the fine consequences of your operations.' He then charged that the vicars apostolic had 'the audacity to make a concordatum with your government, and sacrifice religion to content the unlimited ambition of the Cath. laity'.[55] Macpherson expressed regret at finding the cardinal's mind 'so greatly preoccupied and prejudized [*sic*] by incorrect and false representations'. He then gave an account of the rescript, to which Litta replied by charging that the bishops had agreed to all the clauses in the bill to please the laity.

Macpherson, assuming the cardinal had been indoctrinated by Milner, accused the vicar apostolic of publishing calumnies and falsehoods, though he knew them to be such, and gave the cardinal papers to illustrate his points.[56] And he claimed that the Irish took everything on Milner's word. Litta did admit that Milner was not always consistent and was too fiery, but he praised his learning, zeal and attachment to the Holy See. Macpherson countered by claiming that 'zeal, void of prudence, degenerates into a pernicious vice'. Milner's publications against his colleagues in which he spared neither falsehood nor calumny had damaged religion and tended to raise divisions and schism in Britain more than all the writings of Gaschet and Blanchard put together. Referring to the *Orthodox Journal* and what he called 'other vile pamphlets', which Milner had published, and to his libellous attacks against the other vicars apostolic, Macpherson accused him of pandering to the many Irish in Britain, who like the rest of their countrymen indulged 'a prejudice that approaches to hatred, against Britain and the British government'.

Macpherson found himself on very shaky ground when Litta attacked the Cisalpine Club. To a member of the Roman curia who had lived through the anti-Christian depredations of the French Revolution and Napoleon's spoliations of the church, the very name 'Cisalpine', opposed to the ultramontanism then gaining ground, spelt dangerous hostility to Rome. Litta suggested that all English Catholic gentlemen of note were members, that they were wealthy, funded the vicars apostolic, apart from Milner, and had always been opposed to the Holy See. Had it not been for Milner's exertions against their hideous designs, Catholicism in England would have disappeared. Macpherson replied that the members of the club had suffered many privations for their attachment to Rome, did not retain or bribe the vicars apostolic and performed many works of charity surpassing 'anything of the kind in any other country in Europe'. Nonetheless, Litta insisted that

55 Presumably Litta was suggesting that the vicars apostolic had made some kind of an agreement to accept the terms of Grattan's bill, which they had not done.   56 Cardinal Erskine, had he been alive, would have downed Milner as he had done in 1806, but with his death in 1811 Macpherson had lost a powerful ally.

the vicars apostolic, especially Poynter, were 'too timid; and too much slaves to the nobility'. Clearly some of Milner's accusations had found a willing listener.

Macpherson answered that the documents submitted to the congregation about the disputes concerning de Trevaux and the fifth resolution brought little credit to Milner and his Irish friends. Litta then declared that the great object they should have in mind was to restore peace and harmony to the English mission. To attain that very desirable object, said Macpherson, two resolutions on the part of Rome were necessary: the Irish clergy should be strictly commanded to mind their own business and not, contrary to canonical rules, disturb the peace of other churches, and Milner should be kept in Rome or somewhere other than in Britain to prevent him exercising ecclesiastical jurisdiction there.[57] A joint appeal to Rome by the other vicars apostolic to demote Milner might have been at least considered, but coming from a priest with no jurisdiction in Britain, this appeal to a cardinal who had shown himself well disposed to the combative vicar apostolic of the Midland District, exceeded the limits of diplomacy and common sense. Litta responded that the Irish were entitled to interfere when the faith was in danger but admitted that they had gone too far. The cardinal then asked if Macpherson was trying to prevent Milner from defending the Holy See, only to be told that his so-called defence of it had been hurtful to Rome.

At an audience afterwards with the pope, Macpherson expressed his fear that the congregation that was to examine the rescript might depend too much on the statements of Litta, whose strong prejudices derived from Milner's misrepresentations.[58] Whether or not Litta was apprised of this fear, Macpherson, at their next session, 'found him as violent on every point as on the first day', and, rather mordantly, told him that there was no point in pursuing a subject upon which the eyes of the world were fixed. To Macpherson's great surprise, Litta reminded him that the church always flourished under persecution and that religion would be better served if the penal laws continued, as Rome would then meet with no obstacle from the British court in governing the Catholics. Macpherson replied that the church always sought peace for its mission, and claimed that the church in Britain would suffer more from his decision than from the sanguinary laws of the past. Macpherson submitted further papers for examination by the congregation of Extraordinary Ecclesiastical Affairs, but was nonplussed to be told by the cardinal: 'you defend all the obnoxious clauses of the bill with more eagerness than the Protestants themselves would do'. Macpherson replied

57 Macpherson later told Bishop Gibson that the pope had decided not to allow Milner to return to England. This news was not to be made public until Consalvi returned from Vienna and made arrangements for Milner's placement in Rome (Macpherson to Poynter, copy, 26 Nov. 1814, WDA).   58 This was the new congregation for Extraordinary Ecclesiastical Affairs.

that the vicars apostolic did not approve of the obnoxious clauses of the bill, and he was particularly hurt by the comparison made between himself and Protestants in terms of orthodoxy and veneration for the Holy See, and vowed he would not yield to the cardinal on that point. He insisted that neither he nor the vicars apostolic approved of the clauses in the bill but maintained that they could be tolerated.[59] However, the pope had told Macpherson of his great regard for England and the English Catholics and pledged that whatever the Holy See could grant them would be granted.[60] Perhaps this encouraged Macpherson to make a lengthy submission to Litta in writing.

Explaining that perhaps through incapacity or language difficulties he had not put his case across effectively, he wrote to Litta to put his arguments with greater precision and accuracy. He repeated much of what he had already said but also added a few groundless and astounding claims, which must have strained Litta's powers of comprehension. He claimed that Quarantotti had felt obliged to make a decision partly because the vicars apostolic insisted on it because of the danger of bishops being exiled from all the British dominions if they did not accept the law. The vicars apostolic had written to the vice prefect that the bill would be proposed again when parliament reopened, and, if passed into law, the bishops who did not accept it would be condemned to exile. Quarantotti feared that if this were to happen all the damage would be blamed on him for not having taken precautions. What would have been said if the Catholic religion through his fault had been banished from England?

Though he pointed to the discrimination Catholics suffered – Catholic soldiers and sailors were forced to assist at Protestant services under pain of death,[61] and Catholic couples were obliged to have their marriages conducted at Protestant services – he insisted that the government was not as hostile to Catholics as the opponents of the rescript maintained. With exemplary charity, it had protected and provided for hundreds of French bishops and 8,000 French ecclesiastics, and had also provided schools and teachers for French youth. Should anything hostile to Catholics be proposed after they were admitted to parliament, the Catholic third of the population could

---

59 Macpherson to Poynter in the four conferences with Litta beginning on 11 Aug. 1814, WDA. 60 Macpherson, despite Litta's scepticism, thought he had overcome the impression made by Milner who, he believed 'would have got all overturned to the disgrace of Rome' had he, Macpherson, delayed a week in returning to Rome. He maintained that no alterations would be made to the rescript – an indication of how little he knew about the views of the pope's senior advisers (Macpherson to Hodgson, 8 Sept. 1814, ibid.). 61 In a letter, the vicars apostolic (apart from Milner) explained to Litta that among the oppressive penal laws they would wish to have changed was that which obliged Catholic soldiers and sailors '*cogi possunt and aliquando coguntur*' to attend Protestant services on Sundays (Poynter to Litta, 25 June 1814, APF, CP 146, ff 681r–683v).

protest. But in fact the government looked on Catholics with a benign eye. When Protestants saw Catholics enjoying equality with them, a large number would become Catholic. Arguing that Catholics had often to tolerate much that they were opposed to, he instanced the case of Protestant princes nominating bishops and referred to the influence of the government in Quebec. He also claimed that in Ottoman territories, Catholics received the sacraments from the hands of heretics.

Macpherson reserved a good deal of his venom for Irish Catholics. Maintaining that the rescript was received with enthusiasm and applause by the whole (British) nation and had done more to crush the calumnies that the sectaries had been vomiting against the Holy See for centuries, he went on to lament the monstrous calumnies of the Irish followers of Milner who filled the papers with accusations that Quarantotti and his consultors had been corrupted by English money transmitted to them by Lord Bentinck.[62] The Irish and Milner had so offended the prince regent that the whole nation was disgusted, and the prince – from being a friend of the Catholics – had become the greatest opponent of their cause. Even if approved by the Holy See, the Irish would not want to accept the rescript. The government suspected that they wanted a complete separation from the British crown, and their violent and indecorous behaviour lent force to that suspicion. Should the rescript be revoked, the British court would regard that action as proof that some favoured the rebellious aims of the Irish. A judicious minority among them would accept conditional emancipation, if approved by the Holy See, but that the majority had changed its opinion could only be attributed to the declamations of their bishops.[63]

Some of the exaggerations and falsehoods of this submission could be understood as an attempt on Macpherson's part to bolster his case. The reference to the exiling of the bishops from all British dominions calls into question either his exact knowledge of the bill or his honesty in presenting its terms. Exile was only mentioned as a punishment for bishops who, after the bill had become law, took office without the approval of the king or his ministers. The possibility of Catholicism being banished from England if Quarantotti had not taken action was preposterous. Though Irish Catholics had vigorously opposed the rescript, their motives in doing so had nothing to do with rebellion against Britain. The lay leaders of the Irish Catholics, let alone the bishops, were not then disposed to campaign for separation from Britain.

Macpherson was not alone in exaggerating the situation for Rome. Poynter, astonished and angered by the rumours in the press of the success

---

62 Lord William Bentinck (1774–1839) was commander of the British forces in the Mediterranean from 1811 to 1815. He later became governor general of India.   63 Macpherson to Litta, 5 Sept. 1814, APF, CP 146, ff 345r–361r.

of Milner's representations, wrote indignantly to Macpherson for the benefit of Roman officials. The papers had carried reports of Quarantotti and his consultors having fallen into disgrace and being deprived of their offices, of the rescript being surreptiously bought by money from Castlereagh and Bentinck, and of the bishops, clergy and almost the whole Catholic body being suspect in Rome. Letters from Propaganda corrected these rumours in part, and he had passed on the information to Castlereagh, who, with the other members of the government, had been in a state of consternation.

Reminding Macpherson that he was a witness of the good the rescript had done, and that it contained nothing the Holy See did not tolerate in other countries, Poynter expressed his horror at the prospect of its being rescinded. And he even went to the extreme of predicting that should it be withdrawn, the government would pass laws against Catholicism with clauses even stronger than those in the bill, without conceding emancipation. All the confidence of the government in Rome and its correspondence with the Vatican would end perhaps forever. Milner had lost all esteem and credit with both Catholics and Protestants and had written and printed such false and injurious attacks against bishops, nobles and members of the government that he would have been exiled to Botany Bay, had he not confessed in the presence of peers that he knew what he wrote was calumnious. He had caused all the disturbances that had rocked Catholicism in recent years. If the Holy See did not take action against him, it was very probable that his unhappy conduct would lead to a schism, since all the Irish, a large number of whom lived in Britain, would support him simply because he was an enemy of the government.[64]

The Roman officials must have been somewhat baffled by the threats of schism reported by both parties. And they must have been completely confused by Poynter's fantastic and irresponsible claim that the government, without granting emancipation, would impose further restrictions on the Catholic religion if the rescript were withdrawn. Several petitions for redress had been rejected and the defeat of a bill would have left the Catholics in the same situation as they had been in. However mild many of the offences were for which people were transported to Botany Bay, Milner's antagonism to cabinet ministers could not have been included among them. He could not have been convicted of breaking any law, as he did little more than the parliamentary opponents of the government.

Despite the impression Macpherson gave to Poynter and other correspondents that he was very much au fait with Roman thinking on the whole issue, it seems that he had much less inside knowledge than he claimed. He told Hodgson, the vicar general of the London District, that the pope had

64 Poynter to Macpherson, 6 Sept. 1814, ibid., ff 363r–365v.

sharply reprimanded Litta for letting Poynter and Troy know that the whole question was 'to be examined *ex integro*' and that the pope wanted Litta to give up the prefectship of Propaganda because of his 'scandalous partiality' for Milner.[65] This was wishful thinking, for Litta remained in office until 1818 and played an important role in the whole veto debate. Wishful thinking also accounts for the 'secret' Macpherson revealed to Bishop Gibson. The pope and Cardinal Litta, he maintained, had made up their minds not to alter the rescript. Cardinal Pacca not only compelled him to correct this information, but even reported it to Cardinal Consalvi in Vienna.[66]

Macpherson, whose enthusiasm often outran his discretion, also informed Gibson that arrangements were in train to deprive Milner of his office as vicar apostolic, and sought Gibson's advice on finding a suitable situation for him. Gibson, foreseeing the 'great clamour' such a deprivation would provoke in England, and especially in Ireland, thought Milner should be allowed to return to England, forbidden to interfere in politico-ecclesiastical affairs and then, if it were deemed advisable, asked to resign peaceably and accept the maintenance designed for him by the pope.[67]

Macpherson's defence of the rescript and his advocacy of it with Litta achieved little. All the leading figures of power in Rome – the pope, Consalvi, Litta and Pacca – regarded Quarantotti's issuance of the rescript as both improper and embarrassing, and they had little respect for Quarantotti himself. Milner and Murray had an easier brief to argue. If Milner's exaggerated claims were downplayed by Litta, others took effect and his defence of Roman prerogatives stood him in good stead, and saved him from any serious punishment.

65 Macpherson to Hodgson, 20 Oct. 1814, WDA.   66 Roveri, *La missione Consalvi e il congresso di Vienna*, ii, pp 562–3.   67 Gibson to Macpherson, 1 Jan. 1815, AVEC, 54.2.11.

11

Consalvi and Castlereagh

I

The victors in the struggle against Napoleon invited the pope's chief aide, Cardinal Consalvi, the secretary of state, to join them in London in June 1814. Consalvi was delighted to accept, as he had many problems to discuss with the leaders of Britain, Austria, France, Prussia and Russia, especially the restoration of the Papal States to the pontiff. The pope and his advisers regarded the possession of the Papal States as essential to their mission (and as a source of income). As a sovereign, the pope would be independent and could carry out his spiritual responsibilities freely. As a subject he could be under the control of another sovereign, and even if not actually furthering that sovereign's policy in international relations, could be accused of doing so. Napoleon's ill treatment of Pius VII, whom he wanted in effect to make his subject by moving the papacy to Paris, had made the pope and his advisers determined to regain papal independence. Even Protestant rulers wanted the pope to be independent, as independence would remove the kind of accusations that were or could have been made about his decisions when detained by Napoleon in France.

Consalvi had been secretary of state from 1800 to 1806, when Napoleon forced the pope to dismiss him. He was restored to office in 1814 and set about using all his diplomatic skills not only to regain possession of the Papal States but also to adapt the governance of the church to the necessary changes forced on it by the French Revolution. Possessed of tact and *savoir faire*, he arrived in London on 10 June 1814, shortly after the emperor of Russia and the king of Prussia, and during his sojourn, which lasted nearly a month, he behaved with great discretion.[1] Wearing his cardinalatial robes, he was received by the prince regent, Lord Castlereagh and other ministers, and he believed that they were pleased to see him in full formal dress.

Cardinal Pacca replaced him in Rome as acting secretary of state and Consalvi in his dispatches to him reported on his mission and sought advice and guidance from the congregation of Extraordinary Ecclesiastical Affairs. He was highly pleased with his reception in London and described how he

1 Fischer, *Cardinal Consalvi: Lebens – und Charakterbild des grossen Ministers Papst Pius VII*, pp 294–5.

was brought along to a general audience with other ambassadors to meet the prince regent; he was then received privately and was flattered by his reception. He declared in the most fulsome terms that he was unable to describe 'the goodness, the courtesy, the solicitude, the interest and above all the heartfelt warmth' that the prince had showed him during the audience.[2] The prince, who was not generally associated with the discernment of sanctity, had repeated to him several times that 'a more saintly pope, a greater hero, a more courageous man' than Pius VII did not adorn their age. He yielded to no one in his admiration and esteem for the pope. The cardinal, not to be outdone by the hyperbole of the prince, reported that he was ecstatic and exuberant with joy, but was able to recover sufficiently to refer to the pope's trust in British support for the recovery of all his territories, a goal to which the prince pledged his help. He regarded the disposition of England towards the pope as excellent.

The audience with the prince lasted half an hour and, after a brief preliminary audience with Castlereagh, a second one lasted three quarters of an hour. A further one with the prince lasted an hour and a half. The foreign minister assured Consalvi that Britain would back the pope's claims at the Congress of Vienna and the cardinal in turn pledged papal cooperation in the campaign to abolish slavery. Castlereagh then turned to the religious affairs of Britain and Ireland, and 'demonstrated the greatest reasonableness and moderation in his principles and questions', declaring that he expected nothing from the Catholics that their principles did not permit. But he insisted that emancipation was not possible without a guarantee of the conduct of Catholics in their external communications. Consalvi replied that an oath in some form would be acceptable, and that giving satisfaction to the government in the nomination of bishops in some form would be acceptable, but that the pope could not admit the *exequatur*, though he was forced to tolerate this against his will even in some Catholic states. Castlereagh also stated that if the pope were to express approval of Quarantotti's letter, which might satisfy the nation in opposition to the turbulence and spirit of insubordination of the Irish Catholics, they might then be able to revoke the laws against the Catholics and every difficulty about relations between the two states would cease.

Castlereagh pleased Consalvi (and the cardinal was sure he would greatly please the pope) by suggesting that the Holy See and the British government should exchange representatives, who would not enjoy public recognition until after the abolition of the laws forbidding such contacts. Asked if the representative of the Holy See should be a layman or an ecclesiastic Consalvi

---

2 'E qui mi è impossibile, assolutamente impossibile di riferire in un modo che corrisponda alla cosa, i sentimenti, la bontà, la cortesia, la premura, l'interesse e soprattutto la vera effusione del cuore che dal principio fino alla fine distinsero questa udienza.'

was amazed when the minister replied that he should be an ecclesiastic. But when requested to submit a written statement of his views, Consalvi was reluctant to commit himself to paper – partly because he had not yet heard the pope's plans.

Explaining the religious situation in Britain and Ireland to Pacca, Consalvi made a rather sweeping distinction between two very opposed parties – the English and Scots on the one side and the Irish on the other. Some English and Scots were associated with the Irish, such as Bishop Milner, a man of the soundest principles, who was very attached to the Holy See but very hot-headed, an intriguer very much disliked by the government. The Irish church was very attached to the Holy See and would suffer martyrdom for it. But the Irish were very hostile to England; some of them saw everything coming from England in dark colours and others used the pretext of religion for their political designs against the government, which they hated.[3] With the defeat of the bill in 1813 some Catholics behaved in a way contrary to the law and pushed their displeasure at the defeat of emancipation almost to rebellion.

The Irish clergy and bishops, Consalvi continued, allowed themselves to be dominated in the clubs by laymen who were ambitious to enter parliament. An example of this was the volte-face of the bishops from their acceptance of state pensions.[4] The Irish clergy, dominated by Catholic nobles and by fear of the people, were in their goodness and simplicity behind the times in their knowledge of certain realities, and believed that in both Catholic and non-Catholic countries, the Catholic religion was in the happy condition in which it had been three or four centuries previously.[5] As an example of this backwardness, he instanced the astonishment of the bishop of Cork on hearing of the abuse of the *exequatur*, which was common in all Catholic and non-Catholic states despite the protests of the Holy See. The pope and the sacred congregation should take account of the effects of national enmity towards England in assessing the opposition of the Irish. As a consequence of all this, much less account should be taken of the opposition of Ireland.

According to the Irish, the cardinal contended, the English laity were too

---

3 Agricultural prices had fallen in Ireland in 1813–14 and this with other disputes between landlords and tenants, or farmers and labourers had led to agrarian disturbances in several counties. There was no political movement against Britain at this time. The disturbances were not connected to the defeat of Grattan's bill (Connolly, 'The Catholic question 1801–12', *NHI*, v, pp 56–60). 4 Rome had rebuked the Irish bishops for agreeing to state pensions. 5 Consalvi must have been referring to the angry dismissals of Quarantotti's rescript at the Catholic Board and various meetings throughout Ireland. The Irish bishops, who had all been educated on the Continent, were well aware of the damage done to the church by the French Revolution. Neither the Irish bishops nor clergy were dominated by Catholic nobles. Catholic nobles played a more influential role in England.

well disposed to the government in their desire to obtain positions and seats in parliament and by their influence on the clergy directed them to the same goal. Though he did not have time to acquire an exact knowledge of the laity, he knew that the clergy were very religious, exemplary and attached to the Holy See. Bishop Poynter was without exception the most exemplary of men. The government was very happy with the English and Scottish Catholics, and especially so with Poynter, not because he was subservient, but because of his wisdom and genial character. In fact the English and Scottish clergy were not subservient to the government and had told him in relation to Quarantotti's letter that at all costs they would be guided by the pope. Milner, though basically good, was in conflict with his colleagues – apart from the Irish – and was no friend of Poynter, whose office in London he had sought in vain, and whose failure to get it led to trouble. He was so thoroughly disliked by the government that Castlereagh had said to him that if the pope wanted to do them a favour, he would remove Milner from their midst. In fact Consalvi believed that such was the government's antipathy to him that, had it not been so moderate, he would already have been removed. If he did not alter his ways the government would let him know that he was no longer wanted. As he was then in Rome, perhaps the pope could exhort him amicably to cooperate with the other three vicars apostolic in a spirit of calmness and moderation.

Consalvi believed that the English and Scottish Catholics understood Castlereagh's argument that he needed concessions from Catholics for the security of the state; the Irish did not. He also felt that Quarantotti's rescript went beyond what could or should have been conceded but thought that refusing what in practice was allowed to other states was not feasible. Castlereagh listed the concessions required for emancipation: an oath of loyalty and submission to the state; an assurance that no one could be chosen as bishop who was a hothead (he noted that during the French invasion of Ireland a bishop whose brother or cousin was an enemy general was elected); and the examination of documents from Rome except the exclusively spiritual ones.[6] The government believed that it should not be denied that concessions had been granted to the governments of Russia and Prussia: the right of nomination, in fact if not in name. The cardinal did not know how to oppose this argument, especially if less was sought than what was enjoyed

6 Matthew Bellew, a former officer in the Russian and Austrian armies, joined the Franco-Irish forces in the rebellion of 1798, and was subsequently executed. Dominic Bellew, his brother, who was the bishop of Killala since 1779, in association with the bishops of the province, had previously urged Catholics not to support oath-bound societies or the 'godless' French, if they landed, and after the rebellion proclaimed his loyalty by strongly supporting the union (Hogan, 'Some observations on contemporary allegations as to Bishop Dominic Bellew's (1745–1813) sympathies during the 1798 rebellion in Connaught' in *Seanchas Ard Mhacha*, 10:2 (1982), 417–25).

by Russia and Prussia. Castlereagh did not wish to propose a candidate, as in Russia or Prussia, but to check on the loyalty of the one who was elected. Regarding the inspection of documents from Rome, Consalvi maintained that the Holy See had always protested against this practice, but there was a difference between tolerating it and admitting it. Quarantotti had erred by admitting the *exequatur*.

Rather than comment on Quarantotti's rescript,[7] which would offend either the English or the Irish, Consalvi felt that the pope or the prefect of Propaganda should write to the bishops, and, without mentioning it, let them know what oath they could accept. He believed the government would be satisfied with the one used in the concordat with France (which the Catholics of England admitted but the Irish attacked). The part the government might play in the appointments of bishops should be specified, and the *exequatur* should be excluded but an explanation should be added to the effect that if the complaints of the Holy See against it were not listened to, the measure could be tolerated. He emphasized the necessity of adding that explanation, for, if the government insisted on that article, the whole affair should not be ruined because of it, especially as it was done everywhere.

Castlereagh wanted to enter into a private convention with Consalvi on these questions in Vienna. Though the cardinal was reluctant to take this step (and was later advised by Cardinal Pacca against it, on the pope's instructions), he thought it possible that when the laws against papal representation in England were removed, an agreement made in private could be made in public by the representatives of the pope and the king. As Quarantotti's agreement to a commission which would make inquiries about the qualities of the candidates for episcopal office was neither proper nor prudent, he suggested that before the election a list of candidates could be submitted to the government to see if anyone was not acceptable, or after the election the candidate's name would be presented in confidence to the government before being given to the public or sent to Rome.[8]

Consalvi arrived in Vienna for the congress on 16 September 1814. His overriding goal was to secure the return of the Papal States to the sovereignty

7 Both Consalvi and Pacca strongly disapproved of the rescript and of Quarantotti's part in issuing it. Pacca deplored 'la imbecillità e la facilità del prelato che ha osato di decidere un punto dì dottrina che non era nelle sue facolta' and 'la dichiarazione data da questo prelato con precipítanza in una materia dottrinale riservata al Sommo Pontefice' (Roveri, *La missione Consalvi e il Congresso di Vienna*, i, 159, p. 225).   8 Ibid., i, pp 90–3, 132–5, 163–78, 262–78, 349–53. Ellis, *Cardinal Consalvi and Anglo-Papal relations, 1814–1824*, pp 23–32. Consalvi had few illusions about the difficulty of obtaining emancipation. He referred to 'questo affare gravissimo, e spinosissimo, e delicatissimo, e capacissimo di produrre in un senso o nell altro le più significanti conseguenze' – a most grave, thorny and delicate affair very capable of producing in one sense or another the most significant consequences. Roveri, *La missione Consalvi e il Congresso di Vienna*, i, p. 273.

of the pope. Castlereagh was committed with the other European rulers to redrawing the map of Europe,[9] and he was not interested in spending much time with Consalvi discussing Catholic emancipation. Cardinal Pacca sent Consalvi instructions from the pope which had emerged from the congregation for Extraordinary Ecclesiastical Affairs for his negotiations.[10]

Pius VII ruled out any convention with Castlereagh on the grounds that such an agreement with a Protestant court would be unprecedented. When a new and moderate bill was put forward he would address a letter to the Catholics of Britain and Ireland permitting them to accept it and submit to it, and making clear what duties the Catholic religion imposed on them. Consalvi was encouraged in discussions with Castlereagh to see that the bill was such as Catholics could accept. In the previous bill, the pope was very displeased to find excessive distrust towards Catholicism, towards the Catholics of Britain themselves and towards himself.

Consequently, the pope suggested three formulas for an oath. The first was that of the French concordat, in which the bishop promised allegiance, promised to hold no communication with anyone which could destroy the public peace and promised to let the government know of anything in his diocese damaging to the state. The second oath was that permitted by Clement XI to George I which was a promise to be loyal, not to disturb the peace and tranquillity of the kingdom and not to assist anyone directly or indirectly who was opposed to the king and his government. In the third, a promise was made to be loyal to George III, to defend him against conspiracies, to inform him and his heirs of all plots or conspiracies against them and to be ready to support and defend the succession of his family.

Bearing in mind that some Protestant princes nominated – or rather, recommended – candidates for episcopal office, and regarding this practice as something he had to tolerate from despotic governments, the pope was unwilling to concede a veto that would permit the exclusion of subjects until the government chose one who might damage the Catholic religion to the advantage of the established church. The reply of Benedict XIV in 1748 to the bishop of Breslau declaring that the pontiffs never conceded that right to sovereigns of another religion was quoted. He also ruled out the possibility that the electors, before recommending candidates to the Holy See, should check with the government whether one were unacceptable to it, and, if so, to substitute another and inform the government. Such a right had never been possessed by a Protestant government. The experience of the past and the interest of Catholic subjects should be enough to ensure that candidates who were suspect or hostile to the government would not be proposed. The pope therefore added a new guarantee in the form of an oath for ecclesiastics

9 Bew, *Castlereagh*, pp 370–89.   10 Pacca to Consalvi, in Roveri, *La missione Consalvi e il Congresso di Vienna*, i, pp 487–95.

not to consent to anyone proposed for episcopal orders whom they did not believe to be of irreproachable loyalty and pacific conduct. Any investigation of papal documents was excluded. Otherwise it could happen that the pope could condemn some perverse maxim and the commission, for political reasons, would not permit his condemnation to be promulgated. Then Catholics could be in danger of being exiled if they carried out their duty of publicizing papal decrees.

Fortified by the papal advice, Consalvi soon encountered an unexpected obstacle: Castlereagh continued to show little interest in discussing the Catholic question. In fact the cardinal noticed a coldness in his response very different from his attitude in London, and when he approached the subject was told that it was a matter for the Catholics rather than for the government.[11] The cardinal felt sure that his instructions were bound to fail, as they ran counter to Castlereagh's expectations and desires. He found them too imprecise. He had been told that many clauses in the bill were injurious to the Holy See, but these had not been specified. A similar comment was made on the oath in the bill, but the various parts of it were not examined. The government, as the bill made clear, wanted to be assured of the loyalty of the bishops in Ireland, England and Scotland. The vicars apostolic were nominated directly by the pope and so the suggestion of electors consulting the government would not apply to them. Quarantotti's rescript had called for similar rules for the appointment of deans but it was not clear what role deans played and deans had not been mentioned in the bill.[12]

Castlereagh eventually, in reply to Consalvi, arranged that his chief assistant, Edward Cooke (who had been his undersecretary in Ireland) would hold a conference with him. Being a shrewd diplomat, Consalvi began by asking Cooke what the government sought rather than telling him what the Holy See would concede, but added that it was keen to do all in its power to satisfy English demands. He told Cooke about several clauses in the oath contained in the bill that were disrespectful to the Holy See. Among them he mentioned the rejection of papal infallibility. Cooke thereupon claimed that the Irish bishops, like the Gallicans, denied papal infallibility, but Consalvi contested this. He maintained that the pope could satisfy the government on the oath and on the allegiance of the bishops. Conjecturing that the government was mostly concerned about loyalty to the Hanoverian dynasty, he assured Cooke that Catholics would always be loyal and obedient to it.

11 Roveri, *La missione Consalvi e il congresso di Vienna*, ii, pp 40–1, iii, p. 99. In London he found Castlereagh '*impegnatissimo*', but in Vienna he found '*una certa indifferenza*' and '*una certa freddezza*' – indifference and coldness. 12 There were no deans in the Catholic church in England or Scotland, and very few in Ireland, where it was mostly an honorary title for parish priests. In the Church of England, deans played a much more important role, as they had charge of the cathedrals.

Consalvi mistakenly thought that the bill only required that candidates for the episcopate should be obliged to transmit, to the minister, certificates of their allegiance from five Catholic peers, and so thought that such an arrangement was very acceptable, as it removed from the government the right of excluding or including subjects chosen by the electors. If the candidates did not have a testimony of loyalty, they would not be presented and consequently the government would not exclude them. The cardinal did not put forward the instruction from the pope, but told Cooke that the pope would find no difficulty in accepting the proposal in the bill. Cooke met Consalvi's opposition to the *exequatur* with the argument that it was important for Catholics to show Protestant opponents of emancipation, who feared the damage it could cause to a Protestant government, especially in Ireland, that they had nothing to hide. The cardinal told him that, if such a clause were contained in the bill, the pope could not authorize it, but he feared that the government would pass a separate law claiming a right it saw other states, both Catholic and non-Catholic, claim. Consalvi assured Pacca that he would adhere to his instructions not to enter into a convention, though he did not see why a pact or convention of some kind could not be made with a Protestant government. Though not sure that Castlereagh would have been satisfied with the proposal of a papal brief after the concession of emancipation authorizing Catholics to accept it, if it presented no serious difficulties, he put that suggestion to Cooke.

That evening Consalvi met briefly with Castlereagh, who again asked him for a written statement, but the cardinal was unwilling to commit himself, apart from the three oaths. Then the nuncio at Vienna, Monsignor Severoli, encountered Castlereagh at a dinner and was told that the affair of the Catholics in Britain did not have the good outcome he had hoped for, confirming Consalvi's own view that Rome was not offering enough to satisfy the British government. All it was offering was that the five Catholic peers should testify to the loyalty of the candidate elected but the government, he believed, had altered its demands and wanted a mixed commission of Catholics and Protestants to examine the qualities of the candidate chosen, before including him in those recommended to the Holy See. The government was also being denied the nine paragraphs of the oath in the bill which were not contained in the three formulas sent from Rome. And the pope was not prepared to issue a letter in anticipation of a bill, but would only do so afterwards.

Six weeks after his colloquy with Cooke, Consalvi had to report rather gloomily that he had not had another conversation with Castlereagh: though the foreign minister had once asked him when they could have a further conference, he had not pursued the subject. The cardinal was convinced that this was the result of dissatisfaction on the part of the government with the dispositions of the Holy See. The pope, Pacca informed him, was disappointed that his views were so unfavourably received.[13]

Castlereagh was summoned to London at the beginning of February 1815 and was replaced by Wellington.[14] Though aware of Castlereagh's coldness, Consalvi approached him about the Catholic question before his departure, only to be told that the reason the foreign secretary had not seen him was the fault of the Irish. In the intervening time, the conduct of the Irish had been so refractory, imprudent and ill-disposed towards the government and had so generally upset everyone that the bill, which had been very narrowly defeated the previous year, would not, if proposed again, obtain a third of the members' votes. After what the Irish had done, there was not one Anglican, not one Protestant of the most moderate and well-disposed kind, who had not turned against them. There was therefore no point in talking about the question, and it would be more expedient to postpone it until the Irish calmed down.[15] Castlereagh then remarked that Poynter, for whom he had the highest esteem and who was most acceptable to the government, was then in Rome. He suggested that when Consalvi returned there he should discuss with Poynter what the Holy See could accept and either let Castlereagh know or let Poynter, on his return to London, work for its successful outcome. Consequently, Consalvi asked Pacca to ensure that Poynter would remain in Rome until his return, assuring both himself and the pope of the value of conferring with him.[16] Castlereagh made a gesture of goodwill to Consalvi before leaving Vienna: he gave him a print of his portrait, with a gracious dedication.[17]

Catholic emancipation was the priority neither of Castlereagh nor of Consalvi at Vienna. Castlereagh was concerned with upholding British interests as the map of Europe was being redrawn and was 'inclined to view the pope as an ally'.[18] His negotiations and discussions with the other sovereigns and statesmen consumed most of his time and energy. Consalvi, the greatest

---

13 Consalvi to Pacca, ibid., ii, pp 63–75, 293–8, 562–3. 14 Consalvi described Wellington in terms which the Irish campaigners for emancipation would have treated with scorn: he had *l'aria la più leale, la più franca, la più dolce* – the most loyal, frank and pleasant manner. The cardinal later felt obliged to put on a lavish dinner for Wellington and the other delegates, but, if he hoped thereby to soften Wellington's attitudes to Catholics, the ploy failed (ibid., iii, p. 59). 15 Though Irish priests and laymen had continued to denounce Grattan's bill as infamous, Castlereagh may have been particularly angered by O'Connell's comments on him. O'Connell had said of Castlereagh that he might consent to change one kind of degradation for another but would never consent to Catholics attaining their freedom. He accused Castlereagh of first dyeing his country in blood and then selling her. He went on to describe Castlereagh as 'the master of the Flogging and Torturing Club in Dublin' (15 June 1813, in O'Connell, *Select speeches of Daniel O'Connell, MP*, i, pp 191–208). 16 Consalvi to Pacca, 1, 4, 15 Feb.; 1815, in Roveri, *La missione Consalvi e il congresso di Vienna*, iii, pp 21–136. 17 Consalvi to Pacca, ibid., iii, pp 21, 59, 90–100, 106–8, 267–82, 546–8; Regoli, *Ercole Consalvi: le scelte per la chiesa*, pp 372–84. 18 Zamoyski, *Rites of peace: the fall of Napoleon and the congress of Vienna*, p. 237.

ecclesiastical statesman of the early nineteenth century,[19] was commissioned by Pope Pius VII to obtain the restoration of the Papal States as they existed before the French Revolution. His success in achieving this goal was regarded, perhaps, as his greatest diplomatic triumph,[20] but he was fortunate that the interests of other countries coincided with his aim to win back the Papal States; they did not want Austria controlling most of Italy. He also lent his full support to the abolition of slavery, to which the congress finally agreed.

Castlereagh was very conscious of the opposition of the prince regent and the house of lords to emancipation. He himself had voted for it but had always associated it with the need for securities from Catholics, and so would have welcomed a statement from Consalvi specifying the concessions the Holy See might make. He certainly would not and could not have given any assurances that papal concessions would have led to a change of mind on the part of those who were hostile to emancipation. He was fully aware both of the powerful and influential opposition of the Church of England and also of that of the nonconformists. With that kind of religious opposition allied to the traditional hostility of the English people to Catholicism and their desire not to alter the Protestant settlement of 1688, he knew that emancipation was faced with formidable obstacles. His blaming the Irish for antagonizing and alienating possible supporters of emancipation in parliament was disingenuous. Irish opposition to the bill and the rescript was purely vocal: there were no threats of rebellion or agitation for separation from Britain as a result of it, and Irish hostility to the bill was probably not as extreme as that of English Protestants.[21] Castlereagh doubtless took exception to the noisy protests in Ireland against the bill, but the petitions from the clergy, towns and public bodies in England against the bill and against the Catholic petitions were far more persistent. Castlereagh had given the Catholic leaders of Ireland a promise in all but name in 1800 that emancipation would follow the union, and so they could scarcely be accused of ingratitude when no serious effort was made by the government to fulfil its side of the bargain.

On his part, Consalvi made no effort to find out why the Irish were so opposed to the bill. He could easily have sought guidance from Archbishop Troy, but instead he formed his view of the Irish from his discussions in London with Castlereagh and, perhaps, with Poynter and some of the lay Catholic leaders – less than reliable sources. Given that Irish Catholics were

---

19 Ellis, *Cardinal Consalvi and Anglo-papal relations, 1814–1824*, p. viii.   20 Apart from Avignon, the Comtat Venaissin and Ferrara, the pope recovered all his territories.   21 He later complained to his brother of the damage being done by 'the democracy which is growing amongst the inferior clergy in Ireland' (Castlereagh to Charles Stewart, 20 May 1816 in Bew, *Castlereagh*, p. 425).

far more numerous than those in Britain and were a much more important element in the struggle for emancipation, his failure to acquaint himself fully with their attitudes and responses was negligent. His comment that the Irish clergy were beholden to the aristocracy and his reference to clubs indicate his ignorance of the situation. Undoubtedly the reaction of the Catholic Board in Dublin – which represented the views of the middle classes, not the aristocracy – to the bill and the rescript was extremely hostile, and the bishops could not have stood up to it had they wished to do so. A majority of them would have opposed the rescript without the lay leadership, though in a much quieter way, and they might not have sent a deputation to Rome. The few bishops – like Troy, Moylan and O'Reilly – who were disposed to accept it, realized that they could not resist their confrères, let alone the Catholic public.

Consalvi's opponents in the Roman curia accused him of spending too much time playing the courtier and cultivating statesmen. His office by definition brought him into frequent contact with the aristocrats who ran the governments of Europe, and, as at Vienna, he entertained them in the diplomatic style. However, his need to conform to accepted practices did not diminish the hostility of his critics in Rome, the *zelanti*, many of whom objected to some of his agreements with states in the first instance. He was flattered by the attention of the English nobility, continued to exchange greetings with Castlereagh, and in his will made bequests to Castlereagh's family and to several other English aristocrats.[22] Had Consalvi been allowed a free hand to negotiate with Castlereagh, and had Castlereagh been seriously committed to working towards emancipation, they could possibly have made arrangements that would have satisfied the demands made in the house of commons about the royal role in episcopal appointments, oaths and the *exequatur*. Castlereagh may have wished to see emancipation granted but, even if the 'securities' he had sought had been conceded, it is very doubtful that they would have made much impact on the house of lords. That doubtless explains why he did not hold serious discussions with Consalvi in Vienna. Consalvi was a skilful and flexible negotiator, and he did not regard the traditional obstacle of not granting to a Protestant sovereign the right to nominate bishops or the *exequatur* as permanent impediments. He would have found ways around these difficulties in the distinction between 'tolerating' and 'admitting' to which he had referred in his despatches to Rome.

In the first flush of victory over Napoleon, the pope's refusal to close the ports of his states in Napoleon's Continental blockade won him praise and admiration in British government circles. But this enthusiasm soon cooled and the hard facts of British realpolitik were expressed by Castlereagh in

22 Ellis, *Cardinal Consalvi and Anglo–papal relations, 1814–1824*, p. 177.

June 1815 when he pointed out that he did not wish to have the pope send a regular mission to Britain, though an unavowed resident might be acceptable, that the friends of the pope in the government could not relish anything like a new system, and that the 'religionists' in the country would cry out if Consalvi's red stockings were seen too often in Carlton House.[23]

II

Poynter's visit to Rome was designed both to defend the rescript, which his friends in the Catholic Board had so happily accepted, and to combat Milner. Macpherson had been worried by the inroads made by Milner against the standing of the other vicars apostolic. Poynter, accompanied by his vicar general and confidant, had reached Rome on 19 January 1815. Napoleon's escape from Elba, the march of Murat, the king of Naples, through the Papal States and the flight of the pope from Rome prevented them from remaining in Italy until the Congress of Vienna ended.

While in Rome, they wasted no time in getting down to business with Cardinal Litta. In response to his request, Poynter drew up an account of the situation of the Catholics in England, listing the prejudices against them and the discrimination from which they suffered. In it he showed himself to be as forceful as Milner, even to the extent of rebuking a cardinal – either a courageous or a foolhardy move. Listing the grievances of Catholics, he drew the opposite conclusion from them that the Irish drew, that they were not serious.

Catholics in England, he noted, were excluded from parliament and from voting in elections at all levels; their soldiers and sailors were obliged to attend Protestant services at the risk of fines, imprisonment and even death;[24] many sons of Catholic soldiers were sent to military schools in which they were taught the Protestant religion; the marriages of Catholics were invalid unless celebrated in a Protestant church; their priests were only allowed to visit hospitals with the permission of officials; money given for their charities was sometimes taken from them. The Irish Catholics, on the other hand, were allowed to vote in elections and their marriages could be celebrated by their priests. Their seminary was endowed at public expense to the sum of £8,000 annually.[25]

---

23 Robinson, *Cardinal Consalvi, 1757–1824*, pp 118–20. Carlton House was the residence of the prince regent.   24 'In rebus Religiosis Catholici nautae et milites in Anglia nulla lege patriae violata ad Protestantium Ecclesias aut orandi loca diebus Dominicis cogi possunt et aliquando coguntur, qui si parere recusant mulcta, carcere, et ipsa morte puniri possunt.' This was over dramatizing the situation with a vengeance: despite the regulations, no soldier would have been executed in the nineteenth century for disobeying rules about church attendance.   25 Actually, the grant had been increased to £9,250 in 1808.

Poynter mentioned the prejudices against Catholics about the pope's deposing power over Protestant kings and not keeping faith with heretics. Consequently, Protestants demanded securities and refused concessions unless Catholics took noxious oaths. Knowing the arrangements that both Catholic and Protestant countries had made with the Holy See about the nomination of bishops and communication with Rome, the government thought some similar provisions should be made. But many of the lower classes in Ireland rejected any suggestion that such conditions should be accepted.

Poynter's solution to royal intervention in the appointment of bishops was to recommend the transmission of the names of candidates for episcopal office to the king's ministers to obtain testimonies of their loyalty, and then the transmission of three acceptable names to the pope for appointment. Nothing could please both parliament and the Catholics more than that the pope should thereby show his confidence in the government.

He suggested further that the pope convey to the British people and government his assurance that their fears of evils from his authority were groundless; that he had neither the power nor the will to act against a benefi-cent government; that he wished the Catholics to demonstrate their loyalty, obedience and devotion; that he would order all future bishops to take the oath prescribed for the Irish bishops in 1791;[26] that he would not appoint any bishop who was not a British subject and whose loyalty was not beyond doubt, and not without a testimony from the government; that he would praise George III for the benefits conferred by the relaxation of the penal laws and congratulate the prince regent on the peace that had been achieved after atrocious wars, trusting that Catholics would show reverence, obedience and gratitude to so great a prince; and that he should exhort all Catholics to behave as good Christians, abstaining from any actions, writings or speeches that could disturb public tranquillity or offend the king and his government.[27]

Collingridge, who had been angered by Milner's attacks on himself and his colleagues, addressed a long letter to Poynter, which was translated into Italian and which was obviously intended for direct submission to Litta or some other cardinal. It was a bitter congeries of complaints, many of which had already been aired in Rome, and its style very much resembled Milner's. It contained a few accusations that would have helped Poynter's case but which the London vicar apostolic could not easily have made himself. He brought up Milner's unsavoury intrigue to obtain an appointment to the London District and implied that the frustration of that ambition had led to

26 In the oath to be taken at their consecration, the Irish bishops, according to the formula prescribed for them in June 1791, swore that there was nothing in their obligations contrary to the allegiance due to the king and his successors.   27 Poynter to Propaganda, 18 Feb. 1815, ASV, Segr. Stato, Inghilterra, 1814–56, 29, ff 53r–61v.

his ceaseless persecution of Poynter ever since. It had also led to his frequent charges that London was not properly administered, and to his lambasting Collingridge and the other bishops in his pastorals and writings and in the *Orthodox Journal*. Their characters had been ruined in the press by the malicious references to the tavern where the fifth resolution was signed, giving the impression that the signatories had been a crowd of drunks. They had suffered from Milner's habit of mangling correspondence to create impressions different from those intended. Collingridge also drew attention to a discreditable correspondence between Milner and Coxe-Hippisley, and to improper interventions by Milner in Collingridge's jurisdiction when the bishop was first seeking episcopal office, in which he threatened no longer to be an advocate for Rome, and, in fact, wished to be freed from his ministry, in consequence of the implied rejection of him by the refusal of a mitre. In Collingridge's letter, the Irish bishops were reprobated for their seventeenth resolution (when they praised Milner for his stand against the fifth resolution in 1810) and for their intervention in the de Trevaux case.[28]

Poynter gave a further account of the 'unexpected wound' inflicted by Milner on the vicars apostolic by his exploitation of the fifth resolution. That resolution had already led to bitter arguments and it continued to deepen the antagonism between these two implacable adversaries. He argued that Earl Grey had explained that from the beginning no veto was involved in the resolution, that Lord Stourton had insisted that it only entailed a disposition to negotiate with the government for emancipation so that mutual satisfaction might be obtained, and that Milner had told a couple of lay lords that they might sign it. Milner claimed he could not sign it as he was acting for the Irish bishops, and then 'a vehement clamour was raised in Ireland' among the lower orders of the Irish against it. Poynter complained about this, and about the Irish bishops describing the fifth resolution as 'vague and indefinite' in their resolution of thanks to Milner. He maintained that the Irish bishops' own resolution was similar and questioned their right to pass a sentence on a resolution and act of English Catholics. He also dismissed Milner's charge that the objectionable clauses in the bill in 1813 originated in the fifth resolution, and vehemently rejected Milner's taunt that the laymen who sponsored the fifth resolution had rewarded him with a pension.

Poynter also (very justifiably) lamented Milner's penchant for reviving 'ancient and dormant disputes', citing his habit of referring to Protesting Catholic Dissenters and the Cisalpine Club. Claiming that the former title had not been used since about 1790, he explained that the Cisalpine Club might in its origin have been offensive but was then 'nothing more than a convivial meeting of Catholics'. And he concluded that Milner's writings inflicted the greatest injury on the whole Catholic body of Britain because

28 Collingridge to Poynter (copy), 10 Jan. 1815, WDA.

they disseminated discord between English and Irish Catholics and prevented 'that peace and concord which the other vicars apostolic were endeavouring to establish among all'.[29]

Though Poynter found the pope very kind, he was not prepared to enter into the details of their problems. That was Litta's domain, and for the most part he regarded Litta as harsh and unsympathetic. At their first interview he 'insultingly signified' that Macpherson was not to accompany them, and at the second he attacked Poynter over the fifth resolution. He had read Milner's pamphlets very carefully and 'brought the minutest circumstances against us ... in a very high dictatorial tone'. Poynter and Bramston met another cardinal who was as full of prejudices against them and against all the English Catholics as Litta. Consequently, Poynter set out his defence at length, supporting his case with documents proving 'Bp. M's facts to be fictions', 'charging him with an invasion of their jurisdiction, together with Collingridge's excellent letter' with the accusations against Milner. Angered by Litta's manner, Poynter, after offering an explanation, reported that:

> Mr Bramston and I then rose upon him and we spoke as loud as he did. We then told him that we discovered in some cardinals a disposition to sacrifice the English vicars apostolic to Bp M. and the Irish bishops, and to sacrifice the Catholics of England to the Irish populace. I told him that he protected our aggressor and oppressed the oppressed. We brought him down. We told him that unless the Propaganda would support the other vicars apostolic it would be impossible to govern our districts and he must not be suprised if in less than two years we resigned. He stared and looked pale.

Poynter concluded that this rebuff had changed Litta's tone (though curial cardinals were not accustomed to such treatment and rarely forgot it) and he came to acknowledge how unjustifiable Milner's conduct had been. Bewailing the difficulties he had had to face without one '*efficient*' friend in Rome as he fought the cause of the English Catholic clergy and people, he confessed that he had gone through 'the hardest part of my life'.[30] Macpherson, his agent, had not only annoyed Litta, but had failed to give Poynter the advice and help he expected.

Litta, bombarded by conflicting and contradictory claims, seems to have wavered between them. Milner and he discussed possible plans to allow the government some leeway in approving or disapproving of candidates for the episcopate. Litta had proposed that the civil authorities be restricted to

29 This letter addressed to Cardinal Litta dated 15 Mar. 1815 was published by Charles Butler in 1820 in both Latin and English as 'the apologetical epistle' (copy, DDA). 30 Poynter to Collingridge, 20 Mar. 1815, ClDA.

negatives on two or three candidates, and Milner was prepared to accept that restriction. He agreed that it would be impossible to oblige the government to assign motives for its exercise of a veto. He feared that evil would arise in Ireland depending on how the concession was explained. And so he suggested that Quarantotti's rescript be deprecated, that the bishops, clergy and people be praised for their attachment to the faith and the bishops be praised for their resolutions of the past opposing concessions. His own suggestion was that in a vacancy the metropolitan or senior bishop, after consultation with the bishops of the province, would draw up a list of ten or twelve priests with suitable qualifications who were British-born subjects. The list would then be given by the metropolitan or senior bishop to the lord lieutenant with the freedom to expunge two or three names inside twenty days. A selection of three names would be made by the chapter and clergy of the diocese from the names to which no objection had been made, and subject to the correction of the bishops of the province, would be then recommended to the Holy See. He suggested that coadjutors would not be mentioned because of the certainty that if the bishop asked for one, he would not be in disgrace with the government. As a precaution, Milner stressed the importance of the bishops communicating the pope's orders before the lay orators in Ireland had the chance to provoke agitation among the people.[31]

Milner later regretted taking any part in proposing a veto, however harmless, though his suggestions came close to what was later decided. He escaped any public criticism as Litta changed his mind and did not pursue Milner's suggestions.[32] Poynter's side might have been helped by the arrival in Rome of Edward Cooke, who had negotiated on behalf of Castlereagh with Consalvi at Vienna, and who presumably brought the foreign secretary's high opinion of Poynter with him. But Cooke was in Rome for only a few days when Napoleon escaped from Elba and Murat, Napoleon's brother-in-law, who was king of Naples, hastened to meet him, marching through the Papal States. The pope fled to Genoa, where he was protected by British forces and a British fleet, and the cardinals went with him or followed immediately. Litta was pleased to hear of Cooke's comments and told Poynter and Bramston, who met him at Viterbo, that he was surprised at the Irish bishops' retaining Milner as their agent. He also claimed that he had rebuked Milner for his writings and would order him not to return to England. Poynter and Bramston were very pleased that Litta, whom they regarded as very capricious, had seemingly swung over to their side.[33]

In Ireland, the protests against Quarantotti's rescript showed no signs of abating. Daniel O'Connell's repudiation of it was representative of the views of thousands. O'Connell detected a conspiracy between Lord George

31 Milner to Litta, 18 Feb. 1815, ASV, AES, pos 9a, fasc 7, ff 14r–15r.   32 Ward, *The eve of Catholic emancipation*, ii, p. 125.   33 Ibid., pp 125–31.

Bentinck, the British naval commander at Genoa, Castlereagh and Consalvi, by which the cardinal would give Britain 'effectual supremacy' over the church in Ireland in return for the restoration to the pope of his states. He went on to declare in robust Gallican language:

> I am sincerely a Catholic but I am not a papist. I deny the doctrine that the pope has any temporal authority, directly or indirectly, over Ireland ... In spiritual matters, too, the authority of the pope is limited: he cannot, though his conclave of cardinals were to join him, vary our religion, either in doctrine or in essential discipline in any respect. Even in non-essential discipline the pope cannot vary it without the assent of the Irish Catholic bishops. I do therefore totally deny that Consalvi or Quarantotti or even the pope can claim the submission which the seceders[34] proclaim they are ready to shew ...

He went on to predict that if the clergy were to descend from their high station 'to become the vile slaves of the castle', the people would despise them too much to contribute to their upkeep.[35]

Milner, Poynter and Bramston all made their way to Genoa. Milner sought the pope's verdict on the rescript but received no official answer. Litta, he subsequently reported, tried to persuade him to wait and return with him to Rome, whither the ecclesiastical participants at the Congress of Vienna would go when it ended. But he did not try to force him to do so, and Milner left Genoa on 11 April. The cardinals who, in the congregation for Extraordinary Ecclesiastical Affairs had been giving advice through Pacca to Consalvi, met on 20 April, and, presumably on the basis of the *ponenza* that had been drawn up for the congregation of Propaganda, drew up a letter setting out their views on the role to be assigned to the government in episcopal appointments and on the oaths that might be taken. The pope gave it his approval. Poynter was given copies for himself, Milner and Troy, and he and Bramston left Genoa on 28 April.[36]

If Litta had really wished to prevent Milner from resuming control of his vicariate and to retain him in Rome, which he could only have done with the pope's authorization, he would have insisted on keeping him at Genoa. But he had made no attempt to do so. He could not have foreseen the consequences for the pope of a victory by Napoleon over his former enemies, and in that state of uncertainty, may have decided not to take any draconian steps against Milner.

---

34 The seceders were the aristocratic faction led by Lord Fingall, who had left the Catholic Board. 35 *FJ*, 27 Jan. 1815. 36 Ward, *The eve of Catholic emancipation*, ii, pp 131–3.

Both Milner and Poynter had been given the opportunity to unload their gripes about each other's behaviour on to Litta. Neither had scored a victory, as each regarded the cardinal as vacillating and unpredictable. They were both aggrieved that Litta had not given them a certificate or testimony of his approval. They would have to analyse his comments on their return to England.

12

The Genoese letter

I

The long-awaited papal response to the criticisms of the rescript took the form of a letter addressed by Cardinal Litta to Poynter. In it, the cardinal explained that the pope had been forced to flee from Rome before he could carry out the full examination of the question and did not therefore want to make a solemn judgment on a matter of such importance. However, it was his wish that he, Litta, should make known the pontiff's mind on the conditions that the Catholics of Great Britain could accept, should they be granted emancipation. In that event the pope would address a letter to the Catholics of Britain and Ireland outlining what was acceptable. He then dealt with the three central elements that had formed the core of the rescript: the oath, the involvement of ministers in the nomination of bishops and the *exequatur*.

Litta listed three formulas of oaths that the pope would permit Catholics to take if emancipation were granted, and which he believed would satisfy the government. These had already been submitted to Consalvi in Vienna by Cardinal Pacca. Significantly, they contained nothing about disturbing the Protestant religion or about the pope's temporal power. Nor did they contain any rejection of the claims that Rome found offensive about the pope or council ordering the deposition or murder of princes, the pope not being infallible or about obeying an immoral order from him. The oaths were unexceptionable. Catholics were to swear allegiance and loyalty to the king; to avoid contact with anything or anyone which could harm public order and, if they knew of such in the diocese, to report it to the government; to afford no help to anyone who directly or indirectly was hostile to the government; to defend the king and crown against all conspiracies and to uphold the succession to the crown against all claimants, either inside or outside the kingdom.

Coming to the election of bishops, Litta noted that the pope had always insisted that those who commended candidates for the episcopacy to the Holy See should admit only priests who, in addition to the other pastoral virtues, were distinguished for their prudence, love of peace and loyalty to the king. Though the government could be satisfied with the oath of loyalty of the newly elected bishops, nevertheless for its greater satisfaction he did

247

not hesitate to permit the electors to show a list of the candidates for the episcopate to the king's ministers (as Pacca had already suggested to Consalvi for Castlereagh) so that, if the government found one unsuitable, his name would be removed, but a sufficient number should be left from which the pope could choose those whom he deemed suited for office.[1] Once the decree of emancipation was passed, the pope would forward a brief to the bishops and Catholics of Great Britain and Ireland expressing his gratitude for the clemency and generosity of the British government, would exhort Catholics to show loyalty to their august sovereign and would permit Catholics to accept the oath and the election of bishops, as already laid out.

The *exequatur*, however, could not be conceded, as such permission violated the divinely appointed freedom of the teaching authority of the church, and had never been anywhere permitted. Even when Catholic states arrogated to themselves that right they were guilty of an abuse, which the Holy See was forced to tolerate to avoid greater evils. There was no danger of anything damaging to public order or to the sovereign being transmitted through the independent instructions of the Holy See, and the vicars apostolic did not make reports to the Holy See on any matters concerning politics. It was to be hoped therefore that the government would not persevere in demanding what the Holy See could not concede and which experience showed was detrimental to the government itself.[2]

From the point of view of the Holy See, the Genoese letter was a formal repudiation of Quarantotti's rescript.[3] Two of the three central elements of the rescript were disavowed. The *exequatur* was totally excluded and the oaths were less comprehensive and more innocuous than that accepted by Quarantotti. All three were completely unexceptionable and could have been taken by any Catholic, clerical or lay, in any country. The suspicion or anxiety that Quarantotti's oath might have been used to hinder Catholic evangelical activity among Protestants, or even the freely made decision of Protestants to

---

1 'Sanctitas Sua non dubitabit permittere, ut illi ad quos spectat, exhibeant candidatorum notulam Regiis Ministris, ut Gubernium, si forte quis invisus aut suspectus sit, quamprimum illum indicet ut expugnatur.' This condition obtained in several concordats or agreements. In the concordat between Leo XII and William I of the Netherlands it was laid down: 'Si forte vero aliqui ex candidatis ipsis Serenissimo Regi minus grati extiterint, capitula e catalogo eos delebunt, reliquo tamen manente sufficienti candidatorum numero, ex quo novus archiepiscopus, vel episcopus eligi valeat' (Mercati, *Raccolta di concordati su materie ecclesiastiche tra la Santa Sede e le autorità civili*, pp 704–10).   2 Litta to Poynter, 26 Apr. 1815, ASV, Segr. Stato, Inghilterra, 1814–1856, 29, ff 174r–175r. Richard Hayes later claimed that Litta begged the pope not to write this letter but the powerful Consalvi overrode his unwillingness (Hayes to MacDonnell, 24 Feb. 1816, *Coll. Hib.* 24, ff 133. 7). It is unlikely that Litta would have revealed to Hayes what passed between him and the pope. Milner claimed that the letter was to be ascribed to the 'unconsecrated secretary of state and not to the high church bishop, Card. Litta' (Milner to Scully, 9 Oct. 1815, in MacDermot, *The Catholic question in Ireland and England, 1798–1822*, p. 565).   3 Litta to Troy, 26 Apr. 1815, DDA.

become Catholics, by its demand of a pledge not to disturb the Protestant state or faith had been removed. There was, however, a vagueness about the letter which was bound to lead to trouble. The number of candidates to whom the government could object was not fixed.[4] And in the smaller Irish dioceses, the number of candidates of suitable episcopal timbre within the appropriate age bracket was bound to be small. Clarification would have to wait for a bill, when the pope would give definite answers.

In the meantime the pope and Litta could safely maintain that the role assigned to the state in the nomination of bishops was securely circumscribed. The electors, and here Litta was probably thinking of a chapter of about twelve canons with input from the bishops of the province, were authorized to find out if candidates were rejected by the government and then to send to Rome the names of those against whom no objection had been raised. With a small number of electors, the unfavourable attitude of the government towards two or three could possibly have been kept secret (as distinct from the arrangement accepted by Quarantotti), but, in fact, there was no system in Ireland or in Britain for the official intervention of priests in the selection of names to be forwarded to Rome for episcopal office. Litta obviously felt that the method he suggested was much less objectionable than that proposed in the bill of 1813, in which Catholic lay lords and Protestant officials were involved in testifying to the loyalty of the candidates chosen by the electors, who would then be judged by the king or lord lieutenant. Compared to the French system, where the state named the bishops and the pope gave or withheld canonical institution, or the Prussian system, where the monarch named the candidate whom he wished the diocesan chapter to elect and sought approval from Rome, the system proposed by Litta offered much less influence or power to the state. But that was not how either the bishops or the Catholic Board interpreted the guidance from Genoa.

Archbishop Murray, who had gone to Rome to campaign against Quarantotti's rescript, complained that the most objectionable part of it was retained in the Genoese letter. 'Thus,' he lamented, 'are the hopes of Ireland on the point of being blasted except the hand of God interpose to avert this calamity.' He felt it was a poor 'remuneration for the anxiety with which it was sought for'.[5]

Litta's letter was not officially known to the members of parliament when petitions for unqualified emancipation were presented in May and June 1815, though Murray later claimed the pope's intentions had been made known to the government. The 'seceders', lords Fingall, Southwell and the Bellews did not sign the main petitions, which bore 10,000 signatures,

---

4 In the letter it was stated that if the government found anyone (singular) of whom it had suspicions, that person could be removed from the list; in the concordat with the Netherlands, the reference was to suspect persons (plural).   5 Murray to Coppinger, 18 June 1815, CloDA.

including those of archbishops O'Reilly, Troy and Murray, and other prelates, but Henry Grattan presented one from them. Sir Henry Parnell also presented an English petition. All were rejected. Milner informed Litta of the rejection of the petitions, and added that the concessions in his letter could not satisfy the Protestants.[6]

On his return to London, Poynter wrote to Consalvi to let him know that he had thanked Castlereagh for the complimentary remarks he had made to the cardinal. He told Consalvi that he had shown Litta's letter in confidence to Catholics of distinction, that they were pleased with it and hoped that it would play a happy part in the achievement of emancipation. Without enlarging on the differing attitudes of the grandees who welcomed the letter and the others whom he thought would not, he explained that he had not publicized it for fear that it might excite prejudices against the pope's intentions among the people. Then he went on to bewail at length the prejudices that he found Litta entertained against himself and the principal Catholics, both ecclesiastical and secular, of Great Britain. Though he had refuted Milner's calumnies, Litta had given him no reply in writing to show his satisfaction with the vicars apostolic and the 'injured' Catholics. Milner allegedly had received a flattering letter from the cardinal, assuring him that his past conduct met with the approval of the pope and the cardinals at Rome, with blame being attached only to the asperity of his manner. According to Milner, all his conduct in disturbing the peace, in calumniating his colleagues, invading their jurisdiction and supporting the rabble of Ireland in its revolt against the government had been approved. As his conduct had been known to and condemned by the government, what was it to think of Rome favouring such behaviour? In fact both Poynter and Milner had sought Litta's approval and had been disappointed with the cardinal's impartiality.[7]

Neither the vicars apostolic nor the Irish bishops publicized Litta's letter, but rumours about its content gradually leaked out.[8] In Ireland reports began to circulate of an unfavourable decision from Rome, and Troy informed Litta that he could scarcely describe the ferment which they caused. The pope was accused of making a concession to the British government in return for the restoration of the Papal States. The Irish bishops were blamed for the veto despite their opposition to it, and the English bishops for having favoured it. And the question was being asked how the English bishops prevailed over the Irish and Milner.[9]

6 Milner to Murray, 31 July 1815, DDA.   7 Poynter to Consalvi, 21 July 1815, ASV, Segr. Stato, Inghilterra, 1814–1856, 29, ff 74r–75r. Milner complained to Murray that despite the assurances he had been given by Litta that his conduct in opposing the fifth resolution, the bill, the Blanchard schism and the Cisalpines had met with papal and cardinalatial approval, he never got 'a line *in proof of this*' (Milner to Murray, 31 July 1815, DDA).   8 Bishop Collingridge thought the oaths in the letter amounted to nothing more than those that had already been taken (Collingridge to Poynter, 14 June 1815, WDA).   9 Troy to Litta, 12 Aug. 1815, APF, SC

Milner, writing to Archbishop Murray, his fellow delegate to Rome, about the Genoese letter, admitted that he had revealed the contents of it only to Bishop Murphy of Cork, 'who was not less displeased with its contents than Yr Grace is'. He explained that it was put together at a most unfavourable time, as the papal entourage decided to seek refuge under English protection. At first Litta had desired him to wait and return to Rome, but as the political situation worsened, Milner was told that no letter would be given to him and no change would be made in the English mission. Milner believed that Castlereagh, 'the falsest of all men', was through Consalvi their 'chief antagonist'. He had conveyed to the cardinal that the possibility of a concession had 'produced no sensible effect in favour of emancipation' in parliament and that as the concession would neither satisfy the Protestants nor the Cisalpines, it would 'not answer the grand object of pacifying the Irish and reconciling them to their grievances'. Consequently, he approved of the possibility mentioned by Murray that the Irish prelates should adopt 'a strong expostulation, on the conduct of Rome, in listening more to the representations of the Cisalpines and Protests than to the suffering Irish Caths and their faithful prelates'. And he added that he would be sorry if the Irish bishops appealed to their people against Rome but thought that 'a hint of yr being reduced to do this wd probably have a good effect on a court whose character is *timidity*'.[10]

Three months after receiving the Genoese letter, Troy had shown it neither to the clergy nor to the people, for fear of infuriating them. He therefore sought clarification from Rome. He wanted to know if a government minister could expunge a number of unacceptable candidates from the list given to him. He feared that this would provoke the antagonism of his people, who would suspect that their church was being put under the control of a Protestant ruler. It would therefore be necessary to know how many names of candidates should be left to the pope, from which he would make his selection. He also wanted to know what was meant in the letter by the reference to the electors, whose custom it was to select candidates for office. As there was no custom in Ireland of only a chapter commending names, and as some dioceses did not have chapters, and parish priests had been behaving like chapters, he wanted guidance in this area. He also recommended that metropolitans and the bishops of the province be empowered to expunge the names of those they deemed unsuitable from the list before it was submitted to the minister.[11]

Twenty-three bishops, two coadjutors and the warden of Galway,

(Irlanda), 19, f 347r.   10 Milner to Murray, 31 July 1815, DDA. Milner later told Scully that he was sorry he didn't accept Litta's invitation to stay at Genoa until he could return with the cardinal in his carriage to Rome (Milner to Scully, 9 Oct. 1815 in MacDermot, *The Catholic question in Ireland and England, 1798–1822*, p. 565).   11 Troy to Litta, 7 Aug. 1815 (copy), DDA.

thoroughly alarmed by the vigorous reaction of the laity to the rumours about the letter, met on 23 and 24 August in Dublin to discuss it. Without referring to it, they issued very forthright resolutions against any state involvement in episcopal nominations.[12] The first resolution deplored the interference of the crown, directly or indirectly in the appointment of bishops in Ireland, which they claimed 'must essentially injure, and may eventually subvert' the Catholic religion in the country. Secondly, they stated that they would consider themselves as betraying the dearest interests of their church, if they did not make it clear that they would always and 'under all circumstances, deprecate and oppose, in every canonical and constitutional way, any such interference'. In their third resolution, which Roman officials would have regarded as smacking of Gallicanism, they declared:

> Though we sincerely venerate the supreme pontiff as visible head of the Church, we do not conceive, that our apprehensions for the safety of the Roman Catholic Church in Ireland can or ought to be removed by any determination of His Holiness, adopted, or intended to be adopted, not only without our concurrence but in direct opposition to our repeated resolutions, and the very energetic memorial presented on our behalf, and so ably supported by our deputy, the Most Rev. Dr. Murray, who, in that quality was more competent to inform his Holiness of the real state and interests of the Roman Catholic Church in Ireland than any other with whom he is said to have consulted.

They then resolved that their sentiments, 'respectful, firm and decided', should be transmitted to the Holy See, and they thanked Murray and Milner for zealously discharging the trust that had been reposed in them.[13]

These sentiments may have been firm and decided but they were far from respectful: they were defiant, ungracious and truculent. One can only speculate about which of the bishops forced through this hard-line approach. Both Troy and O'Reilly had been educated in Rome, and as both were far from being firm against some intervention by the government in the appointments of bishops, it seems very unlikely that they took the lead in propounding such a querulous attitude to the Holy See. But Coppinger of Cloyne, O'Shaughnessy of Killaloe and several others such as Plunket, who had

---

12 John Power reported that 'the spirit of resistance (canonical of course) was high and indeed general. The resolutions sufficiently shew it'. He quoted O'Reilly of Armagh's assertion that if the pope ordered him to consecrate a bishop elected on the veto arrangement, 'he would remonstrate and rather than comply resign his crozier' (Power to Bray, 9 Sept. 1815, CaDA). O'Reilly had hitherto been regarded by some of his colleagues as 'soft' on the veto.   13 Resolutions of the Roman Catholic prelates, 24 Aug. 1815, DDA.

spent many years in Paris, were educated in France, where they would have become aware of less subservient attitudes to Rome. The adamantine and entrenched resistance of O'Connell and the members of the Catholic Association, and the cumulative effect of the popular rejection of the rescript and of the rumours about the Genoese letter, had certainly contributed to the firmness of the episcopal sentiments.

Though Pope Pius VII was personally gentle, moderate and mild-mannered, he could also be resolute and determined when he felt ecclesiastical policy demanded it. By redrawing the boundaries of the dioceses of France, dismissing several bishops and appointing a few who had taken the oath of the civil constitution of the clergy, he had overturned the powerful Gallican church. He had signed a concordat with Napoleon by which the French state nominated the bishops and parish priests, leaving him to give them canonical institution. And he was to make similar agreements with other states where ecclesiastical structures had been altered by the French occupation. By 1829 more than four-fifths of the bishops of the universal church were nominated by rulers.[14] Understandably, the pope and his advisers were dismayed by the robust reaction of the Irish bishops to a set of proposals that might be put to the government in the event of emancipation.[15] A consultor at the congregation for ecclesiastical affairs, replying to a request from Consalvi for a comment on the bishops' letter, referred to it as a most thorny affair (*'scabrosissimo affare'*), which could produce very damaging consequences for the Catholic religion and the dignity of the Holy See. The remonstrance had gone beyond the limits of respect due to the Holy See, and he felt the situation should be handled with the greatest delicacy, as he dreaded the greatest of evils – a schism.[16]

Confronted by the wild rumours which circulated about the concessions the Vatican was offering to the British government,[17] the Catholic Association (which had succeeded the Catholic Board),[18] had met in Dublin,

---

14 Of the 646 diocesan bishops in the church in 1829, 545 were appointed by the state: 113 in the Kingdom of the Two Sicilies, 86 in France, 82 in Habsburg Germany, 67 in Sardinia and the Italian duchies, 61 in Spain and its possessions, 35 in Spanish America, 24 in Portugal, 9 in Brazil and 9 in Bavaria. Another 67 in the USA, Ireland, Prussian Germany, the Upper Rhine, Belgium and Switzerland were locally elected by cathedral chapters or some similar arrangement. The pope, as sovereign of the Papal States, appointed 70. He also appointed 24 directly in Russia, Greece and Albania (Duffy, *Saints and sinners*, p. 274). 15 In another unsigned and undated document, which may have been written by an aide of Consalvi, reference is made to the 'small and innocuous variation of the discipline of the church' in the appointment of bishops (ASV, Segr. Stato, Inghilterra 30 Irlanda 1, 1814–1856, ff 527r–529r). 16 M. Fontana to R. Nezio, no date, ibid., 30, ff 511r–512r. 17 The *DEP* reported on 19 Aug. 1815 that, if emancipation were conceded, the pope would issue a brief commanding Catholics to accept the concessions offered by Castlereagh and Grattan. It also claimed that Poynter was to become an archbishop with juris-diction over the Irish prelates. 18 The government, in 1814, in an attempt to curb the meetings for emancipation, had applied the Convention Act of 1793, which prohibited assemblies

just before the bishops' 23–4 August meeting, and decided to call for information from the prelates. A deputation was appointed to make inquiries about any communication from the pope about the nomination of bishops, and about Litta's letter. It was also commissioned to inquire if the hierarchy was recognized in Rome, or if Ireland was a missionary country. The foolish question about the status of the hierarchy was probably designed to test its power of resistance in the face of unwelcome pressure from Rome.[19]

In a strained and hyperbolic letter accompanying their resolutions to the pope, the bishops explained that his 'concession was very full of fatal consequences to the Catholic religion in Ireland', and that, had he foreseen these, he would not have made it. They argued that the merciless and constant hostility of the government to the Catholic religion in Ireland filled both them and their people with fear that the total destruction of Catholicism was not only the object of the politicians who wanted the veto but would be the consequence of it.

Evidence of this hostility was to be found in the multiplication of Protestant churches, and the erection of schools under Protestant patronage, with Protestant teachers, which, though they abjured the intention of proselytism, aimed to achieve that end by the use of heretical translations of the scriptures and of small, poisonous heretical tracts. Force having been tried in vain against the Catholic faith it seemed the government wanted to adopt more insidious means by treating with the Holy See, and these means would certainly be efficacious, if the pope were induced to concede the veto. If the right of the ministry to eliminate one candidate for lack of allegiance were conceded, the ministers would arrogate to themselves the right to eliminate a second, third and so on, 'until the most vile instrument of its choice, the most unworthy and immoral priest' they could find would be chosen. However strongly the principle of limitation was laid down in law, judges would always find in favour of the supremacy of the sovereign. Foreseeing the possibility that the government, to obtain a plausible excuse for its interference, would offer an annual pension to the clergy, the bishops claimed that such payment would deprive them of the trust of their people. Though the Irish were very attached to the Holy See, if forced to accept this pernicious system, they would be driven in their thousands into open schism. Bishops chosen in this way would be the objects of scorn and detestation, would be booed in the streets and no bishop could consecrate a priest so chosen without danger of death from the fury of the people. Though a few vicars apostolic in Great Britain took a contrary view, that made no difference to Ireland, as the circumstances of the two countries were entirely different. In

purporting to represent the people under the guise of petitioning the king or parliament. Most meetings were then held in private houses, including the Dublin house of Lord Fingall.
19 *DEP*, 22 Aug. 1815.

Britain, the number of Catholics was comparatively small; in Ireland, it surpassed 5 million. To point out the evils that could result from giving a Protestant government any involvement in ecclesiastical power, it was sufficient to refer to the recent behaviour of the British government in Canada, Malta and Bombay.[20] Enclosing a translation of their resolutions, they explained that they had adopted them unanimously lest their silence be regarded as connivance in a policy that would spell the ruin of their church, and which, if once accepted, could never be revoked.[21]

When Consalvi returned to Rome and read this letter, he must have been struck by the difference between the Irish view of the government, and the view he had formed in London. The bishops undoubtedly exaggerated the government's promotion of proselytism. Its financial support for the erection of Protestant churches was designed to fill gaps in the parochial structure of the established church. It certainly gave support to proselytizing societies which were conducting schools to evangelize Irish Catholics, but it did not have a grand plan to further proselytism as such. Nonetheless, Irish Catholics took great exception to this practice. Roman authorities would have found it difficult to understand how the difference in the sizes of the Catholic populations in Ireland and England could have affected the result of government intervention, if its motives were as perverse as the bishops suggested.

II

A few days after the bishops drew up their resolutions, a general meeting organized by the Catholic Association took place in Dublin. O'Connell was given a copy of the resolutions to read to the meeting and the gist of Litta's letter. Resolutions were passed thanking the prelates for 'their firm, manly and decided condemnation' of any measure giving the crown control over episcopal appointments. The members further declared that they could never consent to any arrangement by which the British minister could derive from the court of Rome any jurisdiction or power over the conduct in temporal affairs of the Catholic clergy, as they disclaimed any civil or temporal power in the papacy.

O'Connell, whose passionate rhetoric could at times impel him to abuse

20 The bishops of Quebec had been accepted by the governor as 'overseers of the Roman Church' until they were allowed to use their titles in 1811. Before a coadjutor was appointed, the governor's approval had to be granted. After the British took over Malta in 1800, they abolished several ancient clerical privileges, and ecclesiastical jurisdiction was limited to spiritual affairs. In Bombay, the Portuguese clergy and the Italian missionaries disputed jurisdiction and the British authorities divided the churches between them. 21 Twenty-one bishops, including coadjutors, to the pope, 30 Aug. 1815, ASV, Segr. Stato, Inghilterra 30 Irlanda 1, ff 505r–506r.

his opponents, delivered a populist and churlish address. Having argued that the 'seceders' had no justification for their attitudes, and that they should rejoin the other members of the association, and having praised the bishops, he proceeded to give his explanation of the background to Litta's letter:

> Our church was either betrayed or sold to the British minister in Vienna; indeed, the exact amount of price is stated to be eleven thousand guineas. Though a cardinal, the agent was not a priest. Quarantotti and Cardinal Litta were, of course, foreigners. Then the next class in the arrangement of the veto are the English Catholic bishops. First of all, I must mention a name that ought not, though it will surprise you – Doctor Milner. Yes Doctor Milner has performed another truly English revolution.

O'Connell claimed to have information that Milner had written to the bishops to accept Litta's plan, on the grounds that it would never be brought into operation, and they would then have the grace of showing their acquiescence without any danger to the church. Milner then allegedly said that if the candidate was disloyal, everyone would be pleased that he was not appointed, but O'Connell argued that to the government disloyalty in an Irishman was the honest, zealous and pure love of his native land. He then went on to lambaste Poynter:

> The most zealous apostle of the veto is another Englishman (Doctor Poynter). Poor man! His principle means of support depended on the uncertain gratuity of a few of the upper class (as they are called) of English papists; he would prefer the more solid engagement of a permanent pension from government. He exerted every nerve to carry his ruinous measure.

Having told how a deaf prelate used to call Poynter 'Doctor Spaniel', he explained that on being corrected, the prelate commented 'Poynter by name but Spaniel by nature'.

O'Connell then proceeded to spray his vituperation over all the vicars apostolic, with the possible exception of Milner. He argued (wrongly):

> The only scholar amongst them is Doctor Milner; and he appears arrived at dotage. The rest of them by their servility, their pliability, their eagerness to conciliate the favour of their lay patrons and their anxieties for pensions from government have become the ridicule of the country.[22]

---

22 O'Connell, 29 Aug. 1815 in *Select speeches*, second series, pp 18–38. O'Connell, *Life and speeches*, ii, p. 210.

Throughout his political career O'Connell, often allowed his robust attacks on opponents to degenerate into insults and scurrility. On this occasion, both Italian and English clergy felt the blast of his invective. The claims that money had passed in Vienna between Castlereagh and Consalvi, and that Poynter was being bribed by the English gentry were ludicrous, though O'Connell got Consalvi's ecclesiastical status right: he was a cardinal deacon who had never been ordained a priest. Milner promptly wrote to the Irish papers complaining about a 'celebrated orator ... grossly misrepresenting my principles and degrading my understanding'. This orator had relied on hearsay evidence at third hand, and to clear up the misunderstanding, the bishop was willing to let the letter on which O'Connell's claim was based be published. He had suffered more than anyone for defending the principle that it was 'not expedient to alter the discipline of the Catholic church of Ireland'.[23] He maintained that when he saw from the pope's comments in Rome that concessions were inevitable, he expressed his submission, but tried 'to restrain it within the narrowest bounds possible'.[24]

III

Poynter, who had long been irritated by the behaviour both of the Irish bishops and of those whom he called the rabble, was outraged by O'Connell's insults. Adopting the hostile tone of the English press towards the Irish leader, he denounced O'Connell as the 'leader of the opponents to every measure of conciliation', and reminded Macpherson that O'Connell had killed a man in a duel and had challenged Peel, then the chief secretary for Ireland, to a similar contest. He expressed his hope:

> I wish C. Litta would think a little what effect will be produced, if he be known in England to be the supporter of Bp. M. who is the hero of the rabble in Ireland irritated against our own government.[25]

He forwarded copies of O'Connell's speeches to be shown to Litta, and bemoaned the Irish refusal to show patience:

> What a pity the Irish will not be quiet. They are agitated and led on by the duellist orator O'Connell. What a dilemma the Irish bishops will find themselves placed in, when they see these

---

23 Milner, 6 Sept. 1815 in *FJ*, 13 Sept. 1815.   24 Milner to Scully, 1 Feb. 1816, in MacDermot, *The Catholic question in Ireland and England, 1798–1822*, p. 575.   25 Poynter to Macpherson, 25 July 1815, AVEC, 55/4/49.

Jacobinical leaders of the mob supporting themselves on the resolutions of the bishops.[26]

Not content with allowing the bishops to fight their own case, the meeting of the Irish laity decided to present a remonstrance to Rome against any intervention by the government in the nomination of bishops and to send its own agents to convince the pope of the dangers of concessions to secular authority. Only one of the three delegates chosen by the association, Richard Hayes, agreed to go to Rome. This decision of the laity reflected the anger and outrage which the reports about the Genoese letter had provoked. It was almost as if the Catholic Association believed that the bishops were not fully capable of conveying the hurt feelings of the country to the pope. O'Connell drew up the remonstrance, which it was hoped would be presented to the pope by the delegates.

It began by declaring unambiguously that no spiritual grounds were alleged for the proposed alteration in their ecclesiastical system. In fact, it was being proposed in opposition to the advice of their spiritual guides and was being offered 'as an exchange or barter for some temporal aid or concession'. The numerous inducements offered to Catholics and to their children to apostatize, and the oaths blaspheming the Lord's Supper and the Virgin Mary taken by members of parliament and every individual in an official station proved that the government sought to accomplish by intrigue what it had failed to accomplish by persecution. The demand for securities originated 'solely from a desire to enable the enemies of our holy religion … to accomplish the destruction of a church which they have so long ineffectually assailed'. Should a Protestant prince or his ministers be given the right to interfere directly or indirectly in the appointments of the bishops, the Catholic religion would be destroyed. The prelates and priests 'would be shunned and despised' and 'a state of irreligion and immorality would succeed in the country'. All that was sought was the restoration of the temporal rights of Catholics, and therefore they protested humbly but most firmly 'against the interference of your Holiness … in the control of our temporal conduct … and cannot admit any right, on the part of the Holy See, to investigate our political principles, or to direct our political conduct'. Rather than accept emancipation at such a price they would 'prefer the perpetuation of our degraded state in the empire'. And they could not believe that 'their revered pontiff, who had endured so much of suffering in maintenance of his spiritual station, would, knowingly and intentionally invade or oppress the conscientious feelings of a Catholic people'.[27]

26 Ibid., 3 Oct. 1815, 55/4/55 and 19 Mar. 1816, 55/5/71A.　27 J. O'Connell (ed.), *Select speeches*, second series, pp 28–34.

The remonstrance was a firm and unequivocal rejection of any kind of veto and reflected O'Connell's insistence on civil rights. At one level it was a clever piece of advocacy, because of the impressive list of forms of oppression which it emphasized. The oaths taken by members of parliament, judges, and senior military officers against transubstantiation and devotion to Our Lady, which it listed, would have certainly annoyed the pontiff. But where O'Connell erred badly was in his accusation that the veto was 'offered as an exchange or barter for some temporal aid or concession'. The Vatican regarded concessions about the appointment of bishops as a necessary surrender of rights to avoid greater evils, and any suggestion of a shady deal over the Papal States would have been regarded as highly offensive. The protest against the interference of the pope in their temporal conduct was undiplomatic, if not offensive, since he and his advisers did not believe that they had done anything of the kind in making an arrangement that had been made with many states.

The Irish bishops, at their meeting on 24 August, deputed two of their number and a Dublin priest to go to Rome to present their protests against the Genoese letter formally to the pope. Their delegates were Archbishop Murray, the coadjutor of Dublin who had represented them there the previous year, John Murphy, who had recently become the bishop of Cork, and Archdeacon Michael Blake of Dublin. Murray spoke French, Italian and Spanish, Murphy spoke French, and Blake spoke Italian. They called on Milner en route, and arrived in Rome on 23 October 1815.[28] A fortnight later, Macpherson reported that Litta had told them that their business was 'rather extraordinary, and not very respectful to the H. See'. He had further explained that his letter had been written at the command of the pope, 'after the maturest consideration', and could not be altered. The letter was not mandatory and contained only the conditions that could be permitted in the event of emancipation being conceded, and the refusal of parliament to grant emancipation meant that there was no reason to ask for the letter to be changed. Macpherson, who was a hostile observer, also claimed that Murphy was 'very loud and menacing', but admitted that 'great attention is shown to the whole deputation', and that they had dined with cardinals Consalvi and della Somaglia.[29]

They were received by the pope, to whom they presented the letter or remonstrance of the hierarchy. But apart from the intrinsic difficulty of their mission – trying to persuade the pope to reverse a decision – they were hampered by two factors. Consalvi had returned to Rome after successfully obtaining the restoration of the Papal States to the pope's sovereignty, and

28 Significantly, Milner was not chosen on this occasion. Murray, who disliked his aggressive style, may not have wanted him in the deputation. 29 Macpherson to Poynter, 4 Nov. 1815, WDA.

his prestige was at its peak.[30] He resumed full control as secretary of state, and, if Macpherson's view of his relationship with Litta is correct, the chances of a reversal of the policy towards the British government were small.[31] Consalvi, impressed by his reception in London, and always ready to make political compromises where possible with states, saw no difficulty in conceding a limited veto to the government in the appointment of bishops. Given that he believed the Irish were hot-headed, fractious and confrontational, and that he had the highest regard for Poynter's approach to political problems, Murray and Murphy had a near impossible task in seeking to change the pope's mind. The other problem they faced was the presence of Richard Hayes in Rome at the same time. He was the only one of the three deputies chosen by the Catholic Association who had agreed to travel. He arrived in Rome on 25 October 1815, two days after the bishops' delegates.

According to Macpherson, who had his own axe to grind with Litta, Consalvi had a poor opinion of Litta's abilities. He claimed that in conversation Consalvi 'reprobated his conduct in every particular relative to our affairs ... *un vero furioso*', a real firebrand. The cardinal had often made it clear to the pope that Litta's conduct would ruin religion, but 'the *furious* boldness of *that* man terrified the humble and overly meek pontiff from exerting his authority and reprimanding him in an effectual manner'. Consalvi, he also reported, believed the Irish claim that the government was not pleased with the Genoese letter, as he had sent a copy to Castlereagh, who took no notice of it. But he insisted that not an iota of it would be recalled, and was surprised that Irish bishops would think of coming to Rome on such an errand.[32] Even if the Irish deputation were to succeed in convincing Litta of the need to alter his letter, Consalvi's opposition and his commanding influence with the pope would have prevented any change.

---

30 He failed to have Avignon and the Comtat Venaissin restored to the pope, but these failures were not important in view of his other achievements.   31 Macpherson had told Poynter that Consalvi and Litta were 'at open war' (Macpherson to Poynter, 25 Sept. 1815, WDA). 32 Macpherson to Poynter, 7 Dec. 1815, ibid.

13

The delegates in Rome

I

Hayes seems to have owed his selection as a delegate of the Catholic Association to the prominence he had acquired in Cork as an opponent of the veto, but he was an unsuitable and unfortunate choice. Born in Wexford town in 1787, he had received his early education in a local Franciscan school before proceeding in 1802 to St Isidore's College in Rome, where he was ordained a priest in 1810. Luke Concanen, the bishop of New York, was then waiting for a ship to sail to his diocese, and, having heard favourable reports of Hayes' ability, thought of bringing him and another Franciscan to found a school in New York.[1] Reports of a different kind made him change his mind for, as he informed Troy, he had discovered that Hayes was 'a complete trickster'.[2] Forced by the French authorities, as a foreigner, to leave Rome, Hayes made his way home. He reached Wexford in 1811 with a reputation for fluency in languages, and after a spell in pastoral work was appointed to teach in a small local seminary. Scarcely a year later, Patrick Ryan, the coadjutor bishop of Ferns, dismissed him from his teaching post having rebuked him for not observing the school timetable, and refused him permission to preach, as his sermons were considered 'too contentious and outspoken'. He then joined the Franciscan community in Cork, but returned to Wexford shortly afterwards to receive a presentation. When he overstayed his welcome, the bishop forbade him to carry out any spiritual work apart from celebrating Mass in the convent chapel, a concession which he later withdrew. On his return to Cork he again engaged in pastoral work and also did secretarial work on behalf of religious orders, which were involved in disputes with several bishops. This work earned him the suspicion and opposition of several bishops, but the laity who chose him for their mission did so because of his staunch, if not extreme, hostility to the veto.[3] He had

1 Concanen to Troy, 3 Jan. 1810, DDA. 2 Ibid., 18 Apr. 1810. 3 In a letter to James McCormick, OFM, the guardian of St Isidore's, before he was commissioned to go as a delegate to Rome, he referred to 'the villainous scheme' for 'the destruction of the Catholic religion in Ireland'. And he asked McCormick to send him what he could discover of the letters and correspondence of Troy and any other veto bishop, advised McCormick to 'bribe secretaries and every person, if necessary, to obtain information and documents, to send him the document' Poynter got at Genoa and any document signed by the pope or by his orders in favour of the veto. He also bade him to 'watch every manoeuvre of Macpherson'. I am 'a political character of some

told a confrère in Rome that the people would never submit to it, and 'will neither go to Mass or confession to any vetoistical or pensioned clergyman'. He predicted that the contretemps would end in blood.[4]

Bishop Ryan's decisions to dismiss Hayes from his seminary and forbid him to preach or celebrate Mass in public suggest at least that the friar was irresponsible and untrustworthy. More serious charges of a personal nature were later to be levelled against him, but that the bishop should subject him to such severe discipline at a time when priests with his qualifications were so desperately needed to man Catholic schools implies that there was a serious question mark over his sacerdotal behaviour.[5] As his conduct was to prove, he was brash, arrogant and insensitive and his discourteous conduct antagonized both pope and cardinals.

In Rome, Hayes, fortified by a letter from the superiors of the religious orders in Ireland to the procurators of their orders, requesting them to give him every help to block British intervention in Irish ecclesiastical affairs, obtained the first of his five audiences with the pope on 10 November 1815. He presented a petition or summary of the official remonstrance begging the pontiff to permit no interference – direct or indirect – by a Protestant government in the nomination of the bishops. He repeated the arguments used by O'Connell in the remonstrance and implored the pope not to be dazzled by the enemies of Catholicism nor by those employed by them, but to listen to the prayers of a nation that despite bloody persecutions was very attached to the Holy See. Ireland was moved not by politics but by love of religion to present the remonstrance. Hayes was pleased with his first audience with the pope, who, as he deprecated the ferment created in Ireland and expressed surprise and anger that the Genoese letter had not been published there, assured him that it was merely conditional.

Hayes' documents were passed on to Consalvi, and Hayes had a discussion with him and with Cardinal Litta, who likewise told him that the Genoese letter was conditional and that it had been rejected by the English ministers as insufficient. Milner, he claimed, had done much harm to their cause in Rome by 'his wild mode of opposing' the veto and then by yielding to it.[6]

Significantly, the other deputation, which had also been thrice received by the pope refused to act with Hayes. Murray and his colleagues may have feared the friar's rashness, and his hastily formed opinion of Consalvi would have justified this view. He claimed that Consalvi was receiving newspapers from Coxe-Hippisley and the veto faction in England, and he was constantly

celebrity', he concluded (Hayes to McCormick, 11 Aug. 1815 in Giblin, 'Papers of Richard Joachim Hayes', *Coll. Hib.* 21–2 (1979–80), 130–1.   4 Hayes to McCormick, 7 Aug. 1815, ibid. 5 *Coll. Hib.*, 21–2 (1978–80), 82–3.   6 Hayes to O'Connell, 11 Nov. 1815 in *Coll. Hib.* 23 (1982), 19–23.

to charge the secretary of state with treating the whole issue from a political angle and from a desire to placate the government. And he was foolish enough to suggest to the pope that the whole question should not be handled by the congregation headed by Consalvi that dealt with political affairs. He further made a distinction between the pope as king of the Papal States and as supreme pontiff, and he claimed that Castlereagh constantly communicated with the court of Rome, and therefore with Consalvi, and not with the see of Rome.

He also maintained that he lobbied several cardinals for his cause. Then on 22 December 1815 he was received again in audience by the pope, and, forgetting the role of a suppliant in the papal presence, presumed to ask the pope to pass on the papers he had given him to the congregation of Propaganda, so that Irish Catholics would be assured that the matter was not being examined by the political department. He also submitted a letter from the superiors of the religious orders in Ireland against the veto, claiming that, if it were granted, the orders would be suppressed as had happened in Canada.[7] Hayes' desire to have Propaganda examine the remonstrance and other papers reflected his determination to exclude, if possible, Consalvi from influencing the final decision.

Giving an account of his audience to the editor of the *Dublin Chronicle*, Eneas MacDonnell, he maintained that he had said 'much' to the pope against the conduct of Consalvi and claimed that the pope had told his cardinal secretary of state to 'hurry the answers to the remonstrances'. Consalvi then told Murray, Murphy and Blake that he would give them an answer in a fortnight, but Hayes believed that Consalvi was just 'playing on them'. Hayes had a very poor opinion of the bishops' deputation – an attitude that reflects much worse on him than on them – for he maintained that the 'ignorance, impatience, indolence or insincerity of theirs has kept me and the cause back this whole month'.[8] His belief that the cardinal was delaying an answer to gain time for Castlereagh to pass a veto bill before the pope responded to the remonstrances attributed to Castlereagh a power which that statesman did not possess.

Both the pope and Consalvi held discussions with the episcopal deputation. Murray and Murphy were anxious to obtain a response from the pope mitigating the Genoese letter. But as Litta was absent for most of their sojourn in Rome, they sought the help of other cardinals as well. Resorting

7 Hayes to Pope Pius VII, 22 Dec. 1815, ibid., 40–4. Copies of almost 100 documents relating to the veto, in Hayes' hand, are preserved in the Franciscan Library, Killiney, Co. Dublin.
8 Hayes to MacDonnell, 26 Dec. 1815, ibid., 48–9. MacDonnell, a barrister, journalist and campaigner for Catholic relief, was editor of the *Dublin Chronicle* from 1815 to 1817. He later became the agent of the Catholic Association in London and worked with the English Catholic Association and members of parliament in the 1820s.

to the same hyperbole as the bishops had used in their letter to the pope, they described the veto as 'the most insidious measure ever invented' to separate Ireland from the Holy See and make it Protestant, and so they sought Cardinal di Pietro's help in obtaining a reply from the pope, as there was a danger of parliament, due to meet in February 1816, introducing emancipation accompanied by a veto.[9] And they also begged Cardinal Doria to use his influence for the same purpose so that they could bring to their 'afflicted church the consoling reply of the common father of all the faithful'.[10]

On 9 January 1816, Hayes had his third audience with the pope and left with him a proposal for the domestic nomination of bishops in Ireland. He suggested, as the Catholic Association had done, that the pontiff renounce, in a formal document, his right to choose the bishops, and his consent to give canonical institution to those elected by the clergy with the approval of the bishops of the province who had taken the oath of loyalty to the government and had obtained a document certifying that they had done so. By that means the government would be satisfied, unless its goal was the destruction of that Catholicism which had survived miraculously for several centuries despite bitter persecutions. That method would be more acceptable to the bishops and clergy than the hated Genoese letter. Copies of these proposals were also sent to Consalvi.[11]

Hayes, who had an exalted view of his own negotiating skills, complained to Eneas MacDonnell of the inability of the episcopal deputation to obtain longer audiences with the pope, and their failure to obtain any answer to bring home with them. He regretted their unwillingness to tell the pope that the matter should not be settled at 'a political tribunal', and their refusal to protest against holding any communication with Consalvi, who 'both by office, as secretary of state, and by the pledge he gave to Castlereagh at Vienna, was incompetent to decide or examine this ecclesiastical question'. He greatly feared that the pope would do nothing for them because he was dependent for his knowledge of the subject on Consalvi, who kept him in the dark. He had asked them not to report in Ireland Consalvi's statement that 'the letter from Genoa, though permissive in words would be compulsory in its effects, as the pope would not give canonical institution to any bishop not approved by government'. He begged Murray and his friends to stay to enlighten the cardinals and prelates who had frequent access to the pope as their three short audiences were insufficient to do so. As it seems most unlikely that any of the three official delegates revealed anything to him about Troy's directions, the claim that the archbishop 'wrote several times to cow them and make them return' is scarcely credible.[12]

9 Murray to di Pietro, 6 Dec. 1815, APF, SC(Irlanda), 19, f 398rv. 10 Murray and Murphy to Doria, 14 Dec. 1815, ibid., f 404r. 11 Hayes to Pope Pius and Consalvi, 2, 11 Jan. 1816, *Coll. Hib.* 24 (1982), 94–7. 12 Hayes to MacDonnell, 6 Jan. 1816, ibid., pp 97–9, and Murray and

Both the bishops' deputies and Hayes had their remonstrances translated into Italian and, as they were preparing to leave, Murray and Murphy wrote a letter in Italian to the pope. They again referred to the fatal effects a positive or negative power granted to the crown in the nomination of bishops would have, but, unlike Hayes, they did not threaten the pope with turbulence or schism. They doubtless realized that suppliants at Rome should dispense with menacing language, for their appeal to the pope was couched in anodyne terms. Irish Catholics, they predicted would behave in a pacific manner and try to persuade parliament to undo such powers. They merely entreated the pope to formally maintain the current practice and establish it as a rule that those who chose candidates for the episcopate, and the candidates themselves, would be subjects who had sworn fidelity to the crown, and they beseeched him to give an answer that would console the afflicted church of Ireland.[13] They also wrote to Consalvi, trusting that the pope would not approve a law that the Catholics of Ireland would always consider penal, hateful and destructive of true religion.[14]

Understandably, the episcopal deputies were riled by the unsolicited and disdainful counsel from Hayes, and their reply to him was curt, caustic and dismissive. Referring to 'the numerous inaccuracies' of his communications without identifying them, they insisted that they had not applied to a tribunal different from that of the pope and that they had received what they sought – the answer of the pope – and though they had pointed out 'the fatal consequences to be derived from the veto' to his principal counsellors, it was the pope's decision that they had canvassed. Dismissing Hayes' threat of publishing a letter about their premature departure, they reminded him of the failure of his attempts to calumniate the former mission of Muray and Milner in 1814, and predicted that his representations against the present one would be treated with considerable caution, given that a principal object of his journey was 'to blacken before the Holy See the character of the entire episcopate' of Ireland.[15]

Despite this rebuff, Hayes, attributing views to Murray and his colleagues that they had not expressed, tried to convince Consalvi that they had departed disgusted and insulted, rejecting with indignation – or rather with anger – the answer they had been given. Their arrival in Ireland would throw the whole Catholic kingdom into turmoil, and therefore to prevent schism he begged Consalvi to encourage the pope to agree to domestic nomination.[16]

Murphy, 7 Jan. 1816, ibid., 102–7.   **13** Murray and Murphy to pope, 28 Dec. 1815, ASV, Segr. Stato, Inghilterra 30 Irlanda 1, ff 407r–408r.   **14** Ibid., 1 Jan. 1816, f 422rv.   **15** Murray, Murphy to Hayes, 9 Jan. 1816, *Coll. Hib.* 24 (1982), 107–8. Hayes had been commissioned by superiors of the Dominican, Augustinian, Carmelite and Franciscan orders to lay before the Holy See their complaints against the restrictions imposed on their orders by several bishops. **16** Hayes to Consalvi, 11 Jan. 1816, ibid., 108–10. It was necessary for the pope to agree to this

In reply to Murray and his colleagues, he insisted, despite their expressions of satisfaction with the pope's response, that the answer Consalvi had given them was 'so fraught with opprobrious insult against the prelates and people of Ireland' that they had refused to bring it with them, and the pope, alarmed by their refusal and by Hayes' prediction of the ferment that their return would occasion, had ordered Consalvi to draft another answer. What Pius had told them 'was merely the *verbal* political declaration of the king, not the *solemn* ecclesiastical decision of the pope'. Rejecting their accusations against him of seeking to blacken the episcopate in Rome, and informing them that 'the mild permissive, indecisive tone' of the Genoese letter was due to Milner, he begged their forgiveness.[17] Macpherson reported to Poynter that the Irish bishops had left 'not at all pleased with the success of their mission'. The pope, he maintained, had spoken to them in stronger language than he had used to anyone since dealing with Bonaparte. Referring to the quarrel between them and Hayes, Macpherson could not restrain his *Schadenfreude* as he reflected that the Irish clergy were 'a curious set of beings'.[18]

Consalvi, in a letter to Murray and Murphy after their return to Ireland, angrily dismissed the stories Hayes had put out about their comments on the pope's letter as 'unworthy lies'. Seemingly, they had discussed the draft with Consalvi and had called for some expressions in it to be altered. Both he and the pope were anxious to please them, and so he offered to make changes and to send separate replies to the bishops and the laity.[19]

Hayes continued to denigrate the episcopal delegation in letters to Ireland. He complained to MacDonnell of their imprudent conduct in waiting on and dining with Consalvi before they saw the pope and using him as their channel to the pontiff. But, if he denounced Consalvi, he continued to eulogize Litta, who, he claimed, would not of his own will have sent the Genoese letter. He attributed its origin to Bentinck, the British admiral in the Mediterranean, and to Consalvi, who went to Genoa with a commitment to Castlereagh. Cardinal-elect Fontana had said that a key influence in the pope's having it drawn up was Poynter's claim that once emancipation was passed, thousands of Protestants would become Catholics, and that it could only be granted if the pope allowed ministers to reject from the list of candi-

plan so that Hayes could bring it or send it to Ireland before the arrival of the prelates to prevent imminent schism and before parliament could legislate for a veto.   **17** Hayes to Murray, Murphy and Blake, 17 Jan. 1816, ibid., 113–16. In a letter to his brother a few days earlier he accused Murray and his colleagues of lacking *savoir faire* in their dealings with Roman officials and (falsely) claimed that 'they spoke no Italian and but bad French'. One bishop who enthusiastically backed Hayes was the strongly anti-vetoist, William Coppinger of Cloyne and Ross (Coppinger to Hayes, 1 Feb. 1816, ibid., 130–1).   **18** Macpherson to Poynter, 13 Jan. 1816, WDA.   **19** Consalvi (draft) to Murray and Murphy, 1 Feb. 1816, ASV, Segr. Stato, Inghilterra 30 Irlanda 1, ff 464r–467v. Consalvi said of Hayes, 'Egli si è permesso di parlare a SS.mo in una maniera, che la sola bontà estrema di un Papa tanto mite e tanto santo poteva tollerare.'

dates persons to whom they objected. He also maintained that Litta did not want to write the letter at all but was forced to do so.[20] In fact, Consalvi had been disappointed in Vienna that Castlereagh had showed little interest in Catholic emancipation, and Murray and his colleagues had realized that any suggestion to the pope of bypassing Consalvi and seeking to keep the examination of the veto out of the congregation for Extraordinary Ecclesiastical Affairs would have been counterproductive.

While the two bishops were still in Rome, Litta, responding to Troy's request for clarification and presumably also to his tale of woe about the ferment the Genoese letter had created among Catholics, expressed surprise that they were so displeased with his letter, which had been written by papal command. He suggested to Troy that as the bishops had concealed the letter from their people it had been interpreted as being more extensive than it was. In fact, it was not preceptive but preventive, affording instructions in conditions admitted by the pope, should emancipation be granted. But as petitions to parliament for emancipation had since then been twice rejected, the likelihood of it being granted was small. The pope was pleased with having fixed the conditions under which Catholics could accept this change, as otherwise there was a risk of their accepting conditions that did not sufficiently preserve the integrity and safety of the Catholic religion. Turning to the particular queries that had been raised, Litta quoted the text, which said if anyone was unacceptable or suspected by the government his name should be expunged so long as a sufficient number of names was left from which the pope might make his choice. He also made clear that the custom prevailing in Ireland for the recommendation of candidates was to remain.[21]

Murray and Murphy sent an abstract of the formal answer of the pope to the bishops' letter to the archbishops for their suffragans, and they lamented the failure of their mission to convince the pope of the danger to their religion, should he grant to the government the terms contained in the Genoese letter.[22] Almost certainly, the full papal reply was written by Consalvi or his aides, as Litta was absent from Rome for several weeks before it was sent. Pope Pius began by referring to the pain he had experienced in finding that the expedient to which he had recourse had not met their approbation. Repeating the terms of the Genoese letter, he denied that the government would be able to remove the names of the most worthy candidates so that those most subservient to it would be appointed, to the ultimate destruction of religion. There was no reason to fear such a danger. On the contrary, those who proposed the names of candidates for episcopal office would continue to put forward only the names of those who were most

20 Hayes to MacDonnell, 24 Feb. 1816, ibid., 133–9. 21 Litta to Troy, 2 Dec. 1815, DDA. 22 Draft of Murray and Murphy from London to (probably) Archbishop Troy, 10 Mar. 1816, DDA.

suitable, and the government was permitted to erase some but not all of them. Noting that non-Catholic sovereigns claimed a share in the appointments of bishops in those parts of their dominions that still adhered to Catholicism, he wondered if the British government would not consider itself unfairly treated by the refusal of that additional security or whether it would not 'derive from it a motive of doubting the loyalty of the Catholics'. In fact, the arrangement he had made would be a means of averting calamities from the church as well as a 'likely motive towards the obtainment of emancipation'. Without his concession, emancipation might never be granted. In granting to the government that particular indulgence, he had been influenced 'by no political or temporal motives, but induced solely by a consideration of those benefits and advantages, which must flow to the Catholic religion from the repeal of the penal laws'. He wondered what grounds existed for suspecting that the government, which was among the chief of those who had restored him to his office, had designs to destroy the Catholic religion.

Any attempts still made in Ireland to injure the Catholic religion were the acts of private individuals, which would cease when Catholics were placed on the same footing as others with the repeal of the penal laws. 'Was it not feared,' the pope asked, 'that if we had declined adopting the measure already mentioned government would not only lay aside all intention of granting emancipation to the Catholics, but withdraw from them all favour and protection, throughout the whole of its so widely extended dominions?' His concession was harmless, and, from it, the greatest advantages might result to the church, just as heavy calamities might result from its refusal. The pope concluded his letter by making reference to the recall of the Irish nation from the erroneous celebration of Easter in the sixth and seventh centuries,[23] thanks to the strenuous labour of his predecessors, and by inviting the bishops to set an example of docility and allay the 'rising emotions' in the minds of their people.

In his reply to the lay remonstrance, the pope mentioned this letter, whereupon the Catholic Association sought permission to see it. Before passing it on, Troy excised from it a few short remarks and a longer section which, he explained, was confidential to the bishops. The shorter quotations which were eliminated referred to the possibility after emancipation of the Catholic bishops sitting in the house of lords and of many Protestants, even those of noble stock, converting to Catholicism.[24] The longer section which

23 The Celtic churches in the sixth and seventh centuries used a different method of calculating the date of Easter from that used by Rome. The Roman method was adopted at the synod of Whitby in 664. 24 Troy to Litta, 23 June 1818, APF, SC(Irlanda) 21, f 292rv. Troy explained to Litta that he would not have shown the pope's letter to the association had the papal letter to the laity not referred to it.

he withheld was a stern rebuke and censure of the bishops' conduct. In singling out their second and third resolutions,[25] the pope let them know that their threat of opposing any and every arrangement he might make about the appointment of bishops was completely ultra vires. His decisions were not dependent on the consent of the bishops for their legitimacy. The papal disapproval of their resolutions could not have been more pointed and unequivocal, and Pope Pius reminded them forcefully of their duty to give guidance to their people on the exercise of his authority, and to face down all threats of schism:

> We therefore, venerable brothers do not doubt that you all, having considered and duly weighed what we have written will acknowledge the measure adopted by us to be most just and will yourselves conform wholly to it, by acting in a wholly different manner from what you have declared in numbers two and three of your resolutions – declarations which indeed we would have preferred not to read in your letter. And the fear that you have, of the fervour of the people perhaps opposing you, ought not to deter you from this: for firstly, there is clear evidence that this fervour is not so much from the people, whom we trust will be compliant with the teaching of the Holy See, as from a few individuals; secondly even though the people may be deeply averse to that authority which we will exercise, it is, as you see, part of your duty and office no longer to follow unthinkingly the will of the people but to teach them in a suitable and serious manner about the true state of affairs and about those very important considerations which have caused our mind to undertake this expedient. Those threats of schism, which they themselves have often used, are utterly foreign to the purpose and practice of our most holy religion, if in fact the communion of all Catholics with this Apostolic See, the centre of unity, is not such as could be disregarded by the faithful according to what they want or what they think, but has been enjoined upon us all in the strictest terms by our saviour, Jesus Christ. Finally the divine constitution of the church would have to be completely overturned if it were possible for anyone to prefer his own personal view and sentiment to what has been decreed and decided by the successor of blessed Peter, the prince of the apostles.[26]

25 In these resolutions the prelates undertook to oppose in every canonical and constitutional way the interference of the crown in the nomination of bishops, and declared that their apprehensions for the safety of the church could not be removed by any 'determination' of the pope in opposition to their resolutions. 26 Pope Pius VII to the bishops of Ireland, 1 Feb. 1816, DDA (translation, excluding the reserved parts in *FJ*, 2 July 1818). 'Nos igitur, Venerabiles Fratres,

Disconcerted and upset by this papal rebuff, the bishops did not answer for over two months. Their hesitation and delay reflected the embarrassment and perplexity they felt at the firm and uncompromising tone of the pope's letter, which had made no concessions to their anxieties.

II

On his return from Rome to Ireland, Archbishop Murray was annoyed to find that supporters of the veto were actively campaigning for relief based on it. Several nobles and gentry had met at Lord Trimleston's house under the chairmanship of Lord Southwell and drawn up a petition to parliament, which Henry Grattan agreed to present. When the Catholic Association met a few days later, a petition was transmitted from it by William Bellew, designated as that of the Roman Catholics of Ireland. This petition, which opened the way to acceptance of the veto, was roundly condemned and rejected at a general meeting a few days later, and O'Connell declared that he would denounce these seceders as enemies of their religion, their country and their God.[27] At the English Catholic Board, a petition to parliament and an address to the prince regent on Catholic claims were drawn up, and Lord Grey and William Elliott were asked to present them.[28] Murray, in a sermon on Good Friday, was uncharacteristically harsh in his condemnation of those who would excite dissensions in the Catholic body, bewailing those 'mischievous Catholics who would endeavour to bind the mystical body, the church, by pernicious restrictions', as Christ was bound to a pillar for punishment. Conceding that his misguided brethren might be influenced by honourable motives, he denied that the enemies of the Catholic church, who sought the slavery and degradation of the sacred ministry, could be conciliated. He compared the language of the deluded Catholics who would surrender their church to that used by Judas, who asked Christ's enemies how much they would give him for delivering Christ to them.[29]

The gentry or, as the O'Connellites called them, the 'seceders', stung by Murray's outburst, wrote to Troy 'in vindication of our own conduct' and of those who had signed their petition, and 'in order that mistaken notions and principles of a religious description may not from misconception prevail'.

---

minime dubitamus quin Vos omnes, iis perspectis diligenterque perpensis quae huc usque scripsimus, susceptam a Nobis rationem justissimam agnituri, eique prorsus vos conformaturi sitis, alia prorsus agentes ratione ac numeris 2 et 3 Decretorum Vestrorum declaravistis, quas quidem declarationes vestris in litteris legere noluissemus' Troy later admitted that the letter was 'forced' from him by the association (Troy to Milner, 12 Apr. 1819, BDA).   **27** *DEP*, 15 Feb., 27 Feb., 5 Mar. 1816.   **28** Ibid., 8 Feb. 1816.   **29** *DCh*, 12 Apr. 1816. Murray later explained that he had said 'mistaken brethren' not 'mischievous Catholics' (ibid., 15 Apr. 1816).

They asked him whether the petition signed at Lord Trimleston's contained 'matter which renders it such as cannot with a safe conscience be signed by a Roman Catholic' and whether those who had signed it had merited his displeasure. They assured him that they sought answers not to oblige him to commit himself on either petition, but to prevent 'erroneous and unfounded opinion' prevailing on that subject.[30] Troy replied that they could sign their petition without breaking the law of the church or incurring his displeasure.[31] Grattan duly laid the petition of the 'seceders' before the house of commons, but it was quickly dismissed.[32]

To add to the discomfiture of the anti-vetoists, a rumour reached Ireland that Quarantotti had been made a cardinal. The *Dublin Evening Post* reflected their displeasure when it argued that the promotion of such an enemy of the independence of the Irish Catholic church was tantamount to a declaration by the pope of his sentiments in favour of a vetoistical arrangement which Quarantotti had recommended, and though admired by the British cabinet had been rejected by the Irish nation.[33] In the event, Quarantotti did not become a cardinal until the following year, and in appointing him to that dignity the pope was merely following the tradition of 'creating' some of the secretaries of the Roman congregations cardinals, and almost certainly did not intend to reward him for his part in the emancipation controversy. The honour was probably more of a consolation prize in the wake of his colleagues' criticism of the rescript, and of its effective repudiation by Litta's letter.

The bishops met at Kilkenny on 28 April 1816 to consider the pope's letter and to draw up a reply. There was a full attendance. They declared that they were unable to conceal the sorrow that afflicted them on learning that the pontiff was still persevering in the view that the concession he proposed was harmless, when they were aware that it would do much damage to their religion. That their fears were not groundless could be proven both from the behaviour of the government towards Catholics for three hundred years and from its current behaviour: all ministers, members of parliament and Protestant magistrates swore that the invocation of saints and the sacrifice of the Mass were superstitious and idolatrous. And though the Irish parliament, at the suggestion of George III, had granted favours to the Catholics, it had done so not out of benevolence but because principles of justice, the ardent prayers of a deserving people and the peace and security of the empire demanded such relief. Once conferred with the power of the veto, the government would interfere in the appointments of parish priests, curates and even with candidates for holy orders. Furthermore, it would attempt to

30 Trimleston and others to Troy, 17 Apr. 1816, DDA. 31 *DEP*, 23 Apr. 1816. 32 Ibid., 28 May 1816. 33 Ibid., 15 Aug. 1816.

pension both bishops and priests, and those who refused would be accused of disloyalty to the king.

They therefore, on bended knees, begged the pope not to concede any role to their Protestant government, either in the nomination of bishops or in any of their ecclesiastical affairs. Were emancipation to depend upon such grave conditions, the great majority of Catholics would reject it, and, if it were conceded in such a way, it would bind the church in cruel chains and gradually shatter the very healthy bonds of union between the clergy and people. They would therefore urge the government not to pass such a law, and, should one be passed despite their protests, the Irish people would never cease to demand its cancellation. Apologizing for any hurt their resolutions had caused him, they explained that they had never intended to violate the rights of the Holy See or diminish the obedience due to him, but had merely presumed to pour out their fears and bitter sorrow on the breast of their beloved father.[34]

This response to the pope's letter was part apology and part excuse. To defend their case against any kind of veto they emphasized the insulting restrictions and limitations from which they still suffered, and predicted that further circumscriptions of their pastoral freedom would follow the concession of any rights of interference in episcopal appointments. Expressing profound regret that there was anything in their resolutions that the pope would have preferred not to have read, they declared that nothing could have been further from their minds than to mention anything which would damage the rights of the Holy See or diminish the obedience they had always professed towards him.

Murray forwarded the address to Consalvi for presentation to the pope and also sent a copy to Litta. He explained to them both that the bishops and clergy would be presenting a petition to parliament requesting that no legal power be given to ministers to interfere with the appointment of bishops in Ireland.[35] Those who recommended candidates for episcopal office, instead of passing a list to the ministers, would be obliged to take an oath to recommend only those who were loyal to the king and whose conduct was peaceable. Litta, in return, assured him that the pope was much more pleased with their letter than with the previous remonstrance. Both Consalvi and himself believed that Pius would offer no opposition to the petition, and he hoped there would not be dissensions about it.[36]

---

34 Bishops to Pope Pius VII, 28 Apr. 1816, ASV, Segr. Stato, Inghilterra 30 Irlanda 1, ff 455r–456v. The letter was signed by 26 bishops, including coadjutors, and the warden of Galway. Patrick Ryan, bishop of Ferns, dissented from his colleagues, pledged acceptance of the papal letter, argued that the bishops had rejected domestic nomination in 1810, and claimed that by their behaviour they were virtually accomplices of those scoundrels who aimed at cutting off the Irish people from the unity of the church (Ryan to Cardinal Consalvi(?), 15 June 1816, ibid., ff 450r–453r).   35 Murray to Consalvi, 23 May 1816, ibid., ff 454r–457v.   36 Litta to Murray, 29

Meanwhile, Milner was so greatly concerned with the possible conse-quences in parliament of a report produced by Coxe-Hippisley on the methods of episcopal appointments in several European countries, that he complained of the 'unexpected success of the perfidious scheme of Hippisley and of his patron and Orange encourager Castlereagh'. He complained about the blindness of Rome to 'the avowed attempts of Castlereagh & co to restrain her jurisdiction and to cut off her correspon-dence with these islands'.[37] The fear was that 'the ever fraudulent Castlereagh' would command the influence of the crown in the house of lords, and Canning would have similar influence in the commons, and both would be:

> bent from motives of personal honour as well as from their original Pitt-politics to subjugate the Cath. church of Ireland, while Consalvi and through him Pius VII trembling at the thunder of our vessels on both sides of Italy thinks that whatever makes for the interest of the Papal States makes for the good of religion and that we prelates are a disloyal set.[38]

His anxiety about the plans of Castlereagh and Canning duly reached apoca-lyptic levels as he proclaimed that his 'happiness will be in suffering death to oppose the machinations of these men and their coadjutors of every denom-ination'.[39] The Irish bishops' dread of government interference in episcopal nominations paled before this onslaught on these ministers.

Hayes had remained in Rome after Murray and Murphy had gone home, and, according to himself, continued to engage Roman officials on the veto. Encouraged by William Coppinger, bishop of Cloyne, to resist the agents of the veto in Rome,[40] he warned Litta of the dangers of a schism in Ireland.[41] And he claimed that Litta told him that if the remonstrances had been directed to him and not to the pope, he could have settled everything himself and Consalvi could not have interfered. Hayes even maintained that he told Litta that Consalvi had deceived the pope, and he thought his relationship with Litta was so strong that he had won domestic nomination from him.[42] If he was prepared to attack Consalvi to Litta in such an undiplomatic manner, he was much more forthright in his criticisms of Archbishop Troy. He accused Troy of obstinately concealing the Genoese letter from the

Aug. 1816, DDA. 37 Milner to Murray, 31 May 1816, ibid. 38 Ibid., 16 July 1816. 39 Ibid., 8 Dec. 1816. 40 Coppinger to Hayes, 1 Feb. 1816, *Coll. Hib.* 24 (1982), 130–1. Hayes claimed that Poynter constantly wrote lies to Macpherson and had nearly persuaded the Romans that all England would become Catholic if the veto were granted (ibid., 133–7). 41 Hayes to Litta, 18 Feb. 1816, ibid., 131–3. 42 Hayes to Patrick Hayes, 1 June 1816, *Coll. Hib.* 25 (1983), 93–7.

public, which had led to an exaggerated view of it and to the subsequent ferment. He also accused Troy of persistently supporting the veto except when dragged into line by his episcopal colleagues, and complained of the 'kind of papal authority all over Ireland' the archbishop had acquired as the 'regulator of the appointment of Irish bishops'. The 'people judging men's motives from their actions', he made bold to assert, had concluded that Troy 'had entered into some private compact with the government to help it out in the accomplishment of its views ... by *private* correspondence, intrigue, equivocations, doubtful expressions now misleading the public mind by the concealment of innoxious or agreeable documents ...' He signed the anti-vetoist statements of the hierarchy only 'because he would otherwise deprive himself of that patriarchal or semi-papal authority he has by keen manage-ment procured'. He even claimed that Troy's relatives were given highly paid positions by the government.[43]

When Hayes was purportedly preparing to leave Rome in October 1816, he asked Litta for the pope's views on whether the Genoese letter was mandatory when it referred to exhibiting the list of candidates to the govern-ment, whether the direct nomination of bishops, the revision of rescripts, the *exequatur* and the appeal in ecclesiastical affairs to the civil tribunal could with a safe conscience be admitted by Catholics, and whether domestic nomination by the clergy or bishops or both jointly would meet opposition from the Holy See.[44] Litta's answer was brief, cold and factual. He simply referred him to the Genoese letter and to the pope's letter of 1 February 1816, told him he did not know what he could do further in that business and insisted that he did not know enough about domestic nomination.[45] A further fulsome communication from Hayes drew no reply from the cardinal.[46] In his reports home, Hayes had been at pains to present Litta as a patron to whom he could open his heart and who, unlike Consalvi, was always sympathetic to his cause. Consalvi was undoubtedly very interested in maintaining good relations with Britain, but he was not prepared to go beyond the boundaries that the Holy See had set without the pope's author-ization. Litta's laconic response with its curt good wishes for a safe journey would indicate the boredom of a high official with a persistent and tedious suppliant rather than the anxiety of a well-wisher to clarify a situation for a friend. Whatever goodwill Hayes might have enjoyed at the beginning of his mission had been exhausted by the end of it.

However, his sponsors in Dublin continued to offer support, though much less financial help than he would have liked. At a general meeting of the Catholics of Ireland on 17 December 1816, a vote of thanks was passed to

43 Hayes to Litta, 17 Sept. 1816, ibid., 137–50.   44 Litta to Hayes, 29 Sept. 1816, ibid., 154–5.
45 Hayes to Litta, 5 Oct. 1816, ibid., 155–6.   46 Ibid., 12 Oct. 1816, 162–7.

him for 'his zealous, prudent and pious exertions in resisting any species of interference' by the government in the nomination of bishops, and he was encouraged to continue those exertions until the church was rescued from the peril into which the enemies of the faith had placed her.[47]

In the event, Hayes did not leave Rome until the summer of 1817. He had no further messages to communicate to Roman officials, but he may have continued to plague some of them with requests and advice which added nothing new to his case. Growing tired of him, they ordered him to leave Rome in May.[48] Ill health prevented him from obeying this order, and through Cardinal Litta's goodwill, he was allowed an extension to his sojourn, but in July he was brought to the border of the Papal States and sent packing. He reached Dublin in September, and on 13 December 1817 he reported to the Catholic Board, outlining the plan for domestic nomination that he had presented to the Holy See. He claimed that his plan would have been approved had it not been for the successful intrigues of the advocates of the veto, who, through Baron Ompteda, the Hanoverian ambassador, procured his arrest and expulsion from Rome.[49] The newspapers opposed to the veto, which had published rumours of intrigues in Rome in favour of the veto, reported favourably on his mission.[50] Hayes had run up substantial debts,[51] estimated at £470, and various efforts were made to liquidate them. He was the recipient of much praise at public dinners, was toasted enthusiastically by Daniel O'Connell,[52] and received a warm reception. A different complexion, however, was put on his mission when the board received an answer from the pope to a letter it had sent him the previous July.

Before Hayes had actually left the Papal States, but after his sentence of expulsion had become known in Ireland, the Catholic Board, in a somewhat malapert letter to the pope, complained of the treatment Irish Catholics were experiencing from Rome, and, in particular, of that meted out to Hayes. 'The Catholics of Ireland,' they lamented, 'have observed with painful emotions the marked disinclination evinced at Rome to entertain their most humble solicitations for attention.' Nearly two years had passed since they forwarded their remonstrance with Hayes, to which they had received no answer. What made matters worse was their realization that 'an active anxiety [was] evinced to forward the wishes and accomplish the purposes of that power, which persecuted our ancestors and still persecutes their posterity'. Asserting that

47 Resolutions of general meeting of Catholics, 17 Dec. 1816, ibid., 175–6. 48 James McCormick, OFM, the guardian of St Isidore's, claimed that a letter from Hayes published in the *Dublin Gazette* made him many enemies in Rome, England and Ireland. They combined against him in 'revenge' for his making so free with their 'character, reputation and honour' in several letters, and persuaded Consalvi and the pope, both of whom were annoyed by his 'imprudent and provoking words' to order him to leave Rome within twenty-four hours (McCormick to Milner, 7 June 1817, BDA). 49 *DEP*, 16 Dec. 1817. 50 Ibid., 4 Nov. 1817. 51 Ibid., 24 Feb. 1818. 52 Ibid., 25 Apr. 1818.

the 'offensive indignity' suffered by Hayes in being expelled from Rome 'did not arise from any misconduct' on his part, they begged the pope to give 'no credit to the representations' of Coxe-Hippisley, who was strongly prejudiced against the Catholic claims of Ireland. They implored the pontiff to sanction a concordat with the Irish bishops to ensure that a system of domestic nomination would be established, and to revoke the order of banishment imposed on Hayes.[53]

The pope answered this remonstrance six months later. Remarking that he had written to the bishops making his position clear in February 1816, he explained that he thought it unnecessary to repeat to them what they could easily have learned from the bishops. However, he rebuked them for the tone of their letter, pointing out that they had frequently given 'expression to such language and sentiments as seemed, by no means, in unison with that devotion and zeal which the people of Ireland have at all times manifested towards the Apostolic See'. He explained that when he permitted arrangements about the appointments of bishops, if the government would pass an act of emancipation favourable to Catholics, he was induced to do so 'by no temporal considerations or political counsels (of which it would be criminal even to suspect us) but we had solely in view the interests and well-being of the Catholic religion'. In his letter to the bishops, he had proved fully and clearly that his 'proposition was altogether harmless and guarded by such limitations and conditions, that, if they should be observed, no room could remain for abuse'. When he turned to their appeal about Hayes, he did not mince his words about their delegate's conduct. Charging him with having 'furnished us with many and weighty causes of grief and vexation' unbecoming in a member of a religious order, he explained that Hayes' calumnies against himself and the Holy See and his arrogance and audacity had reached such a pitch that he could no longer suppress his sentiments without the abandonment of his personal dignity. Referring to the delegate's report to them the previous December, he concluded that it too was full of falsehoods and calumnies, and therefore undeserving of any credit.[54]

The association must have been taken aback by the severity of this papal reprimand. Not only did the pope hold firm to the terms of the Genoese letter and repudiate any suggestion of political motivation in his conduct, but

53 Remonstrance dated 19 July 1817 in *FJ*, 8 June 1818. Cardinal Severoli, the nuncio in Vienna, sent a copy of a letter Hayes had written to the *Times* on 8 Mar. 1817, and commented that Hayes seemed to be 'indecorously carried away by his own opinion' (Severoli to Propaganda, 31 Mar. 1817, APF, SC (Irlanda), 20 f 46r). Troy reported that Hayes' letters to the papers were 'a farrago of truths and falsehoods' (Troy to Propaganda, 20 May 1817, ibid., f 64rv).   54 Pope Pius VII to Catholic Association, 21 Feb. 1818, in *FJ*, 8 June 1818. Gradwell, the rector of the English College, reported that the letter was written by Mgr Testa, an assistant of Consalvi's. In his report to the Catholic Association, Hayes had attacked Consalvi, the 'political minister' and 'the ardent promoter of every measure prejudicial to me and my mission' (*FJ*, 17 Dec. 1817).

he also reproached them for the impropriety of their language. As he had referred them to his letter to the bishops, they demanded to see it, and Troy felt obliged to let them have it (with a few excisions).

When the letter was read at the Catholic Association, Hayes apologized for his conduct. He was undoubtedly glad that the pope's comments were not more detailed, and so he declared that he would prostrate himself before the pope, expressing his regret that his conduct had given offence, and would implore his forgiveness.[55] Troy persuaded him to modify his apology to the pope to make it less equivocal, and then forwarded it for him to Rome. The archbishop suggested to Cardinal Litta that the pope should pardon him, and remarked that such a letter would be an admonition to the clergy to show proper respect to the Holy See, and to the laity not to get involved in ecclesiastical matters.[56]

The papal letter delicately avoided specifying all the reasons for the grief and vexation that Hayes had caused in Rome. Robert Gradwell, the rector of the English College, spelt them out in his letters to Bishop Poynter: personal immorality and insulting behaviour to the pope in person. Gradwell reported that Hayes rarely wore his habit, and behaved in a scandalous manner by bringing prostitutes into St Isidore's, forcing his superior there to request Cardinal Litta to free the community from his vexations. This was corroborated by an official document given by Consalvi to Coxe-Hippisley.[57] The pope, in response to an insult at an audience, was alleged to have told him: 'You may think yourself well off that I am pope as well as sovereign; otherwise I would throw you out of the window.' The cardinal who passed on this story to Gradwell added, 'You may judge of the insolence and outrage of this man, which could provoke the meekest and humblest of men to use such an expression.'[58] Hayes was ordered to leave the Papal States on 17 May 1817. He refused and barricaded himself in St Isidore's, but the police broke in. When he pleaded illness, he was given a further twenty days before he was escorted to the border of the papal territories and sent on his way to Florence. Gradwell explained that the officer whom cardinals Consalvi and Pacca employed to take statements from the immoral women with whom Hayes associated produced evidence to prove the charges.[59]

55 Declaration of Hayes to Catholic Association, 1 June 1818, ibid., 8 June 1818. Cardinal Litta assured Troy that the pope was pleased by Hayes' apology, forwarded to him the papal response to Hayes and encouraged him to exhort Hayes to maintain his resolution (Litta to Troy, 12 Sept. 1818, DDA). 56 Troy to Litta, 23 June 1818, APF, SC(Irlanda), 21, f 292rv. 57 Undated note, ASV, Segr Stato esteri, ep. Moderna, Rubr 297, busta 659, fasc.1, ff 115r–120r. 58 Gradwell to Poynter, 22 Apr. 1819, WDA. Gradwell explained that the phrase used '*vi butterei dalla fenestra*' expressed resentment mixed with contempt. A milder version of this story has the pope saying to Hayes '*temerario, voi mi offendete, partite dí qua*' (30 Aug. 1819, ASV, Segr Stato estri, Ep. Moderna, Rubr 297, busta 659, fasc 1, ff 6r–7v). 59 Ibid., 7 Feb. 1818, 3 May 1818, 30 July 1818, 22 Apr. 1819, 24, 29 July 1819. WDA. Gradwell also claimed that Hayes' name had

Archbishop Troy may not have known the details of Hayes' misbehaviour in Rome, but the Franciscan's behaviour in Ireland had been sufficient to provoke his contempt. Even before his return, Troy had complained to Litta about the jumble of truths and falsehoods Hayes was passing on, and commented that 'the false and malign representations in the letter of the turbulent Fr Hayes published in the papers disturb the Catholic people a lot and agitate very much the committee or association.'[60] Later, he told the cardinal 'the weird conduct of the eccentric Fr Hayes is condemned by all sensible people. Some laypeople and a very few of the clergy in the province of Cashel defend him because they do not know him. I have always regarded him as unworthy of belief and a crazy impostor'.[61] Though the bishops and their agents bore no responsibility for Hayes' behaviour in Rome, and, in fact, Murray, Murphy and Blake gave him a wide berth at all times, his outrageous conduct and inexcusable discourtesy undoubtedly created a bad image of Irish clergy at the Vatican. He did damage to the cause of the bishops as well as to that of the Catholic Association.

Though Murray, the leader of the episcopal delegation, was the very opposite of Hayes – patient, courteous and gracious – he did not succeed in effecting any change in Roman thinking on the Genoese letter. The pope and Consalvi believed that they had made a minimal concession to the British government, allowing it to erase some names from a list, and they could see no danger in permitting such a compact, if it was linked to emancipation. Contrasted with the concessions the pope was forced to make to other states, those promised in the Genoese letter were indeed small, and the reaction of the Irish bishops must have caused something of a shock at the Holy See. The bishops had gone beyond the bounds of obedience, diplomacy and urbanity, not only by threatening to oppose any form of interference by the crown, but especially by telling the pope that he could not guarantee a safe and secure arrangement with the government. Pius VII may have been mild, but he could also be firm and tenacious, as he showed by overturning centuries of Gallican tradition in France. Doubtless with the urging of Consalvi, he decided that the Irish bishops had taken a step too far,

been put forward for the bishopric of Clogher and for a bishopric in the United States. 'It is a fact,' he wrote, that 'the Irish (heathens to be sure) have recommended ... Hayes' (ibid., 20 June 1818). Towards the end of 1819, Hayes was invited by a group of Catholics in South Carolina to have himself consecrated a bishop by the Jansenist archbishop of Utrecht, bring a few seminarians with him and establish an independent Catholic church in the United States (Giblin, 'Papers of Richard Joachim Hayes, OFM, 1810–24', *Coll. Hib.*, 21–2 (1979–80), 85).   60 Troy to Litta, 18 Aug. 1817, APF, SC(Irlanda), 20, f 144rv.   61 Troy to Propaganda, 3 June 1818, APF, SC(Irlanda), 22, ff 235r–236r. Hayes went to London in 1819, and for two years fought a libel action without success. Poynter withdrew his faculties after three months. He returned to Dublin and there preached sermons in the Capuchin Church which were later printed. He died in Paris in 1824.

and reproached them for their excess. Both the missions to Rome were painful failures.

III

The Holy See was convinced that the Irish bishops had no grounds for fearing that the government, if given the right of rejecting some of those proposed for bishoprics, would have used it to the detriment of the Irish church. Time proved that the bishops were correct in suspecting that the government would have interfered or tried to do so, to their disadvantage. The emancipation act of 1829 made no mention of the right (or otherwise) of the state to be involved in episcopal appointments. Before the act was passed, the congregation of Propaganda had made new arrangements for the recommendation of candidates for bishoprics. When a vacancy occurred, the canons and parish priests of the diocese chose three names, in order of preference, for appointment. These names, with the comments of the bishops of the province, were forwarded to Rome. The pope was free to choose anyone he wished, either from among the three (the '*terna*') or from outside it.

Though not officially empowered to interfere in episcopal appointments, the government, after 1829, decided to do so unofficially. It made use of the British minister to the court of the Grand Duchy of Tuscany at Florence, Lord Burghersh, who had shown an interest in ecclesiastical affairs at Rome and who had met the pope and other prelates there.

Wellington, the prime minister, made use of this contact between the embassy at Florence and the Vatican when the bishop of Waterford died on 8 October 1829. Eleven days later, he wrote to Burghersh, recommending for the vacant see Thomas Weld, an English priest who had been named a coadjutor to a bishop in Canada. Remarking that the 'peace and welfare of Ireland depended in a great degree upon the selection of men appointed to fill the places in the episcopal mission to that country', he invited the envoy to lose no time in discreetly forwarding his suggestion to Rome.[62] Wellington was friendly with the powerful Beresford family in Waterford, and he may have heard that a likely candidate was Nicholas Foran, a leading opponent of the Beresfords, who had been a strong supporter of Villiers-Stuart at the election in 1826. Foran was the first choice of the parish priests of Waterford, and Burghersh had the awkward task of asking the cardinal secretary of state to set him aside. Cardinal Albani replied that Irish Catholics would complain,

---

62 Wellington to Burghersh, 19 Oct. 1829 in Weigall (ed.), *Correspondence of Lord Burghersh, afterwards the earl of Westmoreland, 1808–1840*, pp 264–5.

if, after emancipation, the election of their bishops were ignored, and they were asked to receive a bishop who was not even Irish by birth. He feared they would not quietly accept such an appointment. In the best tradition of Roman compromises, neither Foran nor Weld was appointed, and the office was given to William Abraham, who had been second on the *terna*, and who was the only priest in Waterford who had campaigned for Lord Beresford in 1826.[63]

In October 1832 Archbishop Curtis of Armagh died and the government was anxious to prevent the appointment of Bishop Doyle. Doyle had always behaved in a constitutional manner. He had supported O'Connell's election, was opposed to tithes, wanted arrangements made to support the poor and had made 'ecumenical' proposals about church unity. But he had also predicted that no bishop would excommunicate rebels, or, if a sentence of excommunication were passed, it would have no effect. The British representative who opposed his appointment was told that a coadjutor with right of succession was already in place, and that the see was therefore filled.

Thomas Aubin, an official at the embassy in Florence, was stationed in Rome from 1832 to 1844. He was commissioned to oppose the candidacy of the first name on the list for Cloyne and Ross in 1833. What made his work easier was that the bishops of the province had all supported the second candidate, Bartholomew Crotty, and Crotty was appointed.

A much more important vacancy – that of Tuam – occurred in April 1834, and a much more high-profile candidate hove into sight. John MacHale, the bishop of Killala, was placed second on the *terna* by the parish priests but won the strong support of the bishops of the province. Lord Melbourne, the prime minister, on hearing of MacHale's chances of succession remarked, 'Anybody but him.' Palmerston, the foreign secretary, instructed Aubin to try to prevent the appointment. MacHale had been a forthright critic of the Bible societies, of the Kildare Place Society, of the government's neglect of the poor and of the wealth of the established church. He had written trenchant public letters (which some colleagues regarded as too forceful) on these issues to George Canning, a former prime minister who had died in 1827, and Earl Grey, who was then prime minister.[64] The government regarded him as a political agitator for these reasons and especially because he favoured the repeal of the union. It also wanted to block George Browne, the bishop of Galway, but his name did not figure on the list sent to Rome.

Aubin contacted the cardinal secretary of state and his chief assistant, but his intervention encountered a powerful obstacle in the person of the pope. Gregory XVI had met and been impressed by MacHale in 1832, and on

63 Power, *Waterford and Lismore: a compendious history of the united dioceses*, pp 38–9; Broderick, *The Holy See and the Irish movement for the repeal of the union with England, 1829–1847*, pp 71–4.
64 H. Andrews, *The lion of the west: a biography of John MacHale*, pp 27–68.

hearing of the charges of sedition against him, got his speeches translated into Italian. He found no sedition in them and appointed MacHale, declaring that, if he had appointed anyone else, it would have been evident that he had been swayed by the British government.[65]

After MacHale's appointment, the government did not intervene directly in episcopal appointments, though as late as the 1880s its self-appointed agent, the duke of Norfolk, tried to bring his influence to bear in particular vacancies. The government, however, continued to interfere at a diplomatic level in Rome against repeal and against opponents of its policy on education. Had it been authorized to block candidates for the episcopate, it would certainly have eliminated those who had campaigned against it constitutionally, either for political reasons or in defence of social justice. Doyle and MacHale were widely recognized as the ablest and most learned bishops of their time, and the blackballing of the most capable prelates by the state, had it continued, would have diminished the influence of the Irish church. Those sceptical of the government's intentions would have felt vindicated by the intrigues of the British embassy at Florence.

---

65 Broderick, *The Holy See and the Irish movement for the repeal of the union with England, 1829–1847*, pp 67–99. Broderick quoted from the diaries of Charles Greville, the grandson of a former prime minister, who won fame for the pertinent political comments in his diaries, which were published after his death. 'The law prohibits any intercourse with Rome, and the government, whose business it is to enforce the law has established a regular but underhand intercourse, through the medium of a diplomatic agent, whose character cannot be avowed, and the ministers of this protestant kingdom are continually soliciting the pope to confer appointments, the validity, even the existence of which they do not recognize, while the pope, who is the object of our abhorrence and dread, good-humouredly complies with all or nearly all their requests' (ibid., pp 98–9).

14

Calm after the disaccord

I

A fter its contacts with Murray, Murphy, Blake and Hayes in the wake of the Genoese letter, and its responses to them and to the Catholic Association, the Holy See issued no direct advice or guidance on the question of Catholic emancipation for several years. No new proposals came before parliament that required pontifical counsel and none was sought by any of the bishops in Britain or Ireland.

With the defeat of Napoleon in 1815, the importance of Irish soldiers to Britain greatly diminished, and there was no incentive to make concessions to Catholics to boost military recruitment. In Ireland, the return of agrarian disturbances consequent on the slump in demand for foodstuffs for the army was another factor.[1]

Some prominent lay supporters of emancipation in England were prepared to make concessions about securities. In Ireland, the split between the majority associated with the Catholic Association and the 'vetoists' or 'seceders' ensured that two petitions were presented to parliament in April–May 1816. Only one debate took place. Grattan, offering the terms of the Genoese letter in the 'seceders'' petition, was supported by Castlereagh, the foreign secretary, but opposed by Peel, the chief secretary for Ireland, and his motion was defeated by some thirty votes. In the house of lords, Lord Donoughmore's motion came closer to success but still lost by four votes. A further petition, opposing any alteration in the arrangements for choosing bishops, was signed by most of the bishops and more than a thousand priests, but was withdrawn for procedural reasons.[2] An English petition signed by the leading Catholic aristocrats met a similar fate.

Despite the defeat of the vetoists' petition, O'Connell felt that the anti-vetoists were losing their campaign. Their remonstrances to Rome had been ineffective, and he feared (needlessly) that some bishops and parish clergy

---

1 Connolly, *Union government, 1812–23, NHI*, v, pp 60–2. 2 Ward, *The eve of Catholic emancipation*, ii, pp 234–5. Sir Henry Parnell, a supporter of the Catholic cause, regretted the reaction of the bishops and the renewal of hostility against 'securities'. He maintained that no minister could ever 'succeed in conducting an unconditional measure through parliament' (Parnell to Scully, 31 May 1816 in MacDermot, *The Catholic question in Ireland and England, 1798–1822*, p. 590).

would succumb to vetoism. He assured the Friends of Civil and Religious Liberty, a mainly Protestant group in Belfast, that he had always sought Catholic emancipation on principle and as a matter of right. And that principle, if established, would be equally useful to the Protestants of France and Italy as to the Catholics of Ireland.[3] Castlereagh had let it be known that despite his own support for emancipation, he could not anticipate a majority in the cabinet nor foresee any prospect of success in parliament.[4] The Anglican bishop of Norwich, a consistent supporter of emancipation, was much more optimistic.[5]

Coxe-Hippisley voted against the Irish petition seeking unqualified emancipation. He then declared in parliament that if they needed a motive for seeking securities, it would be found in the Irish petition. Accordingly, he suggested that a committee be appointed to examine the power foreign potentates enjoyed in the appointment of Catholic prelates, and their general practice of inspecting the correspondence between Rome and its Catholic subjects. He maintained that Quarantotti's rescript had given the crown all it required. Peel supported the motion, as did Castlereagh, who explained that he could never tolerate a situation where a foreign power could have contacts with their subjects of which the government had no knowledge. It was monstrous that Rome should have unrestricted intercourse in the realm.[6]

A select committee was appointed to inquire into the nature and substance of laws and ordinances existing in foreign states respecting the regulation of their Roman Catholic subjects and their intercourse with the see of Rome. Castlereagh had already sent orders in 1812 to several British ambassadors to inquire into the appointments of clergy, especially bishops, and the restraints on papal rescripts. A report and lengthy appendix was published, and it found substantially what the vetoists wanted. With minor exceptions, the sovereigns nominated the bishops and the pope gave them canonical institution. In the Austrian empire (Austria, Hungary, Bohemia) the emperor nominated the bishops and papal confirmation was then sought by the Austrian ambassador in Rome. The bishops took an oath of allegiance to the emperor. In Hungary, only native Hungarians could be appointed. The Austrian bishops were also obliged to furnish the provincial governors with the names, places of education, progress and morals of all candidates for ordination. All documents from Rome were submitted to the government before publication and were prohibited unless referring to the legitimate needs of the church. Only cases of conscience coming from the Roman penitentiary were exempted. The only exception to imperial nomination was the archbishop of Olmutz, who was elected by the diocesan canons.

---

3 *DEP*, 25 Jan. 1816.   4 Ibid., 8 Feb. 1816.   5 Ibid., 9 July 1816.   6 *Hansard 1*, xxxiv, 871–8, 28 May 1816.

The same applied broadly to the other countries connected with Austria. In Lombardy, the emperor enjoyed the right of superintendence of seminaries regarding discipline and doctrine, the royal censors censured the books used in them and the *exequatur* was enforced. The Tuscan government presented four names for episcopal appointments, the pope chose one, and the *exequatur* also applied. In Protestant Prussia, the crown nominated the three bishops of Poland, and two German bishops were elected by their chapters on the king's recommendation and confirmed by the pope. The minister of home affairs named the priests to vacant churches, and no bishop could make new regulations without the licence of the state. Male children were baptized by a priest of the father's family and females by a priest of the mother's family. No document from Rome could be published without being submitted to the minister of home affairs, who would modify it to make it conform to the regulations of the state. Royal nominations and the *exequatur* applied in France, Spain, Portugal, Holland[7] and other smaller countries, and in France the parish priests, if first approved by the government, were appointed by the bishops. In Quebec, candidates for the coadjutorships or bishoprics were recommended or approved by the governor and then received their appointments from the pope.[8] The archbishop of Mohilov in Russia was named by the empress. In the Catholic countries, the bishops and clergy received stipends from the states. Attached to this information were copies of Quarantotti's rescript, the Genoese letter, the answers of the six universities in 1788 about the deposing power of the pope and the resolutions of the Irish bishops of 1799.[9]

The power of states throughout the world to nominate bishops was, in fact, greater than that detailed in this parliamentary report. Between the return of Pius VII to Rome in 1814 and 1829, five concordats between the pope and the sovereigns of Tuscany, Bavaria, France, the Two Sicilies, and the Netherlands had been signed. There were also six agreements with rulers about the arrangements ('*circoscrizioni*') of dioceses in Piedmont, Poland, Prussia, the Upper Rhine, France and Hanover. Other accords concerned the administration of ecclesiastical property and episcopal elections in Lucca and the Upper Rhine, and there were special arrangements about bishoprics in Switzerland. The appointments of bishops and clerical pensions were included in nearly all these concordats and conventions.[10]

Milner submitted a petition to parliament on 28 April 1817, signed by

---

7 After the Congress of Vienna, the king of Holland ruled Belgium, the former Austrian province, many of whose inhabitants were Catholics.   8 In 1819, Poynter reported that Lord Bathurst, the minister for the colonies, was extremely displeased when an archbishop of Quebec was appointed without any consultation with the government (Poynter to Gradwell, 10 Sept. 1819, WDA).   9 HC [501] 1816, vii, 3–51.   10 Mercati, *Raccolta di concordati su materie ecclesiastiche tra la Santa Sede e le autorità civili*, pp 585–724.

numerous Catholics of Warwickshire and Staffordshire, objecting to the 'galling restrictions' that Cox-Hippisley's report would inflict on Catholic discipline.[11] He insisted that no layman, sovereign or not, had any right to appoint bishops. The other vicars apostolic requested the historian, John Lingard, to respond to the findings of the report. Lingard argued that the privileges the civil authorities enjoyed, as quoted in the report, were part of arrangements by which the state endowed the church and paid pensions to the clergy. Since no such arrangement existed in England or Ireland, the civil authorities could not lay claim to a role in episcopal nominations, much less to the right of *exequatur*.[12] The state did subsidize Maynooth College, but this was seen by the bishops merely as a gesture of support comparable, though not in size, to the *regium donum* or annual grant given to the Presbyterian clergy.

Poynter, Collingridge and Gibson felt they were required to give some guidance to their people in the wake of Coxe-Hippisley's report about the possible dangers of being asked to pay an unacceptable price for emancipation. Collingridge wrote of his fear that 'emancipation, if ever granted will be accompanied with clauses quite repugnant to essential discipline and even tenets of the Catholic religion', and so he felt that they should publicly declare that they could not submit to many of the regulations in Coxe-Hippisley's report. And so 'we ought, it seems to me for the security of our religion, for consistency's sake and to prevent scandal come forward with an explicit declaration that the terms of the letter from Genoa are to us a *norma agendi* beyond which we cannot and will not go on any consideration'.[13] On the other hand, Bishop Smith, the coadjutor of the Northern District, quoting Murray's view that Rome regretted the Genoese letter, nevertheless believed that 'some caution' should be given to their Catholic people in view of Coxe-Hippisley's 'appalling report'. Though he did not favour domestic nomination, he did not think that any suggestion should be made to Rome in direct opposition to the policy of the Irish bishops.[14] Bishop Gibson, the vicar apostolic of the Northern District, who could not take part in many of these discussions because of illness, nevertheless let Rome know that he had always rejected the veto even before Milner and the Irish bishops had retracted their opinion of it.[15]

Accordingly, Poynter suggested the publication of the Genoese letter, which had never been made public in England, together with a set of protective guidelines. These took the form of resolutions warning Catholics against consenting to regulations that had been made and enforced in other states,

11 Husenbeth, *Life of Bishop Milner*, pp 335–6. 12 Lingard, *Observations on the laws and ordinances which exist in foreign states relative to the religious concerns of their Roman Catholic subjects.* 13 Collingridge to Poynter, 1817, WDA. 14 Smith to Poynter, 25 Mar. 1817, ibid. 15 Gibson to Propaganda, 6 May 1817, APF, SC(Anglia), 6, ff 843r–844r.

noting that several of these regulations had been condemned by the bishops who had been obliged to accept them as inconsistent with the doctrine and discipline of the church, explaining that such regulations were inapplicable where there was no state endowment, and, with a novel and effective argument, pointing out that the nomination of Catholic bishops could not be surrendered to a sovereign who was head of another church and insisting that they could not assent to the interruption of the free intercourse in ecclesiastical matters between the pope and bishops.[16]

The three vicars apostolic could not agree whether to publish these resolutions with a pastoral letter or not. Milner received a copy of them from Bishop Gibson and considered them 'very proper and edifying'.[17] Poynter, who came under more pressure from the Catholic aristocrats and gentry anxious for emancipation, wished to make the Genoese letter the basis of any future policy. Murray believed that the Genoese letter had been given as a concession rather than as part of a fixed policy, and there was no serious commitment to it. Conscious that the Irish bishops and Irish Catholic Association were opposed to it, he thought it should not be put forward as a guideline. Collingridge, agreeing with this view, accepted Murray's opinion that by mentioning it they would be inviting the government to act upon it. He also thought the suppression of any reference to it would please the Irish bishops, and, though 'in reality entitled to no compliment from us, we should give less matter for future exasperation by this sacrifice to peace and leave them full liberty to try their plan of domestic nomination'.[18] Murray's comments were private, and the danger of the Irish bishops commenting on an English response was averted by the decision of the vicars apostolic not to publish the resolutions or the letter. Collingridge did, however, include much of the material of the resolutions in a pastoral letter to his district.[19]

The possibility that Coxe-Hippisley's report would lead to renewed pressure for a veto provoked the vicars apostolic to reflect on the Irish proposal for domestic nomination. The Irish bishops had not spelt out the details of this arrangement to their English colleagues, and it was only in answer to Litta's expression of ignorance of what the proposal meant that Murray told the cardinal that they sought domestic nomination only if the government would accept it in lieu of the veto. If the government would not accept it, the proposal ceased to be practical. And it was to satisfy the government – not priests or bishops – that the plan emerged. It was proposed that within a certain number of days of a vacancy occurring, the diocesan chapter, having taken an oath to recommend no one who was not loyal to the king, would choose the names of three candidates it deemed suitable for appoint-

16 Ward, *The eve of Catholic emancipation*, ii, pp 241–2.   17 Milner to Murray, 10 Mar. 1817, DDA.   18 Collingridge to Poynter, 31 Mar. 1817, WDA.   19 Collingridge's pastoral, 15 Apr. 1817, ClDA.

ment. Those names would then be submitted to the metropolitan, and in the case of his see being vacant, to the senior suffragan, and the majority of the bishops of the province would have a veto. Before exercising this power, the bishops would likewise take the oath of loyalty and would add that they would not reject any candidate except for reasons of conscience. The names of the three candidates approved by the bishops and the chapter of the diocese would then be submitted to Rome, so that the pope might choose one of them for the episcopal office. Murray asked Litta if the pontiff would approve of a law that would grant emancipation on those terms.[20] As distinct from the plan of the Catholic Board, which would have limited the pope's power to the canonical institution of one candidate, similar to the restrictions imposed by rulers, this arrangement would have given the pope a choice among three.

This plan would have preserved the papal right of nomination, and ensured that the bishop chosen was a native of the country, thereby circum-venting some of the difficulties associated with the royal veto. However, it did not meet with the approval of the vicars apostolic (though they did not have detailed information about it). Bishop Cameron of the Lowland District of Scotland maintained that he would prefer any other plan to that of domestic nomination, as he did not believe they should encroach in any way on the pope's prerogative.[21] Bishop Smith, the coadjutor of the Northern District, thought that domestic nomination would only prove to be a source of domestic evil, and would shackle the pope without shielding the vicars apostolic from the dreaded interference of the government. He could not understand why the Irish prelates had embraced that policy.[22] Bishop Collingridge was even more firmly opposed: he opined that the vicars apostolic should have nothing to do with domestic nomination.[23] Poynter declared that he would not support it as he and his colleagues were 'not authorized to propose or to have any concern in such a measure'.[24]

The congregation of Propaganda duly considered the Irish proposal. An official wrote at length of its advantages, both in preventing disputes and in accusations of impropriety in episcopal appointments. He also pointed out that it would negate the charge that the pope, at his pleasure, exerted his authority and therefore had an influence on the nation by directly appointing bishops. Nonetheless the congregation voted not to recommend this method to the pope.[25]

---

20 Murray to Litta, 28 Oct. 1816, APF, SC (Irlanda), 20, ff 502r–503v.   21 Cameron to Poynter, 5 Mar. 1817, WDA.   22 Smith to Poynter, 25 Mar. 1817, ibid.   23 Collingridge to Poynter, 15 Apr. 1817, ibid.   24 Poynter to Collingridge, 26 Apr. 1817, ClDA.   25 Norms for appointing bishops in Ireland, 17 July 1817, APF, SC(Irlanda), 20, ff 103r–106r. A scheme not dissimilar was introduced in 1829, but it did not bind the pope to choose any of the three candidates submitted to him.

Before this decision had reached Ireland, Murray and Patrick Everard, the coadjutor archbishop of Cashel, had been sent by their colleagues to confer with the members of parliament and ministers who would meet them on emancipation. Their commission to negotiate on behalf of the Irish hierarchy was certainly a snub to Milner and seems to have been the point at which they no longer regarded him as their sole agent in England. Murray, who had twice presented their cause in Rome and whose personality and conciliatory manner made him a suitable choice, had in Everard someone of a similar temperament who had spent several years teaching in Lancashire. In choosing them rather than Milner the bishops were attempting to have their case put across in a more diplomatic and less polemical manner. Troy was afraid that the divisions among the Catholics in Ireland, even though only a small minority dissented from the bishops and general body of Catholics, could weaken their influence. But he reserved a more severe judgment for the English board and vicars apostolic: the nobles and most respectable and rich English Catholics were prepared to let their church be enslaved in order to magnify their own importance. The weakness of the vicars apostolic, who signed the famous fifth resolution of 1810, to which Milner was always courageously opposed, was the source of the discord among Catholics and had given the impetus to Coxe-Hippisley and his like to propose to the government innovations in their discipline prejudicial to religion. The most beneficial result of those divisions would be the inducement they would give to parliament to take no action during that session.[26]

The presence of Murray and Everard in London provoked Poynter into venting his exasperation with their colleagues in Ireland. O'Connell's gibes in the wake of the rescript and the Genoese letter, when he denounced Poynter as a vetoist, had riled him, and Poynter obviously felt that the Irish bishops should have offered him an apology. He complained to Collingridge:

> The Irish bps are still here. Should not they do something to repair the injury done me and the encouragement given to every scribbler and refractory man to assail the episcopal character of authority, by the manner in which these bps have treated me after the receipt of Quarantotti's letter and by the speech in 1815 not opposed by one of them when I was called Dr Spaniel etc. They have held me up as a *signum cui contradicetur*.

Strangely, Poynter himself had dismissed O'Connell as an agitator and separatist, and he ought to have known that no one could rein in O'Connell's rhetoric. The Irish bishops were as powerless as British politicians and

26 Troy to Propaganda, 27 Mar. 1817, APF, SC(Irlanda) 20, ff 44r–45r.

cabinet ministers to restrain O'Connell when, in full flight, he engaged opponents of his policies.[27]

The representations of Murray and Everard in London were to no avail. Grattan and Donaghmore again presented their petitions in May 1817 in the two houses of parliament but both motions were lost.[28] Grattan's was translated into Italian and forwarded to Rome. It contained the explanation of domestic nomination.[29] The debates in parliament threw up the usual anachronistic charges which, Troy claimed, revealed the anti-Catholic and anticlerical spirit of some of the members. The Catholic bishops were accused of encouraging mixed marriages to increase their numbers, which was completely contrary to their practice, and a bishop in the house of lords accused Troy of threatening the government with disorders.[30] The members of parliament were not alone in causing Troy annoyance at this time. The Irish Catholic Board, which had been growing more aggressive in its attitude to Rome, asked the bishops to obtain a concordat from the pope that would establish domestic nomination and confirm the Irish church in her national independence.

This public request clearly embarrassed Troy and Murray. They certainly favoured domestic nomination, but had already failed to obtain the approval of the congregation of Propaganda for it. They knew that any request of this nature from the board to Rome would annoy both Litta and Consalvi, who had been displeased by its former intervention. Accordingly, Troy and Murray returned a brief and tart retort. They brusquely rebuffed the board by telling it that the prelates 'need not the admonition of the Catholic Board to be deeply impressed with a sense of the awful trust, which in virtue of their sacred office has been committed to them'. They would always be ready 'to pursue with a firm and steady step the path of duty which their consciences shall point out'.[31]

O'Connell, who always misinterpreted Troy's dealings at Dublin Castle as the policy of a weak-minded prelate keen to cooperate with the government even to the extent of conceding the veto, told Edward Hay, the secretary of the Irish Catholic Board, that 'the pliant Trojan' had turned his coadjutor, Murray, towards the veto. He also misinterpreted their response to Hay as a

---

27 Poynter to Collingridge, 15 May 1817, CIDA. After the publication of the Genoese letter O'Connell criticized Poynter as a 'zealous apostle of the veto'.   **28** Despite these setbacks in parliament, Poynter kept up his contacts with some of the members of the cabinet (Poynter to Gradwell, 30 Dec. 1817, WDA).   **29** APF, SOCG 917, ff 286r–287r (no date). Scully remarked to Sir Henry Parnell that the clergy distrusted and disliked Grattan and that the middle and lower classes viewed him as 'a Trimmer' and with his friends responsible for the 'seceders' (Scully to Parnell, 21 Feb. 1817 in MacDermot, *The Catholic question in Ireland and England, 1798–1822*, pp 605–6).   **30** Troy to Argenti, 20 May 1817, APF, SC(Irlanda) 20, f 64rv. He later identified the bishop as Robert Fowler of Ossory. Lord Donaghmore rebutted his accusations.   **31** Troy to Propaganda, 18 July 1817 (copy in English), APF, SC(Irlanda), 20, ff 97r–98v.

means of intimidating other bishops from their opposition to the veto, and consequently asked Hay to publish the responses of the other prelates.[32] A letter in the *Dublin Evening Post* of 4 October 1817, which pointed out that Coxe-Hippisley was in Rome and was in daily contact with Consalvi, the British consul and the Hanoverian office, must have excited O'Connell's worst fears.

The fear of the veto still greatly exercised William Coppinger of Cloyne. In a strongly worded letter to the congregation of Propaganda he prayed that the pope would reconsider the measure so insidiously suggested to him – presumably to give the government any influence in the appointment of bishops – and claimed that the Irish church was experiencing difficulties worse than the physical persecutions of the past. The Catholic people, already irritated, would be further inflamed if 'their spiritual concerns' were handed over to a secretary for temporal affairs associated with such men as Park and Ompteda (in other words, Consalvi).[33] Expressing total distrust of the motivations of their Protestant government, he instanced the oaths that its members and civic officials took declaring the Catholic religion to be impious and idolatrous. The overthrow of the Catholic religion was still its aim. Protestant churches were being built from general taxation and Protestant translations of the Bible were being widely circulated. Further evidence of its malfeasance was the proselytism it sponsored and financed in poor schools and orphanages, where large sums of money, food and clothing were made available to tempt children to become Protestant. Consequently, Coppinger entreated the pope most fervently to reconsider the proposal to let the government have any influence in the church.[34]

Whatever chance there might have been of persuading the congregation of Propaganda to change its views on domestic nomination was greatly diminished when it was rejected by the congregation for Extraordinary Ecclesiastical Affairs, of which Consalvi was the prefect and which dealt with political questions. It seems that the method was not fully explained to that congregation, and, on the basis of the information it had received, seemed to think that the prelates or metropolitan of the province were not included in the procedure. The secretary for Extraordinary Ecclesiastical Affairs, Lambruschini, told Propaganda that the suggested method gave to the election by clergy the part that freely belonged to the Holy See. Government interference would be strengthened rather than prevented by this method, because the clergy could not resist it with as much authority as the Holy See.

32 MacDonagh, *The hereditary bondsman*, p. 162.   33 John Park was the British consul at Ancona in the Papal States. Baron Ompteda was the ambassador of Hanover to the Holy See. 34 Coppinger to Propaganda, 22 July 1817, APF, SC(Irlanda), 20, ff 115r–117r. Presumably he was warning against Consalvi, the friend of the British consul, Park, and the Hanoverian ambassador, Ompteda, controlling Irish ecclesiastical affairs.

The argument that domestic nomination would remove the disorders associated with the elections of bishops was not valid since the old method did not
cause the disorders in the first place.[35]

Despite the failure of the petitions in 1816–17 and the general rebuffs the
movement for emancipation had received in the last couple of years,
O'Connell was buoyed up by a visit to London in May 1817. He was generously entertained by the leaders of the English Catholic Board – the duke of
Norfolk, Sir John Throckmorton and Charles Butler – and his old vetoist
antagonist, Lord Fingall, joined him on these occasions.[36] The Irish vetoists
had had no success with their recent petition, and so all parties interested in
emancipation realized the need to support each other.

To complicate the issues faced by the English vicars apostolic, and
especially by Poynter, an angry and knotty dispute arose between him and
one of his priests. Peter Gandolphy, a priest of the London District,
ordained in 1804, who later became a chaplain at the Spanish embassy, wrote
two books: *A defence of the ancient faith* and *An exposition of liturgy* (these are
the shorter versions of the titles). Poynter and the other vicars apostolic,
apart from Milner, believed that they contained heretical material. Poynter
notified Cardinal Litta about the errors in both books, adding that Milner
maintained that *An exposition of liturgy* was orthodox, and that Troy had
permitted the author to dedicate it to him. He added wryly that he hoped
that both those prelates had not read it.[37] In writing to Cardinal Litta, Milner
did not claim that the books were free from inaccuracies. He argued that they
could be easily corrected and that there was no point 'in making any stir
about them'.[38] Apprised of this, Gandolphy appealed to Milner and was
allowed to circulate the books in the Midland District. Poynter forbade the
circulation of the work on the liturgy, and of a series of sermons by
Gandolphy in the London District, and so Gandolphy went off to Rome to
defend himself. The dispute should really only have concerned Gandolphy,
Poynter and Rome, but because Milner, and – to a lesser extent Troy –
became involved, it further complicated and embittered the relationships
between all these players in the struggle for emancipation.

In Rome, Gandolphy obtained approval of his books, with some corrections, by two theologians from the office of the Master of the Sacred Palace
and proceeded to circulate them again. Poynter suspended him in September
1816 from ministry, but Gandolphy succeeded in winning the approval of
Cardinal Litta. In July 1817, Gandolphy signed a pledge of obedience to
Poynter, received back his faculties and promised not to circulate his works,
and the suspension was lifted. But Gandolphy continued to allow his works

35 Lambruschini to Propaganda, 9 Sept. 1817, ibid., f 163r. 36 MacDonagh, *The hereditary
bondsman*, p. 164. 37 Poynter to Litta, 23 Nov. 1815, APF, SC(Anglia), 6, ff 687r–688r.
38 Gradwell to Poynter, 14 Dec. 1817, WDA.

to be sold, complete with a note of approval from the Roman theologians. In the midst of this row, the English Catholic Board heard a rumour that Poynter was to be replaced by Milner, passed on to Rome its hope that this would not happen, and was assured by the pope that he had no such plan in mind.[39]

The theologians who treated Gandolphy leniently did not come under the direct jurisdiction of the congregation of Propaganda, but Poynter felt that Cardinal Litta should have overridden them. In his despondency at having to face another difficult encounter with the cardinal he complained to his confidant, Collingridge, that they had no person of 'credit' in Rome to act as their agent and advocate their cause in the Roman curia. Macpherson, he lamented, was 'nothing there', as Litta would not 'admit him into his presence' a couple of years previously. On the other hand his opponents, the Irish, Milner and Gandolphy had their 'Hiberno-Italian agents', and the Jesuits had their influential network.[40]

The stress of his work and the pressure from Gandolphy seems to have worn Poynter down, and he had become obsessive about the alleged power of intermediaries in Rome using their access to Cardinal Litta to his disadvantage. In fact Troy and the Irish did not have an effective agent. Milner, who did not have anyone to speak for him, had advised the Irish to send out a priest to carry out that work in Rome. Presumably he would have used the services of an Irish agent as he had used Luke Concanen. Gandolphy likewise had no friend there.

However, Poynter reserved his most searing criticism for Litta, who, apart from the pope, had full responsibility for English Catholic affairs:

> C. Litta had laboured hard from the time I went to Rome, to prove me guilty of something or other, and his policy in that evidently was that he might say to Bp Milner and me you are both highly blameable, go therefore shake hands without any other satisfaction than a mutual forgiveness. But whilst he on many occasions acknowledged to us *by word of mouth* that Bp Milner was very blameable, he could never prove me to be blameable on any point. Yet whilst Bp Milner's charges were kept in the Propaganda, he would never give me anything in writing to attest the justification of my conduct or of my colleagues ... what will become of us I do not know at least whilst Litta is at the head of the S. Congregation

---

39 The *DEP* reported that the Earl Marshall and several nobles had written to the pope on 31 July 1817 about their fear of Poynter being removed and that the pope in his reply on 30 Aug. 1817 had referred to his high opinion of the vicar apostolic. The *DEP* did not agree, describing Poynter as a vetoist and a 'supple friend' to the Catholic aristocracy of England (*DEP*, 27 Dec. 1817).   40 Poynter to Collingridge, 10 Feb. 1817, CIDA.

... I heard more than once from cardinals a disposition to sacrifice the English Catholics to the Irish.

Poynter then went on to deplore the action of the congregation of Propaganda in letting Milner have copies of the Italian versions of his letters to Macpherson, from which he subsequently published 'garbled passages'.[41]

The vicar apostolic of the London District had a further gripe against Litta when he did nothing to help the English historian, John Lingard, with his research. The Vatican archives were not then open to scholars but Poynter felt that Litta could have allowed Lingard access to some documents in the congregation of Propaganda. Lingard found the cardinal 'civil, but extremely cool', and noted that he made little comment on Milner's use of the extracts from Propaganda in the *Orthodox Journal*. But he reported one defeat for the cardinal, which certainly pleased Poynter: Litta had wanted to annex the English College to Propaganda College, but through Consalvi's influence the pope rejected that proposal.[42]

Gandolphy forwarded a further letter to Rome, and Poynter forwarded Gandolphy's books, which were examined by the congregation of the Index, which was charged with the defence of Catholic doctrine.[43] The books were condemned in July 1818 and Poynter, in December 1818, passed on the verdict to Gandolphy with a formula of submission to be accepted within four months. Archbishop Troy, who had taken a hard line against Blanchard and de Trevaux, assured Cardinal di Pietro in January 1819 that Gandolphy was ready to retract any erroneous statements and advised the cardinal to treat him leniently, as he was highly esteemed and orthodox at heart. A condemnation would cause scandal, produce disputes among Catholics and between Catholics and Protestants, and antagonize the government, which regarded the authority of the congregation of the Index as contrary to freedom and would consider the censure as a form of treason.[44] With the transfer of Litta in 1818 to the office of the cardinal vicar of Rome, Poynter was relieved of the coldness and misunderstanding of his Roman 'superior'. Cardinal Fontana, the new prefect, proved to be more accommodating.[45]

Gandolphy corresponded with Bishop Coppinger of Cloyne but their

41 Ibid., 26 Apr. 1817. 42 Ibid., [unknonwn day] Aug. 1817. 43 To show the difficulties of his situation and win favour in Rome, Gandolphy informed Litta that a deputation consisting of Butler, Jerningham, Silvertop and Blake had gone from the Catholic Board to Lord Liverpool proclaiming the readiness of English Catholics to take the oath of supremacy, if a few expressions such as the accusation of idolatry and superstition were removed (Gandolphy to Litta, 3 Mar. 1818, APF, SC (Anglia), 7, f 55r). Poynter forwarded to Rome Jerningham's denial that such a deputation had ever gone to Lord Liverpool (ibid., 8 May 1818, ff 121r–123r). 44 Troy to di Pietro, 12 Jan. 1819, APF, SC(Irlanda), 22, f 31r. 45 Gradwell reported to Poynter that Fontana and Mgr Testa, Consalvi's assistant, who had written the pope's letter to the Irish, had read the *Orthodox Journal* with horror (26 Sept. 1818, WDA).

letters did not reach the public. It seems that Coppinger congratulated Gandolphy in 1816 at the beginning of his troubles but it is not clear how much of the disputed writings he had read. Later on Gandolphy asked Coppinger to write in his defence to Rome and also to sell some of his books both in Ireland and through his brother in New York. And in the course of their correspondence he attacked those whom he knew were inimical to Irish Catholic aspirations; he suggested the Irish bishops should send a remonstrance to Rome to oust Macpherson, with, if necessary, Milner's help; he denounced Coxe-Hippisley as the furious opponent of Milner and all those of non-Gallican principles;[46] he deplored the persecuting system of Charles Butler and his aristocratic friends.[47]

Poynter also received a plea for reconciliation with Gandolphy and Milner from Patrick Curtis, who was shortly to become archbishop of Armagh and an important player in the struggle for emancipation. Curtis, a former rector of the Irish College in Salamanca and a close personal friend of Archbishop Murray and of Bishop Cameron of the Lowland District of Scotland, may have been encouraged by Murray and by a friend of Poynter's to try a benign intervention in these disputes. Poynter replied that there was no disposition to reconciliation wanting on his part. Curtis admitted that he knew Poynter had been unjustly attacked and ill treated on several occasions. And so he apologized if he had hurt Poynter's feelings, and assured him that he regarded him as far superior in piety, gentleness and conciliating manners to Gandolphy and Milner, 'both remarkable for repulsive manners', but did venture to add that stains had been left on the most eminent characters in history for neglecting reconciliation.[48] In a letter to Milner he complained of his 'virulent attacks' on Charles Butler. He also disapproved of 'the state of open rupture' between Milner and 'other persons' distinguished for their dignity, character and piety', but admitted that he had failed in his attempt to engineer a reconciliation.[49]

The cardinal prefect of Propaganda, Fontana, ordered Poynter to censure Gandolphy.[50] Gandolphy submitted but claimed that he could not withdraw his books as he had sold the rights to publishers. His death in 1821 put an end to the dispute. The intervention of Milner and Troy in this contretemps undoubtedly irritated and angered Poynter. In strict canonical terms, the dispute concerned Poynter and a priest of his district, and though it did not produce the exchange of indignant letters which the Blanchard and de Trevaux cases caused, it must have driven a further wedge between Poynter

46 At an audience with the pope Coxe-Hippisley pointed out 'the vacillations of the Irish bishops and Milner' (Gradwell to Poynter, 17 Dec. 1818, WDA).   47 Gandolphy to Coppinger, 26 Dec. 1816; 8 July, 26 Nov., 24 Dec. 1817; 13 Jan., 15 June 1818, Cloyne DA.   48 Poynter to Gradwell, 31 May 1819, WDA and Curtis to Poynter, 4 Apr. 1819, WDA.   49 Curtis to Milner, 20 Dec. 1819, BDA, c 2329.   50 Statement of facts by Bishop Poynter, 15 Feb. 1820 in APF, SC(Irlanda), 23, ff 125r–126v; Ward, *The eve of Catholic emancipation*, ii, pp 205–20.

and Milner, and Poynter and Troy, who, Poynter always believed, was misguided by his intemperate colleague.

II

The failure of Hayes' mission to produce any papal support for the anti-vetoists may have dampened for several months the enthusiasm of the Catholic Board in Dublin to pursue its campaign for emancipation with any vigour. Hostility to the veto did not diminish in any way. The *Dublin Evening Post* declared that a papal request to submit to the veto would be firmly resisted.[51] Two events early in 1819 encouraged the Irish activists. On 13 January, the English Catholic Board drew up a petition for relief. It was worded courteously – according to those prepared to accept some restrictions – or obsequiously, according to their opponents. It requested parliament to 'grant them such relief as your honourable house shall deem proper for extending to them the enjoyment in common with their fellow subjects of the blessings of the constitution'. Some Catholics, galvanized by Milner's firm line against concession, objected to the terms of this petition, and Jerningham added an explanation that disclaimed any 'concession to the particular measure termed veto'. The petition was signed by some ten thousand people. Still, no debate took place when it was laid before both houses.[52]

Catholics in Dublin were greatly heartened by a large meeting of Protestants held on 11 February 1819 in support of emancipation. Called by the lord mayor, it was attended by some three thousand people, including the high-ranking dignitaries, the duke of Leinster, the earls of Charlemont and Meath, Lord Cloncurry, Sir Henry Parnell and Henry Grattan.[53] The presence of these prominent Protestants sent a message to their co-religionists in England, as well as giving a fillip to the campaign throughout Ireland. Poynter was pleased with the new spirit created among Irish Catholics by the respectable petitions of the Protestants, and believed the union of Catholics and Protestant support had created a good effect in England.[54] Grattan presented a motion for emancipation in the house of commons, which was defeated by only two votes, but Lord Donaghmore's in the lords was defeated by forty-six.[55] The number of votes did not dishearten the advocates of emancipation.[56]

51 *DEP*, 2 June 1818.   52 Ward, *The eve of Catholic emancipation*, ii, pp 249–50.   53 *DEP*, 13 Feb. 1819.   54 Poynter to Gradwell (copy), 2 Mar. 1819, WDA.   55 Ibid., 11 Mar. 1819. The *DEP* continued to accuse Poynter of pronouncing his blessing on the aristocratic vetoists in England – Norfolk, Shrewsbury, Petre, Jerningham and Charles Butler – but noted with satisfaction that another party demanding unqualified emancipation had recently met and had thanked Milner (10 Apr. 1819). Poynter regretted the desire of the Irish that Grattan's motion should come before the English one, and commented despondently that he supposed the English Catholics would, as usual, yield to them (Poynter to Collingridge, 13 Feb. 1819, ClDA).   56 Ibid., 22 May

Despite the rejection of the motion in the house of lords, Lord Grey, who had long been sympathetic to the aspirations of English Catholics, introduced a bill very shortly afterwards to repeal the obligations on those taking up offices to repudiate transubstantiation, the invocation of saints and the sacrifice of the Mass. English Catholics were grateful for Grey's intervention, which was unsuccessful, but in Ireland it met a more sceptical reaction. As it did not extend to the oaths of supremacy and allegiance, it was described as merely relieving Protestants from swearing that the Catholic religion was idolatrous and doing nothing for Catholics.[57] Catholics in Ireland were then confronted with a bill which would have deprived them of their rights of voting at vestry meetings and therefore subjected them to a tax without their consent. There was angry resistance to it in Dublin, and Lord Donaghmore succeeded in having it rejected.[58]

Though Milner continued to rail against any concession by his colleagues on the wording of the oath, he was losing ground in Rome. A new adversary had arrived there in November 1817 to replace his bête noire, Macpherson, as agent for the other English vicars apostolic, and especially for Poynter. Robert Gradwell, a 40-year-old priest from Lancashire, who had studied at the seminaries at Douay and Ushaw, was commissioned to reopen the English College at Rome and to conduct business for the vicars apostolic at the curia. Before his departure from England he was fully briefed by Poynter about the malign role played by Milner and the deleterious interference of Troy in the political and religious affairs of England, and given copies of their correspondence. He proved to be a faithful and diligent intermediary for Poynter and, like Macpherson, passed on to Roman officials his disapprobation of Milner and his Irish friends. He cultivated Consalvi assiduously and succeeded in getting the cardinal to become protector both of England and of the English College. Before the dissolution of the society, the Jesuits had had charge of the English College, and Gradwell fought resolutely to prevent them from regaining control. Reflecting Poynter's determination not to annoy the government by allowing them to re-establish themselves in England, he impressed upon Roman officials the danger such a move would cause.

Coxe-Hippisley also wrote to Consalvi about the harm the re-establishment of the Jesuits in England could cause to the Catholic church by provoking the enmity of Protestants, and thereby gave support to Poynter's rather than to Milner's view. But he caused much more serious harm to the vicar apostolic of the Midland District by referring to the systematic abuse of Consalvi by the *Orthodox Journal*, whom it accused of forging a letter of the pope to the English Catholic Board. Coxe-Hippisley explained that the

1819. **57** *DEP*, 29 May 1819. **58** Ibid., 29 June 1819. The parish vestry of the Anglican church could raise taxes for local needs.

majority of the articles in 'that infamous publication' came from the pen of Milner, and argued that the bishop should be suspended by the Holy See.[59]

Milner's friend William Andrews edited the *Orthodox Journal*. He attacked many of Milner's opponents and gave abundant opportunities to Milner, who wrote under various noms de plume, to do the same. Charles Butler was denounced by both Milner and Andrews, described once as a 'presumptuous layman constantly undermining the church ... and endeavouring to enslave her ministers whom he is otherwise in the habit of flattering'.[60] Poynter was attacked, as were the members of the English Catholic Board. The 'Irish aristocracy instead of appearing in their proper capacity at the head of the people' were accused of having adopted 'the crawling sentiments of the English parasites'.[61] And complaining of statesmen trying to give the state a role in the appointment of bishops, the *Orthodox Journal* referred to 'the intriguing designs of a few treacherous individuals infesting our body'.[62] Milner rehashed all his arguments against the Cisalpine Club, Protesting Catholic Dissenters and the fifth resolution.[63] The language of the journal was always robust, if not intemperate, and it lashed its opponents unceasingly. The middle-class readers of the journal were not unwilling to see the aristocrats, whose control of the English Catholic Board some of them resented, being criticized.

A request from Cardinal Fontana, the new prefect of the congregation of Propaganda, to draw up a report on the church in England afforded Gradwell the opportunity to denounce Milner in all his works and pomps. Maintaining that Milner, when he had 'acquired a great reputation by several learned and useful publications got himself appointed agent by the Irish bishops', Gradwell claimed that he then 'embarked in a sea of politics with his characteristic impetuosity' involving himself in a 'series of contradictions and inconsistencies', alternating between a recommendation of 'an unlimited veto' in the appointment of bishops and the very opposite, and always doing so 'in violent and undignified publications' with 'the address to flatter and the means to terrify the Irish bishops into the adoption of his schemes'. He did not have the ability to cajole the English vicars apostolic into his ways of acting, and so he proceeded to denounce them 'as weak men, sycophants, betrayers of the Catholics, mercenaries who had robbed him and sold themselves to government, fautors of French schismatics, defenders of unsound doctrines, patrons of Bible societies, enemies of the Order of Jesuits and other religious orders'. He misrepresented the other vicars apostolic and betrayed their most confidential secrets, and the vast mass of his contradictory writings was sufficient 'to convict the author of insanity'. The English prelates published no refutations of his calumnies nor vindications of their

59 Gradwell to Poynter, 25 Mar. 1819, WDA. 60 *OJ*, Feb. 1817. 61 Ibid., Mar. 1816.
62 Ibid., June 1816. 63 Ibid., Aug. 1816.

own conduct except in private letters to Rome and, in fact, carried their forbearance to excess. Almost every month the *Orthodox Journal*, which was established under his auspices in 1813, carried defamatory comments on his colleagues. His contributions to the daily papers caught the attention of Protestants, and the frequency and force of his views must have induced people to question the conduct and proceedings of their bishops, and converted the mitres of the vicars apostolic into crowns of thorns.[64]

Consalvi's assistant, Cappacini, discussed the memorial at length with Gradwell and advised him to give a copy of it to the cardinal.[65] Consalvi's response exceeded Gradwell's expectations. A letter was sent to the congregation of Propaganda at the express command of the pope, referring to the scandalous journal in which dissensions among the Catholics of Britain and Ireland were perpetuated, the reputations of other vicars apostolic were defamed, the Catholic people were stirred up against the class of nobility that supported the mission and even the cardinal members of the congregation were accused of trafficking the interests of the Catholic religion with the government. Many of the articles bore Milner's name. The interests of religion, the dignity of the Holy See and the standing of the congregation demanded that the impudence of that vicar apostolic be severely repressed. Accordingly, the pope, being very much under Consalvi's influence and disturbed by Milner's conduct, ordered that he be sharply rebuked by the congregation and commanded to take no further part in the journal. If he disobeyed, his faculties should be withdrawn and he should be removed from office.[66] Apart from instant dismissal, this was the harshest reprimand Milner could have received. Coming as it did with direct papal authority, it was far more powerful than any chastisement from the cardinal prefect.

The secretary of Propaganda replied promptly to Consalvi, assuring him that its officials were already well aware of the scandalous nature of the *Orthodox Journal* and of the dissensions it caused. Even before his letter had arrived, the decision had been taken to reprove that prelate most forcefully and to admonish him to take no further part in that journal, directly or indirectly. Since then a warning letter had been sent to him.[67] Signed by the cardinal prefect, it claimed the authority of the pope and listed all of Consalvi's complaints.

Milner, as was to be expected, did not meekly accept these criticisms. He fought back strenuously against the accusations, which he maintained had wounded him grievously, and, as was his wont, found ammunition in the past activities of his opponents. Dealing firstly with the *Orthodox Journal*, in which he was forbidden to take any part, he argued that it had opposed him

---

64 Gradwell to Propaganda, Aug. 1819, WDA.   65 Ibid., 21 Aug. 1819.   66 Consalvi to Propaganda, 27 Apr. 1820, APF, SC(Anglia), 7, ff 501r–502r and Gradwell to Poynter, 20 Apr. 1820, WDA.   67 Propaganda to Consalvi, 1 May 1820, APF, SC(Anglia), 7, ff 509r–510v.

for the previous twelve months, referring to bitter letters it published against his criticism of a profane historical work written by a priest.[68] It had also attacked him for interfering in politics when, during disturbances in the provinces he had, to the government's pleasure, called for peace.

Returning to the old battles of 1789–91 with the Catholic laity who had called themselves 'Protestant Catholic Dissenters' (in fact they had used the term 'Protesting Catholic Dissenters'), and who denied to the pope the authority to appoint bishops, he recalled that the vicars apostolic of that time had appointed him their defender against these opponents. Cardinal Antonelli had rejected the title and the oath of the Protestant Catholic Dissenters and Cardinal Gerdil had reprobated the antics of those Cisalpine nobles who supported Bishop Berington. Cardinal Litta had read many of his writings about the disputes over the fifth resolution, the schismatical bill of 1813 and the Blanchardist schism, and had assured him that he had carried out his duties without giving offence. His district had been the focus of disputes and schisms and he had altered the ethos of a Catholic college founded by the Cisalpines and based on Enlightment piety. Its style had been changed, clerics were studying in it and some of them had been ordained priests. He had refused to take an oath of the type that Thomas More, John Fisher and over one hundred others had been killed for refusing. The prime minister and lord chancellor insisted on this oath and Earl Grey and many advocates of emancipation had proposed it. Many Catholics at a meeting in London had accepted it, and among the signatories were the names of the other vicars apostolic. And he gave the text of the oath in English, according to which the person taking it swore full and undivided allegiance to the king and acknowledged in no foreign prince, prelate, state or potentate any power or authority to use the 'civil sword' in any cause whatever, whether civil, spiritual or ecclesiastical. Milner insisted that he was not hypocritical; he said and wrote what he felt in defence of the unity of the church and of the rights and dignity of the pope. As a faithful defender of the Holy See for thirty years, he begged that the cardinal's letter, which had been based on false information be regarded as not having been written.[69]

Bishops are not usually dismissed from their sees by the pope, except for serious breaches of morality or the promulgation of unorthodox views. Milner had not done either, but the papal threat must have left him frightened and distressed. Ejection from his vicariate would have been an extremely painful humiliation for someone with such a high profile not only

68 Milner, in the *Orthodox Journal* in 1819, took exception to several opinions expressed by John Lingard in his recently published history of England to 1509. Revd J. Fletcher, writing as 'Candidus', engaged him in sharp exchanges about his criticisms (Husenbeth, *The life of Bishop Milner*, pp 393–407). 69 Milner to Cardinal Fontana, 12 June 1820, APF, SC(Anglia), 7, ff 481r–483.

among English Catholics but also among many Protestants, and, in particular, members of parliament. And it would have provoked a noisy reaction from Catholics, both in England and Ireland. Rejection by the Vatican would have been particularly hurtful to one whose constant refrain was that he was supremely loyal to it, and would have made him look very foolish in the eyes of the Catholic people. But Milner was nothing if not irrepressible, and, while obeying the strictures on the *Orthodox Journal*, he was sure to find some excuse to project an image of himself as the loyal and trustworthy defender of true doctrinal positions in a short time.

Milner's friend, Archbishop Troy, did not escape Gradwell's criticisms, and his part in supporting the Jesuits was deemed to be highly offensive to the English church. Cardinal Litta had ordered Bishop Gibson to ordain Jesuits in his district.[70] When Coxe-Hippisley, at an audience at which he had 'an opportunity to explain and vindicate the consistency of his parliamentary conduct and the vacillations' of the Irish bishops and Milner, drew the pope's attention to this order,[71] the pope, according to Gradwell, expressed his displeasure and explained that he had published the bull restoring the society in such a way 'that it was imperative on no nation, but open to the adoption of any'.[72] Hearing that Lord Sidmouth, the home secretary, and Castlereagh objected strongly to the restoration of the society in England, Poynter and Gradwell used all their influence to prevent it. This became another source of irritation with Milner and Troy. Milner favoured the Jesuits, and Troy, who had welcomed back Irish Jesuits from Palermo to Dublin, could not understand why there should be opposition to them in England.

Gradwell quoted to Poynter an extract from a letter from Troy to Milner that had found its way to Propaganda. The archbishop had remarked that the conduct of the vicars apostolic was 'unaccountable' and explained that the Jesuits had a chapel in Dublin. Gradwell continued angrily:

> Pray what authority had Abp. Troy over the bishops in Engd any more than over the bishops of Ostia or Sabina? The English bishops are in no sense his subjects or inferiors. They know and discharge their duties as well as ever the abp. of Dublin and he has plenty to do in his own diocese without invading his neighbours' grounds.[73]

Gradwell took advantage of his visits to Propaganda to put Cardinal Fontana right about the Irish and Milner. He claimed that he helped unravel a

70 Gradwell to Poynter, 21 Apr. 1818, WDA. The British government did not want to see the Jesuits in England restored to their full canonical rights. Troy could see no reason to object to their restoration.   71 Ibid., 17 Dec. 1818.   72 Ibid., 12 May 1818.   73 Ibid., 6 Feb. 1819.

mystery for the cardinal by letting him know that 'Dr Ty was capable of a bit of dissimulation and duplicity'.[74] He informed Poynter that Fontana had told him that Irish priests wrote very contradictory letters to Rome about candidates for the episcopacy, either lauding or demonizing them.[75] Gradwell helpfully suggested that 'the Irish letters written in a club and signed by several, were generally proposed to the company after a good dinner, and might be supposed to smell of the bottle'. And he further observed that the letters of Troy and Milner against Poynter were 'only a piece of true Irish etiquette'. Fontana, he maintained, was truly disgusted with both those prelates and with the Jesuits. The cardinal then allegedly delivered himself of a remarkable anthropological insight, which unfortunately he did not develop: 'the Orientals and the Irish', he maintained, 'resembled each other in their hotheadedness, their shameless calumnies and rage against one another'.[76]

Notwithstanding or perhaps because of these rebarbative characteristics, which Fontana wanted to correct, he was supposedly contemplating Poynter's appointment as nuncio to Ireland. As nuncios were only assigned to states and governments, and as there seems no reason why Poynter should have been given any supervisory role in the Irish church, Gradwell's report raises the question of his credulity in dealing with the groundless rumours that circulate from time to time in Rome. The prospect obviously pleased him:

> I have learnt from the confidential papers put into my hands by Cardinal Fontana that Propaganda has it in view (hush! This is inter nos) to make Your Lordship apostolic nuncio for Ireland. I could not help smiling when I read this, to think what looks Dr Milner or Cardinal [sic] Troy would put on, if they read this paper of which I am speaking. Your Lordship may expect a long and interesting communication from me soon on the subject to which I am now briefly alluding.[77]

The pope also pleased him by allegedly declaring that Milner was mad, to which he responded with full agreement.[78]

---

74 Ibid., 22 Apr. 1819. Later reflecting on the part played by Troy and his agent, Luke Concanen, in trying to get Milner transferred to the London District, he mused 'would not these sons of St Dominic have spent their time much better in minding their own business or telling their beads' (ibid., 29 Dec. 1821). 75 Irish clergy were far from unique in making extreme comments on candidates for the episcopate. 76 Ibid., 25 Mar. 1819. 77 Ibid., 22 Mar. 1821. 78 The pope said '*lui è matto*' and Gradwell responded '*questo pure è troppo vero*' (ibid., 9 Dec. 1819). Poynter had expressed the same view to Gradwell and wondered why he should be allowed to remain in office (ibid., 7 May 1819).

No long or interesting communication followed from Gradwell's revelation about Poynter's proposed promotion and there is no reference to it in the files of Propaganda. He continued to use his influence to keep the Jesuits out of England, and suggested that a word from Castlereagh to Consalvi, the 'most sensible man in Rome', would be more effective than ten memorials about the problem.[79] Still agonizing about the matter a year later, he mentioned to Poynter that it seemed a fixed point of the government that the Jesuits should not exist in British territories, and he wondered whether the Holy See or the government would ensure this. The pope could dissipate suspicions and complaints. If the government intervened, there was a danger that parliament would hold an inquiry into the state of Catholicism and Catholic colleges, which would lead to injurious measures.[80]

On 26 February 1820, a meeting organized by the Catholic Board was held in a Dublin church to draw up an address of condolence to the new king, George IV, on the death of his father and congratulations to himself on his accession. A deputation headed by Lord Fingall was appointed to wait on the king to present the address. It begged his gracious consideration of the degraded position of the Catholics who were suffering for the right to worship God according to the dictates of their consciences. Recalling their appeal in 1793 and the king's recommendation of their cause to the legislature, they again respectfully implored royal interposition in their favour.[81] Troy was pleased with the gesture, which he regarded as prudent and politic.[82] The English Catholic Board also drew up an address of loyalty to the new king, and followed this up with another petition for emancipation. The terms adopted seemed unobjectionable and the vicars apostolic, apart from Milner, signed it.

Two events prevented petitioning in 1820 from Ireland: the death of Grattan on 4 June and the struggle between the king and Queen Caroline, his estranged wife. Though Grattan had always been willing to yield to the English demand for securities and had made provision for such in the bill of 1813, his petitions to parliament were gratefully appreciated even by those who objected to such concessions. His willingness to travel to London, though sick and frail, to submit a petition, and the memory of his eloquent defence of the Irish parliament, ensured a great outpouring of sympathy at his death – from both English and Irish Catholics.

After the frank and emphatic disapproval of the appeals of the Irish bishops and the Catholic laity of 1817, Rome was not troubled by queries or complaints from Ireland for four years. Both the bishops and the laity had been firmly rebuffed, and their standing and prestige had been damaged by the shameful conduct of Richard Hayes. There was nothing unusual about

79 Ibid., 22 July 1819.   80 Ibid., 16 Mar. 1820.   81 *FJ*, 27 July 1820.   82 *FJ*, 28 Feb. 1820.

the rejection of petitions for emancipation, and no bill for emancipation was drawn up between 1813 and 1821. The Irish bishops may well have been grateful that for some time they did not have to discuss any initiative from Rome or from London.

The English Catholics had not been burdened by the indecorum of a delegate like Hayes, but the unkind acrimony between Milner and Poynter had done some damage to English reputations. Cardinal Litta, rightly or wrongly, had grown tired of the bickering between these two vicars apostolic, and, as Poynter had remarked, his attitude had become 'a plague on both their houses'. Poynter's case had been weakened by Macpherson's undiplomatic and discourteous tactics, and the repetition of the arguments and counter-arguments had wearied the cardinal. Both protagonists were disappointed that he did not give them a letter commending their policies. Had he been tempted to do so, it is unlikely he would have satisfied either of them. The accusations and partial defence of Gandolphy and the hostility of Poynter to the Jesuits added another complication to the mix. In 1818, when Litta became cardinal vicar of Rome, he was doubtless glad to be rid of English and Irish problems. Poynter was surely glad that Litta had moved to another office, and, with Gradwell successfully paying court to Consalvi, he had a more effective method of communicating with Rome. The rebuke to Milner, which Consalvi won from the pope, was a useful consequence of the shifting balance of power.

15

Plunket's bill, 1821

I

A mong those who had supported Grattan in his work for emancipation and helped him prepare the bill of 1813 was the former Irish attorney general, William Conyngham Plunket. Plunket, a veteran defender of the Catholic cause, took up the mantle of his deceased friend and responded to a request to petition the house of commons in 1821.

Two petitions for Catholic relief were presented on the same day: one by Plunket and one by Lord Nugent. Nugent's was signed by upwards of 8,000 English Catholics, including seven peers, sixteen baronets, seven bishops and numerous clergy. The English Catholic Board had presented a loyal address to George IV the previous year in which they had sworn full and undivided allegiance, recognizing the the 'power of the civil sword' in the king alone and acknowledging in 'no foreign prince, prelate, state or potentate any power or authority to use the same, within the said realm, in any matter or cause whatever, whether civil, spiritual or ecclesiastical'.[1] The vicars apostolic, apart from Milner, who objected to 'full allegiance' and the 'civil sword' explained that the denial of ecclesiastical power to a prelate referred only to its enforcement by temporal means. Plunket's petition was signed by thousands of Irish Catholics. He also proposed a motion to set up a committee to examine Catholic claims. In addition to examining the right of Catholics to enjoy the privileges of the state, which they had defended in battle, he also proposed to ensure that effective means would be given to the crown to assure it of the loyalty of the persons who would be elected as bishops. By a majority of six votes, the motion passed.

Peel, the former chief secretary for Ireland, opposed any alteration in the law and maintained that he had never viewed the question other than as a choice of evils. He rejected the view that it was the entitlement of every subject to enjoy the right to every office, and thought that it was proper to exclude those who entertained opinions not in accordance with the tenets of the established church. Castlereagh argued that there was nothing in the state of England or Europe that could justify the continued exclusion of Catholics from the status in society to which their growing prosperity

1 *FJ*, 7 Mar. 1821.

entitled them, and recalled that at the Congress of Vienna agreement had been reached on a policy of not discriminating against anyone on the basis of religion. He insisted that Catholic emancipation had never been held out 'as a pledge for the union' of Ireland and Britain, and explained that 'it was distinctly understood that that question was to be left entirely to the discretion of the legislature'.[2]

With the help of Castlereagh, Sir John Newport, Sir Henry Parnell and a few other supporters of Catholic emancipation, Plunket proceeded to draw up two bills, one establishing Catholics' eligibility for membership of parliament and for appointments to the professions, and one regulating episcopal appointments and relations with Rome. In the first bill, the offices of the lord chancellor, lord keeper of the great seal, and lord lieutenant of Ireland were reserved for Protestants. There was no problem about removing the rejection of transubstantiation and devotion to the Madonna and saints from the oath of supremacy which Catholics would be obliged to take to be eligible for offices. The oath of supremacy presented difficulties, but Plunket wished to keep it to appease Protestant opponents. But he added an explanation of it to make it palatable to Catholics. It ruled out papal deposition of princes and obliged those who took it to swear that no prince, state or prelate had any jurisdiction or power, ecclesiastical or spiritual, in the kingdom. To make the oath palatable the explanation was added that it excluded the power or jurisdiction of any foreign prince or prelate that interfered with full and undivided allegiance to the king.

Poynter, who told Donoughmore that no Catholic could take this oath of supremacy, begged him to insert the word 'civil' to refer to interference by civil means with the oath of allegiance, and submitted a memorial explaining that the pope's claim to spiritual authority on such matters as marriage might diverge from the civil law in Britain but denied that he had any pretensions to civil power. This spiritual authority was seen especially in the election of bishops, in conceding faculties to them for the spiritual governance of the Catholic people, in watching over their religious conduct, and in granting dispensations from matrimonial impediments. Poynter also explained that an oath should be understood according to the mind of those who had drawn it up. He was then presented with the 'legislative explanation' that a Catholic might take along with the oath.[3]

The very term 'oath of supremacy' aroused ancient fears among many Catholics, which Milner was able to exploit. He printed a short theological judgment – which was signed by two of his priests – on the oath before the second reading of the bills on 16 March, had William Wilberforce attack it

2 *Hansard 2*, iv, 961–1034, 28 Feb. 1821.   3 Poynter to Smith, 10 Mar. 1821, LDA and to Gradwell, 6 Mar. 1821, APF, SC(Anglia) 7, ff 614r–620v

in a petition to parliament signed by numerous laypeople from his own district, and then followed this up with a further attack on the oath in a printed letter of thanks to Wilberforce. The other vicars apostolic thought that when Plunket incorporated the legislative explanation of the oath, it could be taken. Poynter asked his agent in Rome to find out if the oath could lawfully be taken when explained in this way. And he informed Gradwell that though they had abjured the belief in 1791 that princes excommunicated by the pope might be murdered, Catholics could not swear that this was a damnable and heretical doctrine.[4]

Before the legislative explanation was attached to the oath of supremacy, Archbishop Curtis of Armagh pointed out that no Catholic could take it, as it claimed that the pope had no spiritual power or jurisdiction in the kingdom, which was not only false but also heretical. Archbishop Kelly of Tuam also rejected it 'in its present shape', and took great exception to the 'unrestricted disapprobation' of candidates for the episcopacy which the bill envisaged.[5]

The second bill, designed to assure Protestants of the loyalty and trust-worthiness of bishops and deans,[6] imposed on all priests an oath obliging them never to elect anyone as bishop or dean who was not of 'unimpeachable loyalty and peaceable conduct', and not to hold any communication with Rome tending directly or indirectly to 'overthrow' the Protestant govern-ment or the Protestant church on any matter which might interfere with the civil duty and allegiance due to the king. Only persons born of British or Irish parents and who had been resident in Britain or Ireland for the previous five years were eligible for the episcopate. The king was authorized to estab-lish two commissions to check on candidates for bishoprics: on each commission there were to be a secretary of state, privy councillors and bishops. Candidates elected as bishops were to notify the commissions, which would issue a report on their loyalty (or lack of it), and the chief secre-tary or secretary of state in England would let them know if they were acceptable. If not, they would be forbidden from exercising their office, on pain of exile. Noting that Catholics themselves had been prepared to offer securities in the form of domestic nomination, Plunket expressed his willing-ness to accept that arrangement but could not see how it could be established, as they themselves were undecided as to whether it should be by dean and chapter or by the clergy. He did not include any proposal to pay the Catholic clergy, as he feared their acceptance of incomes would suggest to the laity

4 Ibid., (copy), 13 Mar. 1821, WDA.   5 McGrath, *The public ministry of Bishop James Doyle*, pp 2–3. Curtis was archbishop 1819–32, Kelly was archbishop 1815–34.   6 There were no deans in the Catholic church in England and in the few dioceses in Ireland where they existed the title was merely an honorary one.

that they were prepared to barter their people's rights for selfish reasons, but he did not exclude the possibility of offering them salaries in the future.

Any person receiving a document, bull or dispensation from Rome was obliged to submit it to the president of the appropriate commission. If the commissioners found anything in the document injurious to the safety of the kingdom they would report it to the king or lord lieutenant. If the document were of a purely spiritual nature, the recipient was obliged to swear that this was so before the president of the commission and it could then be passed on to the senior ecclesiastical commissioner. If he swore that the document was purely spiritual in the presence of the board of commissioners it would then be returned to the person to whom it was sent. A suitable penalty would be attached to the publication of bulls, dispensations or other instruments in violation of the regulation.[7]

At a meeting of the bishops of the Dublin province and of the Dublin diocesan priests on 26 March a resolution was passed permitting the taking of the oath of supremacy as modified in the first bill. Gratitude was expressed to Plunket and his collaborators and, though their motivation was praised, serious exception was taken both to the arrangements in the second bill for dealing with correspondence from Rome and to the unlimited negative on the appointment of bishops which was in effect a right of positive nomination. Troy was called upon to communicate their conscientious objections to Plunket and Donoughmore and to request that the bills should be modified so as to make them acceptable.[8] Donoughmore replied that his opposition to the security clauses was ineffective. He had contacted several colleagues to point out that he could not 'undertake the advocacy of a bill encumbered with such a mass of objectionable matter'.[9] Gradwell passed on the approval of the Dublin clerical gathering to Rome.[10]

The archbishop of Armagh and his clergy also expressed their warmest thanks to Plunket and his fellow advocates of emancipation, and acknowledged that the oath of supremacy as modified in the bill could be conscientiously taken by Catholics. However, without incurring the guilt of schism, they could not consent to the restrictions on contact with the pope, nor could they tolerate the vetoistical interference of persons of other religions in the appointment of bishops or deans. Other diocesan bishops and priests passed similar resolutions.[11]

The milder tone in these resolutions compared to previous such resolutions may owe something to James Warren Doyle, who had become bishop of Kildare and Leighlin in November 1819, and possibly also to the rebuke the bishops had received from the pope in 1816. Doyle was a highly

7 *FJ*, 14, 22 Mar. 1821. 8 *DEP*, 27 Mar. 1821. 9 Donoughmore to Troy, 4 Apr. 1821, WDA. 10 Gradwell to Propaganda, 3 Apr. 1821, APF, SC(Anglia) 7, f 628r. 11 *DEP*, 7 Apr. 1821.

intelligent, thoughtful and able young prelate, who was always ready to bring the fruits of his learning to bear on the pastoral or political situation of his countrymen. As he was to prove by his later writings, he was more liberal and 'ecumenical' than most of his colleagues.[12] He had no objections to ecclesiastics on the commissions checking the correspondence from Rome. Milner was soon to remark ruefully that Doyle 'affirms that nothing will do that comes from me'.[13] Poynter was quick to appreciate the value of the Dublin statement in seeking Roman approval of the oath. He translated the resolution declaring that the oath in the first bill was acceptable, but did not mention the very different comments on the second bill.

Archbishop Kelly of Tuam took a very different approach to the bills from Troy and his suffragans. He regarded them as 'infinitely more objectionable' than that of 1813 because an unrestricted veto had been offered to the crown, and he even depicted the extreme scenario whereby the chief secretary could disapprove of all candidates for episcopal office, and leave Ireland bereft of bishops. The clause that required all briefs and rescripts to be submitted to commissioners was as 'unjust as it is unnecessary', and the precaution of sending documents concerning cases of conscience to the senior ecclesiastical commissioner was 'nugatory' for sometimes 'even that communication would be inexpedient, indecent and improper'. The archbishop rejected Plunket's explanation of the oath of supremacy in the first bill and suggested that its meaning and import should not 'be couched in ambiguous, equivocal or insidious terms'.[14]

Most of the bishops and clergy in the provinces of Cashel and Tuam rejected the bill. Coppinger of Cloyne, who was one of the most determined opponents of the veto, denounced the oath as an abjuration of the Catholic faith. Bishop Costello of Clonfert was prepared to follow Dublin's lead, but at other diocesan meetings the bills were variously described as 'repugnant', 'subversive' and 'obnoxious'.[15] When all the bishops met to discuss what legal arrangements from parliament would be acceptable, if approved by Rome, they could not agree and no public statement was issued.[16]

O'Connell's reaction to the bills was more hostile than that of the bishops. He admitted that the oath contained in the first bill could be taken by Catholics, but he was scathing in his opposition to the second bill. Drawing, as he often did, on his reservoir of contemptuous hyperbole he described it as 'more *strictly, literally and emphatically a penal and persecuting bill* than any or all of the statutes passed in the darkest and most bigoted periods of the reigns of Queen Anne, or of the two first Georges', and went so far as to claim that its title should be 'An Act to "Decatholicise" Ireland'. He asked

12 McGrath, *The public ministry of Bishop James Doyle.*   13 Milner to Curtis, 16 Dec. 1821, DDA.   14 Kelly to Murray, 17 Mar. 1821, DDA.   15 McGrath, *The public ministry of Bishop James Doyle*, pp 2–6.   16 Ibid., p. 7.

scornfully if the Catholic clergy were so notorious as 'brawlers and rioters ... ruffians and bravoes' that it was necessary that those electing them as bishops should swear that they would choose only those of peaceable conduct. He denied that priests could take an oath not to have any communication with the See of Rome tending directly or indirectly to overthrow or disturb the Protestant church, as they were by definition obliged to point out Protestant errors.[17] Cardinal Litta, in his Genoese letter, had already ruled out inspection of Roman correspondence by the state, and the law as it existed already inflicted a punishment on anyone who corresponded with a foreign power to the prejudice of the government.[18]

Not surprisingly, Milner's opposition to Plunket's proposals was similarly intransigent. He told Murray that archbishops O'Hurley and Creagh in Ireland and Fisher and More in England had suffered glorious martyrdom for refusing such an oath and insisted that without apostasy or perjury he could not swear that no foreign prelate had any jurisdiction, ecclesiastical or spiritual that interfered with the allegiance which was due by the laws of the realm to the king. He was aggrieved that the Irish hierarchy, which had been 'so happily united on every question and in every business of a religious nature during the fifteen years that our controversies have lasted are now divided into two parties on the essential head of the *oath of supremacy*', and particularly that the 'high authority of the archdiocese of Dublin stands in opposition to my previously published decision'. He recalled that the king, in his ecclesiastical courts, judged and decided all questions of heresy, impiety and blasphemy, and expressed the hope that Donoughmore would, in consultation with orthodox prelates and learned lawyers, draw up another bill with oaths that were 'unequivocal and translucid'.[19] Milner also argued that the pledge of allegiance to the king in the bill involved recognition of the king as head of the church, even though Poynter had been assured by Castlereagh that it referred only to civil obedience. He also drew up a statement against the bills, which he circulated in printed form, and had a petition signed by nearly a thousand people presented in parliament. Poynter, to make sure that Rome would not judge the bills harshly, explained to his agent that he had worked hard to remove epithets such as 'damnable' and 'heretical' from the oath, and had obtained from Castlereagh an assurance that the pledge of allegiance to the king involved only civil obedience and had no reference to him as head of the Anglican church. He told Gradwell that it was difficult to conceive how 'ardent' the Catholic nobles and gentlemen were to enter parliament.[20]

---

17 Peel, from the opposite point of view, could not see how any conscientious Protestant could subscribe to the oath (*Hansard* 2, 1441–44, 23 Mar. 1821). **18** 17 Mar. 1821 in O'Connell, *Select speeches*, second series, pp 112–25. **19** Milner to Murray, 1 Apr. 1821, DDA. **20** Poynter to Gradwell, 28 Mar. 1821, APF, SC(Anglia) 7, ff 624r–626r.

Milner and the two priests who had signed the theological statement against the bill informed Propaganda that the oath of supremacy was regarded by Catholics and Protestants as a deliberate abjuration of the Catholic religion. They could not agree not to have correspondence that would tend directly or indirectly to overthrow the Protestant religion because their preaching, writing and ministry tended indirectly to that effect. The right of commissioners to investigate documents from the Holy See involved the breaking of the most sacred and inviolable secrets.[21] Milner detected the hand of Charles Butler in the bill and lamented that he and his friends wanted:

> to reduce the power of the pope and the church to *a mere internal belief* which indeed they equivalently express in the bill, to the utter exclusion of all external discipline and laws. Nor would the church be allowed to have it in her power to pronounce even on articles of faith, *in this land of religious liberty*, if all decisions and decrees even of this nature were made subject to the *licet* of a Protestant secretary of state.[22]

Bishop Smith, the coadjutor of the Northern District, wrestled with the terms of the oath, and consulted John Gillow and John Lingard, clerical historians of his district. They both expressed satisfaction with the amendments which Poynter had negotiated and were satisfied that full and undivided allegiance did not exclude submission to papal spiritual authority. Smith was happy with that understanding, though he was much more sceptical about the second bill, strongly disliking the commissions, and suggesting that a secretary of state alone should decide on civil grounds if there was any objection to a particular candidate. He also thought that the power of the state to control correspondence with Rome should be strictly limited, and feared it would be very annoying if it included their dealings with their agent, Gradwell.

Milner, seeking to obtain the support of a vicar apostolic in his opposition to the bill, wrote to Bishop Gibson, insisting that it was their 'bounden duty, as we value our religion and our souls, to lay aside every selfish and private Interest in order to save the jurisdiction and discipline of our H. religion from the profane grasp of worldly politicians Catholics as well as Protestants'. Was it consistent with their duty, he wondered, to tolerate a few lay Catholics and Protestant statesmen making rules for the future administration of their religion without seeking the advice of their spiritual leaders?

21 Milner and others to Propaganda, 13 Mar. 1821, APF, SC(Anglia) 7, ff 663r–664r.
22 Milner to Scully, 26 Mar. 1821 in MacDermot, *The Catholic question in Ireland and England, 1798–1822*, p. 605.

Smith, in reporting this development to Poynter, expressed his dislike of the word 'heretical' in the oath in the first bill, and mentioned that the king had legal rights to which they could not give obedience. But the addition of the explanation to the oath satisfied him of its acceptability. He regarded Milner's 'theological judgment' as 'the most mischievous thing he has ever done'. His advice to Poynter was to avoid passing public judgment on the bill, and, if it became law, then the Irish and English bishops – if not the Holy See – could decide on whether it could be approved.[23]

Gradwell translated Poynter's lengthy letters and the bills into Italian for cardinals Fontana and Consalvi. He told the Roman prefects that he approved of the first bill but disliked the second because he thought it 'needless, troublesome and disrespectful to the Holy See, and casting unjust aspersions on the allegiance and framing unconstitutional penalties against any priest who lived abroad'. Consalvi, Fontana and their officials also disliked the second bill, and were happy that Gradwell shared their opinion. Cardinal Haefflin suggested at one time that he would get the matter properly examined and placed before the pope,[24] and Consalvi and Fontana also thought of getting theologians to submit judgments on the bills. But Consalvi, the Anglophile, who was more prepared to make agreements with states than any of his colleagues, was hesitant about rushing into any decision that could antagonize the British government. Gradwell reported that 'he sees that parliament is going wrong and raises his voice to prevent them from enacting a nullity'. The pope, according to Consalvi, was 'uneasy' about the second bill, and he told Gradwell that several colleagues also had a 'strong aversion' to the oath in the first bill. Fontana had at first been put off by Troy's judgment that the bill would do no good to Catholics and would contain inadmissible clauses and an inadmissible oath. But with the addition to the oath and Troy's change of mind he too altered his view.[25]

Canning, a constant supporter of Catholic emancipation, interpreted the murmurs of the 'more violent Catholic prelates' as a conclusive indication of the probable tendency of the bill, which was to confirm and consolidate the Protestant church in Ireland.[26] Archbishop Murray and Bishop Doyle planned to travel to London to bring their views to bear on sympathetic members of parliament, but then decided not to go because of the division of opinion in the hierarchy.

The duke of Norfolk and lords Shrewsbury, Petre and Arundel – a proud, self-confident and defiant quartet – without waiting for any guidance from Poynter, petitioned the house of commons in favour of the bills and

---

23 Smith to Poynter, 12 Feb.; 8, 15, 21, 22, 24, 27, 31 Mar.; 3, 6 Apr. 1821, WDA. 24 Haefflin, a German member of the curia, had contributed to the concordat with Bavaria in 1817. 25 Gradwell to Poynter, 29 Mar., 31 Mar., 3 Apr., 12 Apr., 21 Apr., 3 May 1821, WDA. 26 *Hansard 2*, v, 1542–8, 2 Apr. 1821.

indicated their willingness to take the oath. The bills, which had been amalgamated on 26 March, passed the house of commons by nineteen votes, but in their united form were defeated in the house of lords by thirty-nine votes. All the Anglican bishops, apart from the bishop of Norwich, lined up in opposition. The bishop of London gave the oath a different twist, insisting that when Catholics took an oath they always kept in view a reservation for the rights and interests of their church. The bill provided no adequate securities for the safety of the Protestant government.[27]

After the success of Plunket's bill in the house of commons, Poynter pointed out that if the pope accepted the commissions, the bill would be of great help to Catholics: the right of correspondence with the pope would be recognized, as would the pope's right to give dispensations (on spiritual matters).[28] He knew he would have to await papal approval, and to his annoyance the Catholic Board could have created a very embarrassing situation for him.

When the debates on the second reading of the bill proceeded, the English Catholic Board presented a petition expressing gratitude for the removal of the bar to the professions and professing their full allegiance to the king. As in 1820, they again acknowledged that the king alone possessed the power of the 'civil sword', and denied that power to any foreign prince, prelate or potentate 'in any matter or cause whatever, whether civil, spiritual or ecclesiastical'. They expressed their readiness to take the amended oath in Plunket's bill and trusted that it would pass into law. The board asked Poynter and Collingridge to sign the petition, but they refused. They had not formally declared that the oath of supremacy, with its legislative explanation, was admissible, and were discomfited by the laity expressing a willingness to take it without spiritual guidance. However, Poynter bent to their wishes and let them know they could take it. But he pointed out that the bishops had no authority to approve the securities for ecclesiastics in the bill. The board nevertheless thanked the government for the whole bill, which would have put the vicars apostolic in a very invidious situation had it been passed.[29] As the bill was lost, Rome did not have to make a formal judgment on the acceptability of the oath. Poynter was happy to let Gradwell know that neither he nor Troy had received any decision from the congregation of Propaganda on the bill.[30]

On receipt of Poynter's accounts of the bill and of his success with the explanatory clause attached to the oath, Consalvi heaped praise on the vicar apostolic of London, but he remained far from enthusiastic about the second bill, which in discussion with the pope he thought 'unlawful and impracti-

27 *Hansard 2*, v, 241–5.   28 Gradwell to Propaganda (Italian translations), 6, 8, 20, 28 Mar., 3, 10 Apr. 1821, APF, SC(Anglia) 7, ff 614r–648r.   29 Ward, *The eve of Catholic emancipation*, iii, pp 70–4.   30 Poynter to Gradwell (copy), 21 Aug. 1821, ibid.

cable', though the right of exclusion of candidates from the episcopate by the state authorities did not differ much from that in the Genoese letter. The *exequatur* had also been an unwelcome element in the bill in 1813. Consalvi was displeased with Milner's 'theological judgment', and on hearing that Hayes was campaigning against the bill in London, described him as 'a great hypocrite and scoundrel'.[31] Gradwell agreed that Poynter, under pressure from Catholic nobles eager for emancipation and Protestant prejudice against any alteration of the status quo, had done very well.

Poynter singled out Milner and Hayes as leading opponents of the bill, who diminished the prestige of the church before parliament. This was astute, as their reputations in Rome were then low. Hayes' opposition was almost guaranteed to produce the effect he did not want among all those who knew about his misbehaviour in Rome. Fontana approved of the suggestion that the other bishops in Britain should write a pastoral letter 'against the aspersions of the arch-schism-maker'. Should Milner then attack their decision, the Holy See should step in and stop the dispute.[32]

Milner, however, was not without advocates in Rome. His support for the Jesuits in England when the other vicars apostolic were opposed to their restoration stood him in good stead. Charles Plowden, the Jesuit superior in Stonyhurst, who was then in Rome, maintained that the oath denied all ecclesiastical power to the pope and that in cases such as divorce the authority of the pope would of necessity be in conflict with the law of the land. The resolutions of the Dublin bishops and clergy, however, had given him pause. Troy, who rarely received any compliments from Poynter's agents, Macpherson or Gradwell, was quoted favourably by Gradwell in support of the innocence of taking 'the oath in opposition to his traditional guide, Milner'. It then became Fontana's turn to question Troy's prudence and wisdom. He assured Gradwell that Troy had been a good bishop 'but he is grown old, his opinion has not now great weight with me'.[33]

Troy's reputation in Fontana's eyes sank lower still with the publication in the Irish papers in July 1821 of an answer he had received from Rome about the lawfulness of an oath of allegiance.[34] Before Plunket's bill was presented

31 Gradwell to Poynter, 22, 29, 31 Mar.; 12, 3 May 1821, WDA. 32 Ibid., 21 Apr. 1821. 33 Ibid., 3 May 1821. Troy's reputation may have been somewhat damaged in Rome by accusations made against the theological views current in Maynooth. The charge that Gallicanism was taught in the college was regarded as very serious in the increasingly ultramontane climate of Rome after the restoration of Pius VII. The bishops would have been expected to prevent staff from teaching it. Archbishop Curtis, responding to this charge, admitted that the French professor of dogmatic theology, Delahogue, followed the opinion of the Paris school on papal infallibility, but insisted that that opinion was not commonly held in the college or in the Irish church. An examination by a consultor of the congregation of Propaganda of the books used in the college did not yield much material deserving of correction, but the fear was expressed that some opinions – perhaps tainted by the Protestant government that had endowed the college – could be a cause for anxiety. 34 *DEP*, 3 July 1821.

in parliament Troy wrote to Fontana about a hypothetical case in a petition which English Catholics had presented to parliament in 1820. Fontana replied that it was not without surprise and sorrow that he learned of the declaration made by many English nobles and Catholics that they did not recognize any power or authority – civil, spiritual or ecclesiastical – beyond that of the king. Should such an oath be proposed, the cardinal continued, it would be manifestly illegal and schismatical. He would not discuss it until it was proposed, and he only wished, in confidence, to prevent it.

In fact, as Poynter was later to point out, the petitioners, in their 7 June 1820 submission to the king, promised to swear full and undivided allegiance to their sovereign, and declared:

> To Your Majesty they swear full and undivided allegiance, in Your Majesty alone they recognize the power of the civil sword within this realm of England. They acknowledge in no other foreign prince, prelate, state or potentate any power or authority to use the same, within the said realm, in any matter or cause whatever, whether civil, spiritual or ecclesiastical.

Poynter was nonplussed to discover that the petition (which was not an oath) had ultimately found its way to Rome in the mangled version produced by Milner, and that Propaganda had been told that the English Catholics were prepared to swear that they did not recognize any authority, civil, spiritual or ecclesiastical beyond that of the king.[35]

Fontana's answer was made known to other Irish bishops and to Milner, and was given to or leaked to the press. It was interpreted as a condemnation of the oath of allegiance that was proposed in Plunket's bill. Gradwell informed Fontana of the interpretation that was put on this letter to Troy. The cardinal explained that he had answered a hypothetical case on 24 March 1821, two days before he had heard anything about Plunket's bill. Consequently, he authorized Gradwell to let Poynter know that the report in the Irish papers stating that the congregation of Propaganda had denounced the bill was 'a downright falsehood and imposition'.[36] As this explanation was not known in Ireland, the many clergy and people who had protested against the 'vetoistical' element in Plunket's bill felt justified. Poynter pointed out that a Catholic layman had written to Troy to ask if Fontana had condemned the bill in this way. He was assured that the archbishop had not known of any decision taken in Rome about the bill and supposed that some people had misunderstood or misrepresented the nature of the petition presented by the English Catholics.[37]

---

35 Poynter to Curtis, 8 Nov. 1821, APF, SC(Irlanda) 23, ff 521r–533v; Ward, *The eve of Catholic emancipation*, iii, pp 314–24.   36 Gradwell to Poynter, 11 Aug. 1821, WDA.   37 Poynter to

The sceptics who met Milner on his visit to Dublin at the end of June would have been gratified by his assurances that their reservations were warranted. But some who opposed the bill or parts of it were not enthusiastic about his presence. The *Dublin Evening Post*, which described him as 'a most imprudent and vacillating divine', who had been a vetoist and had become an anti-vetoist, announced that his coming was ominous and that he would spoil the movement for emancipation, and when he left, it expressed its joy at his departure.[38] Several bishops had grown wary of him by then. Archbishop Murray had told Coxe-Hippisley that he should not be regarded as their agent and Milner himself since his return from Rome in 1816 had begun to realize that the atmosphere had changed.[39]

Nonetheless, the bishops, who were trustees of Maynooth, invited him to join them at their meeting in the college. He there succeeded – almost certainly with the help of the conciliatory Murray – in persuading Archbishop Curtis of Armagh, who was then just two years in office and would not have known much about Milner's tortuous career, that he wanted to be fully reconciled with his brethren in England, whom he might have unintentionally offended, and especially with Poynter. Curtis had already written a friendly letter to Poynter, unburdening himself of some of his local difficulties, praising Poynter for his 'highly creditable and edifying' work and expressing the hope that they would cooperate harmoniously in the future.[40] Milner's plea arose in the context of discussion about the Irish bishops' cooperation with their English and Scottish colleagues in support of a future oath in a bill for emancipation which he had adumbrated.

Before Milner had come to Dublin, he had exhorted Murray to get the Irish bishops to draw up their own oath, which would put the emphasis on allegiance and not on supremacy. He encouraged them to take the professions of faith and oaths out of the hands of lawyers and the 'board of Lincoln's Inn' (Butler) and draw up their own version.[41] In the meantime, he drew up his own formula, the acceptance of which would depend on the response of the Irish bishops.[42] The bishops approved of his oath and so he got fifty copies printed for them and their friends in parliament and fifty for his own friends, clerical and lay. He divided his oath of allegiance into two sections, one for episcopal electors and one for the clergy and laity. As he had

Gradwell, 21 Aug. 1821, APF, SC(Irlanda) 23, ff 471r–472r.   **38** *DEP*, 28, 30 June, 3 July 1821.
39 Coxe-Hippisley to Consalvi, 14 Aug. 1820, ASV, Segr Stato esteri, Rubr 297, Busta 659, fasc 1, ff 35r–38r. Milner in writing to Murray, referred to 'the change in the minds of the Irish prelates in my regard' (Milner to Murray, 26 Mar. 1819, DDA).   **40** Curtis to Poynter, 16 June 1821, WDA. Poynter was suspicious of Curtis' motives. He thought the letter had 'the appearance of a trap ... written with a particular view of engaging me to renew a *confidential* intercourse with Dr Milner' (Poynter to Collingridge, 8 Aug. 1821, CIDA)   **41** Lincoln's Inn was an inn of court where some barristers, including Butler, had their chambers.   **42** Milner to Murray, 14 May 1821, DDA

advised the bishops he placed his emphasis on allegiance. It contained the usual pledges to support the succession to the throne, a promise not to disturb the Protestant church and a repudiation of what he strangely called the 'treasonable doctrine and position' that princes excommunicated by the pope could be deposed or murdered.[43] He still hoped they would have something that would go down better in parliament than 'the crippled veto and clogged oath of supremacy' of Plunket's bill.[44] The substance of Milner's oath was accepted also by the vicars apostolic of the Northern District and Western Districts of England and the Lowland District of Scotland.

Pleased with the result of his journey to unite the prelates of the three countries, he claimed that his oaths would prevent Butler and his counsellors 'from dictating religious tests to bind the consciences of 37 bishops, 3,000 priests and 5 millions of other Catholics'. He felt it was time for Irish Catholics to take the lead in the struggle for emancipation:

> You are the Catholics of the Empire. You form the weight of Catholics in the national scale; you possess the wealth as well as the numbers of the Catholic body ... Is O'Connell beneath Charles Butler in the scale of beings? ... let our friend O'Connell (I presume to call him my friend) exert the talents which God has given him for the benefit of others as well as for his own ... let him say that the final struggle for emancipation shall originate in Catholic Ireland, where the interest of our H. religion is concentrated.[45]

Curtis regretted that there had not been such cooperation on the previous bill, or attempts made by the bishops to inform the parliamentary advocates of emancipation of their views. He was very anxious not to repeat that mistake in the future. He expressed his regrets about this neglect to Poynter and his hope that when future bills for emancipation were introduced all the bishops should let their friends in parliament know what was acceptable. He then referred to Milner's visit to Ireland and his presentation to the prelates of his plan of a bill and an oath, which they regarded as suitable. Milner, he went on to say 'earnestly besought us to employ our influence in order to effect a sincere and perfect reconciliation between himself and any of his brethren, that he might have been unhappy enough to have unintentionally offended'. Consequently, Curtis appealed to Poynter's charity. Milner must

---

43 Ibid., 27 July 1821.   44 Ibid., 14 Jan. 1822. Elsewhere he referred to the 'ambiguous and dangerous, if not heterodox forms of oath which the junta of Lincoln's Inn have successively framed' (30 Sept. 1821).   45 Milner to Scully, 29 Sept. 1821 in MacDermot, *The Catholic question in Ireland and England, 1798–1822*, pp 650–2.

have accompanied his plea with suitably histrionic gestures for, as Curtis wrote, 'he edified, and even drew tears' from Irish episcopal eyes.[46]

Before Poynter answered Curtis, he unburdened himself of his distrust of – and indeed of his anger, against – the Irish bishops to Collingridge, who shared his views,[47] with the remark, 'I might say to the Irish Bps: *medice cura teipsum*', physician heal thyself. He thought it curious that the Irish bishops, who had so long supported Milner against the other vicars apostolic and especially against himself should ask him to renew a confidential intercourse with the agent whom they employed to injure the vicars apostolic and who continued to expose their official conduct in a false and injurious light, as he had recently done in his *Supplementary Memoirs*.[48]

Nonetheless, he replied to Curtis courteously. He took the opportunity to demonstrate how Milner had caused misunderstanding and disharmony between the Irish and English bishops, and to unburden himself of some of the pain and hurt Milner had caused him down the years. He too was keen that the bishops and vicars apostolic should work in harmony, and suggested that they produce a pastoral letter outlining what terms and oath they could accept. He went on to relate how Milner had quoted to him an inaccurate account of how he had approved of the original oath in the bill when it was shown to him by the man who drew it up. On the contrary, he had objected to it as soon as he saw it. He then bewailed the years of misrepresentation and character assassination he had suffered at Milner's hands, recounting how he had been subjected to repeated charges of malfeasance. He instanced the case of the fifth resolution – a long-running sore – and Milner's use of it to discredit him. And he pointed out that charges and accusations against him were made in pamphlets and writings that were disseminated in the London District, and mentioned especially Milner's use of the Roman reply to Troy's hypothetical question about an oath, and his argument that Rome had thereby condemned the oath approved by lay Catholics and others (others being the code for vicars apostolic). He admitted that Milner was right to claim that Poynter had no confidence in him, because he had already witnessed Milner's appeals for pardon being quickly followed by the same offences. He had gone down on his knees to seek forgiveness from bishops Douglass and Gibson, and then shortly afterwards had transgressed against them. Listening to a transient expression of sorrow, Poynter assured Curtis, was very different from constantly experiencing contumely and defamation.

Poynter then rather charitably attributed his misunderstandings with Troy mainly to Milner's influence and guidance, but he also knew that Troy

46 Curtis to Poynter, 22 Oct. 1821, WDA.   47 Peter Augustine Baines, Collingridge's vicar general and future coadjutor, once remarked, 'I know Your Lordship is not partial to the inhabitants of the sister island' (Baines to Collingridge, 10 Aug. 1822, CIDA).   48 Poynter to Collingridge, 28 Oct. 1821, CIDA.

could have kept himself better informed and therefore bore some responsibility for their dissensions. He blamed Milner for giving Troy an inaccurate account of the writings of Blanchard and de Trevaux, and of the significance of the fifth resolution. But he did not absolve the Irish bishops from joining with Milner in condemning the fifth resolution and thereby invading the jurisdiction of the vicars apostolic. He regretted the effects that such criticism by the Irish bishops had had among the thousands of Irish Catholics in England, which separated them from the pastors who laboured for their salvation. Recalling the contribution made by the Irish bishops to the expenses of Milner's journey to Rome in 1814, where he had made use of the opportunity to damage the reputations of his colleagues, Poynter went on to say that he would ask Archbishop Murray if his conduct there was that of an agent or of a principal. He concluded by confessing that Curtis' letter had placed him on the horns of a cruel dilemma: if he renewed his confidence in Milner, he was lost; if he did not renew it, he would be open to the charge of being an enemy of charity and peace.[49]

The vicar of the London District summed up his difficulties and conflicts with Milner by declaring that there was 'something most unaccountable in his character' that could excite charity and compassion but not confidence. Milner was so capricious and volatile that he simply could not be trusted. A less charitable colleague than Poynter would probably have heaped on Milner more derogatory adjectives, such as 'unscrupulous' and 'disingenuous'.

Poynter's reply should have satisfied Curtis that despite his honourable motives there were serious and justifiable reasons for giving Milner a wide berth. The archbishop of Armagh did not challenge any of the London vicar's explanations of his conduct or respond to any of his references to past disputes and misunderstandings. But copies of the correspondence circulated widely among the vicars apostolic and some of the Irish bishops, and Troy duly sent a copy to Milner. It aggravated an already tense relationship by provoking him to an aggressive defence of his conduct and to an attempted rebuttal of many of the claims Poynter had made about his interventions in the London District and his objections to the fifth resolution. He accused his colleague of 'downright falsehoods', referred to Paul Macpherson as 'a practised Scotch intriguer' and to Poynter's 'former libels for obtaining the rescript', denied that the Irish prelates had financed his trip to Rome in 1814 or that he had ever been rebuked there, and suggested that

---

49 Poynter to Curtis, 8 Nov. 1821, WDA and in Ward, *The eve of Catholic emancipation*, iii, pp 314–24. Poynter also informed Curtis that he had sent copies of his letter and of the reply to the vicars apostolic of the Northern District and Western District. Gradwell told Poynter that in response to requests from Consalvi and Fontana, he had translated the letter into Italian, and that Consalvi saw that it was a stratagem by the Irish and Milner 'to catch your lordship in the noose' (Gradwell to Poynter, 11, 26 Jan. 1822 and APF, SC(Irlanda) 23, ff 521r–533r).

he and Poynter stifle their 'selfish passions and unite their 'efforts with those of our brethren in both islands to save our common religion from the danger to which it is still exposed'.[50] In his letter to Troy he did not spare Poynter his customary vituperation, charging his colleague with letting the English Catholic Board know that he approved of the oath in the recent bill, and then subsequently rejecting it so that he had 'two faces and two tongues, one for London, another for Rome'. He dismissed the accusation that he had gone three times on his knees to one or other of his brethren by explaining that he had done so 'to deprecate them not to ask acknowledgment of myself as guilty'. He prayed to God to give his 'unfortunate brother the spirit of *real candour and truth*, instead of the visor of it'. And he concluded that he had received letters recently from the pro-prefect of Propaganda in which he was hailed as the '*true friend of religion and the Holy See*'.[51]

Curtis' well-intentioned intervention had only made matters worse. Milner had been enraged by the accusations Poynter had made and had been provoked into making an intemperate reply. Troy could have summarized Poynter's reaction without letting Milner see the harsher comments. He must have known that it would produce a heated response, and there is a possibility that he was not unwilling to see Poynter being criticized by Milner. Far from contributing to reconciliation, Curtis had unwittingly added to the disharmony between these prelates.

II

Irish hopes had been raised by the visit to Ireland of the newly crowned King George IV from 12 August to 3 September 1821. Not since James II in 1689 had a king come to Ireland and George's gesture was mistakenly believed to represent a change of heart towards his Irish Catholic subjects. O'Connell surprised his colleagues by the enthusiasm with which he welcomed the visit. When the mayor sent an invitation to a meeting of Catholics gathered to address the king, inviting them to join with the corporation in celebrating the occasion, O'Connell enthusiastically agreed. He attended the levee at Dublin Castle, contributed to a fund to erect a palace in Ireland for the king, and, as

---

50 Milner to Poynter, 24 Dec. 1822, in Ward, *The eve of Catholic emancipation*, iii, pp 326–35.
51 Milner to Troy, 22 Oct. 1822, DDA. Almost three years later Curtis wrote to Cardinal della Somaglia, the prefect of the congregation of Propaganda, in defence of Milner, explaining that he did so with the consent of the Irish prelates and out of Christian charity. Regretting that Poynter had rejected his invitation to reconciliation with Milner, and claiming that Milner was excluded from the deliberations of his colleagues and prevented from visiting London, where matters of great moment to the Catholics of England and Ireland were discussed, he invited della Somaglia to correct that situation, without mentioning his name (Curtis to Propaganda, 7 Apr. 1824, APF, SC(Irlanda) 24, ff 234v–235r).

George was leaving, presented him with a crown in the shape of a laurel wreath.[52] Later, praising the king for his wise, gracious and conciliatory actions among them, he enthused that the monarch's departing words deserved to be written in gold, or, if possible, engraved on the heart of every Irishman.[53] George, on his return to England, took no steps to indicate sympathy for Catholic emancipation. The goodwill manifested to him in Ireland did not pay any political dividends.

Hopes were again raised by the appointment of Marquis Wellesley, Wellington's older brother, as lord lieutenant in December 1821. A former governor general of Bengal and foreign secretary, he enjoyed the reputation of being liberal-minded, and, unlike his brother, of being sympathetic to Catholic emancipation. The bishops, in an address that interpreted his appointment as evidence of the king's solicitude for their welfare, expressed their affectionate loyalty to their sovereign and deplored the agrarian outrages then taking place in some parts of the country.[54] The Catholic laity, represented by Fingall and O'Connell, also presented an address. Wellesley gradually introduced some reforms, especially in the magistracy, but there was no sign of movement towards emancipation. William Saurin, the notorious anti-Catholic attorney general for Ireland was replaced by W.C. Plunket, who had given proof of his commitment to emancipation with his bill, but the anti-Catholic Henry Goulburn remained in office as chief secretary for Ireland.

O'Connell, who had strongly criticised much of Plunket's bill, soon admitted that its course through parliament had given them hope and encouragement to renew their petitions. The king had seen his Catholic subjects in a new light and they, in turn, were delighted with 'the delicacy, the tact, the taste and the good feeling' which marked 'the entire personal conduct of the king'. And the ministerial letter that had closed the visit had seemed to be the harbinger of better feelings and better days. Emphasizing his unbending opposition to giving the government a veto over the appointment of bishops, which the late bill would have done, he insisted that the Catholic people, led by their bishops, had 'unanimously, loudly and warmly reprobated it'.[55]

Despite O'Connell's enthusiasm in 1822, Plunket insisted that the time

52 Geoghegan, *King Dan*, pp 189–91; MacDonagh, *The hereditary bondsman*, pp 175–7.   53 *FJ*, 9 Oct. 1821.   54 *FJ*, 9 Jan. 1822. The address of Bishop Tuohy of Limerick to his clergy when he prayed that there would be a conversion of the misguided people from 'their abominable and diabolical designs' was representative of the clerical view of the disturbances in Munster. 55 Ibid., 23 Jan. 1822. O'Connell was greatly embarrassed by the publication of a letter he had written five years previously in which he claimed that the 'gallant Trojan' (Troy) had got Murray's support for the veto, and remarked that Troy's 'traffic at the castle is notorious'. Troy had been accused of using his influence at Dublin Castle to obtain the post of revenue officer in Co. Cork for his nephew. O'Connell was forced to apologize profusely (*FJ*, 23 Feb. 1822).

was not ripe for the presentation of another petition. The English Catholic Association, however, persisted. While the influence of the Irish peers and gentry had waned, their English brothers continued to dominate their association and, as they had shown during the passage of Plunket's bill, were prepared to take little guidance from the vicars apostolic.[56] They persuaded Canning to introduce a bill to permit Catholic peers to become members of the house of lords without taking an oath. This request was based on the claim that the law prohibiting Catholic membership of that house had been passed to exclude the Catholic brother of Charles II, and was not meant to be a permanent law applicable to all members of that religion. Though successful in the house of commons, it met fierce opposition in the lords, led by the prime minister and chancellor, and was defeated.[57]

The English Catholic Association expressed its regret at the failure of Plunket's bill and of the attempt to restore six 'most ancient peers' to their seats in parliament, 'which restoration would have afforded hope, confidence, and satisfaction to a large portion of the united Empire'.[58] The number of people in Ireland to whom hope, confidence and satisfaction would have been restored was minimal, and it seems unlikely that outside the narrow circle of nobles and gentry, much enthusiasm would have been aroused in the Catholic body. The bill simply reflected the determination of the aristocrats to leave their cold exile and gain the positions to which they felt they were entitled. The association went on to resolve that it would use every legal exertion to obtain a repeal of the laws by which 'for conscience sake, we are hourly degraded in society, and constantly deprived, though equally taxed, of every political privilege of the constitution'.[59]

One leading member of the Catholic Board had his own particular problems to deal with. Charles Butler, the lawyer and intellectual who had long provided legal advice and guidance to the board, decided that he could no longer tolerate what he regarded as Milner's unjust charges against him, and unburdened himself of his frustrations in a lengthy letter to Rome. Claiming that Milner had denigrated him for years in various publications – and especially in the *Orthodox Journal*, in which the other vicars apostolic had also been assailed – he maintained that all his efforts to remain on friendly terms with Milner had been to no avail. From 1810, Milner had accused him of deceitful and fraudulent politics, going back to the relief bill

56 Bishop Collingridge and many of his clergy, after the failure of Plunket's bill, approved of Milner's suggestion that the bishops and clergy should draw up an oath and not 'leave to our lay theologians the power of perplexing us with their untheological forms for the future' (Collingridge to Poynter, 14 Oct. 1821, WDA).   **57** Ward, *The eve of Catholic emancipation*, iii, p. 88.   **58** The *Orthodox Journal* took exception to the claims of the Catholic Association to represent the Catholics of England. It pointed out that no one had 'the right to claim to control the concerns of the body at large by reason of their birth, rank, fortune or even of their talents' (*OJ*, Mar. 1814).   **59** *FJ*, 27 June 1822.

of 1791, and of harming the Catholic religion. When the oath contained in that bill was condemned by three vicars apostolic, Butler had maintained that the laity interfered only in temporal and not in spiritual affairs and that the Cisalpine Club only claimed that the state was independent of the see of Rome in temporal affairs.

Butler insisted that it was only in 1808 that he first heard of the veto, which had originated with Castlereagh and the Irish bishops in 1799. And when he asked Lord Grenville who had authorized him to state in the house of lords that the Catholic bishops had agreed to a veto, he was told that it was Milner. He then had a visit from Milner who attempted to stop him writing against the veto. Milner had also tried to get lords Clifford and Weld to defend the veto, and then changed tack and blamed those who supported it. Butler believed that he was among the chief victims of this volte-face, being accused of compiling the clauses which favoured the veto in the bill of 1813, which Milner described as 'infamous' and which he claimed Cecil, Shaftesbury (English anti-Catholics) or Robespierre could not have conceived. The clauses, in fact, were inserted after discussions at the house of George Ponsonby, at the dictation of Castlereagh, and all those responsible for them, though not Catholics, thought they were acting in the best interests of the Catholics.

Milner's wilder charges included the allegations that Butler sought to diminish the authority of the Holy See, that he had defamed the pope, that he was trying to give full spiritual authority to the sovereign and that he was trying to institute a church like the conventicles of the Jansenists at Utrecht. Moreover, Milner accused the Catholic Committee of pensioning Poynter, and its secretary of falsifying a speech by Lord Grey. Butler insisted that in his writings he had repudiated Jansenism, that he had zealously defended the Jesuits and that he had tried in vain to make peace with Milner. And he assured the cardinal that Poynter could testify to his loyalty to and defence of the church, and to his contributions to charities.[60]

Consalvi's reply to Butler was brief, diplomatic and non-committal. He praised his religious sentiments and dispositions and commended his forbearance in putting up with Milner for so long. The cardinal encouraged him to persevere in this patient conduct, which had given much satisfaction to the Holy See. Gradwell, who was a keen disciple of Consalvi, whom he regarded as a most understanding and sympathetic supporter of English Catholics, noted, ominously for his own influence, that Archbishop Pedicini, the secretary of the congregation of Propaganda, believed Consalvi was too

---

60 Butler to Propaganda, 24 Mar. 1822, APF, SC(Anglia) 7, ff 738r–746v. The *Orthodox Journal*, which Milner invariably praised, had often denounced Butler as the author of the Blue Books, 'the founder of Protesting Catholic Dissenters', the contriver of the fifth resolution, and had accused him of trying to get the management of Irish affairs into his hands (*OJ*, Feb. 1817).

indulgent to English interests. Consequently, Consalvi had become more cautious. Gradwell obviously believed that Consalvi had not replied to Butler in the hard-hitting manner he had expected.[61] The *Orthodox Journal*, which reflected Milner's views, had, amid other abusive comments about Consalvi, described him as a 'perfidious minister'.[62] And Milner, undaunted, continued to attack his colleagues. In reply to the refusal of the congregation to comment on the oath of Plunket's defeated bill, he maintained that the chief promoters of Catholic emancipation were Protestants seeking to have the authority of the pope in ecclesiastical, spiritual and civil affairs rejected and to compel Catholics by oath to submit to the royal supremacy.[63]

Despondent because of the defeat of Plunket's bill, the bishops and O'Connell turned their thoughts to some method of satisfying the government about episcopal appointments without the burden of unacceptable conditions. Domestic nomination had been suggested for some years, though the bishops and the Irish Catholic Board had put forward different terms. Troy and Curtis were requested by Rome in 1822 to suggest a plan for the nomination of bishops. Doyle engaged in a controversy with the secretary of the Irish Catholic Association, Edward Hay, who, like many writers in the Irish papers, believed that the clergy had a right to participate in elections. Bishops, if left to themselves, might become more pliant tools of Dublin Castle, Hay argued. Doyle retorted that the Catholic people needed prelates with access to the castle to guarantee their protection. The traditional method of electing candidates by the dean and chapter of the vacant diocese and receiving canonical institution from Rome had been put forward. O'Connell favoured the election of candidates who had taken the oath of allegiance by either the bishops of the province or by the dean and chapter of the vacant diocese. The electors were to take an oath that they would not vote for anyone whose conduct was not strictly loyal and peaceable. Should the government challenge the loyalty of the candidate, it would refer its accusation to the archbishops, who would examine the case and make a decision on it. As many dioceses in Ireland had no chapters, Troy, Curtis, Murray and Doyle favoured election by the bishops, which they believed would put an end to the intrigues and agitation that often accompanied elections. But they realized that compromises in the system would have to be made.[64]

---

61 Consalvi to Butler, 6 July 1822, Husenbeth, *Life of Bishop Milner*, p. 457; Gradwell to Poynter, 27 July 1822, WDA. **62** *OJ*, Aug. 1816. **63** Milner to Propaganda, 13 Nov. 1822. APF, SC(Anglia) 7, ff 798r–799r. Gradwell claimed that Propaganda not only wrote to Milner to order him to stop complaining about the civil-sword oath, but also to rebuke Troy for communicating a confidential letter and exposing it to misrepresentation. This presumably referred to the hypothetical oath (Gradwell to Poynter, 27 July 1822, WDA). **64** McGrath, *The public ministry of Bishop James Doyle*, pp 10–16.

Lord Castlereagh, the foreign secretary, a participant in the discussions about Catholic emancipation since 1799, died on 12 August 1822. His death was not mourned by Irish Catholics nor English liberals, because of the part he had played in putting down the rebellion of 1798 and in bringing about the union, but Poynter regarded it as 'a very important loss to me at present'. Castlereagh, who had recently become Lord Londonderry, had consistently supported emancipation, albeit with the traditional securities. He maintained that the obstacles to emancipation did not come from a spirit of unkindness or monopoly on the part of Protestants, but from the want of securities, without which, it was judged, the constitution, and that venerable fabric the ecclesiastical part of it, might be shaken to its very foundations. If the Catholics insisted on opposing that policy, they had only themselves to blame.[65] Castlereagh had received Consalvi very graciously in London, and assured the cardinal both then and later of his high regard for Poynter. Poynter in turn, believed that Castlereagh's courtesy towards Consalvi had helped nurture the cardinal's sympathy for English Catholics.[66] Milner, on the other hand, never believed that Castlereagh was sincere in his professions of support for emancipation, even with the usual safeguards. Ever afterwards, he spoke of the foreign secretary's death as 'a vile suicide'.[67]

The defeat of Plunket's bill had been a disappointment to the laity. But that outcome had meant that it had not been scrutinized at Rome where objections could have been raised to some of its terms. Grattan's bill of 1813 had been subjected to a full official examination at the congregation of Propaganda. The different treatment of the two bills may be explained by the different circumstances obtaining in Rome at the time they were put forward. In 1814, the cardinals and the prefects of the congregations were with the pope in exile in France. In 1821 the prefects and staffs of the congregations were fully in charge of their offices.

In 1814, Paul Macpherson, Poynter's agent, was able to persuade Michele Galeassi, an official of the congregation of Propaganda, and his superior, Giovanni Quarantotti, the vice prefect, that it was most important to pass judgment on the bill. Macpherson claimed that Poynter was under pressure from the nobility and gentry in England to obtain the agreement of Rome to a measure which would allow them to take seats in parliament. He convinced Galeassi and Quarantotti that a similar bill would be brought forward in 1814 and that it was therefore necessary to know whether terms similar to those in the bill of 1813 could be accepted. When the more experienced prelates,

---

65 Butler to Gradwell, 28 Sept. 1822, AVEC 67.5.28.   66 Poynter to Gradwell (copy), 13 Aug. 1822, WDA.   67 Ward, *The eve of Catholic emancipation*, iii, p. 89.

cardinals Litta, Pacca and Consalvi, returned to Rome, they were upset by Quarantotti's action, which they regarded as ultra vires.

In 1821, the congregation did not submit the bill to a formal examination. No one asked it to do so. Once it was defeated, only six weeks after its introduction, there was no point in sitting in judgment on it. Consalvi, the astute diplomat, would have been well aware of the futility of passing judgment on a bill that would never become law. He would have regarded such a step as pointless and likely to cause annoyance to legislators in London. Commenting on various clauses in the bill as they were submitted to Rome was one thing: issuing a solemn verdict after its defeat was something quite different. Consalvi was too practiced a diplomat to provoke the parliamentarians of a friendly country unnecessarily.

Cardinal Fontana, the prefect of the congregation of Propaganda, and Consalvi were spared the delicate responsibility of pronouncing on the acceptability of the veto and the oaths. They were also spared the unpleasant onus of confronting the Irish bishops, had the issue come to a head. Troy had been hostile to the bill when it was first publicized, but with his suffragans and priests had withdrawn his opposition when the legislative explanation was attached to the oath. But the majority of the bishops remained hostile, as, of course, did Milner in England. The defeat of the bill meant that the anxieties of its opponents disappeared. And so Roman officials did not have to condemn parts of the bill or encourage or placate Milner or the Irish bishops.

16

Increased agitation for emancipation

I

Apart from the failed bill to permit six English Catholic peers to take their seats in the house of lords, parliament did not engage with emancipation in 1822. The defeat of the bill of 1821 had capped a long series of failures. The campaign for emancipation seemed to have stalled, bedevilled by class divisions, confusion over the veto and oaths, and misunderstandings between the churches in England and Ireland. The crown had remained hostile, despite the hopes raised by the royal visit to Ireland of 1821, and the Tory and Orange opponents of concession had remained as implacable as ever. The agrarian violence of the Rockites in Ireland threatened to drag down the Catholic community and bring about repression and further violence.[1] The sectarian bitterness created by the Protestant evangelical societies, and the hostility aroused by the Pastorini prophecies of the end of Protestantism in 1825 deepened denominational ill feelings. O'Connell, reflecting on these bleak circumstances, concluded that some new policy was necessary to lift the Catholics out of their gloom and hopelessness. They needed protection, and attention paid to their grievances.[2]

The formation of a new Catholic Association was first discussed between O'Connell and a former opponent, Richard Lalor Sheil, who had represented the more accommodating approach of the upper classes, in January 1823 – though O'Connell's son, John, claimed that the idea had long been germinating in his fathers' mind.[3] They agreed that a society should be established with a membership fee of one guinea per year, and the first meeting took place at a dinner in Dublin on 25 April 1823. At a general meeting two weeks later, the association was officially founded, to take all necessary legal and constitutional measures to achieve emancipation. The gentry and better-off classes, as represented by Lord Killeen and Sir Edward

---

1 O'Connell maintained that he had long believed that the grievances of the people were unredressed because of disturbances and outrages (*FJ*, 10 Jan. 1825). 2 MacDonagh, *The hereditary bondsman*, pp 205–6; Connolly, *Mass politics and sectarian conflict, 1823–30* in *NHI*, v, pp 73–85. Bartlett, *The fall and rise of the Irish nation*, pp 327–42. 3 O'Connell, *Select speeches*, second series, p. 204. O'Connell himself admitted that the concept of an association supported by a rent from each parish in Ireland had first been suggested by Lord Kenmare to Bishop Moylan of Kerry in 1785 (*FJ*, 5 Feb. 1824).

Bellew, wanted the association confined to campaigning for emancipation, but O'Connell insisted that it concern itself with the grievances of the Catholic people more broadly. He thereby widened its popularity immensely, as the struggle against local injustices had an immediate appeal. Even though the meetings of the association were often poorly attended, reports of its tactics were favourably received and appreciated.[4]

The need for a new and more determined approach was highlighted by the failure of attempts in parliament to obtain for English Catholics what Irish Catholics had enjoyed since 1793 – the right to vote. Bills to introduce relief and to allow Catholics to hold some higher offices were defeated in 1823, and a debate in parliament, which could have examined the right of Catholics to have marriages conducted by their own clergy recognized as valid, ended before this subject was reached.[5]

Almost a year after its institution, O'Connell proposed extending the membership of the association to all who would contribute one penny per month. In the towns, local committees collected this 'rent', and in the rural parishes priests became the chief organizers of the collections. Apart from the increase in finances, this policy drew a huge number of people into interested and active membership. It was proposed to divide the funds among five groups or causes: £5,000 per year would be used to pay an agent in London, who would take charge of petitions to parliament about emancipation and other grievances; support to the extent of £15,000 per year would be given to the liberal press of Dublin and London to enable it to counter the Orange press; £15,000 was to be set aside for the legal protection of Catholics assailed by Orangemen; £5,000 was to be given to Catholic schools to enable them to compete with the proselytizing schools conducted and financed by the Kildare Place Society; and £5,000 was to pay for the education of priests to serve the Irish emigrants in America. The remainder, which was expected to be £5,000, would be applied to the provision of churches and parochial houses for priests in Ireland.[6]

The financial support for Catholic schools instantly appealed to the bishops and clergy. The 'Second Reformation' was making extensive provision for schools in which the scriptures were read without note or comment, or a Protestant interpretation was given to them, and the Catholic clergy found themselves under pressure to make Catholic schools available to prevent children from attending proselytizing schools. Help given to the poorer Catholic parishes for education won immediate local approval.[7]

4 Connolly, *Mass politics and sectarian conflict, 1823–30, NHI*, v, pp 84–95.   5 Ward, *The eve of Catholic emancipation*, iii, pp 92–3.   6 Geoghegan, *King Dan*, p. 203.   7 In the 'Second Reformation' of 1822–7 the evangelical preachers, who were making great efforts also to win over Catholic adults, had the support of prominent landlords: Farnham, Roden, Powerscourt, Lorton, Gosford (Whelan, *The Bible war in Ireland*, pp 134–70). Curtis lamented to Bishop O'Kelly the

Partly because of failures in parliament to obtain any relief and partly in imitation of the Irish example, the English Catholic Board responded to the suggestion of Lord Petre, one of its active members, and set up a new Catholic Association in 1823. Petre believed that Catholics needed a more vigorous body to conduct their affairs and 'repel in a temperate but decided manner the numerous calumnies which were thrown out against them'. The association would bond them together and act as a stimulus to their friends in parliament. Unlike the Catholic Board, which had been dominated by nobles and gentry, the association would be open to all who paid £1 per year, and clergy would be admitted free of charge. The vicars apostolic and the nobles, together with fifty elected members, would form the committee of the association, which was to meet quarterly. This rule was altered to permit monthly meetings, and, in addition, an open meeting would be held annually. Edward Blount, the secretary of the old board, was appointed secretary of the committee, and in a public letter of September 1823, he announced that their aim was to recover their rights as Britons under the constitution, to ensure that no slander remained in the Protestant press without a temperate reply, and to establish a Catholic daily paper.[8]

The Catholic Association in England, impressed by the efficiency and effectiveness of the Irish association, passed on its desire to act together for their common goal. Pleased, O'Connell agreed that the associations should act in concert, but worried that the English provincial Catholic associations were acting illegally by being linked with the national association. By forming themselves into independent societies, they could escape the charge of illegality. Though Orange branch societies had long existed with impunity, he was not sure that Catholic associations could escape the rigours of the law. He moved at a meeting of the Irish Catholic Association that he be allowed to make his reply to that effect, and his motion was accepted.[9] A month later, the committee of the English Catholic Association in London resolved that, in response to the wish of the Irish body for cooperation, it would 'unite all efforts for the advancement of the common cause'. The secretary was instructed to convey its thanks to the Irish association for its 'devoted zeal and successful efforts', and to work out the best way of advancing their interests and objectives.[10]

The Irish association, which highlighted the numerous grievances it wished to combat – the influence of Orangeism, the abuses of power by landlords' agents and tithe proctors, the biases of magistrates – soon won the approval of Archbishop Murray and Bishop Doyle.[11] Doyle's powerful

rejection by Irish members of parliament of the bishops' complaints of proselytism in the Bible schools. One of them claimed it was the duty of the Bible schools to give not only literary but also religious instruction (Curtis to O'Kelly, 3 May 1824, DrDa).   8 *CM*, June, Dec. 1823.   9 *FJ*, 4 Oct. 1824.   10 Ibid., 4 Dec. 1824.   11 In the administration of justice there were 257 posts

response to attacks on Catholicism and criticism of the 'monstrous estab-lishment' of the Church of Ireland in his *Vindication of the religious and civil liberties of the Irish Catholics* had made headlines at a national level. At the meeting of the association on 10 April, a lengthy letter from Doyle was read to loud applause. It detailed the educational situation in his diocese, in response to an attack against the attitudes of the clergy to education by a member of parliament. Defending the endeavours of the Catholic clergy to provide and supervise schools for their children, he rejected the charge that 'immoral and seditious books' had been used in their schools until replaced by tracts from the Kildare Place Society. And by commending parishioners for collecting the rent, the monthly fee of the association, he gave powerful encouragement to this initiative. Several other bishops also submitted accounts of the state of education in their dioceses.[12]

Doyle's support of the association boosted its standing in Ireland, but a highly injudicious remark in a letter to Alexander Robertson, an English MP, allowed opponents of emancipation in England to depict the Catholic church as untrustworthy in its attitude to the state, and its members therefore as not worthy of playing a part in parliament. Robertson had mentioned the possi-bility of 'ecumenical' union between the Catholic and Protestant churches as a possible solvent of political antagonisms. Doyle welcomed this suggestion, and with a totally unrealistic optimism, declared that such a union would not be difficult and that it should be attempted. He listed the major issues that would have to be examined (issues, which, in a much more ecumenical age, have still proved intractable), and he also passed a preposterous compliment about the king, whom he described as 'wise, liberal and enlightened'. But the fatal flaw of his argument was the claim that the Catholic priesthood would not help the state in a conflict with Irish Catholics:

> If a rebellion were raging from Carrickfergus to Cape Clear, no sentence of excommunication would ever be fulminated by a Catholic prelate or if fulminated, it would fall as Grattan once said of British supremacy, like a spent thunderbolt 'some gazed at it the people were fond to touch it'.[13]

Not only was this analysis wrong – Catholic prelates would certainly have used both spiritual and political means to save the lives of their people fighting legitimate authority against hopeless odds – but it was a totally

from that of lord lieutenant to sub-sheriff from which Catholics were barred by law. Of the 1,314 lower offices for which they were eligible by 1828 they held only 39. They were excluded from 653 offices of civil rank or honour such as MPs or officers of corporations, and of 3,033 minor offices to which they could aspire they held only 134 (Reynolds, *The Catholic emancipation crisis in Ireland, 1823–1829*, p. 65).   12 *FJ*, 31 May 1824.   13 *DEP*, 24 June 1824.

unnecessary comment. Had he limited himself to bewailing the condition of his people and called for redress, he would have made his point much more effectively and less provocatively. While many Catholics and church leaders, including Milner, were stunned by the proposal for the reunion of the churches, Archbishop Curtis sought to mend fences by writing to his old friend, the duke of Wellington, with whom he had been in occasional contact since they met in Salamanca in 1812.[14] Curtis assured the duke that in all the bishop's writings there was no passage 'as harsh, unreasonable or reprehensible'. He went on to claim that

> It has caused an extraordinary sensation here, but in general, a feeling of deep regret and of an irritation against the bishop, who among many other absurdities has clumsily placed the Roman Catholic prelates and clergy in a very awkward predicament ... But what gives us most pain is that the letter in question must be offensive to government ... It is possible your grace may here exclaim, Why do you not yourselves disavow silence, suspend, and put down such a man at once? You may depend, my lord duke, it will end in that, and very soon, if the aggressor does not come forward and make speedy, full and sincere atonement for his error.[15]

This stern condemnation of Doyle's imprudent démarche may not have been known much beyond the cabinet. But a group of five professors from Maynooth – led by the old Gallican Louis Delahogue, who was personally appalled by the remarks – issued a statement or manifesto proclaiming the duty of obedience to lawful authority and the allegiance of Maynooth to its sovereign. Doyle himself realized he had overstepped the line of obedience to constituted authority and, perhaps regretting making the proposal for 'reunion' without consulting the Roman authorities, penned a letter of resignation to the pope – but he did not send it. Doyle received some support from Peter Augustine Baines, the coadjutor to the vicar apostolic of the Western District, who agreed that 'Catholic bishops would no longer support oppression by ecclesiastical censure', but the Irish bishops maintained their silence. Doyle's comments were not easily forgotten, and the fact that he was known in English political circles meant that influential Englishmen remained wary of the trust that could be placed in Irish prelates.[16]

Not all clergy were such enthusiastic advocates of the association as Doyle, Coppinger and O'Shaughnessy, though the majority gradually took

---

14 Curtis, as rector of the Irish College in Salamanca, met Wellington there during his campaign against the French. The Irish students acted as guides to the British forces. 15 Quoted in McGrath, *The public ministry of Bishop James Doyle*, pp 24–5. 16 Ibid., pp 25–7.

part in the collection of the rents. One prominent priest who remained aloof was William Crolly, the parish priest of Belfast, who in February 1825 was appointed bishop of Down and Connor. He was afraid that some of the activities of the association would antagonize Presbyterians, who were sympathetic to emancipation, and thought that Catholics, who were a minority in many parts of Ulster, could not afford to irritate their neighbours. But where Catholics constituted substantial majorities the reaction of Protestants to the rents was of less concern.

Archbishop Curtis, who was always loath to say or do anything that might give offence to the government, made no public statement about the work of the association for several months. Then on 7 November 1824, rowing with the tide, he sent a letter of warm approval to the secretary. He maintained that he had always entertained strong hopes of its success, despite the misgivings of 'many respectable Catholics' and the tide of opposition it encountered from anti-Catholic militants. He noted that:

> even the free and voluntary contribution itself, called the Catholic rent, with the perfectly lawful, prudent and necessary objects on which it was proposed to be expended, were represented by an adverse party in an alarming point of view, but with so little sincerity, argument or common sense, that I did not delay a moment in subscribing my mite (the utmost then allowed but which I shall augment more than fourfold in future) to that salutary fund.

Though he recommended the rent to his clergy, he abstained from proposing it as 'an ecclesiastical measure' lest their opponents would regard it as 'odious and objectionable'. He explained that he never meddled in politics or secular affairs except when they fell indirectly into his sphere, and instancing examples of general principles, he claimed that 'religion as well as human prudence requires that all such affairs, how important soever they may be considered, should always be restrained and guided by great moderation and calmness, as well as with profound respect for government, and submission to the existing laws'.[17]

O'Connell immediately hailed Curtis' intervention as vitally important, being as it was the 'unbiased testimony and approbation of the venerable and most amiable and distinguished prelate', which 'speaks trumpet-tongued for the merits and utility of the association'.[18] He paid a glowing tribute to the contribution Curtis had made in Spain to the military successes of

17 *FJ*, 15 Nov. 1824. 18 A few days earlier O'Connell had hailed the 'venerable' bishop of Meath, Patrick Joseph Plunket, who had circularized his clergy to obtain their support for the rent. Plunket had then been bishop of Meath for 46 years (ibid., 4 Nov. 1824).

Wellington, and even alleged that he had 'by his influence and character, preserved a great portion of the British army from perishing by starvation'.[19]

Curtis shortly admitted to Bishop Poynter, with whom he had become a friendly correspondent, that he had come under pressure to declare his hand to the Catholic Association, and comment on the Catholic rent. Having spent most of his life in Spain and been well aware of the relationship of the church there to the king, his instinct was not to get involved in any movement that smelt of opposition to properly constituted authority. He had seen the expulsion of the Jesuits from Spain for no just reason and was wary of provoking the civil power in any way. But the force of public opinion pulled him along with it. Expressing satisfaction with the cooperation of the English association, he remarked that the Irish prelates wished to cooperate in a similar way with the vicars apostolic. He admitted that he had not sent any lists of the schools to the association,[20] and had not approved of that body asking for such lists from the clergy except through their respective prelates, 'whose exclusive province it was to judge, of the doctrine and propriety of instruction, so afforded'. He explained that the lay members of the association should have given 'ample testimony of the existence and salutary effects of such schools, and of exemplary labours of our clergy in promoting and directing them'. Assuring Poynter that he was most reluctant to appear 'in the public prints', he claimed that he had been forced to do so by:

> the atrocities and horrid imputations made on us, without a shadow of foundation, but daily teeming from a large portion of a venal and most corrupt press, as well as the proselyting [*sic*] attempts, and now latterly, the openly avowed mission, and incredible exertions of itinerant biblical fanatics ... that the ordinary duties of our ministry and private instruction are become insufficient without some more public appeals to stem this torrent of iniquity.

He invited Poynter to suggest expedient measures for the next session of parliament, as a resident of London would have better opportunities for finding out the most suitable policy. The Catholics of Ireland were coming under attack from many British papers, which confounded 'the unguarded expressions of a few intemperate individuals with those of the whole body', and labelled all advocates of parliamentary reform as partisans of the British radicals, who were supposed to harbour more obnoxious views than that of reform.[21]

19 Ibid., 15 Nov. 1824.   20 It had sought this information so that it could help the poorer parts of the country.   21 Curtis to Poynter, 24 Nov. 1824, WDA.

The hostility of the British and much of the Irish press, as Curtis claimed, had become intense and bitter. Though O'Connell and other leading officials of the Irish Catholic Association were sincere and profuse in protestations of loyalty to the crown, the association was depicted as disloyal and even revolutionary. Every one of its aims was fully constitutional. Nonetheless, the duke of Wellington, with a blend of pessimism and aggression, 'prophesied civil war, if the association were not put down', and Peel, the home secretary, also believed in the need to suppress it.[22] It was the very success of the association in collecting money that could be used in fighting against a biased judiciary and giving strength to the Catholics by uniting them to fight for their rights and improve their status by education that provoked excessive and unwarranted fears.

O'Connell was afraid that the association could be damned by the violence of those for whom it bore no responsibility. He believed that the police were paying agents provocateurs 'to prevail upon the wretched peasantry to continue and to revive the system of Ribbonism'.[23] These agents spread the rumour that the association secretly favoured violence. Consequently, he called for a committee to issue an address to the people repudiating Ribbonism and explaining that Ribbonmen were the greatest enemy of Ireland.[24]

Anxiety about being tainted with lawlessness was so great that the association devoted a petition to parliament presented by Francis Burdett to clearing its name of that and similar charges. Referring to accusations made in the *Morning Chronicle* and other newspapers, it repudiated the claim that the association had usurped the privileges of parliament, that it had taxed the country, and that it was exciting the people to hatred and contempt of the laws of the land and almost directly provoking them to take up arms.[25] However, the government got its chance to prosecute O'Connell when he claimed that if Ireland was provoked by persecution 'he wished that a new Bolivar may be found'.[26] The case failed, but Peel, the consistent and determined opponent of Catholic emancipation, had decided that the association should be banned. He told Goulburn, the chief secretary, an intransigent Tory concerned to allay the fears of his Irish Tory and Orange friends, that

22 Gash, *Mr Secretary Peel*, pp 389–94.   23 The Ribbonmen were a secret society of Catholics with vaguely nationalist objectives who, in Ulster, engaged in sectarian conflict with Protestants. A fall in agricultural prices in 1818–22 had led to sporadic violence in Munster, and a poor potato crop in 1821 had led to famine conditions in Connacht in 1822.   24 *FJ*, 14 June 1824. At the same meeting, another member of the association claimed that a work entitled *Pastorini*, designed to poison the minds of the English people, and containing monstrous calumnies on the Catholic religion, was circulating in the north of Ireland. *Pastorini* was in fact a work by Bishop Walmesley of the Western District predicting the violent destruction of Protestantism in 1821 or 1825. Different dates were given.   25 *FJ*, 22 June 1824.   26 Simón Bolivar (1783–1830) fought for the liberation of the north-western states of Latin America from Spanish rule.

he should put down the association when it took some illegal step, or have it suppressed by law. He favoured the latter course.[27]

The success of the association and an increase in the weekly rents it was collecting produced opposite reactions in O'Connell and the government in London. From £8 in the first week of February 1824, they had risen to £1,032 in the last week of November.[28] By March, 1825 they had brought in £16,836.[29] O'Connell feared that their campaign would be sullied by the outrages that the very oppression of the people was provoking. He hoped that the discipline created by the association would counteract such dangers, and that the rent collectors would serve 'as a police of affection, warning the people against spies, informers and incendiaries'. Unless there was a cessation of turbulence and outrage ministers would suppress the association.[30] One form of violence he continued to excoriate: that of the Orangemen. The British Catholic Association took up his case and wrote to the secretaries of the provincial associations, advising them to mention in their petitions 'the unpalatable conduct of the Orange party in Ireland'.[31]

In Rome, a new pope, Leo XII, was elected in April 1823. Cardinal Consalvi, the all-powerful secretary of state and master diplomat, who had long been an admirer of Poynter and a critic of Milner, was transferred from his influential office to the prefecture of the congregation of Propaganda. He died on 24 January 1824. Poynter bemoaned his loss 'as an almost irreparable blow'.[32] He had played a highly significant role in arranging church-state relations in several European countries since 1800, and was widely credited with the restoration of the Papal States to the pope at the Congress of Vienna, but had not had any success in furthering Catholic emancipation in Britain and Ireland. Though Gradwell, Poynter's agent, reported that the new pope esteemed the vicar apostolic of the London District, it does not seem likely that he could have known much about him. The pope interested himself in British politics and the movement for emancipation, but he had no adviser of Consalvi's calibre, with a knowledge of and curiosity about the British system and an instinct for realpolitik.

Archbishop Troy died on 11 May 1823. For the last five or six years of his life he had handed over the reins to Archbishop Murray. But for some thirty years he had been the spiritual leader of the Irish Catholics. Clever, learned and diligent, he was Rome's principal informant on Irish affairs and the channel of Roman instructions to the Irish church. He was the first prelate whose views and advice were sought by Dublin Castle, and, though accused

---

27 MacDonagh, *The hereditary bondsman*, pp 214–15.   28 Ibid., 213, *FJ*, 3 Dec. 1824.
29 Connolly, *Mass politics and sectarian conflict, 1823–30* in *NHI*, v, p. 84.   30 *FJ*, 14 Jan. 1825.
31 Ibid., 28 Dec. 1824.   32 Poynter to Collingridge, 11 Feb. 1824, CIDA. By a strange coincidence Richard Hayes died in Paris on the same day as Consalvi.

by critics of cultivating powerful officials at the castle, he regarded his contacts there as important means of advancing ecclesiastical interests.

Realizing that he could not exercise that kind of personal influence with the administration in London after 1801 and believing that Bishop Milner could play the role in London that he had played in Dublin, he had made the mistake of trying to interfere in English ecclesiastical affairs to bring about this arrangement. It was an intervention that created ill feeling between himself and Bishop Poynter, a relationship that was further damaged by the resolutions of the Irish bishops on the alleged veto contained in the fifth resolution and on Milner's part in opposing it. Troy was never at heart an opponent of the principle of royal involvement in episcopal elections, unlike several of his colleagues, and the repudiation of the fifth resolution by the Irish prelates was most likely not inspired by him. Nevertheless, he defended it and further antagonized Poynter in so doing.

He came under attack for his hostility to violence, both political and agrarian, and had to bear the brunt of Protestant reaction to the part Catholics played in the rebellion of 1798. A dedicated pastor, he made every effort to provide churches and schools for his parishes, and gave his money to the pastoral and charitable needs of his people.

II

The English Catholic Association was not deterred by accusations of violence in Ireland from drawing closer to its Irish counterpart. Branch associations were established in Manchester, Liverpool, Blackburn, Preston and Wigan. When it became known that this arrangement was illegal, the Catholics of the Midlands formed their own independent association. The central association, dominated by the aristocrats and gentry, was no longer the sole representative body of the Catholic people. Milner's reputation stood higher in the Midland and Northern associations than in London. The Midland association circulated tracts expounding Catholic beliefs and repudiating false views attributed to Catholics. The success of the Irish association helped draw it and the English association closer, and at a meeting in London in January 1825, sympathy was expressed for O'Connell who had been unsuccessfully charged with treasonous threats. The English association offered its most cordial congratulations to 'that zealous, efficient and undaunted champion of Catholic emancipation'.[33] The chairman insisted that the aim of all Catholics was to preserve peace and tranquillity as they sought emancipation. In the petition they drew up they repudiated the

33 *DEP*, 11 Jan. 1825.

accusations of the bishop of Peterborough that they 'owed a sort of divided allegiance', insisting that they owed allegiance only to the king, and gave 'a true spiritual reverence' to the pope. Tributes were paid to the eloquent advocacy of their case by O'Connell, Sheil and Bric,[34] and 'to the glorious conduct of the Irish people, who, by their pecuniary aid, had created a gigantic engine for the attainment of Catholic emancipation'.[35]

In February 1825, an address of the Catholics of Ireland to the people of England, signed by Nicholas Purcell O'Gorman, the secretary of the Irish association, firmly repudiated the charges of ignorance, idleness and seditiousness often made against the Irish people, and pointed out that their aim was the full removal of the penal code. In a similar address to the house of commons the vigour of the Orange party after the arrival of Wellesley as viceroy was deplored,[36] as the bill of 1823 about secret societies did not affect them.[37] Peel, the home secretary, who regarded as anamolous the possibility of admitting Catholics to a share in the essential Protestant character of the constitution under which they had enjoyed 'more liberty, more glory, more character and power' than any other country, opposed the association for its interference with the magistracy and its assumption of political authority.[38] Goulburn, the heavy-handed Tory chief secretary for Ireland, on 10 February 1825 introduced a bill to suppress the Catholic Association, charging that it represented a great part of the country, thereby violating the convention act of 1793, and claiming that it raised funds by 'an onerous and grievous tax', which was often collected by means of intimidation. Priests virtually compelled people to contribute by keeping records, not only of those who paid, but also of those who refused and who were consequently held up to scorn. The association interfered with the administration of justice by sending its agents to interfere in the courts of petty sessions, and attempts had been made to load the Protestant with crimes he might not have committed. To create the impression of impartiality, all societies which were affiliated to or corresponded with others, which excluded persons of any faith or who took oaths other than those prescribed by law, were included in the bill.[39]

In the house of lords, Donoughmore presented yet another petition from the Catholics asking for a restitution of their rights, signed by 100,000 faithful subjects, and Lord Lansdowne presented a petition from Protestant landowners, merchants and bankers of Dublin for the same purpose. O'Connell took the view that, if the Dissenters in the north of Ireland would join with them in a petition, they would ask the legislature to extend to the

34 John Bric, a former clerk of O'Connell's, was an active agent of the Irish Catholic Association. 35 *FJ*, 24 Jan. 1825. 36 Marquis Wellesley was viceroy from 1821 to 1828. He married an American Catholic in 1825. 37 *CM*, Jan. 1825. 38 Gash, *Mr Secretary Peel: the life of Sir Robert Peel to 1830*, pp 209, 393. 39 *Hansard 2*, xii, 168–86, 10 Feb. 1825.

Dissenters of England the privileges enjoyed by the Dissenters of Ireland,[40] but this view was not shared by Bishop Poynter. Other petitions were presented in both houses from the bishops of Exeter and Bath and Wells, the lord chancellor, and from the University of Cambridge and others, denouncing the violent language used by Catholics both in Britain and elsewhere which proved that their principles were hostile to religious liberty.[41]

Meetings spearheaded by parishes in Dublin were promptly called to object to Goulburn's legislation, and 'to raise their voices against the monstrous principle, of punishing a people, because of the tranquillity of their country, and their submission to the laws'. Speakers argued that the 'object' of the association was 'peace and good order' and that it had been punished in a vengeful way for 'applying its funds to the constitutional protection of the lower and poorer orders against magisterial oppression, delinquency, and factious violence'. On the other hand, Orange associations were fostered and protected, and had a general licence to do what they pleased.[42]

At a general meeting in Dublin, it was decided that parliament was to be petitioned against the suppression of the association. A deputation, including O'Connell, the Catholic archbishops and, if possible, the Catholic peers and gentry, was to proceed to London to plead the cause of the association at the bar of the house of commons.[43] When the deputation was first mooted Curtis suggested to Poynter that he convey to it 'such instructions and salutary precautions, as they may stand in great need of, to restrain and moderate the natural warmth and impetuosity of their dispositions and for avoiding any close connexion with men of dangerous principles, or rash politics'. He admitted that O'Connell was the only one he knew (and probably had him in mind when seeking Poynter's guidance) and praised him as a sincere and practical Catholic.[44]

The delegation, consisting of O'Connell, Killeen, Sheil and four others, was refused permission to speak in the house. But O'Connell and Sheil were invited to address the English Catholic Association, which met in the Freemason's Tavern. The duke of Norfolk, as chairman, rejoiced in the company of Catholic gentlemen from Ireland and England, and of Protestant friends 'whose cooperation would, he trusted, succeed in producing those concessions and benefits for the Catholics which were unjustly withheld from them'. Lord Stourton repudiated the aspersions cast upon the Catholic Association, maintained that the Catholics claimed the right of religious liberty and said that if they were in power they would

---

40 *FJ*, 29 June 1824. 41 *Hansard* 2, xii, 642–8, 936–7, 964–5, 1030, 1270–8, 1335, 24 Feb., 7, 9, 15, 28 Mar., 4 Apr. 42 *FJ*, 14 Feb. 1825. 43 Ibid., 17 Feb. 1825. 44 Curtis to Poynter, 17 Dec. 1824, WDA.

extend to Protestants what the Catholics sought from them. Blount, the secretary, read their resolution claiming that all peoples had a right to worship God according to conscience. O'Connell spoke for three hours, reviewing the grievances of Catholics and the consequences of the penal laws, and was loudly and robustly cheered. He explained that he had come to England to appeal to the common sense, the honesty and the generosity of the British people. Referring to the promise of liberty of conscience made by King William to Irish Catholics, he described it as 'a lasting memorial of Irish honour and of English shame'. He paid tribute to George III but noted that their kind reception of George IV had been repaid by 'the rejection of their rights'.[45] The Catholic nobles and others entertained O'Connell and his friends lavishly and generously. He proudly recounted the dinners hosted by Henry Brougham and the duke of Norfolk: at the first he sat near three dukes, and at the second there were four dukes, four earls, six other peers and two baronets present.[46]

A few days previously, Sir Francis Burdett had moved that the house of commons resolve itself into a committee to consider the state of the laws by which oaths and declarations were required to be taken as a qualification for office and whether it was expedient to allow them as they affected Catholics. In cooperation with Plunket, the attorney general, he then started work on a bill to give effect to this motion. O'Connell was invited to work with them. In it, a more acceptable form of scrutinizing candidates for the episcopate was put forward: a commission of bishops was to be appointed to examine the loyalty of the candidates proposed, to report to the government if they found any whose loyalty could not be guaranteed and to ensure that foreigners were excluded from the prelacy. O'Connell, coming under pressure from English advocates of emancipation to make concessions to the prejudices of legislators, agreed to the addition of two 'wings' to the bill. These 'wings', which were to prove highly controversial, involved the disfranchisement of the forty-shilling freeholders and the payment of stipends to the clergy.[47] The 'genteel atmosphere' of the lobby in parliament

45 *FJ*, 1 Mar. 1825 and *CM*, Feb. 1825. At a meeting in Dublin several months later, O'Connell stated that his hopes for emancipation were based 'on the royal word of the present king, who in the year 1805, declared to Lord Kenmare his firm conviction that the emancipation of the Catholics was a measure due to justice as well as policy' (*FJ*, 31 Oct. 1825).   **46** MacDonagh, *The hereditary bondsman*, pp 215–16. On his way home later, he addressed the British Midland (Catholic) Association and was given a very warm reception (*DEP*, 5 May 1825).   **47** The *Freeman's Journal*, which was always critical of O'Connell, published an anonymous piece on 7 June 1826 sardonically called 'Mr O'Connell's consistencies', in which it was claimed that from 1810 onwards O'Connell was the most determined opponent of any arrangement by which the crown might be brought into contact with the clergy. In 1823, he described Dr Troy as the 'pliant old Trojan' because he seemed disposed to discuss how arrangements could be made to meet the wishes of parliament. But by March 1825, he wished to bind the clergy to the state by a 'golden link'. Bishop Doyle was annoyed with O'Connell for claiming his support for payment of the

and Norfolk's dinner parties softened the 'demagogue ... [and made him] amenable to the compromise', which seemed so essential in the light of English party politics, if emancipation were to pass.[48]

A few days after O'Connell met Plunket and Burdett to draft the bill, he was examined by the parliamentary committee investigating the state of Ireland. There he elaborated on his attitude to the 'wings'. He thought that raising the voting qualification to £5 or £10 would not cause dissatisfaction. The forty-shilling freeholders were under the power of the landlords and in some counties they could be sold as regularly as cattle. Questioned about state payment of the Catholic clergy, he declared that, if there was full equality for Catholics, 'it would be very desirable in that case that the government should possess a legitimate influence over the Catholic clergy, that in all relations of the state with foreign powers the government should be as secure of the Catholic clergy as they are now of the Protestant clergy'. With emancipation, the clergy would be ready and willing to receive state provision; without it, they would have been supposed to have sold their religion, to have 'trafficked' for themselves and attached themselves to a government the people regarded as hostile.

O'Connell, who had once violently denounced any form of veto by the government on the appointment of bishops, had mellowed considerably in his opposition to ministerial interference. He favoured a system of domestic nomination whereby electors in the Irish dioceses would choose three names to submit to the pope, from which he would choose one. He did not approve of passing those names to the government with a right of rejection, but with the successful working of an act of emancipation, the government could make known to Rome its objection to particular candidates, and he approved of the suggestion that it might have an agent in Rome to conduct this business.[49] His 'concession' on these issues was strenuously challenged by John Lawless, a prominent journalist. The board of Catholics, which was to report to the government on the characters of persons seeking ecclesiastical promotion and to provide details of their backgrounds, was allegedly to be 'an innocent, harmless establishment, exercising a wholesome control' over the clergy. Lawless, on the contrary, charged that it would be 'a source of perpetual hostility – a species of ecclesiastical inquisition into the political as well as moral conduct of every Catholic clergyman, and a powerful instru-

clergy. He later declared that, if the prelates approved of that measure, he would not cause dissension, but 'sooner than that my hand should be soiled by it, I would lay down my office at the feet of him who conferred it, for if my hand were to be stained with government money, it should never grasp a crozier, or a mitre ever afterwards be fitted to my brow' (Fitzpatrick, *Correspondence of Daniel O'Connell*, i, pp 114–15).   **48** Reynolds, *The Catholic emancipation crisis in Ireland, 1823–1829*, p. 40.   **49** Report of the select committee of the house of lords on the state of Ireland, 4, 9 Mar. 1825, HC 1825 (181, 521) 107–33, 123–71.

ment of corruption in the hands of an artful minister'.[50] Ironically, Lawless was expressing opinions O'Connell had long held, for O'Connell's great fear of the veto was that it would produce an episcopate that the government regarded as politically reliable and respectable, and which might try to advance the political views of the government against those of its own people. Lawless was far from alone in expressing bewilderment at what was regarded as O'Connell's volte-face.

The Irish association was formally wound down on 18 March. Observing all legal requirements, the funds it held were transferred to Lord Killeen, who was to hold them in a non-official capacity, and the quest for emancipation was to be confined to separate general meetings and separate societies lasting no more than fourteen days. The bishops and priests were thanked for their support, and O'Connell was to be informed that he continued to enjoy the confidence of the members of the association in his 'splendid and disinterested exertions on behalf of the Catholic people of Ireland'.[51] He later denounced the law forbidding the association to exist as spurious and meretricious:

> We consider the law of the suppression of the Catholic Association as the greatest injury and insult that Catholic people have ever sustained. For every other enactment, however perfidious or atrocious, there were found some plausible though elusive pretexts. For this nothing could be discovered but the example of the unconstitutional law of 1793, and some idle and weak pretences, to influence the conduct of mere children.[52]

The Catholic Association of Britain had also come to recognize and acknowledge O'Connell's 'splendid and disinterested services' on its behalf as well.[53] Several of its leading members had once, like Bishop Poynter, regarded him as a dangerous separatist, who was using the campaign for emancipation for improper and even revolutionary ends. The distance that had separated the campaigners for emancipation in England and Ireland had been bridged, and both parties would henceforth march forward together.[54]

---

50 *FJ*, 18 Mar. 1825. The paper blamed Lawless for entering unnecessarily on this discussion, and remarked that his eccentricity and the warmth with which he promulgated his opinion was well known.   51 Ibid., 19 Mar. 1825.   52 Ibid., 17 Nov. 1825.   53 Bishop Baines, the recently appointed coadjutor of the Western District, apologizing to the secretary of the association for his inability to attend a meeting, expressed the hope that it would continue to work with vigour and zeal, and 'continue to cooperate as far as possible with the great association in Ireland' (Baines to Edward Blount, 16 Jan. 1825, WDA).   54 O'Connell, reporting his oratorical success to his wife, quoted Lord Stourton as saying that neither Pitt nor Fox was his equal, and Charles Butler as saying that he had heard nothing like it since the days of Lord Chatham (Fitzpatrick, *Correspondence of Daniel O'Connell*, i, p. 104, about 28 Feb. 1825).

Burdett's relief bill passed the house of commons with a comfortable majority of twenty-seven. Not only was O'Connell optimistic about the proximate success of emancipation, but its strongest and most persistent opponents, Lord Liverpool and Peel, the prime minister and home secretary, became pessimistic about the future. Both threatened to resign, and then Liverpool attacked Catholics' questionable allegiance and the baneful influence of their clergy.[55] O'Connell's optimism was to be brutally punctured in the house of lords. The king's brother, the duke of York, appealed yet again to the coronation oath as constituting an inviolable impediment to the granting of emancipation, and his influence helped turn enough waverers against the bill to ensure its defeat on 18 May. O'Connell felt humiliated and betrayed. The concession of the wings had been in vain.

The duke of Wellington, who had always opposed Catholic emancipation on the grounds that Catholics were subservient to their priests – who were loyal to the pope rather than to the king – feared that there could be civil war in Ireland if the Catholic Association were not put down, and felt that the government would have to come to terms with the Catholics. He believed that the opportunity of taking practical steps had presented itself. A settlement could not be made between the government and the Catholics alone, as they were under the control of Rome. The solution was therefore to be found by agreement with the Vatican in the form of a concordat. In other European countries, such agreements had successfully settled the relationships between church and state, and the power of the church had been diminished. Neither Liverpool nor Peel was prepared to abandon their support for Protestant supremacy.

Wellington's plan for a concordat was not properly worked out. There is no evidence that he had studied the conditions and demands which were normally involved in agreements of this nature between states and the Holy See. The significance of his initiative was that he had realized that, however much he may have disliked emancipation, it could not be resisted indefinitely.[56] He got some support from Bishop Doyle, who in a public letter suggested that the government and the church should together propose domestic nomination to Rome.

Dismayed and disgusted by the defeat of Burdett's bill, the normally placid archbishop of Armagh, Curtis, unburdened himself to Bishop Poynter. His friendship with the vicar apostolic of the London District had been strengthened by the hospitality which Poynter had recently shown him and his colleagues, Murray and Doyle, when they were in London giving evidence to the select committee of the house of commons on the state of

55 Gash, *Lord Liverpool*, p. 234. 56 Muir, *Wellington: Waterloo and the fortunes of peace, 1814–1852*, pp 139–40, 220–7.

Ireland. He supposed that Poynter's feelings had, like his own, been deeply wounded:

> with those of the whole Catholic body, and many others of this country, that have seen with utter disappointment, dismay and irritation, not alone, the unexpected rejection of the C. relief bill by the lords, but still more, the intolerant and repulsive sentence pronounced from a high official quarter, of the eternal reprobation and exclusion of that boon, unless we renounce the religion we profess, which is declared incompatible with our emancipation.[57] And all this decisive anathema daringly founded, on the weak clumsy repetition of the same old, and often convicted bigotry, that canting innovators have been for ages croaking in their national mud.

He asked in surprised indignation how the premier could have avowed such sentiments, given that he had been distinguished for 'his manly, fair and statesmanlike line of moderation even in his former speeches against us?' (The question doubtless surprised Poynter, who would have had no illusions about Lord Liverpool's feelings.) He wondered how a marquis could challenge Catholics to rebel at that time when they could be conveniently fought.[58] What he feared more than the refusal of emancipation were the denunciations and insults 'calculated and seemingly meant, to irritate, and drive a too-warm and high-spirited people, to despair and to fatal extremities'. The marquis and his friends miscalculated the effects of their provocative language if they imagined that the Irish would be quiet in the face of overwhelming force. He was greatly concerned that the 'ungovernable party' would not take wise precaution into account, and under experienced leaders might go very far.

He begged Poynter to recommend to their friends in parliament to have something done to heal these wounded feelings. And he asked him to add his thanks to those who had advocated relief for Catholics, mentioning in particular the duke of Devonshire, lords Lansdowne and Grey. He was particularly grateful to the duke of Norfolk for his kindness, and extolled Poynter's 'condescension' and 'seasonable display' of Christianity in assisting at the recent consecration of Milner's coadjutor.[59]

In his reply, Poynter urged the necessity of bearing their disappointment

---

57 Lord Liverpool, the prime minister, backed the duke of York's claims about the coronation oath. At a meeting at which the duke of Norfolk complained of being accused of having a divided allegiance, O'Connell accused Liverpool of insulting them with his nonsense about the coronation oath (*DEP*, 26 May 1825).   58 Lord Anglesey had challenged Irish Catholics to rebel, as the time was ripe to defeat them.   59 Curtis to Poynter, 25 May 1825, WDA.

with patience and resignation, and Curtis thanked him for this advice, which corresponded to his own opinions. He was hopeful that at the general Catholic meeting arranged for Dublin on 8 June nothing of a violent tendency would be proposed, and under this heading he included the advice given by Wiliam Cobbett and 'British Radical Reformers' that they should join the reform movement. He would not wish to gain emancipation:

> by such means of resistance and intimidation, or by any other than the lawful channel marked out by duty, honour and conscience; and it may, at length, be quietly obtained, when our separated brethren become more convinced, than they are at present, that we deserve it, and that they would rather secure, than injure their own interest, by granting it.

Curtis then went on to recall the painful shock he and his colleagues had experienced when Plunket, in Poynter's presence, had insisted on the expediency of making a suitable provision for the Irish clergy, but had refused to consider extending the same concession to the British prelates and clergy. The attorney general had justified this distinction by reference to the difference between their church leaders: the Irish had canonically instituted bishops, whereas the English had vicars apostolic removable at any time by the pope. Curtis suggested that the legislature could be easily convinced that such an objection was of no practical consequence but, if not, the Holy See would doubtless constitute a hierarchy with an archbishop in London and make the other vicars apostolic diocesan bishops.[60]

Among those examined by the select committee of the house of commons on the state of Ireland in March 1825, along with Curtis, Murray and Doyle, were bishops Kelly of Tuam and Magauran of Ardagh. Leading figures in political life, including O'Connell, and prominent bishops and clergy of the established church were also questioned. The prelates were queried about papal power, the appointments of bishops, payment of the clergy and the correspondence of churchmen with Rome. They again stressed the limitation of papal authority to the purely spiritual sphere, emphasizing their full civil allegiance to their sovereign and the inability of the pope to absolve subjects from that allegiance. They objected to any interference by the crown in the appointment of bishops. Doyle and Murray claimed that Protestant rulers were never permitted to appoint bishops directly or to exercise a veto over appointments, but they agreed that compromises had been found in Prussia and Russia. Doyle and Murray saw no problem in preventing foreigners from being appointed.

60 Ibid., 6 June 1825.

Asked about state payment of the clergy, they all agreed that in the absence of emancipation it was unacceptable. Though they preferred the voluntary system, they were prepared to discuss state payment, if it were part of the concession of emancipation. Curtis maintained that state provision would be desirable as long as people did not think that the church depended on the state or that the government might later rule the church. If no attempt were made to overturn or impair religion, such payment would be a great boon. Strangely, neither Doyle nor Murray had serious objections to the submission of official Roman documents – bulls, briefs and rescripts – to the scrutiny of the government, provided highly personal and confidential material of a spiritual nature were excluded. They both agreed that Quarantotti, for whom they had little respect, had overstepped the bounds of his authority in conceding a veto to the government in 1814 over the appointments of bishops.[61]

Doyle put very strong emphasis on the duty of allegiance by declaring that, should the pope interfere with the rights of the king, the bishops would oppose him with every means in their power, even making use of their spiritual authority to do so. He was also prepared to oppose the exclusive right of the pope to appoint the bishops in Ireland by advocating domestic nomination based on a concordat and, in effect, bringing about an episcopate over which the pope would have as little control as he had in many of the Continental countries.[62] He also maintained that they should not be prepared to accept any document from Rome that would 'entrench on our rights as a national church'.

Doyle's comments reassured some of those in parliament who were dubious about papal influence, but Gradwell reported from Rome that they did not impress a few prelates there, who censured what he had said about the pope's power and oaths. Those who baulked at the pledge not to disturb or weaken the Protestant religion doubtless disliked any suggestion of weakening or diminishing papal control of the church. But when Gradwell told the pope about a favourable change in public opinion towards the Catholics and the good impression created by Doyle's views on the payment of the clergy, he was glad to hear the pope speak approvingly of the good

---

61 Reports of the select committee on the state of Ireland, HC (129) viii, 173–264; ix, 223–58. McGrath, *The public ministry of Bishop James Doyle*, pp 36–8.   62 Doyle's plan, which would have had the pope confirm the choice made in Ireland, put a greater limit on the pope's input into the election of bishops than that which had been proposed by Archbishop Murray in 1816–17. According to Murray's proposals, the chapter, having taken an oath to choose no one disloyal to the king, would select three names which would be passed to the bishops of the province. They, in turn, would swear to accept only loyal and suitable candidates and the three names would be sent to Rome. The pope would then choose one of the three (Murray to Litta, 28 Oct. 1816, APF, SC(Irlanda) 20, ff 502r–503v).

sense, ability and integrity the Irish prelates had shown before the parliamentary committees.[63]

Curtis passed on an account of Burdett's bill to Cardinal della Somaglia, Consalvi's successor. Claiming that emancipation was soon to be conceded, he explained that the loyalty of candidates for the episcopate was to be attested by a commission consisting of bishops, and that the government was anxious that the clergy accept state pensions. The commission of bishops was to examine all papal documents to check if they contained anything contrary to the laws or supreme civil authority and though it was known that this was an odious imposition, nevertheless it was deemed necessary to calm Protestant fears. They had been asked if they would accept a nuncio from the Holy See, and consequently Curtis sought guidance from Rome.[64]

According to Lord Burghersh, the British minister to the court of the Grand Duchy of Tuscany at Florence, the issue of state pensions of the clergy had been raised with him during discussions in Rome. He reported to Canning, the foreign secretary, that in meetings with the cardinal and other influential persons, he had learned that the court of Rome 'would be anxious to reduce [the Irish clergy] to more orderly conduct' towards the government and its own authority. To do so, it would agree to the payment of the priesthood and a renunciation of the ancient establishment, would grant 'a power in the election of bishops and other church dignitaries' and would then issue a bull which would override opposition. The court of Rome, he continued, would welcome this connection, which 'would lead the Catholic priest to look to the approbation of government as a means of advancement'.[65] If the statues which restricted communication with the Vatican were removed, it could establish a link with the British state, which would enable it to bring the clergy and 5 or 6 million Catholics to a new relationship.

The Irish bishops and clergy regarded the campaign of the Catholic Association for emancipation as a struggle for social justice, but in Rome public participation in political movements by clergy was regarded as improper. It was held that the clergy should stay in their churches. Cardinal Fransoni spelt out this obligation to Archbishop Crolly in 1844: 'ministers of the king of peace ... should not be involved in secular matters but should concern themselves with furthering among their people quiet tranquillity

---

63 Gradwell to Poynter, 17 May 1825, WDA. 64 Curtis to Cardinal della Somaglia, 15 Apr. 1825, APF, SC(Irlanda), 24, ff 452r–453r. 65 Burghersh to Canning, 2 Apr. 1825. NA FO 79/44. Burghersh sought Canning's pardon for entering upon 'a subject so replete with difficulties'. He did not make clear to whom he had spoken. Consalvi might well have made comments like these but he had ceased to be secretary of state in 1823 and had died in 1824. Burghersh may have been referring to meetings before 1823. It seems unlikely that Cardinal della Somaglia, Consalvi's successor, would have spoken about exchanging ancient endowments for payment of the clergy or threatened to override opposition by a ruling from Rome.

and peace ... and inculcate due obedience to the temporal order in civil affairs and preach only Christ crucified'.[66]

Burghersh most likely did hear complaints from 'the influential persons' at the Vatican about the behaviour of the Irish clergy. English newspapers had been criticizing them for their participation in organizing the Catholic rent, and rumours about such activity would have been badly received in Rome.[67]

The British Catholic Association, though disappointed with the rejection of Burdett's bill, was not defeatist. It was determined to carry on the fight for relief. At a meeting in early June, it was decided to appeal for more money to fund the publication and circulation of pamphlets promulgating the Catholic cause. Already, numerous tracts and a recent speech by O'Connell at Birmingham had been published. The association planned to create a special fund and to seek contributions to enable it to extend this work. A resolution was passed calling for the establishment of more associations in other parts of England. It was agreed that the union and harmony of the Catholics of England and Ireland should be promoted. The support of the Unitarians for liberty of conscience for all was welcomed. One member optimistically claimed that their cause was gathering strength daily and the only question was 'whether the claims should be granted today or tomorrow'.[68] Towards the end of the year, the British association announced that it had circulated some 90,000 tracts, most of which were replies to those of Bible societies attacking Catholicism.[69]

In Dublin, Catholics prepared for a general meeting, and O'Connell adverted to the resolutions of sixty-five peers who had met at the duke of Buckingham's, and, in calling for honest legislation for Ireland, had recommended that Catholics act with unanimity, firmness and temperance. Temperance, O'Connell explained, meant keeping within the law. Firmness in pursuing their goal would be shown by holding simultaneous meetings in all parishes before the next session of parliament, to prepare their petitions.[70] In July 1825, the New Catholic Association was established. Those matters which had not been declared beyond the legal compass of the former association were to be dealt with by the new one – especially works of charity, education, agriculture and evictions. The new association would not deal with political questions and would not petition parliament. Each aspiring member was to submit his name to the secretary before 1 November and pay

66 Fransoni to Crolly, 15 Oct. 1844, APF, LDB 331, ff 794r–795v.   67 Canning to Burghersh, 20 Apr. 1826, ibid., 79/47/1. Burghersh passed on some further information to the Foreign Office, including a copy of the concordat between 'the court of Rome and the King of the Netherlands', of 18 June 1827 (FO 79/49/133). The pope assured Burgersh that if he could be of any service to the English government, 'he should most anxiously desire the opportunity'. 68 *FJ*, 3 June 1825. 69 *DEP*, 15 Nov. 1825. 70 Ibid., 13 July 1825.

an annual subscription of £1. The clergy were admitted to membership free of charge.[71] As they had fourteen days to draw up grievances, Richard Lalor Sheil also called for the nobility, clergy, merchants and barristers to meet in the new metropolitan church in Dublin. The Catholic peers of England might also be asked to attend, and he wondered would not such a great assembly be attended with 'signal consequences'.[72] Though O'Connell continued to rail against the suppression of the Catholic Association as 'a causeless and despotic addition to the oppression of the penal code', he remained optimistic.[73] He had the prohibition of Goulburn's bill forbidding the association to hold meetings for more than fourteen days to ensure that the new association kept within the law. He had done what the government feared and, in effect, had beaten it at its own game.

III

The New Catholic Association set about pursuing its goals with vigour and determination. An indication of the closeness which O'Connell had helped to create between the Catholic associations of Ireland and England came in the invitation to the duke of Norfolk to preside at the meeting of the Irish association on 10 January 1826. Enjoying a much higher rank in the peerage than Fingall or Killeen, and possessed of vast estates in England, the officials of the association thought that he would be a more impressive figurehead at their proceedings than the Catholic peers who customarily presided. He refused the invitation, pointing out that he had no property or title in Ireland, but assured them that he would help in any way he could.[74] O'Connell noted in advance of this meeting that the English association had made no decision about petitioning, but urged Irish Catholics to meet soon to draw up their petitions. He suggested that all the parishes of Ireland should meet simultaneously on three successive occasions, and predicted that they would thereby constitute such a moral force as would convince the ministry that it would be unwise to exclude them from the rights enjoyed by their fellow subjects.[75]

He continued to excoriate Lord Liverpool, the prime minister, for his hostility to Catholic relief. Referring to his charge that the allegiance of Catholics was divided, he maintained that 'the man was not fit for Christian society who charged Catholic millions with perjury, and yet such a man continued as prime minister of England'. Commenting on the condition of many Irish poor, he complained that it was a sad country 'when the potatoes of the wretched cottier are tithed to support the indolent, bloated man of God'.[76] He regretted that among the English people there was 'the worst of

71 *FJ*, 25 July 1825. 72 *DEP*, 22 Aug. 1825. 73 Ibid., 31 Oct. 1825. 74 *FJ*, 4 Jan. 1826.
75 Ibid., 9, 21 Jan. 1826. 76 Ibid., 17 Jan. 1826.

ignorance with respect to the Catholic question; not merely negative ignorance, but prejudice and calumnies against the Catholic religion, and its professors [*sic*], have been instilled into their minds at all ages, and through all mediums, from the ponderous folio to the two–penny schoolbook'.[77]

O'Connell was somewhat disappointed at the inactivity of some English Catholics. Those whom he had met the previous year were the rich aristo-crats or from the comfortable middle class, and he mistakenly thought that they constituted a larger proportion of the Catholic population than they did. O'Connell believed that the English Catholics should have exploited the press for the purposes of propaganda:

> there was a great want of energy amongst the English Catholics, many of whom were exceedingly affluent, and almost all in comfortable circumstances; and they should tax themselves and make some sacrifice to obtain a legitimate influence in that great organ of public opinion – the press; they should avail themselves of those opportunities when shares of the English papers are at market, and obtain the opportunity of disseminating their wants and wishes, their political objects, their religious principles and they should appeal to the gratitude the English nation should owe to their Catholic ancestors, who procured them their enviable constitution.[78]

It was strange that O'Connell should have suggested that the memory of a Catholic ancestral past would have moved the English people, when he ought to have known that most Protestants heartily repudiated the Catholic elements in their past. Historical sentiment of that kind held no attraction for them.

In contrast to O'Connell, Blount was pleased with the activity of the English association. Inside the last three months, it had distributed some 32,000 publications to counter the prejudice existing against them and at the meeting on 31 Jan. 1826, reference was made to the 'criminal apathy' of the nobility and gentry.[79] At their meetings in London, English Catholics complained of their difficulties in raising money. The nobility, who had contributed £258, did not subscribe as generously as their resources would have suggested. The poorer people had given £116.[80]

O'Connell was pleased with the pastoral letter the Irish bishops issued on 25 January. A third of it was given over to the plan for national education, which a commission of inquiry had recently produced. Another third concerned mistaken views about the sacraments and devotions. The final

---

77 Ibid., 27 Jan. 1826.   78 *FJ*, 27 Jan. 1826.   79 *CM*, Feb. 1826.   80 Ibid., 3 June 1825.

third dealt with matters which figured in the campaign for emancipation. The bishops explained that they would not agree to a state provision for the clergy until their people had been emancipated. They pointed out that:

> at no period can we accept any such legal provision unless our acceptance of it be found by us consistent with the independence of our church and the integrity of its discipline as well as with the cordial union and affectionate attachment which has hitherto subsisted between the Catholic clergy and that faithful people from whose generous contributions we and our predecessors have, for centuries, derived our support.

Then to remove the false imputations, which, they believed, were frequently cast upon their faith and discipline, they emphasized the fact that the Catholic religion was 'reconcilable with every regular form which human governments may assume'. They then formally dealt with the questions of Catholic allegiance to the British state, which had been a source of contention for decades.

The Catholics of Ireland, the bishops solemnly declared, detested as unchristian and impious the belief that it was lawful to murder or destroy anyone on the grounds of heresy, or that an immoral or wicked act could ever be justified under the pretence that it was done for the good of the church or in obedience to any ecclesiastical power. Furthermore, Catholics were not required to believe that the pope was infallible or to obey any order that was immoral, irrespective of the authority giving it. They also proclaimed full allegiance to King George and repudiated the charge that princes excommunicated by the pope or by any ecclesiastical authority might be deposed or murdered by their subjects. The pope, they added, had no temporal or civil jurisdiction within the realm. Having made this declaration without any mental reservation or dispensation from Rome, the prelates expressed their mystification that they could be charged with a divided allegiance towards their sovereign. Rejecting any engagement to overturn 'the arrangement of property in this country', Catholics also excluded any intention of subverting 'the present Church establishment for the purpose of substituting a Catholic establishment in its stead', and of exercising any privilege to which they might be entitled 'to disturb and weaken the Protestant religion and Protestant government'. In conclusion, the bishops expressed their readiness to provide 'authentic and true information upon all subjects connected with the doctrine and discipline' of their church.[81]

This was the first formal pronouncement by all the bishops of Ireland on

---

81 *FJ*, 21 Feb. 1826. The address was dated 25 Jan. 1826.

the disputed issues of loyalty, allegiance and obedience to their sovereign. In the various oaths that had been linked to the petitions and bills for emancipation, similar expressions of loyalty had been used, and attempts had been made to scotch the ancient prejudices and shibboleths that many Protestants associated with the Catholic church. The pastoral offered to those fearful of Catholic power all the reasonable assurances they could require, and it had comforting words for those who feared that their church or property would be threatened by Catholic emancipation. Milner had baulked at a previous pledge not to disturb and weaken the Protestant religion; the bishops here pledged themselves fully to this policy. Apart from tackling the thorny issue of state interference in the process of episcopal appointments, the bishops had dealt fully with the other disputed issues. At the next meeting of the Catholic Association, the suggestion that the pastoral be circulated was made, and a vote of thanks was proposed to Bishop Doyle, who had written most of it, for his valued exposition of Catholic doctrine.[82] The bishops, in fact, had made use of the terms employed in various oaths and given their official approval to them. Michael Blake, the rector of the Irish College in Rome, had the pastoral carefully translated into Italian and added his own explanatory notes. The pope disliked some elements of the letter and Cardinal Cappellari, the prefect of Propaganda (and a future pontiff of strongly conservative views), believed that the pope was being required to countenance a suspicion of ordering or demanding obedience to something that was unjust, immoral or wicked.[83]

Writing to Poynter about their statement of Catholic faith and political principles, Curtis apologized for not consulting Poynter before their pastoral had been issued, and assured him that he had the highest opinion of his 'learning and prudence'. As it concerned matters of interest to all the Catholics of the British empire, the Irish prelates had hoped that Poynter or one of his colleagues would have attended their meeting, but because some of their friends in parliament had called on them urgently to give them a clear and brief explanation of 'certain points ... of Catholic faith and political principles', they had felt obliged not to delay their response. Copies had been sent to all members of both houses of parliament. Though happy with the reception of their document, the archbishop felt that it would have carried much more weight, had it also borne the imprimatur of the vicars apostolic of Britain, and he feared that the absence of their names might be misinterpreted.

He then referred to a letter of Robert Wilmot Horton, a member of parliament, to the duke of Norfolk, a copy of which had been passed to him by Lord Killeen. Assuming it had been written before the statement of the

82 Ibid., 27 Feb. 1826.   83 Blake to Murray, 31 Dec. 1826, DDA.

Irish bishops was published, he had sent an answer to Killeen for Norfolk, but was disappointed by subsequent letters of Horton complaining that Protestants did not know what Catholic faith and political principles entailed. He found this baffling in view of the clarifications they had recently given, as well as those made at the parliamentary inquiry in the previous year. They had accepted the decisions of the Catholic universities on loyalty to the state forty years previously, and continued to take the oath of allegiance. Perhaps Horton awaited an authoritative and combined reply from all the bishops of Britain and Ireland. In the meantime Curtis wondered why Charles Butler, who was 'always ready to enter the lists on less momentous occasions', had remained silent.[84] Poynter then, at the behest of the British Catholic Association, also drew up a statement on the beliefs of Catholics. All the vicars apostolic of England and Scotland signed the statement, which, in addition to its explanation of their loyalty to the king, disclaimed any intention of infringing the rights or property of the established church.[85]

Poynter replied to Curtis' letter and enclosed copies of his pamphlet for all the Irish bishops. Though delivery was delayed by the courier, Curtis was very grateful for both the letter and pamphlets, and explained that the bishops had not sent theirs to Britain in case it would have been regarded as 'a sort of dictation'. He may well have heard from Murray that Poynter had objected to 'dictation' from Troy. He was also afraid that their statement might have been viewed in Rome as something that should not have been published without prior approval. Praising the English contribution as 'exact, elegant and accommodated to the present exigencies', he added that the Irish prelates joined cordially with Poynter in 'glorying and triumphing in this impressive and invincible production'. Hence they adopted it in preference to their own.

Surprisingly, Curtis then proceeded to reflect on emancipation and to express his opinion that it was not 'the whole or even the chief feature, of the Catholic question'. The Catholic cause consisted principally:

> in convincing the public, high and low, that our doctrine is perfectly sound in theory, and safe in practice. Without such persuasion, we can hardly expect a full restitution of our civil rights, nor would it be of almost any advantage. For we are already, long since, admissible by law to many rights, from which, however, we are constantly excluded in practice, on the old pretence of our dangerous and unsocial principles. We must then effectively prove these charges to be groundless, and unjust; and I think we have done so, to some purpose.[86]

84 Curtis to Poynter, 17 Apr. 1826, WDA. 85 *CM*, June 1826 and Ward, *The eve of Catholic emancipation*, iii, pp 169–70. 86 Curtis to Poynter, 25 Sept. 1826, WDA.

Few Catholic activists, including the bishops, would have agreed with Curtis that convincing the public about the soundness of their doctrine was their priority. They would have felt that the public had been given as much evidence as it needed.

The British Catholic Association was anxious to rebut the groundless charges made against them. In an address to their Protestant fellow countrymen they drew attention to the declarations of the bishops in England and Ireland, and asked rhetorically if they were joined in a perfidious league to deceive their neighbours. They rejected the accusations of not keeping faith with heretics, of divided allegiance, of idolatry, of the deposing power of the pope and of his alleged authority to absolve anyone. They feared they were being punished for excesses in which they had played no part, and drew attention to the situation where 6 or 7 million people were deprived of the benefits of equal chances in life. They also complained of the proselytism which operated through premiums for apostasy. This appeal was signed by the leading members of the Catholic aristocracy – Norfolk, Surrey, Shrewsbury, Stourton, Kinnaird and Petre – and some sixty others. Copies of this address and of the bishops' address were sent to the royal family, the Anglican bishops, the heads of the universities and many others and 100,000 were distributed free of charge.[87]

By mid 1826, there was some optimism among the clergy and laity striving for emancipation. The responses of the Irish bishops at the parliamentary inquiry and the statements of both hierarchies on Catholic beliefs had cleared away some of the prejudices about Catholic doctrine and claims. The intervention of the duke of York in the house of lords had helped torpedo Burdett's bill and showed the power of the obstacles in the way of emancipation. Hope, however, was given a new boost by an election in Waterford.

87 *CM*, June 1826.

17

The Waterford election

I

Discussions at the Irish Catholic Association about the presentation to parliament of a further petition seeking emancipation took account of the possibility of an election. The decision to proceed with a petition was left in abeyance until the date of the election was made known. But a resolution was passed calling for support at the election for those candidates:

> who have declared their intention of advocating the question of emancipation unqualified and unrestricted by any condition whatever, and in particular such individuals as shall declare their determination to give their support to no administration but one that will give its official and avowed advocacy to the great measure of total and unconditional emancipation.[1]

This resolution was put to the test sooner than expected.

The election was called for June. The diocese of Waterford had been one of the first to carry out the census of population that O'Connell had called for, which had shown that the Protestant portion of it was very small compared to the Catholic. Portlaw, the parish in which Lord Waterford, the head of the Beresford family, had his seat, returned a figure of 5,567 Catholics to 337 Protestants.[2] The Beresfords, a powerful family with many influential connections, had long dominated politics in the county, and had antagonized many other prominent families, including the rising Catholic family of the Wyses. The forty-shilling freeholders had been successfully mobilized in 1818 for pro-emancipation candidates in Wexford, Leitrim and Sligo, and Thomas Wyse and a group of liberals decided that it was time to engage the Beresfords in a trial of strength. With the help of the clergy they set up committees and agents throughout the county to support their candidate, Henry Villiers-Stuart, a young Protestant landlord. The agents and parish clergy seeking to motivate the Catholic voters, especially the forty-shilling freeholders, made a note of their names and offered to support them, if their landlords took revenge after the election. Lord George Beresford's

1 *FJ*, 10 May 1826. 2 Ibid., 17 Jan. 1826.

supporters not only offered bribes but also tried to persuade the voters to deny on oath that they had done so. The clergy who campaigned tirelessly for Villiers-Stuart, a liberal, pro-emancipation landlord, not only denounced the bribery and the accompanying oaths but also emphasized the harsh, heartless tradition of the Beresford family. O'Connell arrived before the polling to encourage the voters to hold firm.

Despite fears of reprisals, Catholic voters held firm, and with the help of skilful organization, succeeded in overwhelming Beresford. He withdrew from the race when Stuart was leading by 1,356 to 527, and it has been calculated that the final result, had the vote continued, would have favoured Villiers-Stuart by a margin of three to one.[3] As one speaker at the association commented, 'the miracle was, how these poor people could make head or at all succeed against a leviathan aristocratic power, which had wielded so long and so powerfully the monopolised ascendancy in that County'. Waterford was not alone in overturning the expectations of the traditional ruling classes. A hasty mobilization of the Catholic voters in Louth, Westmeath, Monaghan and Armagh ensured victories for pro-emancipation candidates over the anti-emancipation members who had held the seats.

Sheil, who had campaigned in Louth, exulted over 'the general resurrection' that had taken place:

> We have roused the most potent and indomitable spirit – we have awakened the people to the noble consciousness of their religious and political duty – we have taught them "how to know their rights" ... we have kindled this great, this wide, this expansive flame, which envelopes the country ... Look, for example, at Louth. In forty-eight hours notice, we beat the whole Protestant aristocracy to the ground.[4]

Sheil's conclusion was widely accepted. The Catholic Association had become aware of the power it possessed through the votes of the forty-shilling freeholders. In the large majority of county elections, only supporters of emancipation could expect to win seats.

The British Catholic Association immediately recognized the significance of the Waterford result. Its members sent their thanks to the bishops, clergy and forty-shilling freeholders for the electoral victory. At a later meeting, a vote of thanks was passed to the Irish agent, Eneas MacDonnell, who took an active part in the British association, for his 'manly efforts to stem the tide of prejudice and advance the great cause of civil and religious liberty',

---

3 MacDonagh, *The hereditary bondsman*, pp 224–5. Connolly, 'Mass politics and sectarian conflict, 1823–30', *NHI*, v, pp 99–100; Wyse, *Catholic Association of Ireland*, i, p. 270; Reynolds, *The Catholic emancipation crisis in Ireland, 1823–1829*, p. 93.   4 *FJ*, 6 July 1826.

through which he had proved himself to be a 'worthy organ for expression of the feelings of 6 million of a deeply injured and suffering people'.[5]

II

Before the Waterford election, the death occurred at Wolverhampton of the most prominent and best-known English ecclesiastical player in the struggle for emancipation. John Milner died on 19 April 1826. His influence in that struggle, and certainly in the Irish part of it, had waned several years previously. As Archbishop Troy had begun to take a less prominent part in public affairs and had handed over more responsibility to Archbishop Murray, Milner was no longer consulted as chief adviser on the English side of the emancipation movement. As far back as 1817, Murray had remarked that the Irish bishops no longer looked to him for guidance, and Milner himself regretted the change in their relationship. His biographer noted Milner's disquiet in 1824 over Bishop Doyle's proposal for the union of the Catholic and Protestant churches in Ireland (which Milner was not alone in regarding as too simplistic). Milner took exception to Doyle's judgment that on the chief points of doctrine there was no essential difference between Catholics and Protestants, and that division was maintained by pride and points of honour rather than a love of Christian humility, charity and truth. He attacked the proposal under a pseudonym, denouncing it not only as 'useless and inexpedient [but also as] wrong and productive of mischief'. He feared that ill-informed laypeople would be tempted to wonder which doctrines they could exchange in 'consideration of temporal advantages'. And he recalled the failures of prominent theologians in the past to achieve Christian unity.[6]

Though influential cardinals at Rome deprecated some of the reports of his abusive comments about his opponents, they (apart from Consalvi) were inclined to pardon many of his faults because of his constant support for the Holy See in his writings. In his later years, he remained as indomitable a controversialist as ever. He took issue with his bête noire, Charles Butler, over his attitude to William Cobbett. Butler had opposed a proposal to make a presentation to Cobbett in which O'Connell had acclaimed him as a 'powerful, honest and disinterested friend of Ireland'. Milner also juxtaposed the opinions of Butler and O'Connell on Lord Castlereagh, who had taken his own life in 1822. Butler had extolled Castlereagh as the friend of Catholics, but O'Connell had denounced him with the full force of his rhetoric, declaring that if it were ever lawful to stamp on 'the grave of any

5 Ibid., 15 Dec. 1826. 6 Husenbeth, *The life of the Right Revd John Milner, DD*, pp 495–7.

man, that man was Castlereagh', who had 'spread corruption far and wide [and] tampered with all classes, the rich and the low, the noble and the ignoble, the church and the law, the mitre and the robe [which] were all tributary, not to the ascendancy of his genius, but to the ascendancy of his debasing corruption'.[7]

Ever scornful of the alleged pro-Catholic sympathy of Canning – who had asked in 1812 if the papists were to receive everything and give up nothing – he had been unimpressed by Burdett's bill of 1825. Though he had considered it less objectionable than some of those that had preceded it, he had thought it nonetheless contained 'a quantity of deleterious matter'. He had feared that Catholics could become too careless about the demands of their religion as they glimpsed the prospect of success in their struggle for emancipation.[8]

His biographer paid tribute to Milner's pastoral activity and to his zeal and exertions in attending to all his duties and commitments as a bishop. He lived frugally and drove himself hard as he attended to the care of his people in his extensive vicariate. In consequence, his writings often bore the signs of hasty composition. A more leisurely and reflective approach might have enabled him to excise hurtful comments about those who did not share his views. Bishop Poynter was invited to preach at his requiem but declined the offer.[9] That was the final, symbolic representation of the differences that had long separated them. Milner's bitter opposition to Poynter's views – frequently expressed in the most aggressive, uncompromising and intemperate manner – had often tried the patience of his colleagues. His disagreements with their attitudes, his desire not to submit to the dictation of the nobles and gentry, his fear and anxiety that the Catholic people might surrender too much in their desire to conciliate the government – these they could have understood and accepted. But the manner in which this opposition to them was expressed, in effect his public questioning of their orthodoxy, his frequent insinuations that he was protecting the Catholic people from the dangers into which his colleagues were allowing them to drift – all this they found insufferable. The virulence of his language and the harshness of his criticisms made the controversies into which he frequently entered unnecessarily caustic and hurtful.

Undoubtedly there was personal animus between Milner and Poynter, going back to Milner's attempts to oust Poynter from the succession to the vicariate of the London District. Milner had wanted that office, as he had wanted to be at the centre of political life. He was a priest of the London

---

7 Ibid., pp 499–501.   8 Ibid., pp 506–7.   9 Poynter, however, had attended the consecration of Milner's coadjutor in May 1825. According to Gradwell, Poynter claimed that on that occasion he and Milner were '*amicissimi*', and all passed off in an atmosphere of '*pace, armonia, concordia*' (Gradwell to Propaganda, 10 May 1825, APF, SOCG 939, ff 58r–59r).

District, and he felt more at home in that district than in his own. His failure
to obtain that office was a major disappointment. Troy's involvement in that
hapless intrigue with Milner had contributed to the sullenness of the
archbishops' relationship with the vicar apostolic of London and to the
misunderstandings, antipathy and acrimony that had existed between those
prelates for nearly twenty years.

Poynter, often the undeserving victim of Milner's barbed attacks, likewise
did not live to see the last part of the struggle for emancipation. He was given
a coadjutor in 1823 and died on 26 November 1827. As the resident vicar
apostolic in London, Poynter had come into closer contact than the other
vicars apostolic with the nobles and gentry who ran the Catholic boards and
associations. He had also dealt occasionally with ministers when issues arose,
such as the appointments of bishops to the colonies, in which both parties
had an interest. Because of the opposition of lords Castlereagh and
Sidmouth to the full restoration of the Jesuits to England, he fought for years
through his agent at Rome to prevent the Jesuits at Stonyhurst from enjoying
the rights of their order, including the right to ordain new members. He
came under pressure from both the ministers and Catholic grandees to agree
to securities in return for emancipation, pressure from which the other vicars
apostolic were freer. He was not popular with many working-class Catholics
of the London District, and indeed may have been 'held in opprobium'.[10]

Being based in London, he carried more responsibility on political issues
than his colleagues, even though they were all technically equal in status.
Apart from Milner, the others looked to him for guidance and reassurance.
Poynter had a difficult role to play balancing the demands of Rome and the
desires of the Catholic aristocrats and gentry, and the ever watchful and often
hostile Milner made his task more difficult. He was therefore obliged to write
lengthy explanations of the various bills and oaths both to the congregation
of Propaganda and to his Roman agents. His Scots friend, Macpherson, may
have been a zealous and committed executant who successfully persuaded
Quarantotti and his chief assistant to approve of the bill of 1813, but he
lacked diplomatic finesse and subsequently antagonized influential and
powerful Roman prelates. His later agent, Robert Gradwell, was more astute
and was able to build on the favourable opinion of Poynter which Consalvi
had formed in London in 1814. Poynter also enjoyed the respect of politicians like Castlereagh, whose favourable comments on him to Consalvi stood
him in good stead in Roman circles. He usually suffered the unjust antagonism of Milner and the unjustified interventions of Troy with commendable
patience, but on occasions allowed his exasperation free rein. It was only
when he felt forced to clear his name that he unburdened himself to the

10 Leighton, 'John Milner, history and ultramontanism', *Arch. Hib.*, 63 (2010), 346–74.

congregation of Propaganda about Milner's hostility. His commitment and dedication to his work for the Catholics of his own district and of England were wholehearted.

III

As parliament resumed at the end of 1826, the British Catholic Association decided to present another petition. They widened it to include freedom for the Dissenters as well as themselves, declaring that they wanted to see their countrymen of every religious persuasion united in participating in every right and blessing that they solicited for themselves. They went further. They claimed that 'any boon not possessed by any other denomination of our fellow subjects would render our enjoyment of it imperfect'. The vicars apostolic took exception to this broad-minded approach, which had also long been espoused by O'Connell.

Bishop Collingridge of the Western District wrote to Poynter, reminding him of his previous dissatisfaction with a petition of that nature, remarking that Catholics could not stand on higher ground than when they stood on their own. But he feared that a tone and spirit more imbued with infidel philosophy than with Catholic or Christian principles had crept in among the members of the association. Though their favourite theme – religious and civil liberty – might hold good in the abstract, it seemed to him pregnant with the most disastrous consequences:

> The idea goes to upset immediately all religious national endow-ments, as tyrannical, whether Protestant or Catholic, and whatever may be the wishes of the great majority of the nation. It goes to deprive all civil power of any interference in matters not strictly of a civil nature, whether they relate to faith or morals, at least where morals are not immediately connected with civil order: v.g. the cessation from servile works on Sundays, polygamy, preaching the most blasphemous doctrines against the Xtian religion, Socinianism, Arianism, deism and even atheism.

He went on to argue that civil liberty meant that no man should be subjected to the will of other men, or should be forced to obey laws emanating from a power in which he had no share. Soon it would extend to 'the wild theory of the rights of man, the *contrat social*'. To maintain in the text of the petition that they wished to see the Dissenters share in every right and blessing which the Catholics desired for themselves:

is certainly *directly* wishing that no law may restrict them from preaching their blasphemous doctrines, that of course they may be at full liberty to do so; and not barely as our laymen say that *if* they do preach these doctrines they may not *on that account* be subjected to penalties.

Collingridge was therefore unwilling to sign the petition unless it was stripped 'of all that fashionable jargon about *religious and civil liberty*'.[11]

Poynter and Bishop Smith of the Northern District also objected to being associated with Dissenters in the petition. Poynter declared that a Catholic bishop signing it would in effect be proclaiming that he was not content to teach the doctrines of the Trinity, the divinity of Christ or the necessity of baptism unless the Unitarian was allowed to preach against the Trinity, the Socinian against the divinity of Christ or the Quaker against baptism. He protested to the association but it only removed the second part, which argued that a concession to Catholics but not to other denominations would diminish their enjoyment of such a concession. The part asking that all denominations share the same rights remained.[12]

O'Connell and the Irish association would not have understood these objections. The appeal to civil and religious liberty was often heard at their meetings. O'Connell was heartily cheered when, at a Catholic meeting in October 1827, he declared that he would petition for freedom of conscience for the English Dissenters. 'It would be worthwhile, if it were only for the sake of example,' he claimed, 'to see a union of English Catholics and Irish Protestants to procure freedom of conscience for the English Dissenters'.[13] And, in fact, after emancipation was won, O'Connell encouraged Jewish friends to demand the same rights as Christians. The vicars apostolic feared that slogans about liberty would lead to a form of licence in the religious field reminiscent of the abuses of such slogans in the French Revolution. They virtually identified civil and religious liberty with the freedom to preach blasphemy and to denounce Christianity, as had happened in Paris in 1793. But neither O'Connell nor the Catholic Association foresaw or were frightened by such a prospect in Britain. They believed that Dissenters were entitled to preach what they believed in their churches and to enjoy the same rights as Anglicans in political affairs.

The Irish bishops petitioned the house of lords for emancipation for the first time in February 1827. They insisted that no legislation could remove the evils affecting Ireland while the disabilities under which Catholics suffered continued. Pointing out that they were deeply interested in the

11 Collingridge to Poynter, 17 Oct. 1826, WDA. 12 Ward, *The eve of Catholic emancipation*, iii, pp 173–4. 13 *FJ*, 1 Nov. 1827.

peace and happiness of Ireland, and devoted to their king and country, and that they had again recently disclaimed the disloyal opinions so gratuitously imputed to them, they then quoted a part of the formal declaration they had made a year previously. They begged the members of the house of lords 'to concur in repealing those laws which continue to aggrieve the Roman Catholics of the United Kingdom'.[14]

Sir Francis Burdett moved on 5 March that the house of commons should go into committee on the Catholic claims. But his motion was narrowly defeated. A solemn resolution of complaint was promptly passed at the next meeting of Catholics a week later. It was resolved with 'the deepest feelings of regret and most awful forebodings for the future' that they observed the refusal of the house to even consider the prayers of 7 million 'oppressed, injured and highly discontented subjects'.[15] The British Catholic Association declared that it was not disheartened by this setback. That 'men of ability and property' (members of parliament) had favoured emancipation was seen as an encouraging sign.[16] The duke of Norfolk thought their position was better than it had been two years previously, and trusted that their government would not drive 6 million of their countrymen to extremes. He repudiated Peel's endeavour 'to fix the stamp of idolatry on us' by claiming that Catholics did not observe the second commandment.[17]

Lord Liverpool, under whose watch emancipation would never have been willingly given, resigned the premiership in March 1827, and was succeeded by George Canning. As O'Connell was prepared to give Canning time to show his sympathy for Catholics, so too was the British Catholic Association. At its meeting in May, a resolution that the Catholics should not embarrass the ministry by bringing forward petitions was passed by a narrow majority. But Eneas MacDonnell thought they should 'not put their question in connexion or collision with any party of the state, and not regulate their proceedings with a reference to any ministerial cabals'.[18] Canning's premiership lasted a mere four months. After the short premiership of Lord Goderich, Wellington became prime minister in January 1828, with Peel, the persistent opponent of emancipation, as home secretary. O'Connell was angered that no significant change took place at Dublin Castle. He argued that the English people were sympathetic to the Catholic claims and that the only class hostile to emancipation was the clergy. (The signatures on the recent petitions against emancipation did not bear out this assertion.)

14 Ibid., 25 Mar. 1827.   15 Ibid., 14 Mar. 1827.   16 *CM*, Mar. 1827.   17 *DEP*, 22 Mar. 1827. Eneas MacDonnell, the Catholics' agent in London, had alerted Archbishop Murray to a newspaper report in which Peel accused the Irish bishops of being untruthful in their statement of January 1826, since they claimed that the Catholic church accepted ten commandments, whereas their catechism showed that they did not accept the second commandment. Though Murray could scarcely believe that Peel would hold such an opinion, he explained in his reply how mistaken that claim was (Murray to MacDonnell, *FJ*, 25 Mar. 1827).   18 *FJ*, 4 May 1827.

At the last meeting of the Irish Catholic Association for 1827, O'Connell proposed that they should have three petitions ready for the opening of parliament on 22 January: one in favour of the Dissenters of England, one for emancipation and one for the repeal of the sub-letting act. He insisted on fighting for the rights of Dissenters, and emphasized the importance of assisting them, even if they did not reciprocate, as this would show that Irish Catholics were always the friends of civil and religious liberty.[19]

A plan to hold parish meetings throughout Ireland met with a highly favourable response. About two-thirds of all the parishes in Ireland held meetings in January 1828. Archbishop Curtis of Armagh, who, far from being an ardent advocate of emancipation, had gone along with the public enthusiasm for it, realizing that he had no choice, was called upon to preside at the meeting in Drogheda. He did so with some hesitation, as he feared that the opponents of emancipation would exploit his chairmanship to claim that the bishops and clergy dictated the political agenda to the people. He wanted to give them no opportunity for taunting the Catholics with the smear that the laity 'pay a blind and implicit obedience' to the clergy and are 'not allowed to think or judge for themselves, but forced to adopt what they look upon as indifferent or unjust'. He was anxious to provide no evidence for such aspersions:

> The very calumniators who repeat these imputations well know them to be false and ridiculous; but in Great Britain, and even in Ireland, they will be believed by very many, merely on the testimony of their faithless informers. I am so far from wishing to dictate to you, gentlemen, that I only consent to take the chair as one of the inhabitants of this town and by no means as Catholic archbishop or primate; which situation, however, would give me no right to interfere in your meetings or other temporal concerns, except alone, so far as to admonish you not to assert or prosecute even your just rights, otherwise than with due moderation and Christian charity, that will rather fortify and recommend rather than weaken them: and to remind you that a good cause may suffer, and even become a bad one, by being unduly conducted.[20]

The advent to power of the high Tories, Wellington and Peel – or as O'Connell called them, 'a vile faction' – cast a cloud over those struggling for emancipation. They feared that they would be subjected to further obstruction and delay. Nonetheless, Catholics went ahead with their new petitions to parliament. They maintained that in the present enlightened age, denomina-

---

19 Ibid., 1 Jan. 1828. 20 Ibid., 23 Jan. 1828.

tional differences should not exclude Catholics from parliament, and reminded the house that in its military, naval and commercial treaties with neighbouring powers it recognized the title 'Most Christian' for the princes and monarchs who performed the same rites and ceremonies as they did. They asked that the charges of blasphemy, superstition and idolatry recorded against them in the statute book be expunged, and insisted that they felt as great an attachment to king and country as all other subjects of the crown.[21]

The repeal in April 1828 of the Test Act and the Corporation Act, which enabled Dissenters to take their seats in parliament, was warmly welcomed by Catholic activists, who saw it as a step in the right direction.[22] The arrival of the marquis of Anglesey as lord lieutenant was also interpreted as a felicitous omen. As Sheil remarked, he might once have been 'obnoxious to the people of Ireland' but he had become a friend to religious liberty. Sheil concluded that with the liberation of the Dissenters, there was evidence of a general sentiment that no disqualification from office should be imposed on the basis of religious differences.[23]

O'Connell, who was buoyed up by the increased activity of the English Catholics, was disconcerted by the suggestion of one member of the English association. Michael Joseph Quin, an Irish barrister, journalist and friend of O'Connell's, had suggested at a meeting that the government should make a concordat with the pope.[24] A concordat usually involved the church making concessions to the state in return for guarantees of certain rights in education and public organizations, and freedom of evangelization. The concessions which the states demanded often involved participation in episcopal appointments and some control over publications and communications with Rome. Mention of a concordat immediately conjured up in O'Connell's mind the veto and the *exequatur*. These he had vigorously denounced for the threat they posed not only to the church, but also to the Catholic people of Ireland, at a political and social level.

Lamenting Quin's introduction of the possibility of a concordat between the British government and Rome, O'Connell maintained that Catholics should not concern themselves with such questions:

> They sought for their rights, not as Catholics, but as citizens. They would not allow the pope, nor any spiritual authority, to interfere with their civil rights. They would meet the armies of the pope,

---

21 Ibid., 13 Feb. 1828. 22 These acts, dating to the seventeenth century, required officers in boroughs, military officers and other crown officers to take the oaths of supremacy and allegiance and receive the sacrament according to the rites of the Church of England. 23 *FJ*, 3 Mar. 1828. 24 Michael Joseph Quin (1796–1843) practiced for a time as a lawyer in London, but later turned to journalism. A supporter of O'Connell he contributed to the *Morning Chronicle* and *Morning Herald*. He later became a travel writer and co-founder of the *Dublin Review*.

and drive them back, as they would the armies of any other potentate. Their hostility would be as direct. To Caesar they would give
what belonged to Caesar, and to God what belonged to God. Their
spiritual allegiance should never interfere with their civil duty. It
would only make them better citizens.

Warning Quin 'not to fling a firebrand amongst Catholics', he argued that
the democracy of England did not 'amalgamate with the higher orders'.
Catholics in Ireland were united as also were those of England, and they had
very few opponents apart from the dignitaries of the established church.[25]

Rumours about a concordat continued to circulate in Rome, England and
Ireland for the next year. To what extent Wellington's government was
involved is not clear. In May 1828 Michael Blake, the rector of the Irish
College,[26] informed Archbishop Murray that he had been assured by
Cardinal Cappellari, the prefect of the congregation of Propaganda, that no
negotiations had taken place between the British cabinet and the Holy See on
that subject.[27] But a short time later Robert Gradwell, the rector of the
English College, was appointed coadjutor bishop in the London District and
let it be known that he had to hurry to England as the pope and the congregation of Propaganda wished that he might be their agent in any negotiations
about a concordat.

Bishop Baines, the coadjutor of the Western District, had then been in
Rome for two years and had met many of the English aristocrats and gentry
who visited the city. He regarded Gradwell as an intriguer who was ambitious
for promotion to the London District and he dismissed the agent's claims.
He maintained that the proposal from the government for a concordat had
been given to him and that he was:

> commissioned by his Holiness to return the official answer to the
> person applying on the part of the ministers which was that
> though nothing would give his Holiness greater pleasure than to
> re-establish an intercourse with England, yet until the laws which
> prohibit that intercourse are solemnly abrogated, the Holy See will
> not enter into any negotiation whatever.[28]

Baines' view of Gradwell's boasts was endorsed by Christopher Boylan, the
new rector of the Irish College. He reported that before leaving Rome,
Gradwell had maintained that the general principles of new arrangements
between the government and the Catholics had been agreed and that the

25 *FJ.*, 17 Apr. 1828. 26 Blake had returned to Rome in 1824 to reopen the Irish College.
27 Blake to Murray, 10 May 1828, DDA. 28 Ward, *The eve of Catholic emancipation*, iii, pp
203–4. Gilbert, *This restless prelate: Bishop Peter Baines, 1786–1843*, pp 61–70.

settlement of details would be easy. Boylan advised the Irish bishops to be vigilant and to be ready to refuse their authority to any of Gradwell's projects. He feared that despite the pope's repeated declarations that he would not entertain the idea of a concordat as long as Catholics were 'under disgraceful laws', Gradwell might have got an understanding from some people of power and influence in Rome.[29]

Boylan later surmised that O'Connell may have got information from an Irish student at Propaganda College about the concordat. The pope had told a group of Irish students there that there could be no concordat while the existing laws prohibited contact with Rome.[30] Nonetheless, O'Connell was perturbed by the rumours that reached him. He had heard that the duke of Buckingham was in Rome and, though he was not sure that Buckingham was an intermediary for the government, he was annoyed by the report said to be circulating there that Irish Catholics would rebel if they were not granted emancipation, and that Irish Protestants would rebel if emancipation were not accompanied by a concordat.[31]

Ever ready to bolster his case with the strongest possible arguments, even if they were not always accurate, O'Connell claimed that seven bishops, all of whom were under ecclesiastical censure, had been chosen by the government of the Netherlands to fill vacant sees. He concluded with sardonic hyperbole that if a concordat like the one between the Netherlands and Rome were put into effect in Ireland, the government might appoint the Monaghan magistrates to fill the sees.[32] The Monaghan magistrates had blocked the political tour of the journalist John Lawless, but concordats always made provision for the pope to authorize canonical institution of the candidates chosen by states, and consequently O'Connell need not have bothered with that nightmare scenario. Maintaining also that the ambassador of Hanover had been acting on behalf of the British government, he drew an indignant denial from the Hanoverian embassy. Writing to Cardinal Bernetti, the secretary of state, the ambassador quoted references to this claim of O'Connell's from English newspapers, and insisted that it was a pure invention on O'Connell's part that three negotiations had taken place on that subject since 26 October. He accused O'Connell of pursuing a policy of separatism from Britain.[33]

Contact on this issue, if not by the Hanoverian ambassador, was made by an English go-between with a Roman official or officials. This intermediary of the British government or of someone associated with the government was Sir Robert Wilmot Horton, the member of parliament for Newcastle-under-Lyme and former undersecretary for war and the colonies. He spent

29 Boylan to Murray, 25 Oct. 1828, DDA.   30 Ibid., 5 Jan. 1829, DDA.   31 *CJ*, 4 Jan. 1829.
32 *FJ*, 31 Dec. 1828.   33 August Kentner to Cardinal Bernetti, 14 Dec. 1828, ASV, Segr Stato Esteri, Rubr. 271(26), Busta 585.

time in Rome in 1828. It is not clear what precise authority he had or whether his role was merely to take soundings about the possibility of some arrangement with Rome in case of a decision to grant emancipoation.

An exchange of letters between Horton and Bishop Baines took place in December 1828, though the letters were not published in the Irish papers until February 1829.[34] In his first letter, Horton remarked that the ancient law of praemunire prevented contact with the see of Rome, and, consequently, he could understand how Rome would be unwilling to enter into any such arrangement until that law was repealed.[35] Horton also wished to know if an answer of the pope to the duke of Norfolk 'contained expressions of admonition against any Catholics, English or Irish, who might be prepared to receive emancipation coupled with any security whatever'. Baines explained that in answering hypothetically he would state that if arrangements could be made, which 'leaving the Catholic church wholly untouched' would allay the groundless apprehensions of Protestants, 'it would be a most injurious libel upon the head of the Catholic church to insinuate his disapprobation was to be apprehended'. Horton asked Baines if it was true that – as O'Connell had been reported as claiming – the pope had said no treaty could be made between Britain and Rome until the Catholics of Ireland were emancipated. Baines answered that he did not believe that the pope had made this statement.

Boylan seems to have believed that Horton was the government's intermediary. Unimpressed by him, and likening him to Coxe-Hippisley, Boylan thought he was trying 'to make himself of weight', both by his scheme and his correspondence.[36] Though Boylan later feared that after emancipation had been passed, efforts would be made to impose a concordat, he was 'delighted that Mr Wilmot Horton's plan has been passed by, though I understand the ingenious author feels considerable mortification at its rejection'.[37]

The proposals about a concordat could have got no further than friendly discussions with some cardinals or Roman officials. There is no mention of negotiations in the relevant Roman archives. If the British government had been made aware of the need to repeal the statutes of praemunire before any concordat could have been signed, it would have backed off, rather than risk hostile reaction from Protestant extremists.

Apart from Baines, Horton consulted Chevalier Bunsen, the Prussian

34 *FJ*, 3 Feb. 1829. The letters are dated 10, 13, 15, 17 Dec. 1828.   35 Praemunire was the title of statutes passed between 1353 and 1393 to resist the encroachments of the papacy in England. The statutes were later used to prevent any official relations with Rome.   36 Boylan to Murray, 5 Jan. 1829, DDA.   37 Ibid., 2 Apr. 1829. Horton's 'plan' could only have been some right of intervention by the government in episcopal appointments and the concession of some vague security in return for emancipation. Wellington had by then given up the idea of concordat.

minister at Rome, and Bunsen sent him a lengthy memorandum. In it, he explained the influence exerted by Protestant German states over the Catholic church, making clear that they enjoyed powers beyond what was officially and publicly acknowledged by Rome. He noted that since Frederick the Great's time, the canons in Breslau had been informed of the king's choice for the bishopric and then proceeded to elect him. All German Protestant states examined the communications between the bishops and Rome, except those on matters of conscience. He suggested that it would be expedient to negotiate with the pope after the civil question had been settled, and inexpedient to negotiate before that. He thought that the English state could then impose its will in many ways on the Catholics, and he approved of Horton's view of not allowing Catholic members of parliament to vote on matters concerning the Protestant church. This (rather naive) advice came too late, as emancipation was then being drawn up.[38]

Boylan advised the Irish bishops to be ready to fight against any restrictions on their rights that might be made with the consent of Rome. He did not believe that they enjoyed much influence or prestige at the Vatican. Commenting on Roman impressions of them, he told Murray that most of them were 'looked upon as too deficient in their qualities of coolness, sagacity and penetration to entitle their opinions to much weight in the question of arrangements, whether antecedent or consequent in the contemplated settlement of the Catholic grievances'. Those impressions were mainly to be ascribed to the effort industriously made by Gradwell to extol Dr Poynter at the expense of the English, and more especially the Irish bishops. Poynter's timidity was well-known, and, moreover, he was the intimate – or rather the tool – of Lord Bathurst:

> and was constantly transmitting to this city the views and wishes of that illiberal nobleman and of that government of which he formed a part regarding the affairs of the English or Irish Catholics. His diligent and active agent lost no opportunity of magnifying his influence with the ministry, and it was more than once imagined that he was the means of averting their heavy displeasure from the heads of the Roman Catholics.[39]

Consequently, the Irish bishops would need to watch Gradwell's 'motions with utmost vigilance' as he would walk in the footsteps of Poynter.

The Ultra-Tories would have baulked at the repeal of the old praemunire

---

38 Bunsen to Horton, 30 Dec. 1828, 7, 17 Jan. 1829, DRO, D3155/WH2935. 39 Boylan to Murray, 28 Oct. 1828. Ibid., Lord Bathurst was the secretary of state for war and the colonies from 1812 to 1827. Poynter had negotiated with him about the appointments of bishops in the colonies, and about the restoration of the Jesuits in England.

legislation, and if any attempt had been made by the government to impose a settlement in which it obtained a significant role in the appointment of the bishops, it would have provoked outrage and fury from O'Connell and the multitudes who supported him. Too much had been invested in opposition to such an outcome over too many years to allow the subject even to be calmly considered. The bishops, despite the frosty papal reply to their complaints about the Genoese letter, would have had no option but to throw their full weight against a veto, even if any of them were hesitant about doing so. Pope Leo XII was personally conservative, and there was no cardinal in Rome with Consalvi's outlook and experience even to attempt to push him in a direction that suited the government. Gradwell and English Catholic aristocrats who visited Rome may have succeeded in conveying to Vatican officials a picture of Irish clergy as politically troublesome and unnecessarily confrontational, but trying to curb them by imposing a veto or establishing any form of concordat would not have been practical or possible. The risk implicit in any such attempt would have far outweighed any potential advantage.

18

Emancipation wrested from the government

I

Even after the motion of Sir Francis Burdett for Catholic emancipation in May 1828 comfortably passed the house of commons only to be lost by forty-four votes in the lords, and resistence to emancipation in parliament was weakening, Peel's opposition to it was as firm as ever. He declared that the admission of Catholics to parliament would destroy every link that bound the constitution to the Protestant faith, apart from that of the crown.[1]

At a meeting of the British Catholic Association, the duke of Norfolk expressed its satisfaction at the repeal of the Test Act and Corporation Act, and argued that, even if it operated against the Catholics, they should rejoice in the recognition of the principle of civil and religious liberty. O'Connell had sent a message to Edward Blount, the association's secretary, that the granting of securities would produce a rupture between English and Irish Catholics.[2] Blount, in his report, stated that 'to conciliate the love of 6 million men was the best mode of security, and for their future allegiance they referred to their past fidelity'. If the British Catholic were called upon 'to purchase by his religion or his honour, his advancement, he would reject the offer with scorn'.[3]

O'Connell's close associate, Richard Lalor Sheil, commenting on a book, partly religious and partly political, by Lord Shrewsbury, enthused about the recent change in the English Catholic mentality. Hitherto the English Catholics had been pusillanimous and servile, their proud spirit had fallen, but they had 'recently raised themselves to a noble attitude' and were demanding the restoration of their rights in more becoming language.[4] Sheil would not have included anyone prepared to offer securities among the manly cohort whom he praised, and at the discussion of Blount's report, William Petre, one of the Catholic gentry, declared his readiness to give securities. Though maintaining that they ought to have 'free and unshackled emancipation', he argued that 'if the securities were consistent with the principles of religion and faith', he would not say that they should not be

---

1 Gash, *Mr Secretary Peel*, p. 514. 2 O'Connell to Richard Bennett, 27 May 1828 in MacDonagh, *The hereditary bondsman*, p. 248. 3 *FJ*, 5 June 1828. 4 Ibid., 17 June 1828.

given. His request that the British association seek total, unqualified and unconditional repeal of all laws disabling Catholics was defeated.[5]

The whole question of emancipation was raised to a new and exciting level in Ireland by a by-election in Clare in July 1828. Vesey Fitzgerald, the member for that county, was appointed president of the board of trade, prompting an election in the constituency. The Irish Catholic Association was determined to put forward a candidate committed to the Catholic cause, and Major MacNamara, O'Connell's second in his ill-fated duel with John Norcot D'Esterre, was approached to stand. When he refused and no other suitable candidate was forthcoming, O'Connell offered to contest the election. As Catholics could not take the oaths required of members of parliament before taking their seats, O'Connell's action provoked amazement and fury among his enemies and opponents, and delight and enthusiasm among his supporters. He had only two weeks left to campaign, but threw himself into the contest with vigour and brio.

The Catholic Association mobilized the clergy, who, in turn, rallied the forty-shilling freeholders. All the clergy of the diocese of Killaloe apart from James Coffey, the parish priest of Kildysart, backed O'Connell. Terence O'Shaughnessy, the dean of Ennis, whose nephew was Fitzgerald's agent, absented himself during the election, and his uncle, James, the bishop of Killaloe, stayed silent.[6] Fitzgerald, who had been in favour of Catholic claims, was quickly subjected to O'Connell's powerful disdain and brutal provocation. He was denounced as the ally and colleague of Wellington and Peel, 'the most bitter, persevering and unmitigated enemies of the Catholics'. Appealing to his own past disinterested service to the religion and liberties of Catholics, O'Connell committed himself to voting for 'every measure which can strengthen the right of every human being to unrestricted and unqualified freedom of conscience'. He also gave a pledge to vote for radical reform in the representative system of the house of commons, and to oppose local measures that annoyed Catholics.[7]

Apart from the priests in Clare, who led their people to vote in Ennis, O'Connell enjoyed sympathy from the clergy countrywide. The most scholarly member of the hierarchy, Bishop Doyle, wrote a warm, appreciative letter of encouragement to him, espousing the hope that the lovers of civil and religious liberty would do their duty to one who had committed his talents, fortune and life to the sacred cause.[8]

---

5 Ibid., 18 June 1828. 6 Murphy, *The diocese of Killaloe, 1800–1850*, pp 77–84. O'Connell later remarked that neither the dean nor his uncle, the bishop, were his friends, but they cost him no votes (*FJ*, 28 July 1828). 7 *FJ*, 26 June 1828. 8 Ibid., 28 June 1828. Doyle had already written to Wellington supporting domestic nomination of the bishops, and suggested that the pope might vest in an Irish prelate the powers in matters of conscience and discipline then exercised by some of the congregations in Rome (Fitzpatrick, *The life, times and correspondence of the Right Revd Dr*

O'Connell's overwhelming victory made news not only throughout Britain but also on the Continent. The government now faced the difficulty of how to respond to the likely election of numerous Catholics who were not eligible to take their seats. Some solution had to be found to the constitutional crisis that such a development would provoke. The British Catholic Association was delighted with the result, and its leading lawyer, Charles Butler, set to work investigating the legal right of a Catholic to become a member of parliament. He concluded that no law of Ireland disabled Catholics from sitting and voting in parliament, and as the Act of Union had not altered that situation, O'Connell was 'not disabled by any act of the English, Irish, or united parliament from sitting for any place in Ireland'.[9] The Irish association had been encouraged by the new energy that the British association, galvanized by its newspaper, the *Catholic Journal*, had begun to exhibit.[10] The British association extended its warmest thanks to its sister body, congratulating it on advancing the cause of emancipation, and congratulated the Irish Catholics 'on their most exemplary forbearance under unparalleled provocation'.[11]

The distance Wellington would have to travel was shown by his private view that the conversion of Lord Anglesey (the viceroy who had been wounded at Waterloo) to the need for emancipation was a sign of madness.[12] Though neither Peel nor Wellington commented publicly on the Clare election, they both realized the significance of it. Peel understood the difficulties of resisting a movement that did not use violence or break the law, but he also realized that between the excitement of the Catholics and the increasing truculence and violence of the Brunswick clubs, which had been founded explicitly by Orangemen to resist emancipation, the peace of the country was undoubtedly endangered. Wellington informed the king on 1 August of the danger of rebellion in Ireland and got permission to discuss the concession of emancipation with Peel and the chancellor. They soon agreed that emancipation had to be granted.[13] Wellington hoped that the Catholic clergy could be licensed and paid by the state, and the Anglican church could be protected by banning the use of church titles by the Catholics – a plan with which Peel disagreed.[14]

The support of influential Protestants, headed by several nobles, calling for an end to the disqualifying laws at a meeting in Dublin gave further

Doyle, ii, pp 70–5).   9 Ibid., 10 July 1828. Butler, encouraging the circulation of a pamphlet establishing the validity of O'Connell's election, remarked: 'it is impossible to feel stronger wishes for the success of the Irish in their endeavours to obtain emancipation than the British Catholics do' (*FJ*, 13 Aug. 1828). He was extremely grateful to the Irish association for its vote of thanks (*FJ*, 16 Jan. 1829).   10 *DEP*, 1 May 1828.   11 Ibid., 14 Oct. 1828. 12 MacDonagh, *The hereditary bondsman*, p. 259.   13 Gash, *Mr Secretary Peel*, p. 532. 14 Muir, *Wellington: Waterloo and the fortunes of peace, 1814–1852*, pp 326–7.

encouragement to O'Connell.[15] And the British Catholic Association, stimulated by O'Connell's success, circulated addresses calling for emancipation as
a just right at an outdoor meeting organized by the Brunswick club in
opposition to emancipation in October 1828 at Pennenden Heath in Kent.
Though greeted with hostility, Lalor Sheil addressed some of the participants. The duke of Norfolk, at a meeting of the Catholic Association, later
claimed that this initiative had been beneficial, as it had stimulated enquiries
among the participants, and all enquiries would ultimately prove helpful to
their cause.

But the duke also threw an apple of discord into the relations between the
two associations by expressing a willingness to concede securities to the
government. As there was some support for this policy, O'Connell felt
obliged to have the Irish association 'put upon record our total dissent from
the measures they seem willing to adopt'. O'Connell indignantly dismissed
securities as merely furthering contempt on one side and discontent on the
other, and he praised Eneas MacDonnell, the Irish agent, who had made
clear at the meeting in London that the Irish would not agree to any
tampering with church discipline. Praising the duke of Norfolk, he regretted
that they had to part on the issue of securities, and asked:

> Does he not feel that he is himself a living and most striking
> example of the unrelenting severity and the monstrous injustice of
> the penal laws, and can he think of crouching to that bigotry which
> robs him of his share in that constitution which was the work of
> his own glorious ancestors? ... But the duke of Norfolk if we are
> to credit the reports of his speech, does not wait to have the
> question put to him, but is himself considering how much he will
> proffer to those who are withholding what belongs to him. I know
> the purity of his heart, and I respect it; but if he holds such senti-
> ments as these, I should not be sorry to see him retire into private
> life.

'The duke of Norfolk is a high name,' O'Connell maintained, but it was the
Irish Catholics who had 'given him so much importance'. 'The English
Catholics,' he insisted, 'would be powerless as a political party, but for their
communion in a constitutional struggle with the Catholics of Ireland'.

Edward Blount, the secretary of the British Catholic Association, also
provoked O'Connell's ire with his plan to petition for unconditional emancipation, but, if conditions were offered, to accept them. O'Connell had
already sent a message to him that willingness to agree to the concession of

15 *DEP*, 7 Oct. 1828.

securities would produce a rupture between the two associations. Blount protested against 'wanton imputations being cast on most honourable men' who sincerely believed that 'securities ought to be entertained' and maintained that if the government offered them the rights of British subjects and the glorious privileges of freemen on terms consistent with their principles, they would gratefully accept them. O'Connell, however, insisted that they would never consent to an emancipation that would trench on their religious principles. Concluding that these views were bad signs of the weakness of spirit among some English people, he consoled himself with the view that there was still 'a body of noblemen and gentlemen in England, who, with the earl of Shrewsbury at their head, would make a bold stand for the liberties of their country'. Nonetheless he did not wish to separate the Catholics of the two countries.[16]

When analysing possible securities, O'Connell ruled out any scheme to pension the clergy, as the cost – £600,000 – would be prohibitive and would meet as much resistance in England as in Ireland. The other possibility was a concordat, which presumably would include some arrangement about the appointment of bishops (about which he had already repeatedly complained). He claimed that by 25 October the government had made no less than three applications to Rome for a concordat. They had not done so directly; as the law forbade such an approach, but had operated through the Hanoverian ambassador in Rome. A reply 'couched in terms of kindliness and friendship towards the British government' made clear that until the Catholics of Ireland were emancipated, no such treaty could be drawn up. O'Connell therefore argued that 'if a man wanted to retard emancipation to an indefinite period, the best course he could adopt would be to broach the subject of securities'.[17]

Eneas MacDonnell, who usually attended the meetings of the British Catholic Association, was extremely concerned about the danger of bad blood being created between the two associations on the question of securities. Reminding the Irish association that the recent petition drawn up by their British counterparts called for unconditional emancipation, he maintained that that request was a true reflection of the sentiments of the English body. Paying tribute to the courtesy and kindness he had always received from British Catholics, he noted that they had always expressed their fullest sympathy for the condition of Ireland, and had gone 'to very considerable expense in exposing the falsehood of her calumniators, and justifying the character and conduct of her people'. And no one had manifested more sincerity or zeal in that regard than the illustrious duke of

16 *FJ*, 15, 19 Nov. 1828; *CJ*, 16, 23 Nov. 1828.   17 *FJ*, 20 Nov. 1828, Ward, *The eve of Catholic emancipation*, ii, p. 243.

Norfolk. Nothing short of absolute necessity would warrant the dissolution of their compact against a common enemy, and he was convinced that no such necessity existed, as the great majority of the English Catholics were as opposed in principle to securities as their Irish equivalents.[18]

Blount, hearing of the hostile reaction in Ireland to any form of conditional emancipation, wrote to MacDonnell to assure him of the desire of his association to continue to work harmoniously with the Irish. But he confessed that if it were 'blameable to hold that it is inexpedient to reject all conditions before they are tendered', his association would plead guilty. Nonetheless, he hoped that no differences would arise between them which would weaken their common cause. When this letter was read out at a meeting of the Irish association, O'Connell was in no mood to tolerate any possible deviation from the demand for full emancipation. Believing that the government would have to yield in the wake of the Clare victory, he was very anxious to give it no excuse to minimize the terms of relief. Responding to Blount's communication, he indignantly declared that he would submit a motion calling on Eneas MacDonnell to relinquish all connection with the British Catholic Association, questioning its ignorance of the Hanoverian embassy in Rome, and the rumour that a concordat had been arranged on the same basis as that of the Netherlands. Designating 'the measure of conditional emancipation proposed by the British association [as] one of Wellington's feelers', he maintained that they wanted none of the feelers of that 'worthless' man.[19] O'Connell developed this point a few days later, declaring:

> The English Catholics have had their quarterly meeting and the duke of Norfolk commenced the proceedings by stating his readiness to go into securities … It is therefore our duty to prevent so mischievous a topic being at all introduced … It remains then that we must call on the British Catholics to disavow this opinion … I do not want a separation from the English Catholics, but I want that we shall not be committed with them in their mischievous measures.[20]

Eneas MacDonnell passed on to Nicholas Purcell O'Gorman, the secretary of the Irish Catholic Association, the claim of the *Times* that the duke of Norfolk, as head of the lay Catholics of England and a respectable ecclesiastic, whom it supposed to be a representative of that church, had announced 'in the most public manner their willingness to accept emancipation upon terms'. MacDonnell admitted that he had been unable to ascertain if the

18 Ibid., 21 Nov. 1828.   19 Ibid., 26 Nov. 1828.   20 Ibid., 10 Dec. 1828.

editor had been authorized by the duke or the ecclesiastic to make that statement. On the contrary, he maintained that all the accounts given in England
of the speech made reference to the duke distinctly and emphatically
declaring that he was merely expressing his own individual opinion.

MacDonnell identified the ecclesiastic as a Dr Collins, an Irish priest
stationed in London, and he was at pains to point out that Collins, 'far from
being the representative of the British Catholic evangelical body, is not the
representative of a single member of that body, nor authorized, I verily
believe, to speak on behalf of anyone amongst them'. And his views on
securities were at variance with that body of which he was erroneously
described as a representative. In fact, if it were generally believed in England
that the British Catholic prelates and clergy authorized Collins to identify
them with the feelings he had expressed, 'it would be unreasonable to expect
that the union, now so happily subsisting, could be retained'. Before writing,
he had hoped that the statement in the *Times* would have been officially
contradicted, but was unwilling to delay lest great harm be done to the
relationship of the two associations at the upcoming aggregate meeting in
Dublin.[21]

MacDonnell did not stop at explaining the attitudes of English Catholics
to securities. He went on the offensive against them in the British press. In a
long letter to the *Morning Chronicle*, he attempted to show why Catholics
regarded them as 'unnecessary, offensive and mischievous'. If the government were made aware of the feelings of Catholics and introduced measures
hostile to those feelings, the government and not the Catholics would be the
aggressors. But if the Catholics waited until the measures were proposed and
then opposed them, they would be the aggressors. Listing the elements that
securities might contain – the intervention of the crown in episcopal
appointments and in the correspondence between the bishops and Rome,
payment of the clergy and the disfranchisement of the forty-shilling
freeholders – MacDonnell dealt extensively with the first. He quoted the
firm rejection of the intervention in appointments in the various statements
of the Irish bishops, starting from 1808. He also quoted the hostile view of
Bishop Collingridge on the bill of 1813. And from the previous century, he
drew on the forthright and vigorous dismissal by Edmund Burke of the
proposal that the members of one religious sect should appoint pastors to
another. Burke had predicted that the lord lieutenant, not knowing which
priests were fit to be made bishops, would pass on the choice to 'lords
lieutenants of counties, justices of the peace, and other persons, who, for the
purpose of vexing, and turning to derision this miserable people, will pick
out the worst and most obnoxious they can find amongst the clergy to set

21 Ibid., 4 Dec. 1828.

over the rest'. MacDonnell concluded by quoting the most recent opponents of emancipation – Peel and Liverpool – both of whom attached no value to the veto.[22]

The danger of the two associations going their separate ways was averted by the government not pursuing the need for securities of an ecclesiastical nature.

II

Towards the end of the year, the duke of Wellington received a letter urging the concession of emancipation from a friend or acquaintance of former days. Patrick Curtis had been rector of the Irish College in Salamanca during the Peninsular War, in which Wellington defeated the French. On three occasions between 1808 and 1813, Curtis was driven from Salamanca by the French occupying forces, and on one occasion his life was endangered by his communicating with Wellington. He allowed his students to act as guides to the British forces in the Salamanca region. A tradition has it that he presented Wellington with a cloak, which the commander later wore and his soldiers regarded as a sign of luck in battle.[23] He subsequently sought Wellington's help in claiming compensation for the damages done to the property of the Irish College.[24] When in 1819 Curtis' name was put forward by several Irish bishops for appointment to the archbishopric of Armagh, he let Wellington know, so that he might 'have it communicated to such department as you may deem expedient', even though he had no desire for such promotion. Wellington replied that he considered the appointment 'so honourable and advantageous to the country' that he had passed on the information to Lord Castlereagh, and, in a letter to Lord Sidmouth, the minister of home affairs, he described Curtis as:

> a very honest, loyal man [who] behaved remarkably well throughout the war. He has none of the modern notion of religion or philosophy, and altho' a zealous and probably a bigoted Roman Catholic, he is not inimical to the British government and in my opinion there is no person who it would be more desireable [*sic*] to see in the situation to which it is proposed to appoint him.[25]

Wellington contacted Castlereagh, who informed Cardinal Consalvi that the government would view with pleasure Curtis' appointment to Armagh.

22 Quoted in *FJ*, 14 Dec. 1828. **23** Coleman (ed.), *Historical memoirs of the city of Armagh by James Stuart*, p. 285. **24** Curtis to Wellington, 9 Jan. 1813, MS 61, 1/364, Wellington Papers, University of Southampton. **25** Wellington to Sidmouth, 8 Feb. 1819, ibid., MS 1/619/13.

According to Robert Gradwell, Consalvi 'strongly solicited' Cardinal Fontana, the prefect of the congregation of Propaganda, to that effect.[26] It would be inaccurate to suggest, however, that Curtis owed his nomination solely to Wellington or to the government, as he enjoyed the support of several bishops, including that of the influential archbishop and coadjutor of Dublin.[27]

So, several years later, Curtis as archbishop believed that he ought to approach his former acquaintance who, as prime minister, enjoyed the power and influence to advance the cause of emancipation. So he wrote to Wellington on 4 December 1828, stating that it was generally assumed that the question of emancipation would be settled in the next session of parliament, and that a concordat with Rome was said to be envisaged. He repeated the views he had expressed to Wellington nearly a decade earlier about 'the deference, respect and submission' that he believed church authorities should show to state authorities. But his proposal went much further than those of either British parliamentary or Roman officials: after his selection and institution by the pope, the bishop would be presented to a government commission, and, if he could not satisfy any legitimate objections raised by it, he could not take possession of his see.[28] This would have placed a bishop in a far more painful and embarrassing position than that of a candidate who was excluded from office before being officially appointed by the pope, and illustrates the subservient *ancien régime* views of the archbishop. Almost certainly these were purely personal views and he had not obtained the approval of colleagues for them.

In fact, Curtis, though he went along with the campaign for emancipation, did not really believe that the goal was worth the effort and struggle it required. Shortly before writing to Wellington, he had made the staggering confession to a Scottish acquaintance:

> My own firm opinion is, and I wish I could get Catholics to adopt
> it, namely that said emancipation is a contemptible thing and not
> worth the tenth part of the struggle, labour, expense and irritation
> it has cost already, and is likely still to be attended with; its value is
> quite mistaken and overrated, as it can do very little good or harm
> on either side, Yet not this, but the very reverse is the general
> opinion ...[29]

26 Gradwell to Poynter, 5 May 1819, WDA.   27 Macaulay, *The appointments of the archbishops of Armagh in the nineteenth century*, pp 1–39. On 4 Feb. 1819, he had told Wellington that 'if any doubts should be there entertained [by the government] concerning my principles, connexions or conduct, the nomination made in my favour should be there set aside'.   28 Curtis to Wellington, 4 Dec. 1828 quoted in McGrath, *The public ministry of Bishop James Doyle*, p. 66.   29 Curtis to Sir John Sinclair, 22 Oct. 1828, ibid.

Had any of his colleagues seen this letter, not to mention O'Connell and the leaders of the Irish Catholic Association, they would have been appalled and mystified. They would have been completely baffled by his description of the campaign as 'contemptible'. To have the primate of their church calling into question what they had striven for despite colossal obstacles, delays and frustrations would have shaken their confidence in ecclesiastical leadership.

Wellington's answer was far from a positive commitment to carry a bill of emancipation, but, on the other hand, it was not the kind of rejection which would have dashed the hopes of the Catholics. Remarking that he was 'sincerely anxious to witness the settlement of the Roman Catholic question, which by benefiting the state, would confer a benefit on every individual belonging to it', he then added the bleak prediction that he saw no prospect of such a settlement. He explained that the issue had been so bedevilled by party passions that it was impossible to have it considered disinterestedly. Consequently, he begged for patience: 'if we could bury it in oblivion for a short time, and employ that time diligently in the consideration of its difficulties on all sides (for they are very great), I should not despair of seeing a satisfactory remedy'. Catholics could have concluded from the letter that the duke, who had long been recognized as an opponent of their claims, and excoriated by O'Connell as such, had at least moved into a neutral gear, and, depending on circumstances, would be prepared to accommodate them. The question left to trouble them was the length of time the duke expected them to wait. Feeling that the tide was with them since the Clare victory, they did not relish the prospect of a further delay of three or four years.[30] Curtis shared the duke's answer with a few friends and with O'Connell, and it was later published in the newspapers.

Curtis replied to the duke a week later. Explaining that he was forced to publish the letter since it was franked by the writer and word would soon have got around Drogheda about its source, he paid a fulsome tribute to Wellington's liberal and benevolent sentiments. But he took issue with the duke's suggestion that the question should be buried in oblivion for a short time. Such views might be understandable in a private individual, but should not trouble a powerful prime minister who had distinguished himself as a most successful general. The archbishop added that his friends had assured him that no opposition could resist the application of the premier's general prerogative, and furthermore that the prospect of 'burying the Catholic question in oblivion for the purpose of considering it more at leisure' would exasperate those strongly desiring it, and encourage their bitter opponents, the Orangemen and members of the Brunswick clubs. Disclaiming any desire to interfere in politics, he explained that he involved himself in

30 *FJ*, 26 Dec. 1828. Wellington's letter was dated 11 Dec. 1828.

the question from an obligation to contribute to charity, moderation and forbearance.[31]

Lord Anglesey, the lord lieutenant, on discovering that Wellington's answer to Curtis was authentic, recommended its publication widely in the newspapers. Wellington and Peel had already decided on his dismissal, being dissatisfied with his response to the Catholic agitation. Consequently, he was free to advise Curtis that 'the Catholic should trust to the justice of his cause – to the growing liberality of mankind', and regret that, he (the Catholic) had 'lost some friends and fortified his enemies, within the last six months by unmeasured and unnecessary violence'.[32]

III

As 1828 ended, the Irish and the British associations passed resolutions demanding that their rights be granted. Referring to the anticipated bill for emancipation, the British association expressed a wish that, if it contained conditions derogating from the general and received discipline and canons of the church, the committee hoped that it would be rejected by every sincere Catholic. Contemplating with regret the symptoms of discord between the British and Irish associations, the executive aspired to see the association resist all securities in any proposed bill, to stand by the words of the recent petitions and thereby render themselves worthy of the confidence of their Catholic fellow countrymen. The society believed that no better security could be offered than that of the oath of loyalty to the sovereign and the state.[33]

In Ireland, the dismissal of Lord Anglesey caused serious disappointment to churchmen and to politicians. Archbishop Murray, at a meeting of the Catholic Association at which an address was presented to Anglesey, emphasized that it was not by 'personal or irritating insinuations' that the retiring viceroy should be honoured or the interests of the country promoted. 'A more steady hand,' the archbishop declared, 'never held the destinies of Ireland.' He had devoted himself to the general interests of the island. Murray expressed the widely held Catholic view when he declared that the viceroy's recall was 'a national misfortune, and a new infusion into the cup of Irish calamity'.[34]

The Irish association was again embarrassed by the wavering of its sister association in Britain on the disputed issue of unqualified emancipation. A meeting attended by some 500 people was held in London on 21 January

31 *FJ*, 3 Jan. 1829. The letter was dated 19 Dec. 1828.   32 Anglesey to Curtis, 23 Dec. 1828, *FJ*, 2 Jan. 1829.   33 Ibid., 19 Dec. 1828.   34 Ibid., 12 Jan. 1829.

1829 in response to the Irish association's repudiation of securities. The peers and the leading English members of the association did not attend but many Irish members who were resident in England turned up, and took part in the heated discussions. Eneas MacDonnell, in a lengthy speech, pointed out that the majority of prelates and laity, both in England and Ireland, had protested against securities for the previous twenty years. He proposed resolutions demanding the total, unqualified and unconditional repeal of all laws restricting civil and religious liberty, and calling for resistance to the imposition of any securities or conditions attached to any bill for Catholic relief. Though he won considerable support, an amendment was proposed offering full approbation of Blount's sentiments on concessions and assuring Blount of their indebtedness to him for his services to the Catholic body. A prolonged and noisy debate ensued, and Blount complained about 'the dictatorial tone assumed by Mr O'Connell and the Irish association'. After ten hours of discussion, which understandably proved too much for the stamina of many of those present, the amendment was put and it was carried by eighteen votes to seventeen.[35]

O'Connell, indifferent to the charges against him, was outraged by the verdict of the meeting, believing, as he did, that it was Irish activists who had virtually won emancipation. With burning indignation he asked at the next meeting of the Irish Catholic Association 'what have the cringing English Catholics got by their subserviency. They have been the most time-serving crouching creatures that ever lived ...'[36] He planned to bring forward resolutions asserting that the Irish Catholics demanded unqualified emancipation, whereas, when the English Catholics petition for unqualified emancipation 'and express their readiness to take it qualified, they belie us and involve themselves in utter absurdity'. Consequently, as the English Catholics had virtually separated themselves from the Irish, they should be left to their own fate and the Irish should try to manage their own cause as best they could. Eneas MacDonnell was therefore to be requested to hold no further communication with the British association (a threat that was not carried out).[37]

In January 1829, Wellington brought to the king's attention the dangers deriving from the heightened agitation in Ireland, and sought his permission to have the question discussed in cabinet so that a solution satisfactory both to the Protestant establishment and to the Catholics could be found. George IV reluctantly consented, as Peel had already withdrawn his threat to resign if emancipation were granted, and so the proposals for legislation could be drawn up.[38] O'Connell decided to go to London to try to influence the

---

35 *FJ*, 26 Jan. 1829; *CJ*, 25 Jan. 1829.   36 A few days earlier Bishop Doyle had given O'Connell some salutary advice, which he did not always take: 'the *suaviter in modo* and *fortiter in re*, so little suited to us Irish, would be always useful to you' (McGrath, *The public ministry of Bishop James Doyle*, p. 69).   37 *FJ*, 28 Jan. 1829; *CJ*, 1 Feb. 1829.   38 Ward, *The eve of Catholic emancipa-*

situation, which he felt was promising, and in his absence the Catholic Association was dissolved.

At the last meeting of the Catholic Association before his departure on 6 February, O'Connell enthused about the bill for emancipation, which he claimed was already prepared, though, in fact, the details were still under discussion. Confident that it would be free of conditions, he declared that there would be no need for the government to suppress the association, as it would voluntarily cease to exist, but he promised that he would rather 'die on the scaffold than even consent to an abolition of that brave, that noble, and generous body',the forty-shilling freeholders. Attributing their ultimate success to the appeal of the Protestant peers, gentry and prominent citizens, he called for vigilance lest Peel, whose whole life had been 'one uninter-rupted scene of antipathy and malignant prejudice against Ireland', would be unable to shake off his anti-Irish qualities and 'close his career of opposition by one splendid act of political regeneration'. He had harsh words for his English co-religionists, whose conduct he claimed had been very unfortu-nate, and he maintained that if any securities were introduced into the bill the fault would lie with the British Catholics. Theirs had been 'a most infelici-tous connection', and he mused on the possibility of a different association arising in England 'to counteract the mischievous consequences that may grow out of the cringing conduct of the British association and to avert the evils that may be done by Mr Blount and his supporters'. Then, referring to his former reference to a concordat, he quoted a letter from Bishop Baines to Wilmot Horton in which Baines denied that the pope had given the answer to which he (O'Connell) had referred, and he accepted Baines' comment that the pope would not negotiate with a court that had a law forbidding commu-nication with the Holy See. He accepted the denial of the Hanoverian ambassador of having acted as an intermediary with the Holy See, but he still maintained that contacts on that subject had been made by a minister.[39]

At a meeting of the British association arguments continued about the concessions to be made by the government, and to some extent there was an English-Irish split on the issue. Lord Anglesey, the ex-viceroy, then acted as an intermediary between O'Connell and the British association, many of whose members had been hurt by O'Connell's criticism. Consequently, Norfolk, Blount and other members of the association called on O'Connell at his hotel and the ill feelings were set aside.[40]

When parliament met on 5 February 1829, the king's speech outlined the government's plans.[41] The house of commons supported the cabinet's proposal of linking emancipation with the dissolution of the Catholic

tion, iii, pp 240–2; Muir, *Wellington: Waterloo and the fortunes of peace, 1814–1852*, pp 332–4. 39 *FJ*, 4 Feb. 1829. O'Connell also dismissed Horton's proposal that Catholics in parliament should not be allowed, directly or indirectly, to discuss the established church.   40 *FJ*, 27 Feb. 1829, quoting the *Morning Chronicle*.   41 Wellington had already discussed emancipation with the archbishop of Canterbury and the bishops of London and Durham. The Anglican bishops

Association and the disfranchisement of the forty-shilling freeholders. The duke of Cumberland, the king's brother, galvanized the opposition of the Ultra-Tories in the house of lords, and some of the Anglican bishops lent their influential support. Nonetheless, the bill passed its third reading on 10 April, and on 13 April, the king signed it into law.[42]

Now Catholics could at last become members of parliament. All offices, civil and military, except that of the monarchy, the lord chancellorships of England and Ireland and the lord lieutenancy were opened to Catholics. The offensive oaths repudiating Catholic beliefs which members of parliament were obliged to take were replaced by a general one of allegiance. The core elements of the previous oaths about the royal succession, the pledge not to disturb or weaken the Protestant religion or government, the denial of the papal deposing power of princes excommunicated or deprived by the pope, and the denial of papal jurisdiction in the civil or temporal affairs of the realm were retained. The pope's alleged dispensing power from all oaths, which greatly exercised some Protestants and was mentioned in the bills of 1813 and 1823, was also included. There was no mention of papal infallibility or forgiveness of sin. As a sop to Protestant prejudice, Catholic bishops were forbidden to use the titles of their sees, and the Jesuits and religious orders were forbidden from entering the country. Those already resident were obliged to register, and Jesuits and other orders were prevented from admitting new members. No mention was made of the appointments of bishops or of the submission of Roman documents to governmental inspection. Peel was credited, once he had changed his mind, with getting the cabinet to approve of this 'clear-cut radical solution'.[43]

O'Connell was not disturbed by the clauses prohibiting the ingress of the Jesuits and the religious orders. He claimed that he would 'drive a coach and six' through that restriction. He regarded the prohibition on Catholic bishops using the titles of their sees as 'absurd and childish', and he was happy to tell a colleague that he had always known that when emancipation came 'they would not care a bulrush about those vetoistical arrangements which so many paltry Catholics from time to time pressed on me as being useful to emancipation'.[44]

The oath of allegiance prescribed in the act was forwarded to Rome and was examined at the behest of the pope by Carlo Vizzardelli, an official of the congregation for Extraordinary Ecclesiastical Affairs.[45] This oath included a

---

were strongly opposed to the measure. When news of the king's speech spread, no less than 720 anti-Catholic petitions were sent to parliament. One from Glasgow had 37,000 signatures, one from Kent had 81,400 signatures and one from Ireland 168,000 signatures (Brown, *The national churches of England, Ireland and Scotland, 1801–46*, p. 143). **42** Muir, *Wellington: Waterloo and the fortunes of peace, 1814–1852*, pp 337–47. **43** Gash, *Mr Secretary Peel*, p. 586. **44** O'Connell (ed.), *O'Connell correspondence*, iv, p. 23. **45** Carlo Vizzardelli (1791–1851) became a cardinal in 1848 and prefect of the congregation of Studies.

pledge not to make use of any privilege to disturb or weaken the Protestant church and government – a pledge which English Catholics had not previously taken but which the Irish had been obliged to take since 1793.

Vizzardelli disapproved of the conclusion about taking the oath 'without any evasion, equivocation or mental reservation', but felt that, if it referred to a faultless formula, it was harmless. But if the government wanted to show that Catholics admitted mental reservations in the oath, and, by doing so, did an injury to their doctrine, the result was that the man who took the oath did something absolutely wrong. It would be necessary to point out, he concluded, that those who swore to that clause or their ecclesiastical superiors were protesting to the public that they were doing so to satisfy others and not because the church did not condemn mental reservations.

He also disliked the pledge to swear to the succession of the family of the Princess Sophia, being Protestant, but regarded it as tolerable on the grounds that it was not a new constitutional arrangement excluding Catholics from the throne, but rather a promise to defend the Protestants who, by a previous act, were the only people called to the throne. One also should take account of the fact, he thought, that a Catholic in good conscience could not succeed as long as the constitution, which obliged the king to actions opposed to the Catholic religion, was not changed.

Vizzardelli recalled that his suggestion about tolerating these elements in the oath coincided with the decision of the congregation of Propaganda in 1794 to tolerate them in the oath prescribed for the English and Scottish Catholics. Dealing with the promise to defend the laws of property, abjuring any intention of subverting the establishment of the Anglican church and not use any privilege to disturb or weaken the Protestant religion and government, he noted that the clause relating to the defence of property tended to sanction the ancient usurpation of the goods of Catholics, and especially of the church. But the Irish bishops had agreed to this in their declaration of 1826, and a less offensive interpretation could be given to the words by recollecting that the church had no hope of regaining the possession of those goods which had long been in the hands of others. The same would apply to the intention not to subvert the Anglican church, which could be interpreted as the wish not to use dangerous means to do so. And the promise not to use privileges would not include the commitment to abstain from the fulfilment of obligations, when the Catholic was bound in conscience to take actions that disturbed or weakened Protestantism. In confirmation of this view, he recalled that the preaching of Catholic truths and the refutation of opposing errors had always been carried out by Catholics even when they made similar promises in the past, and the government had never considered that conduct as a violation of the oath.

Nonetheless, he found in the whole context of this promise something perverse – or at least a dangerous and scandalous element. And bearing in mind that the oath was to be taken without any evasion, equivocation or mental reservation, he could not but find in the promise about not disturbing the Protestant church and government an inexcusable offence. Recalling the decision of the congregation of Propaganda on the oath of 1793 that it was reprehensible and should not be taken by Catholics, he maintained that the judgment then passed concerned that part of the oath.

However, given the dangerous circumstances then prevailing, the congregation decided not to issue a condemnation but to write to the Irish bishops warning them that Catholics should not take the oath. He thought that, if there was to be a condemnation, it should be directed principally against the declaration of the Irish bishops of 1826. He believed that a doctrinal declaration made by a respectable bench of bishops to recognize as lawful and good those promises later sanctioned in the bill was the most reprehensible and the most scandalous act of all those seen in recent times in Great Britain.

He was convinced that the time was not suitable for issuing a condemnation of an oath which had been delayed for thirty-six years, in the case of the preceding formula, and had not been applied in the previous three years to the declaration of the Irish bishops. They were in a time of crisis and they hoped that the divine mercy would increase the number of Catholics in Great Britain. A solemn act against the oath, or the declaration of the bishops to which for the most part the oath conformed, would at that time annoy the Protestants, who would become more difficult to convert, and would encounter opposition from the Catholics. Humanly speaking, it was not to be hoped that Catholics would cease to take an oath which they had taken without difficulty on other occasions, or that their bishops could be induced to repudiate what they had approved of a few years previously in a solemn declaration. Consequently, they should maintain the moderate system adopted in 1794. Nevertheless, it might be appropriate for the Holy See to seek an opportunity to let it be known that it was displeased about the oath, and, much more so, that it was disturbed by the bishops (or at least the Irish bishops) approving – for the most part – those articles contained in it.[46]

If Vizzardelli had found parts of the oath reprehensible, the bishops and the vicars apostolic, had they seen his *votum* or judgment, would have found it incomprehensible. As he admitted, the clauses to which he most strongly objected formed part of the oath of 1793 and had been taken by Irish Catholics since that time. The Irish bishops, quite rightly, had always recognized that the pledge not to disturb and/or weaken the established church and government referred – and could only refer to – avoiding the use of violent or improper means to do so. There was never any suggestion that Protestant individuals might not become Catholics as a result of peaceful

46 Vizzardelli, *votum*, 18 May 1829, ASV, Segr Stato, Inghilterra, 1814–1856, 29, ff 314r–321r.

evangelization, persuasion and conviction. The vast majority of Catholics would have regarded the prospect of a wholesale conversion of Protestants to Catholicism in the wake of emancipation, which some Roman officials like Vizzardelli seemed to think likely, as fantasy. Catholics would not have thought of provoking trouble by publicly preaching in the streets of towns or cities. Consequently, they did not believe that any serious restriction was being imposed on them.

Though Vizzardelli had castigated the Irish bishops for their declaration of 1826, in which this promise not to subvert the established church and government was given, it had also been included in the bills of 1813 and 1821. Only Milner had taken exception to it; the other vicars apostolic, like their Irish colleagues, had not complained about it. Vizzardelli at least had the wit not to call for a condemnation of the oath. Had he done so, and had his recommendation been acted upon, the reaction among both British and Irish Catholics would have far surpassed in anger and venom the hostility shown to the veto in 1814.

The pope to whom this *votum* or opinion was addressed was Pius VIII, who had been elected on 31 March 1829. Lord Burghersh, the envoy in Florence, had been instructed by Lord Aberdeen, the foreign secretary, to go to Rome for the conclave but to take no part in it, and to express no 'lively interest' in the success of any particular candidate.[47] Burghersh was received by the new pope two weeks after the election and found him enthusiastic about the relief bill. Pius, he reported, was delighted to find 'it was not clogged with any of those restrictions, which had been thought of on previous occasions, some of which during Lord Castlereagh's administration he had been called upon to examine'.[48] He was not disturbed by the clauses forbidding Catholic bishops to use the titles of the clergy of the established church, and he was anxious 'about any measure which would prevent the great and respectable body of clergy of the established Church for looking with jealousy at their Catholic brethren'.

Burghersh quoted the pope as saying that the king could rely on the gratitude and devoted loyalty of the Catholics. As obedience to their sovereign was the first duty of true Catholics, and as obedience was due to a Nero, how much more so was it due 'to a most Christian king, such as the present sovereign of the British Empire'? he asked. There was no exertion that Pius would not make 'to render the great benefit he [the king] was conferring upon the Catholics a blessing to himself and a source of strength and happiness to his empire'. Burghersh was also welcomed by Cardinal Albani, the secretary of state, who also expressed sentiments of friendship and assurances of Catholic loyalty to their country.[49]

47 Aberdeen to Burghersh, 20 Feb. 1829, NA, FO 79/53.   48 Pius had been a student – and later, vicar general – of Archbishop Devoti, the canonist who had examined Grattan's bill of 1813 for Quarantotti.   49 Burghersh to Aberdeen, 14, 23 Apr. 1829, NA, FO 79/53. Burghersh had

Pius was more liberal in his thinking than Leo XII, who had reigned from 1823 to 1829, and who had not had to pass judgment on the bills for relief once they were defeated. Though Leo XII had been conservative and had undone some of Consalvi's reforms, he had continued the policy of Pius VII by arranging concordats or agreements with Hanover and the Netherlands. In each case, the chapters of the diocese sent to the ministry a list of the candidates from which the choice of a bishop would be made, and the ministry could strike out the names of those it found unacceptable.[50] Reports about these concordats had enabled O'Connell to speculate with some plausibility about some similar arrangement for Britain and Ireland, and had comparable terms been suggested for Ireland, he would have objected to them, as he had objected to the Genoese letter. Some of the Irish bishops would have gone along with him, but the vicars apostolic would have found it more difficult to resist the nobility and gentry of the Catholic Association, who would most likely have been happy to accept them.

Though oaths for Catholics to secure their toleration by the state had been proposed in the first half of the eighteenth century, the oath put forward by Lord Limerick in 1756 could be regarded as the first one of any significance in the campaign for Catholic relief. From then until 1829 several oaths were included in the bills for relief, and, though some were longer than others all included the core elements of allegiance to the king and the Hanoverian succession, defence of the sovereign against conspiracy, the repudiation of the lawfulness of not keeping faith with heretics or of murdering them, the rejection of the pope's and others' power to dispense from the obligations of an oath and of the papal power to depose princes or to exercise civil jurisdiction in the state. The person taking the oath swore to do so without any evasion or mental reservation. The oath of 1774, which English Catholics could take from 1791, included the rejection of the Stuarts' claims to the throne, but by 1793 the Pretender had died and there was no specific mention of him.

The oath of 1793 contained a denial of papal infallibility and of the power of any pope or priest to forgive sins without sorrow on the penitents' part. It also introduced the clause obliging those who took it to abjure any intention of subverting the church establishment and of using any privilege accorded by law to disturb and weaken the Protestant religion and Protestant government.

taken an interest in ecclesiastical affairs and had made some comments about them to the Foreign Office. He had forwarded a copy of the concordat between the Holy See and the king of the Netherlands (22 Sept. 1827, NA, FO 79/49).   50 In the case of the dioceses of Hildesheim and Osnabruck in Hanover, the agreement stated: 'ac si forte aliquis ex Candidatis ipsis Gubernio sit minus gratus Capitulum e catalago eum expunget, reliquo tamen manente sufficienti Candidatorum numero, ex quo novus Episcopus eligi valeat' (Mercati, *Raccolta di concordati*, pp 689–96).

This last clause exercised the minds of the Roman authorities at the highest level more than any other. According to Vizzardelli, the cardinals of the congregation of Propaganda had it expressly in mind when they issued their hostile judgment of the oath in 1794. And the consultors who examined the bill of 1813 for Quarantotti also raised questions about it, though they accepted the view that it only referred to the use of violence. Vizzardelli's appraisal of it was pedantic, pernickety and wrong-headed. No body of bishops in England, Ireland or anywhere else would have approved of terms that prevented people from becoming Catholics, and the mention of not subverting the Protestant government and Protestant church could only have referred to the use of violent means. The danger of violence being used against the government was chimerical.

Apart from this clause, the opposition of Rome to other elements of the oaths must have been based on historical reasons or originated from the view that the papacy was being insulted by offensive language. The implication that Catholics would carry out evil acts and justify this by claiming that they were done for the good of the church, or were bound to obey immoral acts or believe that sins could be forgiven without sorrow was regarded as insulting to both the pope and the church. In the oath of 1821, before it was revised, the person who swore it expressed his abjuration of that 'damnable' doctrine and position that excommunicated princes could be deposed or murdered as impious and heretical. Milner, in his proposed oath of 1821, referred to this claim as a treasonable doctrine and position. But because popes had declared sovereigns in the past deposed, it was deemed improper and a form of condemnation of them to suggest that their actions or decisions had been wrong. And when reference was made in oaths to the 'damnable and heretical' doctrine that princes might be deposed by the pope, an overly scrupulous or myopic interpretation of that clause could have charged popes from Gregory VII to Paul V with heresy. No British statesman or politician would have seriously considered the possibility of the pope deposing their sovereign.

Vizzardelli's strictures against the oath, as he suggested, led to no action from Rome. Archbishop Oliver Kelly of Tuam visited Pope Pius VIII within two months of his election and some six weeks after the bill became law, and reported that he said many things on emancipation and 'on the oath which he does not much relish'.[51] No doubt he too was perplexed by the pledge not to disturb and weaken the established church, but his reservation was not translated into action.

The government, in fact, needed none of the guarantees which it demanded in the oaths. The pope could not have exercised any power or

---

51 Kelly to Murray, 27 May 1829, DDA.

significant influence in Britain or Ireland. Catholics in Britain were a very small minority, and though they were numerous in Ireland, no pope would have encouraged or approved of any violent action by them against their government. Papal influence, if used at all, in Ireland would have been used in favour of the government. There was no danger whatever of seditious documents being sent to the bishops in Ireland or Britain, and no likelihood of a rebellious or disloyal priest being chosen as a bishop. The reaction of the bishops to the rebellion in 1798 had given clear and unmistakeable proof of their loyalty and of their hostility to violent insurrection. Castlereagh and his assistants in Dublin Castle appreciated the part played by the bishops in denouncing all violations of the law, and Castlereagh must have known that there was no danger to the state from Irish prelates, and even less from the vicars apostolic of Britain. Yet he always insisted on 'securities'.

What he really meant was that Protestant sentiment demanded some 'concession' of that nature. Protestant attitudes to the papacy were still governed by the perceptions and images of the Reformation and of James II, and the pope, in the wild imaginations of some people, was credited with powers and ambitions which he did not possess. Though Pius VII behaved impeccably as far as the British government was concerned during the Napoleonic wars, the fear of papal craft remained. Numerous petitions from Anglican bishops, nonconformist clergy and Protestant laity were presented to parliament against emancipation. And it was to accommodate these prejudices and opinions that restrictions on bishops and on their contacts with Rome, and the obligations of the oaths were proposed.

The Roman Catholic relief bill became law when signed by King George IV on 13 April 1829. The long campaign for Catholic relief had ended but the immediate victory was more psychological than practical. Most Catholics in Ireland did not have the education – or means to obtain it – which would have made them eligible for high professional or public office. Old-boy and other networks also conspired to deprive them of promotions. Catholics in Britain were a small percentage of the population, and apart from the upper classes could not have been expected to figure prominently in high office. In the parliament of 1830, five English Catholics were elected to the house of commons, and eleven Irish Catholics won seats. In the parliament of 1831, the number of English Catholic members increased to eight, and Irish Catholic members to thirteen.[52]

The leaders of the English Catholics – the duke of Norfolk and Edward Blount – acknowledged O'Connell's preponderant role in obtaining Catholic relief and equality with their Protestant fellow citizens, and treated him with courtesy and consideration after the bill became law. Not all the better-off

52 Ward, *The eve of Catholic emancipation*, iii, p. 276.

Catholics showed him the same gratitude. When he applied to join their club, the Cisalpine, he was blackballed, though it later transpired that only two members had opposed his membership. He contented himself with remarking that 'it was a strange thing of them to do; it was a comical "testimonial" of my services in emancipating them'.[53]

The Irish bishops issued a formal expression of gratitude for the great boon of emancipation in February 1830. Written by Doyle, it expressed their thanks in the adulatory manner that was probably expected on such an occasion. Praise was heaped on the king and Wellington, and the Catholic people were bidden to respect the constitution, the king and the legislature, and were encouraged to avoid religious discord and party dissensions and to labour for the pacification and improvement of Ireland. The bishops strongly expressed the hope that the clergy would not have to continue the role they had played in politics, but they did not – as their successors would – issue an order forbidding such intervention. Doyle was thought to have suggested this pastoral as a means of obtaining goodwill, with a view to an appeal to parliament on education. Copies sent to Peel and Wellington did not elicit replies, but the lord lieutenant and chief secretary were pleased with the gesture.[54]

O'Connell, writing on the day after the act of emancipation became law, 'the first day of freedom', hailed the measure as a 'bloodless revolution more extensive in its operation than any other political change that could take place'.[55] It was an appropriate comment on the happy ending of a long and tortuous but peaceful struggle.

---

53 MacDonagh, *The hereditary bondsman*, p. 270.   54 McGrath, *The public ministry of Bishop James Doyle*, pp 77–8.   55 Ibid., 74.

Bibliography

MANUSCRIPT SOURCES

Belfast
Public Record Office of Northern Ireland
Papers of Lord Castlereagh
Papers of Lord Donoughmore

Birmingham
Birmingham Diocesan Archives
Papers of Bishop John Milner

Bristol
Clifton Diocesan Archives
Papers of Bishop Peter Bernardine Collingridge
Papers of Bishop Gregory Sharrock
Papers of Bishop Charles Walmesley

Carlow
Kildare and Leighlin Diocesan Archives
Papers of Bishop James W. Doyle

Cork
Cloyne Diocesan Archives
Papers of Bishop William Coppinger

Cork and Ross Diocesan Archives
Papers of Bishop Francis Moylan

Dublin
Dublin Diocesan Archives
Papers of Archbishop Murray
Papers of Archbishop Troy

National Library of Ireland
Papers of Archbishop Bray (on microfilm)
Papers of Lord Gormanston

Edinburgh
Scottish Catholic Archives
Papers of Bishop Alexander Cameron

Leeds
Leeds Diocesan Archives
Papers of Bishop Matthew Gibson
Papers of Bishop William Gibson
Papers of Bishop Thomas Smith

London
National Archives
Reports to the Foreign Office from the British embassy to the Grand Duchy of
    Tuscany in Florence

Westminster Diocesan Archives
Papers of Bishop James Yorke Bramston
Papers of Bishop John Douglass
Papers of Revd Robert Gradwell
Papers of Bishop William Poynter

Matlock
Derbyshire Record Office
Papers of Sir Robert Wilmot Horton

Newry
Dromore Diocesan Archives
Papers of Bishop Michael Blake

Rome
Archives of the Sacred Congregation for the Evangelization of Peoples
Correspondence, recommendations and decisions relating to Ireland
Papers of Cardinal Consalvi

Archives of the Sacred Congregation for Extraordinary Ecclesiastical Affairs
Papers relating to England and Ireland

Archives of the Sacred Congregation for the Doctrine of the Faith
Papers relating to oaths in the legislation for the relief of Catholics

Vatican Archives
Papers of the Secretariat of State relating to Ireland

NEWSPAPERS

Catholic Journal	*Freeman's Journal*
Catholic Miscellany	*Northern Whig*
Dublin Chronicle	*Orthodox Journal*
Dublin Evening Post	

PRINTED PRIMARY SOURCES

Berington, J., *The state and behaviour of English Catholics from the Reformation to the year 1780* (London, 1780).

—— *The rights of dissenters from the established church in relation principally to English Catholics* (Birmingham, 1789).

—— *The memoirs of G. Panzani; giving an account of his agency in England in the years 1634, 1635, 1636 ...* (Birmingham 1793).

Blue Books, *Papers of the Catholic Committee of England ...* 3 vols (London, 1789–91).

Burke, T., *Hibernia Dominicana, sive historia provinciae Hiberniae ordinis praedicatorum* (Cologne, 1762; supplement 1772).

Butler, C., *Historical memoirs respecting the English, Irish and Scottish Catholics from the Reformation to the present time*, 4 vols (London, 1819–21).

Clergyman of Massachusetts, *The works of Revd Arthur O'Leary, OSF* (Boston, 1868).

Doyle, J.W., *A vindication of the religious and civil principles of the Irish Catholics in a letter addressed to his excellency, the Marquis Wellesley, K.G., lord lieutenant general and governor general of Ireland* (Dublin, 1823).

—— *A defence by J.K.L. of his vindication of the religious and civil principles of the Irish Catholics* (Dublin, 1824).

—— *Letters on a reunion of the churches of England and Rome from and to the Rt. Revd Dr Doyle, RC, Bishop if Kildare, John O'Driscoll, Alexander Knox and Thomas Newenham* (Gloucester, 1824).

—— *An essay on the Catholic claims addressed to the Right Honourable the Earl of Liverpool, KG* (Dublin, 1826).

—— *A letter to the Duke of Wellington on the Catholic claims* (Liverpool, 1828).

England, T.R., *Life of the Reverend Arthur O'Leary* (London, 1822).

Fitzpatrick, W.J., *The life, times and correspondence of Dr Doyle*, 2 vols (Dublin, 1880).

Giblin, C. (ed.), 'The papers of Richard Joachim Hayes, OFM' in *Coll. Hib.*, 21–5 (1979–83).

Grattan, H. (ed.), *Memoirs of the life and times of the Rt. Hon. Henry Grattan*, 5 vols (London, 1839–46).

Hussey, T., *A pastoral letter to the Catholic clergy of the united dioceses of Waterford and Lismore* (Waterford, 1797).

Lingard, J., *A review of certain anti-Catholic publications* (London, 1813).

——*Observations on the laws and ordinances which exist in foreign states relative to the religious concerns of their Roman Catholic subjects* (London, 1817).

MacDermot, B. (ed.), *The Catholic question in Ireland and England, 1788–1822: the papers of Denys Scully* (Dublin, 1988).

—— *The Irish Catholic petition of 1805: the diary of Denys Scully* (Dublin, 1992).

McCarthy, D., *Collections on Irish Church history from the Mss of the late V. Revd Laurence F. Renehan* (Dublin, 1861).

Miller, D.W. (ed.), *Peep O'Day boys and Defenders: selected documents on the county Armagh disturbances, 1784–96* (Belfast, 1990).

Milner, J., *The divine right of episcopacy addressed to the Catholic laity of England in answer to the Layman (Sir John Throckmorton) and Second letter to the Catholic clergy of England* (London, 1791).

—— *The end of religious controversy* (London, 1796).

—— *A letter to the Rt Revd John Douglass, vicar apostolic of the London District* (London, 1797).

—— *Dr Milner's appeal to the Catholics of Ireland deprecating the attacks made upon him by Sir R. Musgrave* (Dublin, 1809).

—— *An elucidation of the veto in a threefold address to the public* … (London, 1810).

—— *Letter to a Roman Catholic prelate of Ireland in refutation of C. Butler's letter to an Irish Catholic gentleman* (Dublin, 1811).

—— *An explanation with the Rt Revd Dr Poynter, coadjutor LD* (Wolverhampton, 1812).

—— *A brief memorial on the Catholic bill* (London, 1813).

—— *Supplementary memoirs of English Catholics addressed to C. Butler* … (London, 1820).

—— *Letters to a prebendary being an answer to reflections on popery by Revd J. Sturges* … (London, 1833).

Moran, P.F. (ed.), *Spicilegium Ossoriense, being a collection of original letters and papers illustrative of the history of the Irish church from the Reformation to 1800*, 3 vols (Dublin, 1874–84).

O'Connell, J. (ed.), *The life and speeches of Daniel O'Connell, MP*, 2 vols (Dublin, 1846).

O'Connell, J. (ed.), *The select speeches of Daniel O'Connell, MP* (Dublin, 1855).

O'Connell, M. (ed.), *The correspondence of Daniel O'Connell*, 8 vols (Shannon, 1972–80).

Parker, C.S. (ed.), *Sir Robert Peel from his private papers*, 2 vols (London, 1891).

Plowden, C., *An answer to the Second Blue Book* … *addressed to the Roman Catholics of England* (London, 1791).

—— *Remarks on the writings* … *of Revd J. Berington addressed to the Catholic clergy of England* (London, 1792).

—— *A letter from C. Plowden to C. Butler, W. Cruise, H. Clifford, W. Throckmorton, supporters of the Cisalpine Club* … (London, 1796).

Plowden, F., *A historical review of the state of Ireland, from the invasion of that country under Henry II to its union with Great Britain*, 2 vols (London, 1803).

Plunket, D. (ed.), *The life, letters and speeches of Lord Plunket*, 2 vols (London, 1867).

Redesdale, Lord, *Correspondence between the Right. Hon. Lord Redesdale, Lord High Chancellor of Ireland and the Right Hon. the earl of Fingall* (Dublin, 1804).

Ross, C., *The correspondence of Charles, first marquis Cornwallis*, 3 vols (London, 1859).

Select committee on the state of Ireland, Report and evidence 1825 (129), viii.

—— Minutes of evidence taken before the lords' committee 1825 (181), ix.

Stafford clergy, *An appeal to the Catholics of England by Catholic clergy of the county of Stafford* (Wolverhampton, 1792).

Throckmorton, J., *A letter to the Catholic clergy of England on the appointment of bishops. By a layman* (London, 1790)
—— *A second letter addressed to the Catholic clergy of England on the appointment of bishops. In which the objections to the first letter are answered* (London, 1791).
Troy, J.T., *A pastoral instruction on the duties of Christian citizens* (Dublin, 1793).
—— *Pastoral instructions to the Roman Catholics of Dublin* (Dublin, 1798).
Vane, C. (ed.), *Memoirs and correspondence of Viscount Castlereagh* (London, 1850).
Ward, C.C. and R.E., *The letters of Charles O'Conor of Belanagare*, 2 vols (Ann Arbor, 1980).
Wellington, Duke of (ed.), *Despatches, correspondence and memoranda of Field Marshal Arthur, duke of Wellington*, 8 vols (London, 1867–80).
Wyse, T., *Historical sketch of the late Catholic Association of Ireland*, 2 vols (Dublin, 1829).

SECONDARY SOURCES

Akenson, D.H., *The Irish education experiment: the national system of education in the nineteenth century* (London, 1970).
—— *The Church of Ireland: ecclesiastical reform and revolution* (New Haven, CT, and London, 1971).
Anglesey, marquis of, *One leg: the life and letters of Henry William Paget, first marquis of Anglesey, 1768–1854* (London, 1961).
Aspinall, A., *Lord Brougham and the Whig party* (Manchester, 1927).
Aubert, R., Beckman J. and R. Lill, *Tra rivoluzione e restaurazione, 1775–1830* (Milan, 1977).
Auchmuty, J.J., *Sir Thomas Wyse: the life and career of an educator and diplomat* (London, 1939).
Bartlett, T.,'Defenders and Defenderism in 1795', *IHS*, 24 (May 1985), 373–94.
—— 'The origins and progress of the Catholic question, 1690–1800' in T. Power and K. Whelan (eds), *Endurance and emergence: Catholics in Eighteenth Century Ireland* (Dublin, 1990).
—— *The fall and rise of the Irish nation: the Catholic question, 1690–1830* (Dublin 1992).
—— *Ireland: a history* (Cambridge, 2010).
——'Defence, counter-insurgency and rebellion: Ireland, 1793–1803' in Bartlett, T. and K. Jeffrey, *A military history of Ireland* (Cambridge, 1996), pp 247–93.
——'The penal laws against Irish Catholics: were they too good for them?' in Rafferty, O. (ed.), *Irish Catholic identities* (Manchester, 2013).
Bartlett, T. and D.W. Hayton, *Penal era and golden age: essays in Irish history, 1690–1800* (Belfast 1979).
Bellenger, A. (ed.), *Fathers in faith: the Western District, 1688–1988* (Bath, 1991).
Bence-Jones, M., *The Catholic families* (London, 1992).
Bew, J., *Castlereagh: enlightenment, war and tyranny* (London, 2011).
Bew, P., *Ireland: the politics of enmity, 1789–2006* (Oxford, 2007).
Bossy, J., *The English Catholic community, 1570–1850* (London, 1975).

Bowen, D., *The Protestant crusade in Ireland, 1800–70: a study of Catholic-Protestant relations between the Act of Union and disestablishment* (Dublin, 1978).

Brady, J. and P. Corish, 'The church under the penal code' in P.J. Corish (ed.), *A history of Irish Catholicism* (Dublin, 1971), iv: ii.

Broderick, J.F., *The Holy See and the Irish movement for the repeal of the union with England, 1829–1847* (Rome, 1951).

Brooke, P., *Ulster Presbyterianism: the historical perspective, 1610–1970* (Belfast, 1994).

Brown, M., P. Geoghegan and J. Kelly, *The Irish Act of Union, 1800* (Dublin, 2003).

Brown, S., *The national churches of England, Ireland and Scotland, 1801–1846* (Oxford, 2001).

Burkard, D., *Staatskirche, Papstkirche, Bischofskirche: Die Frankfurter Konferenzen und die Neuordnung der Kirche in Deutschland nach der Sakularisation* (Rom, Freiburg, Wien, 2000).

Burns, R.E., 'The Catholic relief act in Ireland, 1778', *Church History*, 32 (1962), 181–207.

—— 'The Irish popery laws: a study in eighteenth century legislation and behaviour', *Review of Politics*, 24 (1962), 485–508.

Buschkühl, M., *Great Britain and the Holy See, 1746–1870* (Dublin, 1982).

Butler, I., *The eldest brother, the Marquess Wellesley, the duke of Wellington's eldest brother* (London 1973).

Chadwick, O., *The popes and European revolution* (Oxford, 1981).

Chinnici, J., *The English Catholic enlightenment* (Shepherdstown, 1980).

Clark, S. and J. Donnelly (eds), *Irish peasants: violence and political unrest, 1780–1914* (Manchester, 1983).

Cogan, A., *The diocese of Meath, ancient and modern*, 3 vols (Dublin, 1870).

Coleman, A. (ed.), *Historical memoirs of the city of Armagh by James Stuart* (Dublin, 1900).

Colley, L., *Britons: forging the nation, 1707–1837* (New Haven, CT, 1992).

Comerford, R.V. et al., *Religion, conflict and coexistence in Ireland: essays presented to Monsignor Patrick J. Corish* (Dublin, 1990).

Connolly, S.J., *Priests and people in pre-Famine Ireland, 1780–1845* (Dublin, 1982).

—— *Divided kingdom, 1690–1800* (Oxford, 2008).

—— 'Aftermath and adjustment', 'The Catholic question 1801–12', 'Union government 1812–23', 'Mass politics and sectarian conflict 1823–30', *NHI*, v, *Ireland under the union*, i (Oxford, 1989), pp 1–106.

Coppa, F., *Controversial concordats: the Vatican's relations with Napoleon, Mussolini and Hitler* (Washington, 1999).

Corish, P., *The Catholic community in the seventeenth and eighteenth centuries* (Dublin, 1981).

—— *The Irish Catholic experience: a historical survey* (Dublin, 1985).

—— *Maynooth College, 1795–1995* (Dublin, 1995).

Couve de Murville, M.M.L., *John Milner, 1752–1826* (Birmingham, 1986).

Curran, K.J., 'Dr Michael Blake and the re-establishment of the Irish College, Rome', *Repertorium Novum*, 2 (1956), 434–42.

Curtin, N., *The United Irishmen: popular politics in Ulster and Dublin, 1791–1798* (Oxford, 1984).

Davis, R.W., 'The Tories, the Whigs and Catholic emancipation, 1827–1829', *English Historical Review*, 98:382 (1982), 89–98.

Dickson, D., Keogh, D. and K. Whelan, *1798: a bicentenary perspective* (Dublin, 2003).

Dickson, D., *New foundations: Ireland, 1600–1800* (Dublin 1987).

Dockery, J.B., *Collingridge: a Franciscan contribution to Catholic emancipation* (Newport, 1954).

Donnelly, J.S., 'Pastorini and Captain Rock: millenarianism and sectarianism in the Rockite movement of 1821–4' in Clark and Donnelly (eds), *Irish peasants, violence and political unrest* (Dublin, 1988).

—— *Captain Rock: the Irish agrarian rebellion of 1821–1824* (Cork, 2009).

Duffy, E.,'Ecclesiastical democracy detected' (3 parts), *Recusant History* (1970–1).

—— *Saints and sinners, a history of the popes* (New Haven, CT, and London, 2006).

Ehrmann, J., *The younger Pitt* (London, 1920).

Elliot, M., *Wolfe Tone: prophet of Irish independence* (New Haven, CT and London, 1989).

Ellis, J.T., *Cardinal Consalvi and Anglo-Papal relations, 1814–1824* (Washington, 1942).

Fagan, P., *Divided loyalties: the question of an oath for Irish Catholics in the eighteenth century* (Dublin, 1997).

Fagan, W., *The life and times of Daniel O'Connell* (Cork, 1847–8).

Fenning, H., *The undoing of the friars of Ireland* (Louvain, 1972).

—— *The Irish Dominican province, 1698–1797* (Dublin, 1990).

——'The archbishops of Dublin, 1693–1786' in Kelly, J., and D. Keogh (eds), *History of the Catholic diocese of Dublin* (Dublin, 2000).

Fischer, E.L., *Cardinal Consalvi: Lebens und Charakterbild des grosseu Ministers Papst Pius VII* (Mainz, 1899).

Fitzpatrick, W.J. (ed.), *Correspondence of Daniel O'Connell, the liberator*, 2 vols (London, 1888).

Flood, J.M., 'Dr Plunket, Bishop of Meath, 1779–1827' in *IER*, 72 (1949), 234–42.

Gash, N., *Lord Liverpool* (London, 1984).

—— *Mr Secretary Peel: the life of Sir Robert Peel to 1830* (London 1985).

Gatz, E., *Die Bischöfe der deutschsprachigen Länder, 1785–1945: Ein biographisches Lexikon* (Berlin, 1983).

Gaunt, R.A., *Sir Robert Peel: the life and legacy (London, 2010)*.

Geoghegan, P.M., *King Dan: the rise of Daniel O'Connell, 1775–1829* (Dublin, 2008).

—— *The Irish Act of Union* (Dublin, 1999).

Gibbons, L. and K. O'Conor (eds), *Charles O'Conor of Ballinagare* (Dublin, 2015).

Giblin, C., 'The Stuart nomination of Irish bishops, 1687–1765', *IER*, 105 (1966), 35–47.

——'Nunziatura di Fiandra' in *Coll. Hib.*, 11 (1968), 64–6.

Gilbert, I., *This restless prelate: Bishop Peter Baines, 1786–1843* (Leominster, Herefordshire, 2006).

Gillow, J., *A literary and biographical history or bibliographical dictionary of the English Catholics*, 5 vols (London, 1885–1903).

Gough, H. and D. Dickson, *Ireland and the French Revolution* (Dublin, 1990).

Hales, E.E.Y., *Revolution and papacy, 1769–1846* (London, 1960).

Hempton, D., and M. Hill, *Evangelical Protestantism in Ulster society, 1740–1890* (London and New York, 1992).

Healy, J., *Maynooth College: its centenary history, 1795–1895* (Dublin, 1895).

Hinde, W., *George Canning* (London, 1973).

—— *Castlereagh* (London, 1981).

Hogan, P., 'Some observations on contemporary allegations as to Bishop Dominic Bellews' (1745–1813) sympathies during the 1795 rebellion in Connaught' in *Seanchas Ard Mhacha*, 10:2 (1982), 417–25.

Holmes, J.D., *More Roman than Rome: English Catholicism in the nineteenth century* (London, 1978).

Huber, E.R. and W., *Staat und Kirche im 19 und 20 Jahrhundert: Dokumente des deutschen Staatskirchenrechts*, 2 vols (Berlin, 1973).

Hughes, P., *The Catholic question, 1688–1829: a study in political history* (London, 1929).

Husenbeth, F.C., *The life of the Right Revd John Milner, DD, Bishop of Castabala, vicar apostolic of the Midland District of England* (Dublin, 1862).

Jenkins, B., *Era of emancipation: British government of Ireland, 1812–1830* (Kingston and Montreal, 1988).

Johnson, C., *Developments in the Roman Catholic Church in Scotland, 1789–1829* (Edinburgh, 1983).

Jupp, P., *British politics on the eve of reform: the duke of Wellington's administration, 1828–1838* (Basingstoke, Hampshire, 1998).

Keenan, D., *The Catholic church in nineteenth century Ireland* (Dublin, 1983).

——*The grail of Catholic emancipation, 1793–1829* (Philadelphia, 2000).

Kelly, J., *Prelude to union: Anglo-Irish politics in the 1780s* (Cork, 1992).

Kelly, J. and D. Keogh (eds), *History of the Catholic diocese of Dublin* (Dublin, 2000).

Keogh, D., *The French disease: the Catholic church and radicalism in Ireland, 1790–1800* (Dublin, 1993).

——'Thomas Hussey, bishop of Waterford' in W. Nolan, T. Parker and D. Cowman (eds), *Waterford: history and society* (Dublin, 1992).

Keogh D. and K. Whelan, *Acts of Union: the causes, contexts and consequences of the Act of Union* (Dublin, 2001).

Larkin, E., *The historical dimensions of Irish Catholicism* (New York, 1976).

Leighton, C.D.A., *Catholicism in a Protestant kingdom: a study of the Irish ancient regime* (Dublin, 1994).

—— 'Gallicanism and the veto controversy: church state and Catholic community in early nineteenth century Ireland' in R.V. Comerford, M. Cullen, J. Hill and C. Lennon (eds), *Religion, conflict and coexistence in Ireland: essays presented to Monsignor Patrick J. Corish* (Dublin, 1990).

Longford, E., *Wellington: the years of the sword* (London, 1969).

Macaulay, A. *The appointments of the archbishops of Armagh in the nineteenth century* (Cumann Seanchais Ard Mhacha, 2008).

MacCaffrey, J., *History of the Catholic church in the nineteenth century*, II (Dublin, 1910).

MacDonagh, O., 'The politicization of the Irish Catholic bishops, 1800–1850', *Historical Journal*, 18:1 (1975), 37–53.

—— *States of mind: a study of Anglo-Irish conflict, 1780–1980* (London, 1983).

—— *The hereditary bondsman: Daniel O'Connell, 1775–1829* (London, 1988).

Mac Giolla Phádraig, B.,'Dr John Carpenter, Archbishop of Dublin (1770–86)', *Dublin Hist. Rec.*, 30:1 (1976), 2–17.

Machin, G.I.T., 'Canning, Wellington and the Catholic question', *English Historical Review*, 99 (1984), 94–100.

—— *The Catholic question in English politics, 1820–1830* (Oxford, 1964).

Malcomson, A.P.W., *John Foster: the politics of the Anglo-Irish ascendancy* (Oxford, 1978).

Mansergh, D., *Grattan's failure: parliamentary opposition and the people in Ireland, 1779–1800* (Dublin, 2005).

Mathew, D., *Catholicism in England: the portrait of a minority, its culture and tradition* (London, 1955).

McCluskey, R. (ed), *The Scots College Rome, 1600–2000* (Edinburgh, 2000).

McDowell, R.B., *Ireland in the age of imperialism and revolution, 1760–1801* (Oxford, 1979).

—— *Grattan: a life* (Dublin, 2001).

——(ed.), *The writings and speeches of Edmund Burke*, ix:ii, *Ireland* (Oxford, 1991)

——'Colonial nationalism and the winning of parliamentary independence' in *NHI*, iv, *Eighteenth-century Ireland, 1691–1800* (Oxford, 1986), pp 196–235.

McGrath, T., *Politics, interdenominational relations and education in the public ministry of Bishop James Doyle of Kildare and Leighlin, 1786–1834* (Dublin, 1999).

—— *Religious renewal and reform on the pastoral ministry of Bishop James Doyle of Kildare and Leighlin, 1786–1834* (Dublin, 1999).

McNally, V., *Reform, revolution and reaction: Archbishop John Thomas Troy and the Catholic church in Ireland, 1787–1817* (Lanham, New York and London, 1995).

McRoberts, D., *Abbé Paul Macpherson, 1756–1846* (Glasgow, 1946).

Mercati, A., *Raccolta di concordati, su materie ecclesiastiche tra la Santa Sede e le autorità civili* (Vatican, 1954).

Muir, R., *Wellington, Waterloo and the fortunes of peace, 1814–1852* (New Haven, CT, and London, 2015).

Mullet, M.A., *Catholics in Britain and Ireland, 1558–1829* (Basingstoke, 1998).

Murphy, I., *The diocese of Killaloe in the eighteenth century* (Dublin, 1991).

—— *The diocese of Killaloe, 1800–1850* (Dublin, 1992).

Norman, E.R., *The English Catholic church in the nineteenth century* (Oxford, 1984).

O'Brien, C.C., *The great melody: a thematic biography and commented anthology of Edmund Burke* (London, 1992).

O'Brien, G., 'The beginning of the veto controversy in Ireland', *Journal of Ecclesiastical History* (Jan. 1987), 80–94.

—— (ed), *Catholic Ireland in the eighteenth century: collected essays of Maureen Wall* (Dublin, 1989).

O'Ciardha, E., *Ireland and the Jacobite cause, 1685–1766: a fatal attachment* (Dublin, 2004).

O'Donaghue, P., 'The Holy See and Ireland', *Arch. Hib.*, 34 (1976–7), 99–108.

—— 'John Thomas Troy, archbishop of Dublin, 1786–1823: a man of his time' in J. Kelly and U. MacGearailt (eds), *Dublin and Dubliners* (1989), pp 25–35.

O'Ferrall, F., *Catholic emancipation: Daniel O'Connell and the birth of Irish democracy, 1820–30* (Dublin, 1985).

O'Flaherty, E., 'The Catholic convention and Anglo-Irish politics, 1791–3', *Arch. Hib.*, 40 (1985), 14–34.

O'Hogartaigh, M., *Edward Hay: historian of 1798* (Dublin, 2010).

Pakenham, T., *The year of liberty: the story of the great Irish rebellion of 1798* (London, 1969).

Peel, H., 'The appointment of Dr Troy to the see of Dublin' *Repertorium Novum*, 4:1 (1965), 5–16.

Power, P., *Waterford and Lismore: a compendious history of the united dioceses* (Waterford, 1937).

——'The Most Rev. James Butler, DD, Archbishop of Cashel, 1774–1791' in *IER*, 3rd series, 13 (April 1892), 302–18, 522–38.

Power, T.P. and K. Whelan (eds), *Endurance and emergence: Catholics in Ireland in the eighteenth century* (Dublin, 1990).

Rafferty, O., *The Catholic church and the Protestant state: nineteenth century Irish realities* (Dublin, 2008).

Regoli, R., *Ercole Consalvi: le scelte per la chiesa* (Rome, 2006).

Reynolds, J.A., *The Catholic emancipation crisis in Ireland, 1823–1829* (Newport, CT, 1970).

Roberts, M., *The Whig party, 1807–12* (London, 1939).

Rogers, P., *The Irish volunteers and Catholic emancipation, 1778–1793: a neglected phase of Ireland's history* (London, 1934).

Roveri, A., *La mission Consalvi e il congresso di Vienna* (Rome, 1970–1), i, ii.

Roveri, A., Fatica, M. and Cantu, F., *La missione Consalvi e il congresso di Vienna* (Rome, 1973), iii.

Schofield, J. and G. Skinner, *The English vicars apostolic, 1688–1850* (Oxford, 2009).

Senior, H., *Orangeism in Ireland and Britain, 1795–1836* (London, 1966).

Smyth, J., 'Popular politicisation, defenderism and the Catholic question' in H. Gough and D. Dickson (eds), *The men of no property* (London, 1992).

Stewart, A.T.Q., *The summer soldiers: the 1798 rebellion in Antrim and Down* (Belfast, 1995).

Swords, L., *A hidden church: the diocese of Achonry, 1689–1818* (Dublin, 1997).

Walsh, J.R., *Frederick Augustus Hervey, 1730–1803* (Maynooth, 1972).

Ward, B., *The dawn of the Catholic revival in England*, 2 vols (London, 1909).

—— *The eve of Catholic emancipation*, 3 vols (London, 1911–12).

Watkin, E.I., *Roman Catholicism in England from the Reformation to 1850* (London, 1957).

Weigall, R. (ed.), *Correspondence of Lord Burghersh, afterwards eleventh earl of Westmoreland, 1808–1840* (London, 1912).

Whelan, I., *The Bible war in Ireland: the 'Second Reformation' and the polarization of Protestant-Catholic relations, 1800–1840* (Madison, WI, 2005).

Whelan, K., 'Catholics and the 1798 rebellion' in R. O'Muiri (ed.), *Irish church history today* (Armagh, 1991).

—— *The tree of liberty: radicalism, Catholicism and the construction of Irish identity, 1760–1830* (Cork, 1996).

Yates, N., *The religious condition of Ireland, 1770–1850* (Oxford, 2006).

Zamoyski, A., *Rites of peace: the fall of Napoleon and the congress of Vienna* (London, 2007).

Index